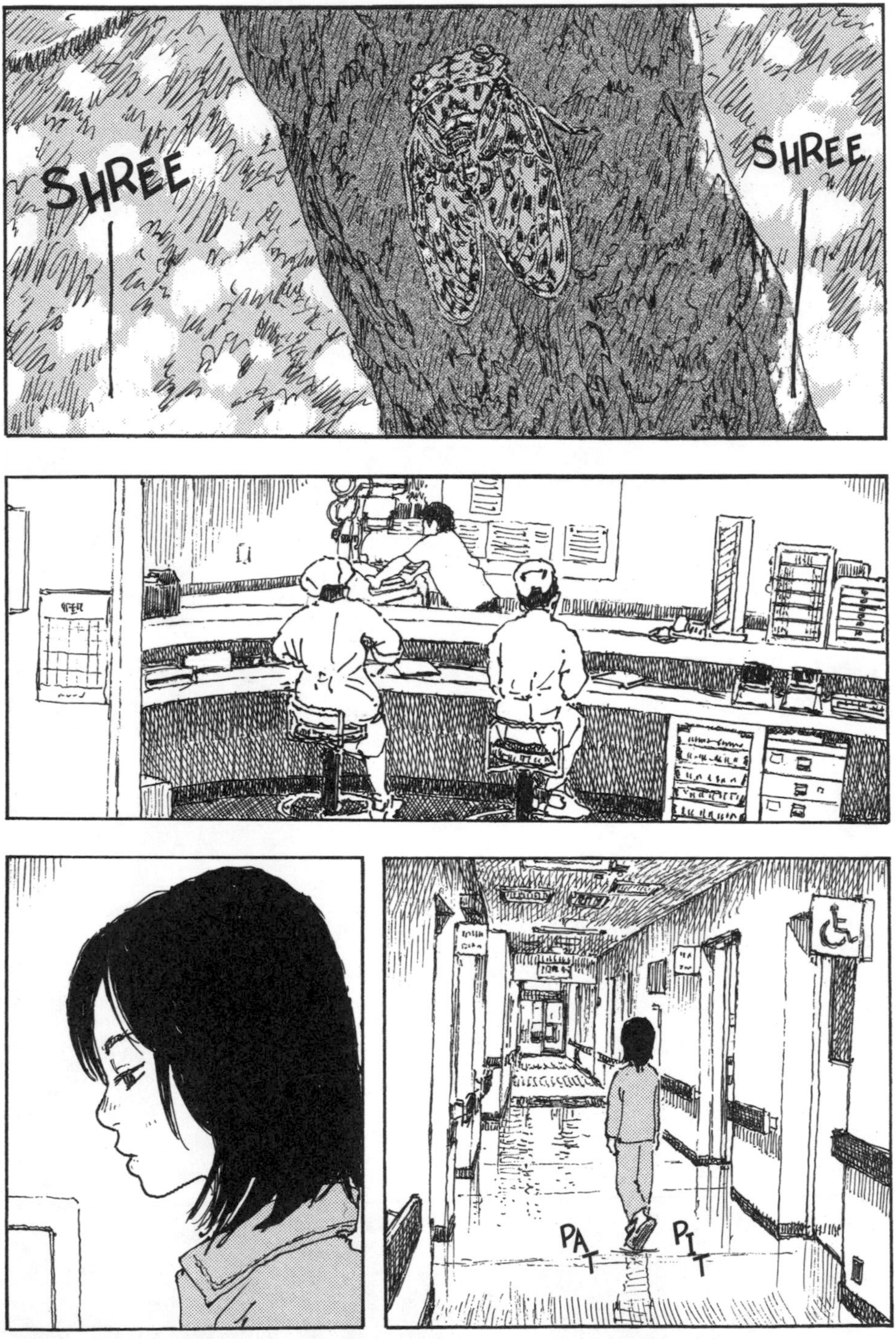
SHREE
SHREE
PAT PIT

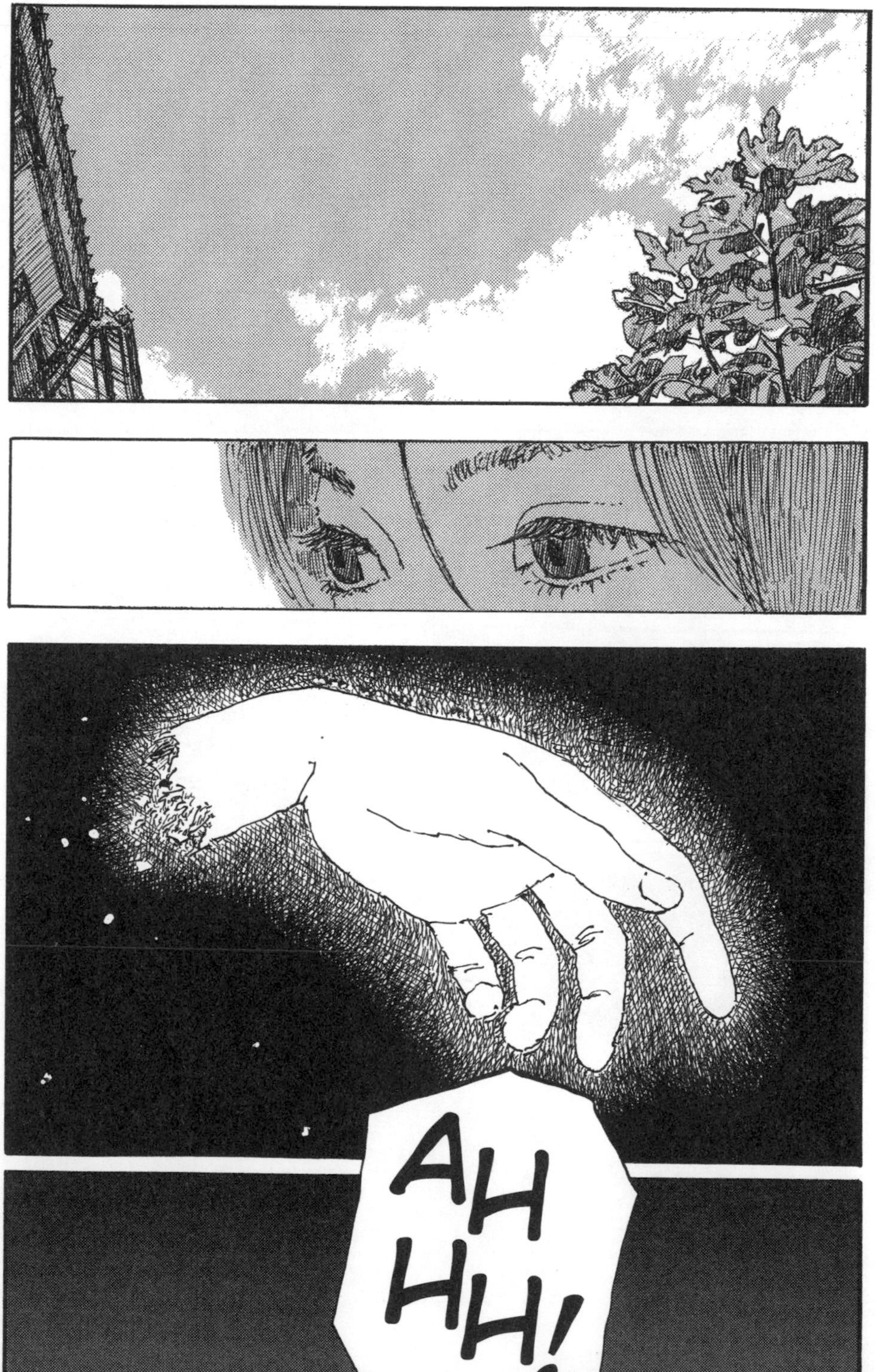
AHHH!

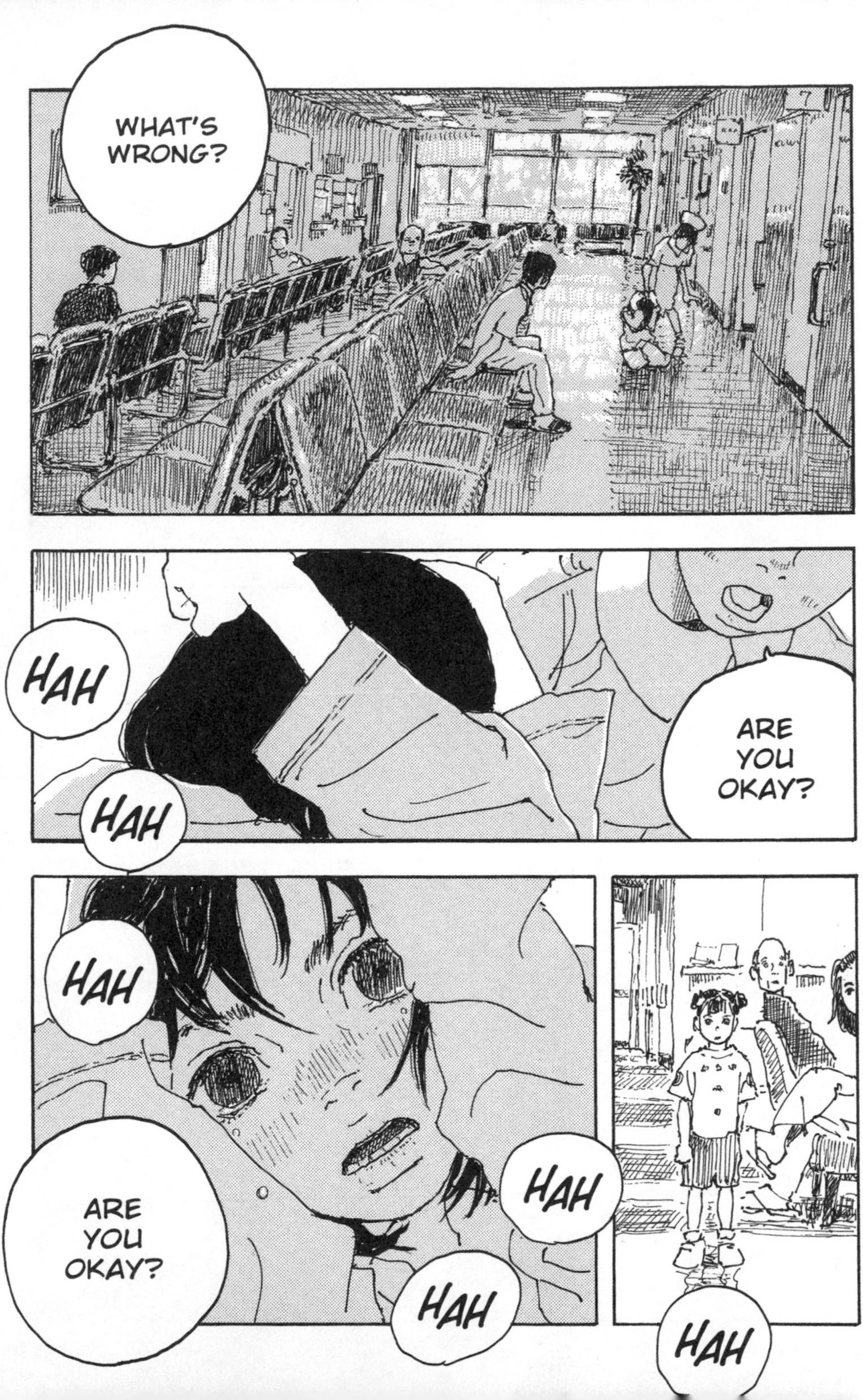
WHAT'S WRONG?
ARE YOU OKAY?
HAH
HAH
HAH
HAH
HAH
ARE YOU OKAY?
HAH

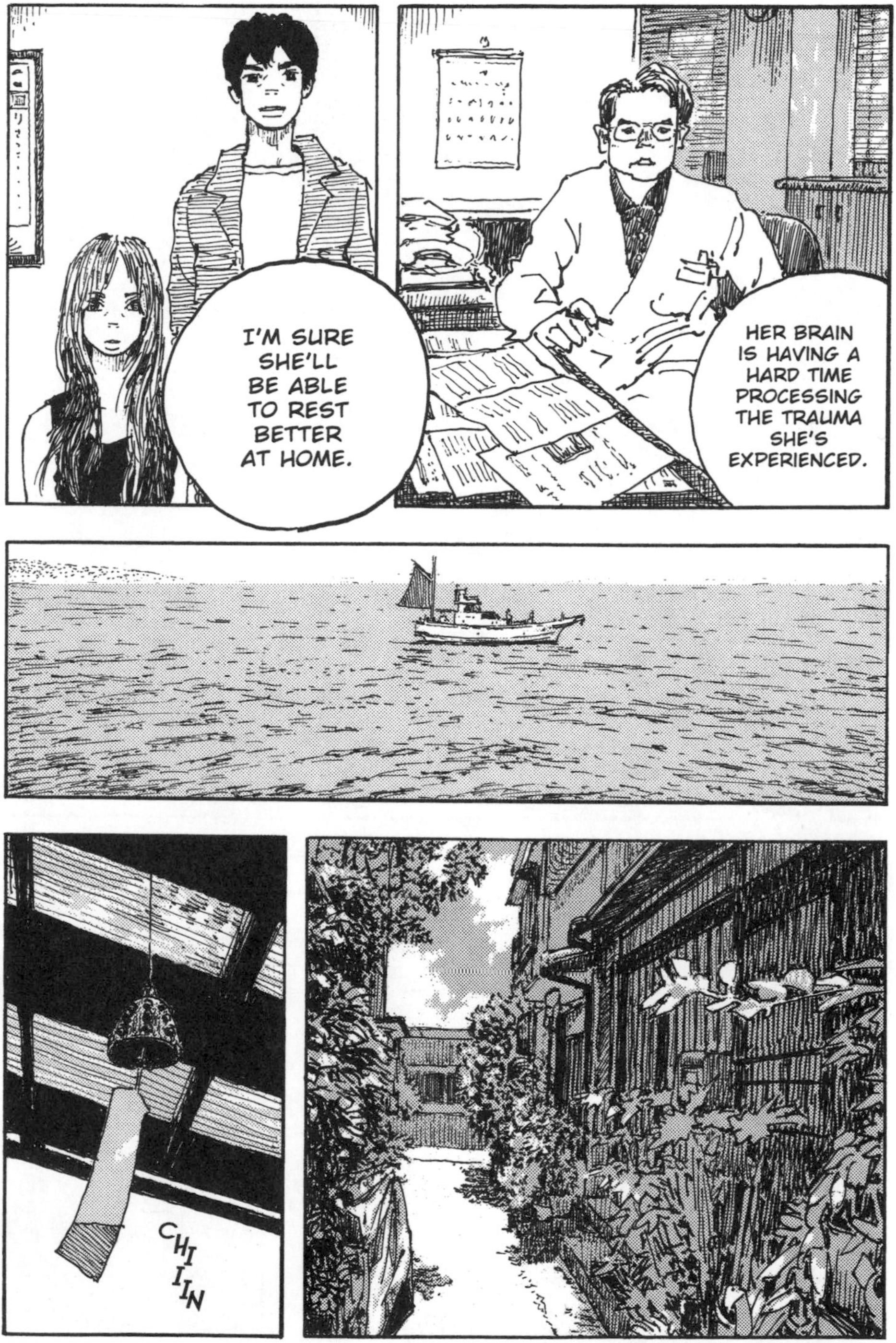
HER BRAIN IS HAVING A HARD TIME PROCESSING THE TRAUMA SHE'S EXPERIENCED.
I'M SURE SHE'LL BE ABLE TO REST BETTER AT HOME.
CHIIIN

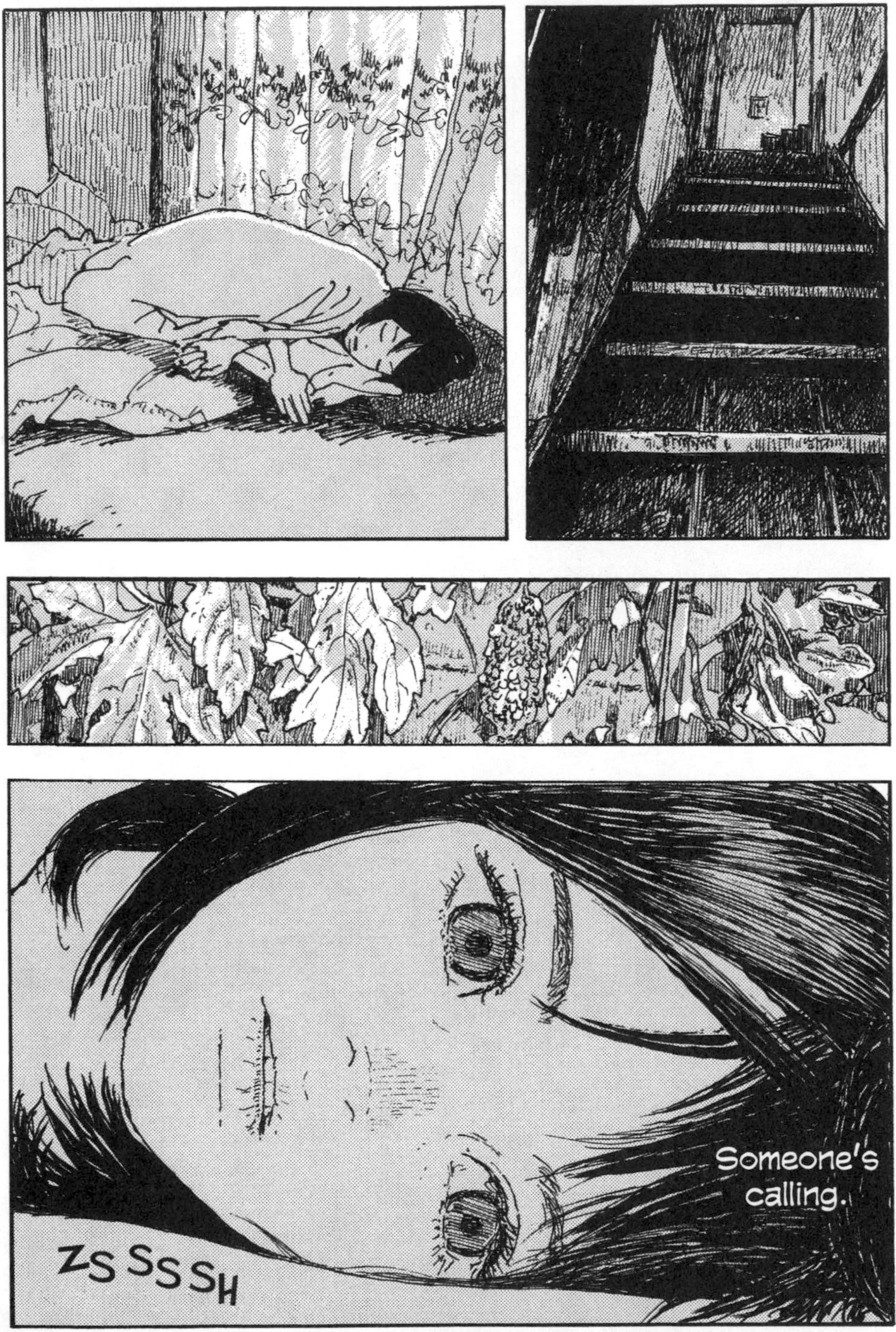
Someone's calling.
ZSSSSH

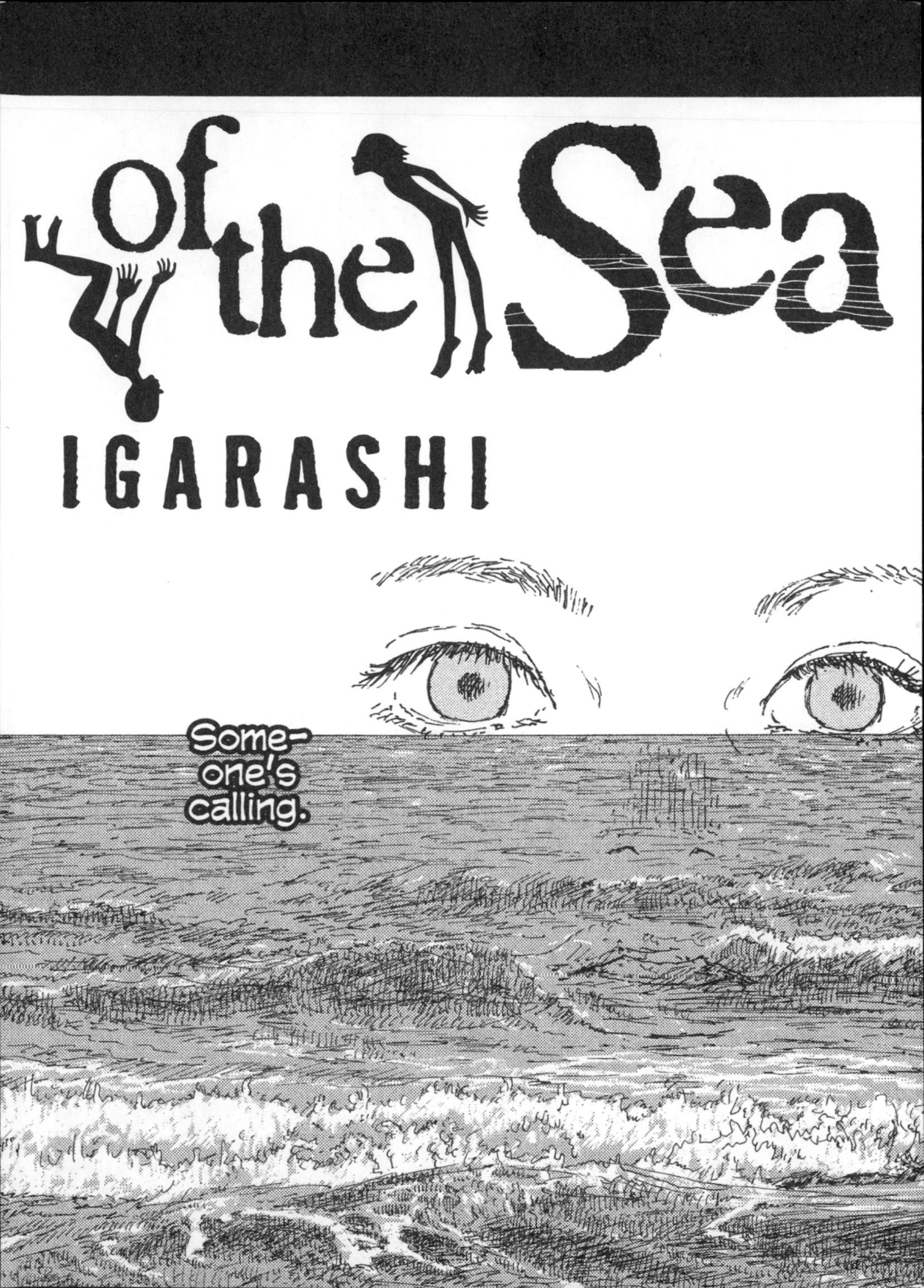
of the Sea
IGARASHI
Some-one's calling.

Children

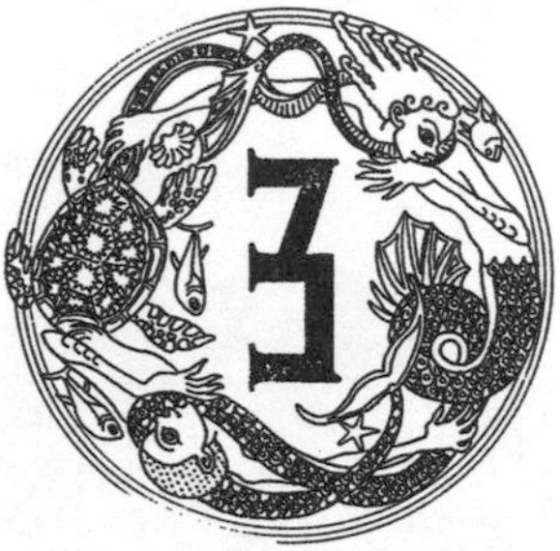
3

DAISUKE

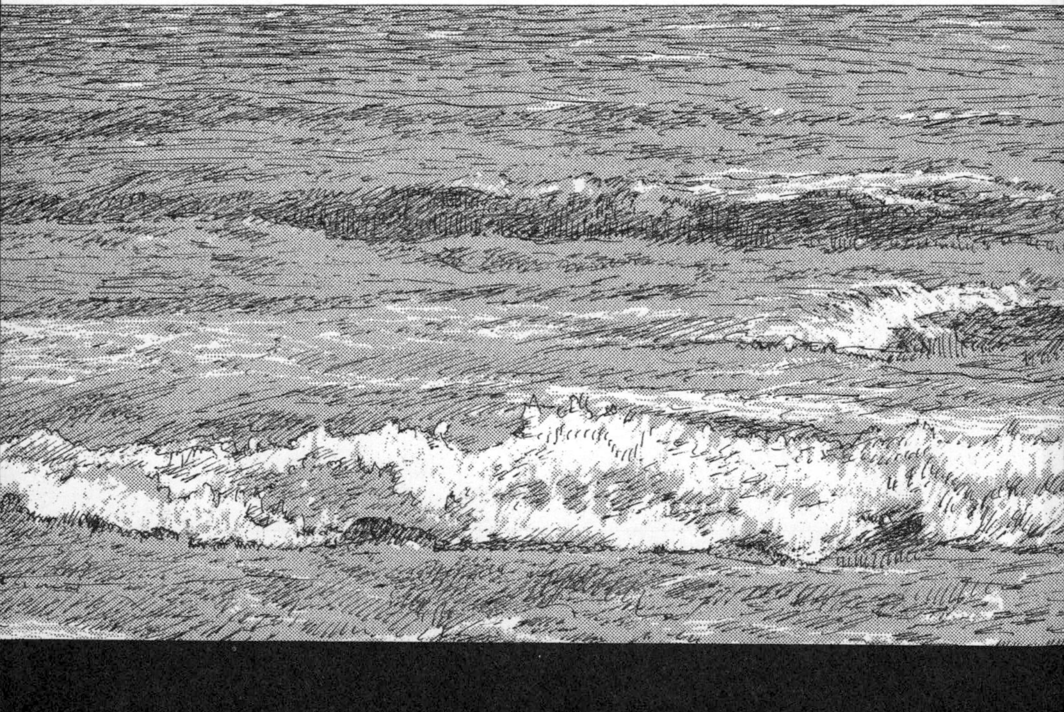

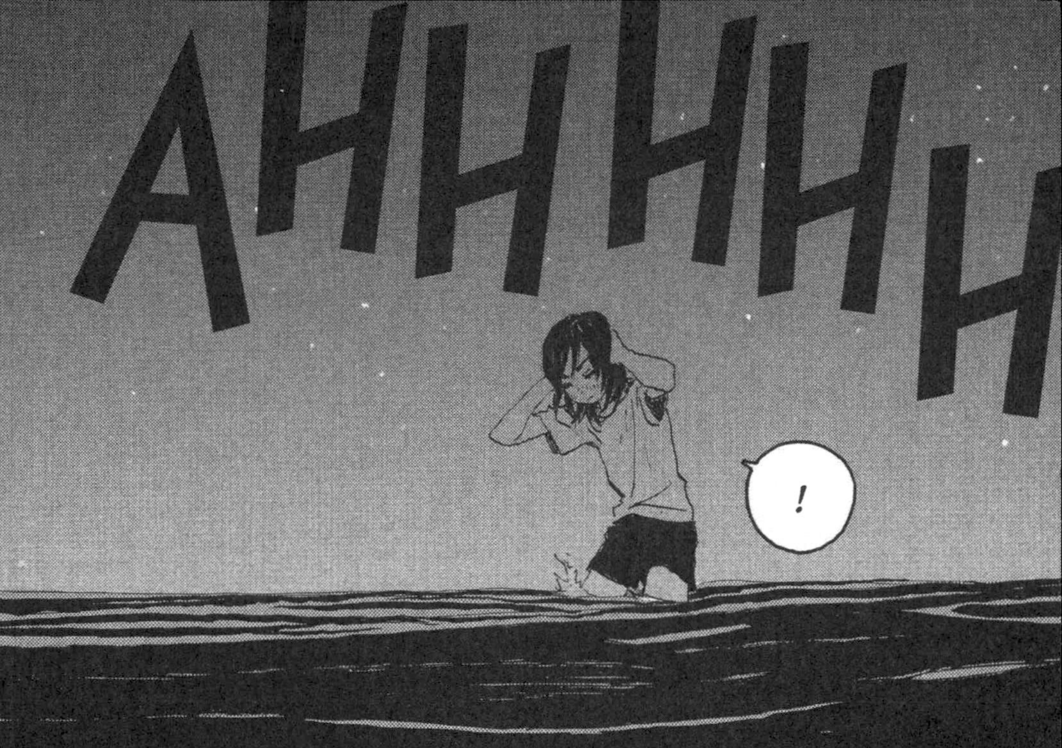
AHHHHHH
!

out of your stomach and give it to him."

Children of the Sea

THE STORY THUS FAR

During summer vacation Ruka meets Sora and Umi, two boys who were raised by dugongs. After meeting the boys, strange things begin to happen. A mysterious shooting star appears, fish turn into light and disappear...

Sora runs away with Anglade to discover the secret of his birth. Ruka and a depressed Umi, who has lost his ability to speak, travel to the Ogawara Islands to find them. That night Sora gives Ruka the meteorite he was keeping. Soon after, his body starts to glow and he disappears in front of Ruka's eyes. Meanwhile, mysterious things are happening in the oceans all over the world...

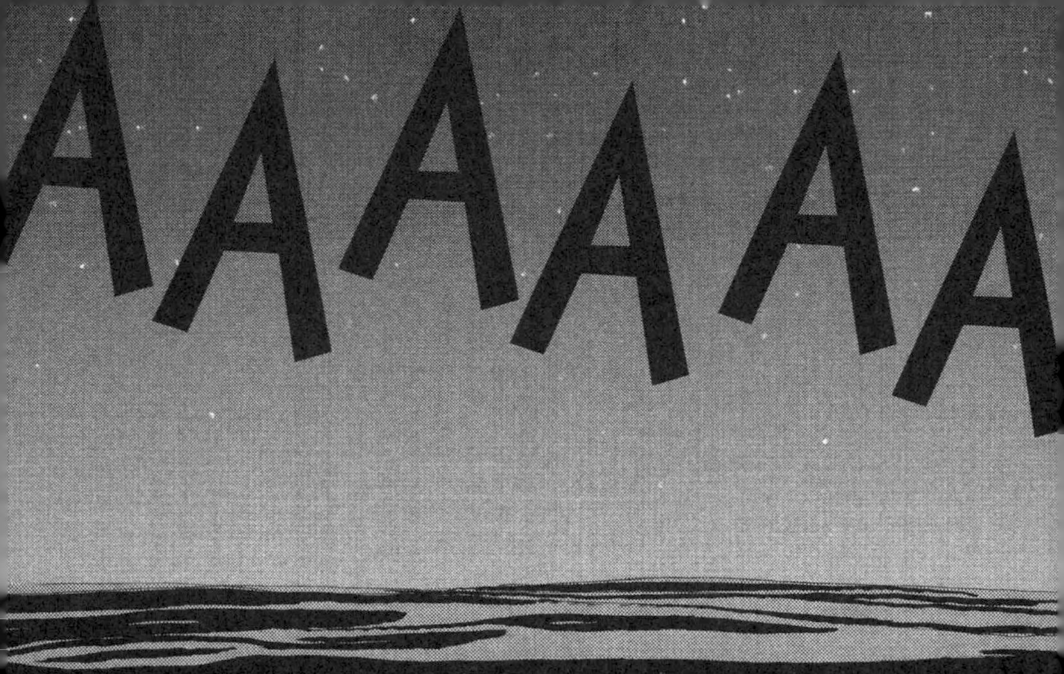
AAAAAA

"If Umi ever needs the meteorite, cut it

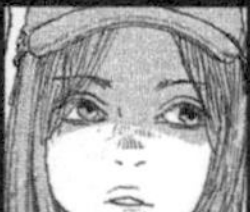

KANAKO AZUMI

Ruka's mother. She used to work at the aquarium.

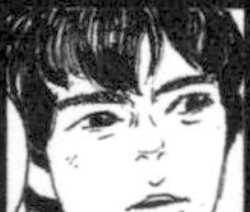

MASĀKI AZUMI

Ruka's father. He works at the aquarium.

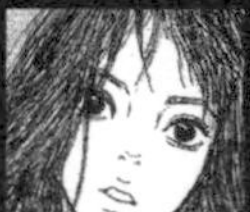

ANGLADE

A gifted young marine biologist. He was Jim's partner once, but now has different priorities.

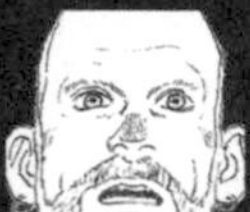

JIM CUSACK

A marine biologist. Forty years ago he was responsible for the death of a young boy who looked like Sora. Since then he has been pursuing the mystery of the ocean children.

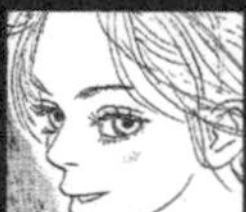

SORA

Raised as Umi's older brother. He is physically weak and is often in the hospital. He disappeared with Anglade.

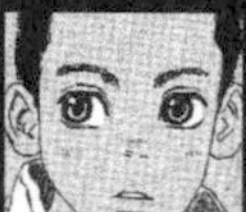

UMI

A boy found off the Philippine coast over ten years ago. The aquarium has been taking care of him and Sora. He has opened up to Ruka.

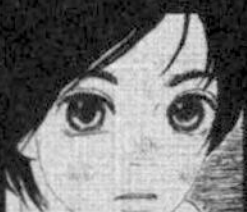

RUKA AZUMI

A middle school student who has a hard time articulating her feelings and tends to use her fists and not her words. Her parents are separated and she lives with her mother.

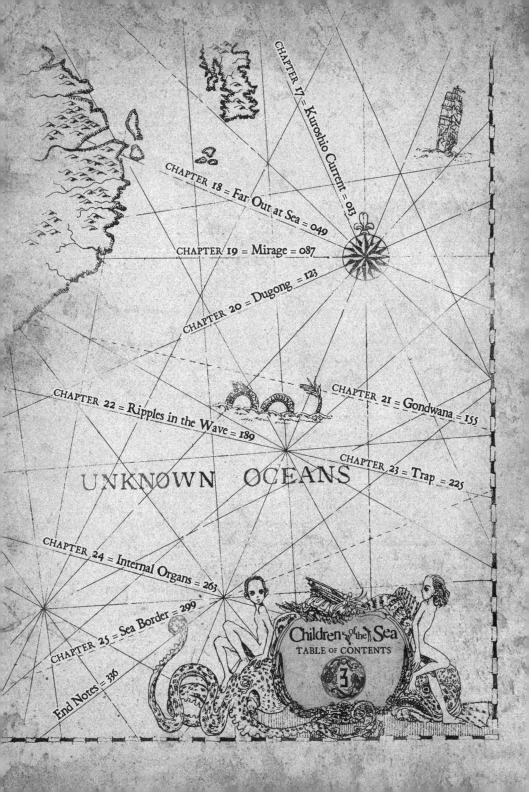

UNKNOWN OCEANS

Children of the Sea

TABLE OF CONTENTS

3

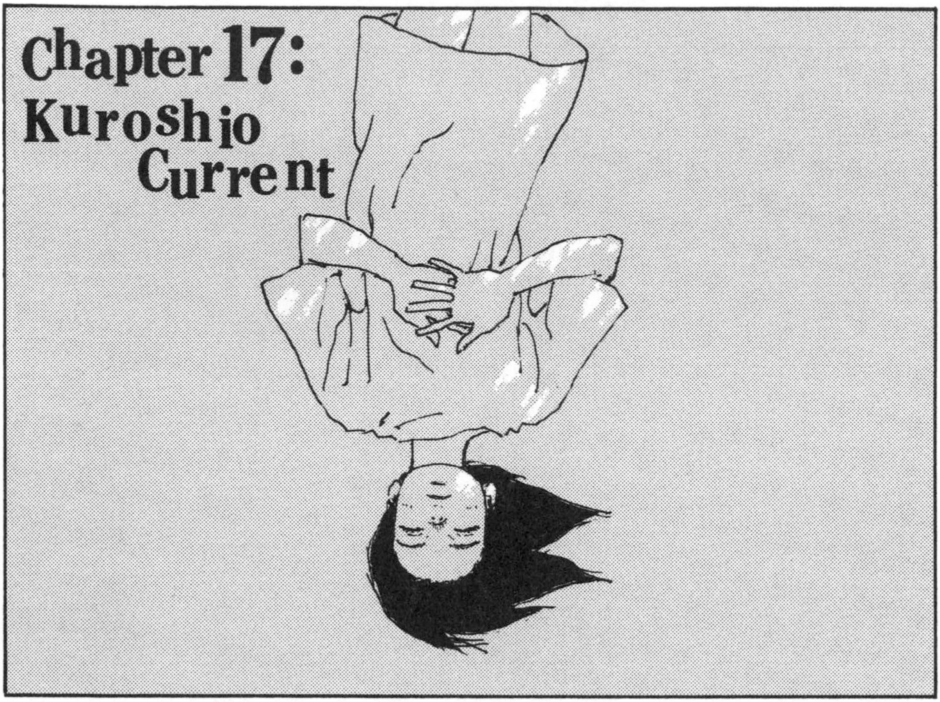
Chapter 17:
Kuroshio Current
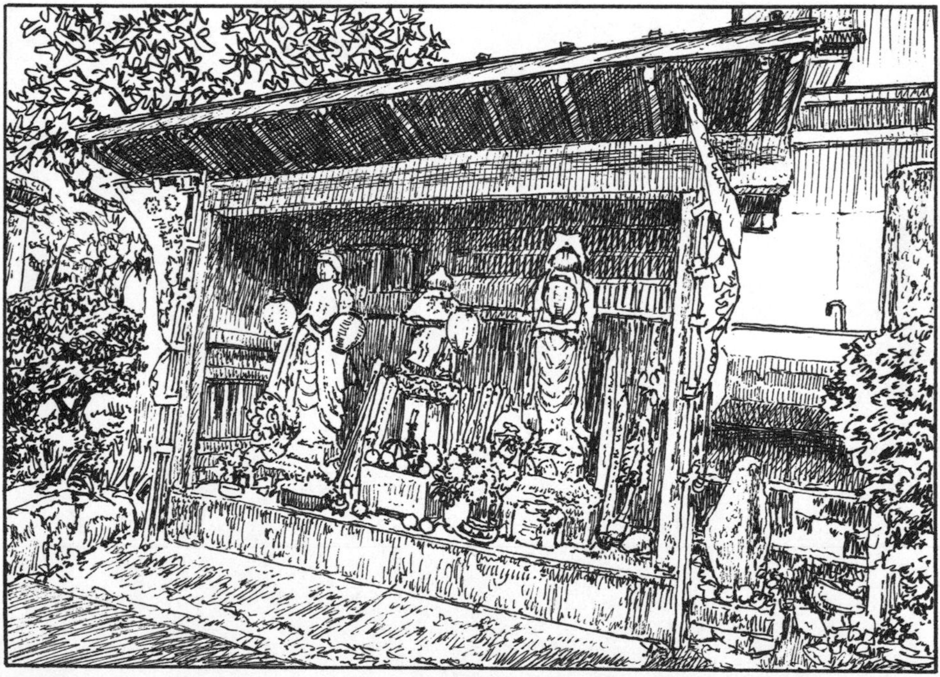

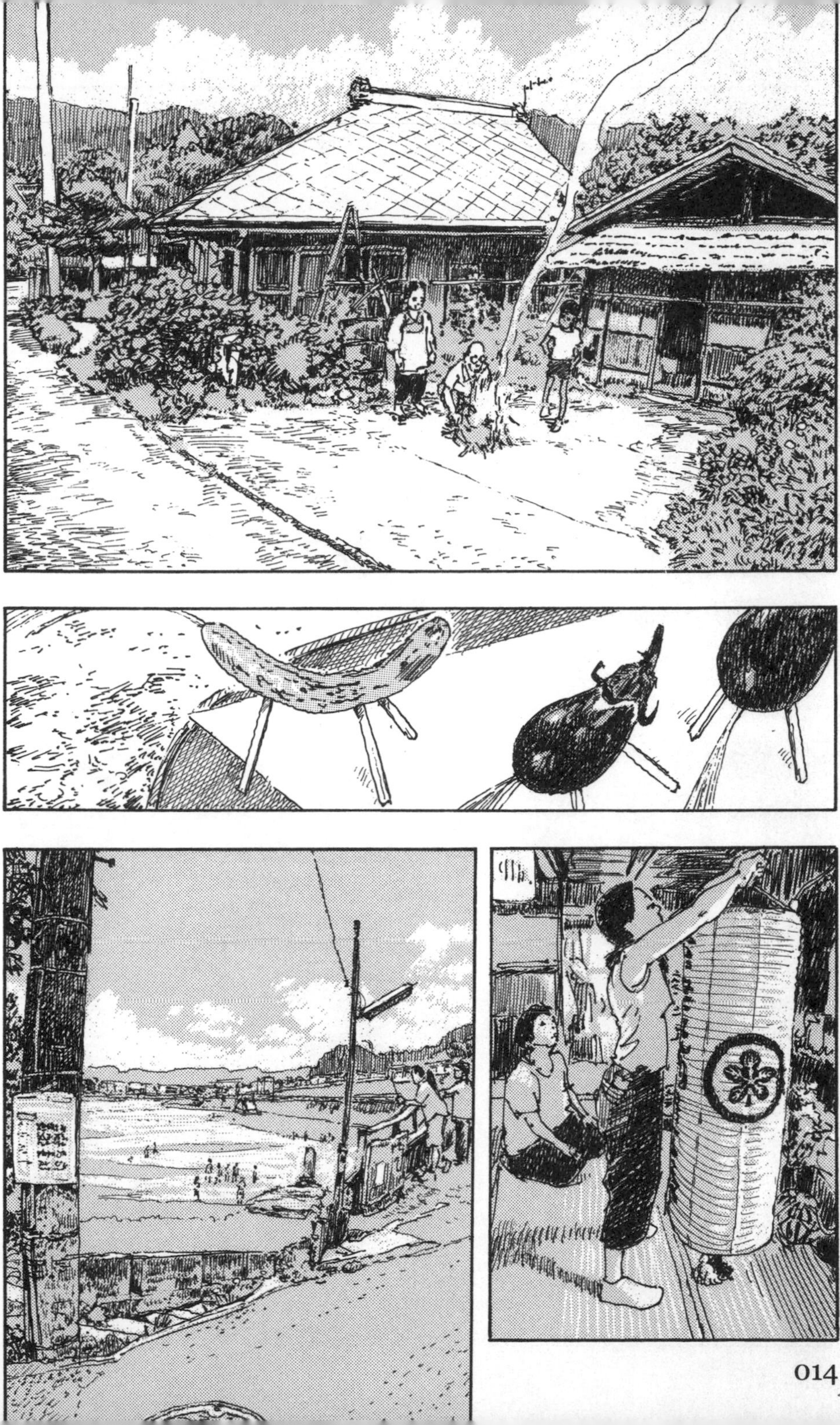

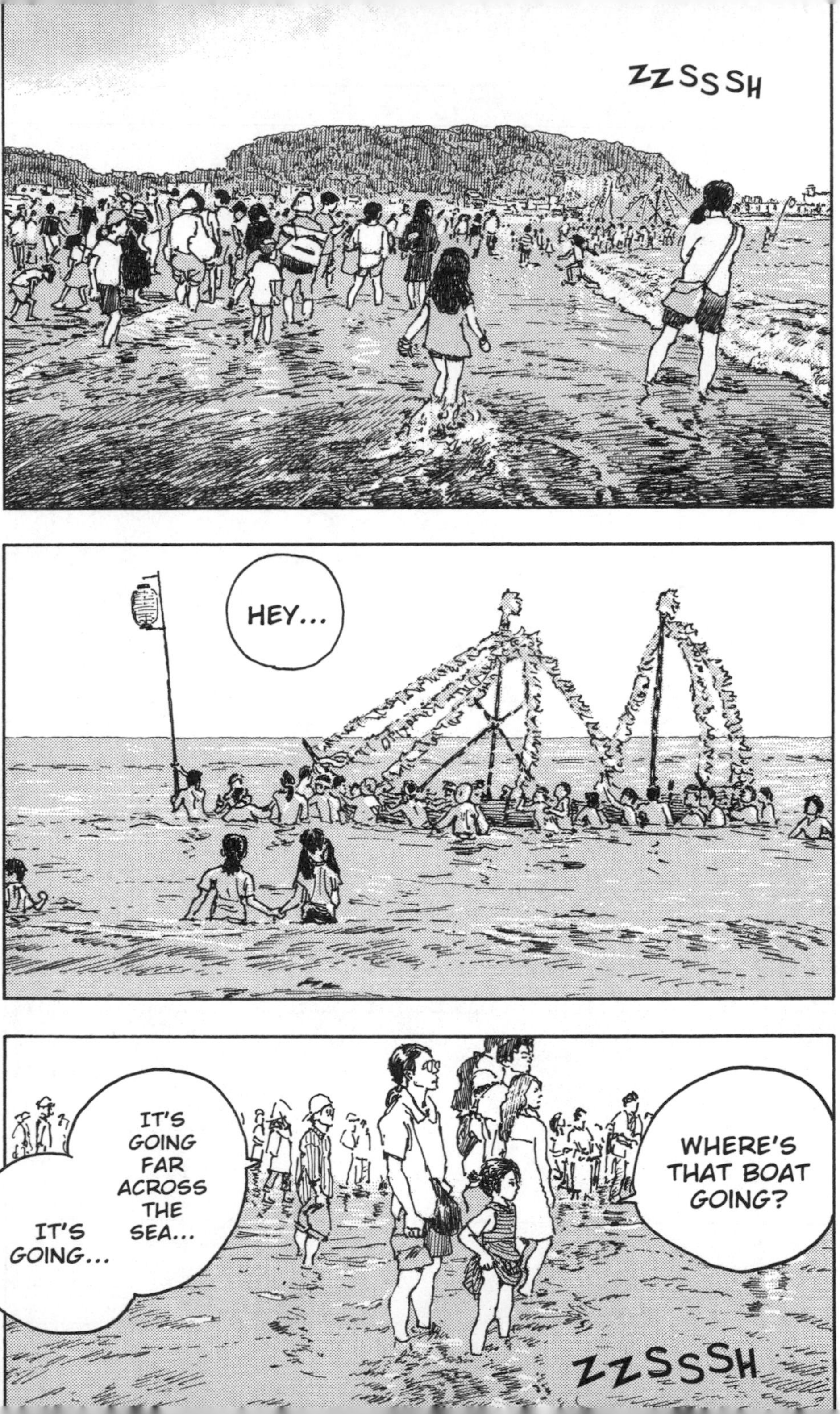
ZZSSSH
HEY...
WHERE'S THAT BOAT GOING?
IT'S GOING FAR ACROSS THE SEA...
IT'S GOING...
ZZSSSH

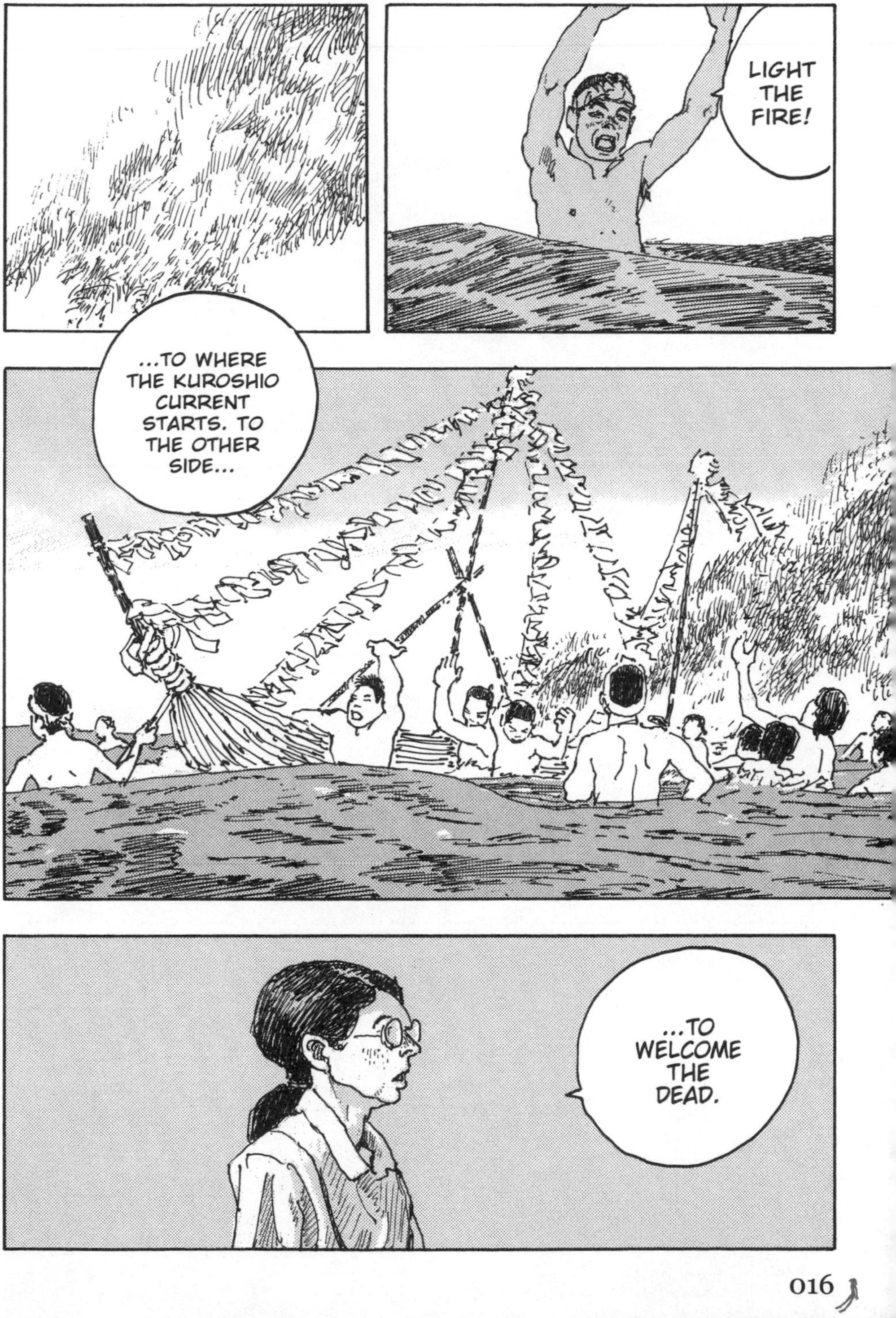
LIGHT THE FIRE!
...TO WHERE THE KUROSHIO CURRENT STARTS. TO THE OTHER SIDE...
...TO WELCOME THE DEAD.

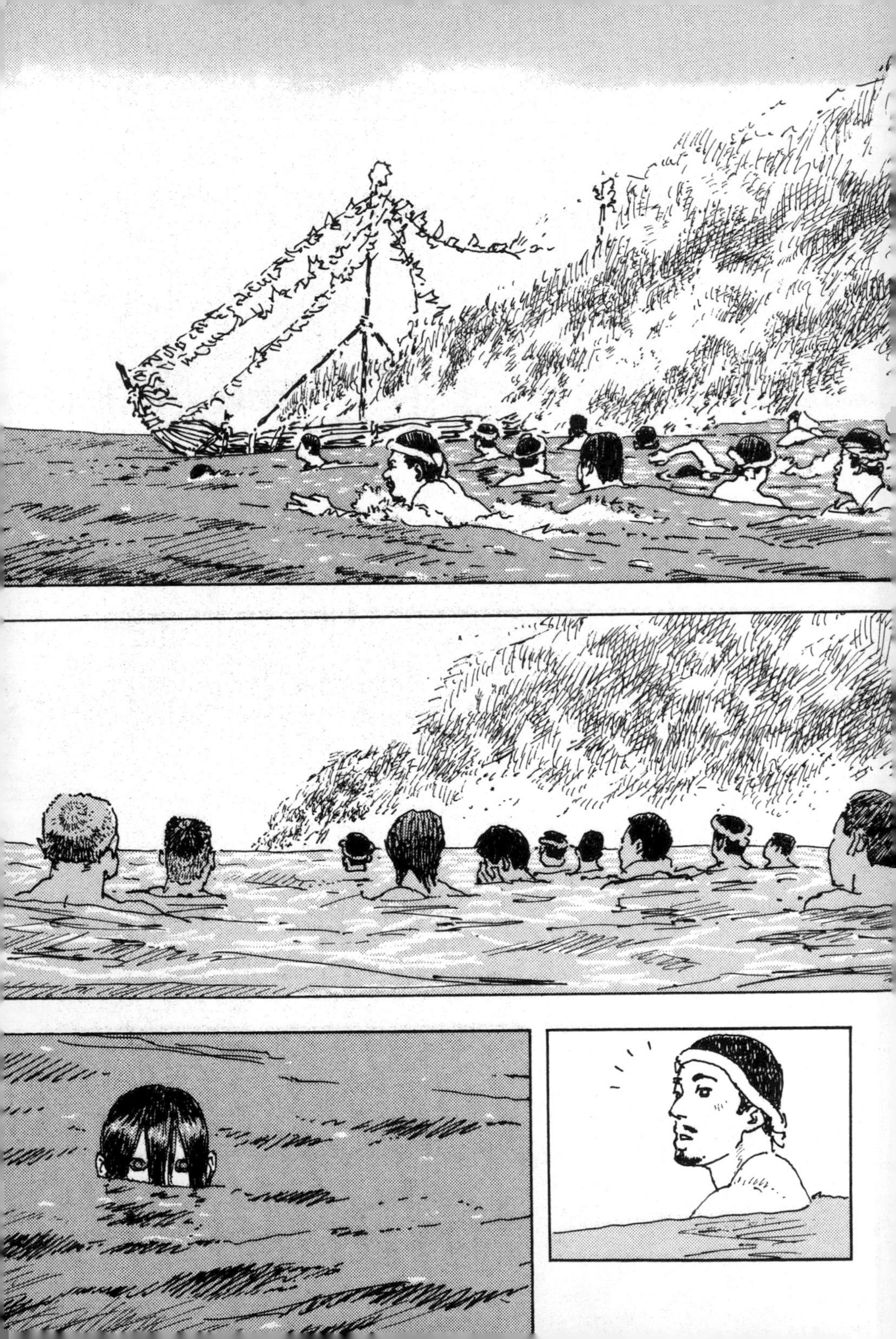

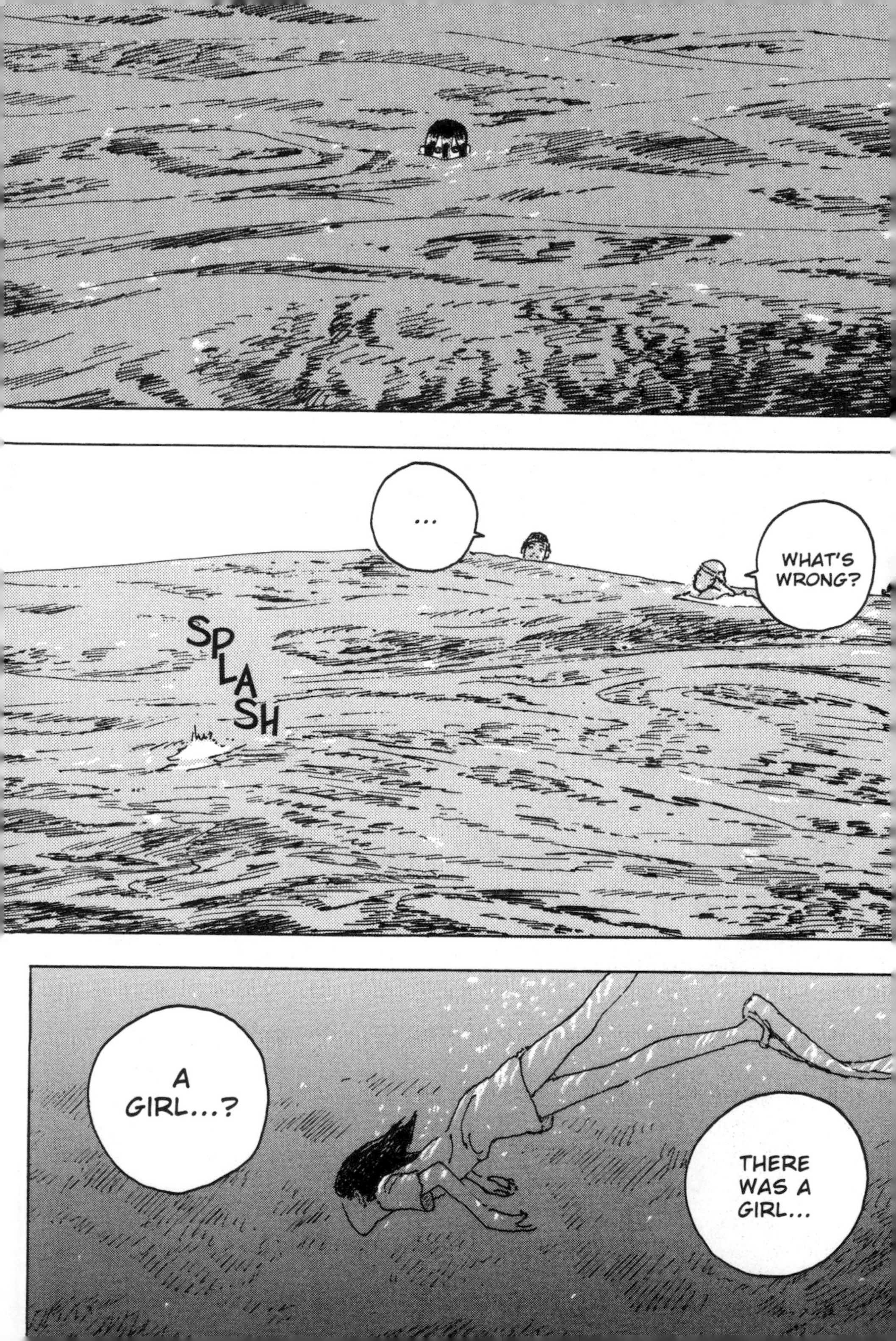
WHAT'S WRONG?
...
SPLASH
THERE WAS A GIRL...
A GIRL...?

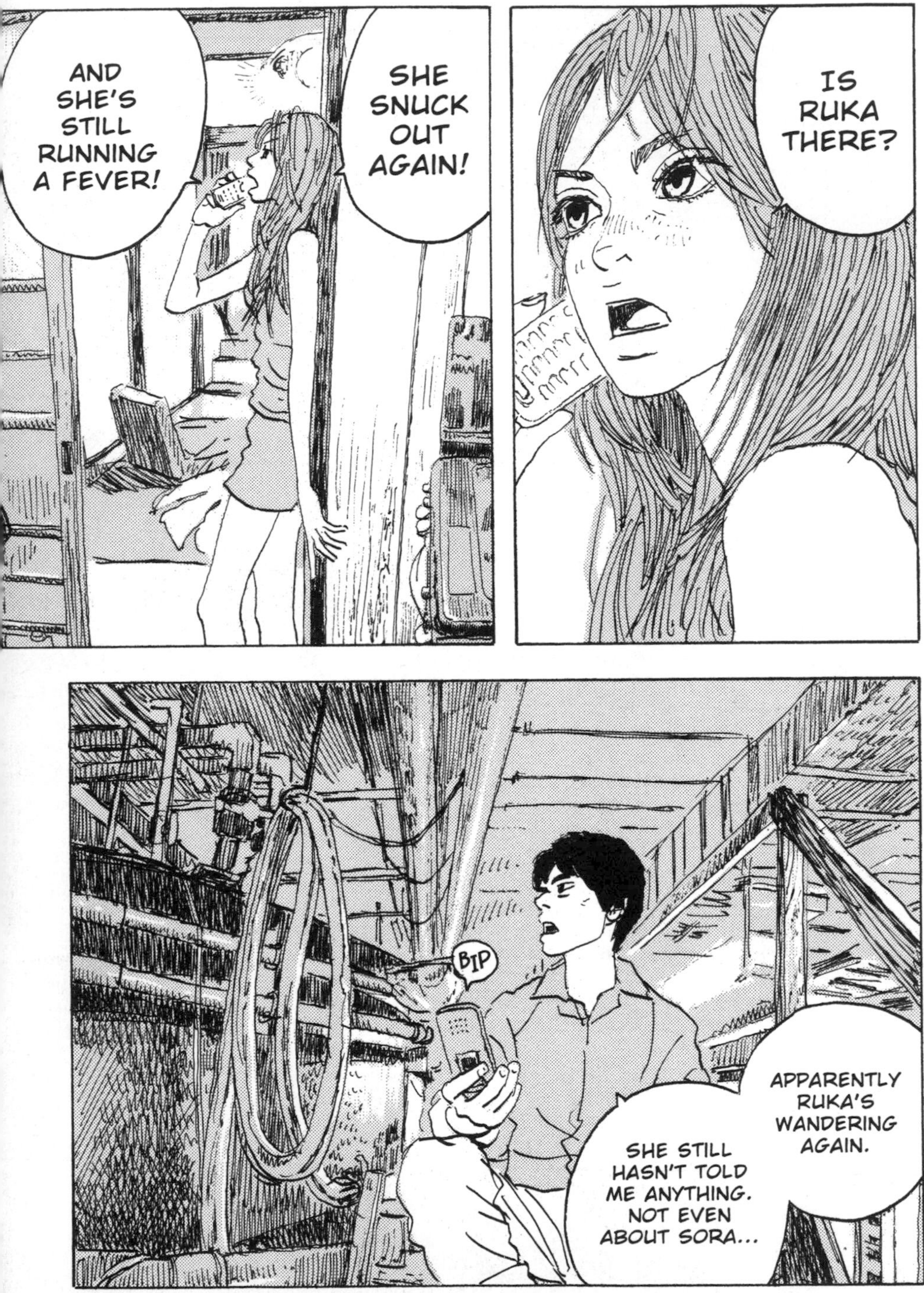
IS RUKA THERE?
SHE SNUCK OUT AGAIN!
AND SHE'S STILL RUNNING A FEVER!
BIP
APPARENTLY RUKA'S WANDERING AGAIN.
SHE STILL HASN'T TOLD ME ANYTHING. NOT EVEN ABOUT SORA...

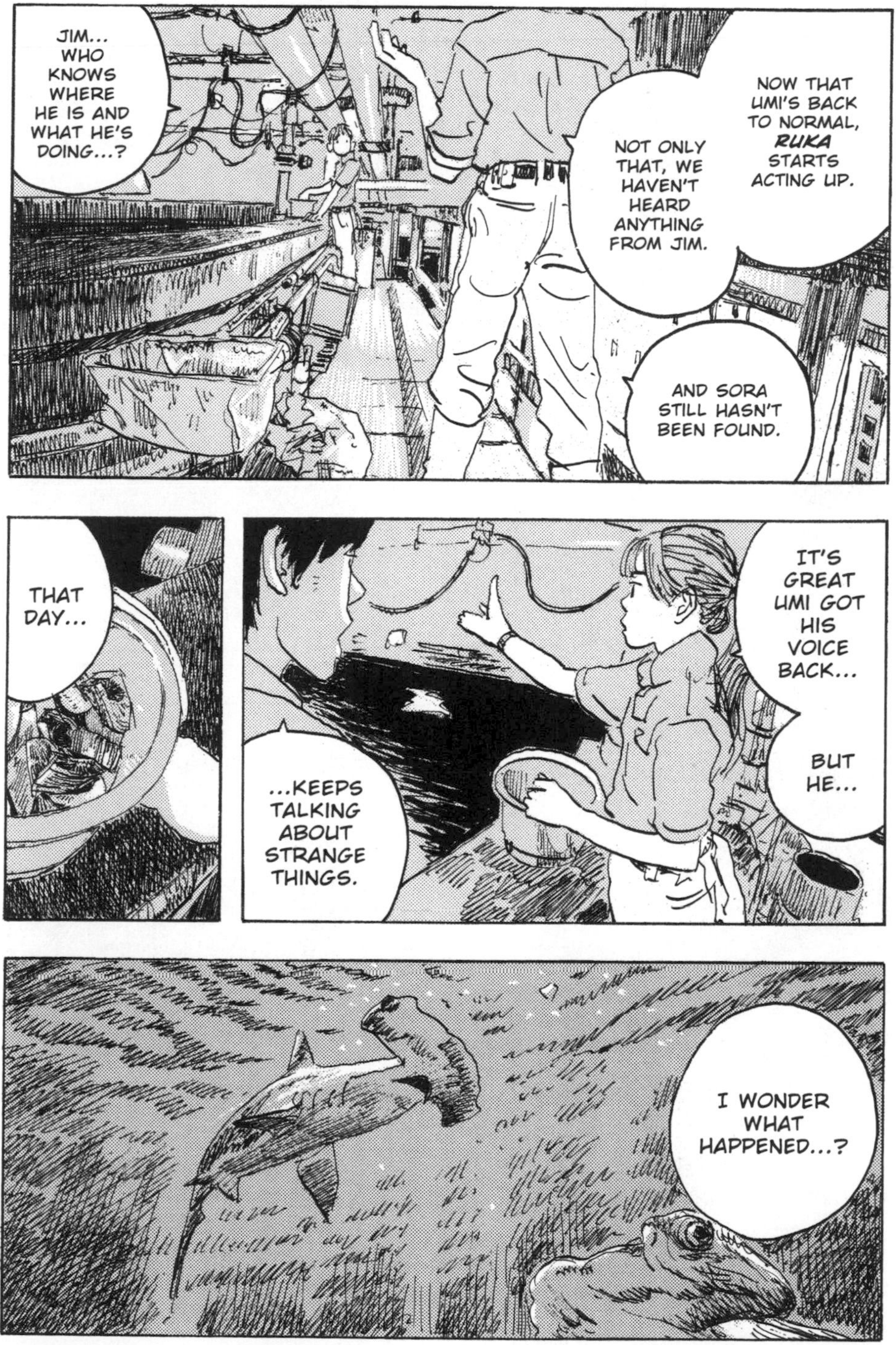
NOW THAT UMI'S BACK TO NORMAL, **RUKA** STARTS ACTING UP.
NOT ONLY THAT, WE HAVEN'T HEARD ANYTHING FROM JIM.
JIM... WHO KNOWS WHERE HE IS AND WHAT HE'S DOING...?
AND SORA STILL HASN'T BEEN FOUND.
IT'S GREAT UMI GOT HIS VOICE BACK...
BUT HE...
...KEEPS TALKING ABOUT STRANGE THINGS.
THAT DAY...
I WONDER WHAT HAPPENED...?

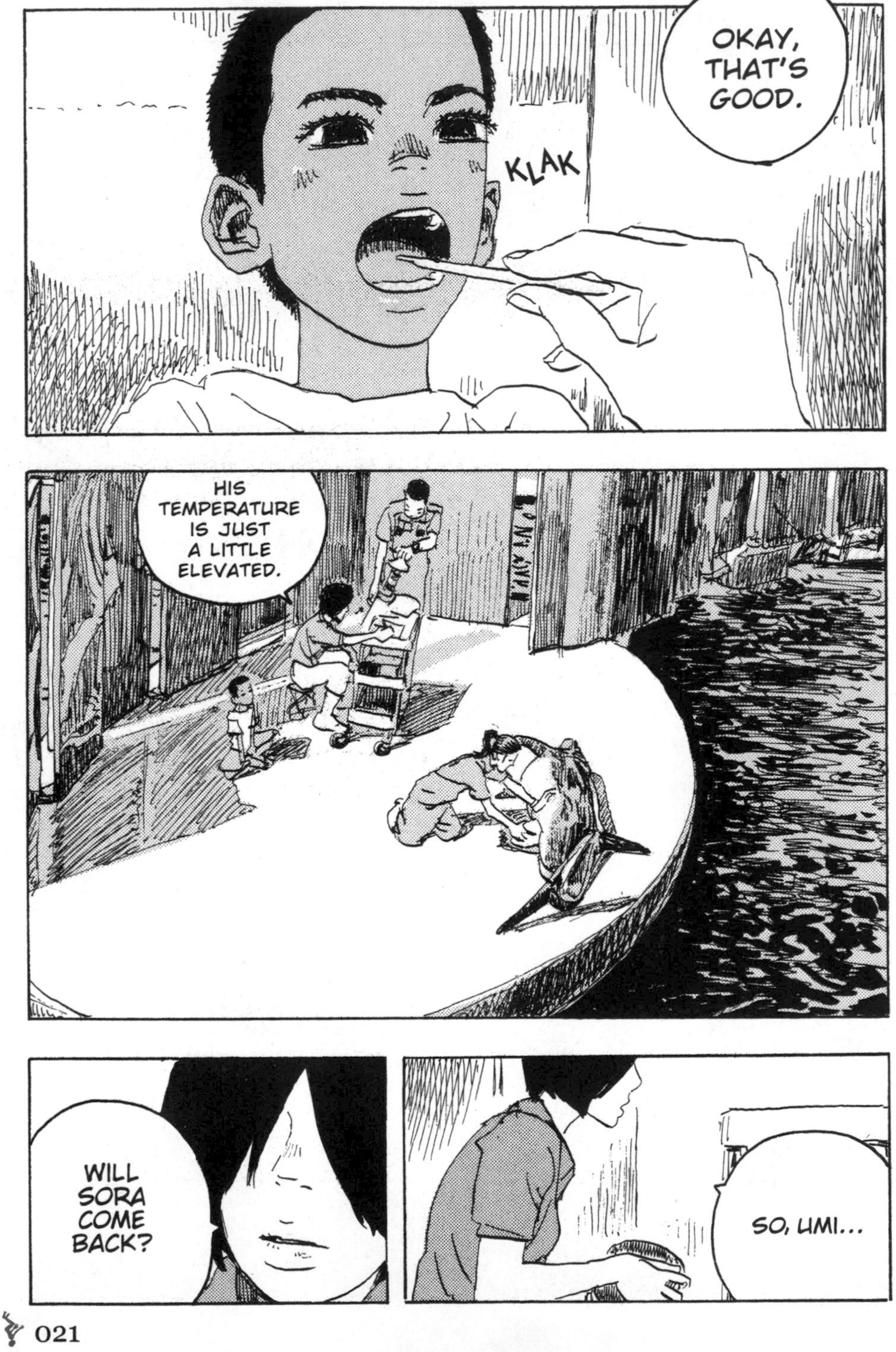
OKAY, THAT'S GOOD.
KLAK
HIS TEMPERATURE IS JUST A LITTLE ELEVATED.
SO, UMI...
WILL SORA COME BACK?

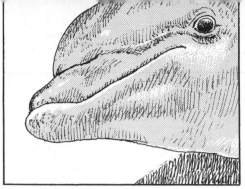

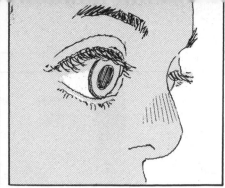

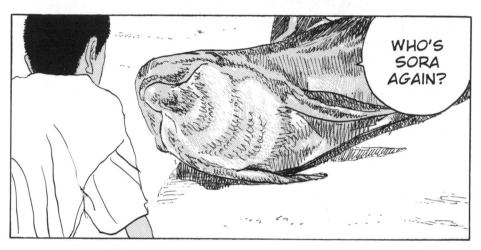

WHO'S SORA AGAIN?
HUH?
OH...BUT I REMEMBER SOMETHING...
I woke up in complete darkness.
It was pitch-black and cramped.
I knew immediately ...

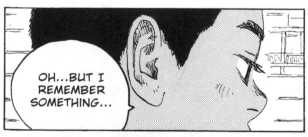

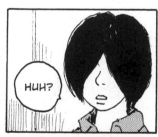

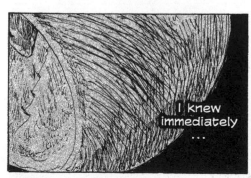

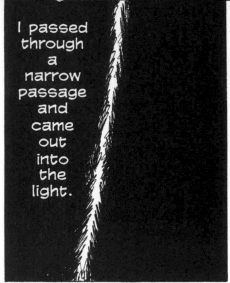

...that I had to be born.
That it was my turn.
I passed through a narrow passage and came out into the light.
It's cold!

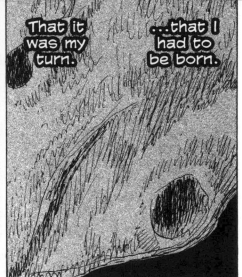

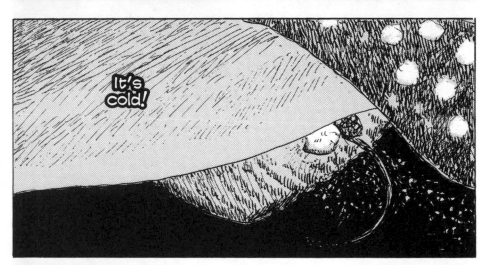

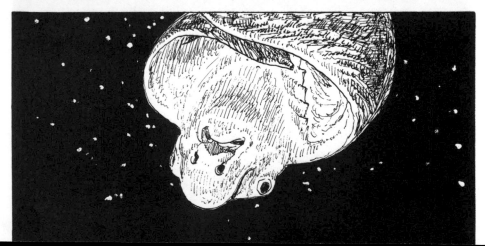

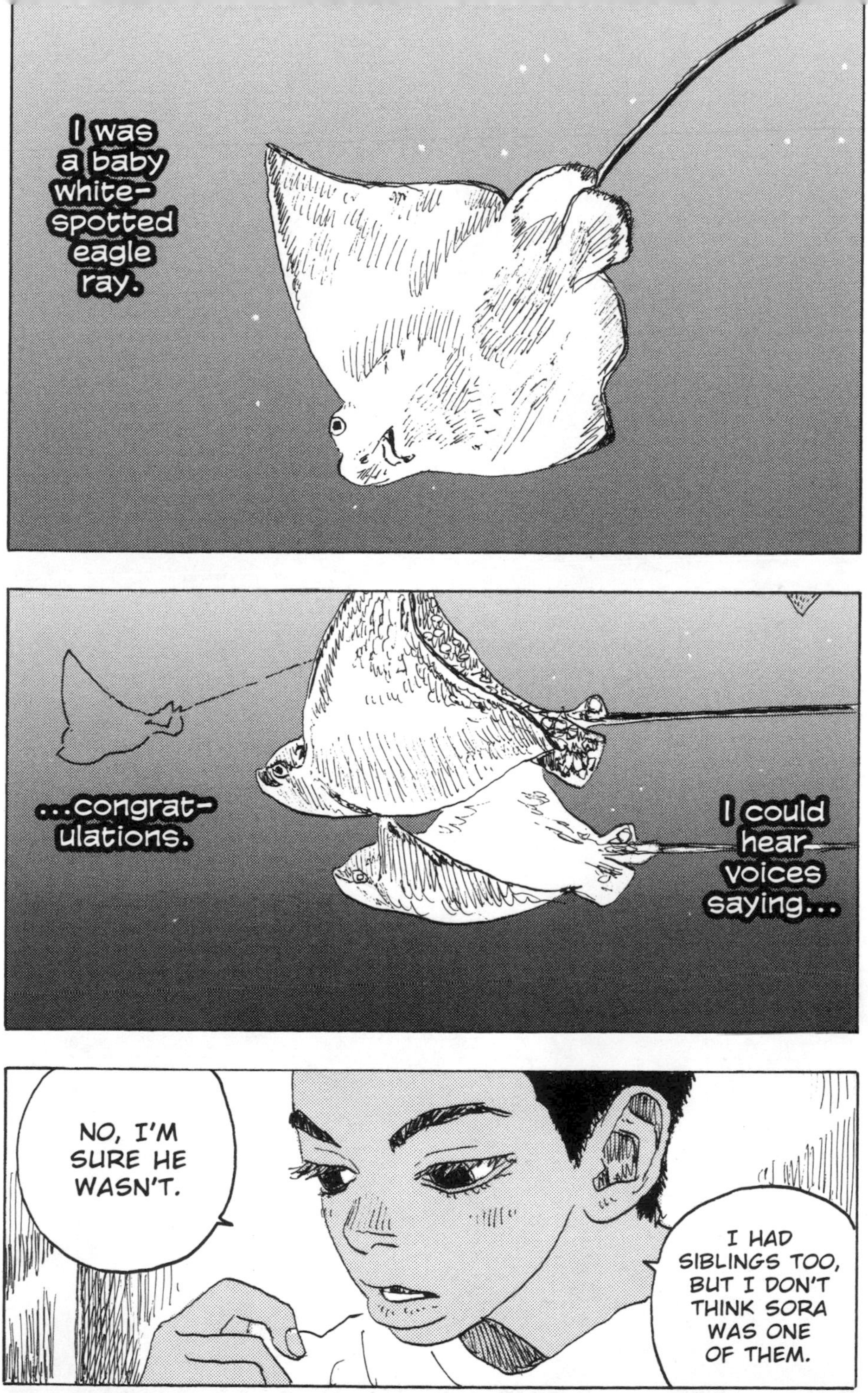
I was a baby white-spotted eagle ray.
I could hear voices saying...
...congrat-ulations.
I HAD SIBLINGS TOO, BUT I DON'T THINK SORA WAS ONE OF THEM.
NO, I'M SURE HE WASN'T.

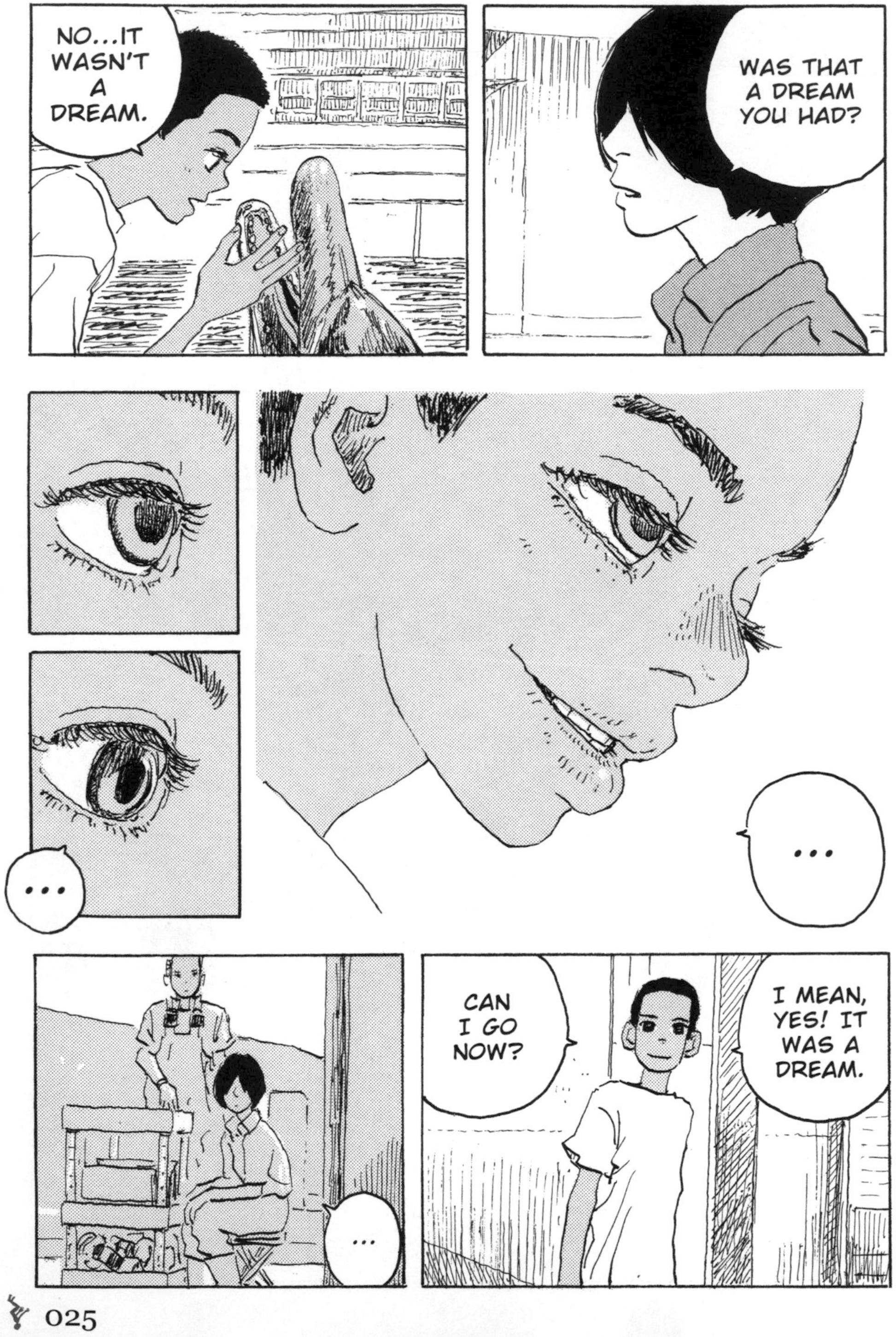
WAS THAT A DREAM YOU HAD?
NO...IT WASN'T A DREAM.
...
...
I MEAN, YES! IT WAS A DREAM.
CAN I GO NOW?
...

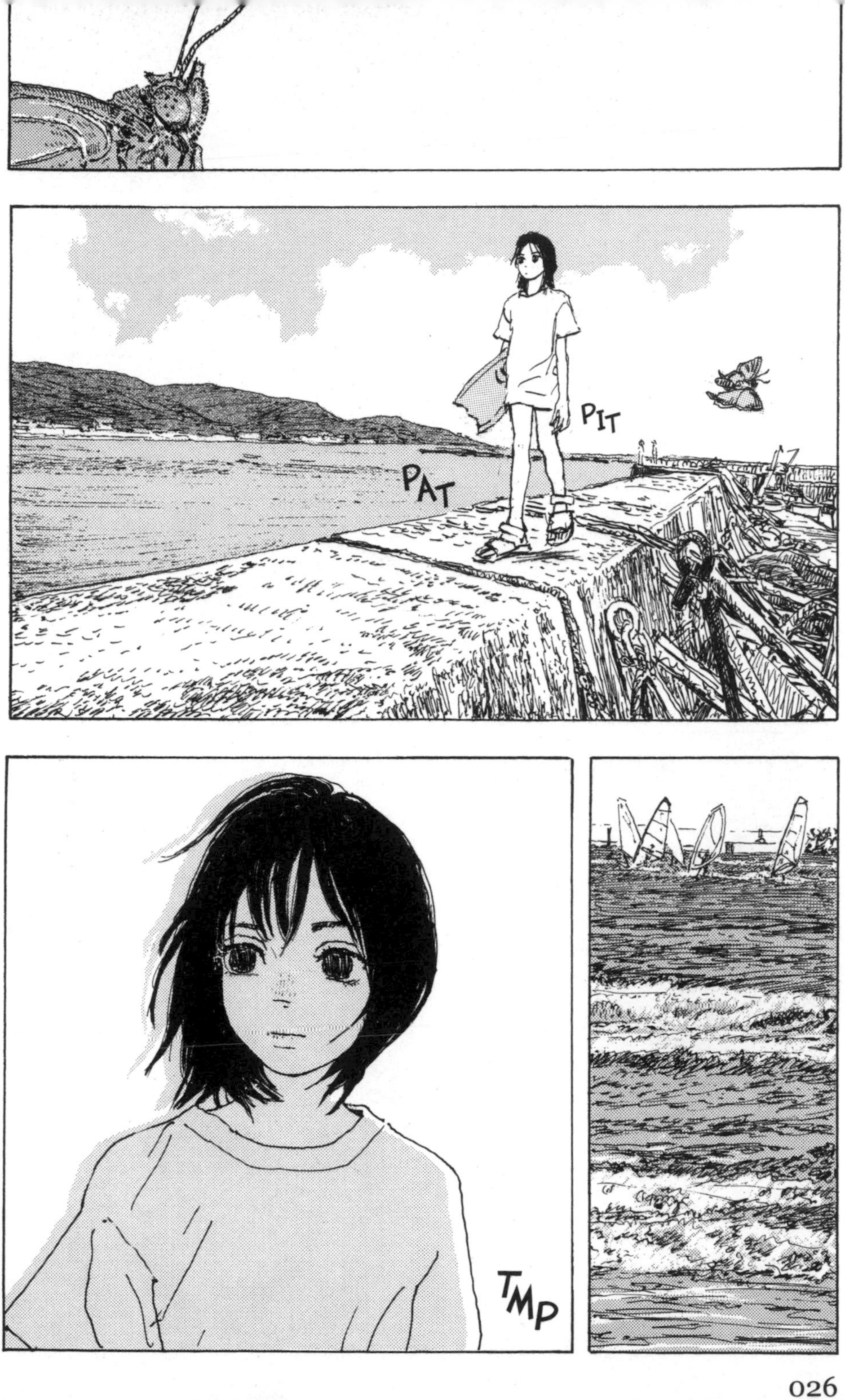
PIT
PAT
TMP

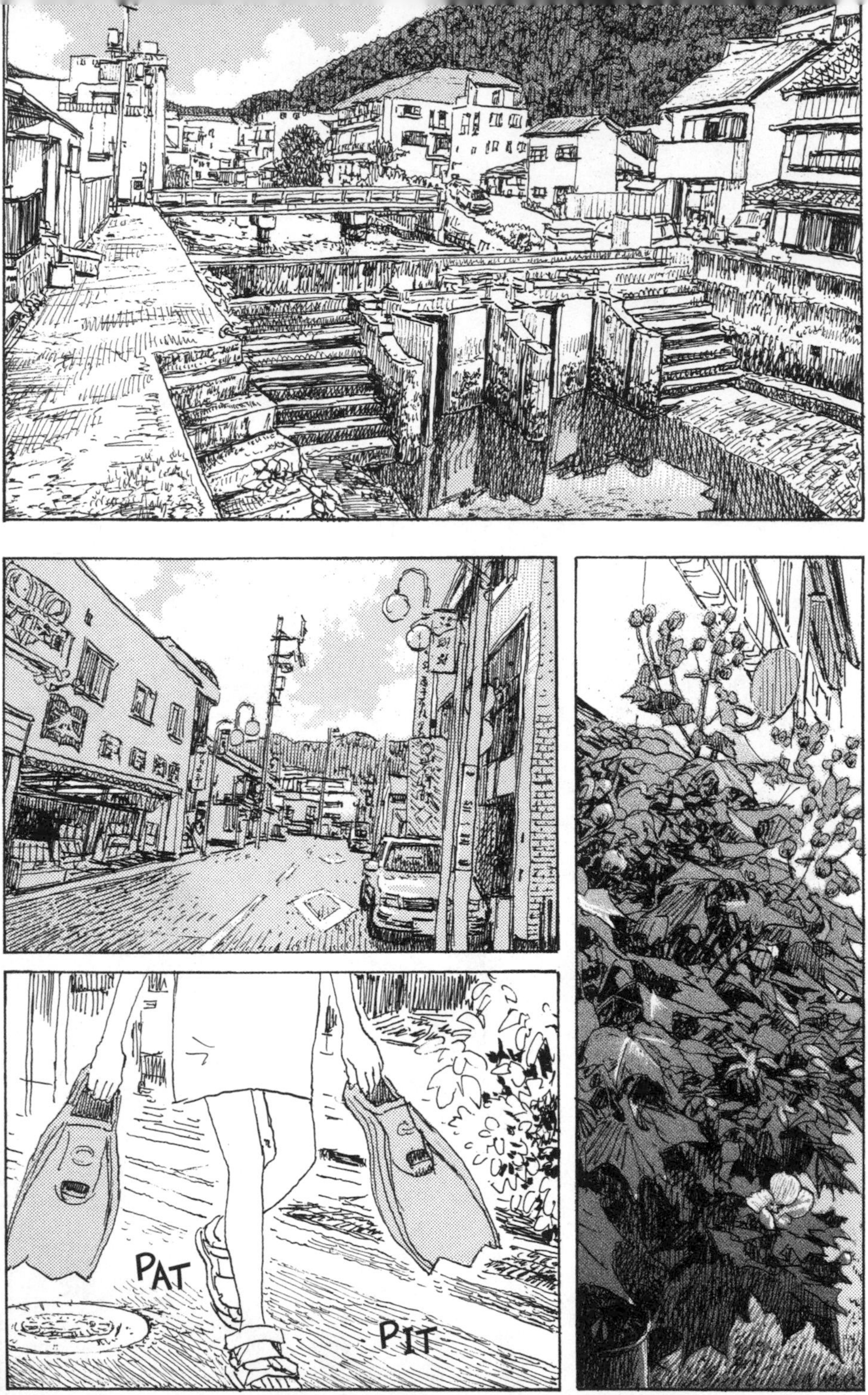
PAT
PIT

JING
JING
JING

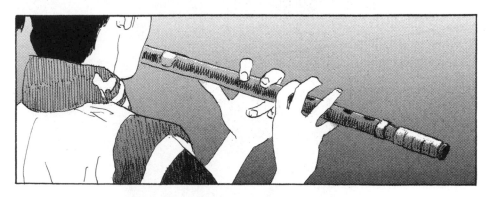

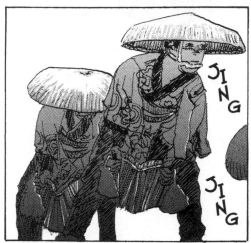

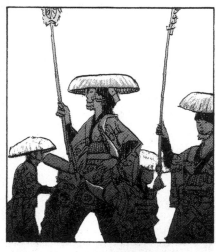

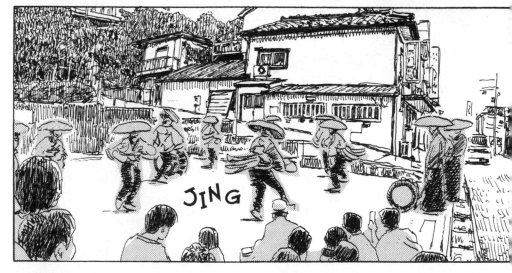

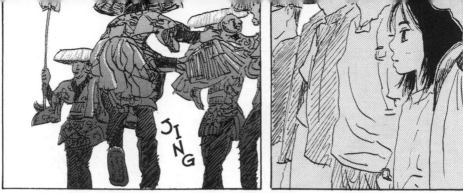

JING

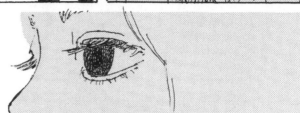

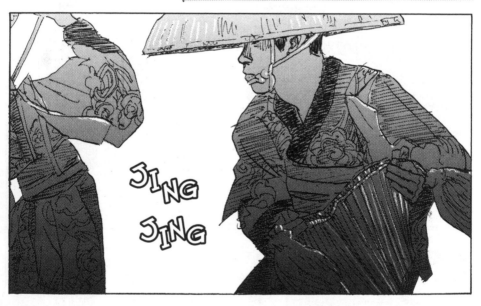

JING
JING

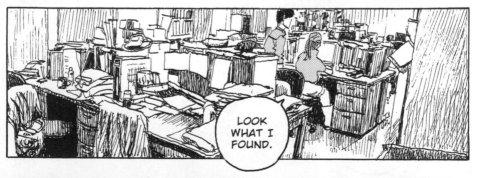

LOOK WHAT I FOUND.

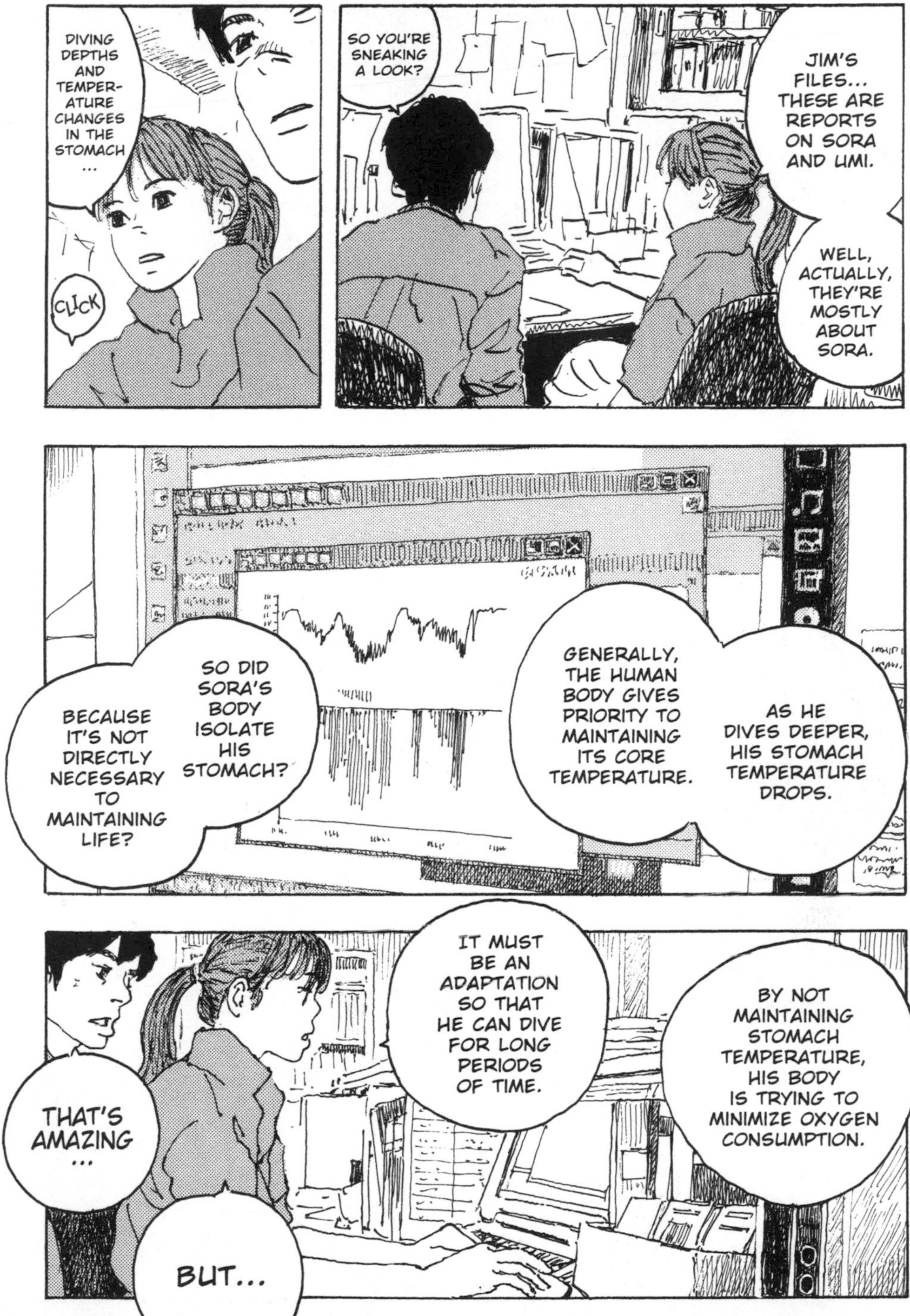
JIM'S FILES... THESE ARE REPORTS ON SORA AND UMI.
SO YOU'RE SNEAKING A LOOK?
WELL, ACTUALLY, THEY'RE MOSTLY ABOUT SORA.
DIVING DEPTHS AND TEMPER-ATURE CHANGES IN THE STOMACH ...
CLICK
AS HE DIVES DEEPER, HIS STOMACH TEMPERATURE DROPS.
GENERALLY, THE HUMAN BODY GIVES PRIORITY TO MAINTAINING ITS CORE TEMPERATURE.
SO DID SORA'S BODY ISOLATE HIS STOMACH?
BECAUSE IT'S NOT DIRECTLY NECESSARY TO MAINTAINING LIFE?
BY NOT MAINTAINING STOMACH TEMPERATURE, HIS BODY IS TRYING TO MINIMIZE OXYGEN CONSUMPTION.
IT MUST BE AN ADAPTATION SO THAT HE CAN DIVE FOR LONG PERIODS OF TIME.
THAT'S AMAZING ...
BUT...

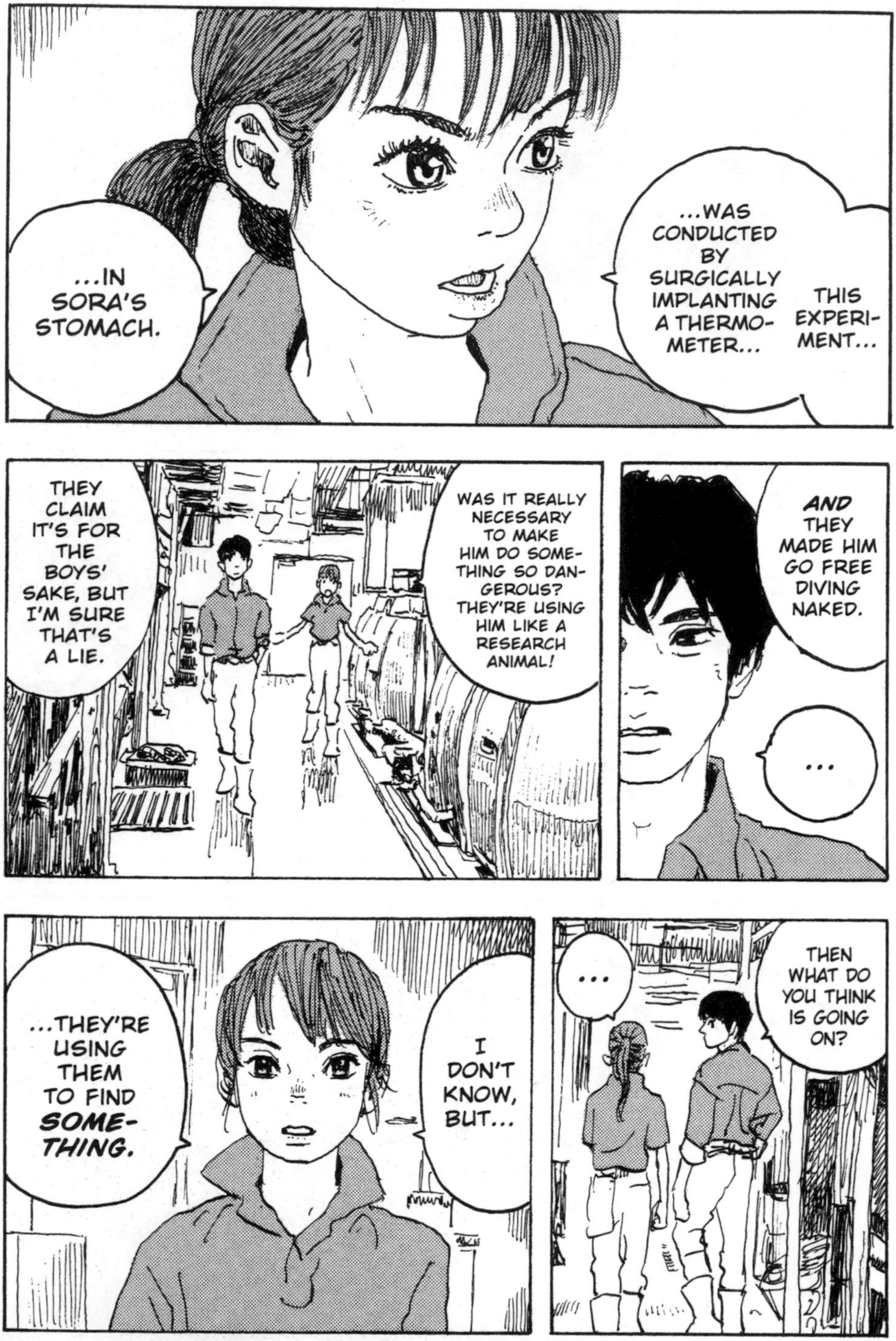
THIS EXPERIMENT...
...WAS CONDUCTED BY SURGICALLY IMPLANTING A THERMOMETER...
...IN SORA'S STOMACH.
AND THEY MADE HIM GO FREE DIVING NAKED.
...
WAS IT REALLY NECESSARY TO MAKE HIM DO SOMETHING SO DANGEROUS? THEY'RE USING HIM LIKE A RESEARCH ANIMAL!
THEY CLAIM IT'S FOR THE BOYS' SAKE, BUT I'M SURE THAT'S A LIE.
THEN WHAT DO YOU THINK IS GOING ON?
...
I DON'T KNOW, BUT...
...THEY'RE USING THEM TO FIND ***SOMETHING.***

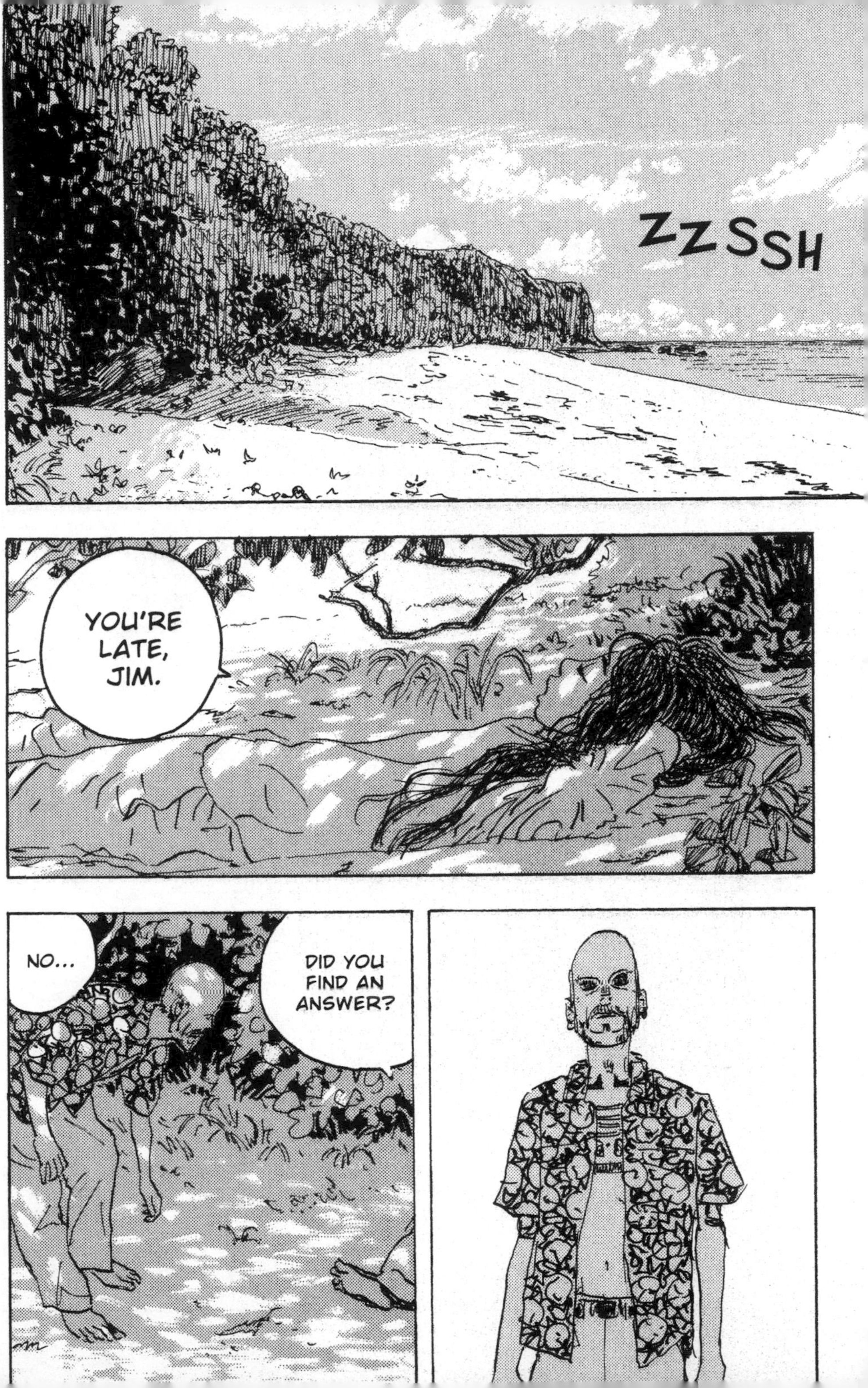
ZZSSH
YOU'RE LATE, JIM.
DID YOU FIND AN ANSWER?
NO...

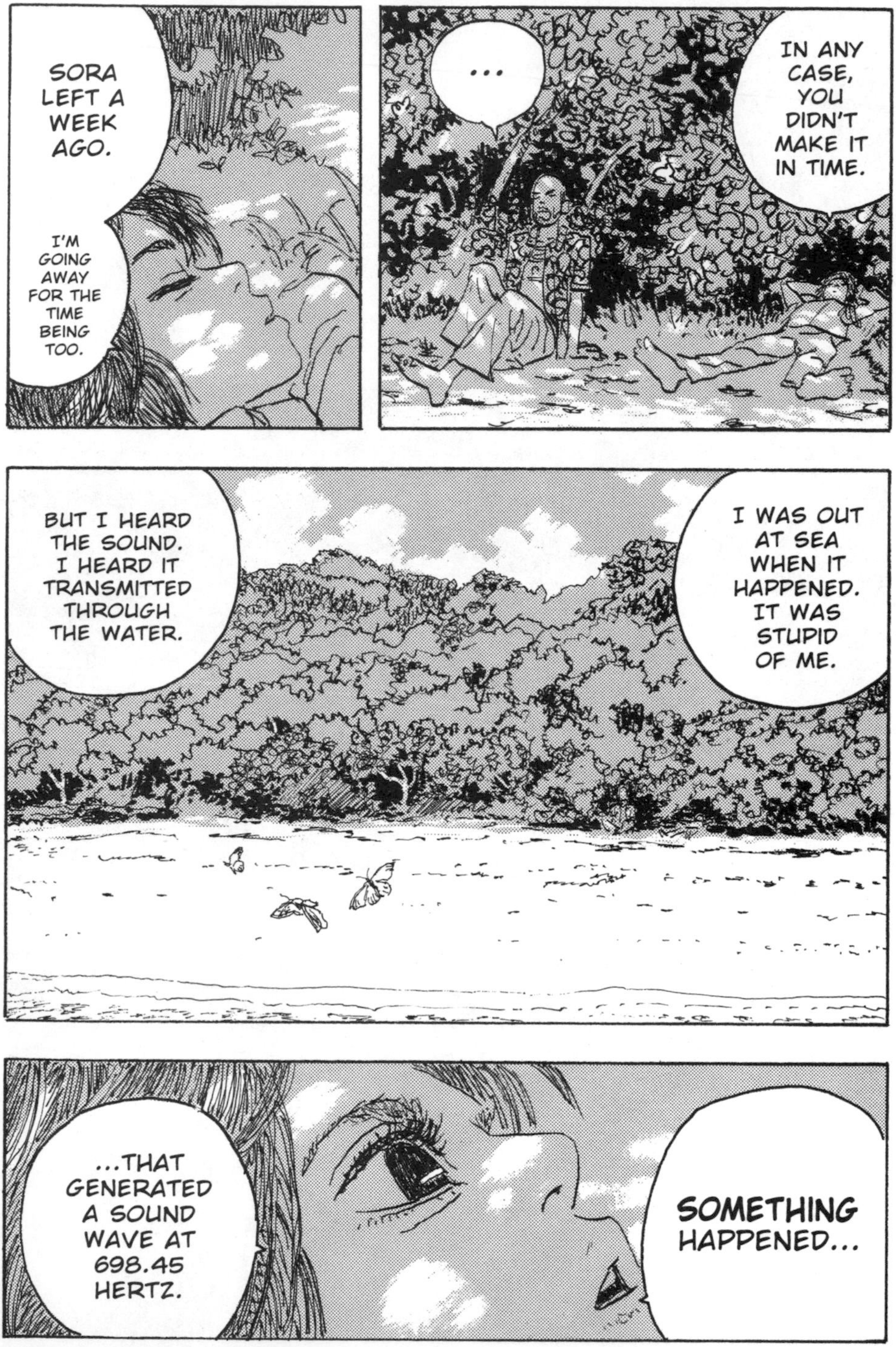
IN ANY CASE, YOU DIDN'T MAKE IT IN TIME.
...
SORA LEFT A WEEK AGO.
I'M GOING AWAY FOR THE TIME BEING TOO.
I WAS OUT AT SEA WHEN IT HAPPENED. IT WAS STUPID OF ME.
BUT I HEARD THE SOUND. I HEARD IT TRANSMITTED THROUGH THE WATER.
SOMETHING HAPPENED...
...THAT GENERATED A SOUND WAVE AT 698.45 HERTZ.

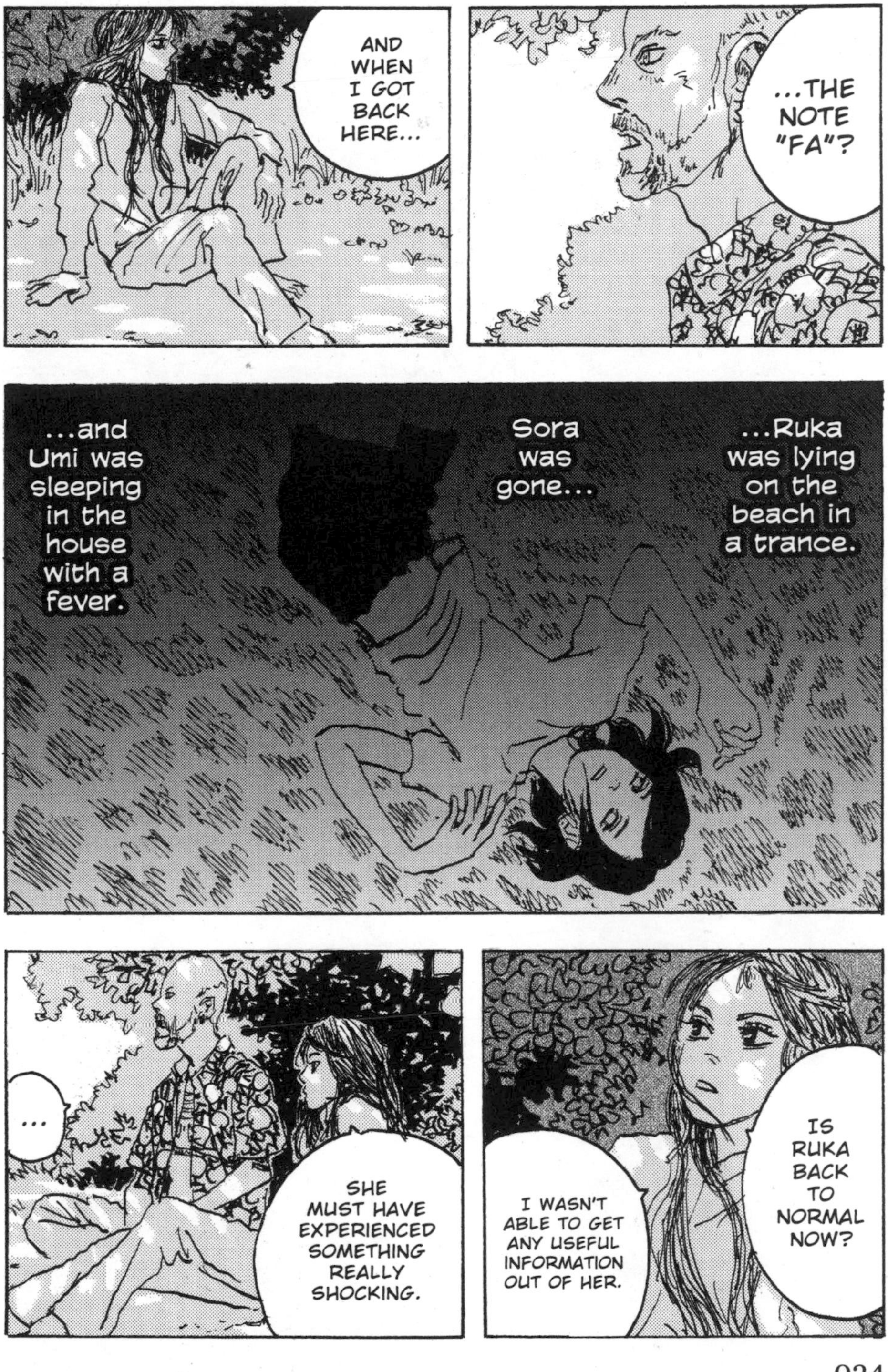
...THE NOTE "FA"?
AND WHEN I GOT BACK HERE...
...Ruka was lying on the beach in a trance.
Sora was gone...
...and Umi was sleeping in the house with a fever.
IS RUKA BACK TO NORMAL NOW?
I WASN'T ABLE TO GET ANY USEFUL INFORMATION OUT OF HER.
...
SHE MUST HAVE EXPERIENCED SOMETHING REALLY SHOCKING.

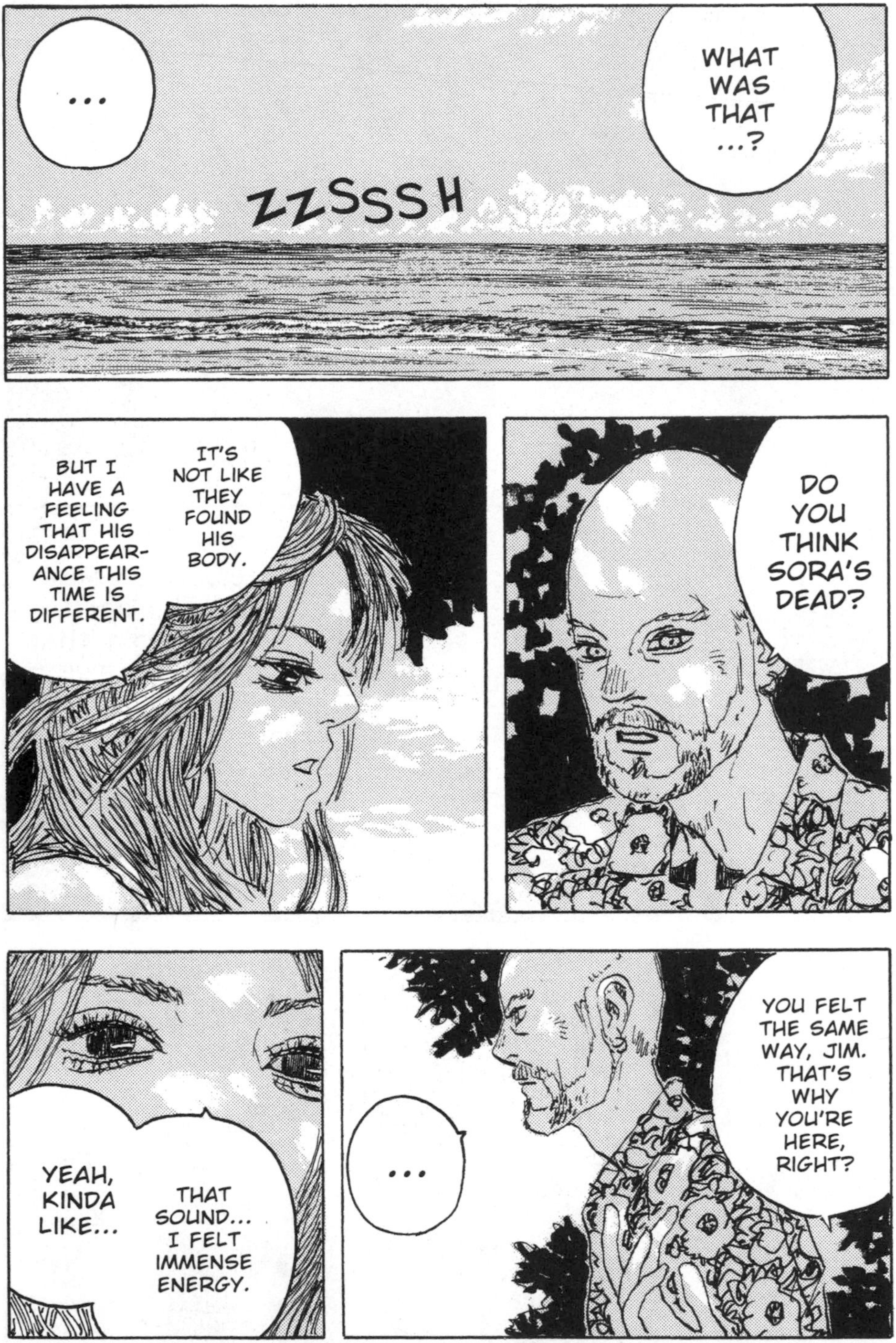
WHAT WAS THAT ...?
...
ZZSSSH
DO YOU THINK SORA'S DEAD?
IT'S NOT LIKE THEY FOUND HIS BODY.
BUT I HAVE A FEELING THAT HIS DISAPPEAR-ANCE THIS TIME IS DIFFERENT.
YOU FELT THE SAME WAY, JIM. THAT'S WHY YOU'RE HERE, RIGHT?
...
THAT SOUND... I FELT IMMENSE ENERGY.
YEAH, KINDA LIKE...

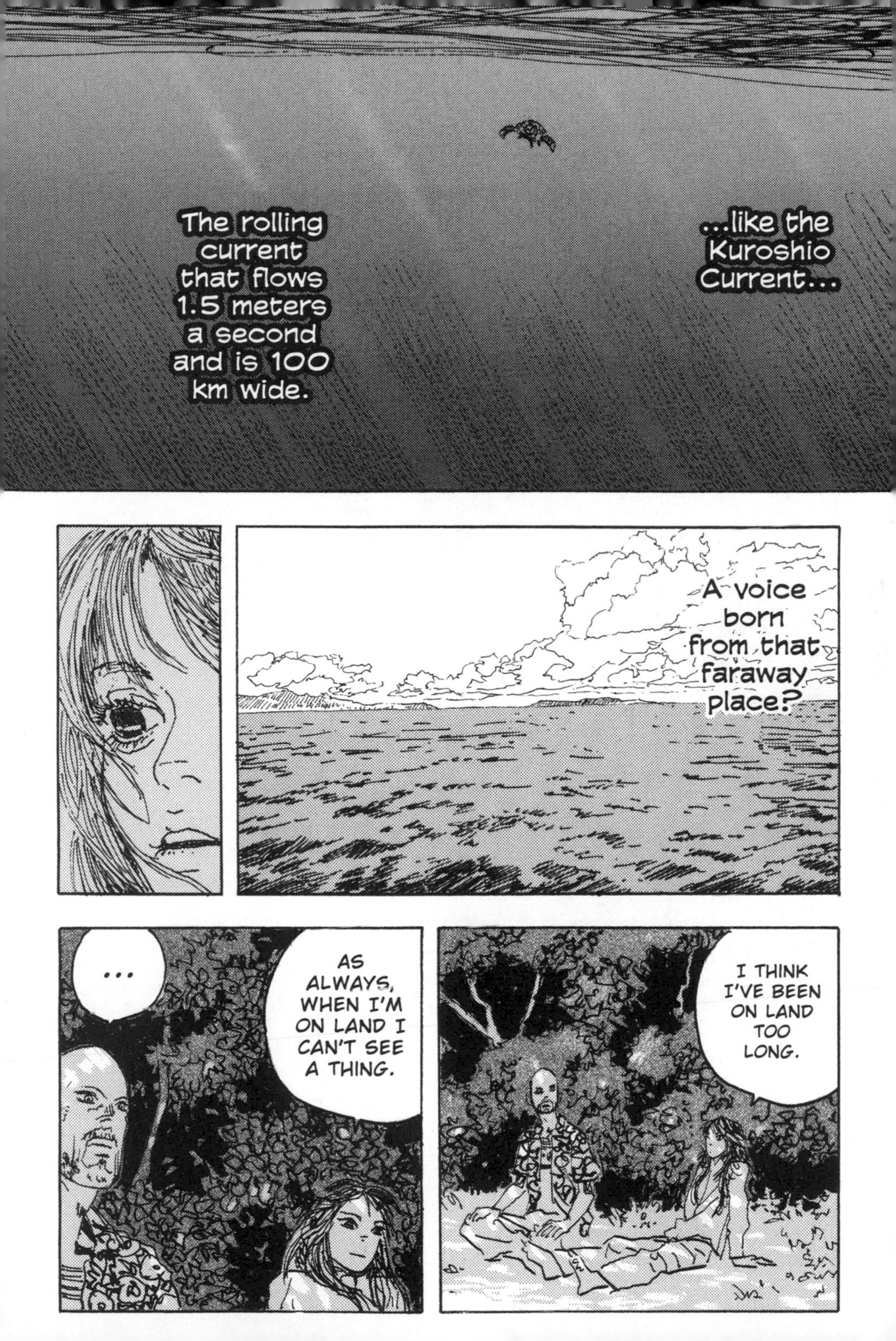
...like the Kuroshio Current...
The rolling current that flows 1.5 meters a second and is 100 km wide.
A voice born from that faraway place?
I THINK I'VE BEEN ON LAND TOO LONG.
AS ALWAYS, WHEN I'M ON LAND I CAN'T SEE A THING.
...

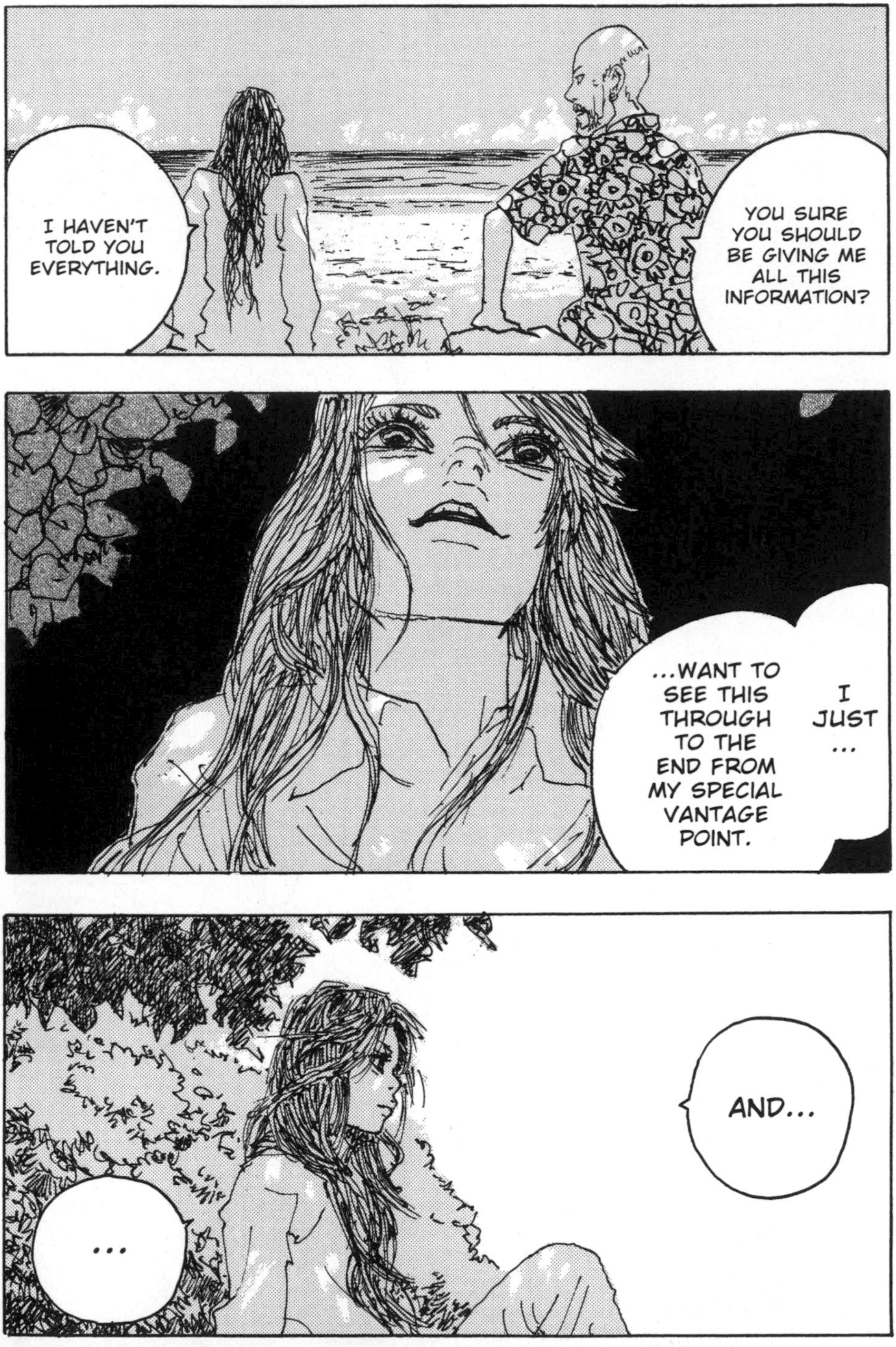
YOU SURE YOU SHOULD BE GIVING ME ALL THIS INFORMATION?
I HAVEN'T TOLD YOU EVERYTHING.
I JUST ...
...WANT TO SEE THIS THROUGH TO THE END FROM MY SPECIAL VANTAGE POINT.
AND...
...

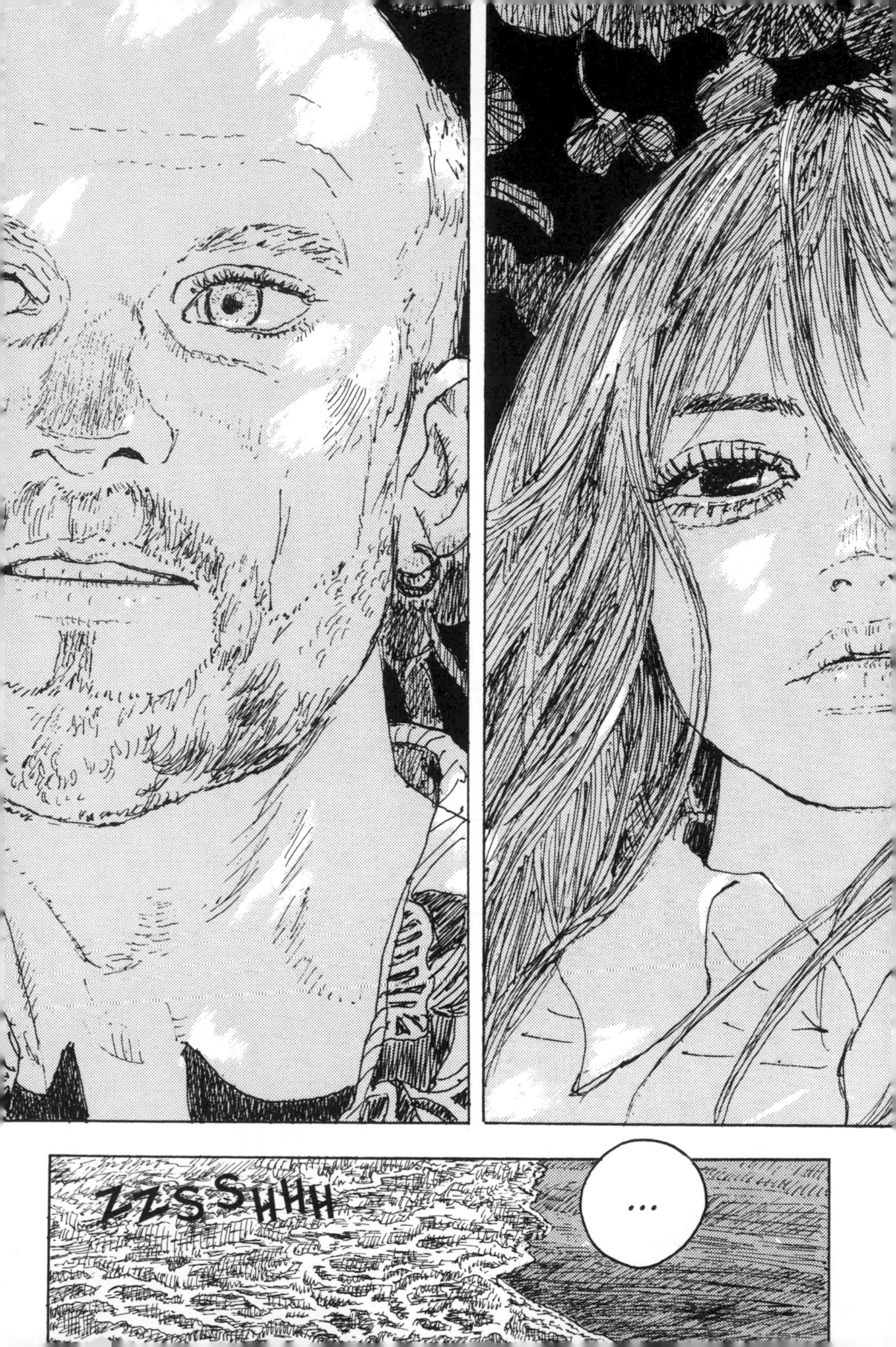
ZZSSHHH
...

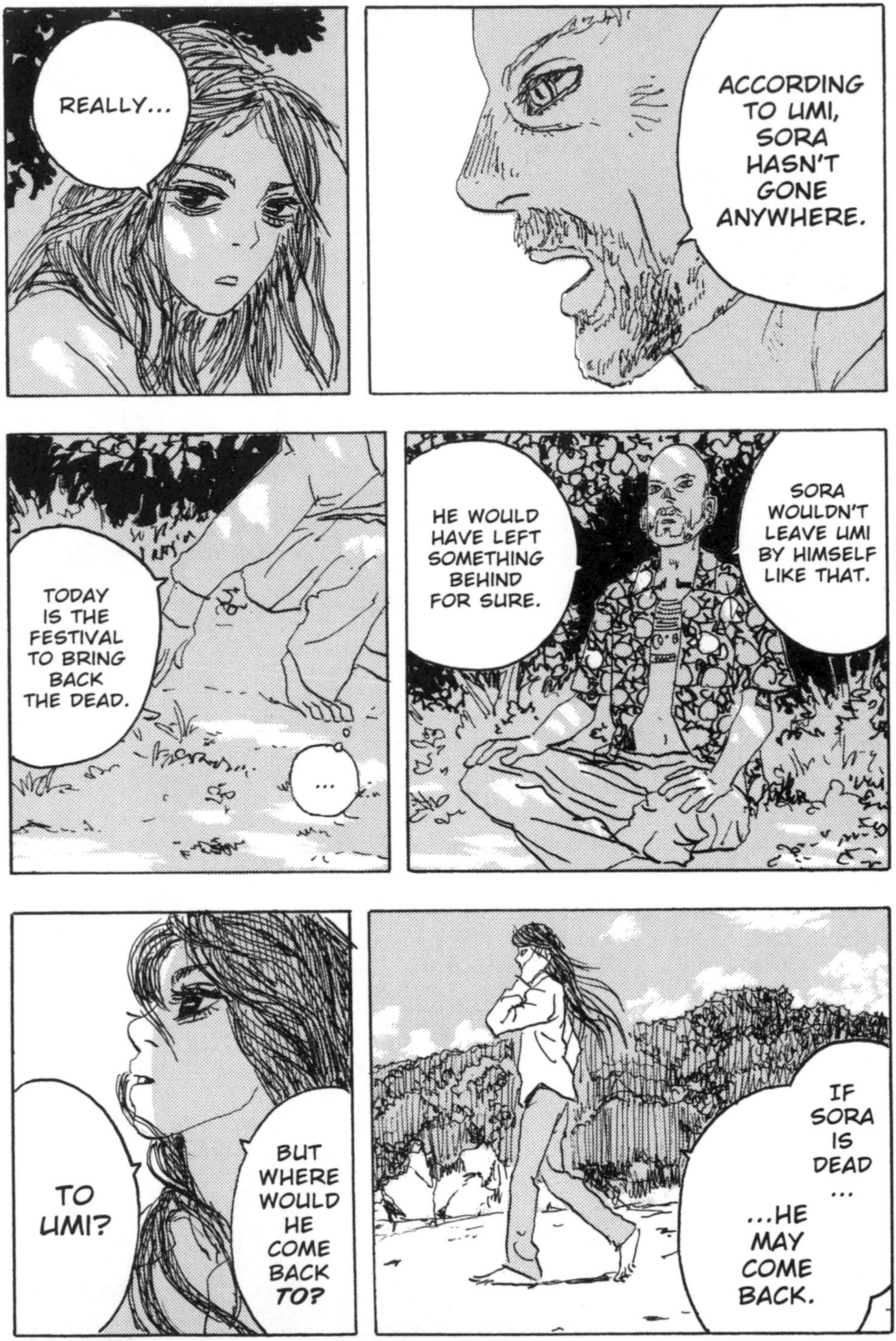
ACCORDING TO UMI, SORA HASN'T GONE ANYWHERE.
REALLY...
SORA WOULDN'T LEAVE UMI BY HIMSELF LIKE THAT.
HE WOULD HAVE LEFT SOMETHING BEHIND FOR SURE.
TODAY IS THE FESTIVAL TO BRING BACK THE DEAD.
...
IF SORA IS DEAD ...
...HE MAY COME BACK.
BUT WHERE WOULD HE COME BACK *TO?*
TO UMI?

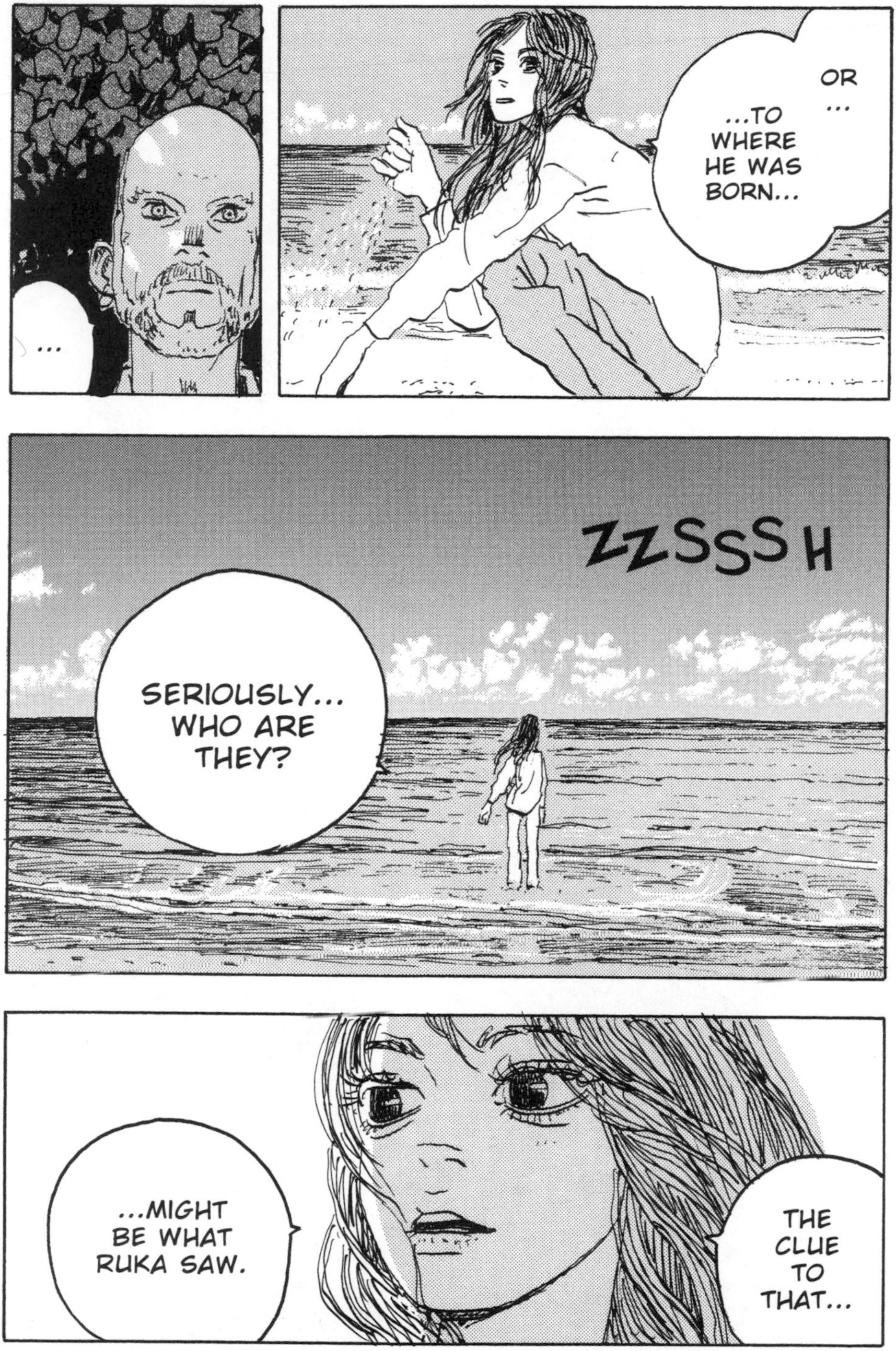
OR ...
...TO WHERE HE WAS BORN...
...
ZZSSSH
SERIOUSLY... WHO ARE THEY?
THE CLUE TO THAT...
...MIGHT BE WHAT RUKA SAW.

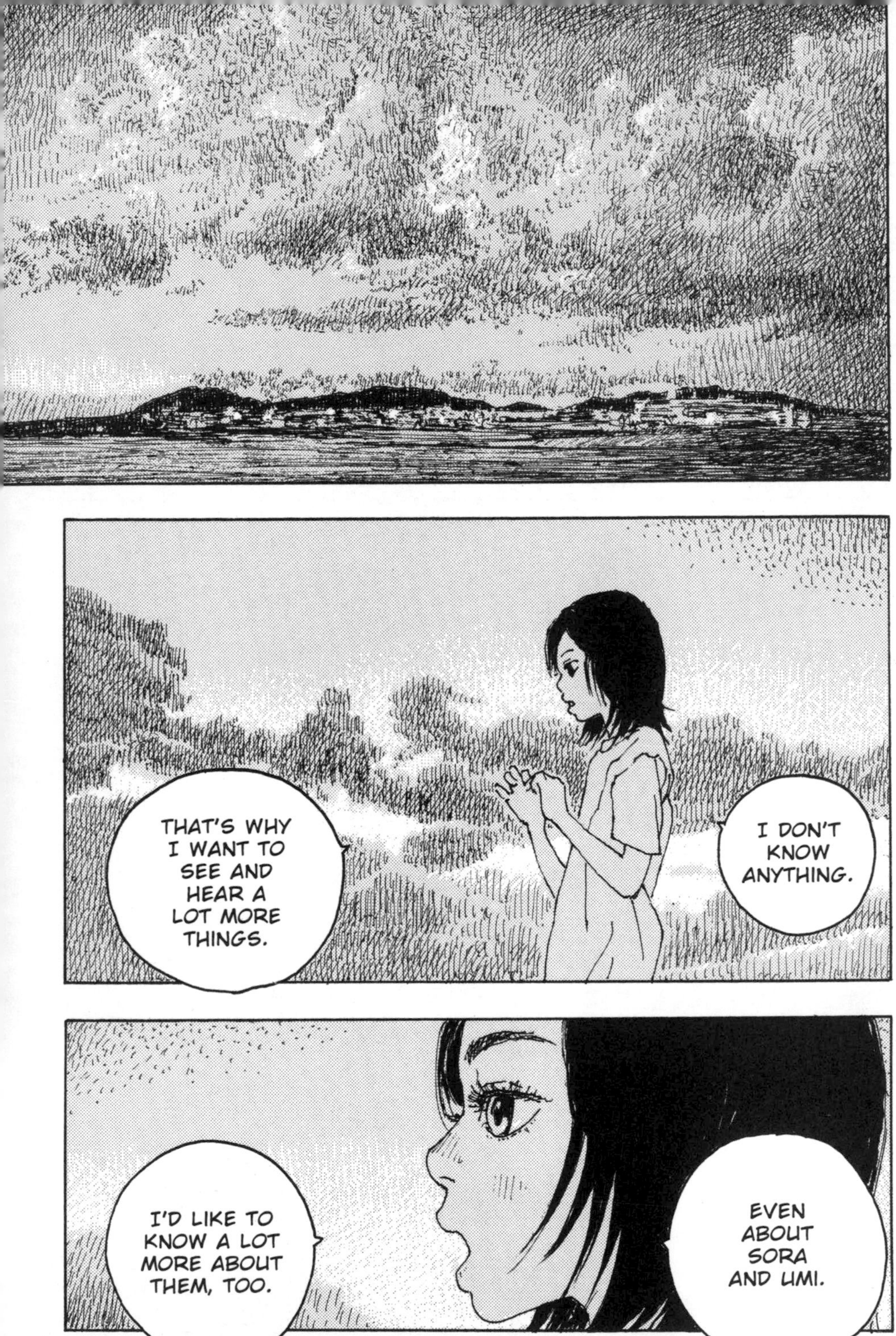
I DON'T KNOW ANYTHING.
THAT'S WHY I WANT TO SEE AND HEAR A LOT MORE THINGS.
EVEN ABOUT SORA AND UMI.
I'D LIKE TO KNOW A LOT MORE ABOUT THEM, TOO.

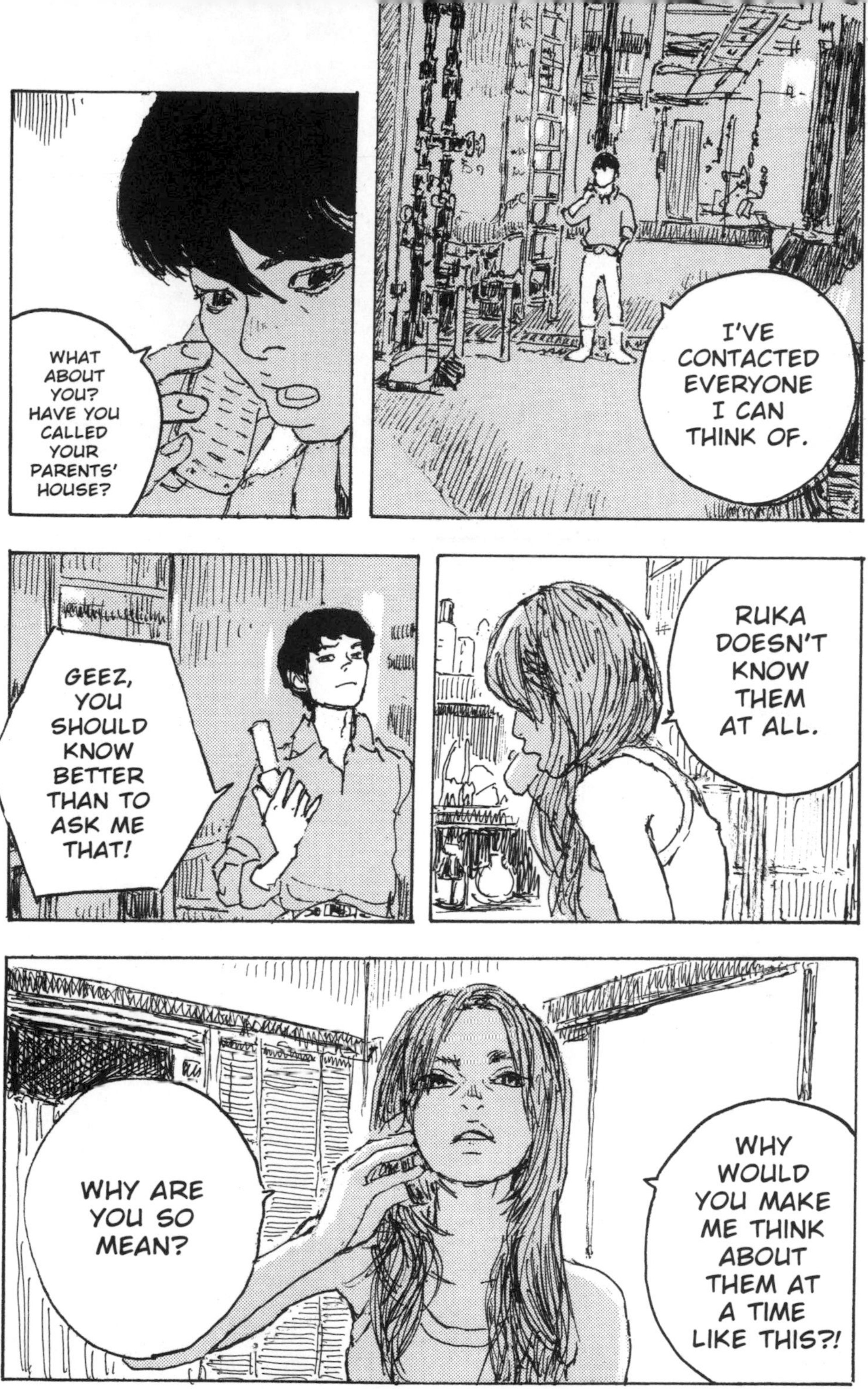
I'VE CONTACTED EVERYONE I CAN THINK OF.
WHAT ABOUT YOU? HAVE YOU CALLED YOUR PARENTS' HOUSE?
RUKA DOESN'T KNOW THEM AT ALL.
GEEZ, YOU SHOULD KNOW BETTER THAN TO ASK ME THAT!
WHY WOULD YOU MAKE ME THINK ABOUT THEM AT A TIME LIKE THIS?!
WHY ARE YOU SO MEAN?

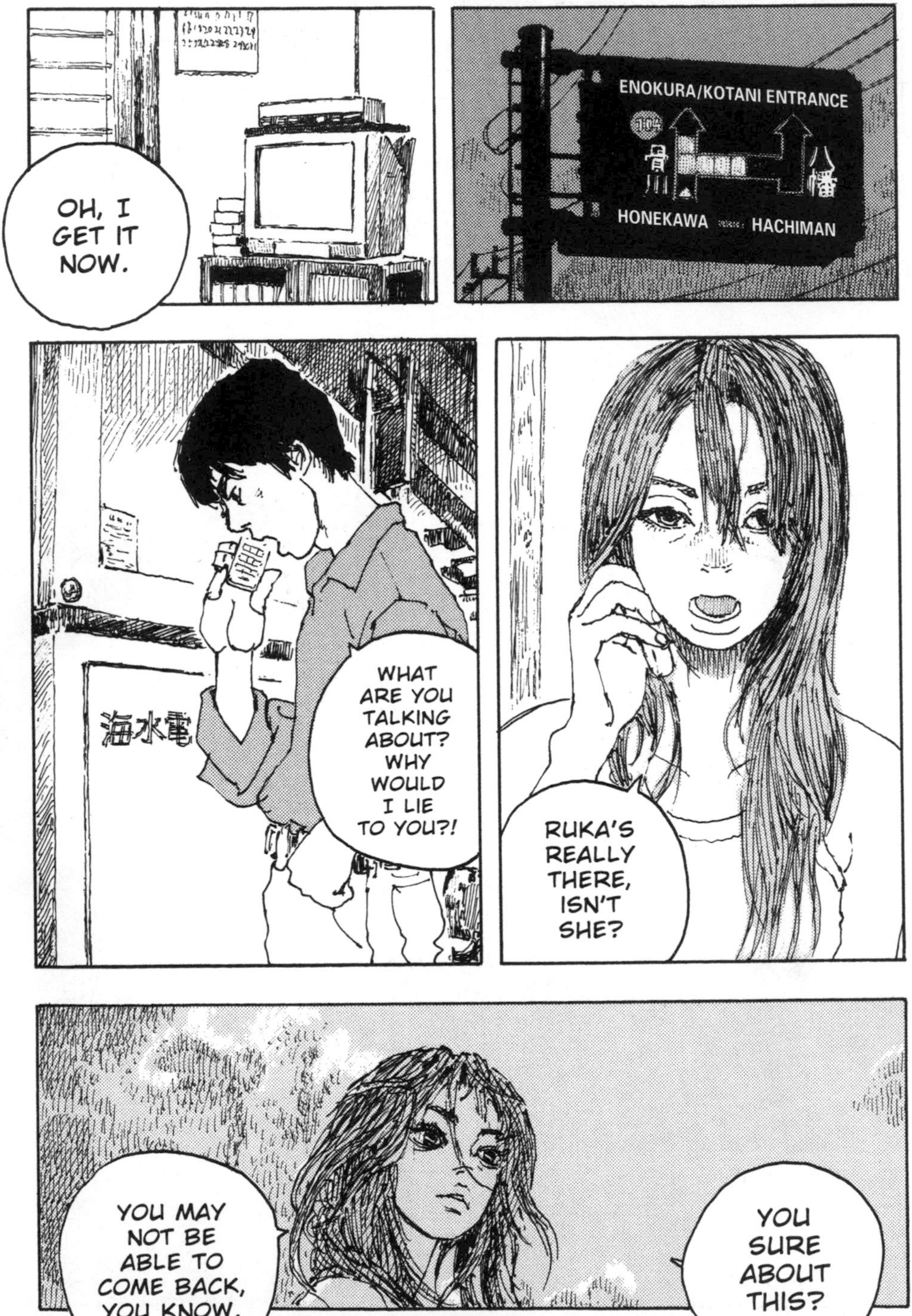
ENOKURA/KOTANI ENTRANCE
104
骨川
八幡
HONEKAWA
HACHIMAN
OH, I GET IT NOW.
RUKA'S REALLY THERE, ISN'T SHE?
WHAT ARE YOU TALKING ABOUT? WHY WOULD I LIE TO YOU?!
YOU SURE ABOUT THIS?
YOU MAY NOT BE ABLE TO COME BACK, YOU KNOW.

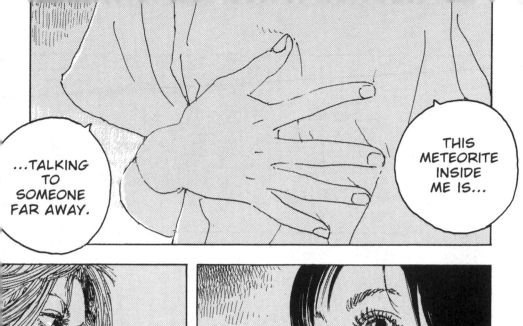

THIS METEORITE INSIDE ME IS...
...TALKING TO SOMEONE FAR AWAY.
I...
...HAVE TO GO.
WHRR RRR RRR

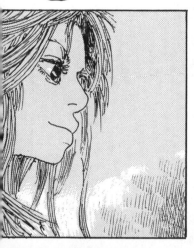

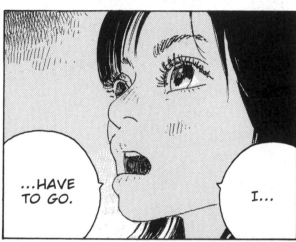

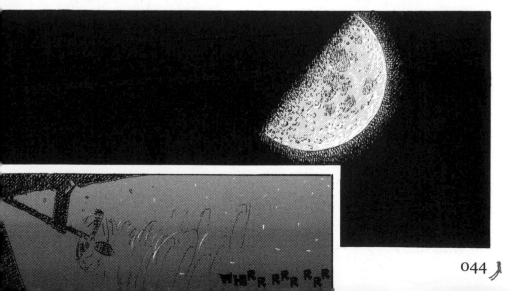

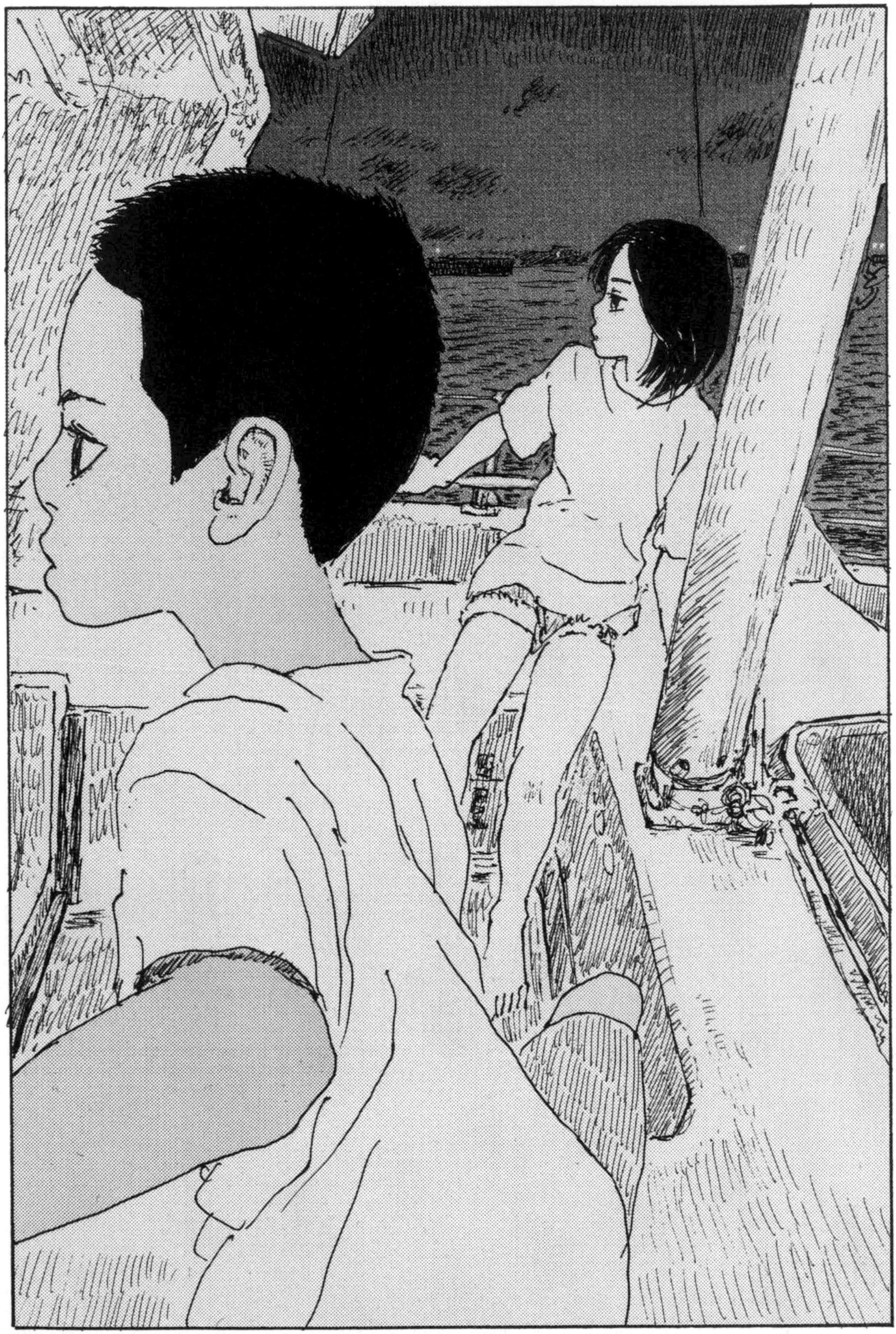

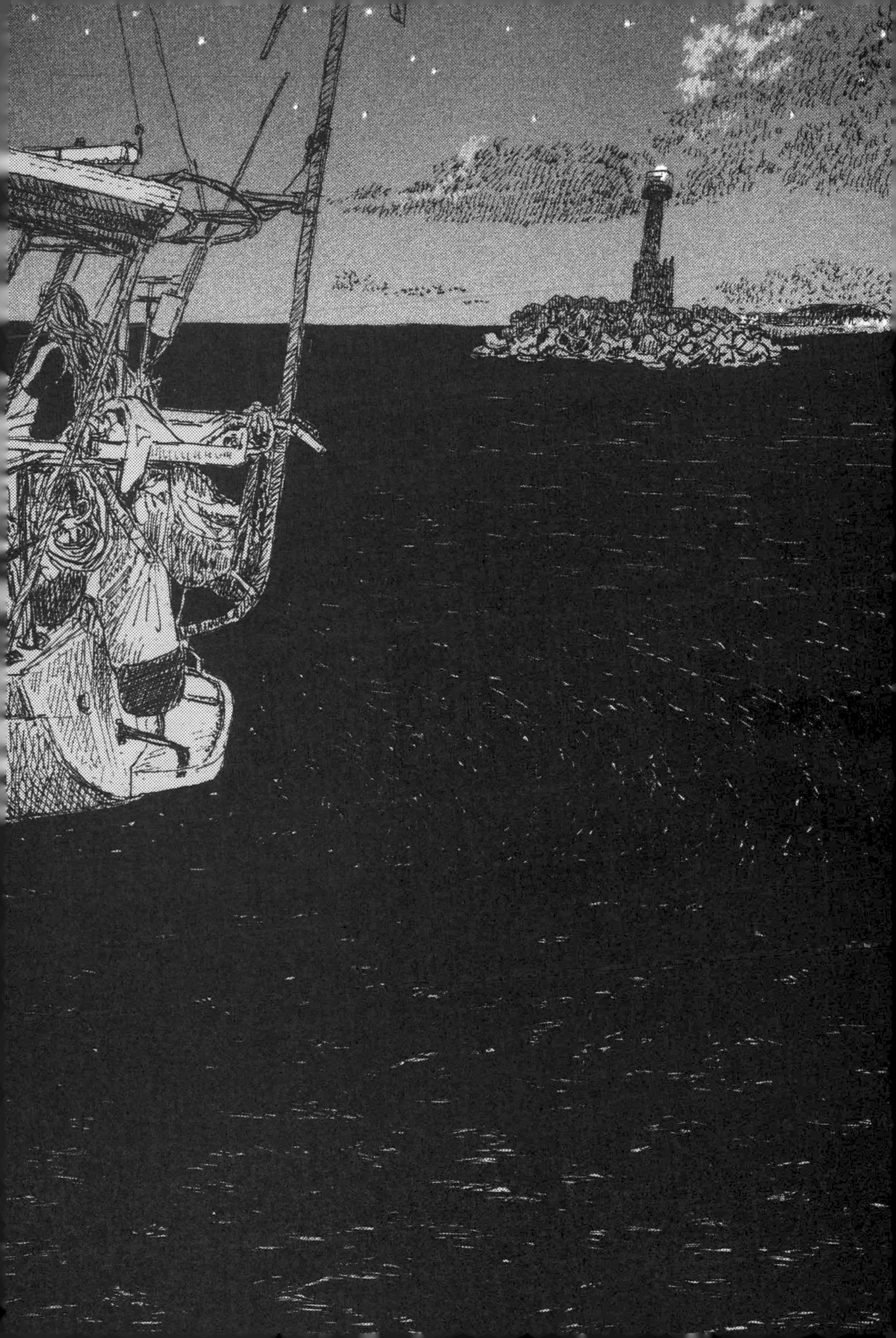

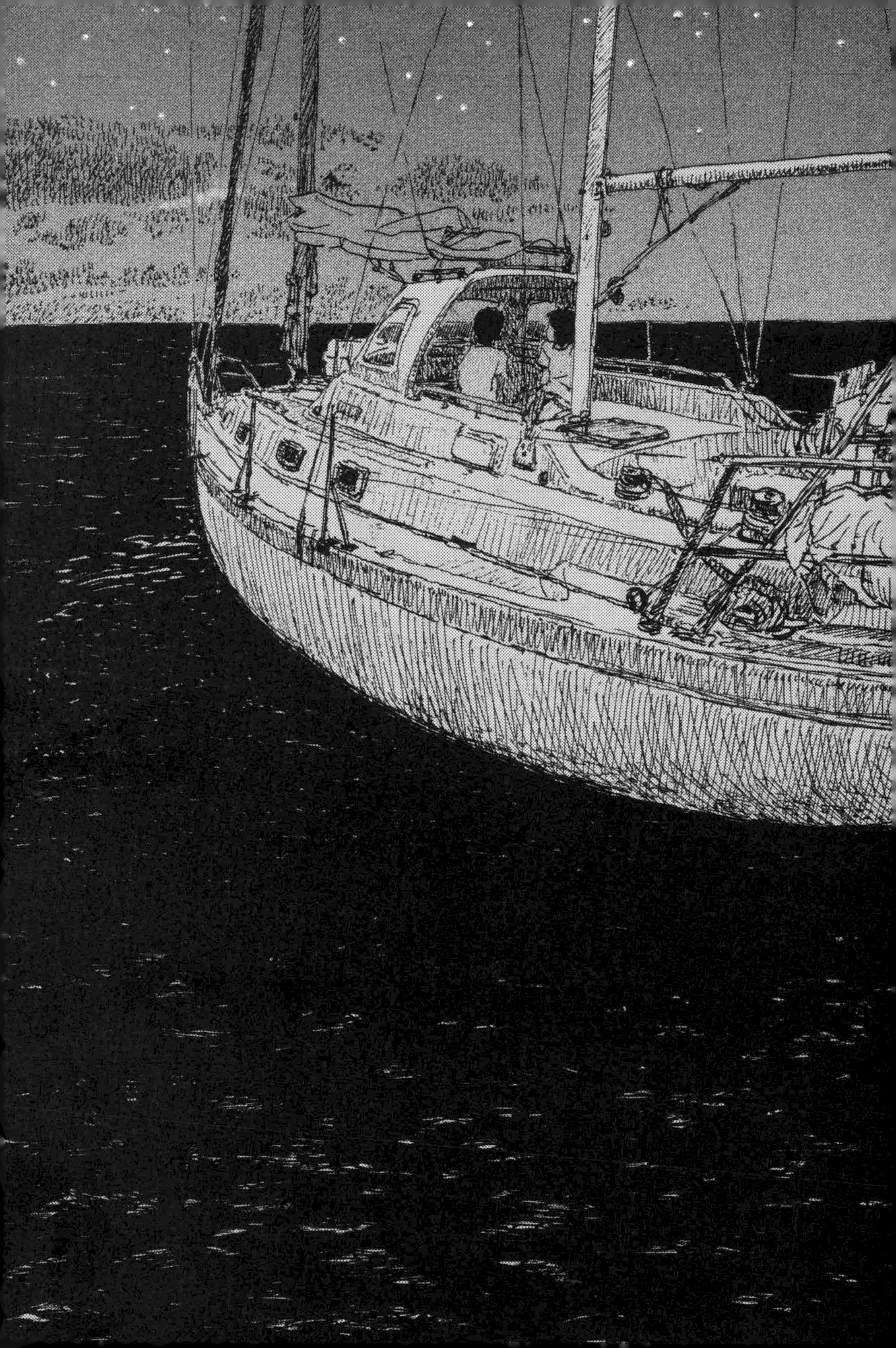

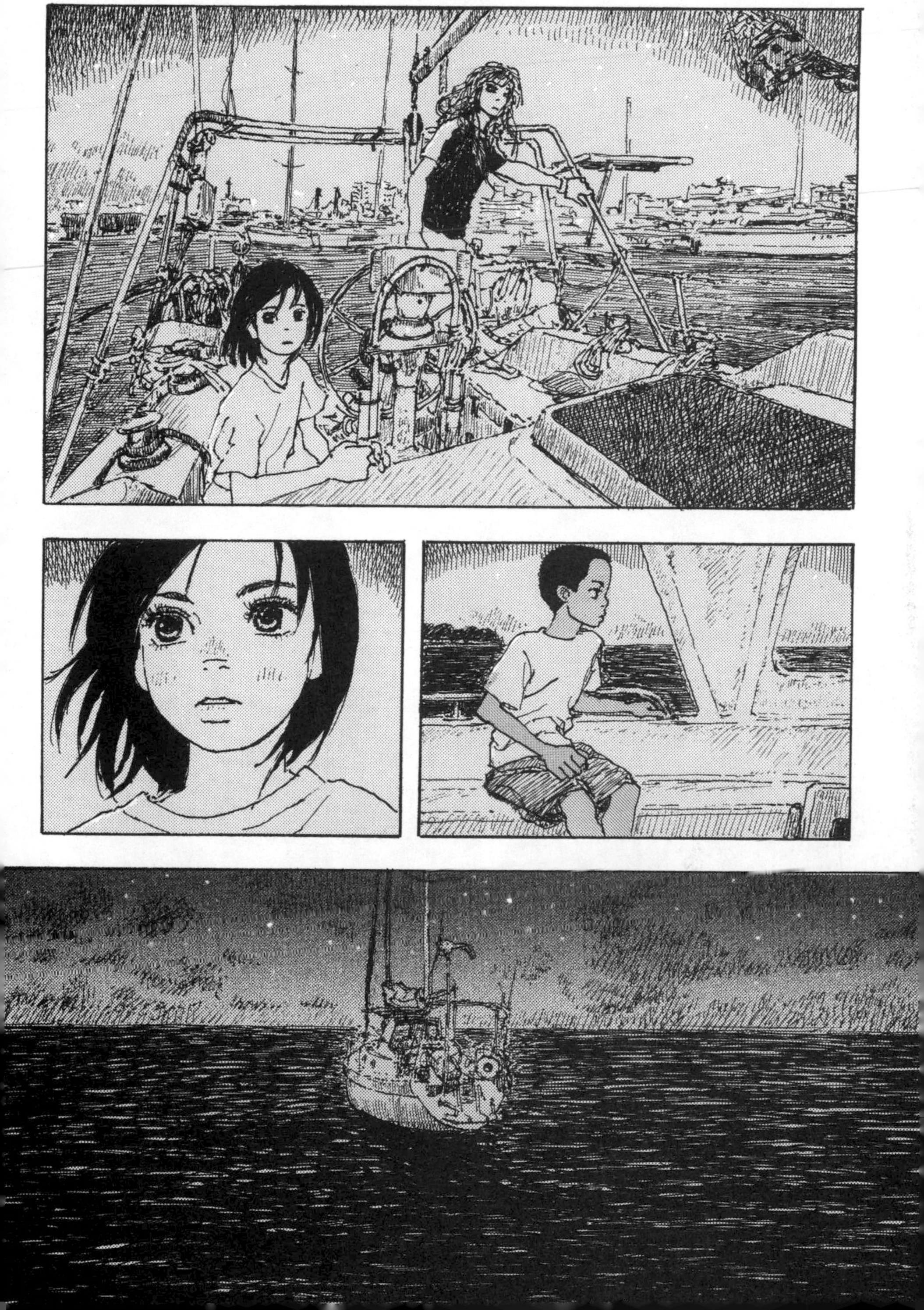

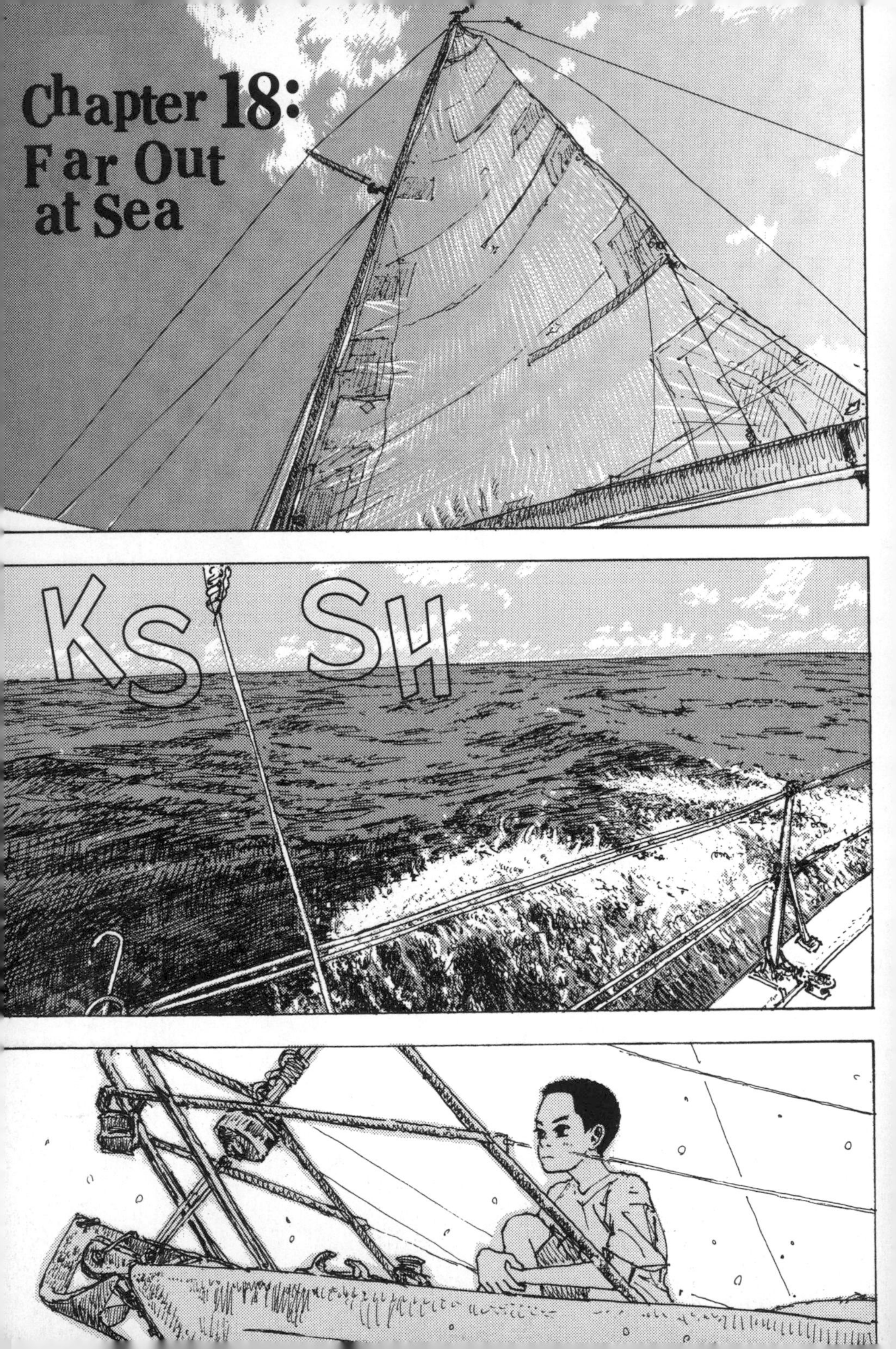
Chapter 18: Far Out at Sea
KS SH

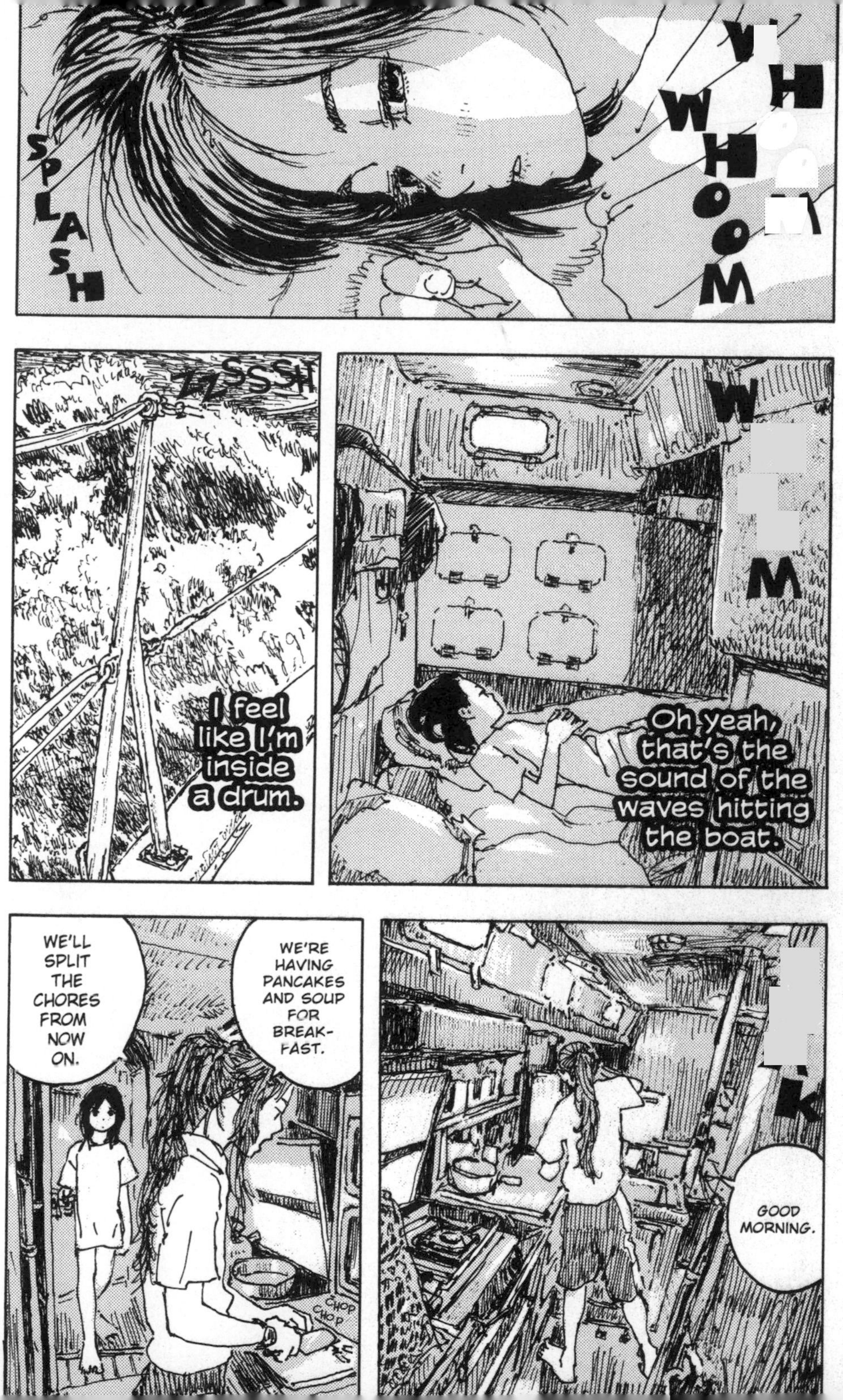
WHOOM
SPLASH
Oh yeah, that's the sound of the waves hitting the boat.
ZZSSSH
I feel like I'm inside a drum.
GOOD MORNING.
WE'RE HAVING PANCAKES AND SOUP FOR BREAKFAST.
WE'LL SPLIT THE CHORES FROM NOW ON.
CHOP CHOP

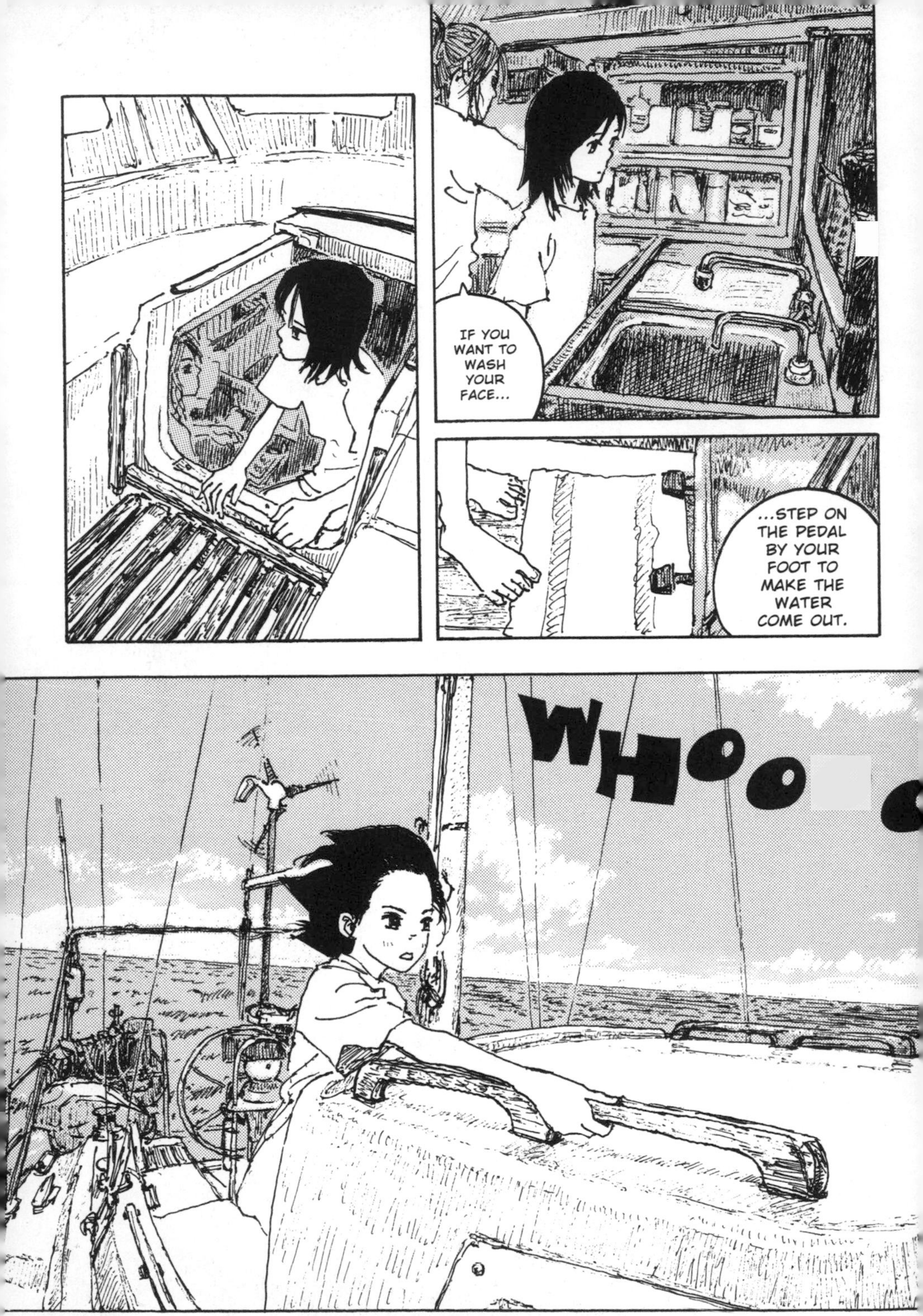
IF YOU WANT TO WASH YOUR FACE...
...STEP ON THE PEDAL BY YOUR FOOT TO MAKE THE WATER COME OUT.
WHOO

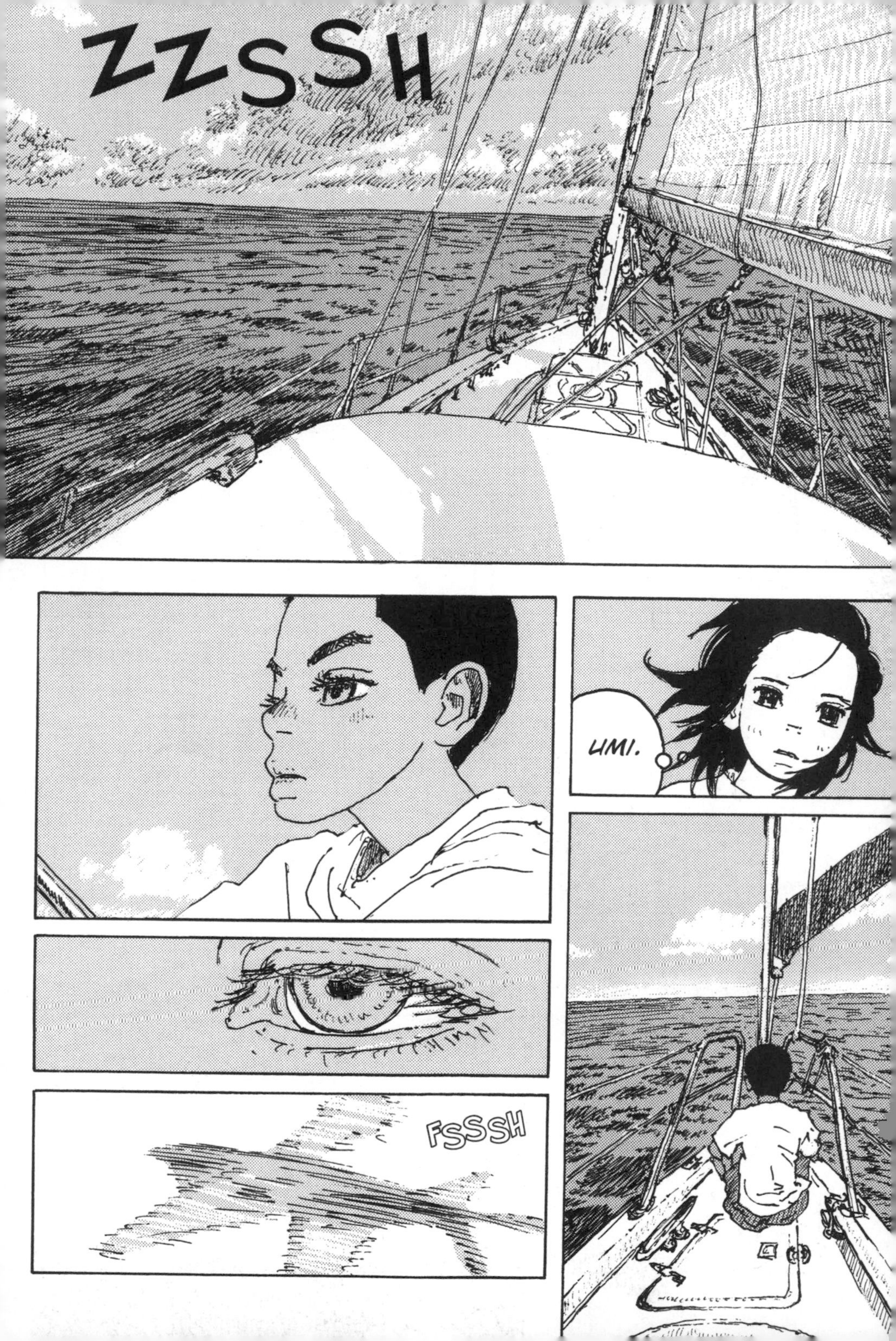
ZZSSH
UMI.
FSSSH

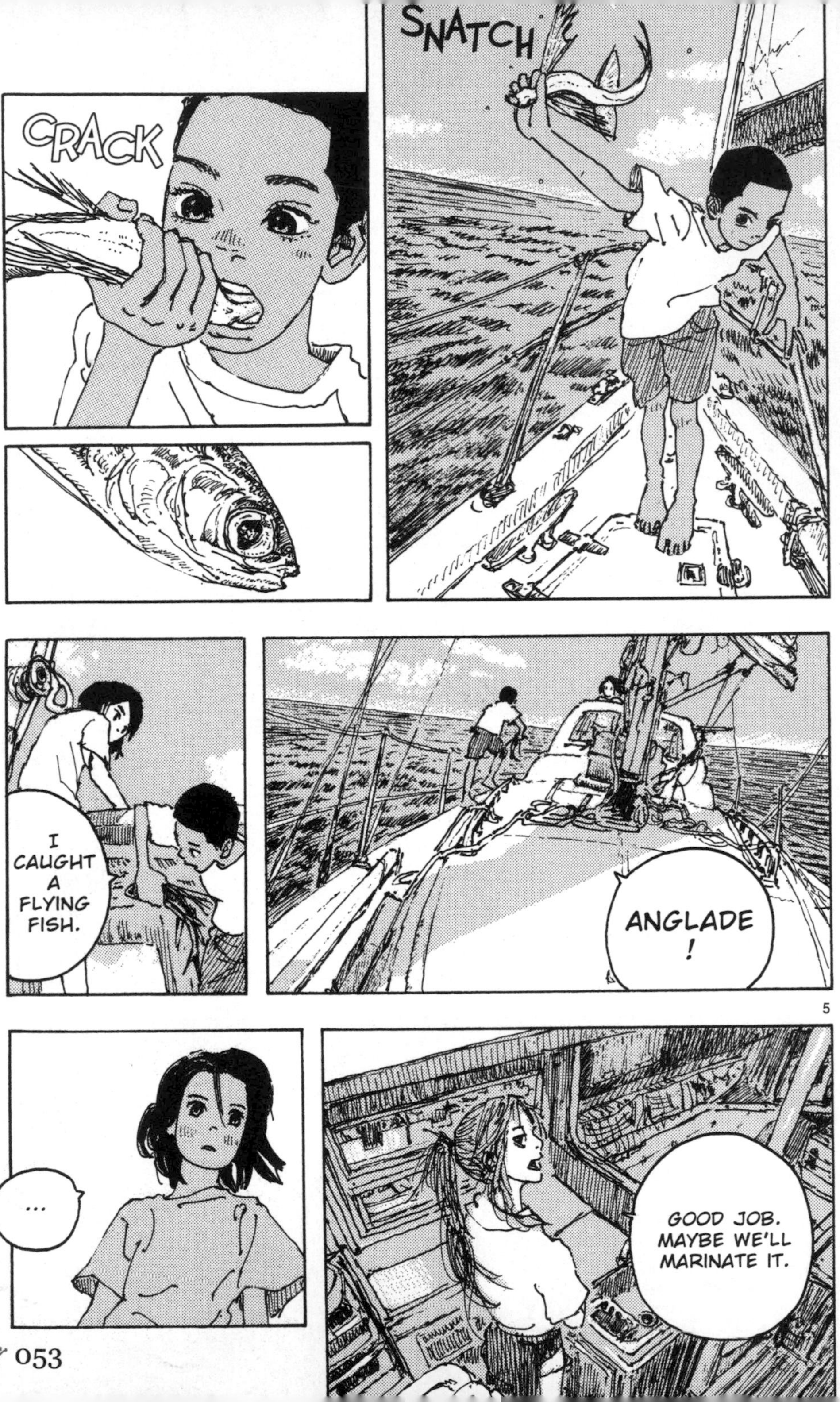
SNATCH
CRACK
ANGLADE !
I CAUGHT A FLYING FISH.
GOOD JOB. MAYBE WE'LL MARINATE IT.
...

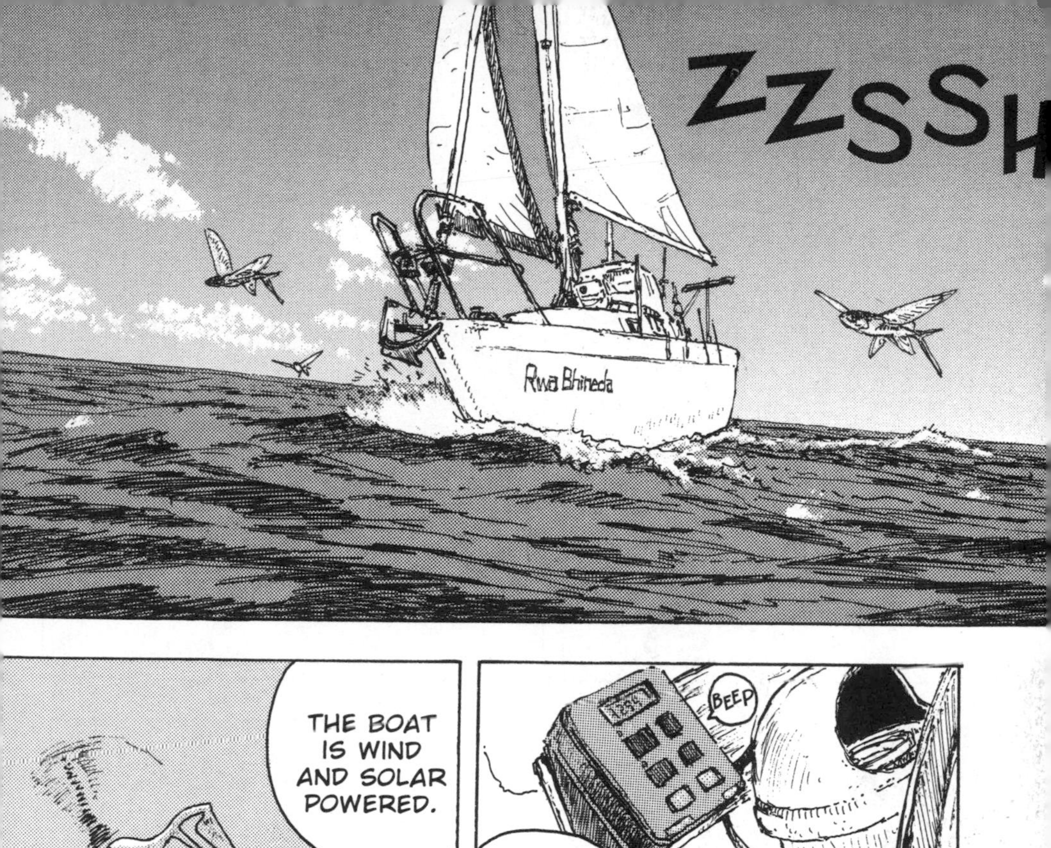
ZZSSH
Riwa Bhineda
BEEP
IT'S GOT AN AUTOPILOT. JUST INPUT THE COORDINATES.
VRR
VRR
VRR
VRR
THE BOAT IS WIND AND SOLAR POWERED.
VRRR

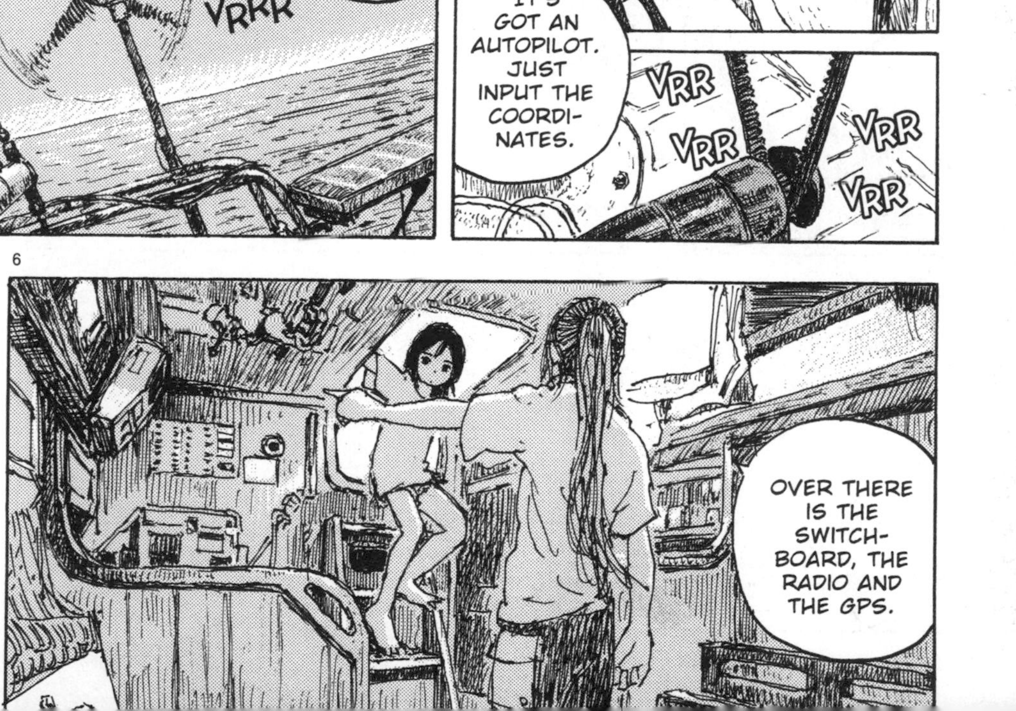
OVER THERE IS THE SWITCHBOARD, THE RADIO AND THE GPS.

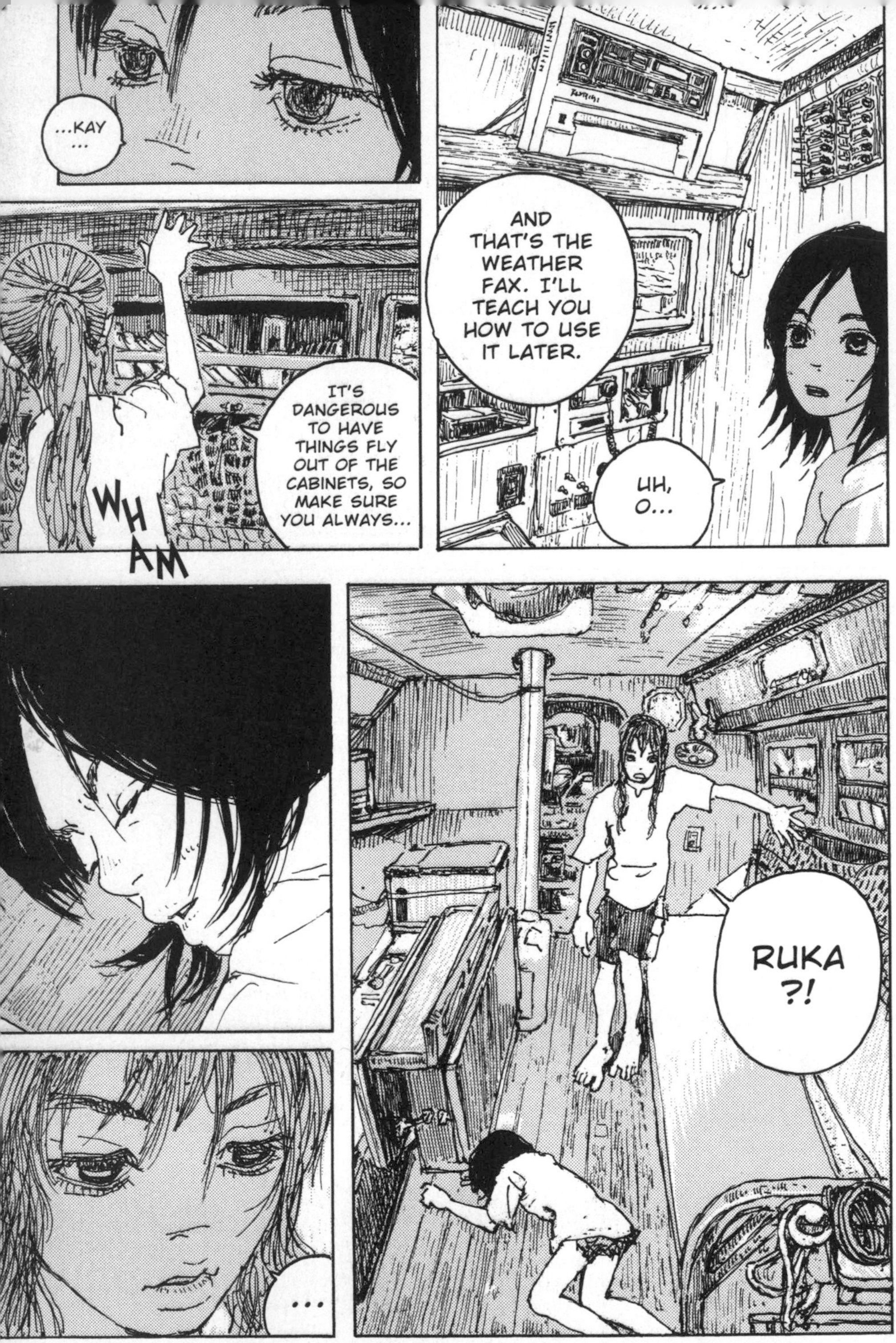
AND THAT'S THE WEATHER FAX. I'LL TEACH YOU HOW TO USE IT LATER.
UH, O...
...KAY ...
IT'S DANGEROUS TO HAVE THINGS FLY OUT OF THE CABINETS, SO MAKE SURE YOU ALWAYS...
WHAM
RUKA ?!
...

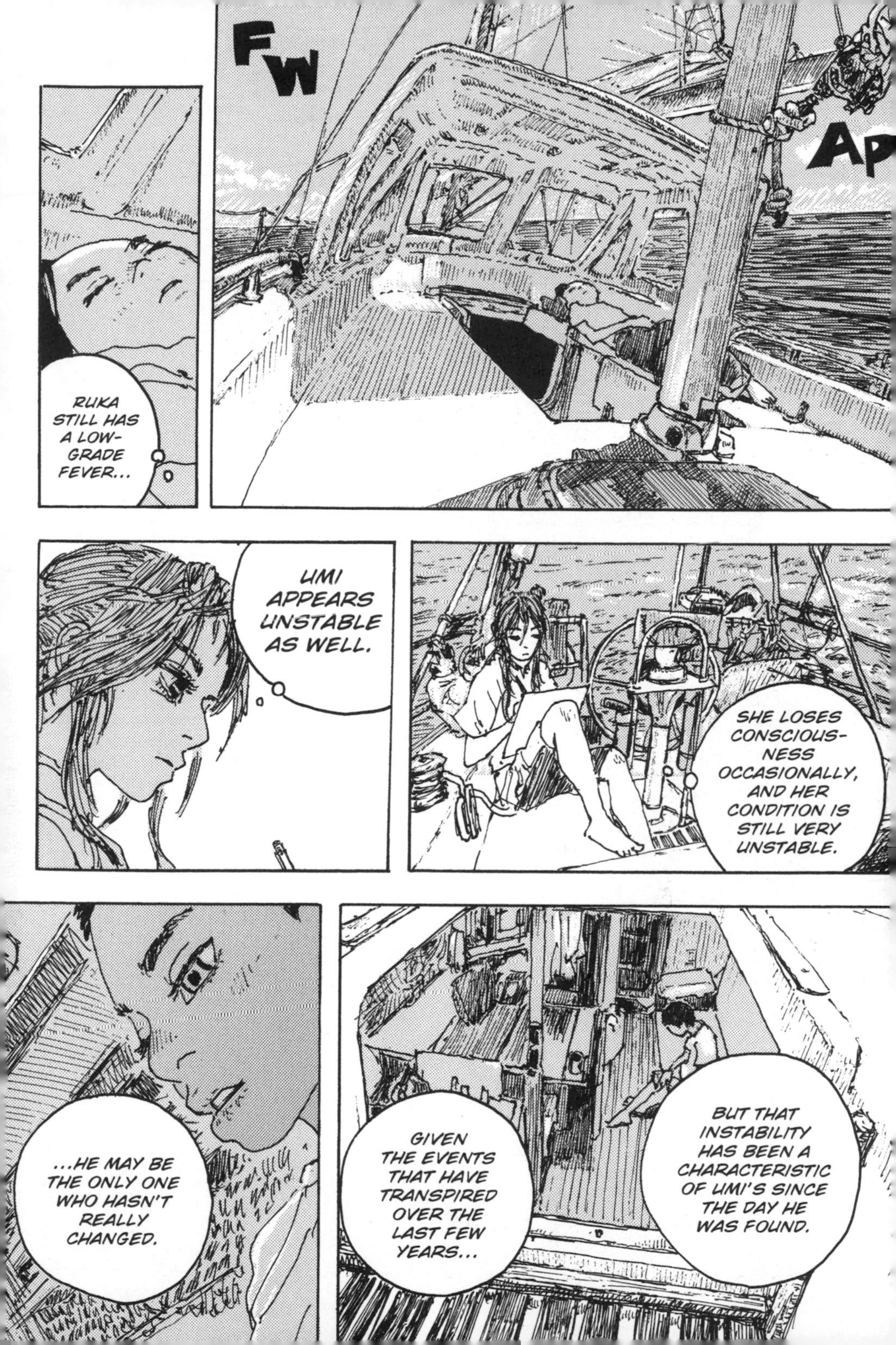
FW
AP
RUKA STILL HAS A LOW-GRADE FEVER...
SHE LOSES CONSCIOUSNESS OCCASIONALLY, AND HER CONDITION IS STILL VERY UNSTABLE.
UMI APPEARS UNSTABLE AS WELL.
BUT THAT INSTABILITY HAS BEEN A CHARACTERISTIC OF UMI'S SINCE THE DAY HE WAS FOUND.
GIVEN THE EVENTS THAT HAVE TRANSPIRED OVER THE LAST FEW YEARS...
...HE MAY BE THE ONLY ONE WHO HASN'T REALLY CHANGED.

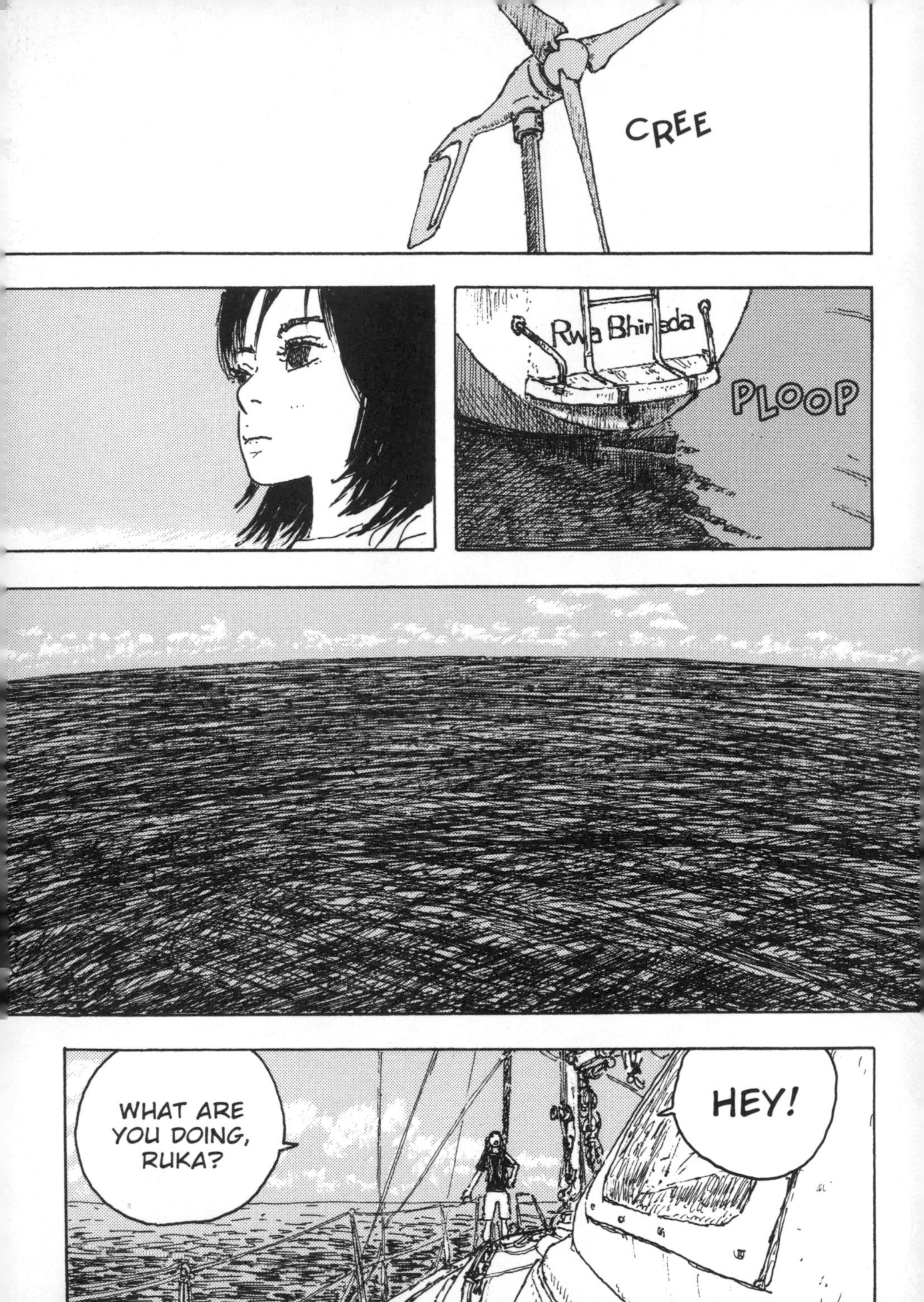
CREE
PLOOP
HEY!
WHAT ARE YOU DOING, RUKA?

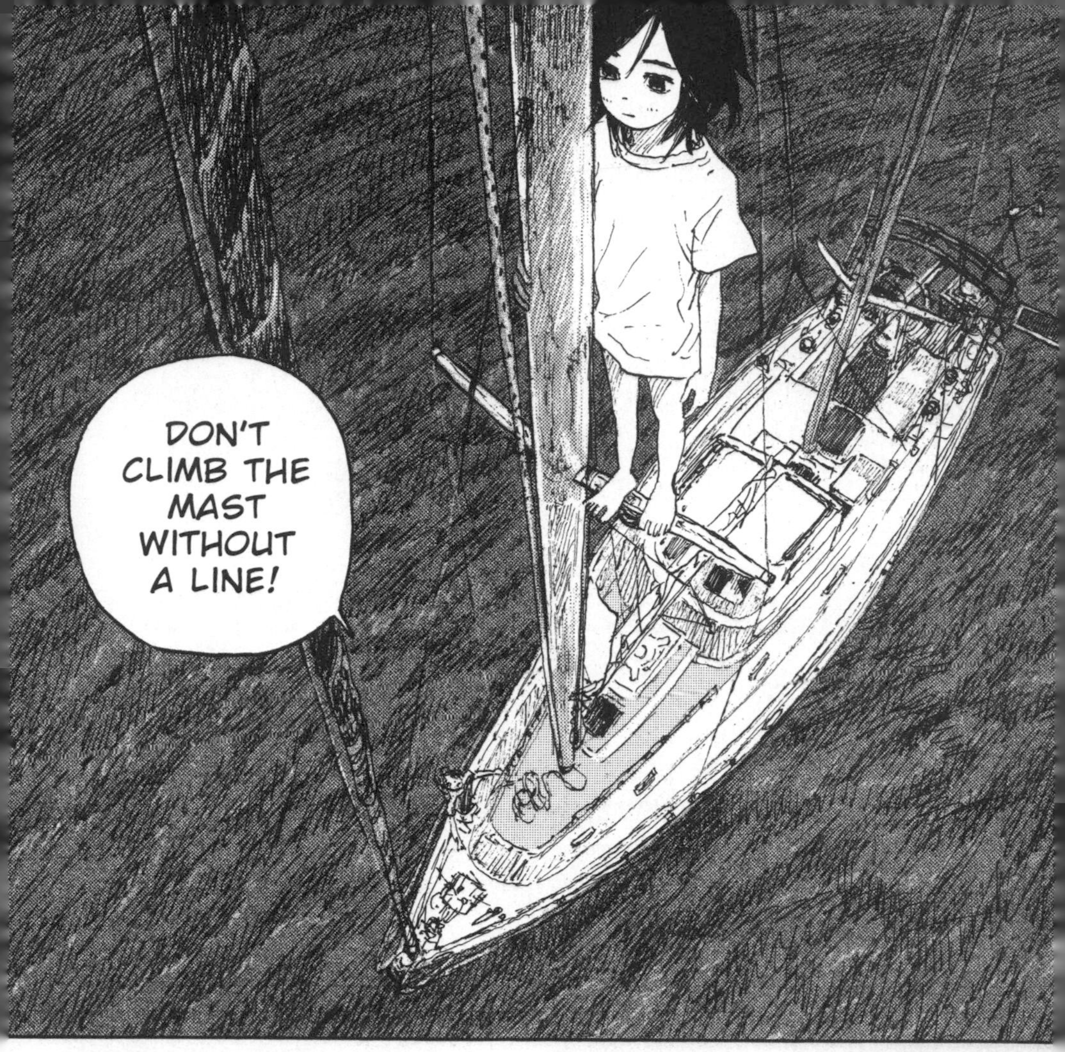
DON'T CLIMB THE MAST WITHOUT A LINE!
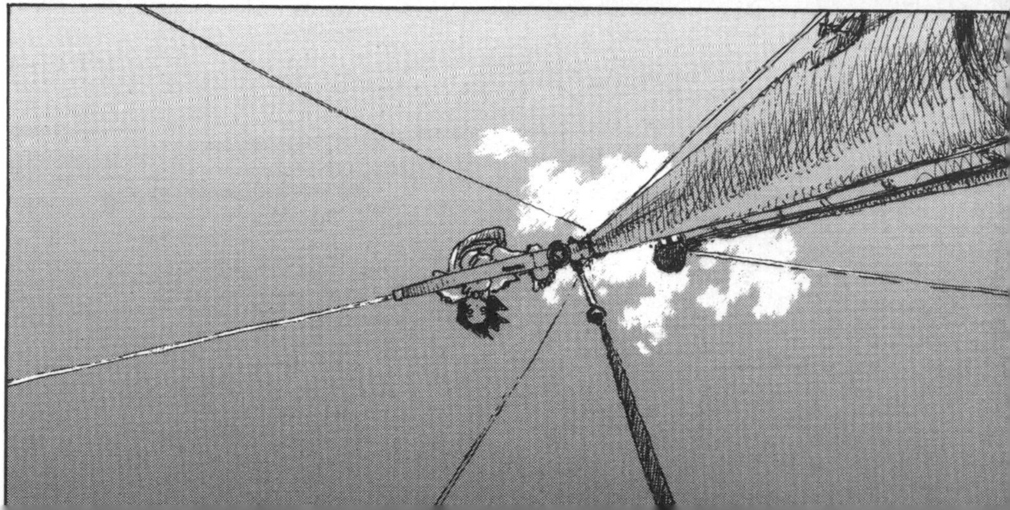

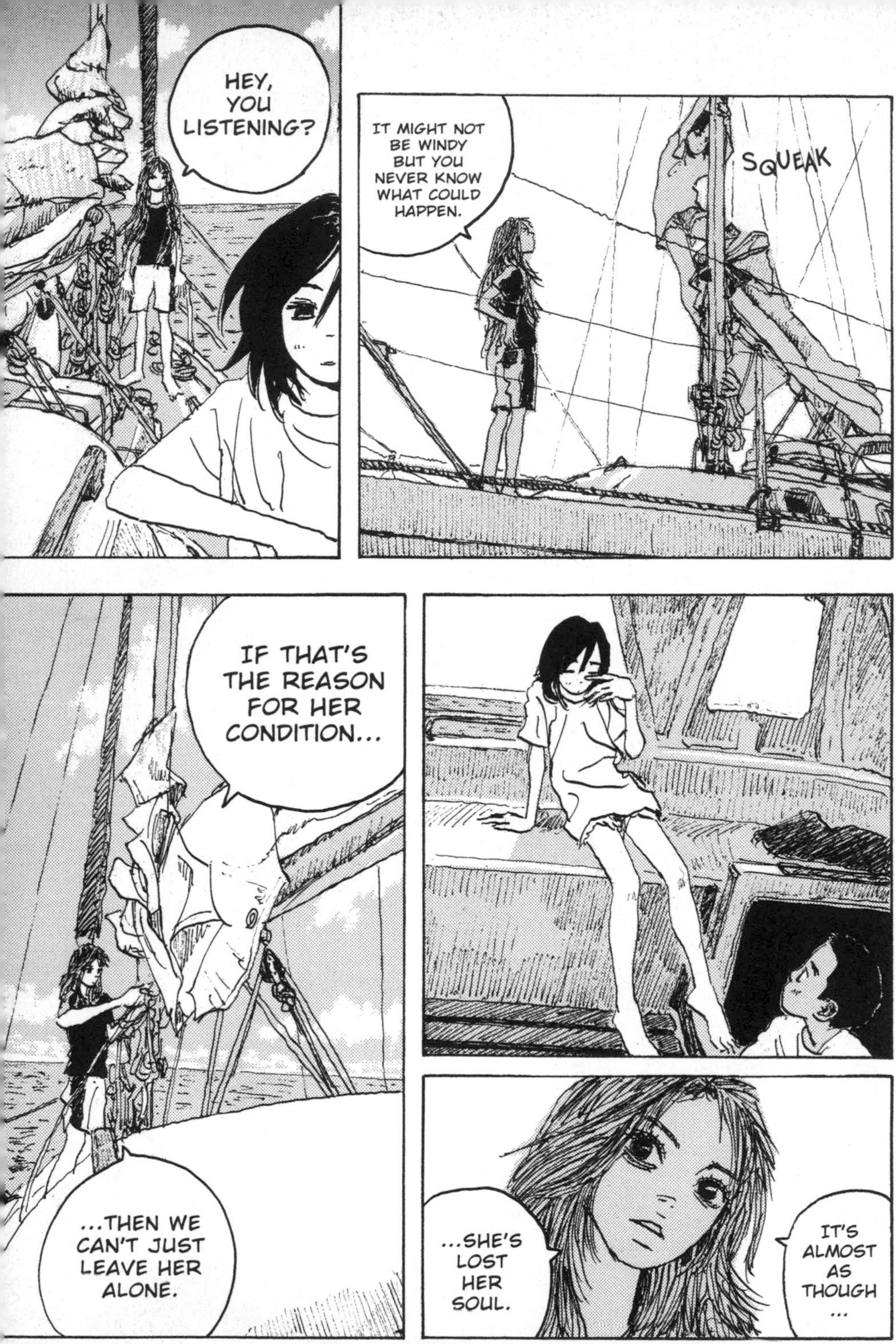
SQUEAK
IT MIGHT NOT BE WINDY BUT YOU NEVER KNOW WHAT COULD HAPPEN.
HEY, YOU LISTENING?
IT'S ALMOST AS THOUGH...
...SHE'S LOST HER SOUL.
IF THAT'S THE REASON FOR HER CONDITION...
...THEN WE CAN'T JUST LEAVE HER ALONE.

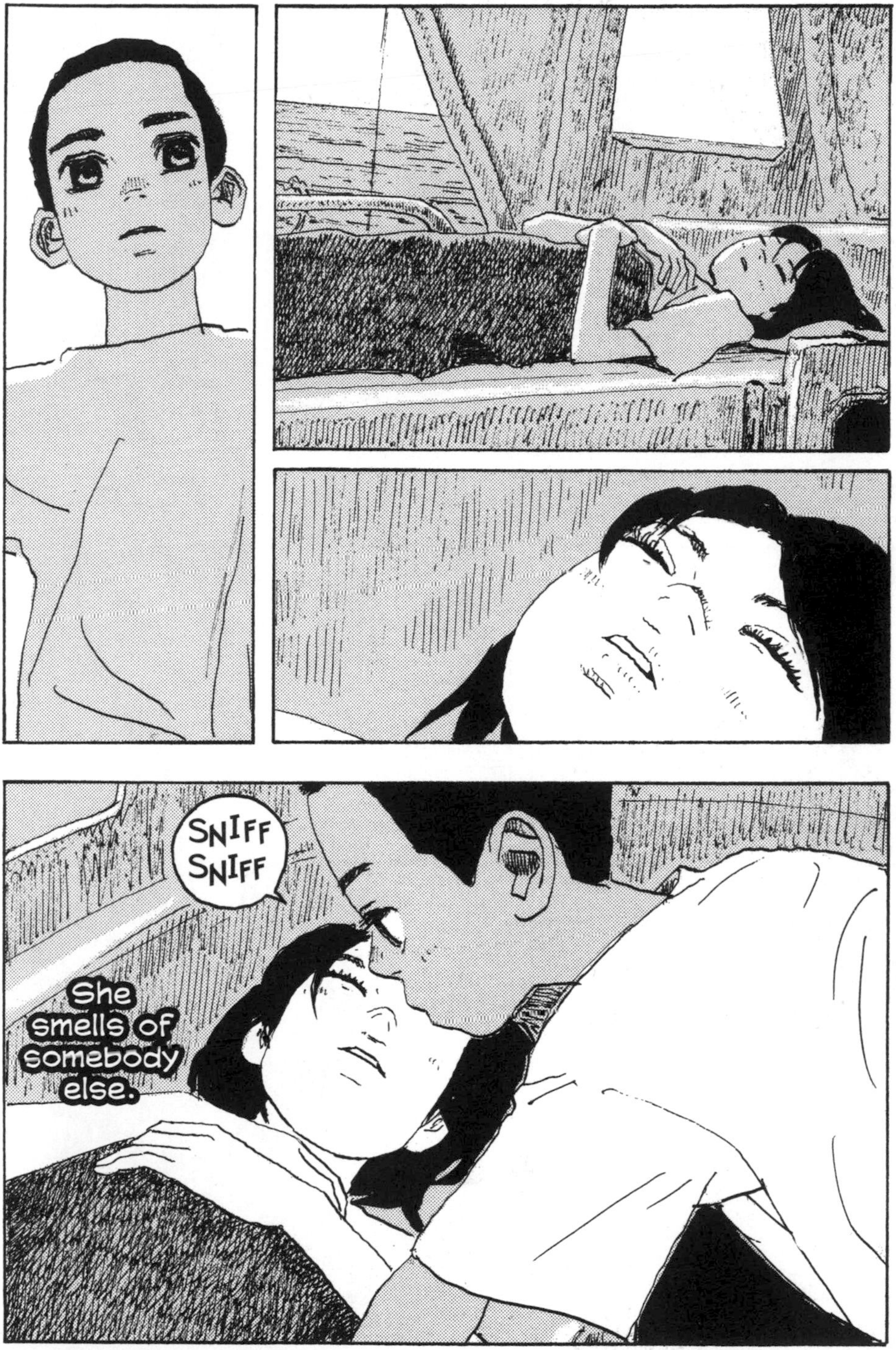
SNIFF SNIFF
She smells of somebody else.

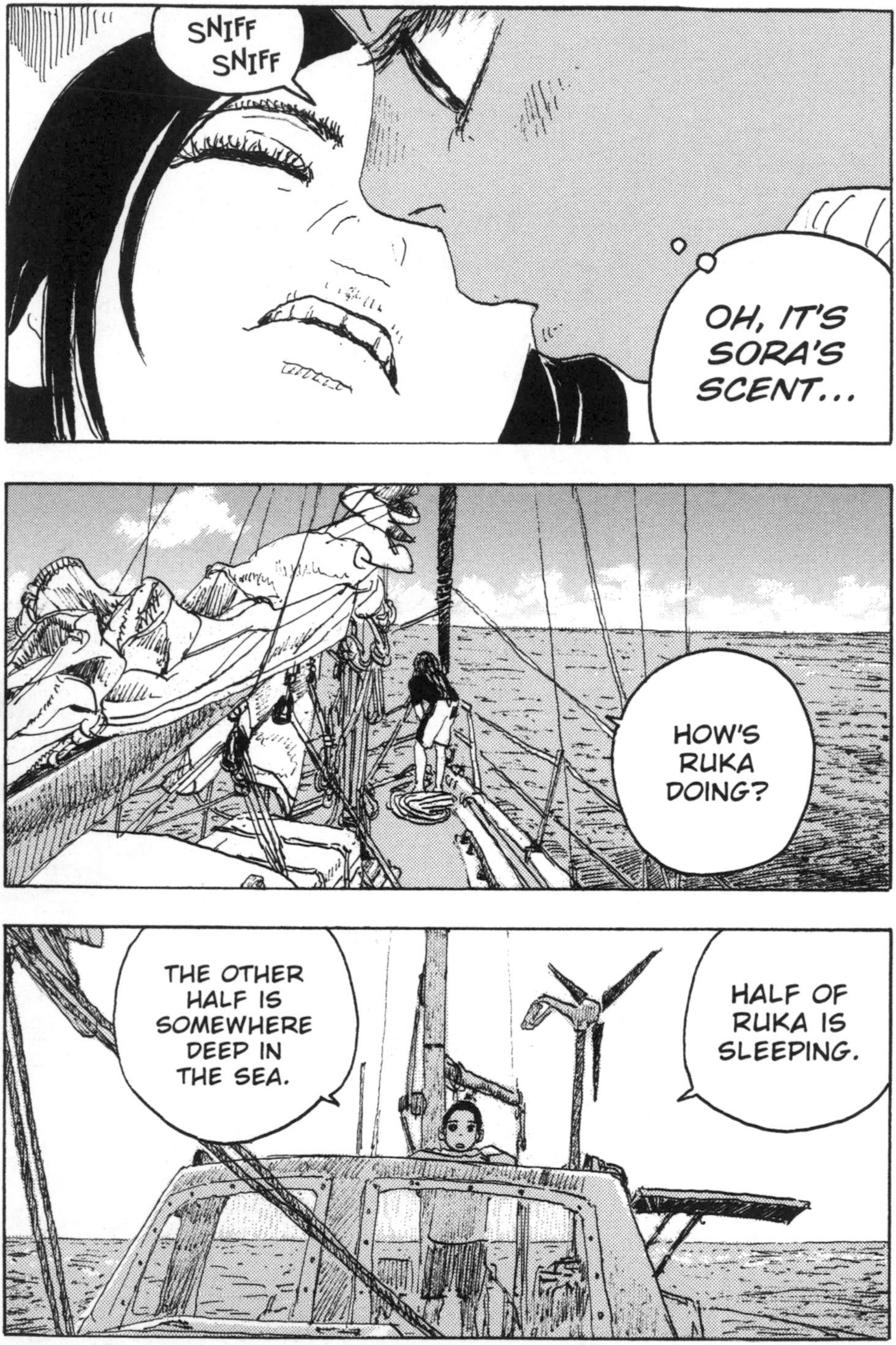
SNIFF SNIFF
OH, IT'S SORA'S SCENT...
HOW'S RUKA DOING?
HALF OF RUKA IS SLEEPING.
THE OTHER HALF IS SOMEWHERE DEEP IN THE SEA.

I'LL GO DIVING AND BRING HER BACK.
HUH?

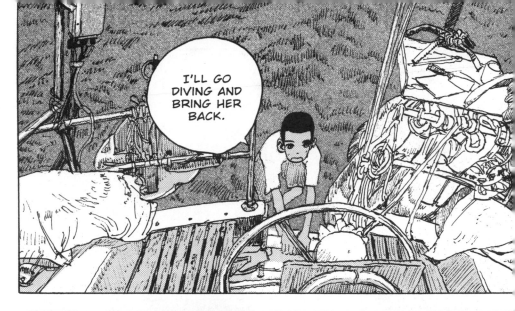

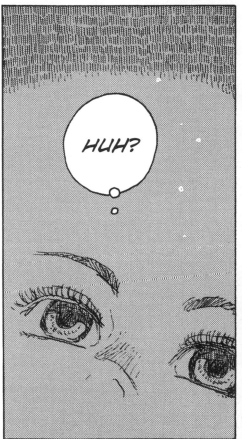

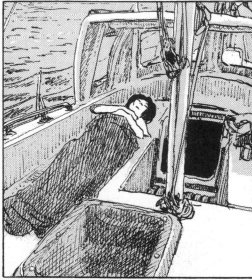

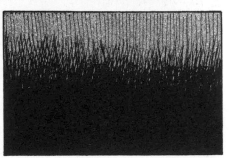

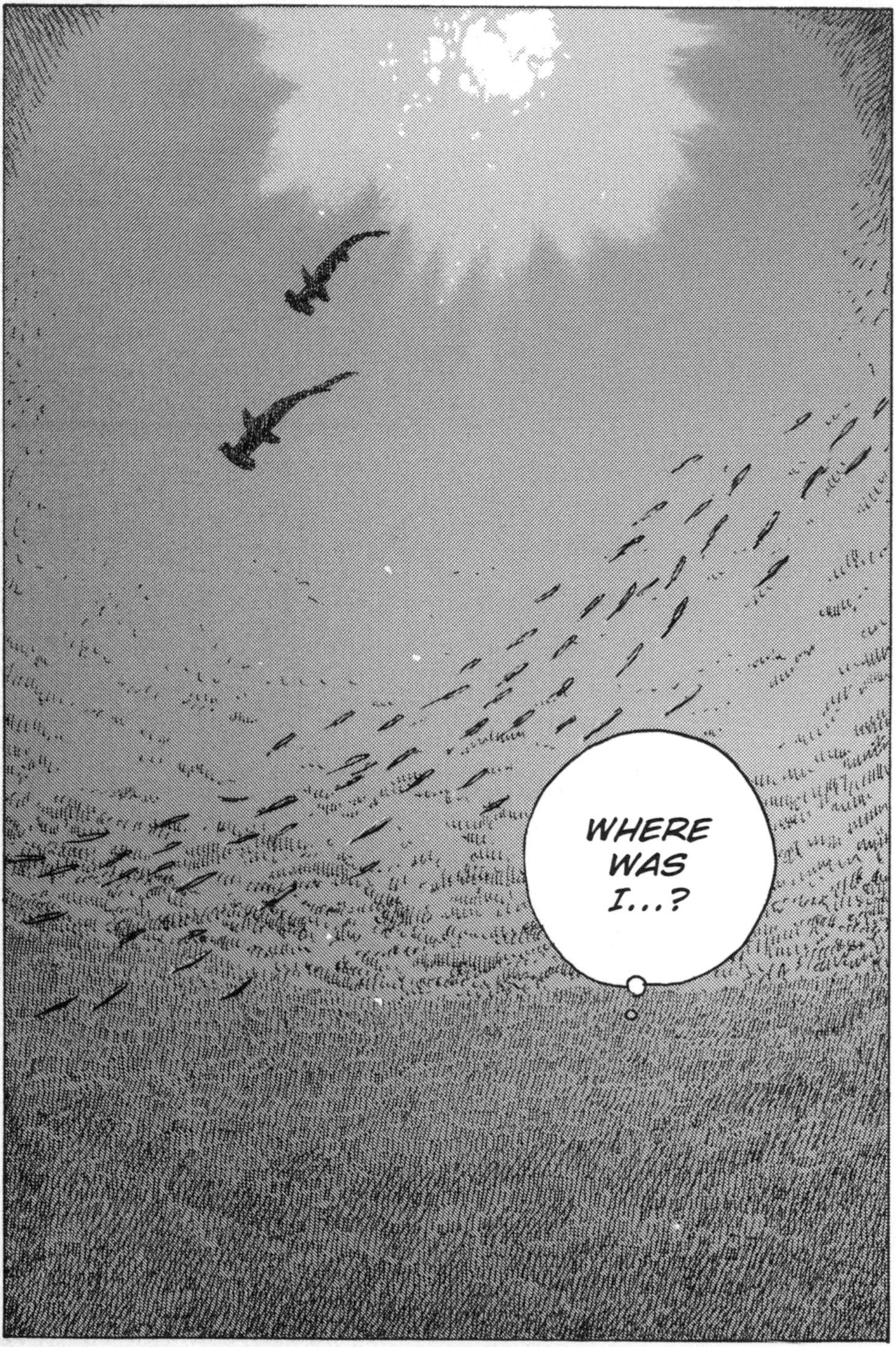
WHERE WAS I...?

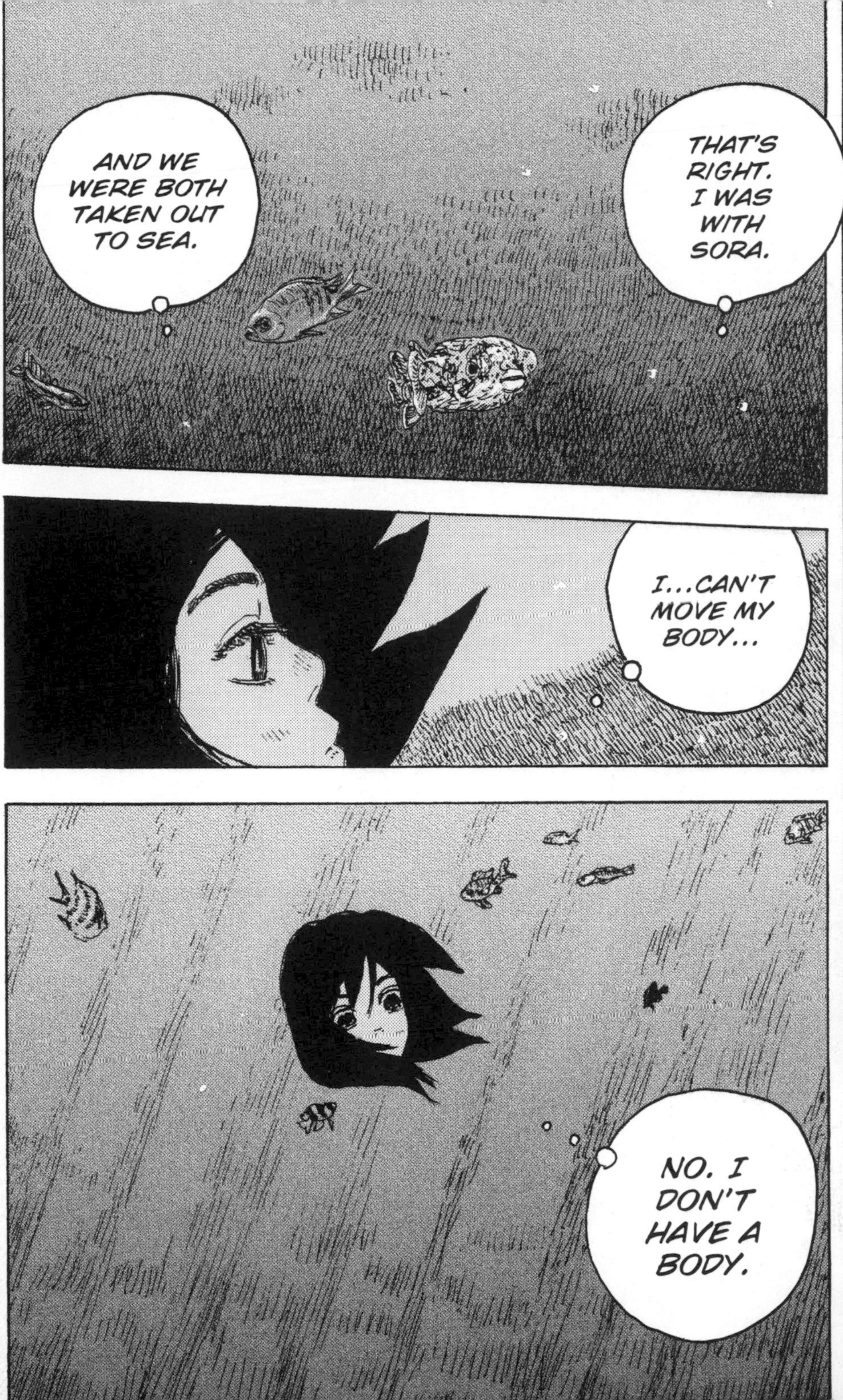
THAT'S RIGHT. I WAS WITH SORA.
AND WE WERE BOTH TAKEN OUT TO SEA.
I...CAN'T MOVE MY BODY...
NO. I DON'T HAVE A BODY.

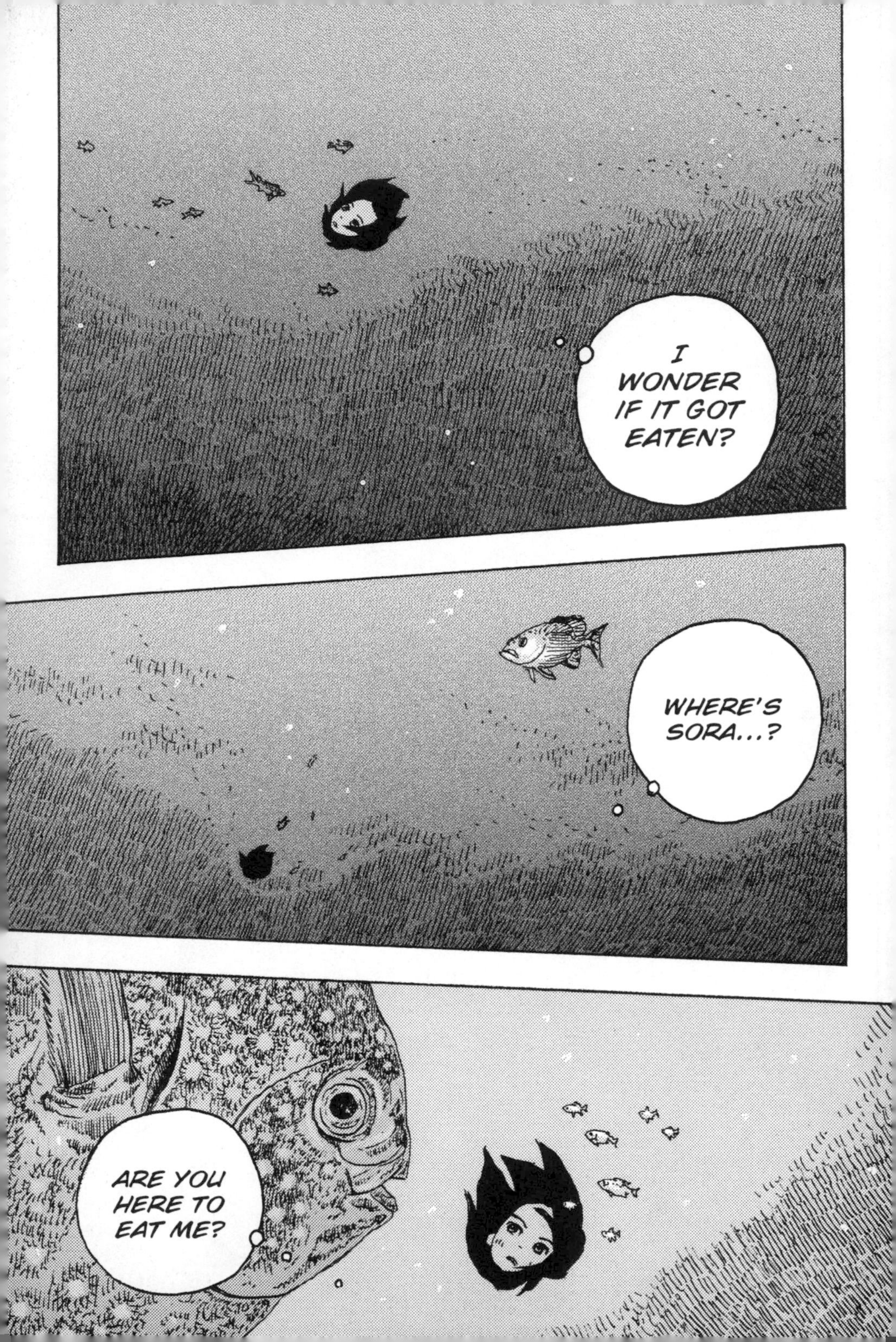
I WONDER IF IT GOT EATEN?
WHERE'S SORA...?
ARE YOU HERE TO EAT ME?

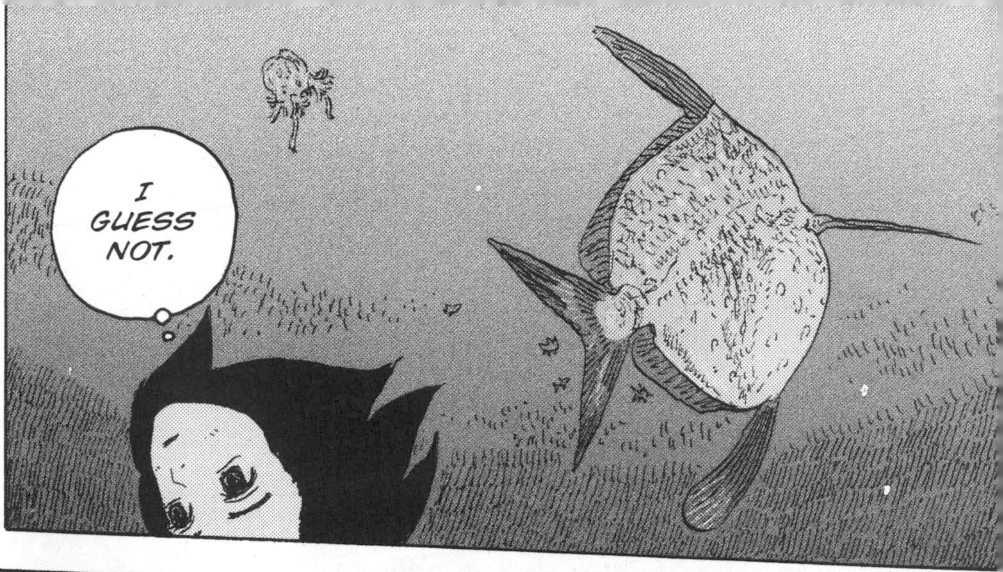
I GUESS NOT.
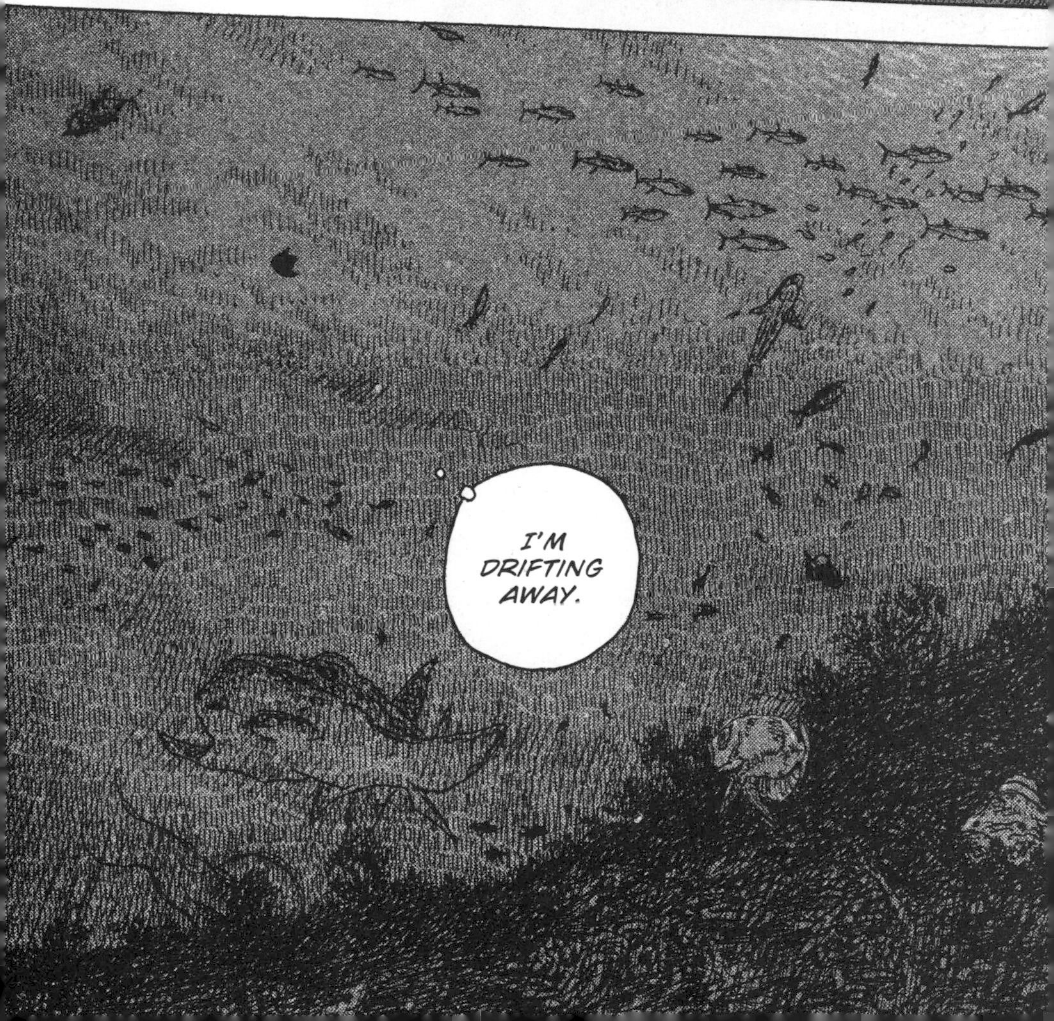
I'M DRIFTING AWAY.

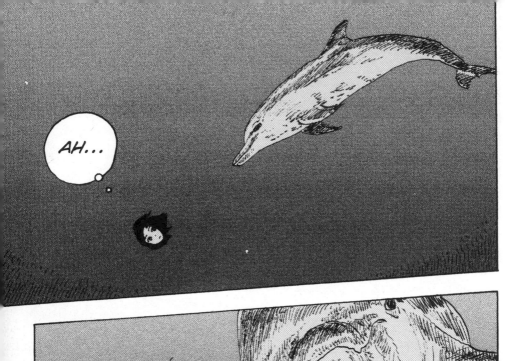

AH...

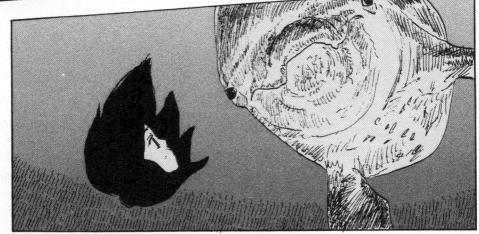

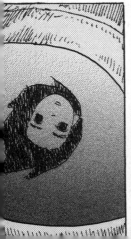

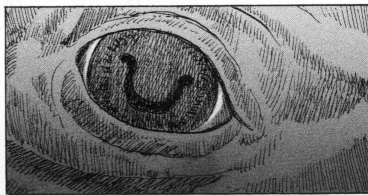

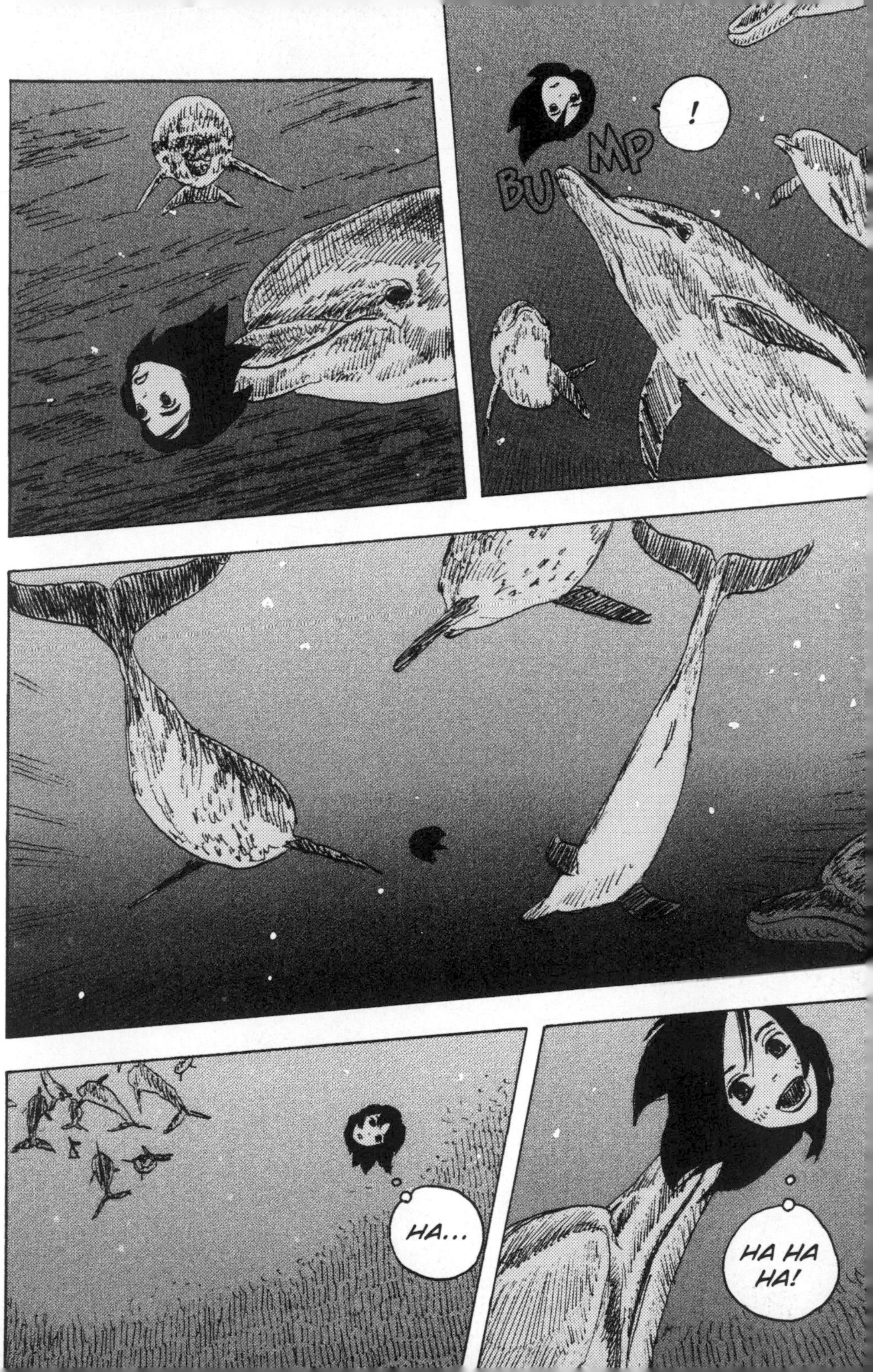
BUMP
!
HA HA HA!
HA...

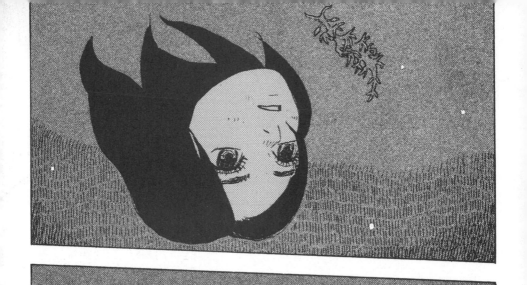

What's
that?

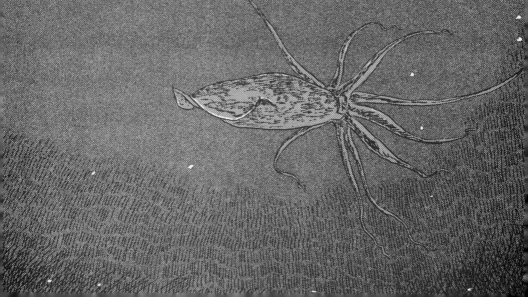

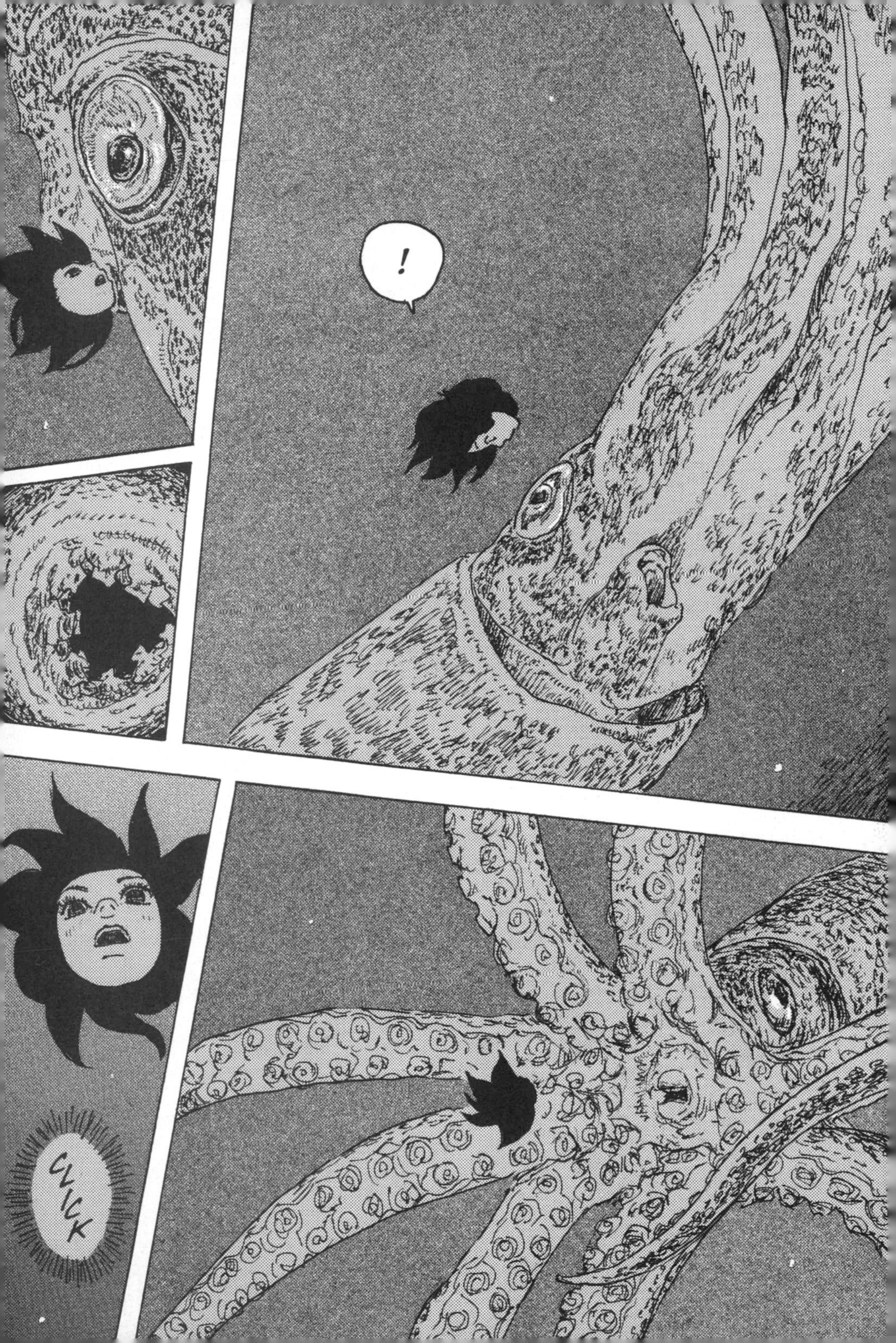
!
CLICK

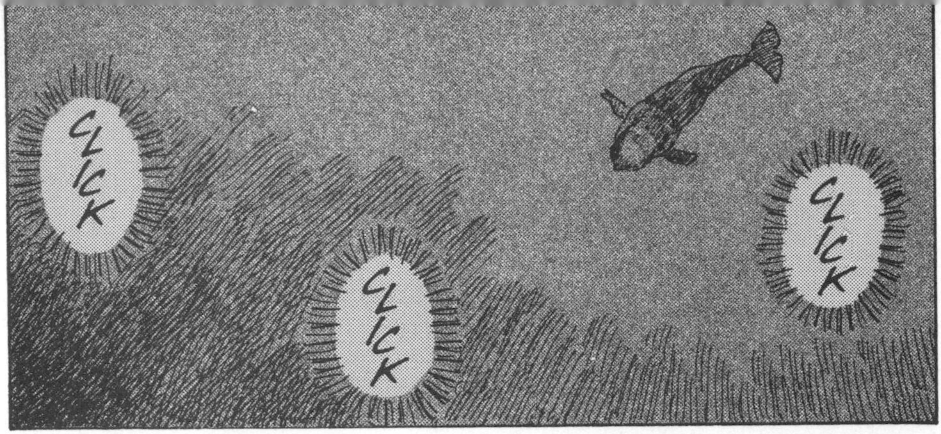
CLICK
CLICK
CLICK

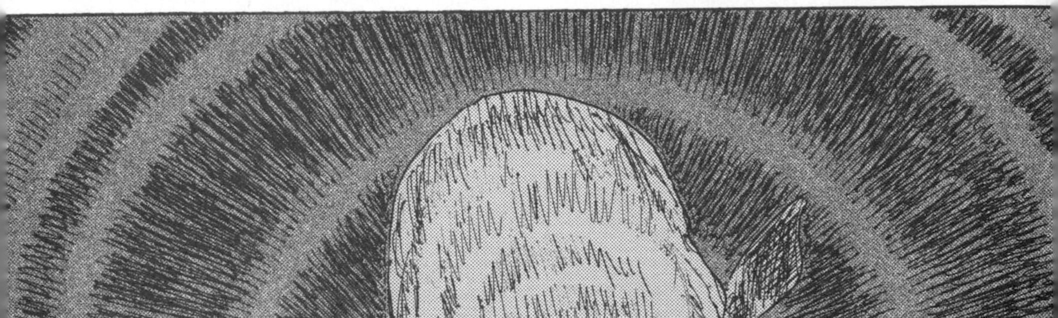

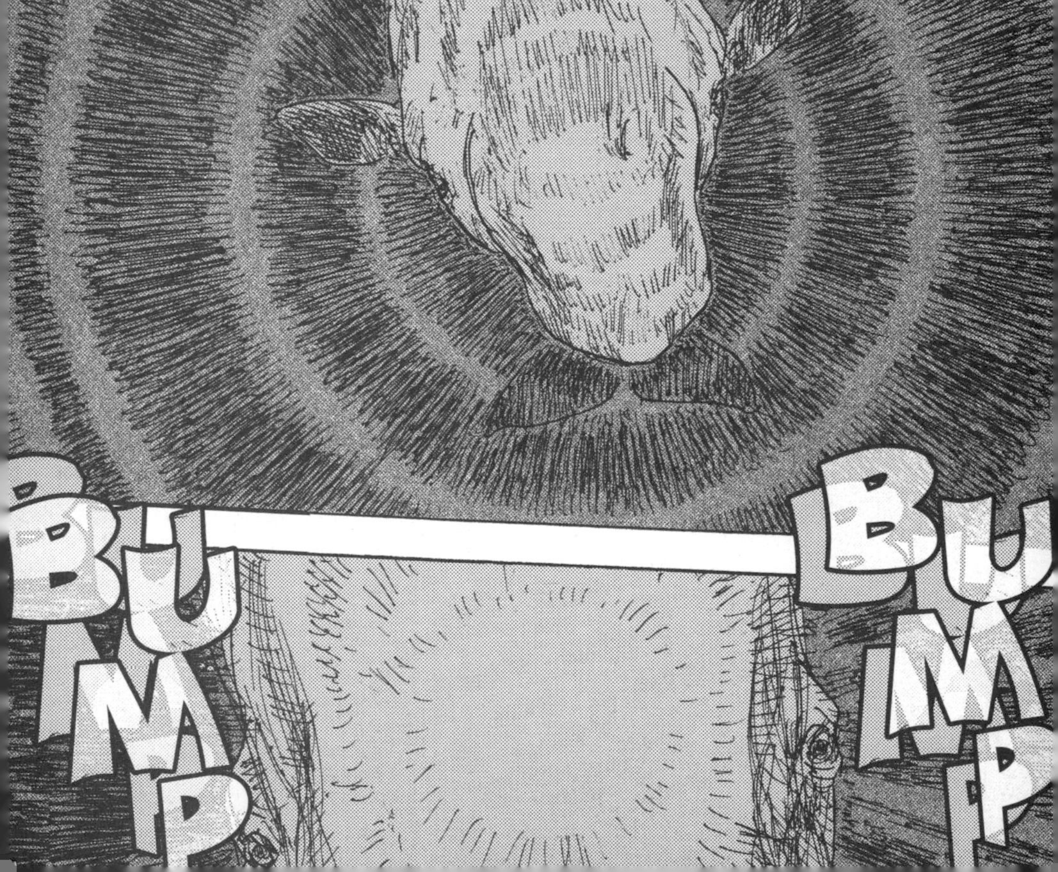
BUMP
BUMP

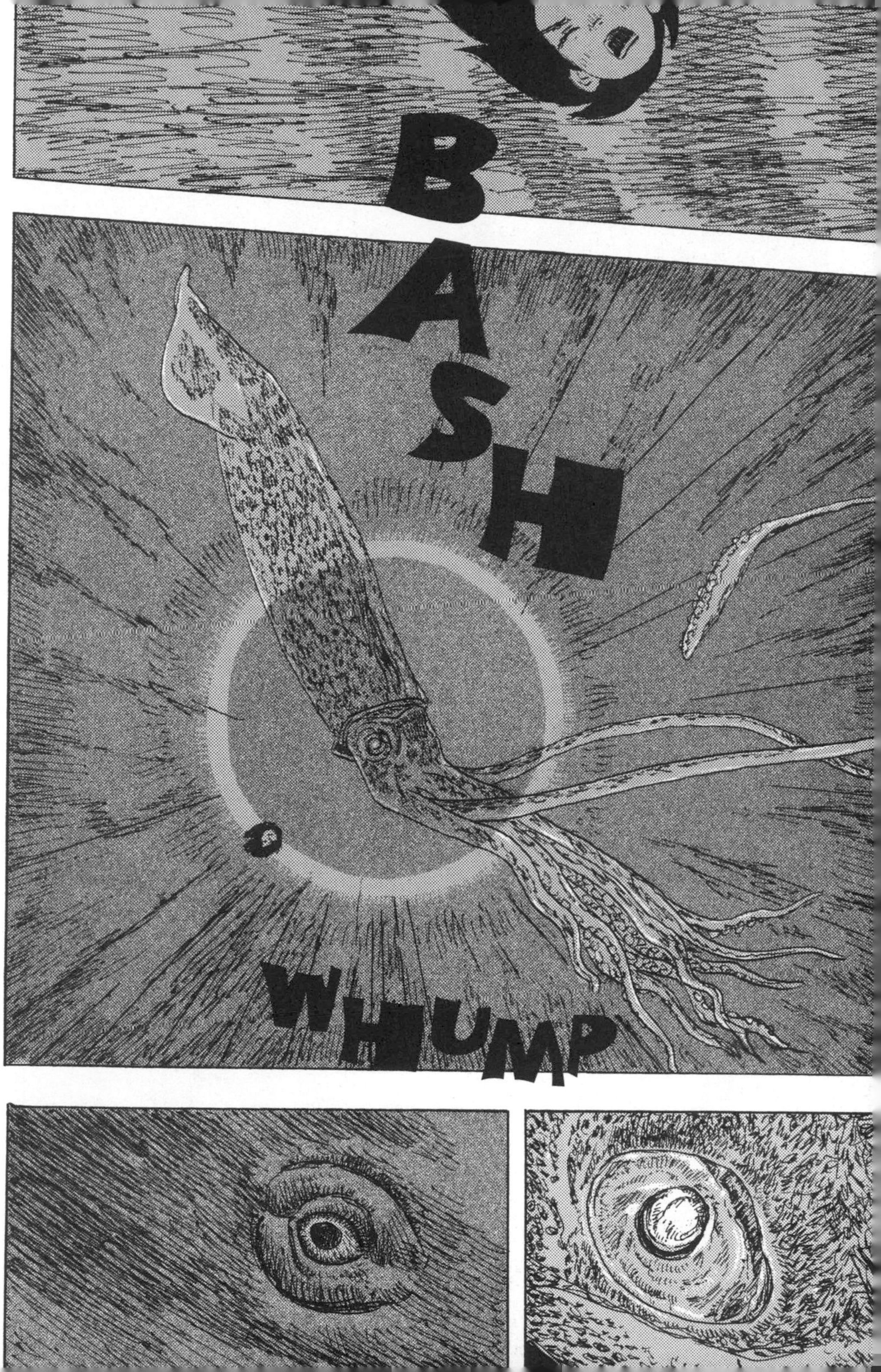
BASH
WHUMP

WHUMP

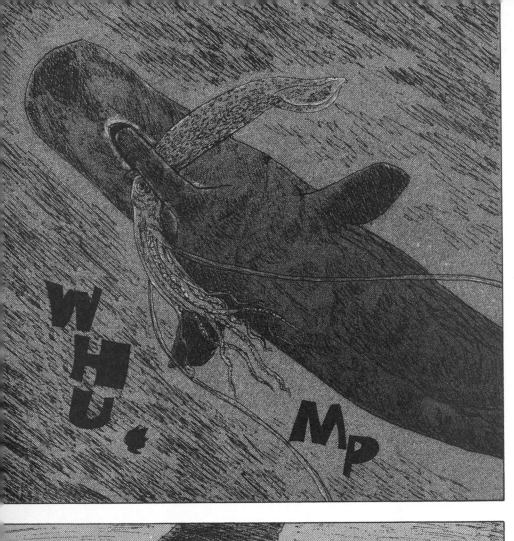

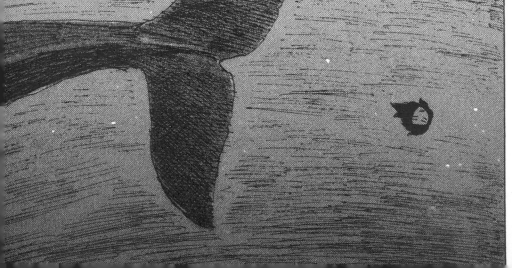

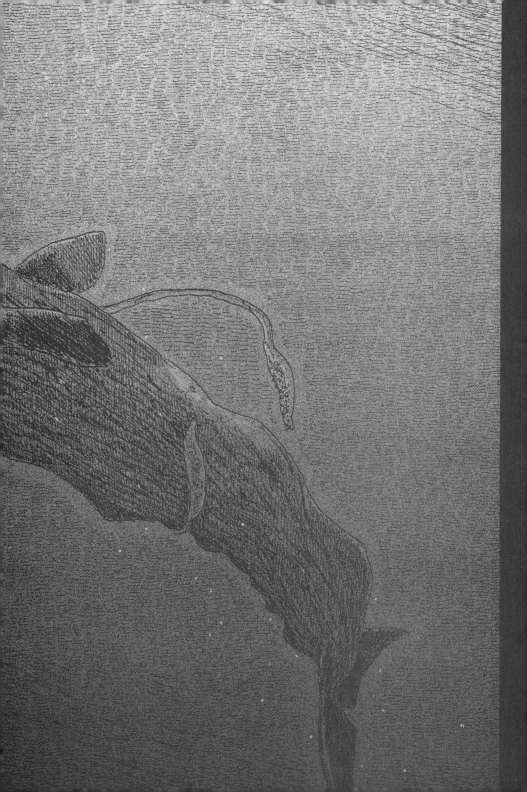

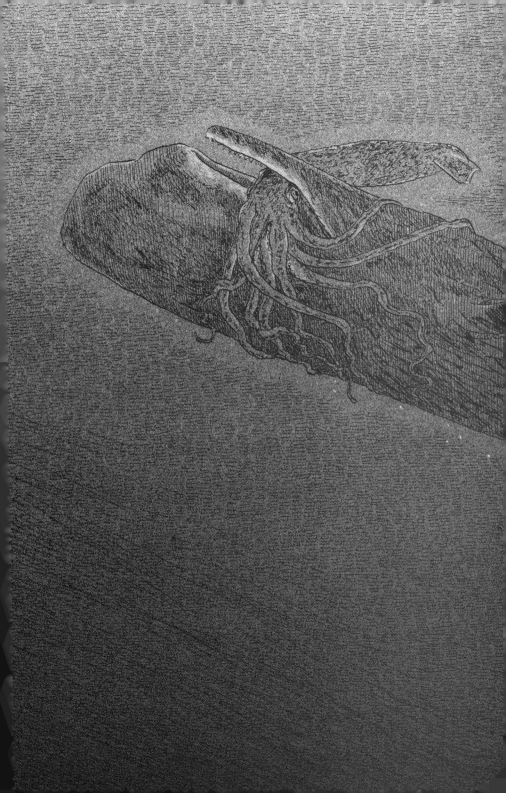

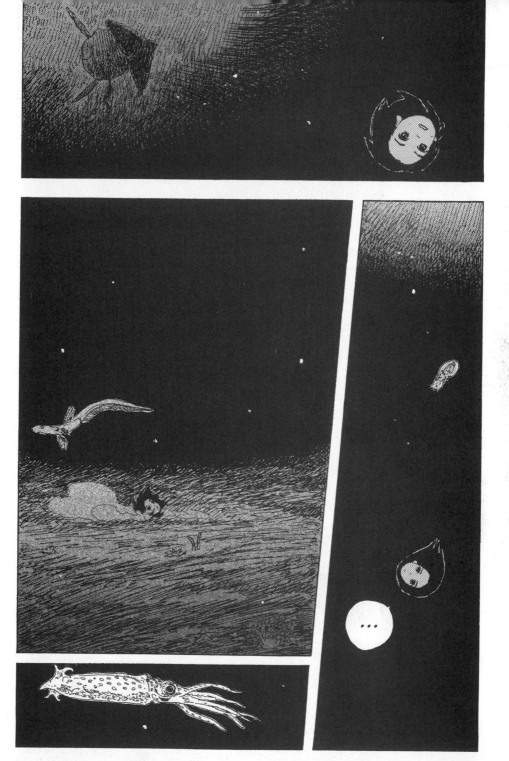

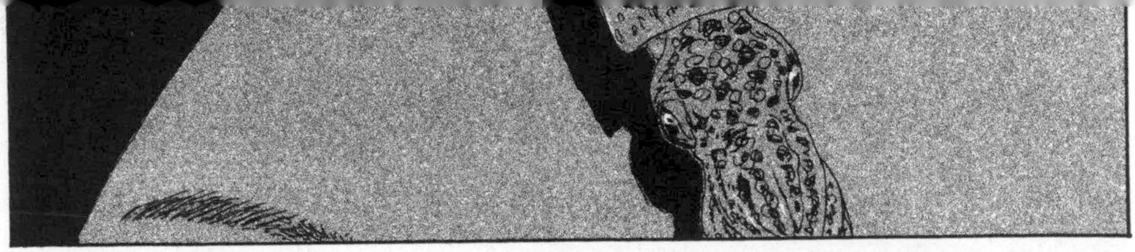
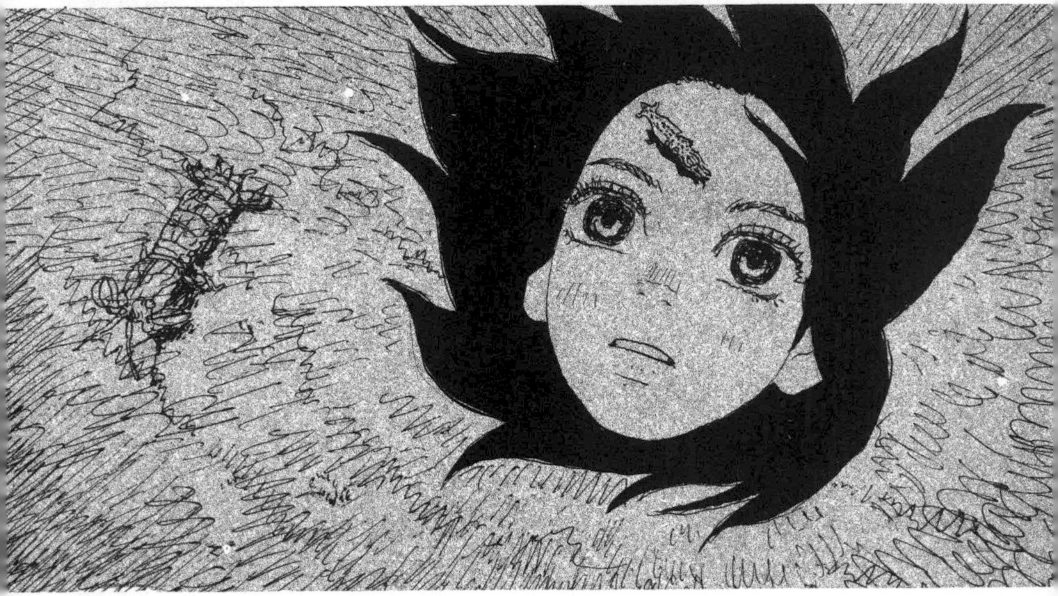
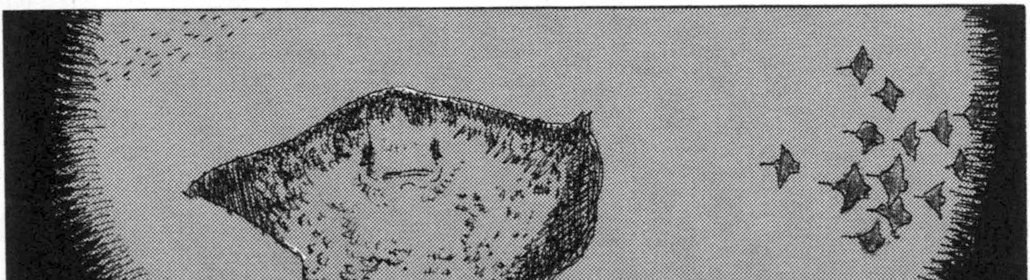
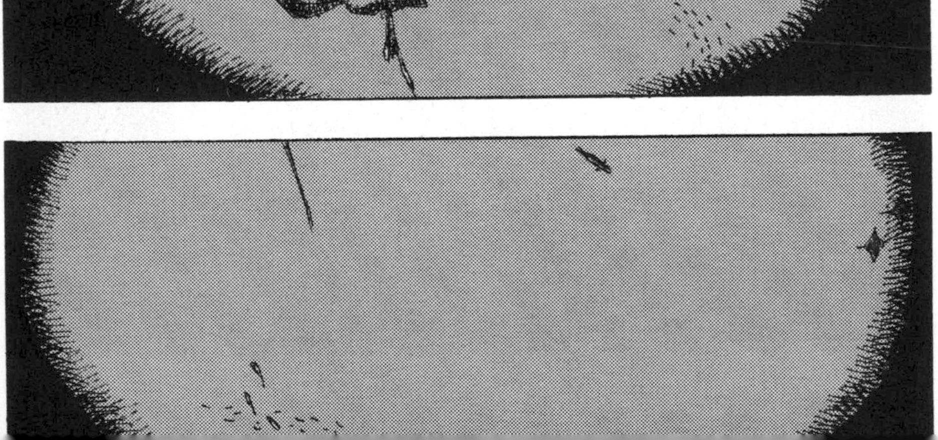

IT'S BLUE...
OH?

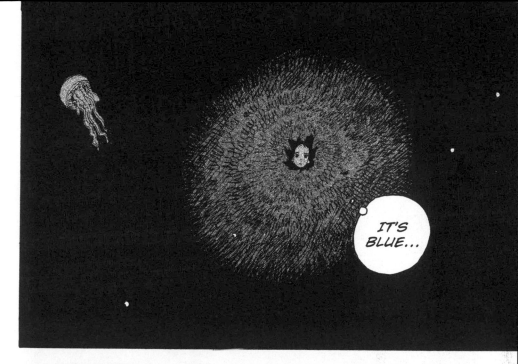

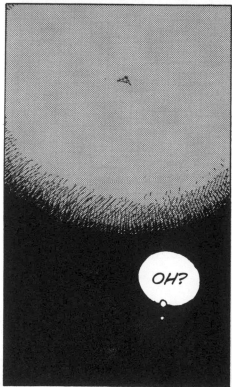

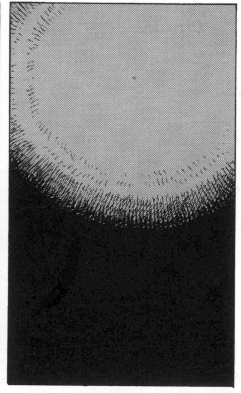

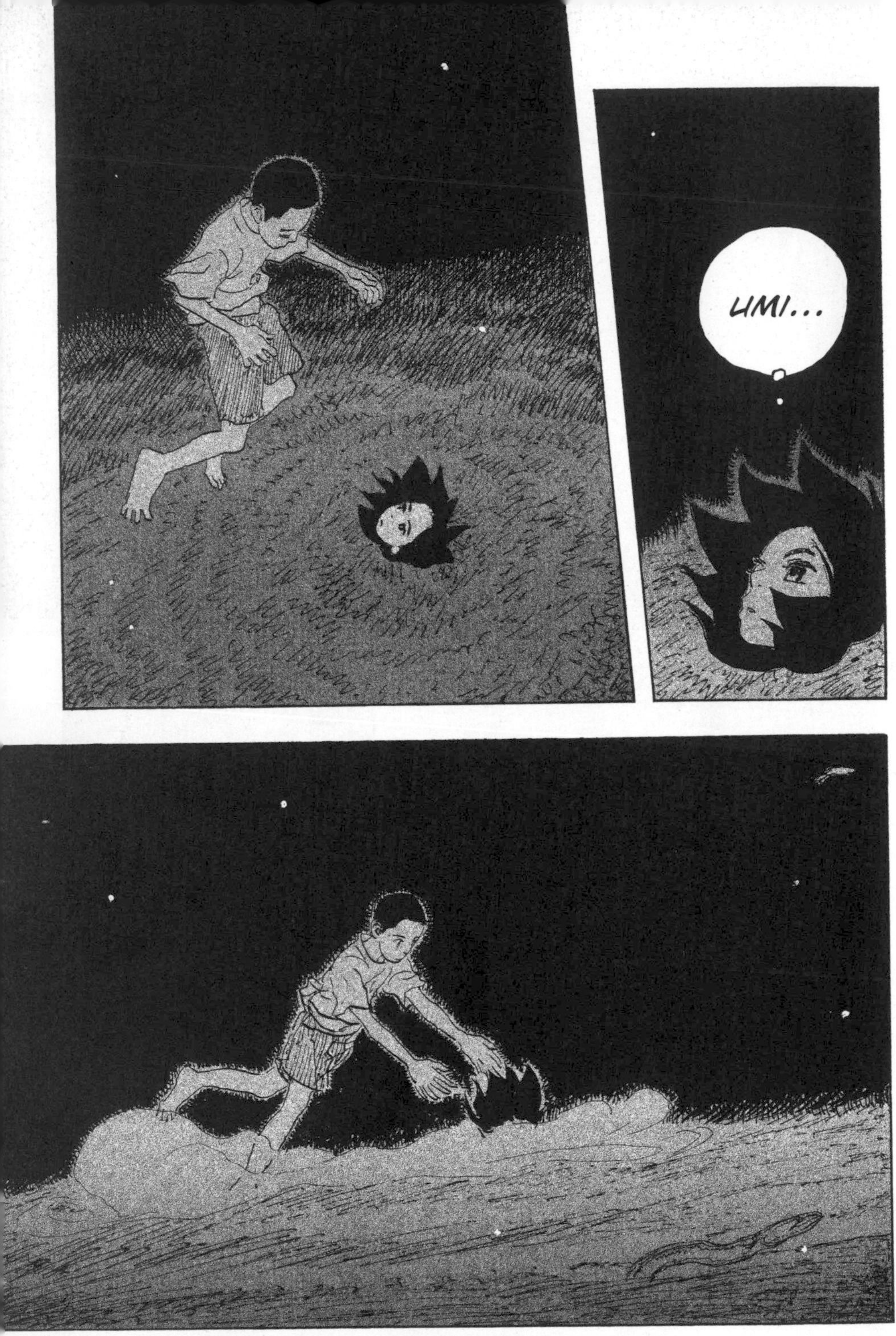
UMI...

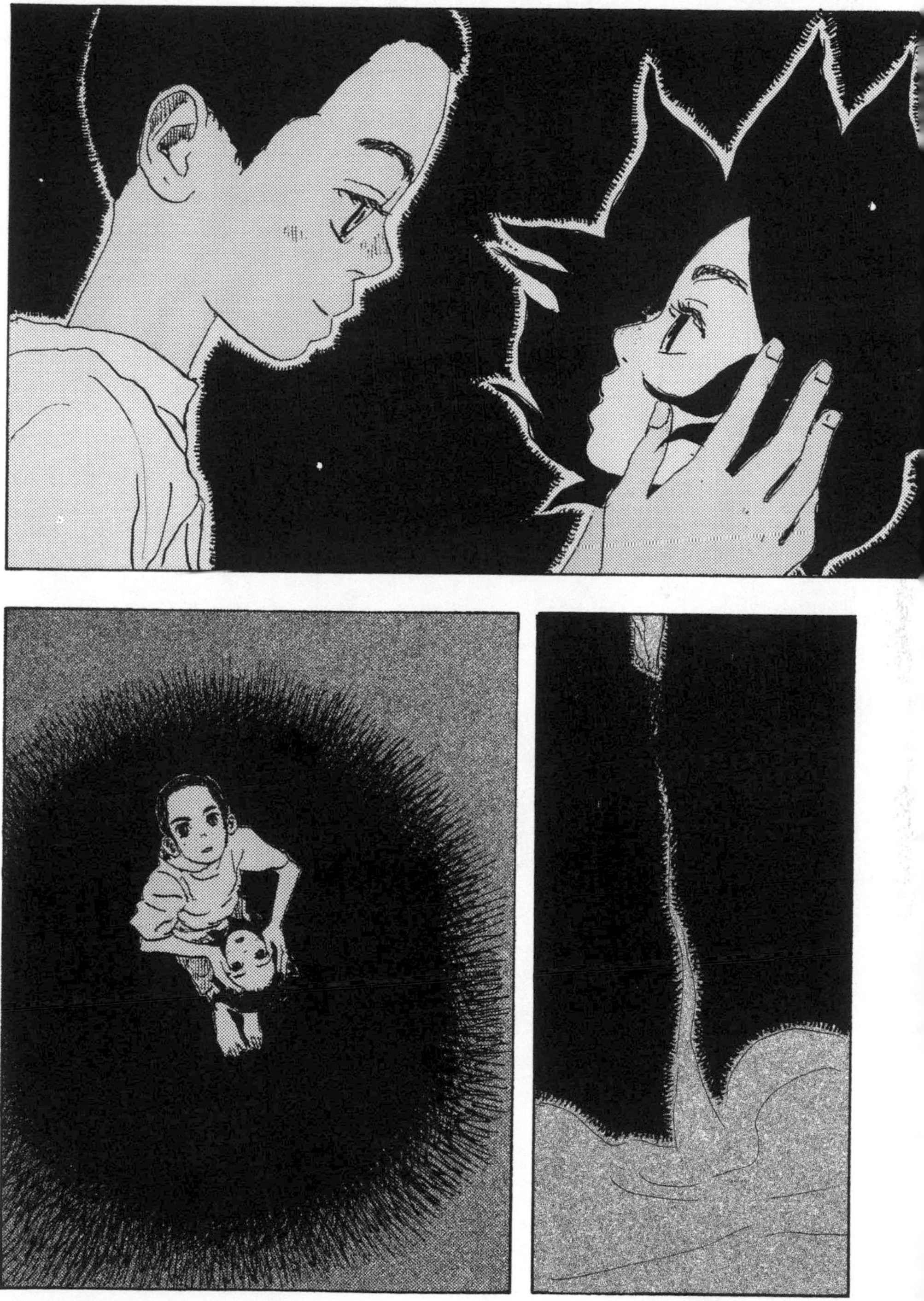

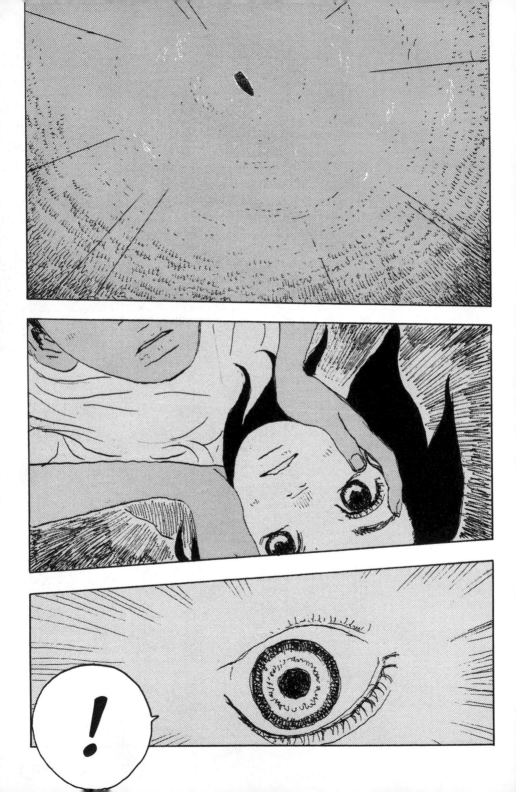

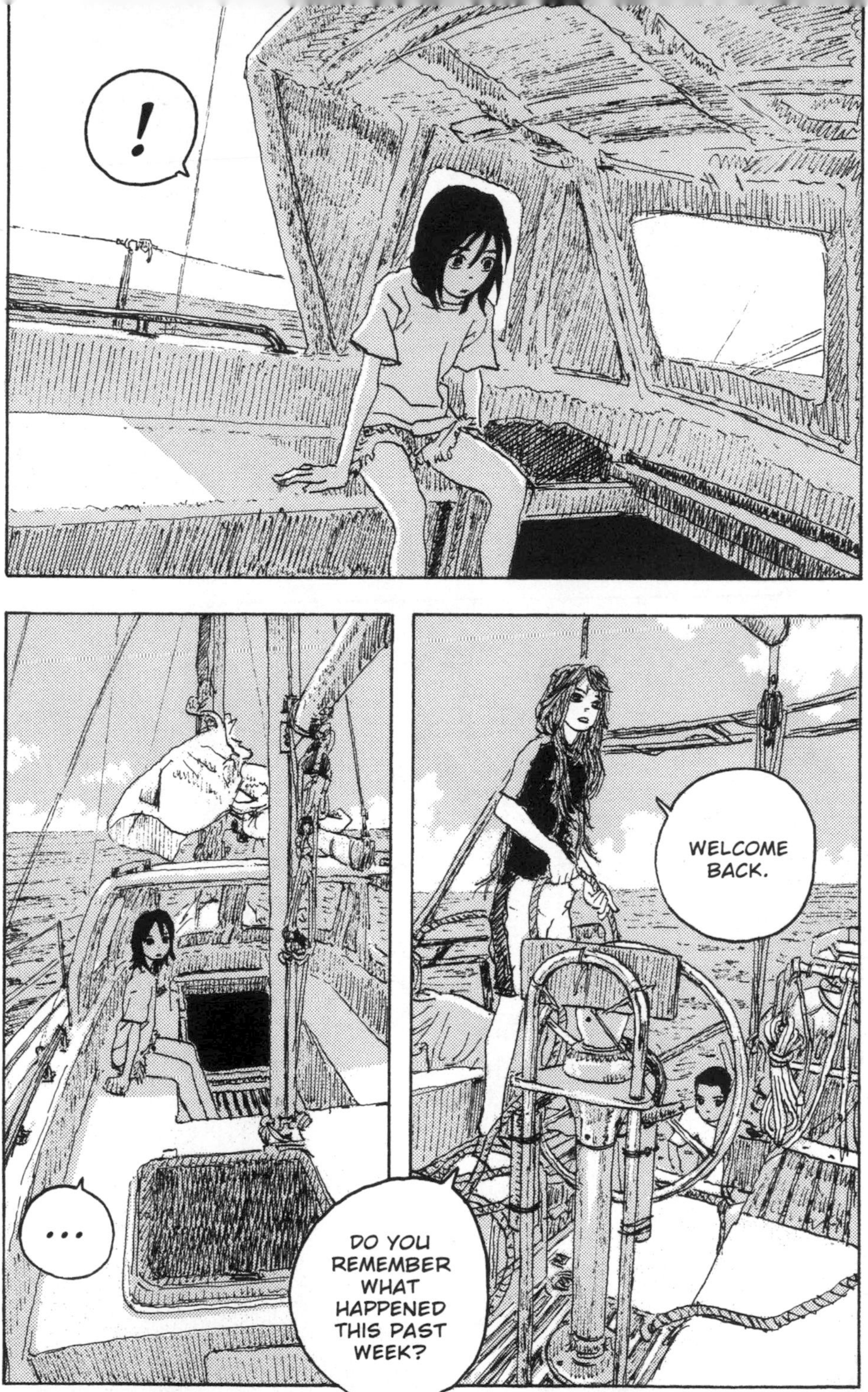
!
WELCOME BACK.
DO YOU REMEMBER WHAT HAPPENED THIS PAST WEEK?
...

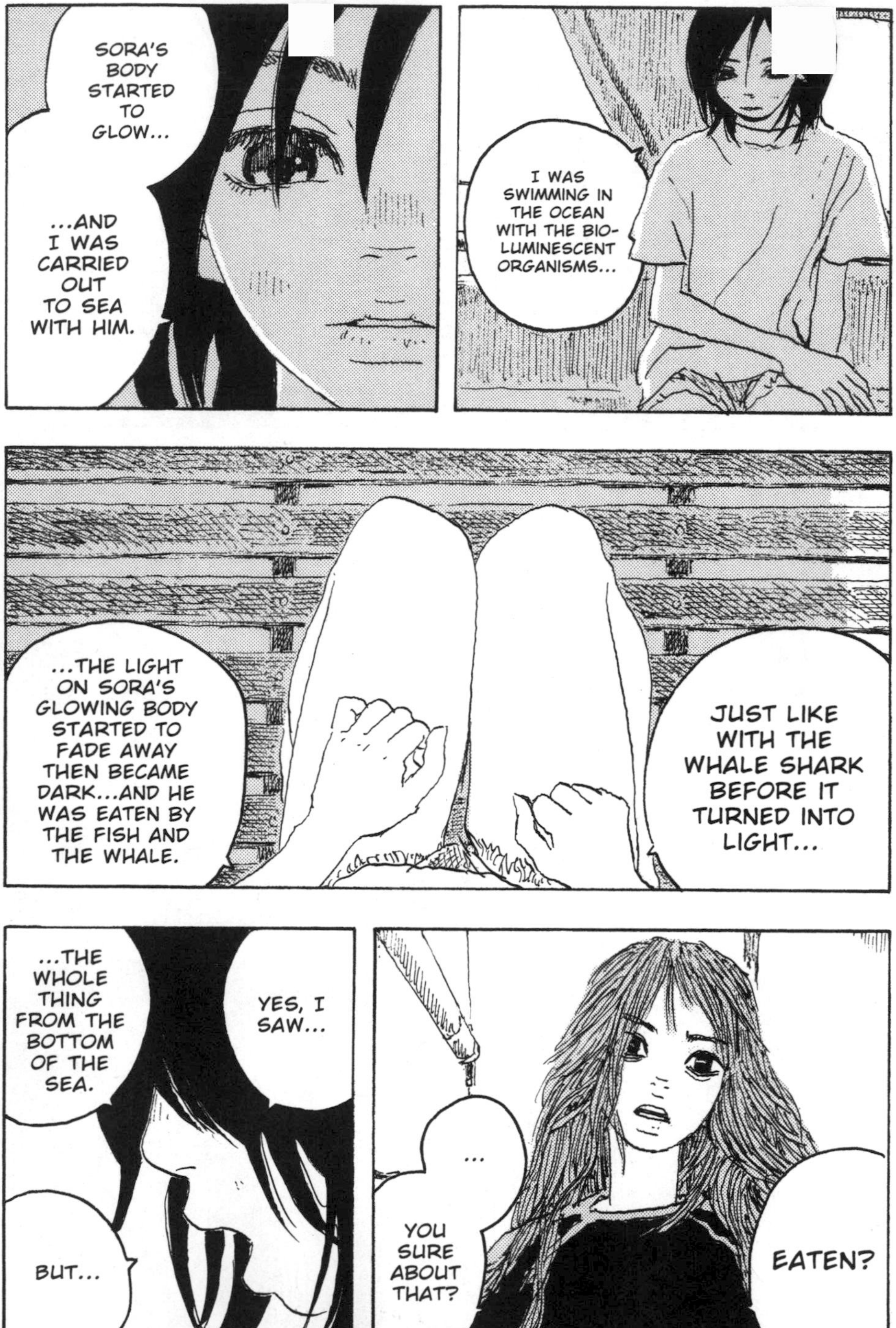
I WAS SWIMMING IN THE OCEAN WITH THE BIO-LUMINESCENT ORGANISMS...
SORA'S BODY STARTED TO GLOW...
...AND I WAS CARRIED OUT TO SEA WITH HIM.
JUST LIKE WITH THE WHALE SHARK BEFORE IT TURNED INTO LIGHT...
...THE LIGHT ON SORA'S GLOWING BODY STARTED TO FADE AWAY THEN BECAME DARK...AND HE WAS EATEN BY THE FISH AND THE WHALE.
EATEN?
...
YOU SURE ABOUT THAT?
YES, I SAW...
...THE WHOLE THING FROM THE BOTTOM OF THE SEA.
BUT...

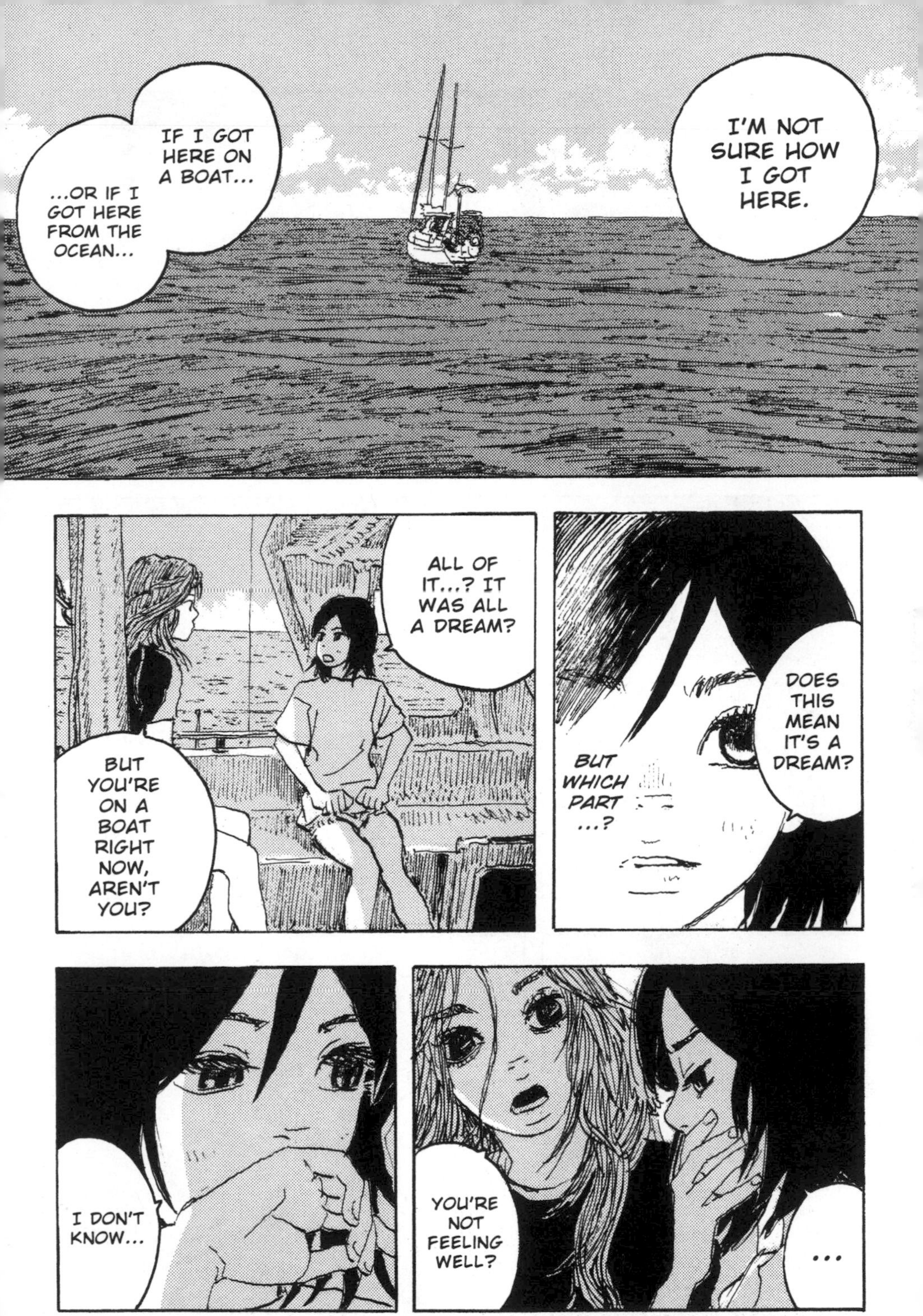
I'M NOT SURE HOW I GOT HERE.
IF I GOT HERE ON A BOAT...
...OR IF I GOT HERE FROM THE OCEAN...
DOES THIS MEAN IT'S A DREAM?
BUT WHICH PART ...?
ALL OF IT...? IT WAS ALL A DREAM?
BUT YOU'RE ON A BOAT RIGHT NOW, AREN'T YOU?
YOU'RE NOT FEELING WELL?
...
I DON'T KNOW...

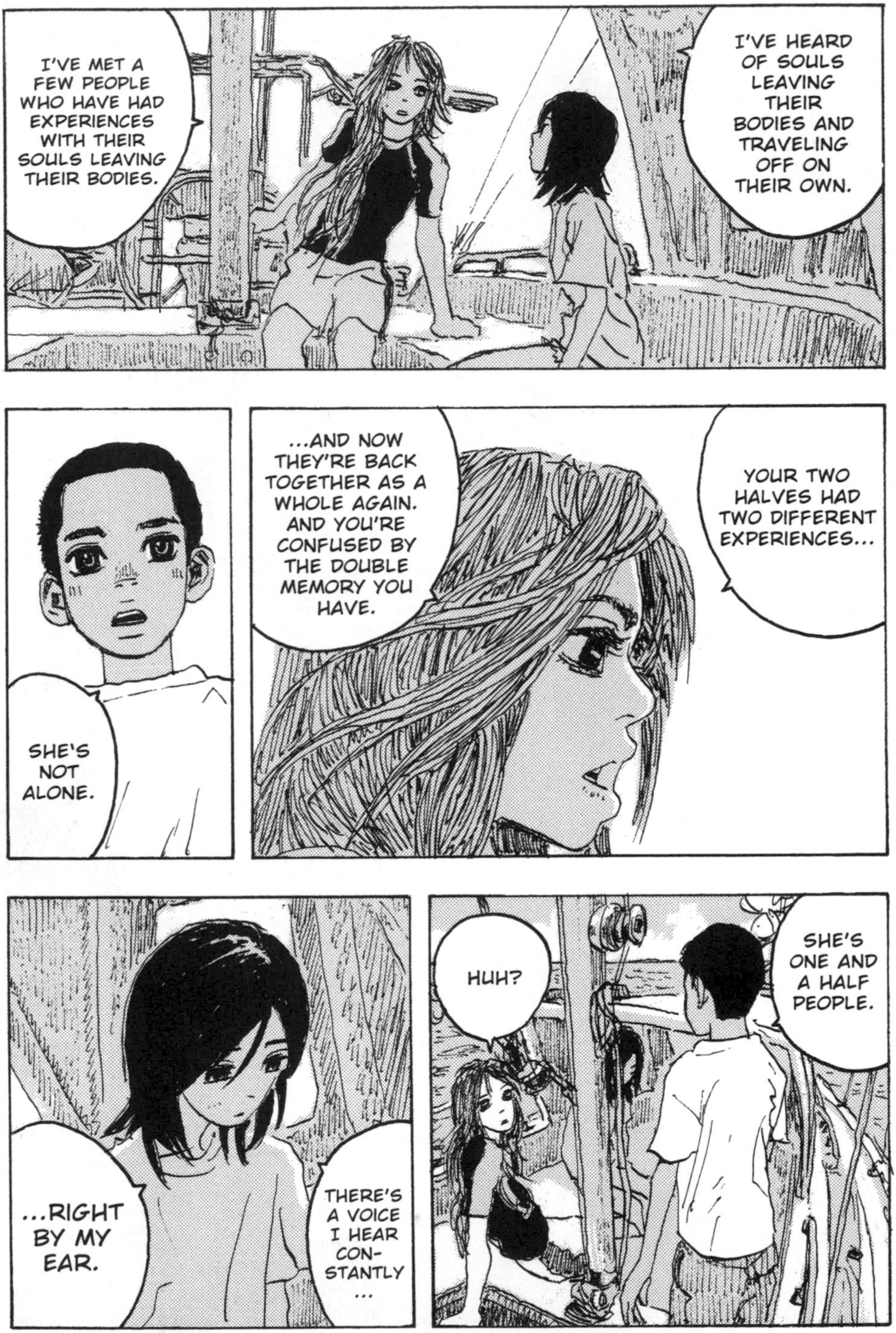
I'VE HEARD OF SOULS LEAVING THEIR BODIES AND TRAVELING OFF ON THEIR OWN.
I'VE MET A FEW PEOPLE WHO HAVE HAD EXPERIENCES WITH THEIR SOULS LEAVING THEIR BODIES.
YOUR TWO HALVES HAD TWO DIFFERENT EXPERIENCES...
...AND NOW THEY'RE BACK TOGETHER AS A WHOLE AGAIN. AND YOU'RE CONFUSED BY THE DOUBLE MEMORY YOU HAVE.
SHE'S NOT ALONE.
SHE'S ONE AND A HALF PEOPLE.
HUH?
THERE'S A VOICE I HEAR CON-STANTLY...
...RIGHT BY MY EAR.

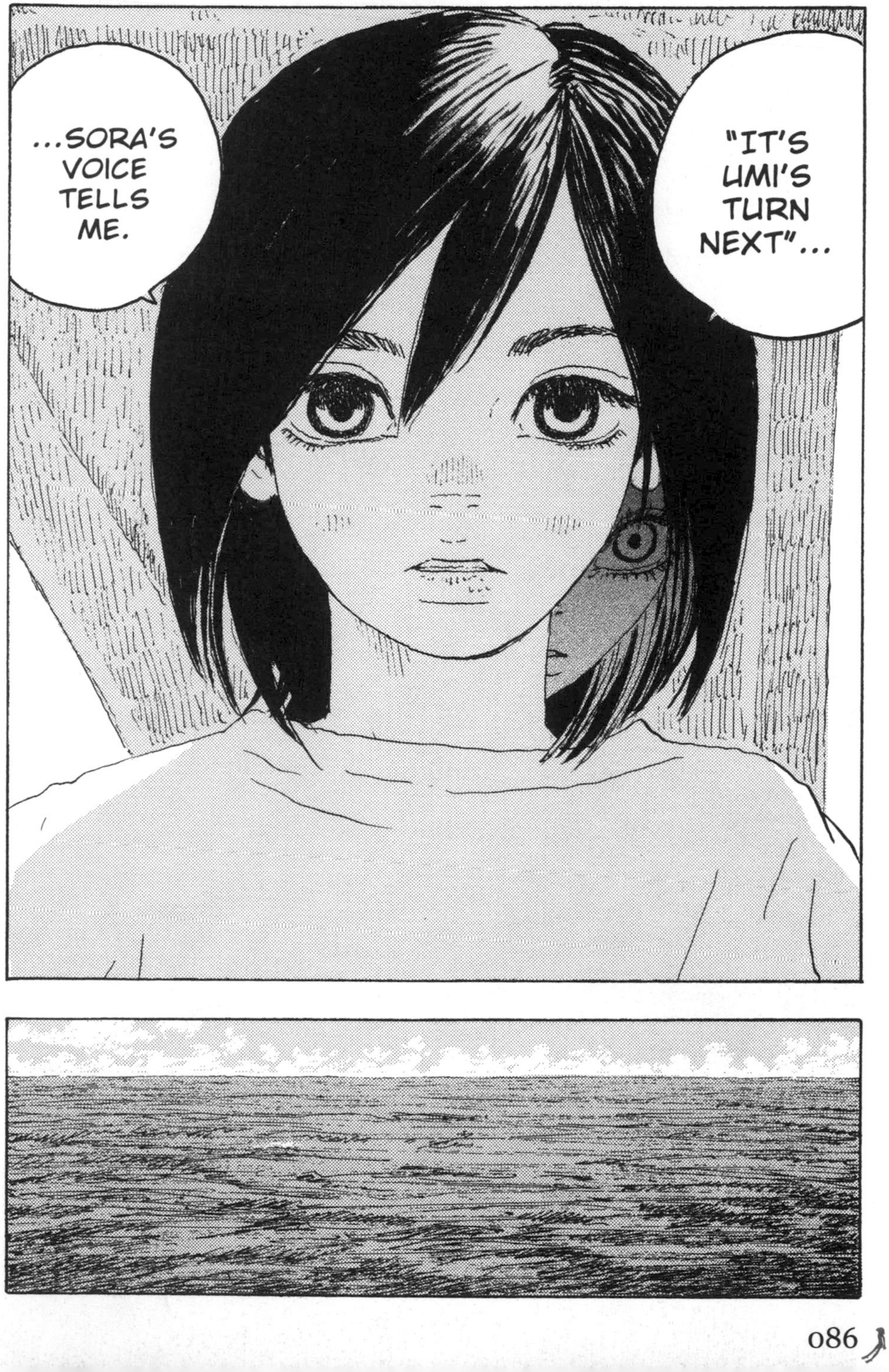
"IT'S UMI'S TURN NEXT"...
...SORA'S VOICE TELLS ME.

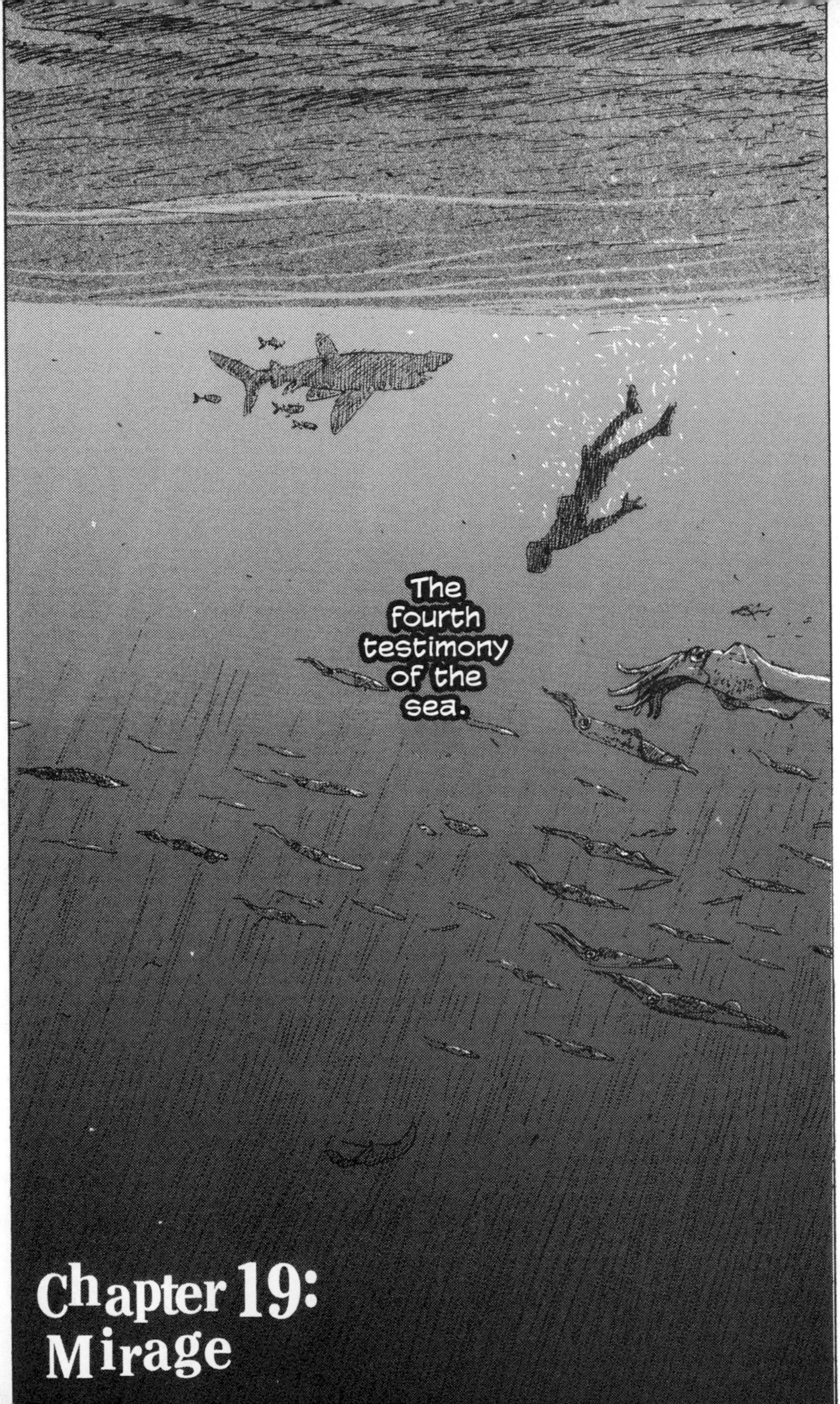
The fourth testimony of the sea.
Chapter 19:
Mirage

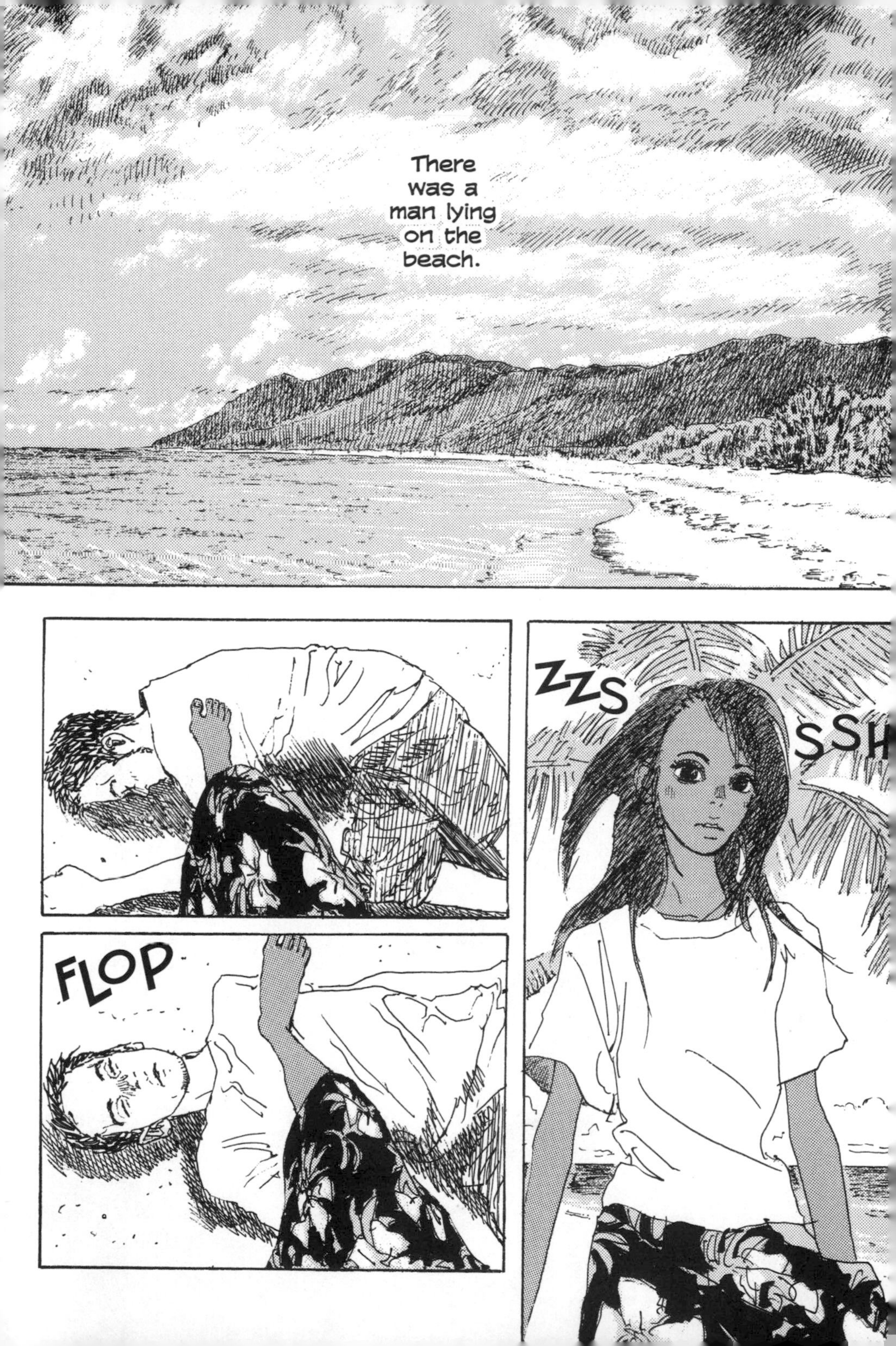

There was a man lying on the beach.
ZZS
SSH
FLOP

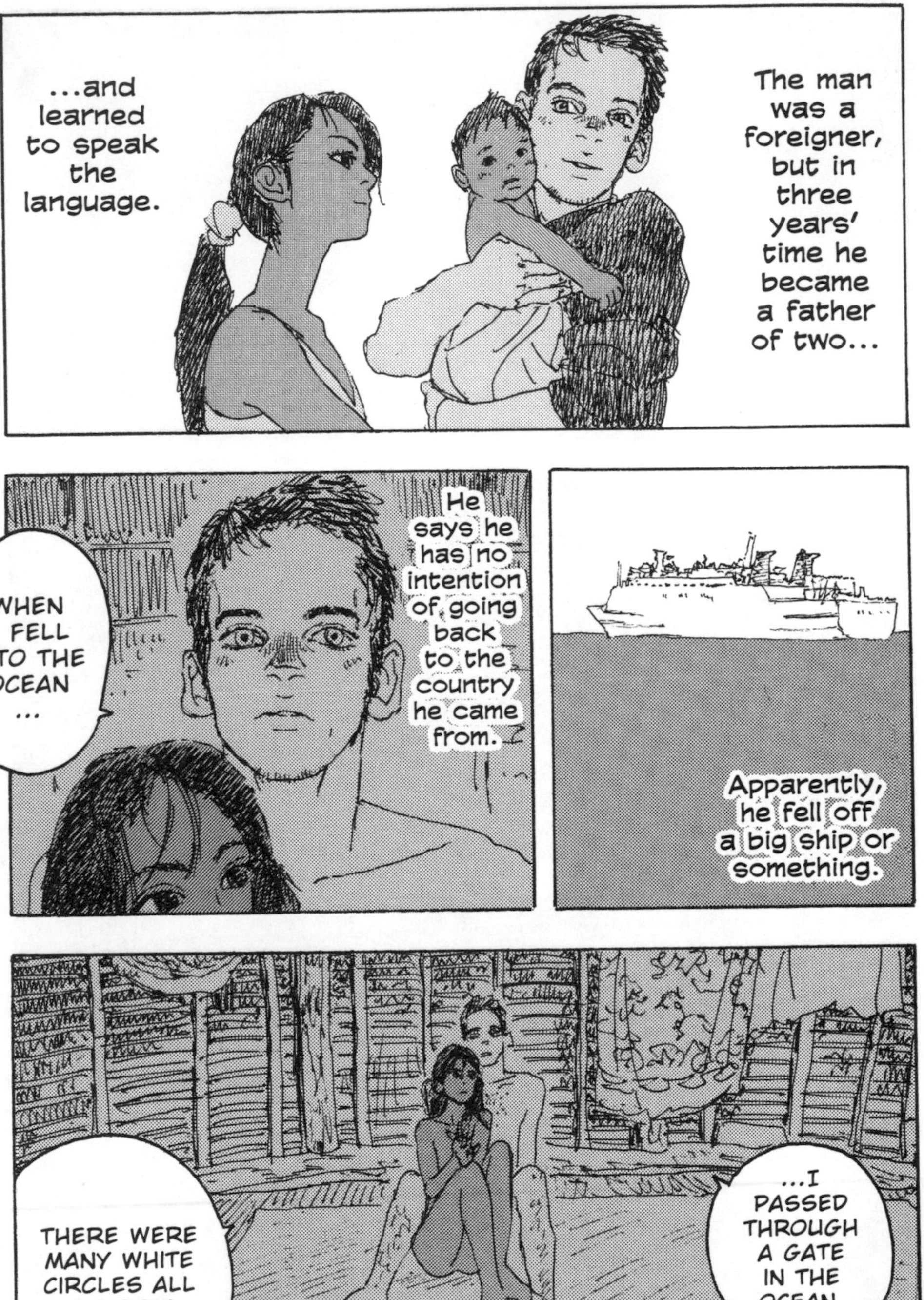
The man was a foreigner, but in three years' time he became a father of two...
...and learned to speak the language.
Apparently, he fell off a big ship or something.
He says he has no intention of going back to the country he came from.
WHEN I FELL INTO THE OCEAN ...
...I PASSED THROUGH A GATE IN THE OCEAN.
THERE WERE MANY WHITE CIRCLES ALL IN A ROW.

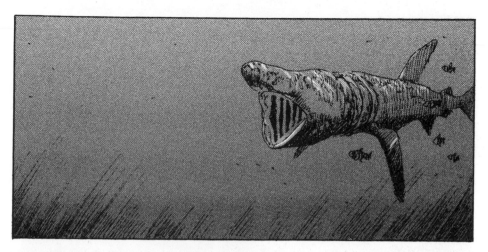

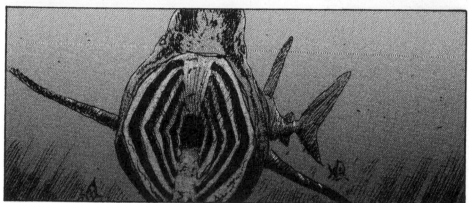

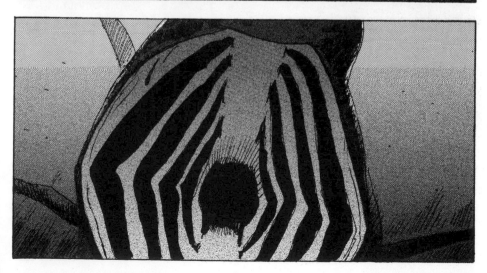

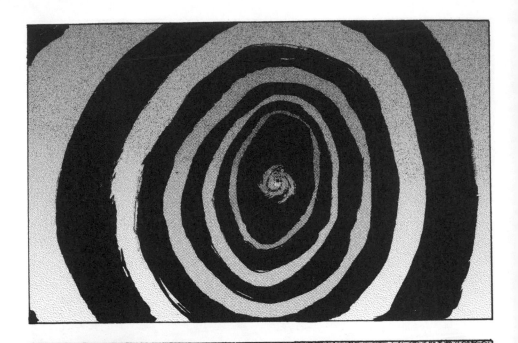

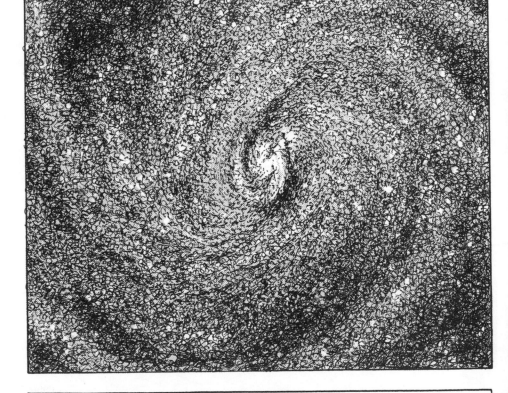

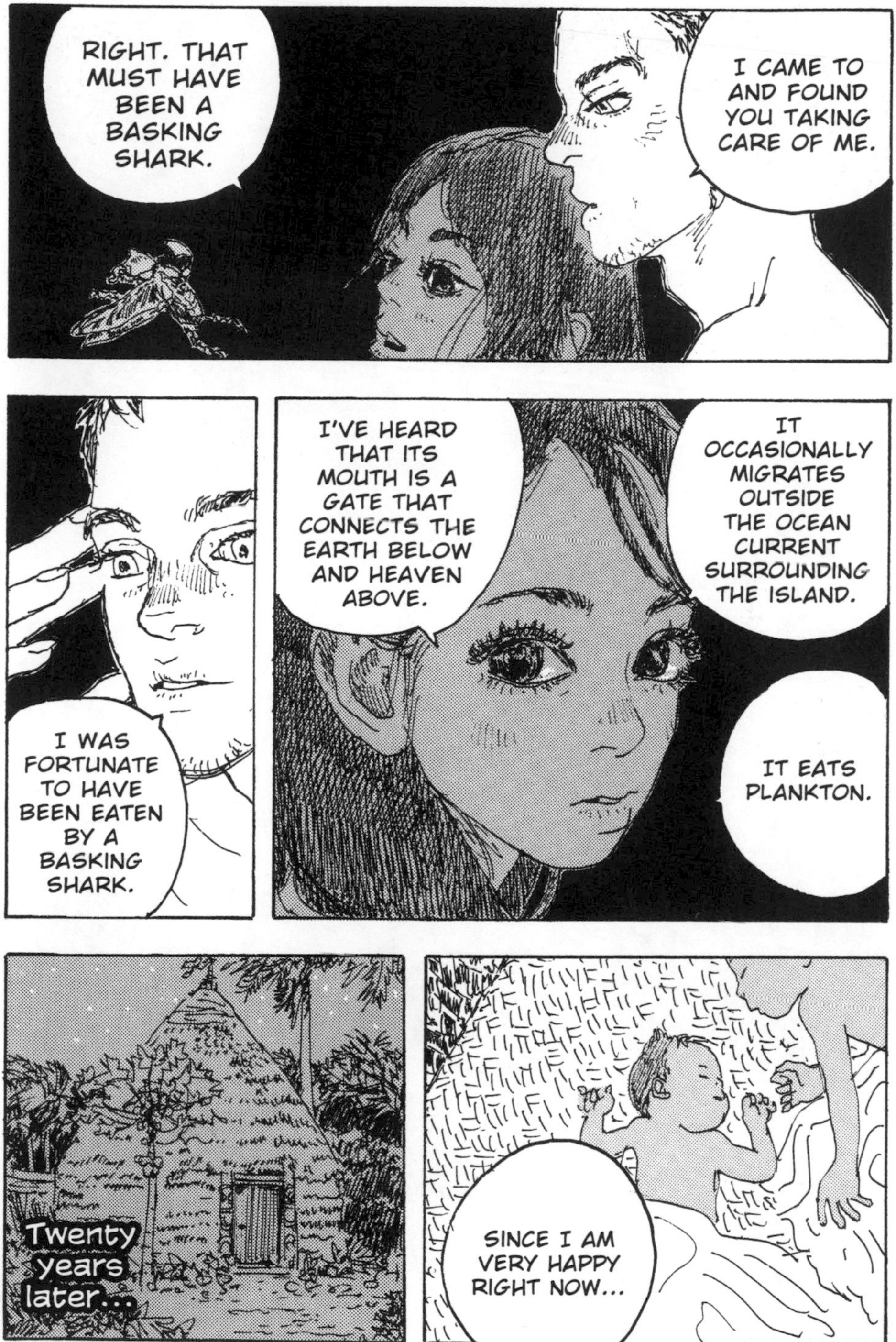
I CAME TO AND FOUND YOU TAKING CARE OF ME.
RIGHT. THAT MUST HAVE BEEN A BASKING SHARK.
IT OCCASIONALLY MIGRATES OUTSIDE THE OCEAN CURRENT SURROUNDING THE ISLAND.
I'VE HEARD THAT ITS MOUTH IS A GATE THAT CONNECTS THE EARTH BELOW AND HEAVEN ABOVE.
IT EATS PLANKTON.
I WAS FORTUNATE TO HAVE BEEN EATEN BY A BASKING SHARK.
SINCE I AM VERY HAPPY RIGHT NOW...
Twenty years later...

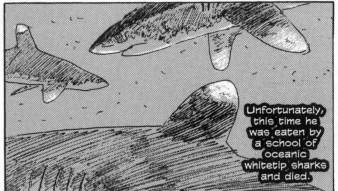

The man was injured while fishing.

Unfortunately, this time he was eaten by a school of oceanic whitetip sharks and died.

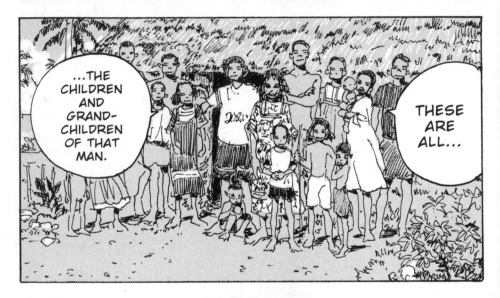

...THE CHILDREN AND GRAND-CHILDREN OF THAT MAN.

THESE ARE ALL...

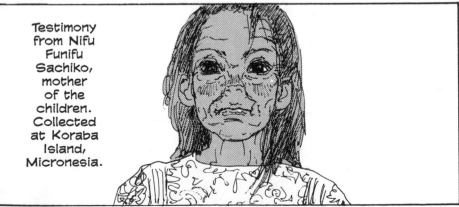

Testimony from Nifu Funifu Sachiko, mother of the children. Collected at Koraba Island, Micronesia.

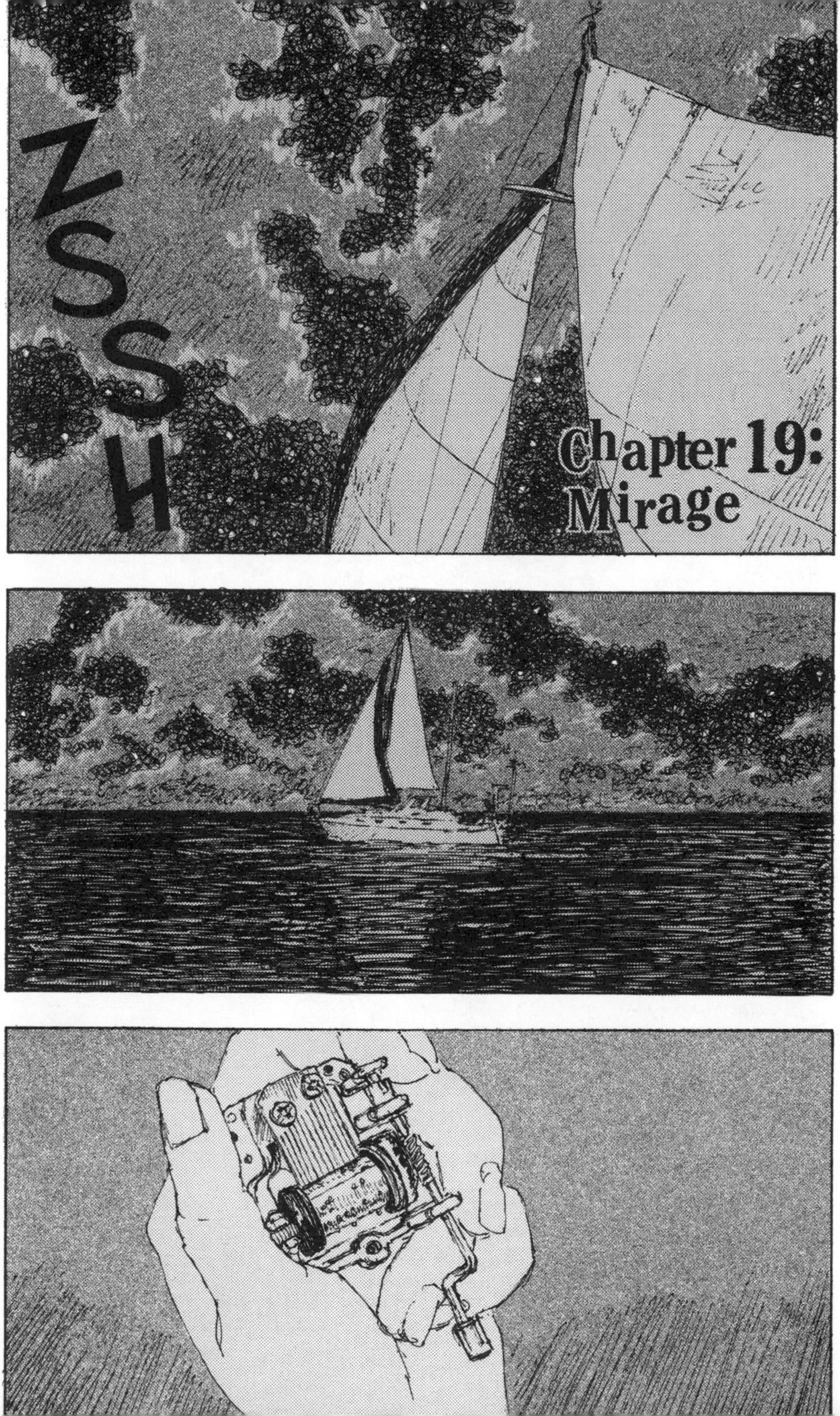
ZSSH
Chapter 19:
Mirage

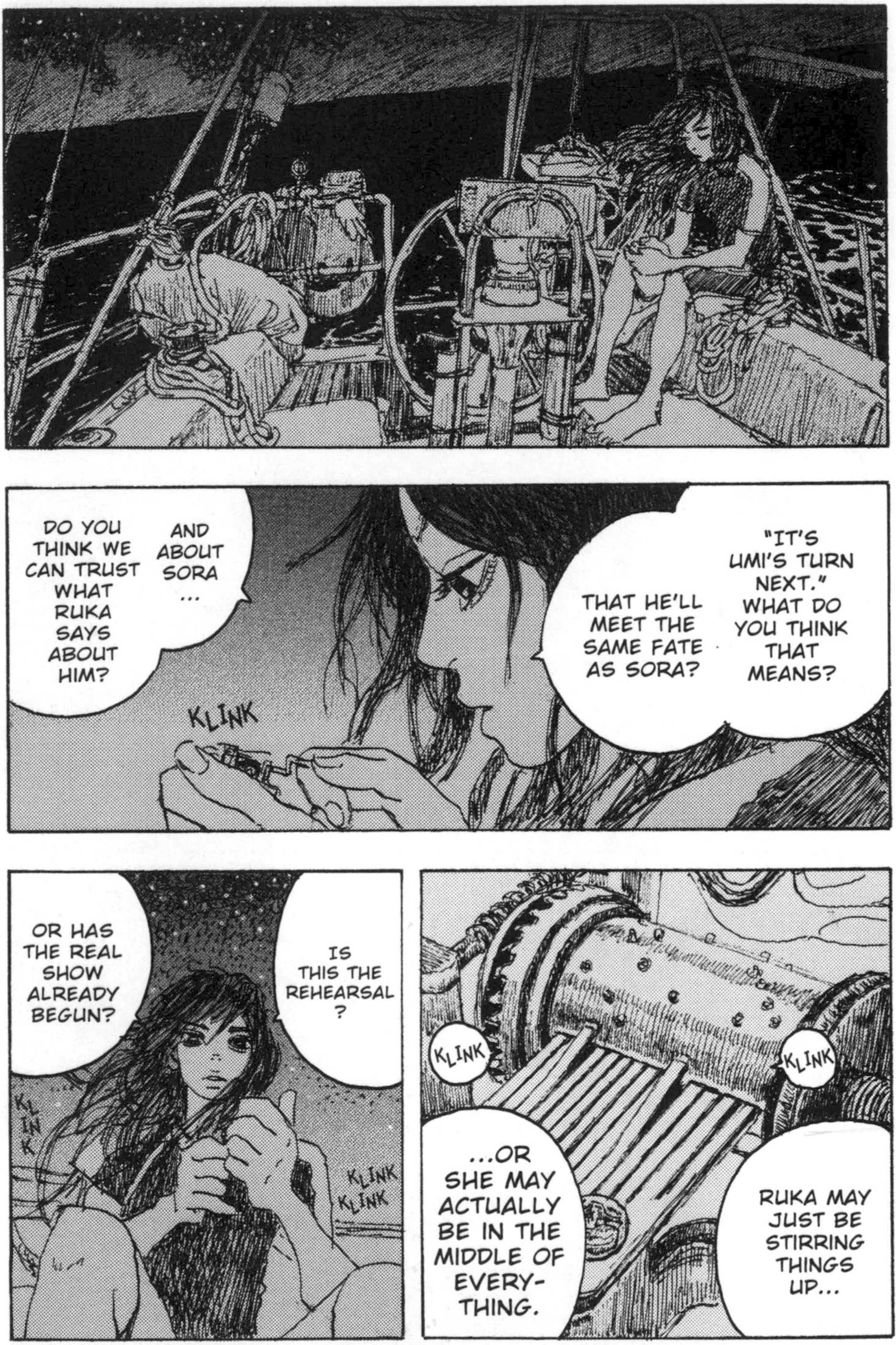
"IT'S UMI'S TURN NEXT." WHAT DO YOU THINK THAT MEANS?
THAT HE'LL MEET THE SAME FATE AS SORA?
AND ABOUT SORA...
DO YOU THINK WE CAN TRUST WHAT RUKA SAYS ABOUT HIM?
KLINK
KLINK
KLINK
RUKA MAY JUST BE STIRRING THINGS UP...
...OR SHE MAY ACTUALLY BE IN THE MIDDLE OF EVERY-THING.
IS THIS THE REHEARSAL?
OR HAS THE REAL SHOW ALREADY BEGUN?
KLINK
KLINK KLINK

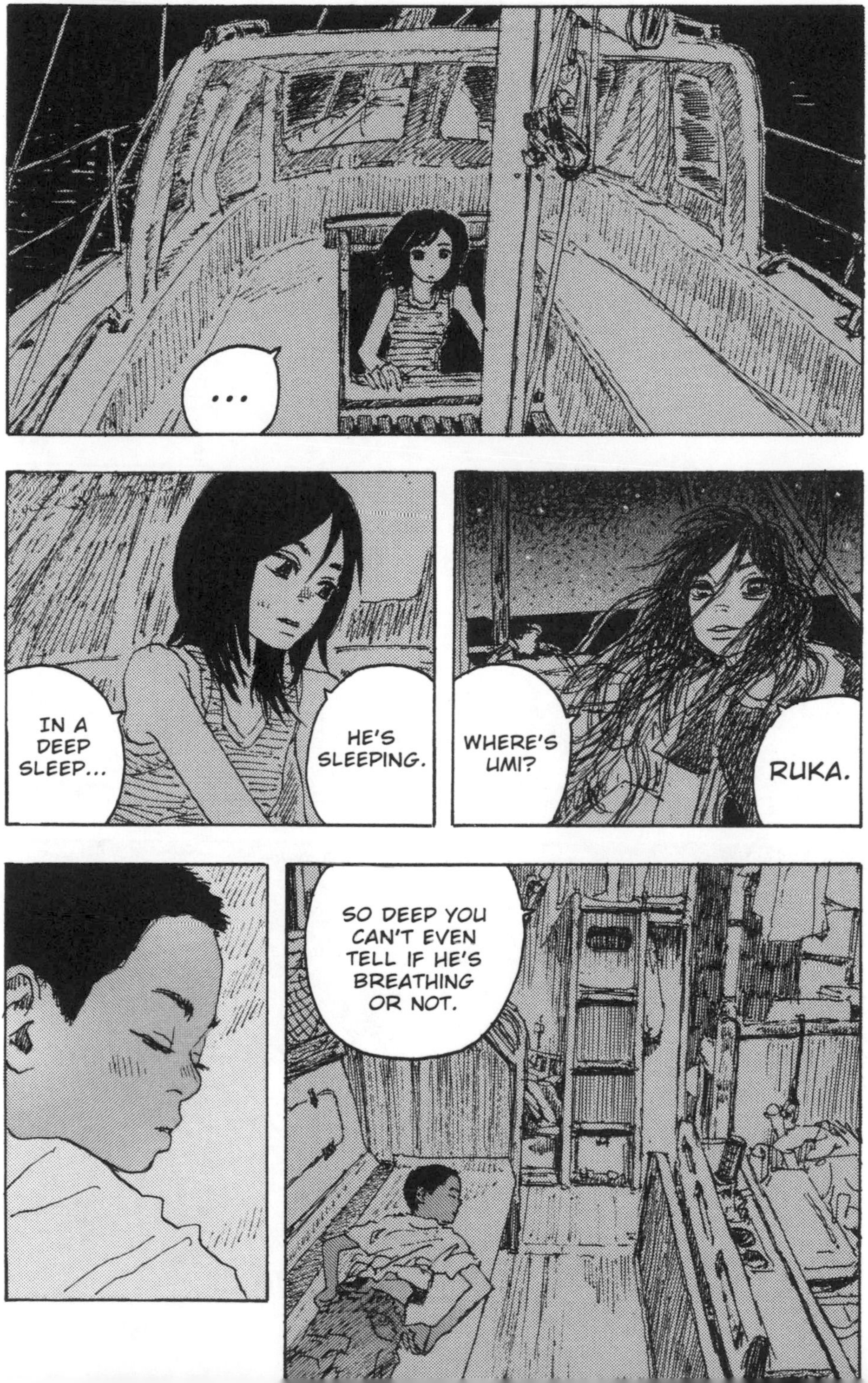
...
RUKA.
WHERE'S UMI?
HE'S SLEEPING.
IN A DEEP SLEEP...
SO DEEP YOU CAN'T EVEN TELL IF HE'S BREATHING OR NOT.

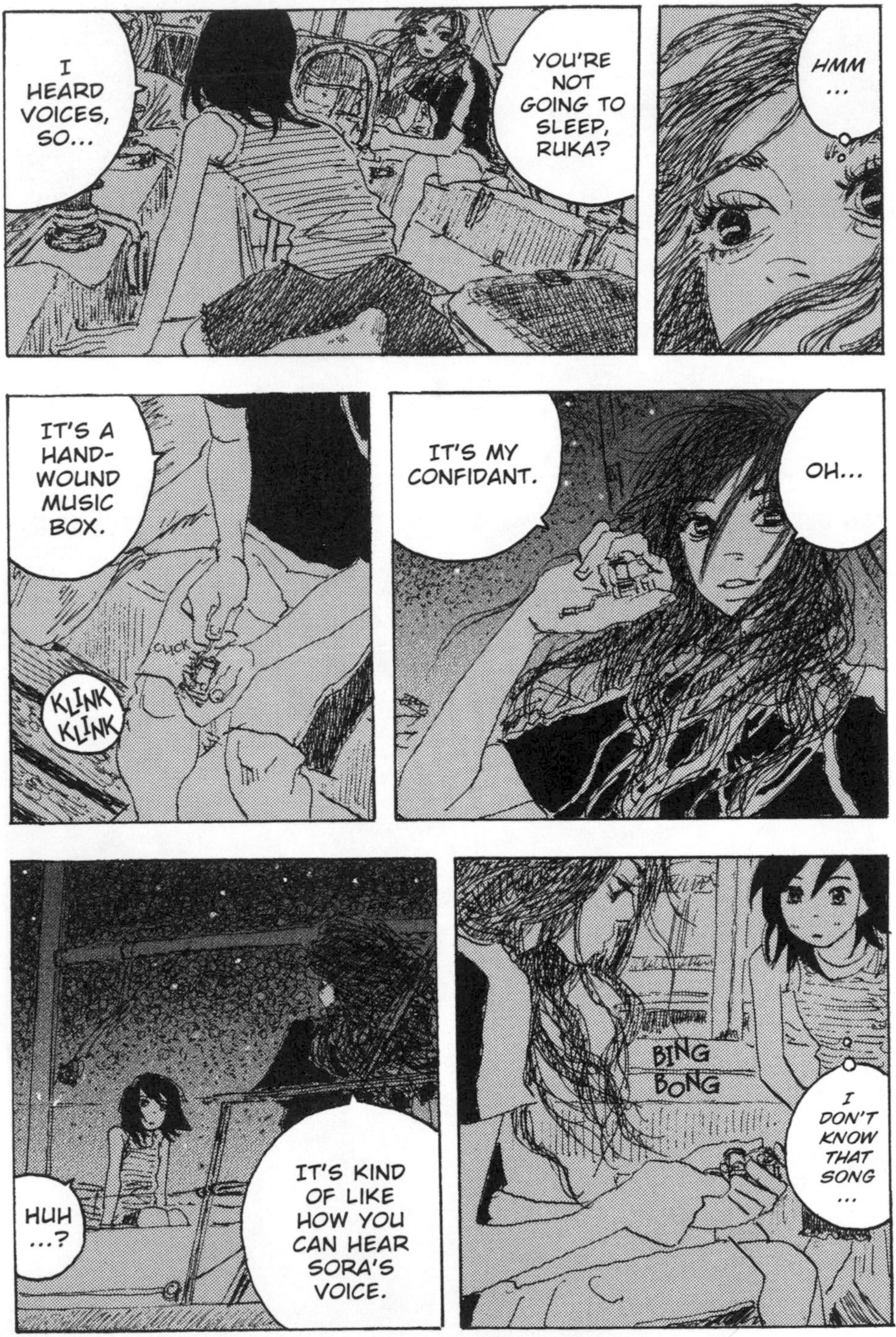
HMM ...
YOU'RE NOT GOING TO SLEEP, RUKA?
I HEARD VOICES, SO...
OH...
IT'S MY CONFIDANT.
IT'S A HAND-WOUND MUSIC BOX.
CLICK
KLINK KLINK
BING BONG
I DON'T KNOW THAT SONG ...
IT'S KIND OF LIKE HOW YOU CAN HEAR SORA'S VOICE.
HUH ...?

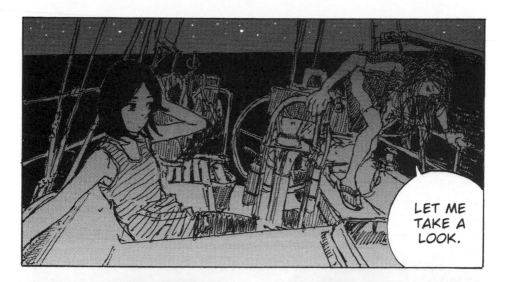

LET ME TAKE A LOOK.

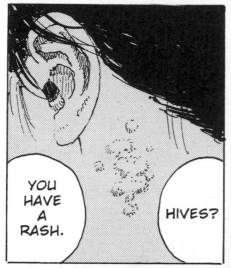

YOU HAVE A RASH.

HIVES?

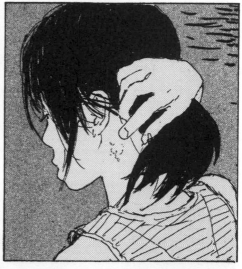

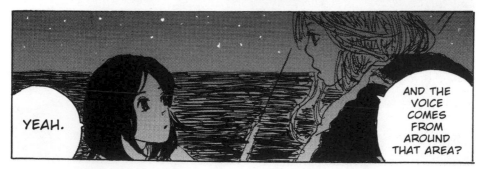

YEAH.

AND THE VOICE COMES FROM AROUND THAT AREA?

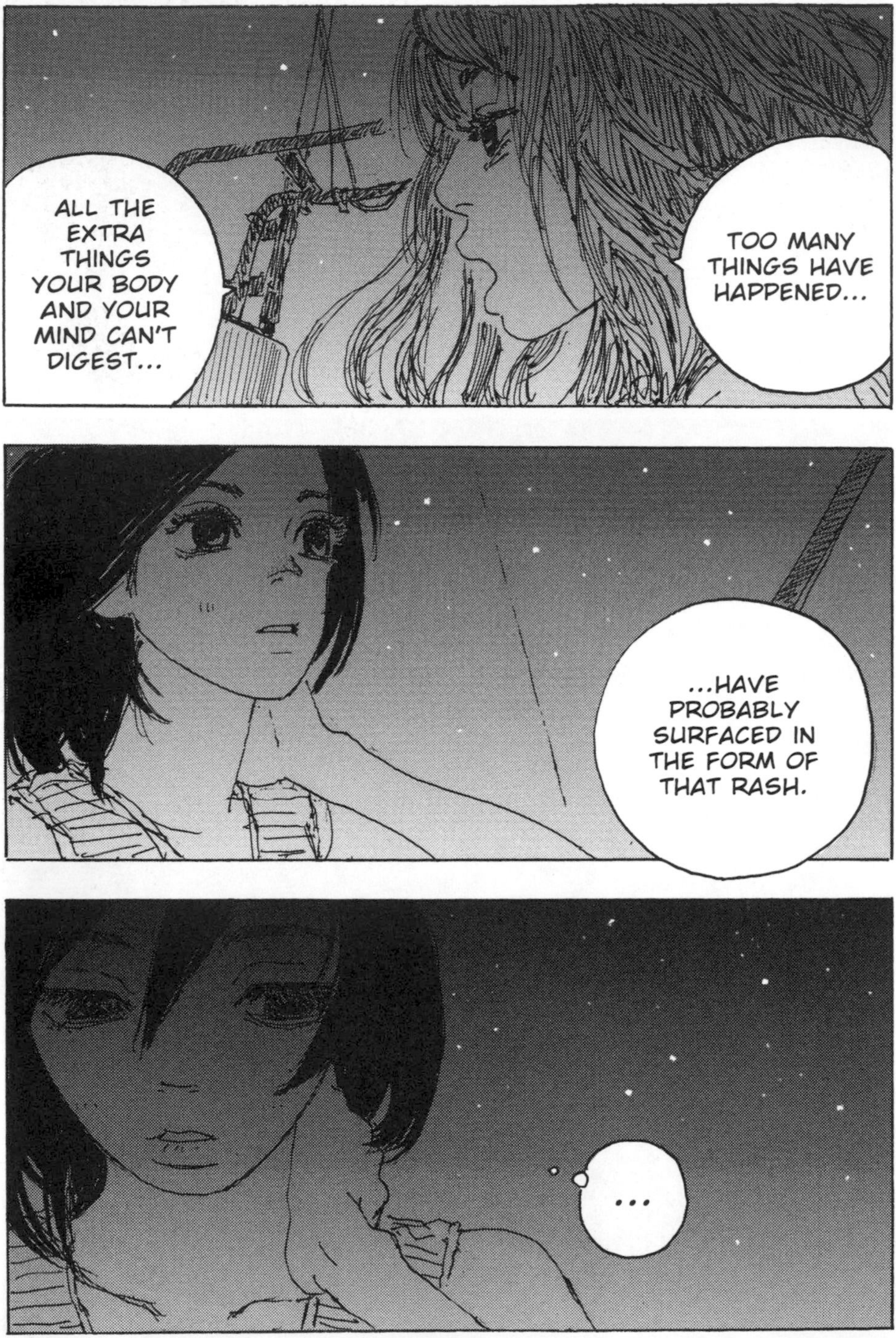
TOO MANY THINGS HAVE HAPPENED...
ALL THE EXTRA THINGS YOUR BODY AND YOUR MIND CAN'T DIGEST...
...HAVE PROBABLY SURFACED IN THE FORM OF THAT RASH.
...

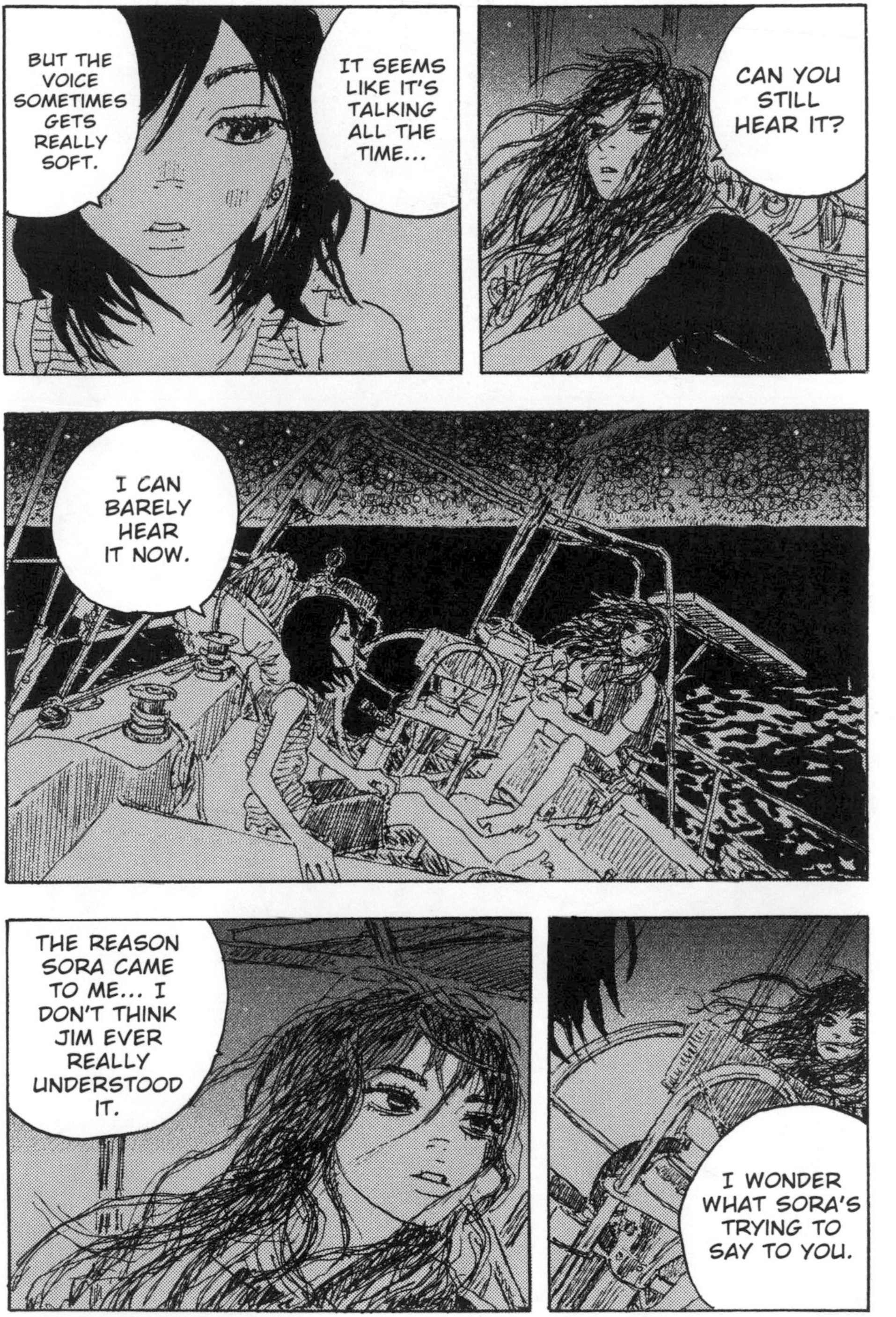
CAN YOU STILL HEAR IT?
IT SEEMS LIKE IT'S TALKING ALL THE TIME...
BUT THE VOICE SOMETIMES GETS REALLY SOFT.
I CAN BARELY HEAR IT NOW.
I WONDER WHAT SORA'S TRYING TO SAY TO YOU.
THE REASON SORA CAME TO ME... I DON'T THINK JIM EVER REALLY UNDERSTOOD IT.

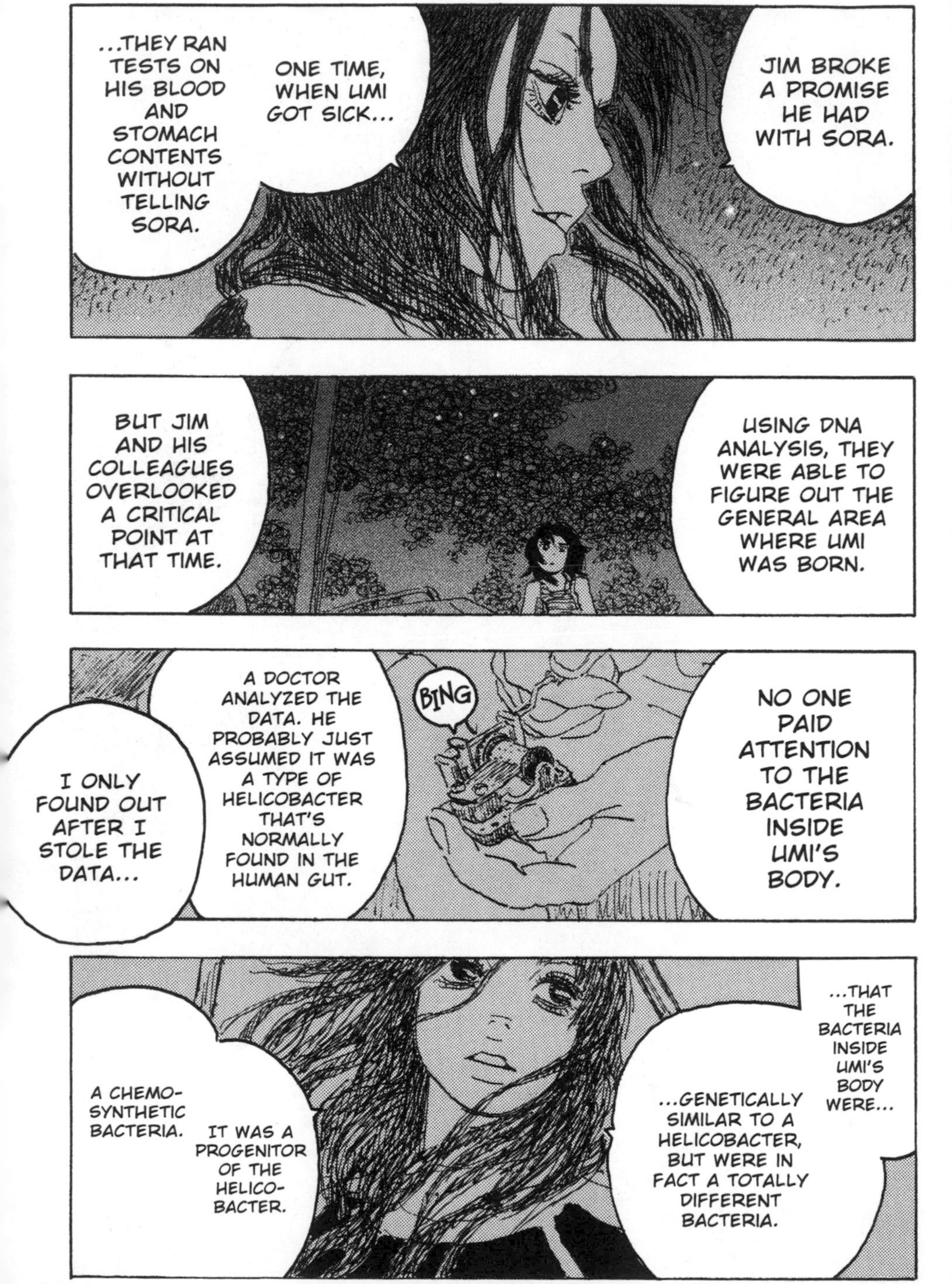
JIM BROKE A PROMISE HE HAD WITH SORA.
ONE TIME, WHEN UMI GOT SICK...
...THEY RAN TESTS ON HIS BLOOD AND STOMACH CONTENTS WITHOUT TELLING SORA.
USING DNA ANALYSIS, THEY WERE ABLE TO FIGURE OUT THE GENERAL AREA WHERE UMI WAS BORN.
BUT JIM AND HIS COLLEAGUES OVERLOOKED A CRITICAL POINT AT THAT TIME.
NO ONE PAID ATTENTION TO THE BACTERIA INSIDE UMI'S BODY.
BING
A DOCTOR ANALYZED THE DATA. HE PROBABLY JUST ASSUMED IT WAS A TYPE OF HELICOBACTER THAT'S NORMALLY FOUND IN THE HUMAN GUT.
I ONLY FOUND OUT AFTER I STOLE THE DATA...
...THAT THE BACTERIA INSIDE UMI'S BODY WERE...
...GENETICALLY SIMILAR TO A HELICOBACTER, BUT WERE IN FACT A TOTALLY DIFFERENT BACTERIA.
IT WAS A PROGENITOR OF THE HELICO-BACTER.
A CHEMO-SYNTHETIC BACTERIA.

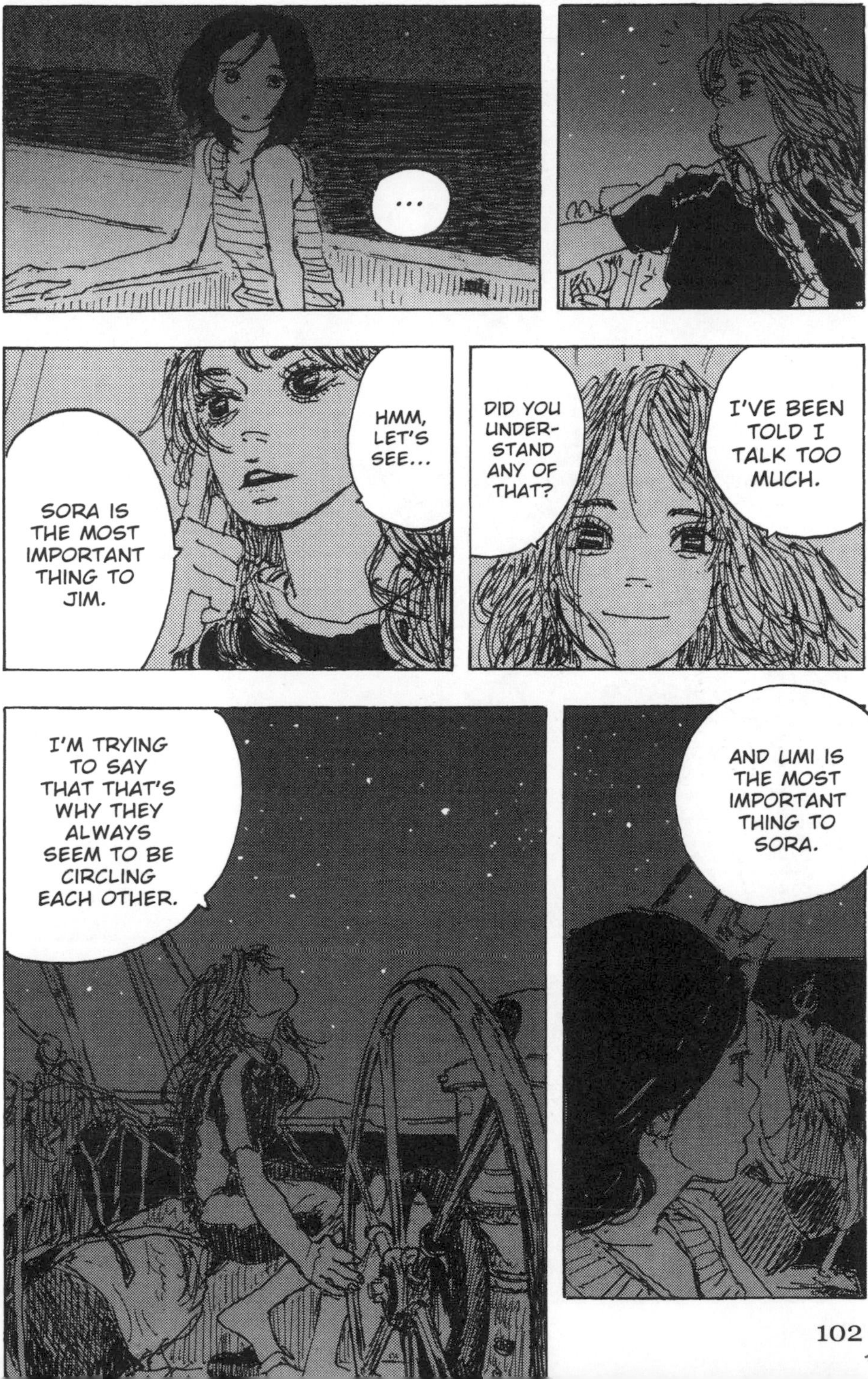
...
I'VE BEEN TOLD I TALK TOO MUCH.
DID YOU UNDER-STAND ANY OF THAT?
HMM, LET'S SEE...
SORA IS THE MOST IMPORTANT THING TO JIM.
AND UMI IS THE MOST IMPORTANT THING TO SORA.
I'M TRYING TO SAY THAT THAT'S WHY THEY ALWAYS SEEM TO BE CIRCLING EACH OTHER.

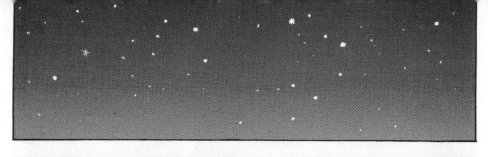

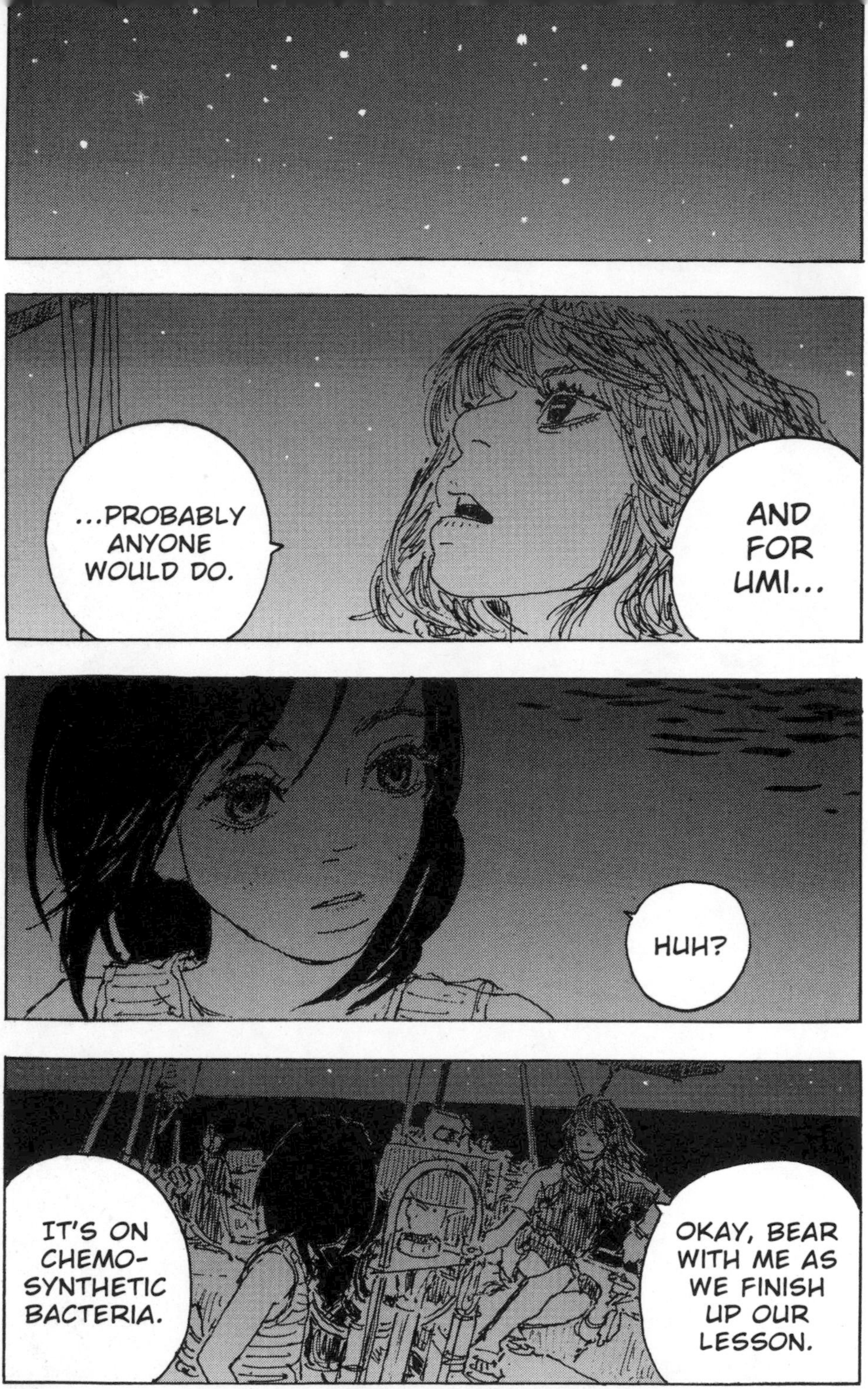
AND FOR UMI...
...PROBABLY ANYONE WOULD DO.
HUH?
OKAY, BEAR WITH ME AS WE FINISH UP OUR LESSON.
IT'S ON CHEMO-SYNTHETIC BACTERIA.

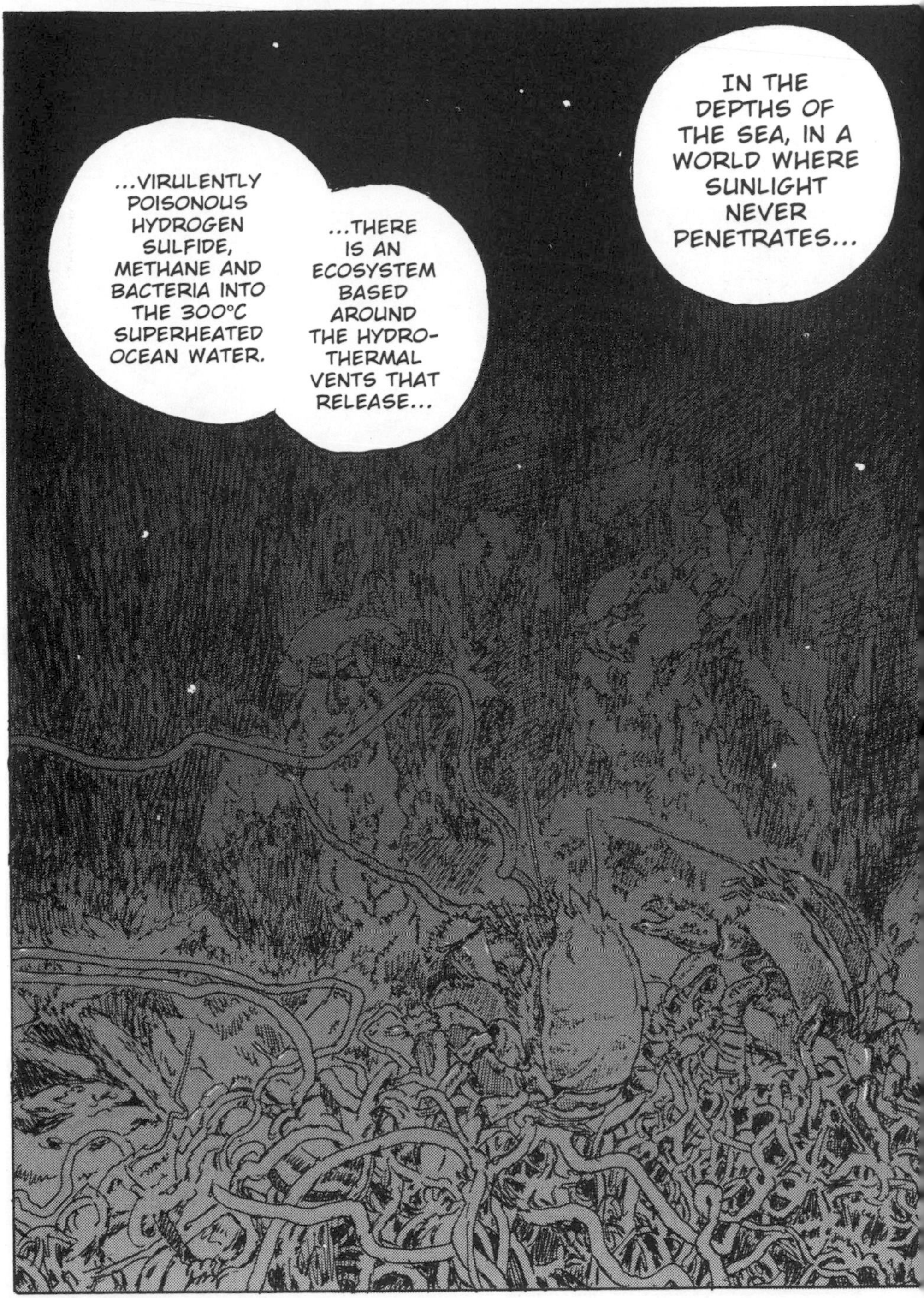
IN THE DEPTHS OF THE SEA, IN A WORLD WHERE SUNLIGHT NEVER PENETRATES...
...THERE IS AN ECOSYSTEM BASED AROUND THE HYDRO-THERMAL VENTS THAT RELEASE...
...VIRULENTLY POISONOUS HYDROGEN SULFIDE, METHANE AND BACTERIA INTO THE 300°C SUPERHEATED OCEAN WATER.

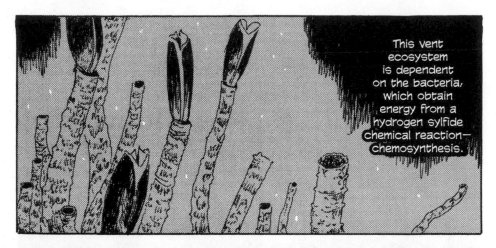

This vent ecosystem is dependent on the bacteria, which obtain energy from a hydrogen sylfide chemical reaction—chemosynthesis.

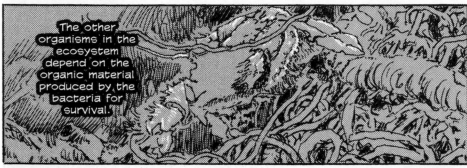

The other organisms in the ecosystem depend on the organic material produced by the bacteria for survival.

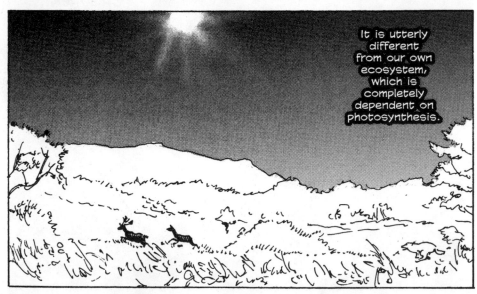

It is utterly different from our own ecosystem, which is completely dependent on photosynthesis.

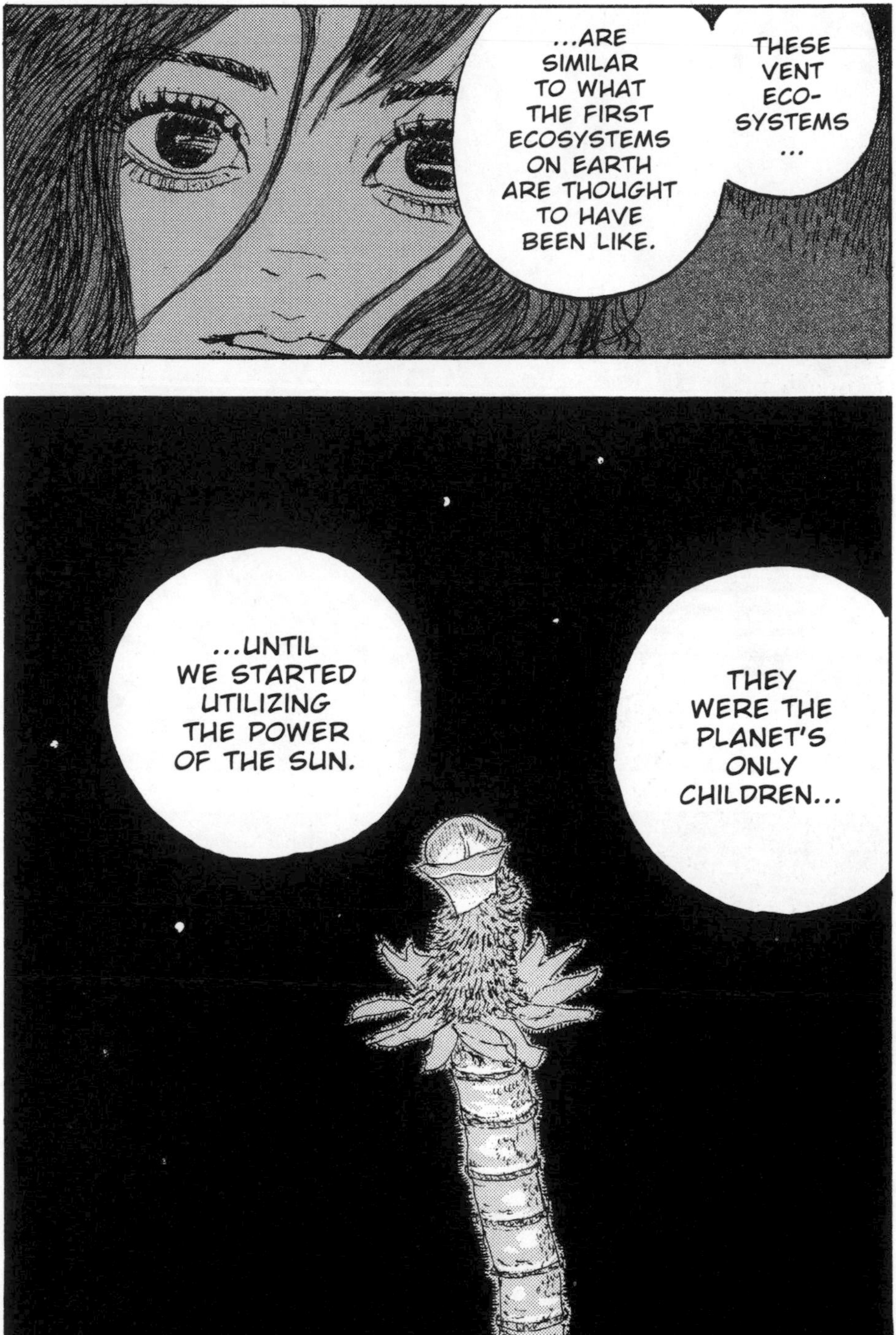
THESE VENT ECO-SYSTEMS ...
...ARE SIMILAR TO WHAT THE FIRST ECOSYSTEMS ON EARTH ARE THOUGHT TO HAVE BEEN LIKE.
THEY WERE THE PLANET'S ONLY CHILDREN...
...UNTIL WE STARTED UTILIZING THE POWER OF THE SUN.

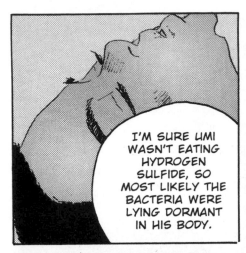

THE BACTERIA THE VENT ECOSYSTEM IS BASED ON WERE FOUND IN UMI'S BODY.
ISN'T THAT THOUGHT JUST THRILL-ING?
I'M SURE UMI WASN'T EATING HYDROGEN SULFIDE, SO MOST LIKELY THE BACTERIA WERE LYING DORMANT IN HIS BODY.
WERE THEY ACTIVE AT ONE TIME?
OR ARE THEY WAITING FOR THE RIGHT TIME TO BECOME ACTIVE ...?
I'M COM-PLETELY INTRIGUED.
WHEN YOU HEAR A STORY LIKE THIS...
...YOU CAN'T HELP BUT WONDER...

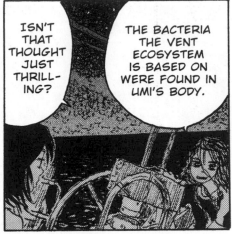

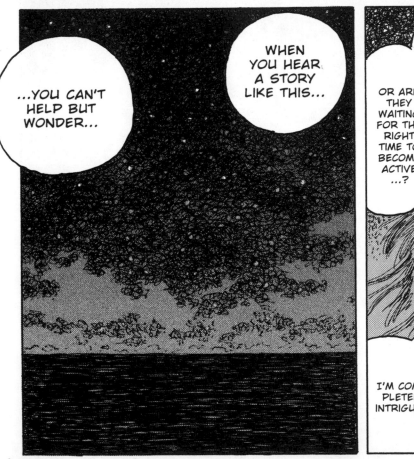

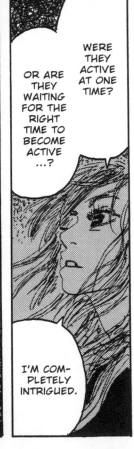

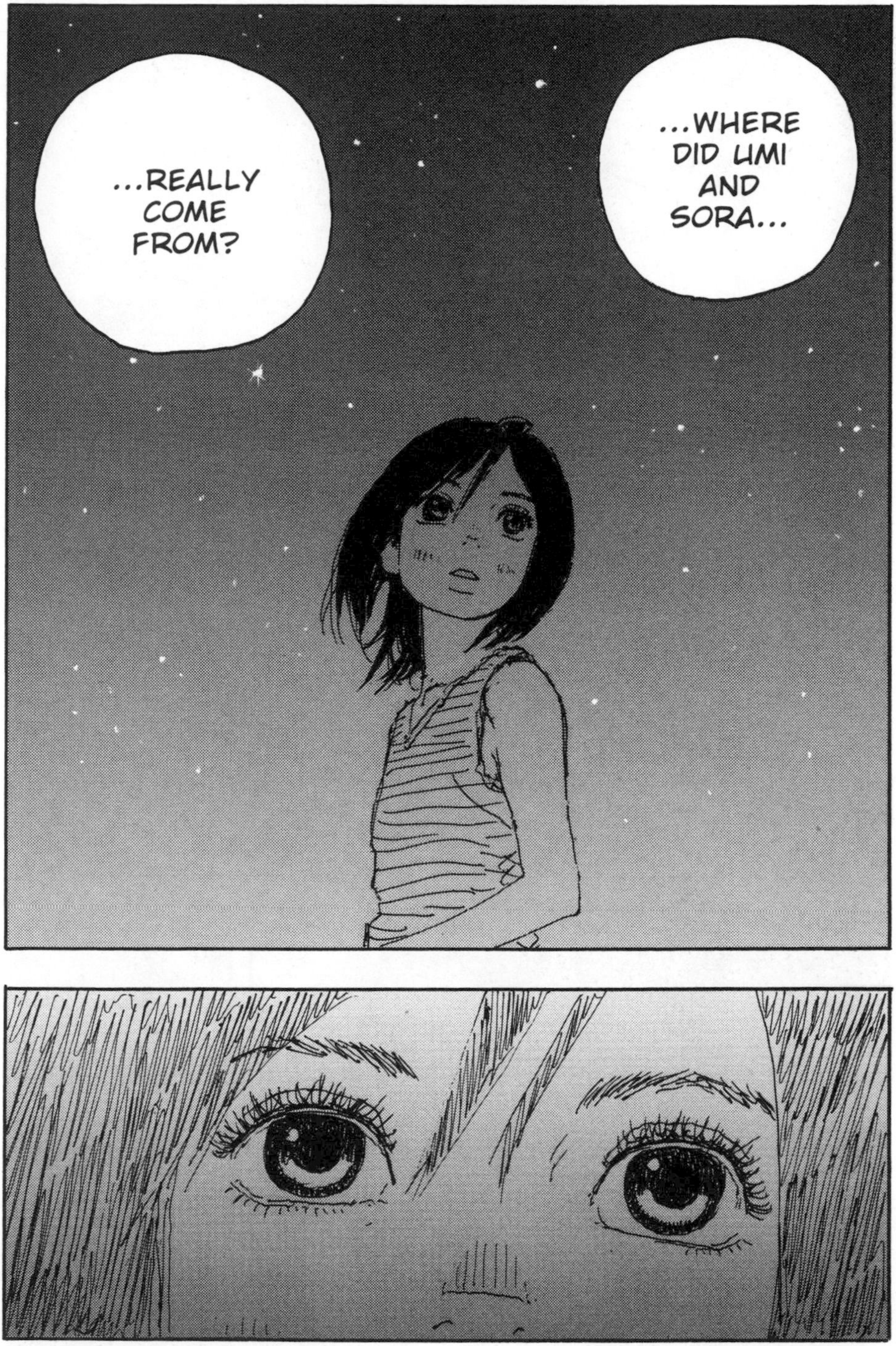
...WHERE DID UMI AND SORA...
...REALLY COME FROM?

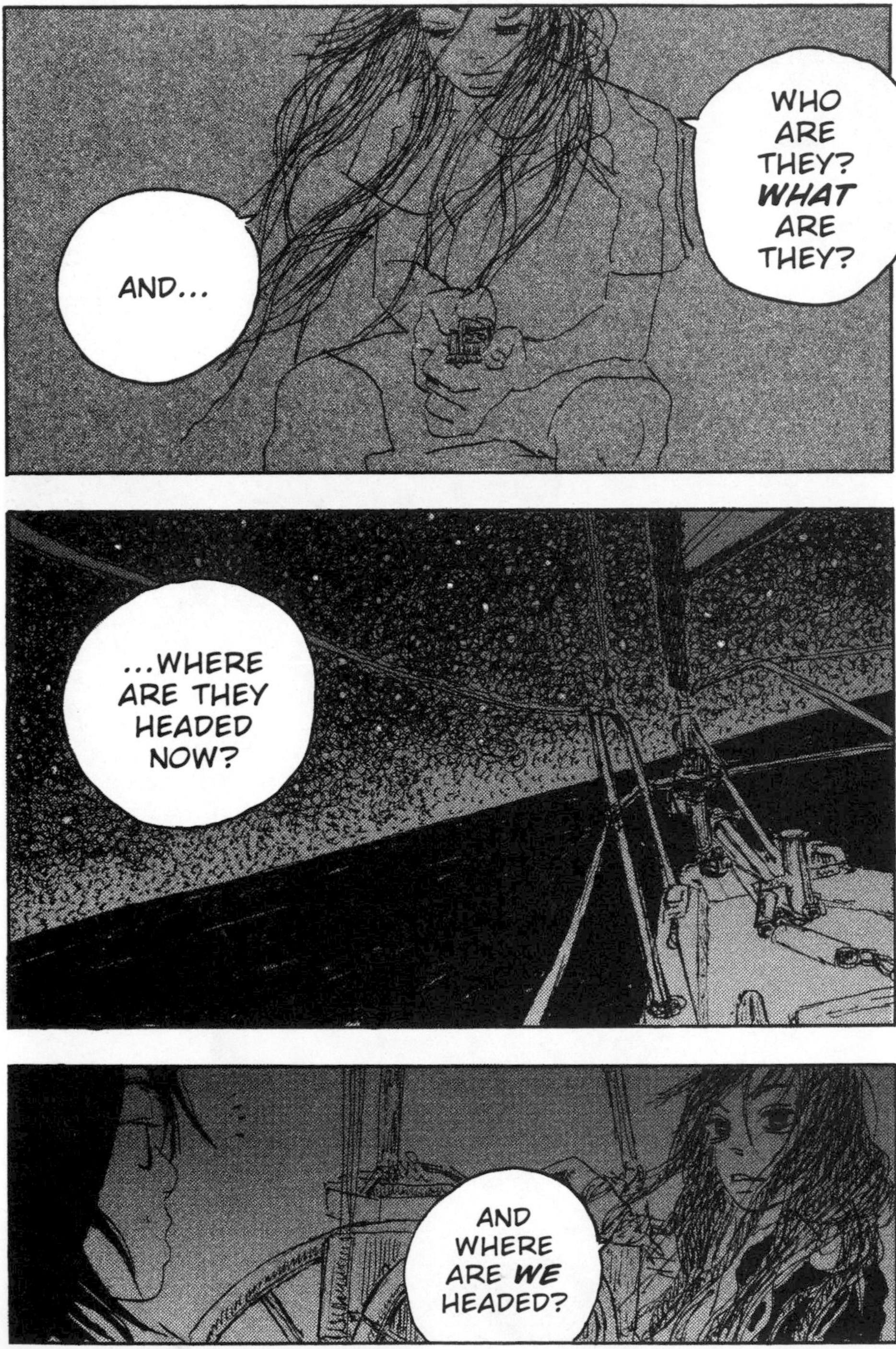
WHO ARE THEY? WHAT ARE THEY?
AND...
...WHERE ARE THEY HEADED NOW?
AND WHERE ARE WE HEADED?

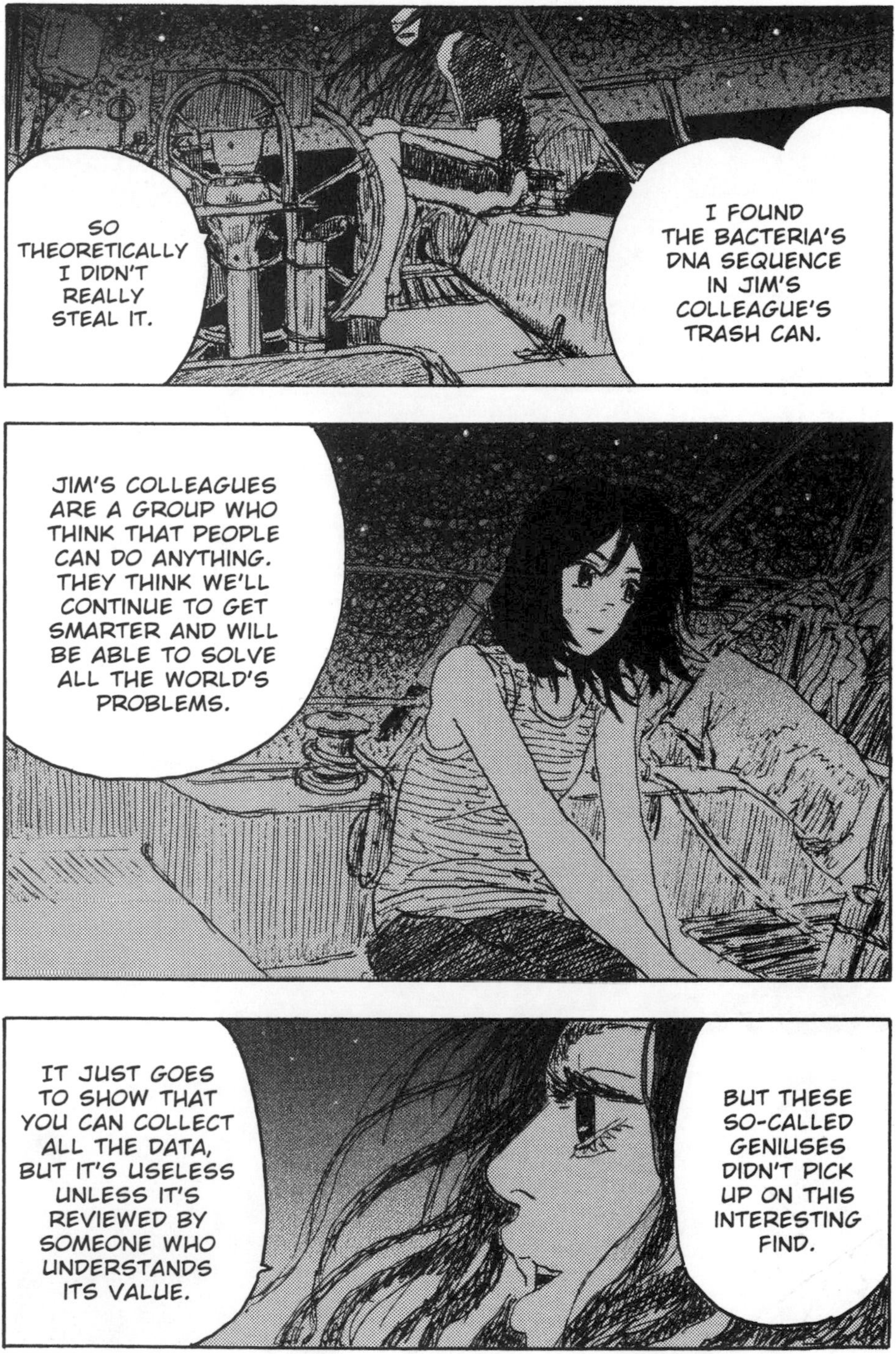
I FOUND THE BACTERIA'S DNA SEQUENCE IN JIM'S COLLEAGUE'S TRASH CAN.
SO THEORETICALLY I DIDN'T REALLY STEAL IT.
JIM'S COLLEAGUES ARE A GROUP WHO THINK THAT PEOPLE CAN DO ANYTHING. THEY THINK WE'LL CONTINUE TO GET SMARTER AND WILL BE ABLE TO SOLVE ALL THE WORLD'S PROBLEMS.
BUT THESE SO-CALLED GENIUSES DIDN'T PICK UP ON THIS INTERESTING FIND.
IT JUST GOES TO SHOW THAT YOU CAN COLLECT ALL THE DATA, BUT IT'S USELESS UNLESS IT'S REVIEWED BY SOMEONE WHO UNDERSTANDS ITS VALUE.

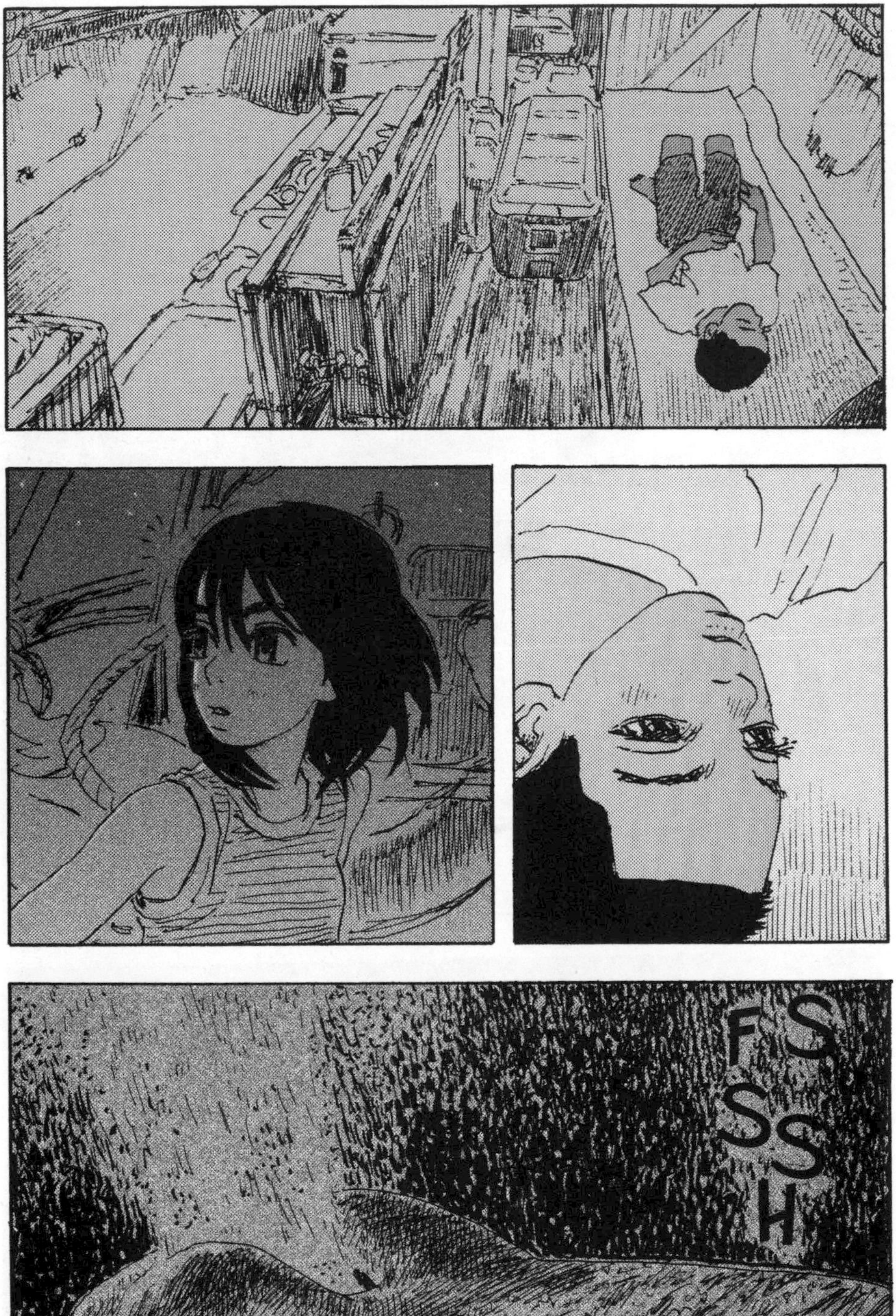
FSSSH

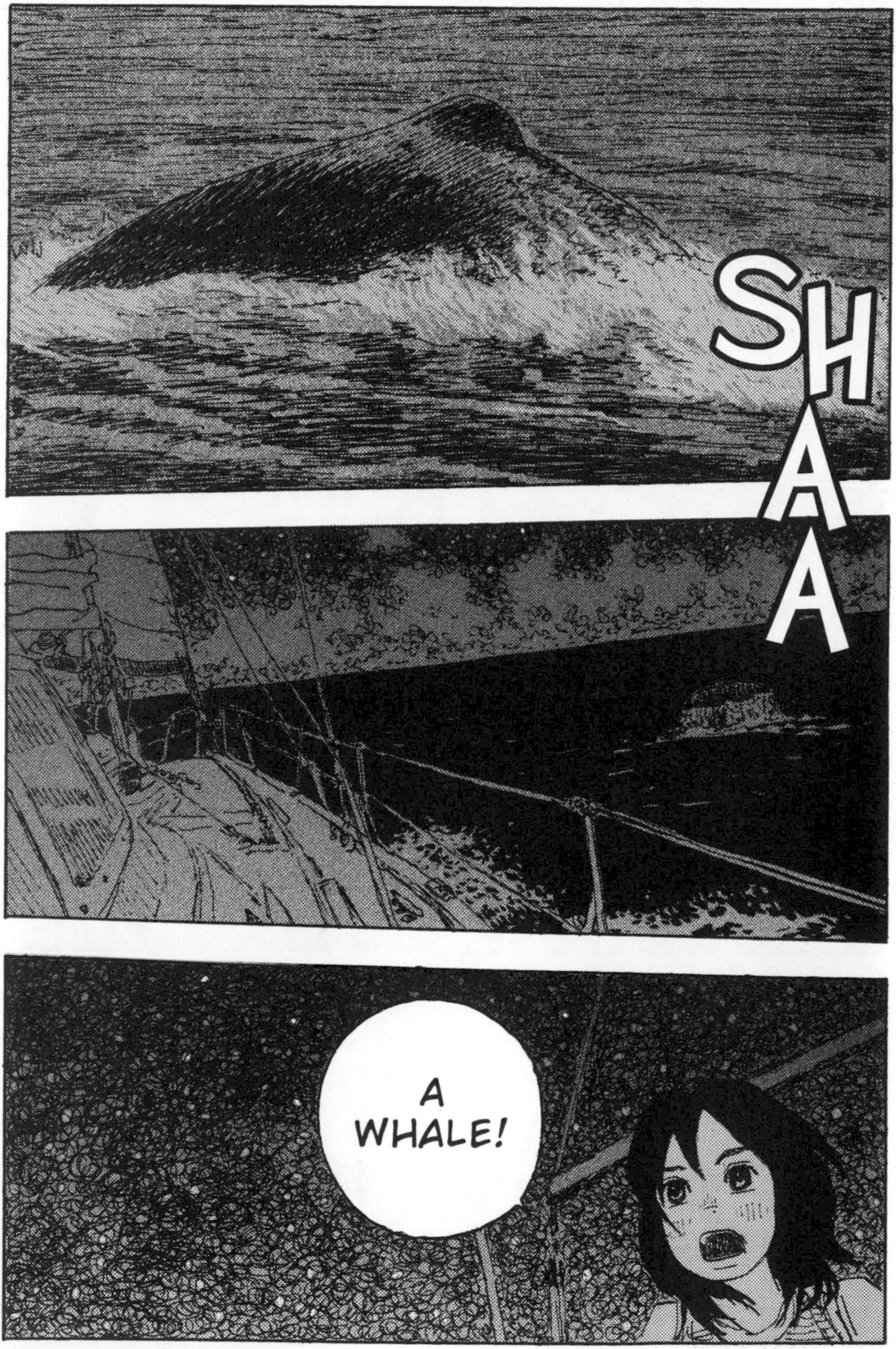
SHHAAA
A WHALE!

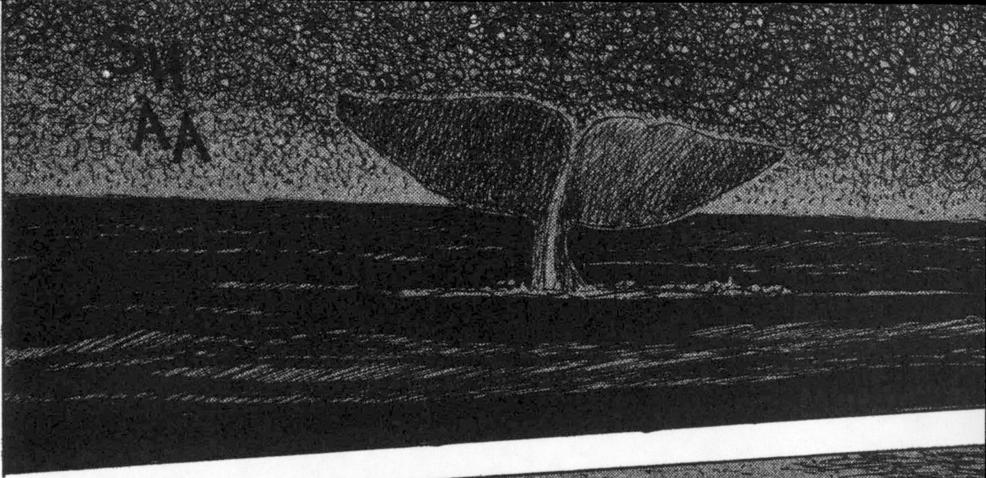
SWAA
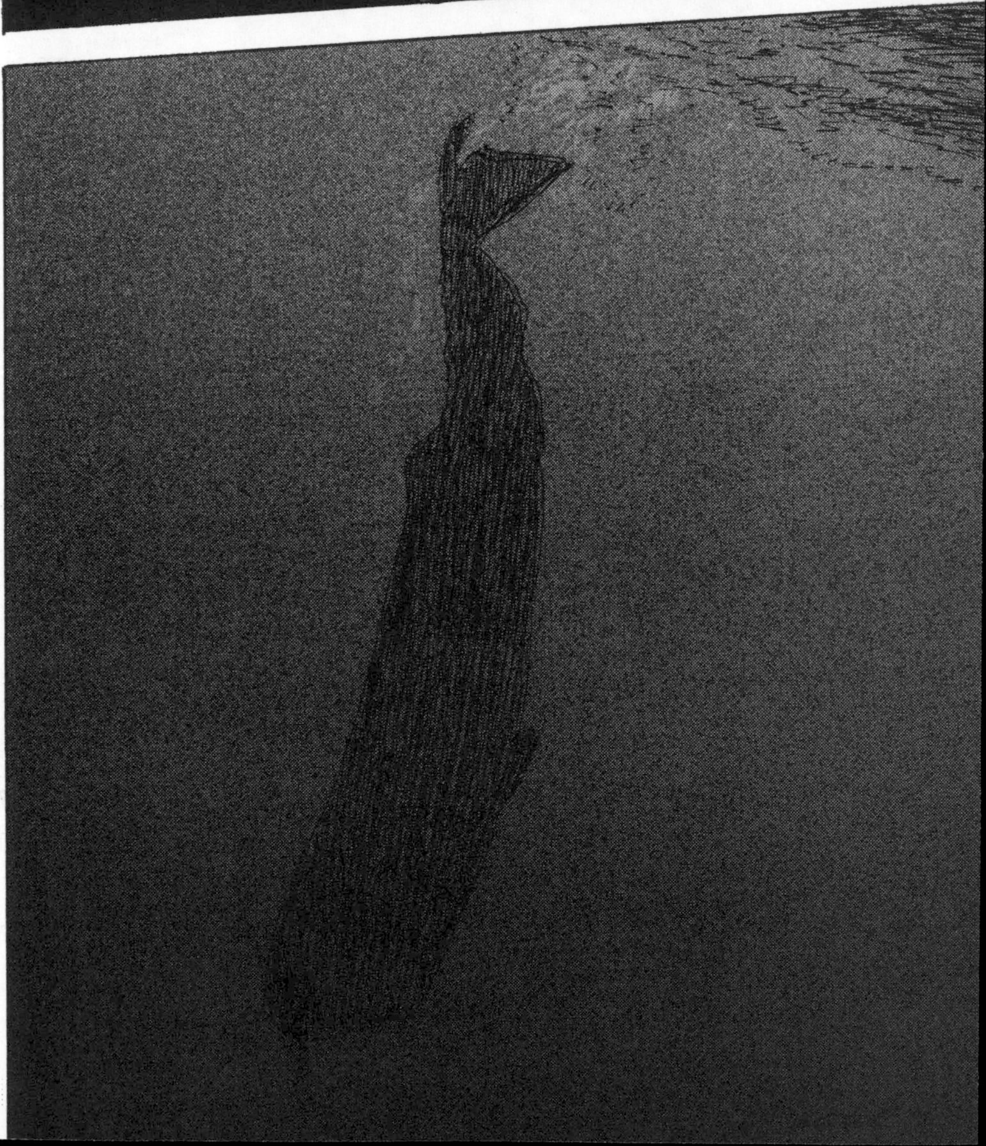

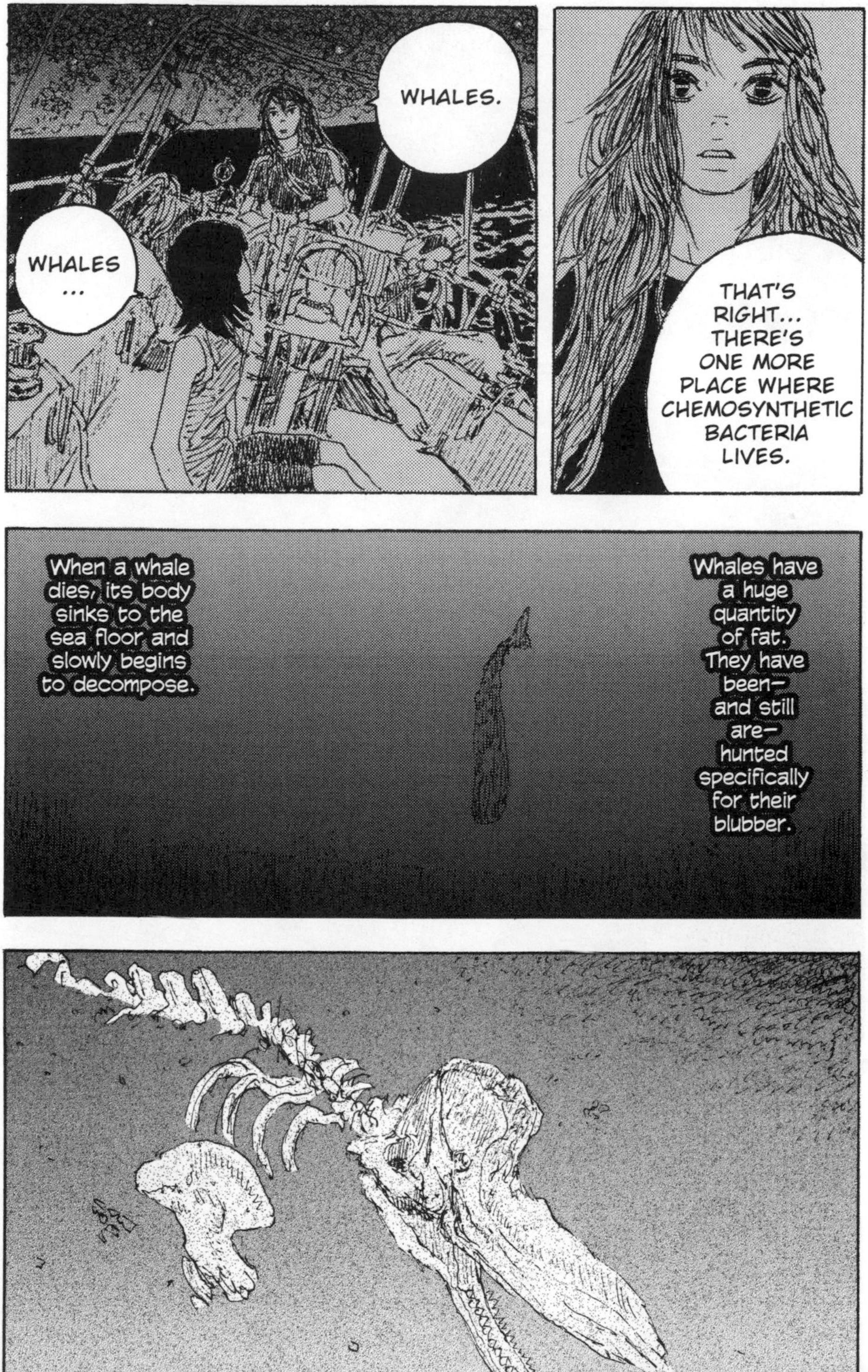
THAT'S RIGHT... THERE'S ONE MORE PLACE WHERE CHEMOSYNTHETIC BACTERIA LIVES.
WHALES.
WHALES ...
Whales have a huge quantity of fat. They have been— and still are— hunted specifically for their blubber.
When a whale dies, its body sinks to the sea floor and slowly begins to decompose.

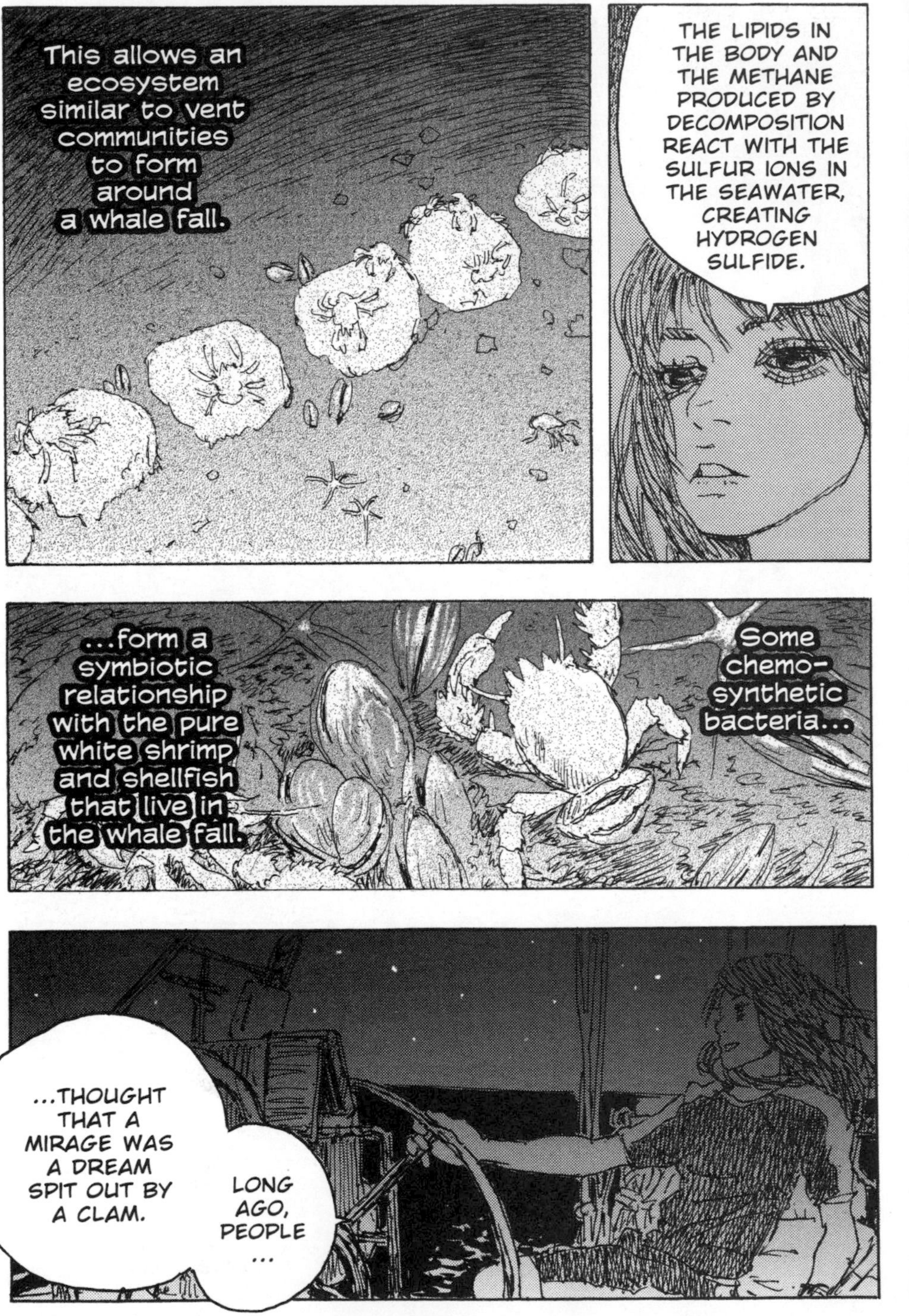
THE LIPIDS IN THE BODY AND THE METHANE PRODUCED BY DECOMPOSITION REACT WITH THE SULFUR IONS IN THE SEAWATER, CREATING HYDROGEN SULFIDE.
This allows an ecosystem similar to vent communities to form around a whale fall.
Some chemo-synthetic bacteria...
...form a symbiotic relationship with the pure white shrimp and shellfish that live in the whale fall.
LONG AGO, PEOPLE ...
...THOUGHT THAT A MIRAGE WAS A DREAM SPIT OUT BY A CLAM.

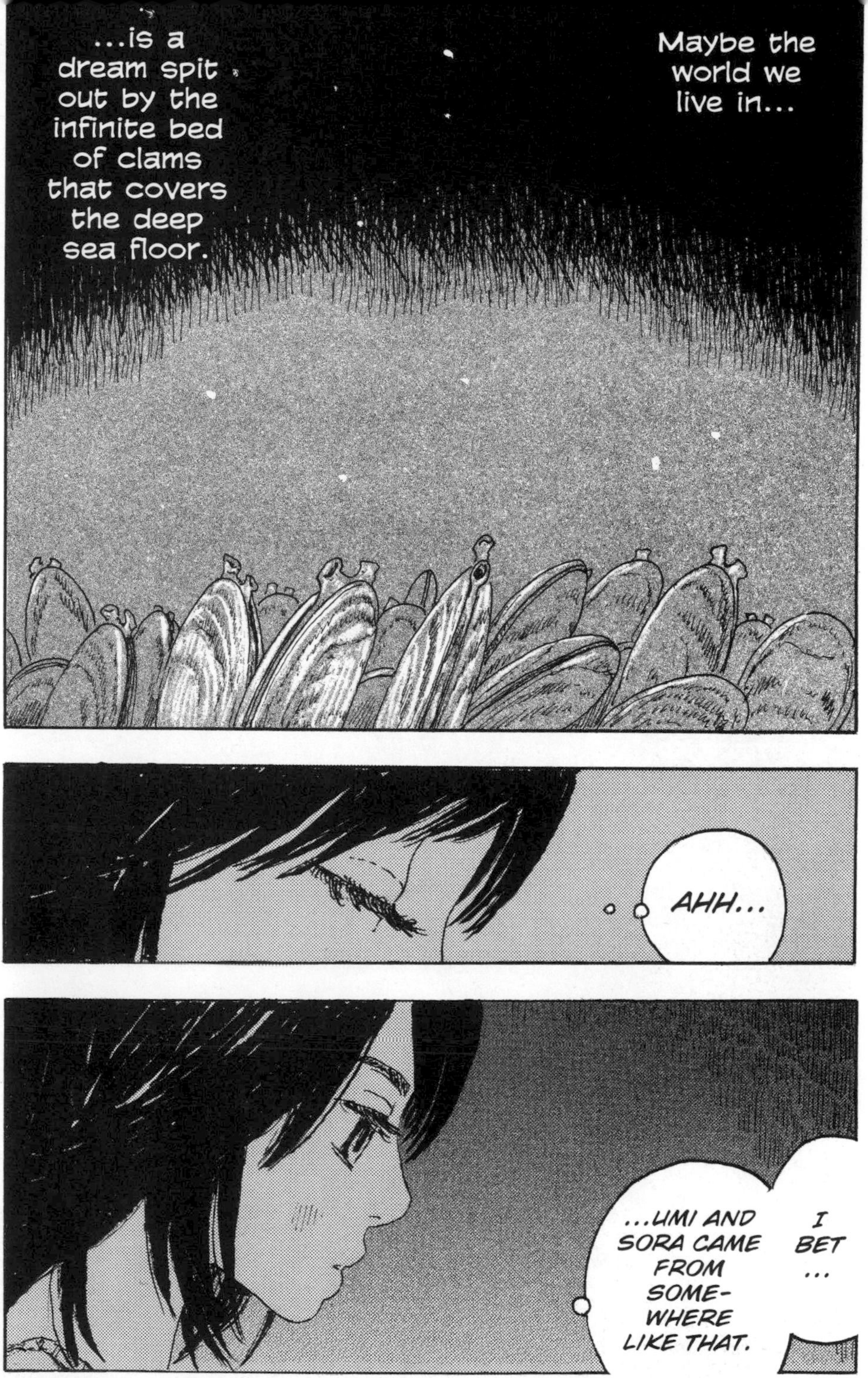
Maybe the world we live in...
...is a dream spit out by the infinite bed of clams that covers the deep sea floor.
AHH...
I BET...
...UMI AND SORA CAME FROM SOMEWHERE LIKE THAT.

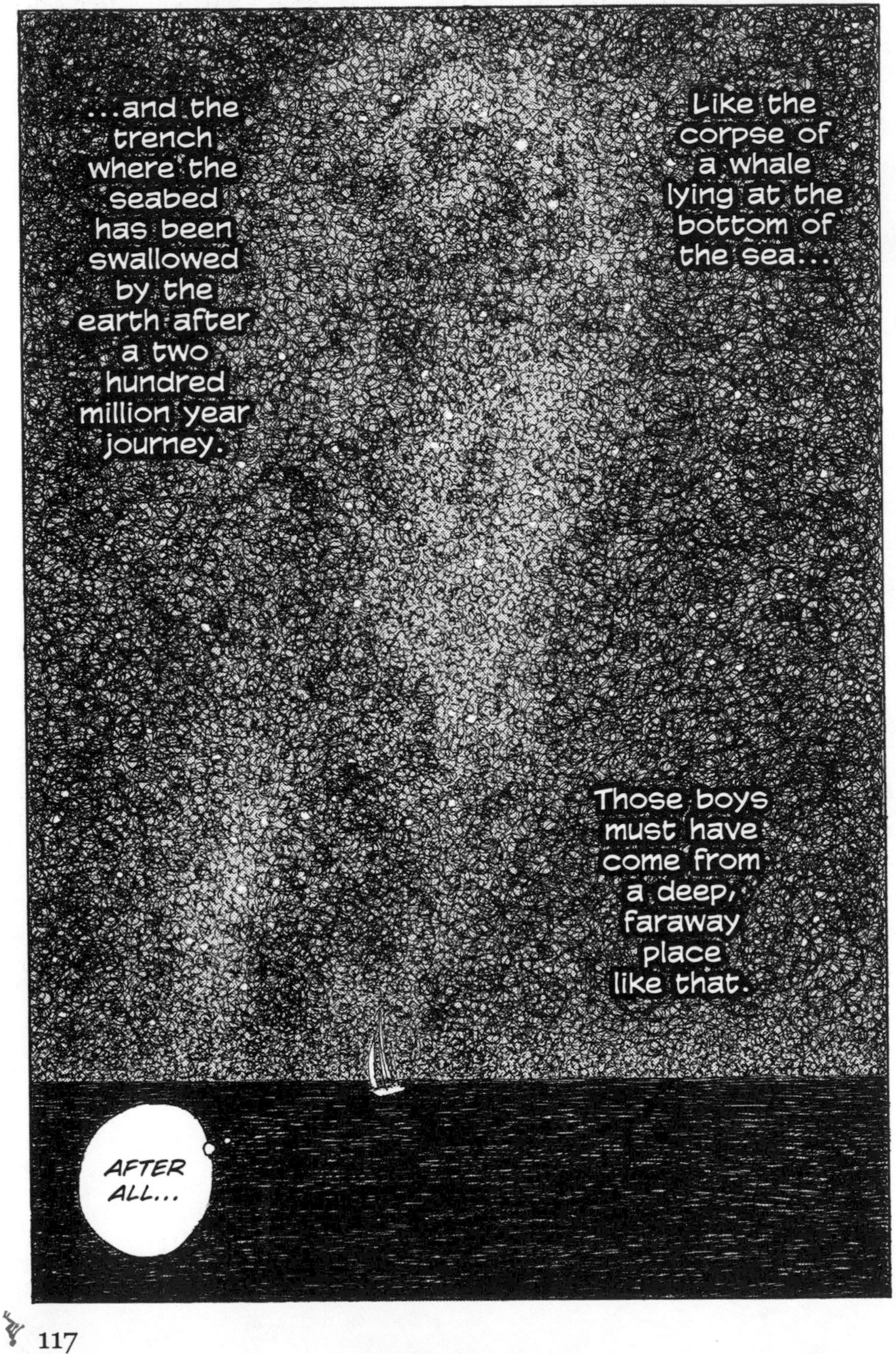
Like the corpse of a whale lying at the bottom of the sea...
...and the trench where the seabed has been swallowed by the earth after a two hundred million year journey.
Those boys must have come from a deep, faraway place like that.
AFTER ALL...

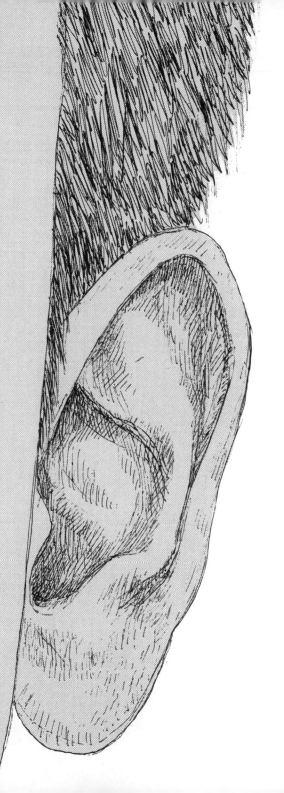

Their eyes
are always
focused
somewhere
someplace
far away,
not here.

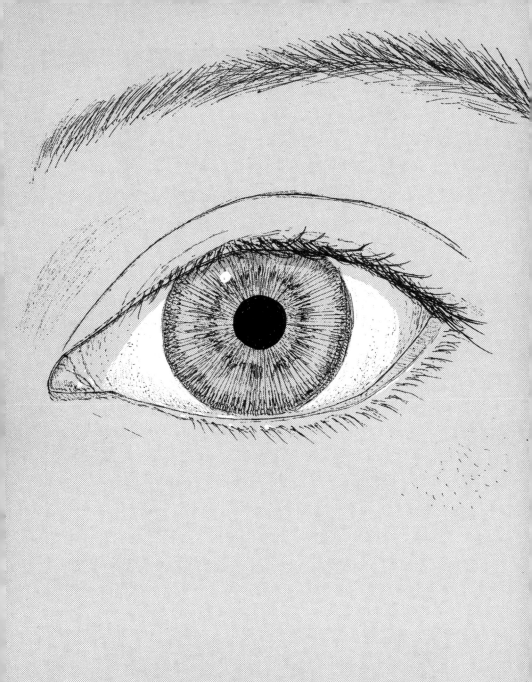

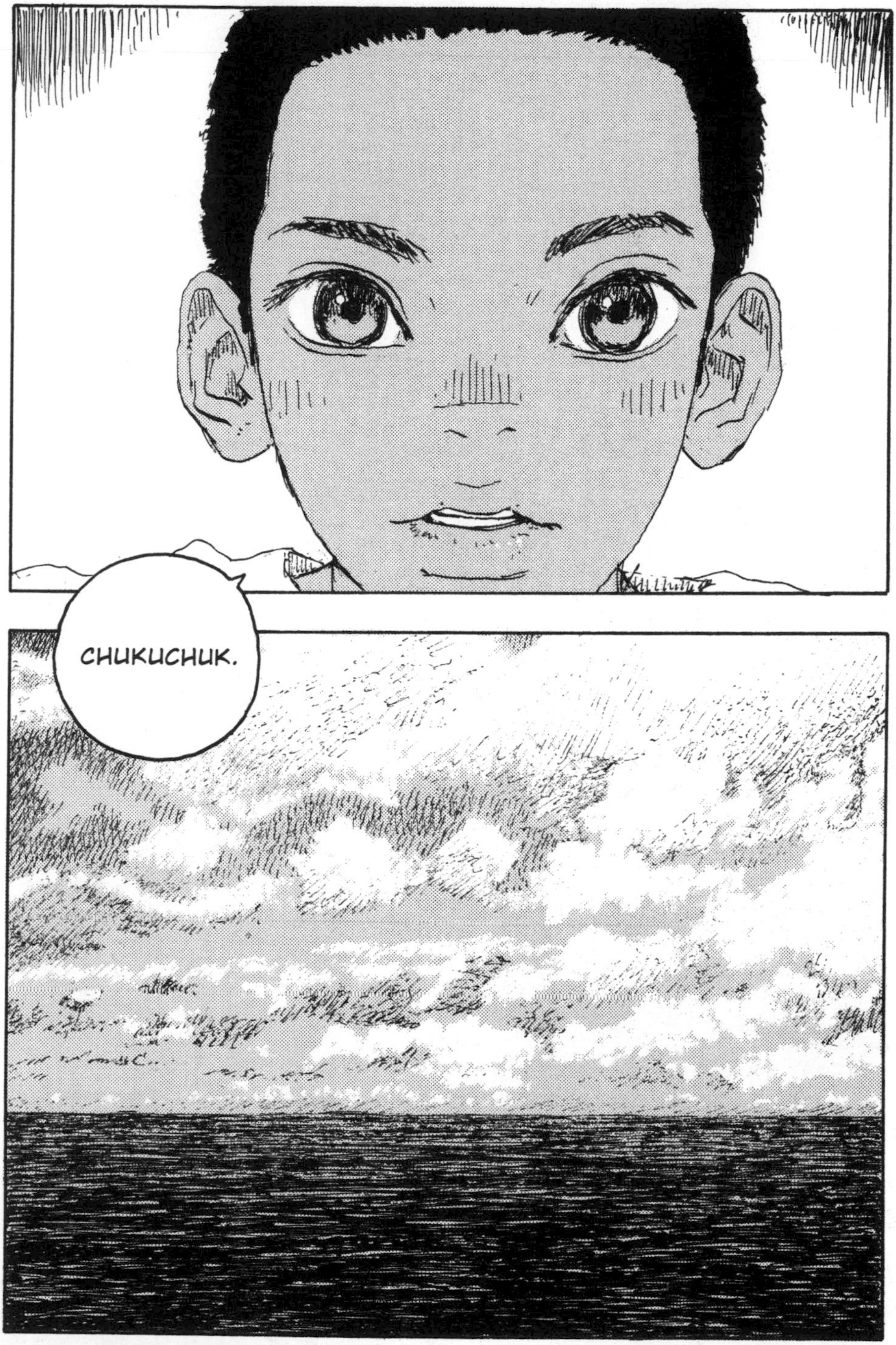
CHUKUCHUK.

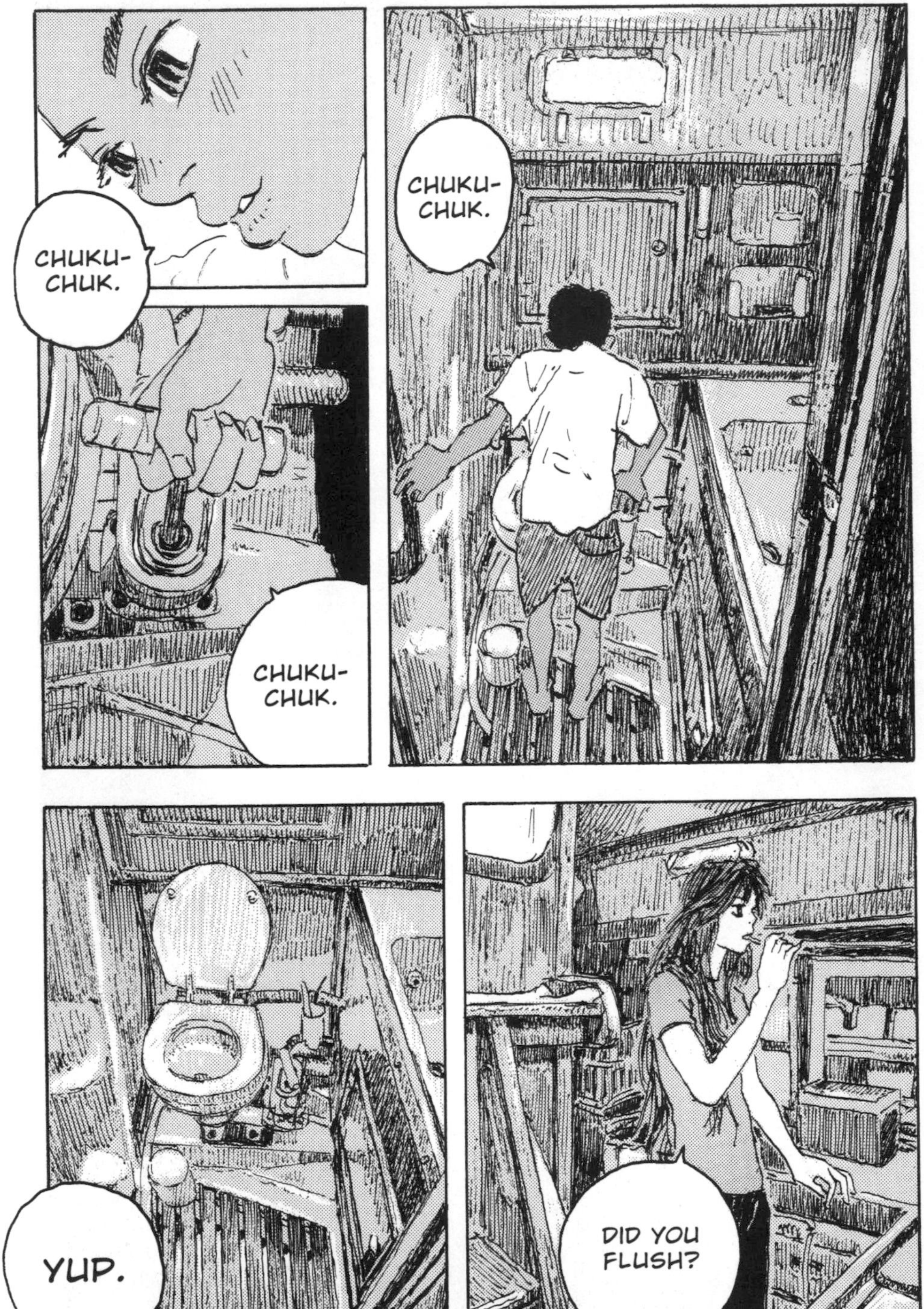
CHUKU-CHUK.
CHUKU-CHUK.
CHUKU-CHUK.
DID YOU FLUSH?
YUP.

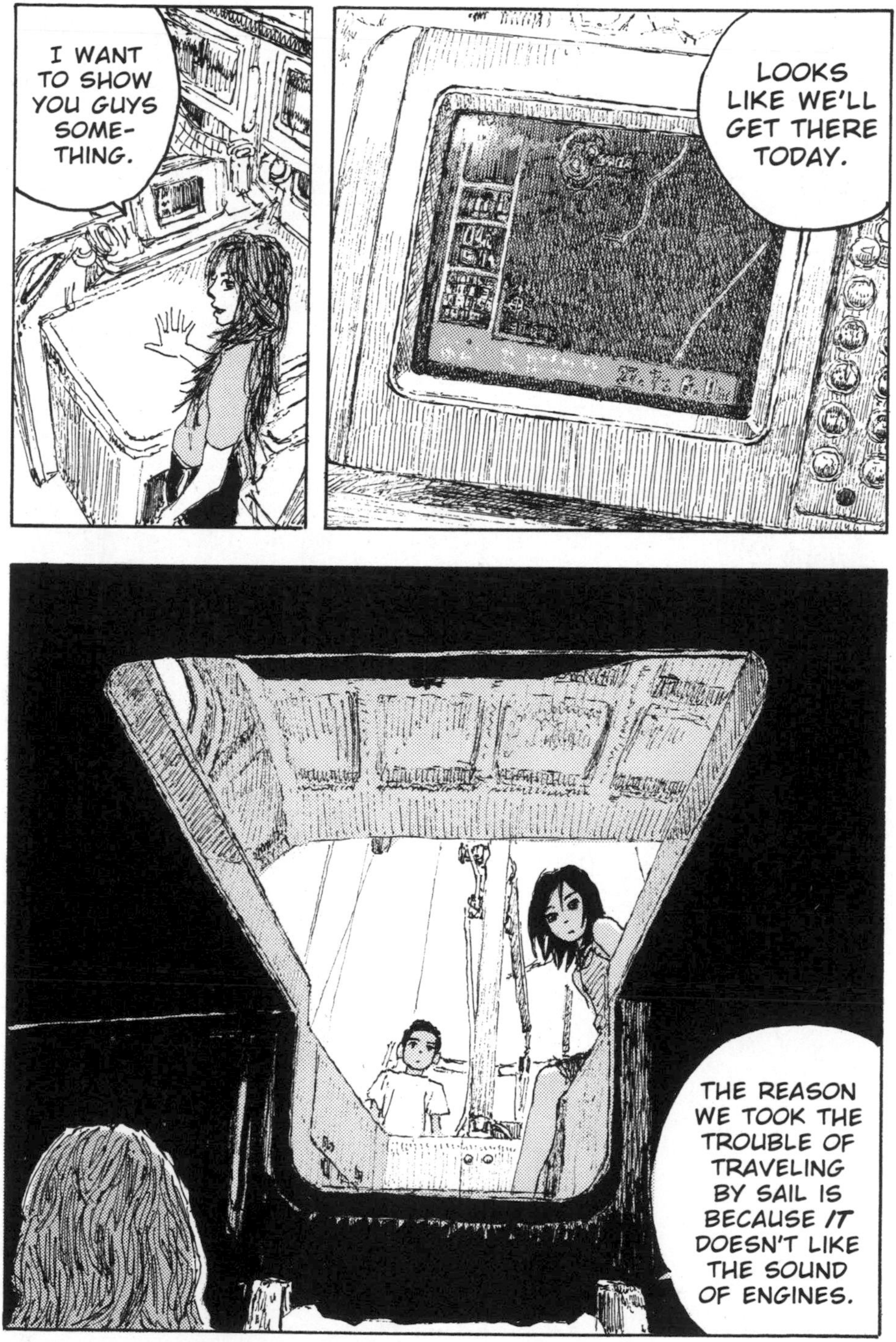
LOOKS LIKE WE'LL GET THERE TODAY.
I WANT TO SHOW YOU GUYS SOME-THING.
THE REASON WE TOOK THE TROUBLE OF TRAVELING BY SAIL IS BECAUSE *IT* DOESN'T LIKE THE SOUND OF ENGINES.

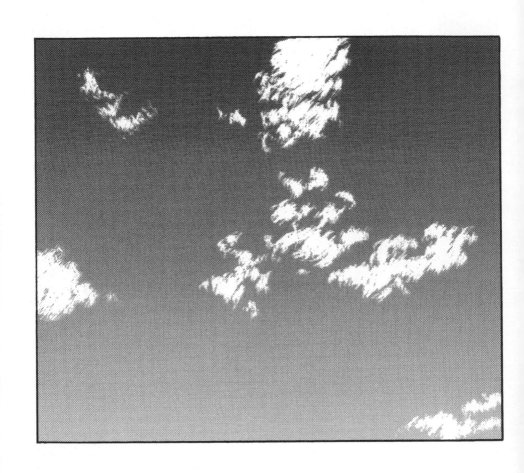

Chapter 20: Dugong

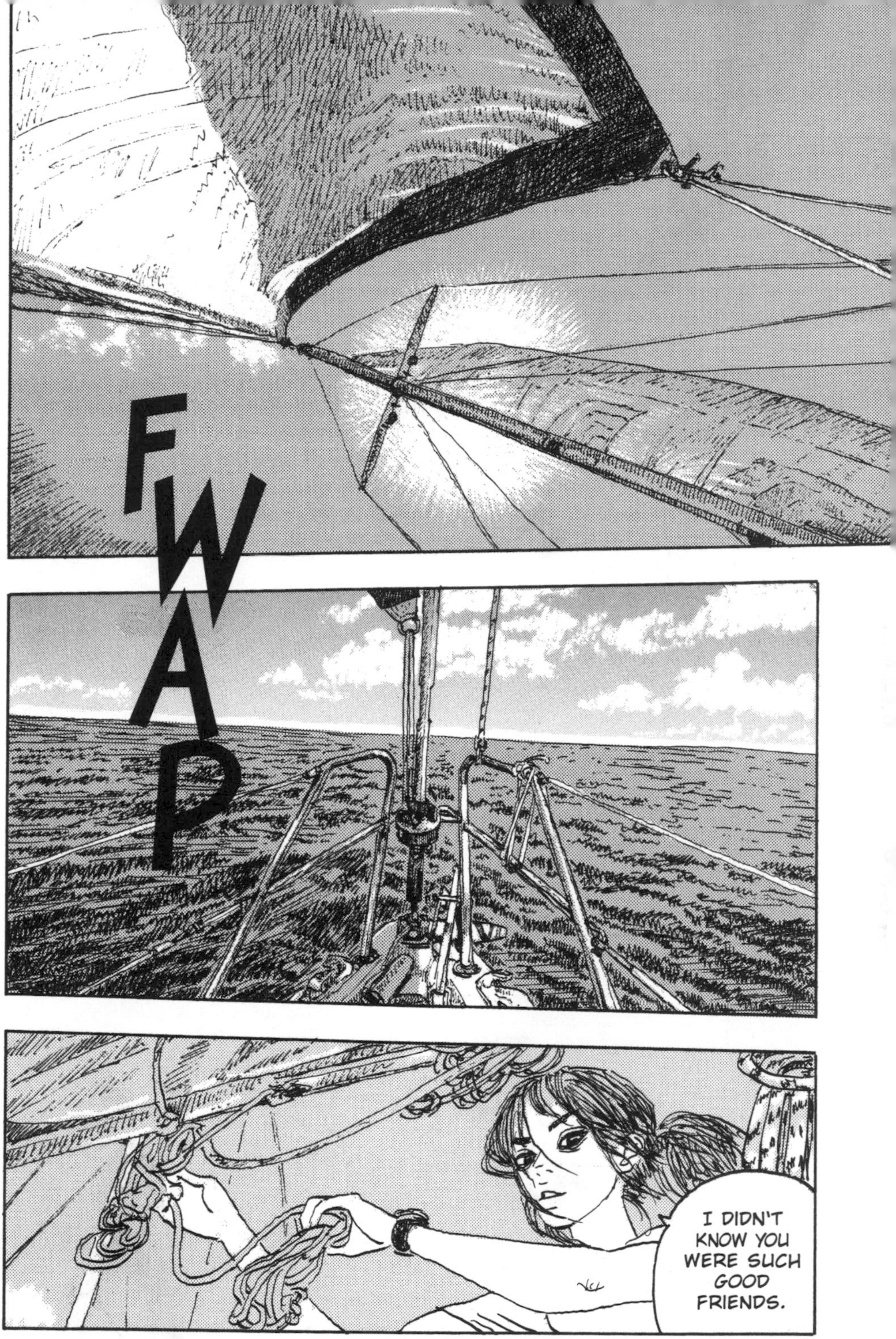
FWAP
I DIDN'T KNOW YOU WERE SUCH GOOD FRIENDS.

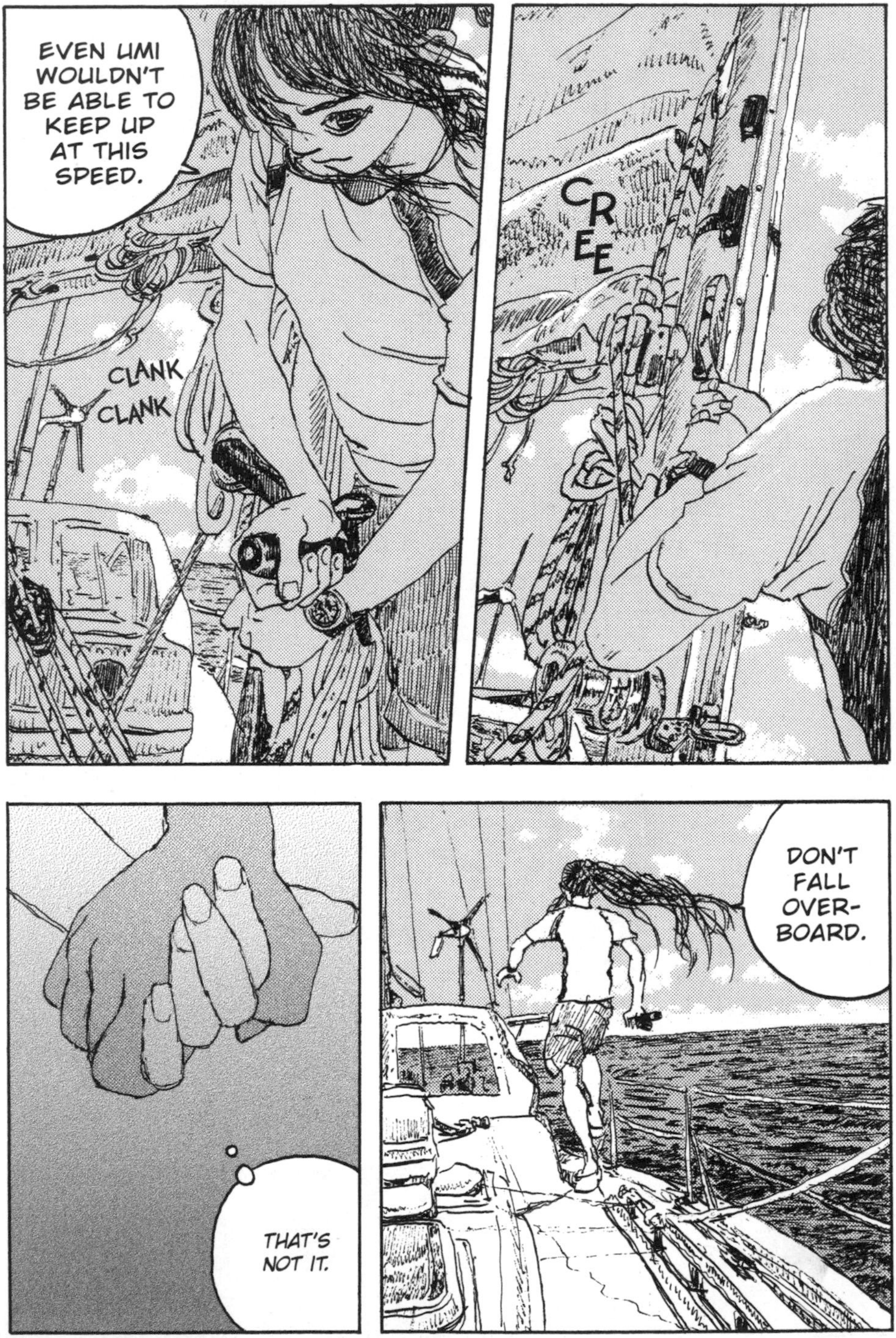
CREE
EVEN UMI WOULDN'T BE ABLE TO KEEP UP AT THIS SPEED.
CLANK CLANK
DON'T FALL OVER-BOARD.
THAT'S NOT IT.

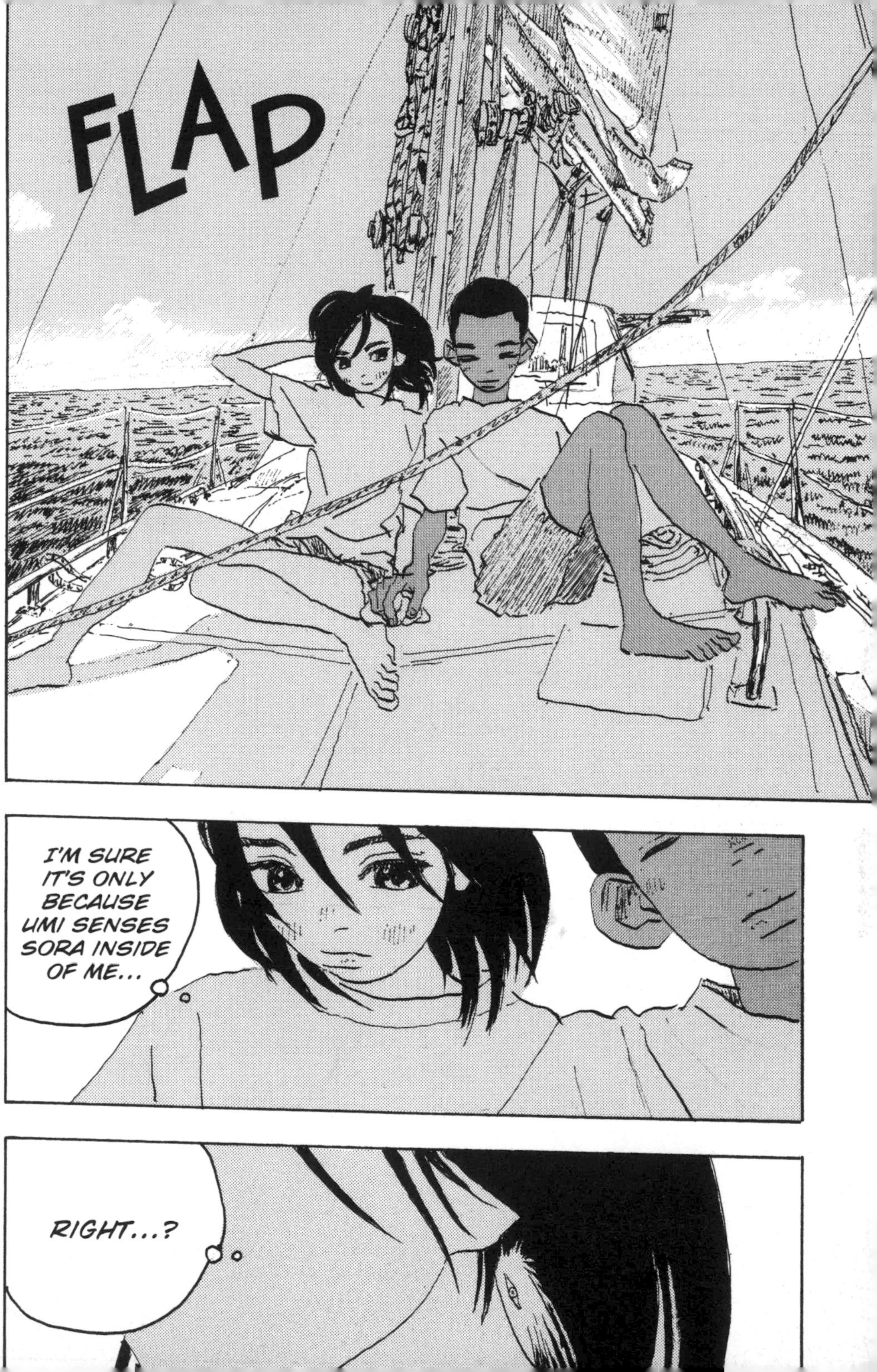
FLAP
I'M SURE IT'S ONLY BECAUSE UMI SENSES SORA INSIDE OF ME...
RIGHT...?

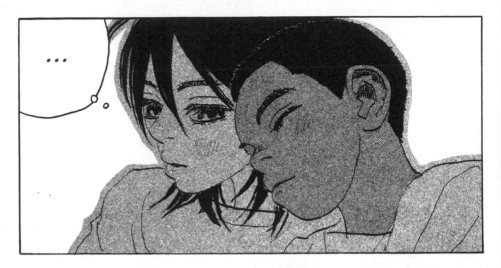

...

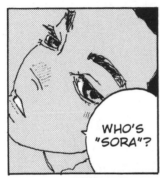

WHO'S "SORA"?

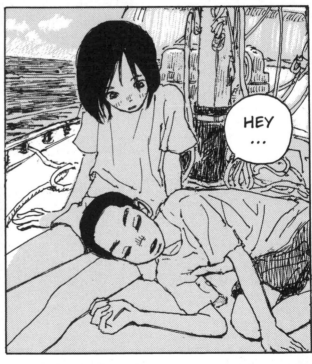

HEY ...

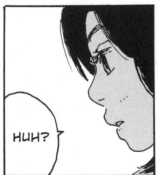

HUH?

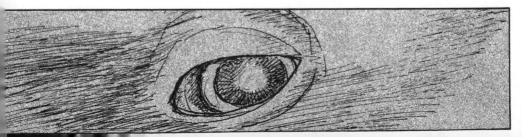

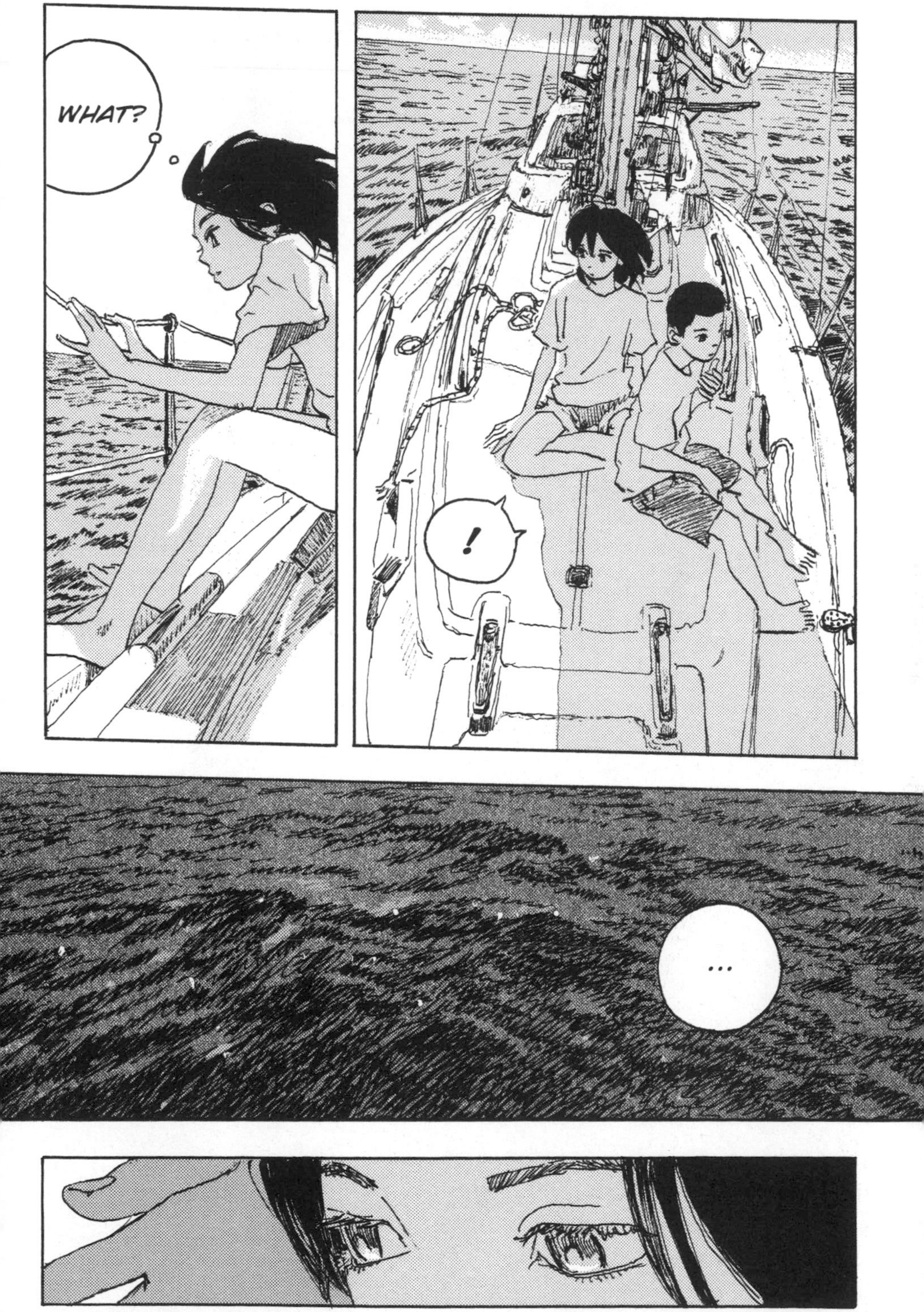
!
WHAT?
...

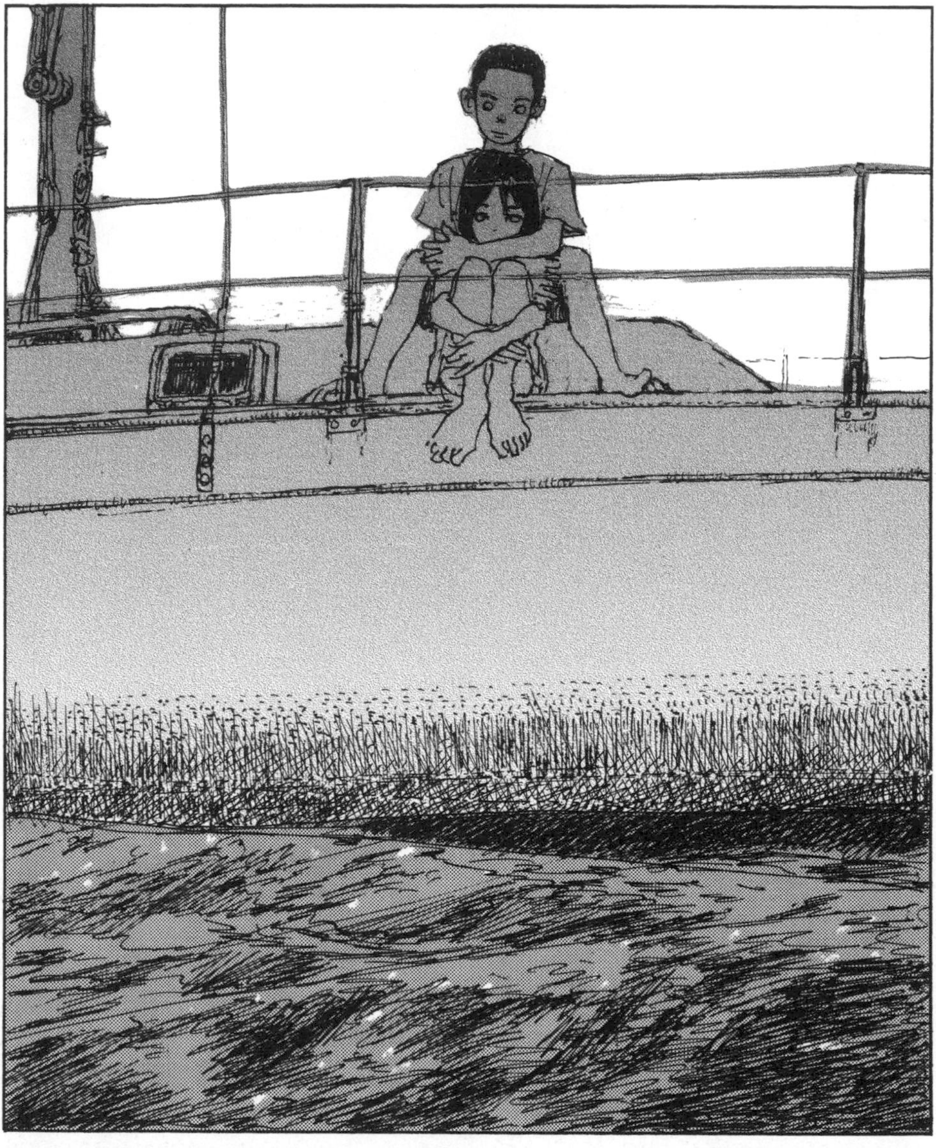
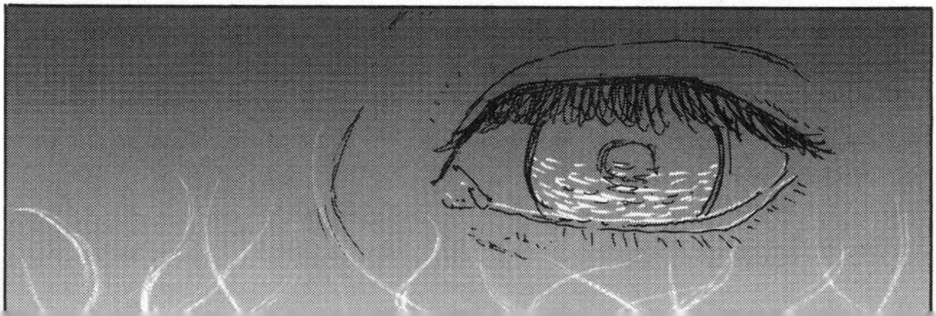

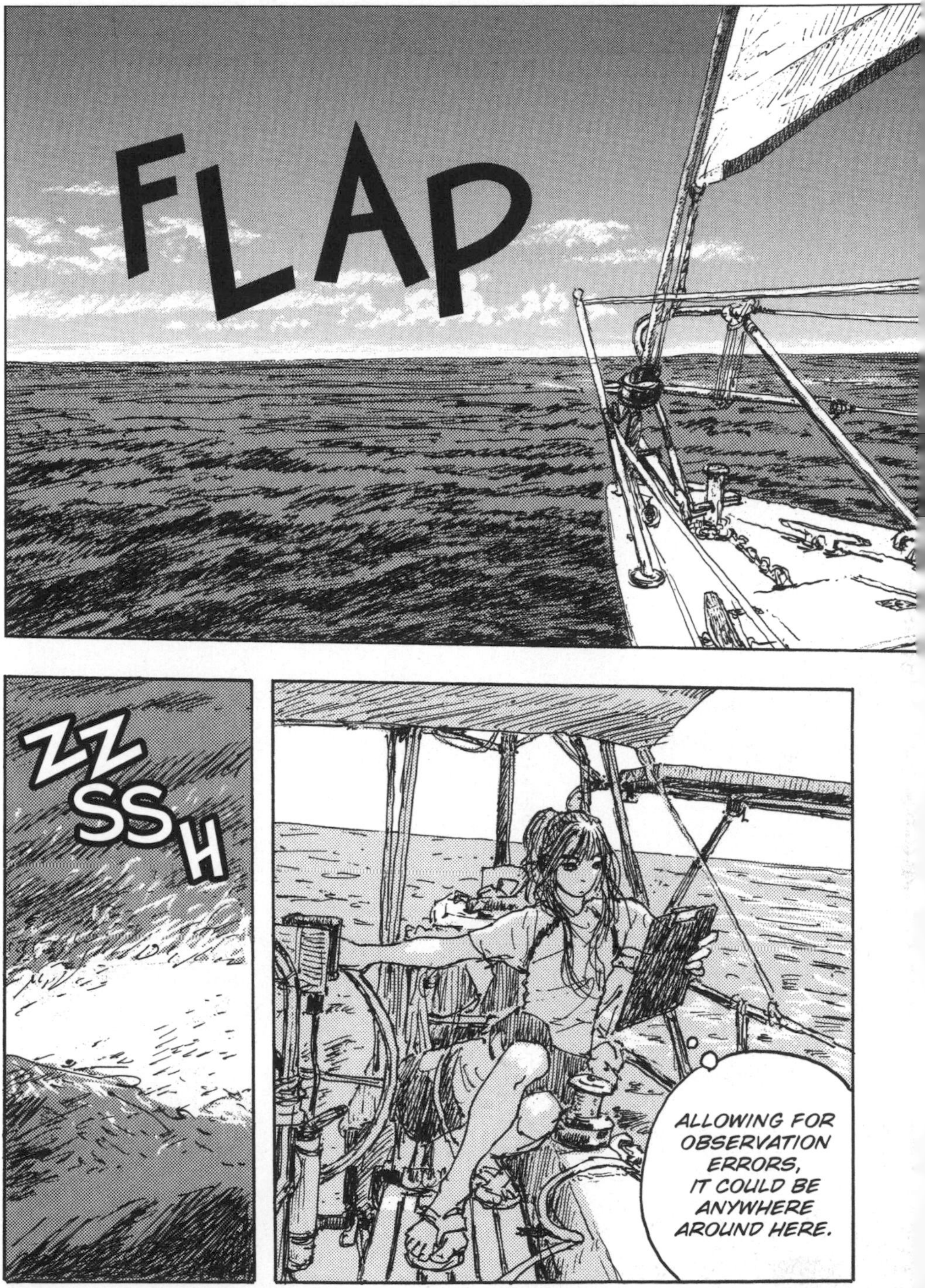
FLAP
ALLOWING FOR OBSERVATION ERRORS, IT COULD BE ANYWHERE AROUND HERE.
ZZSSH

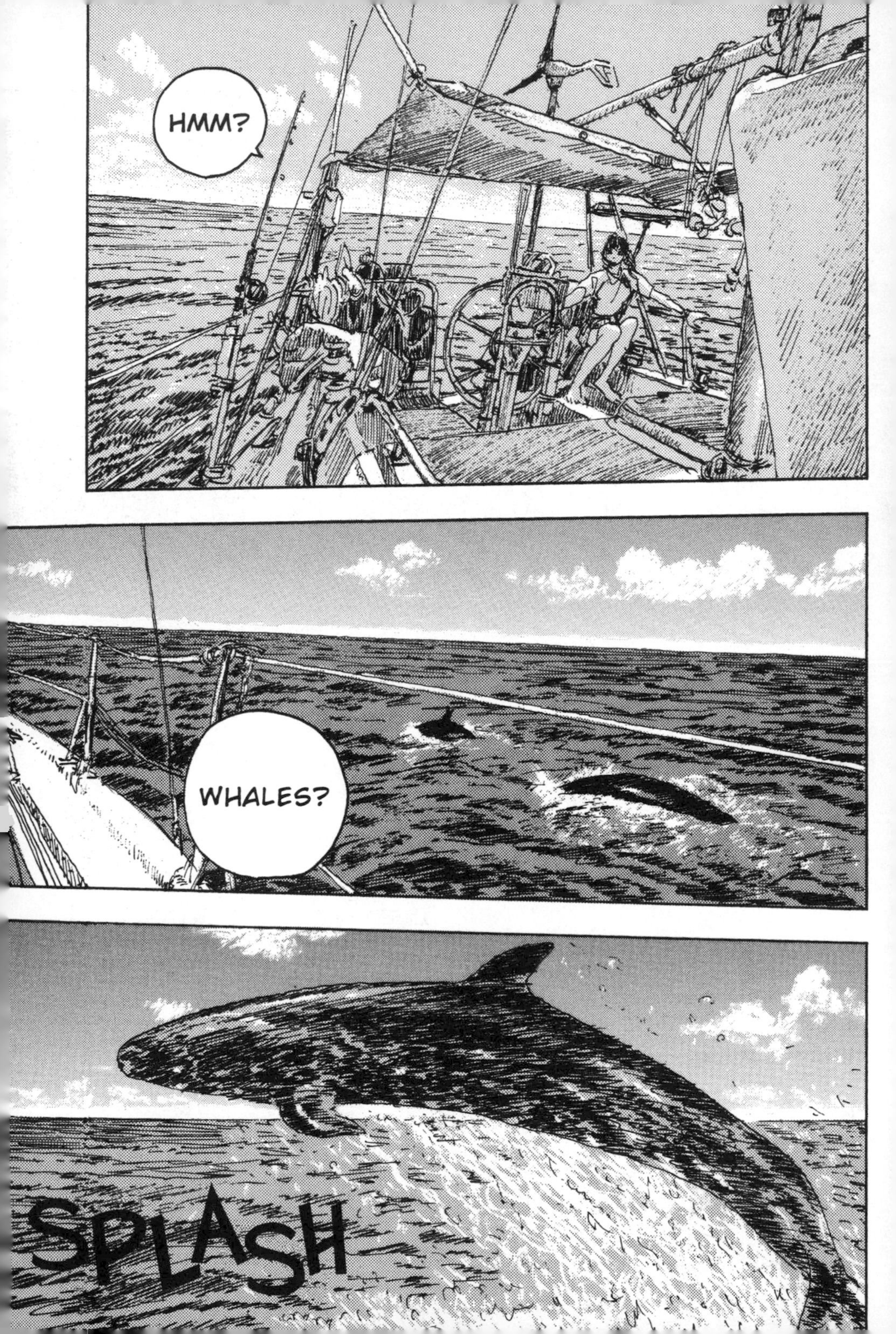
HMM?
WHALES?
SPLASH

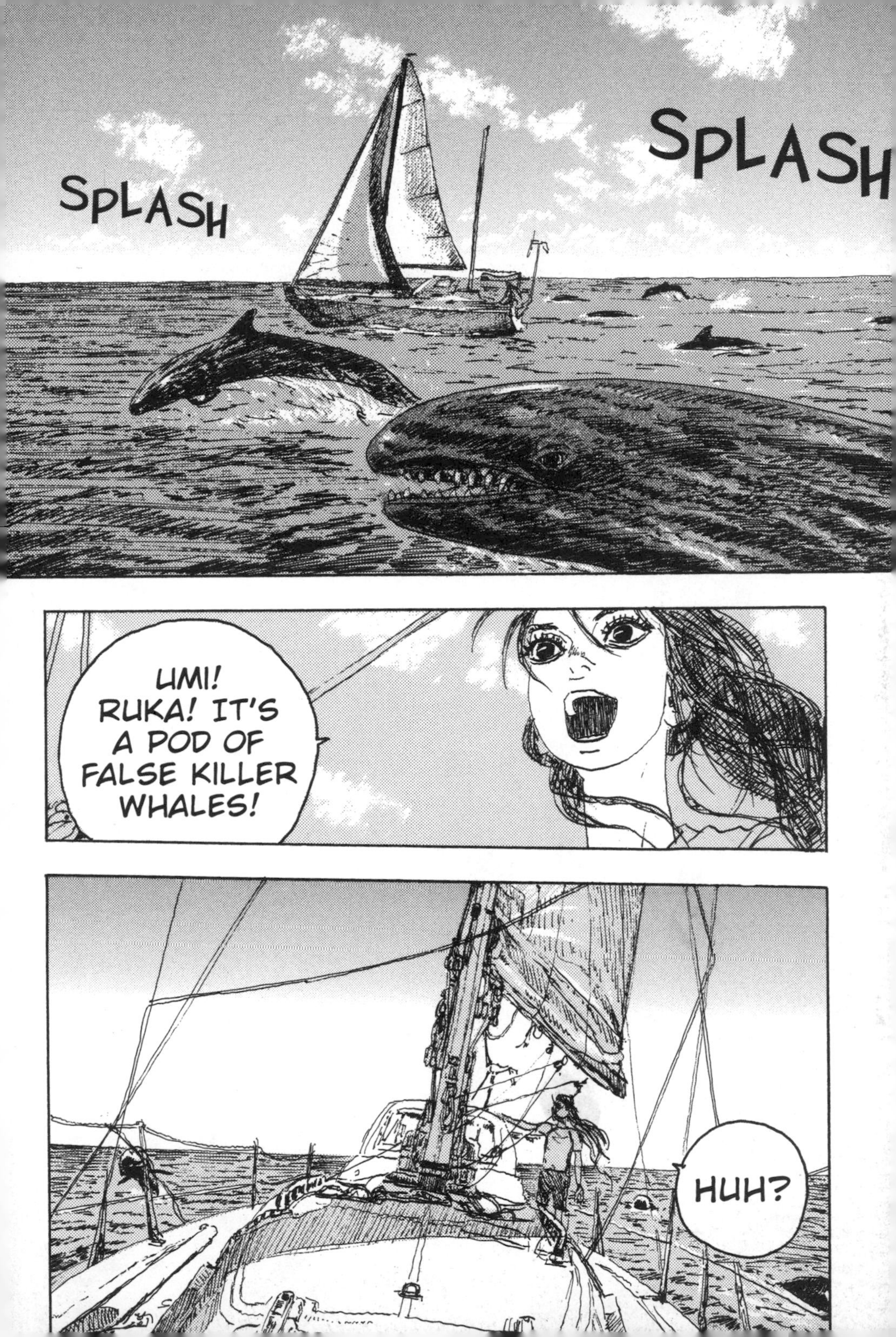
SPLASH
SPLASH
UMI! RUKA! IT'S A POD OF FALSE KILLER WHALES!
HUH?

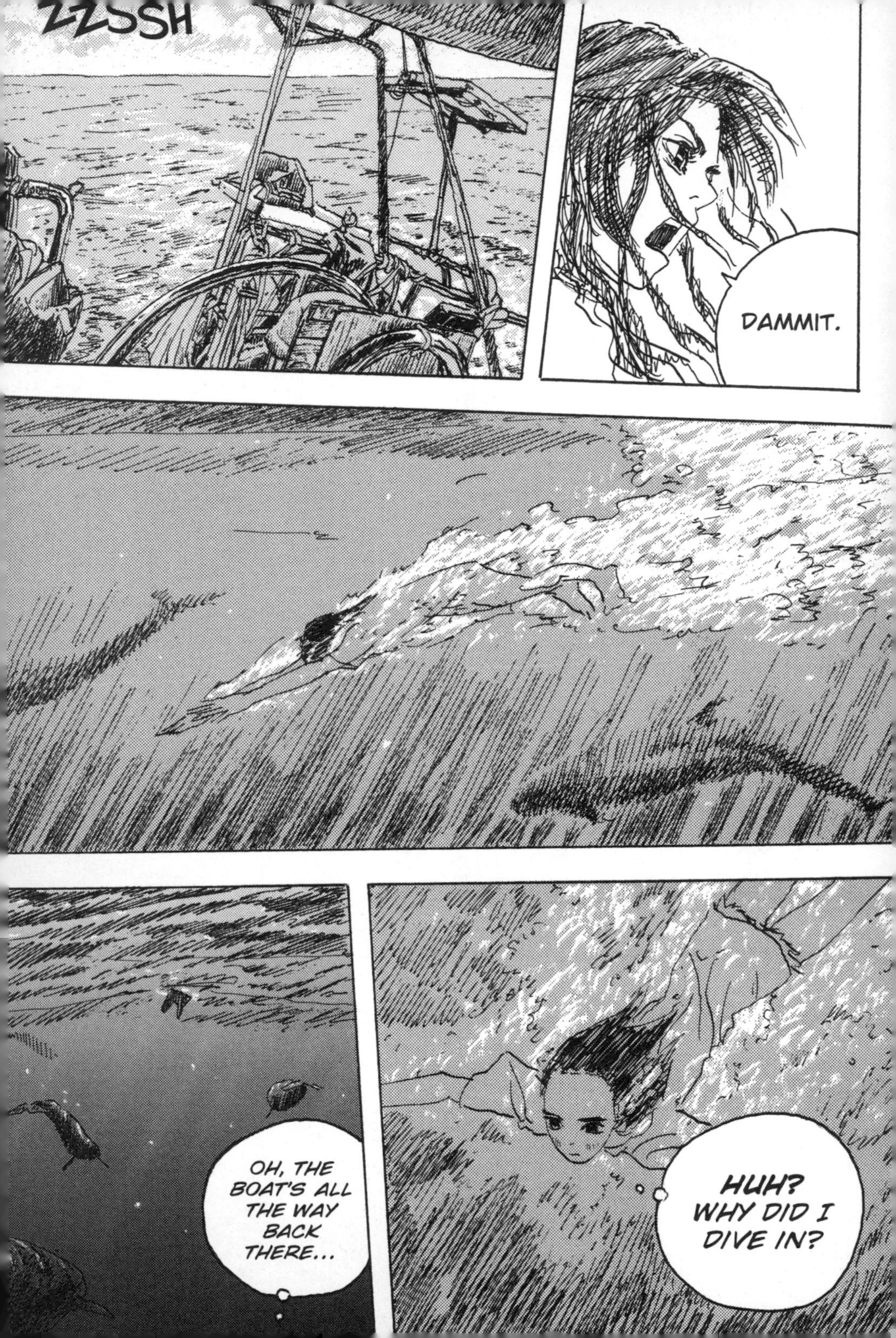
DAMMIT.
ZZSSH
HUH? WHY DID I DIVE IN?
OH, THE BOAT'S ALL THE WAY BACK THERE...

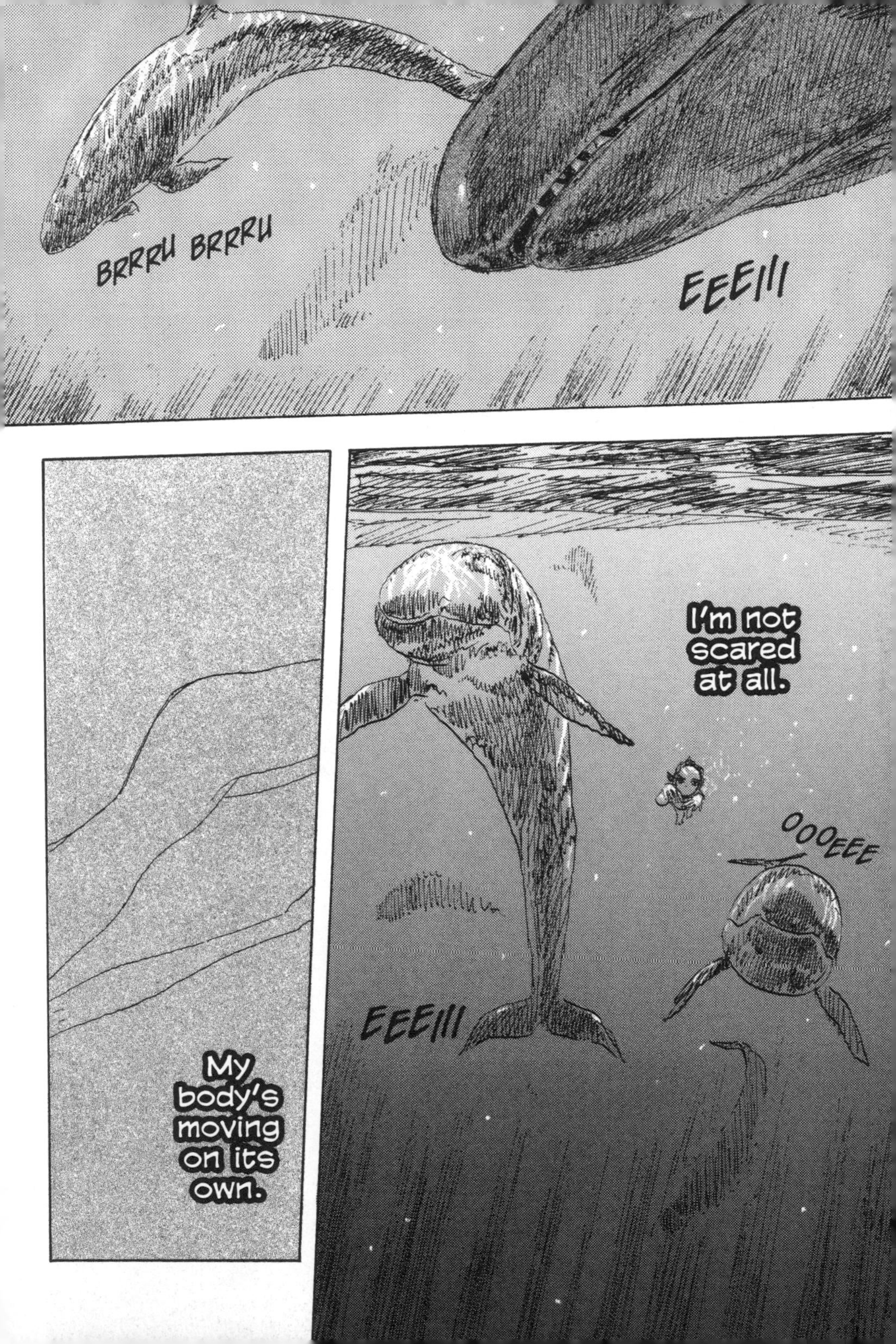
EEEIII
BRRRU BRRRU
I'm not scared at all.
OOOEEE
EEEIII
My body's moving on its own.

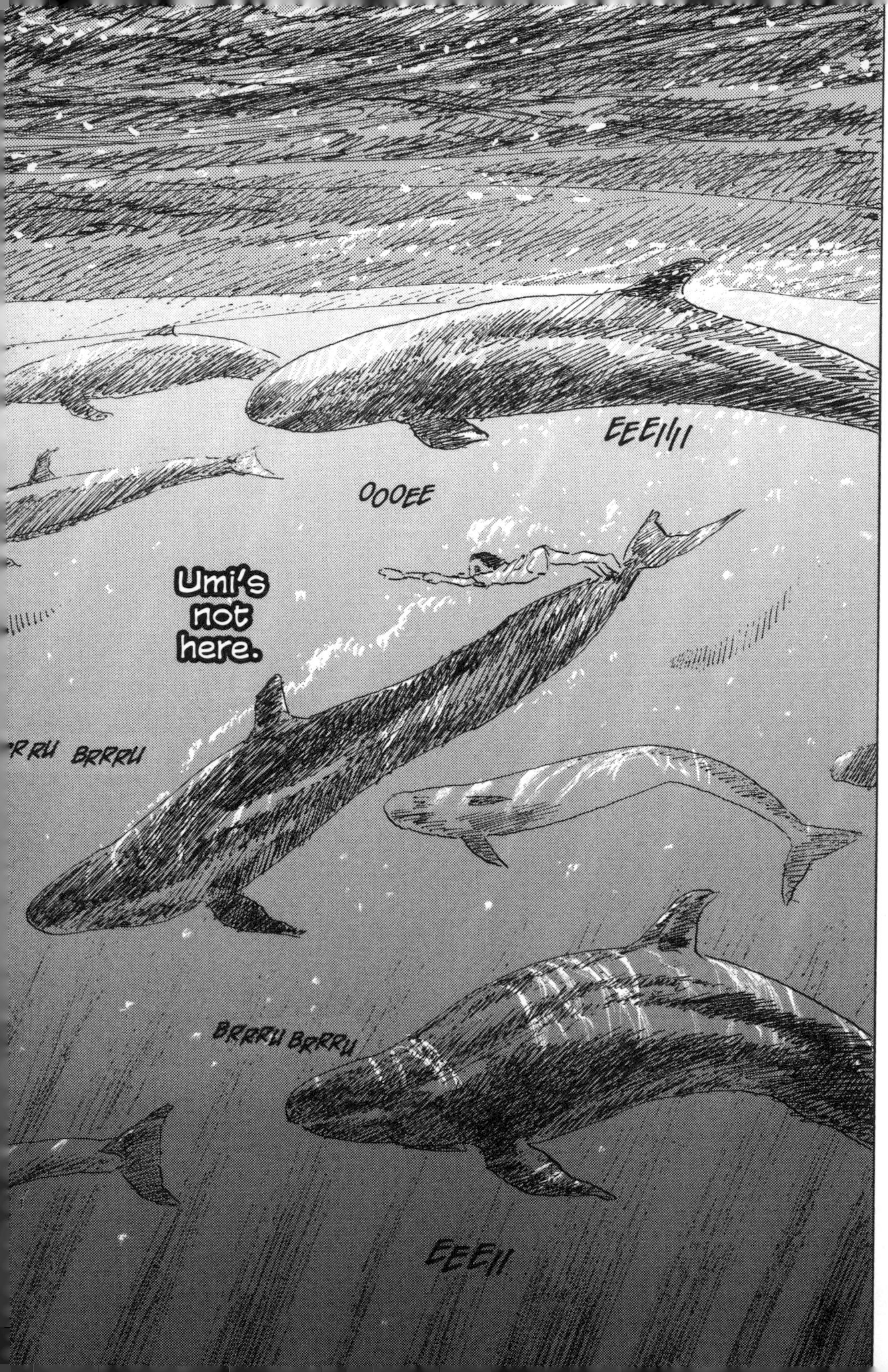
EEEIIII
OOOEE
Umi's not here.
BRRRU BRRRU
RRRU BRRRU
EEEII

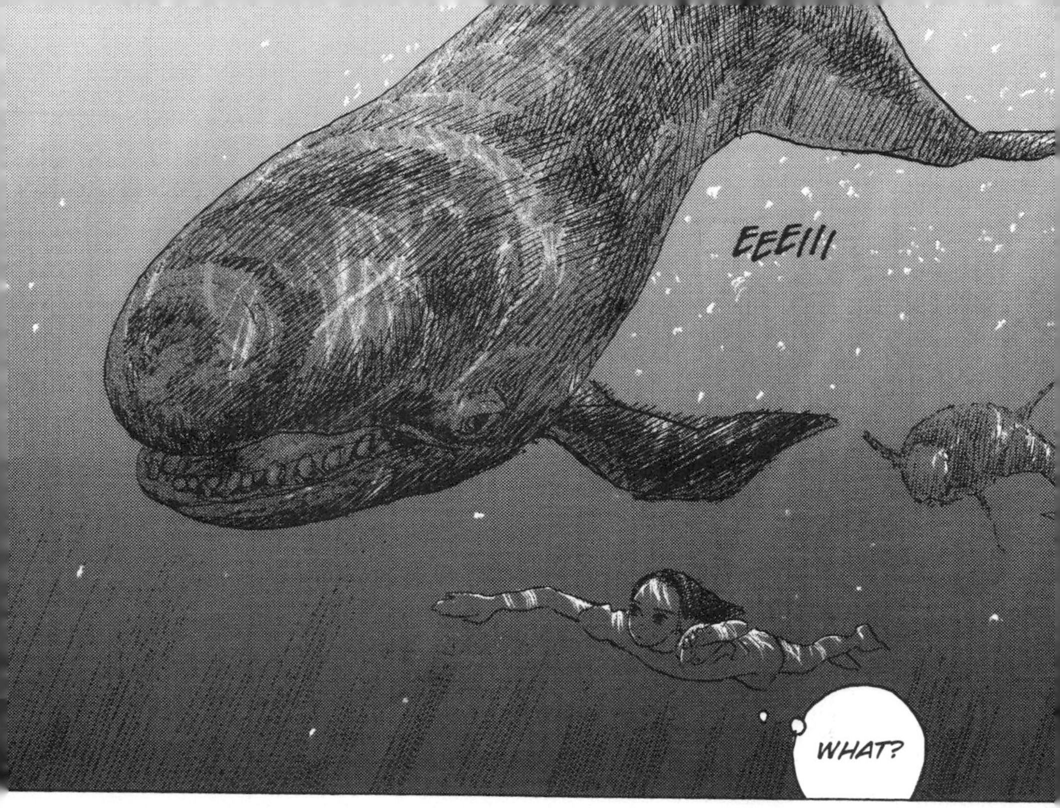
EEEIII
WHAT?
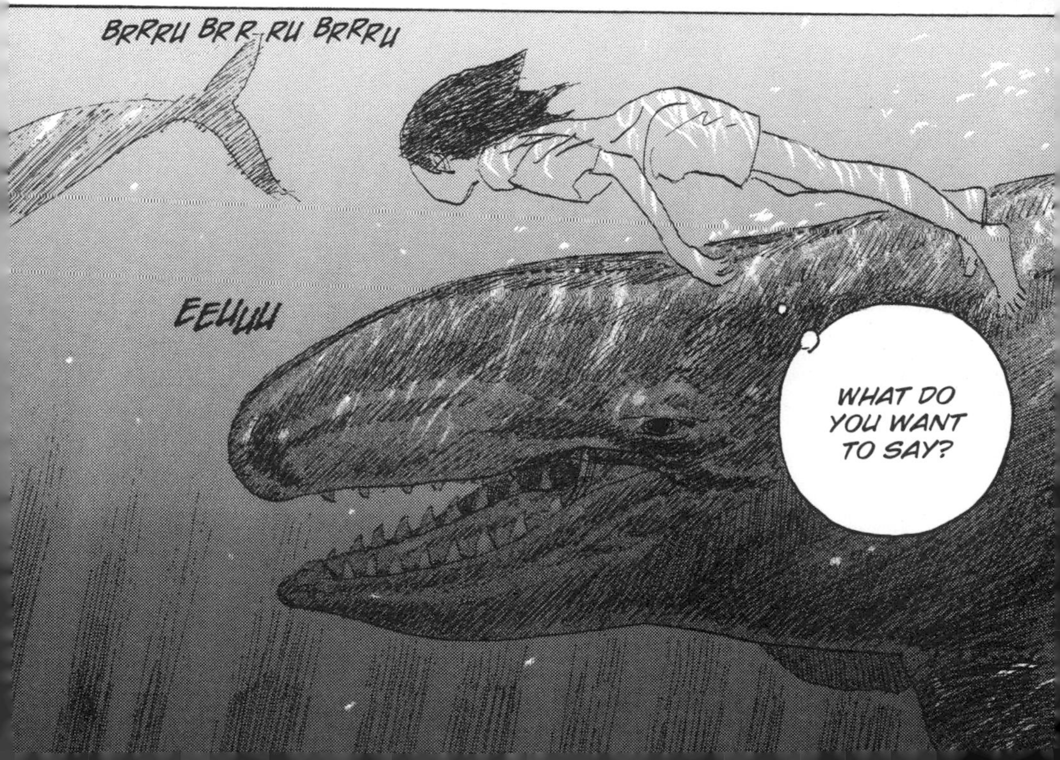
BRRRU BRR-RU BRRRU
WHAT DO YOU WANT TO SAY?
EEUUU

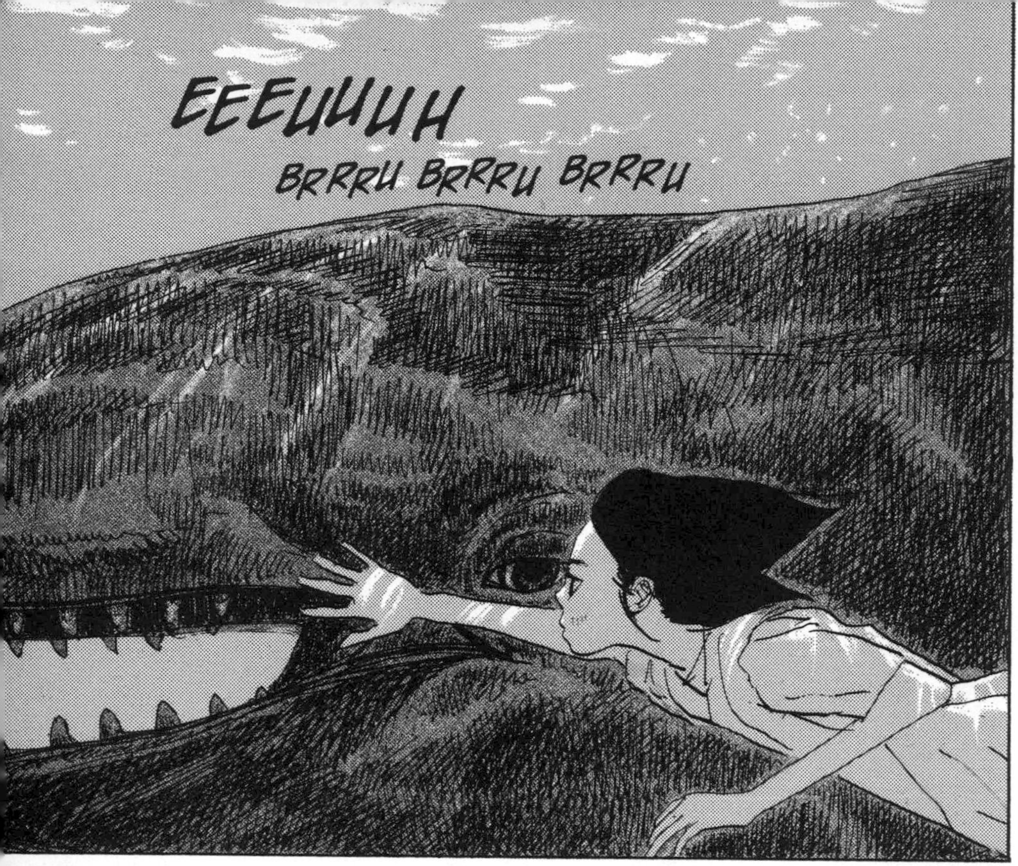
EEEUUUH
BRRRU BRRRU BRRRU

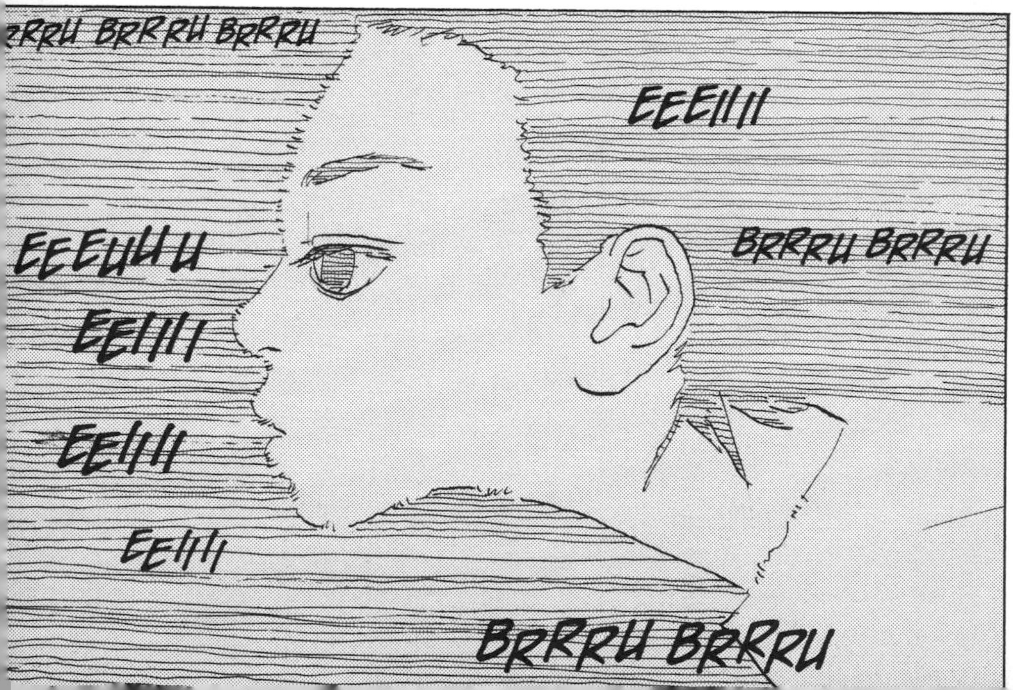
RRRU BRRRU BRRRU
EEEIII
BRRRU BRRRU
EEEUUU
EEIII
EEIII
EEIII
BRRRU BRRRU

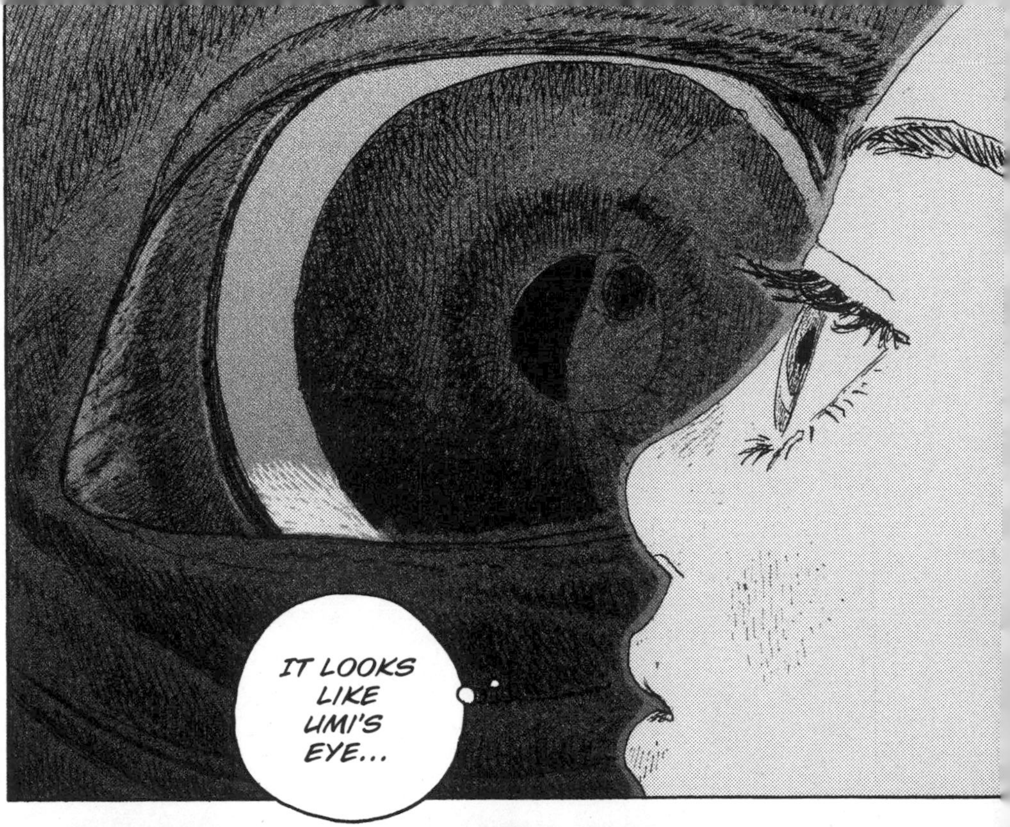
IT LOOKS LIKE UMI'S EYE...

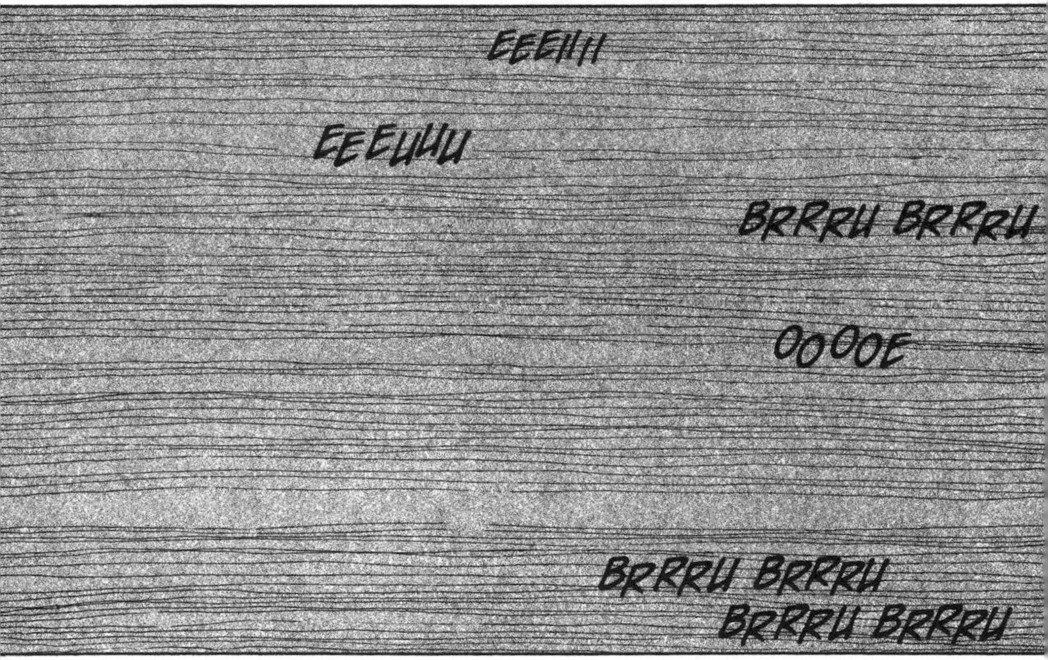
EEEIIII
EEEUUU
BRRRU BRRRU
OOOOE
BRRRU BRRRU
BRRRU BRRRU

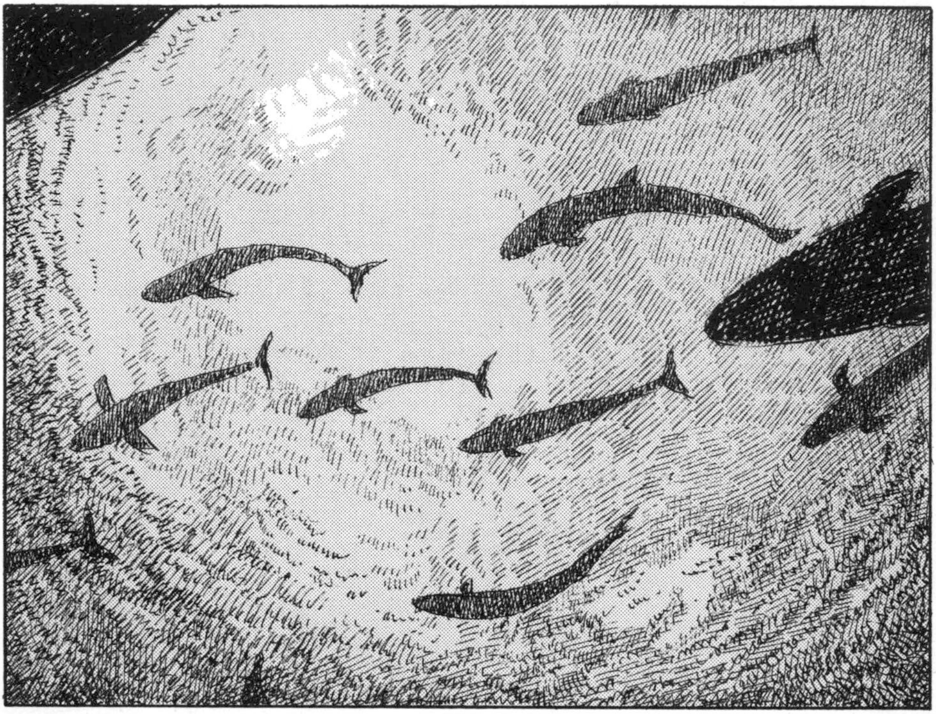

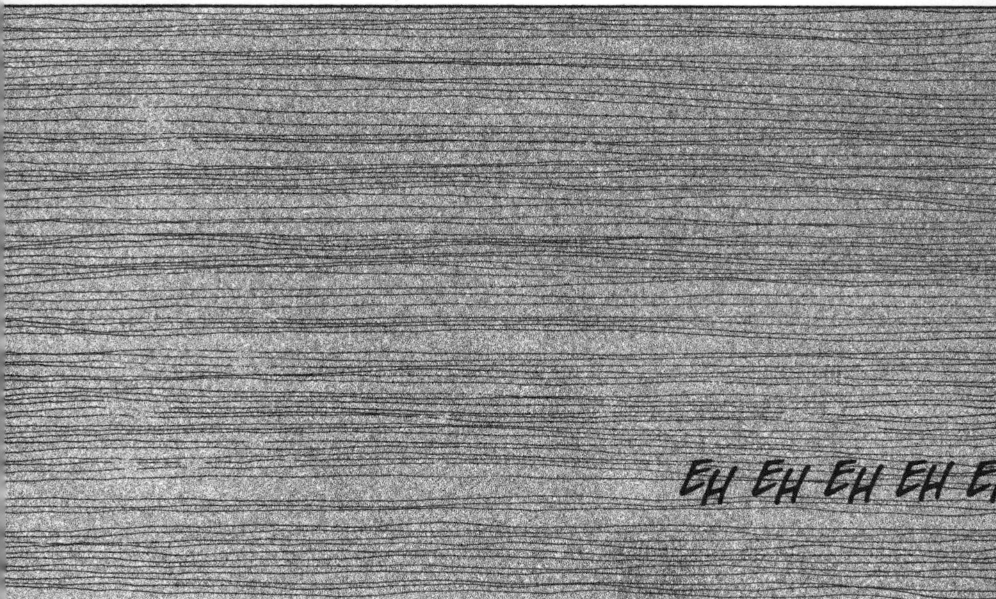
EH EH EH EH EH

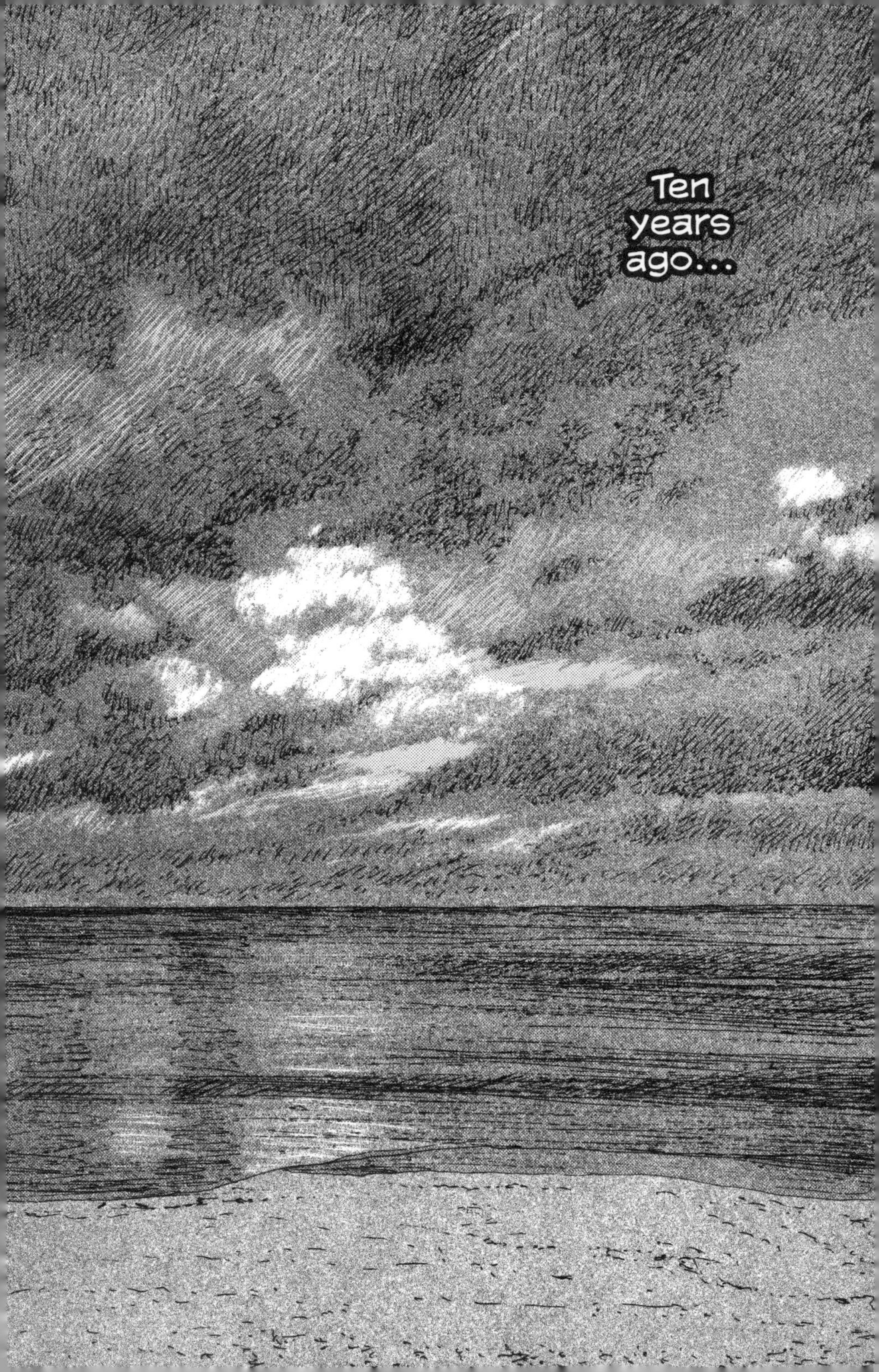
Ten years ago...

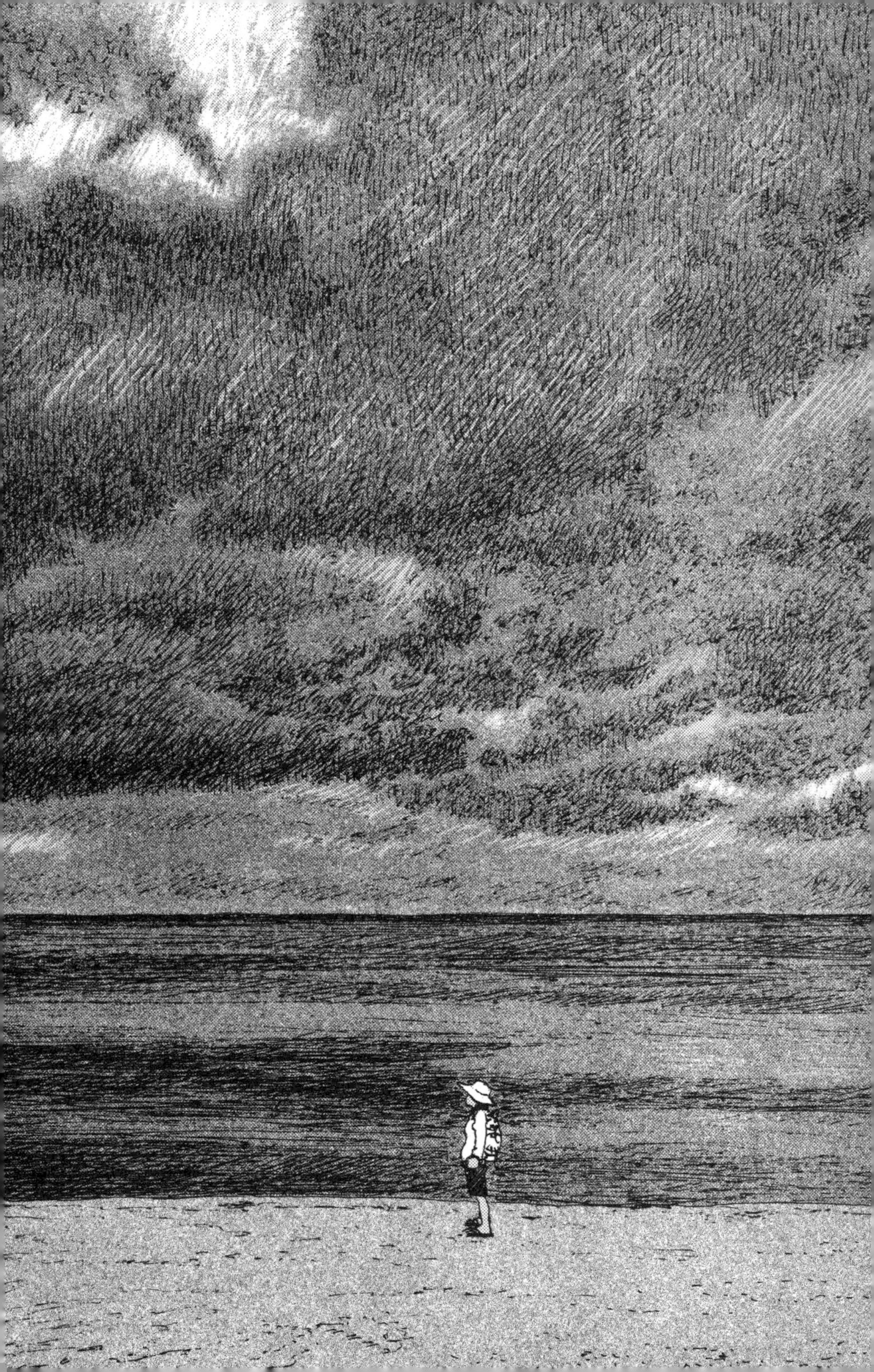

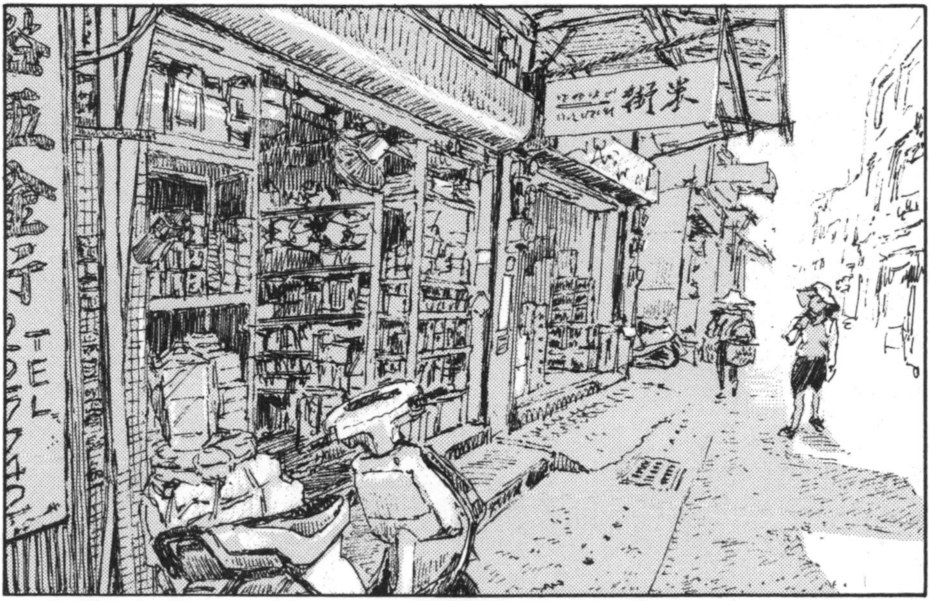
TEL

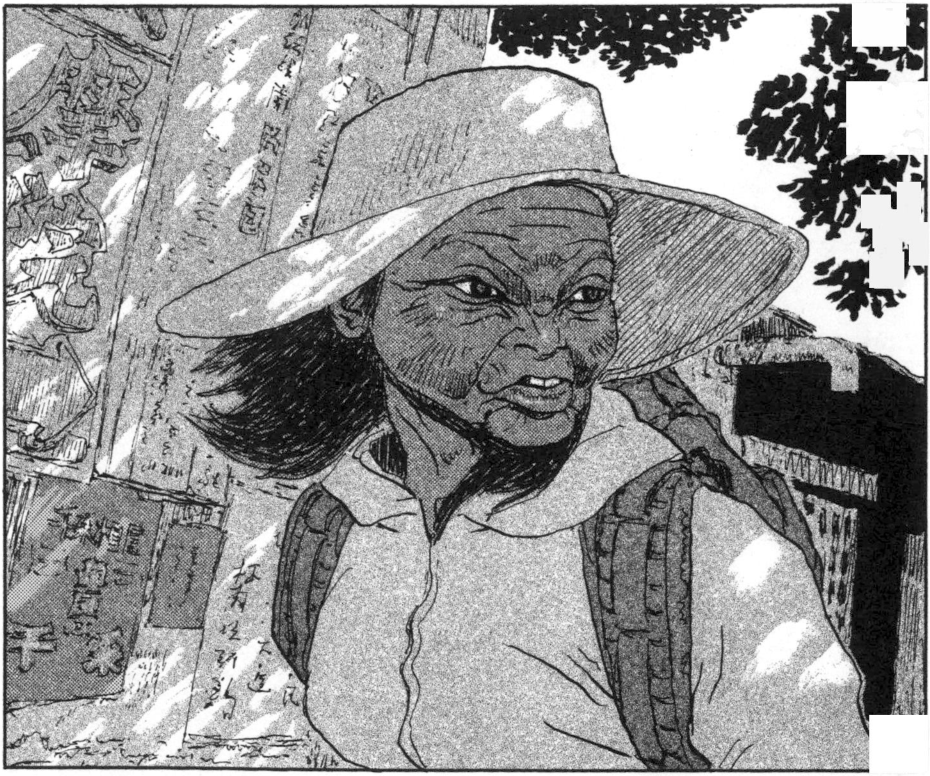

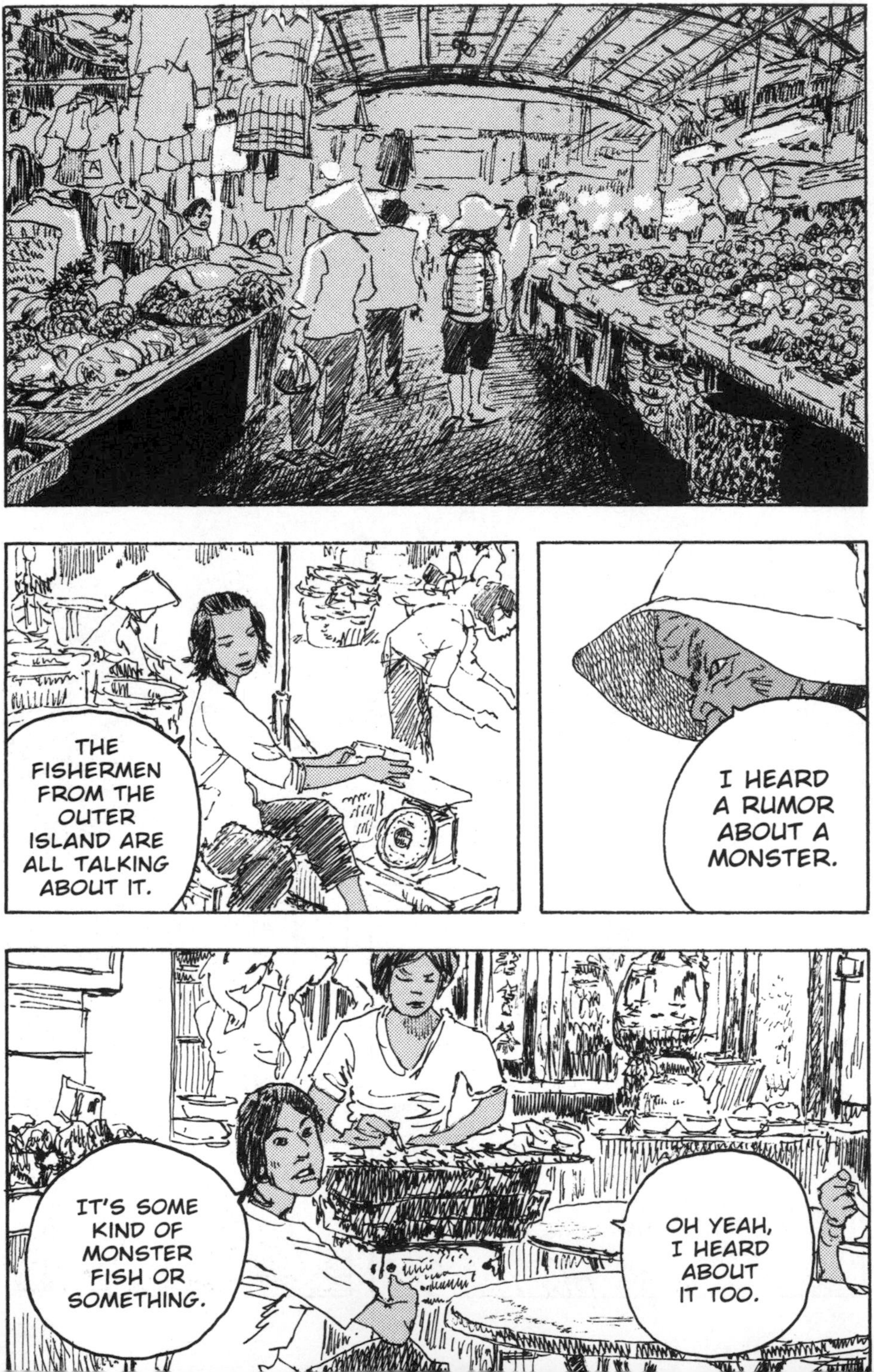
I HEARD A RUMOR ABOUT A MONSTER.
THE FISHERMEN FROM THE OUTER ISLAND ARE ALL TALKING ABOUT IT.
OH YEAH, I HEARD ABOUT IT TOO.
IT'S SOME KIND OF MONSTER FISH OR SOMETHING.

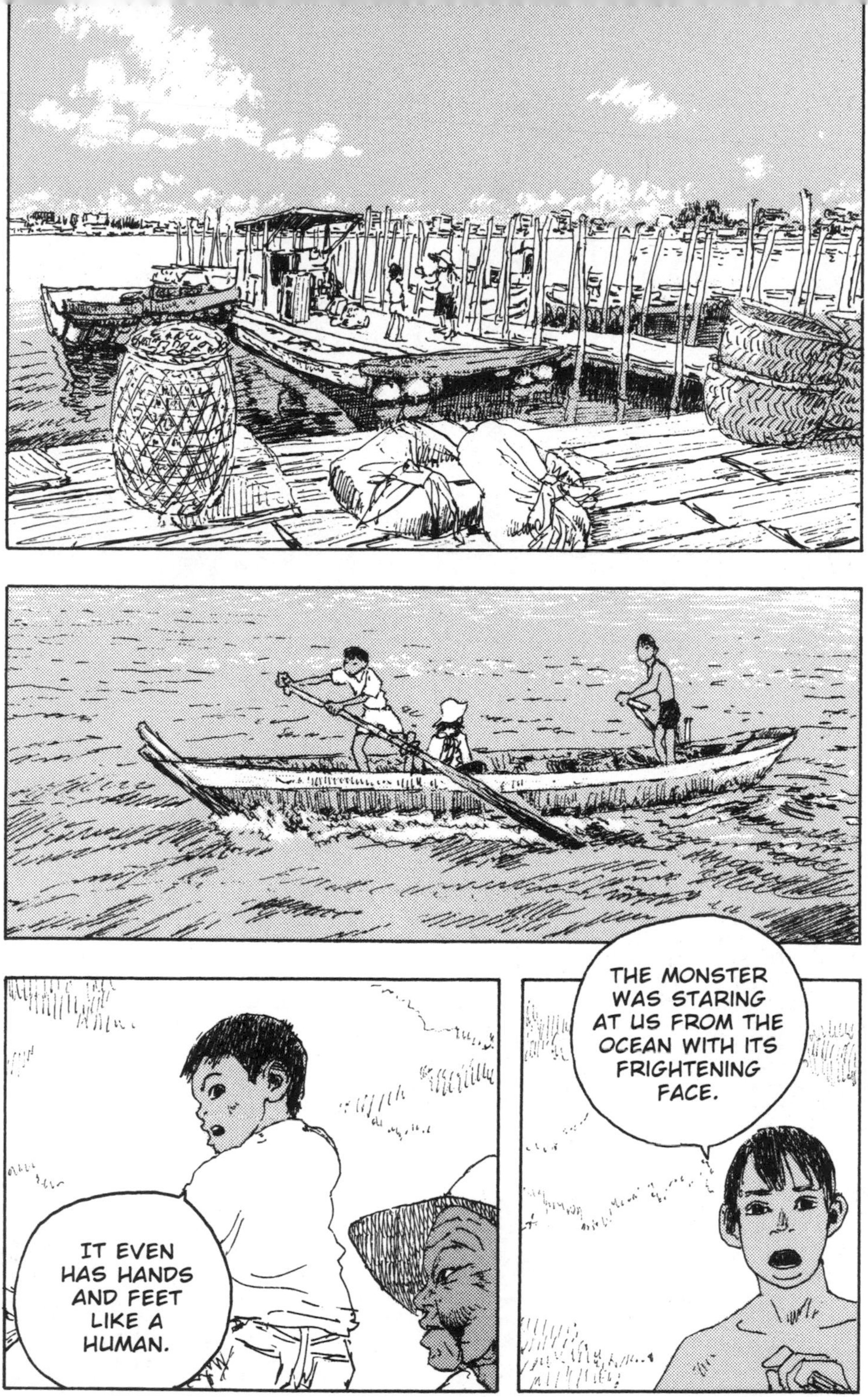
THE MONSTER WAS STARING AT US FROM THE OCEAN WITH ITS FRIGHTENING FACE.
IT EVEN HAS HANDS AND FEET LIKE A HUMAN.

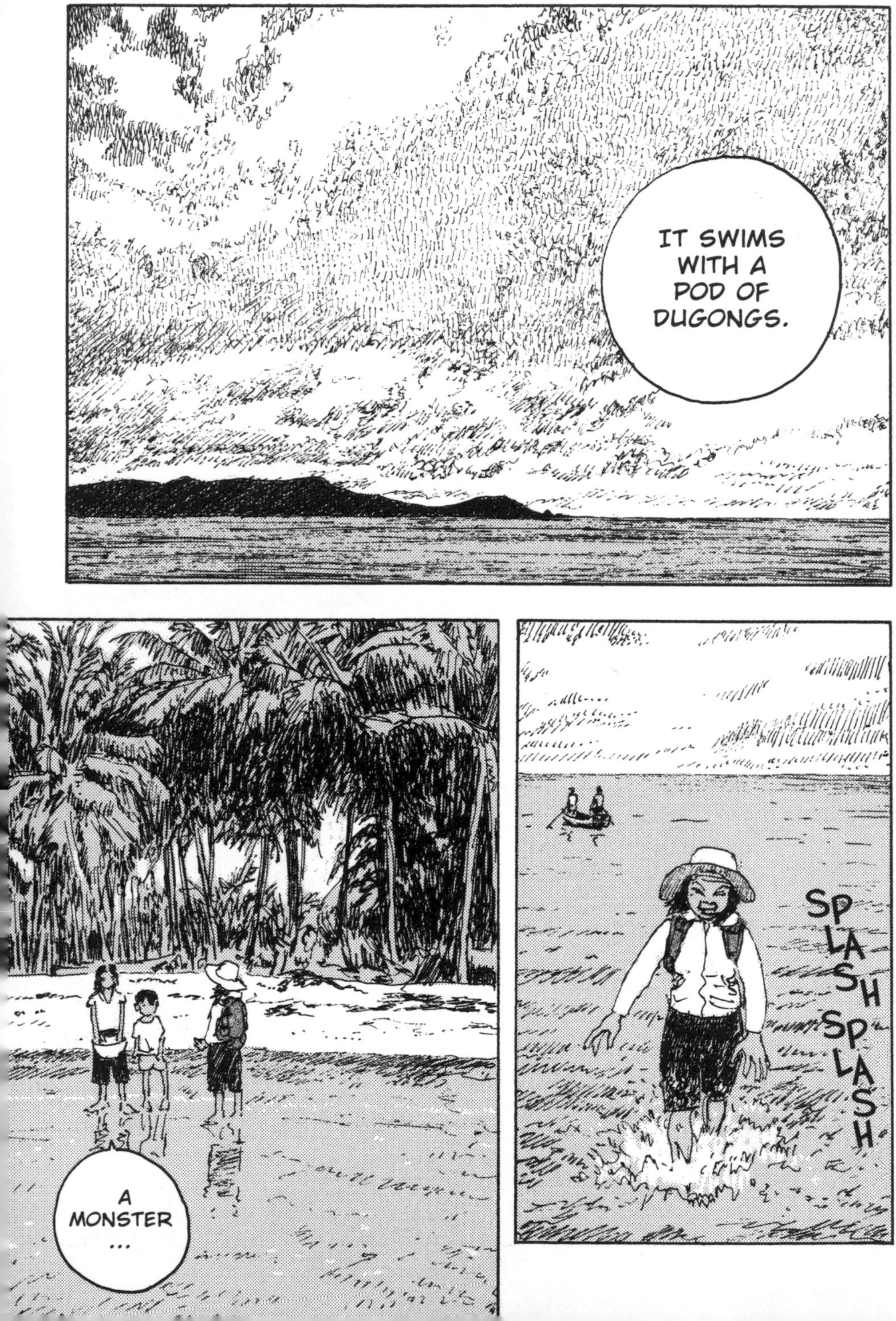
IT SWIMS WITH A POD OF DUGONGS.
SPLASH SPLASH
A MONSTER ...

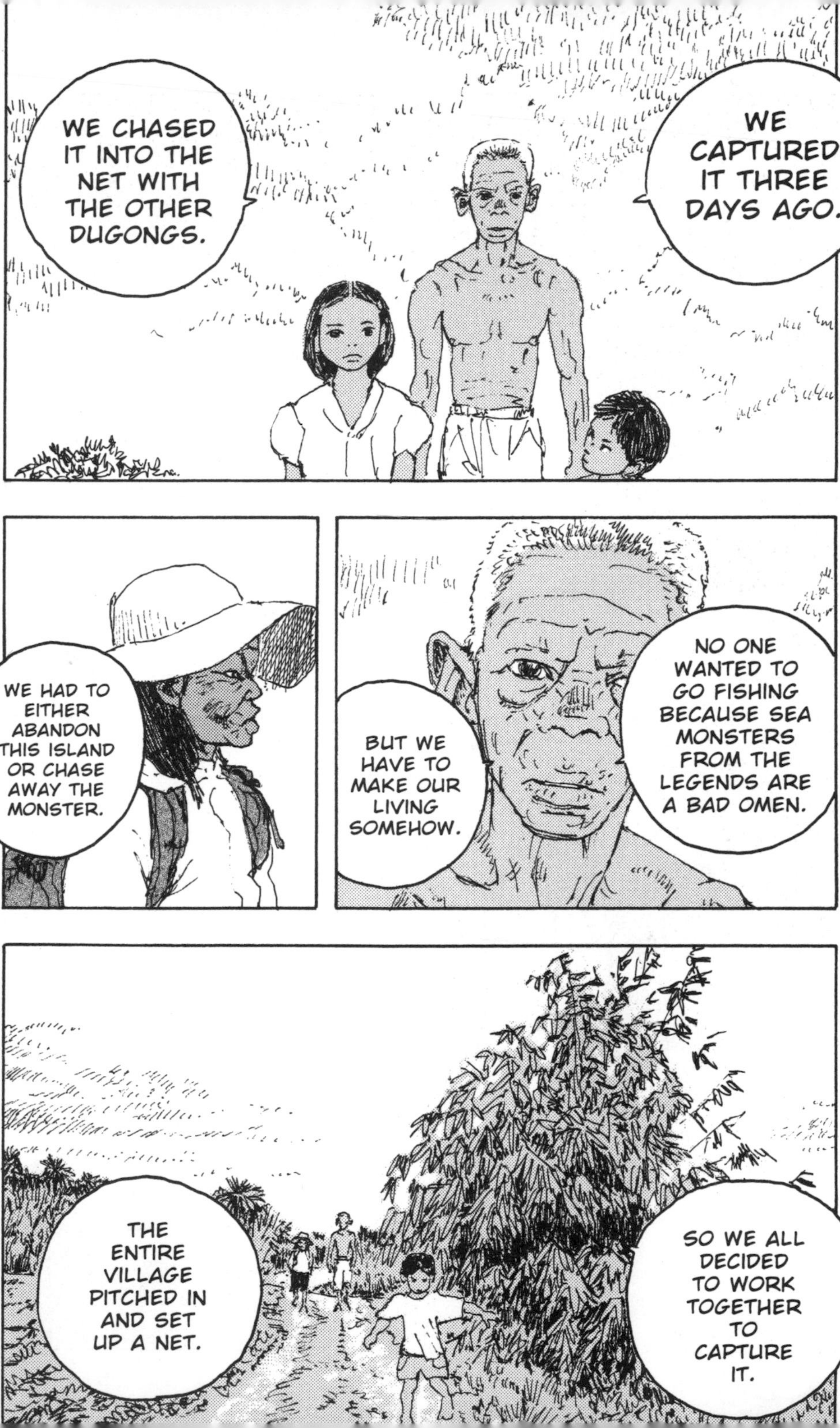
WE CAPTURED IT THREE DAYS AGO.
WE CHASED IT INTO THE NET WITH THE OTHER DUGONGS.
NO ONE WANTED TO GO FISHING BECAUSE SEA MONSTERS FROM THE LEGENDS ARE A BAD OMEN.
BUT WE HAVE TO MAKE OUR LIVING SOMEHOW.
WE HAD TO EITHER ABANDON THIS ISLAND OR CHASE AWAY THE MONSTER.
SO WE ALL DECIDED TO WORK TOGETHER TO CAPTURE IT.
THE ENTIRE VILLAGE PITCHED IN AND SET UP A NET.

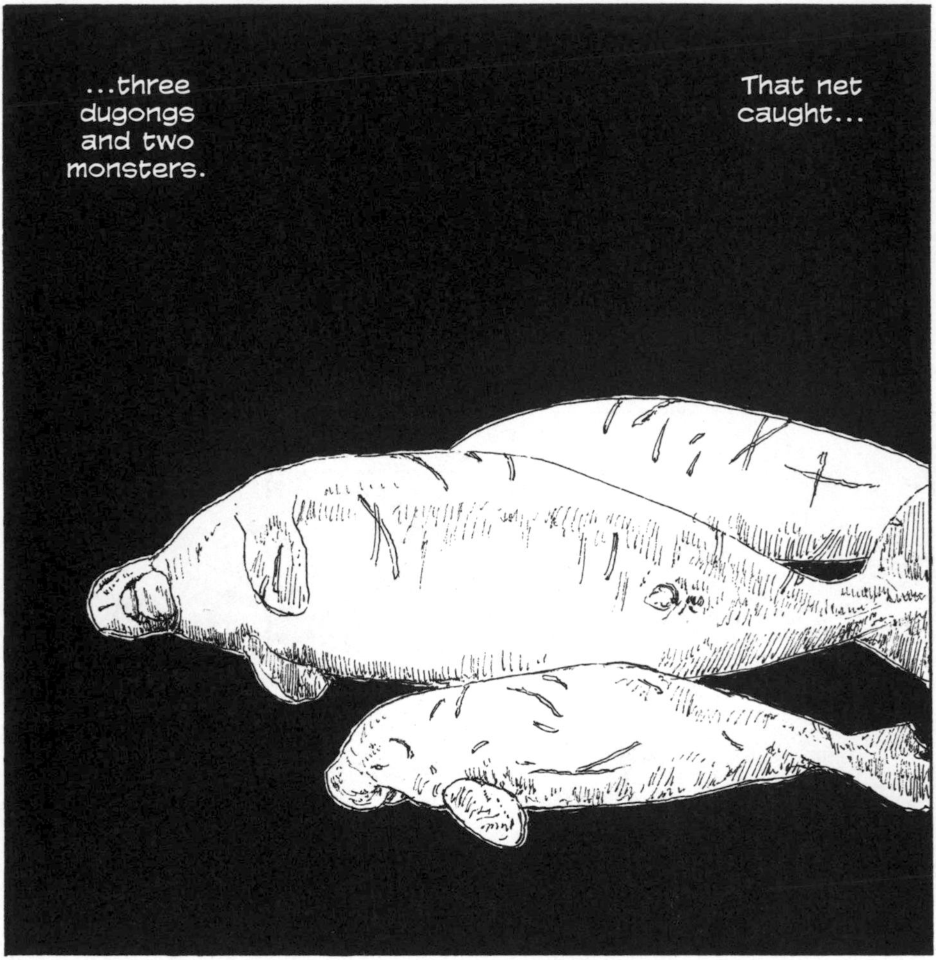
That net caught...
...three dugongs and two monsters.

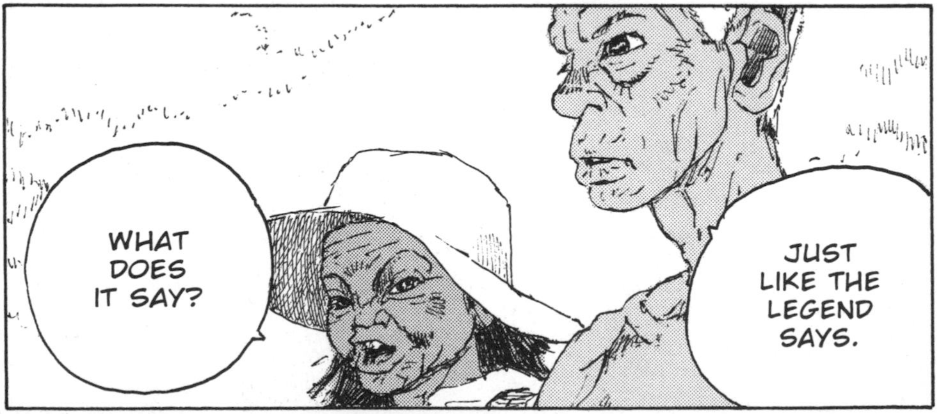
JUST LIKE THE LEGEND SAYS.
WHAT DOES IT SAY?

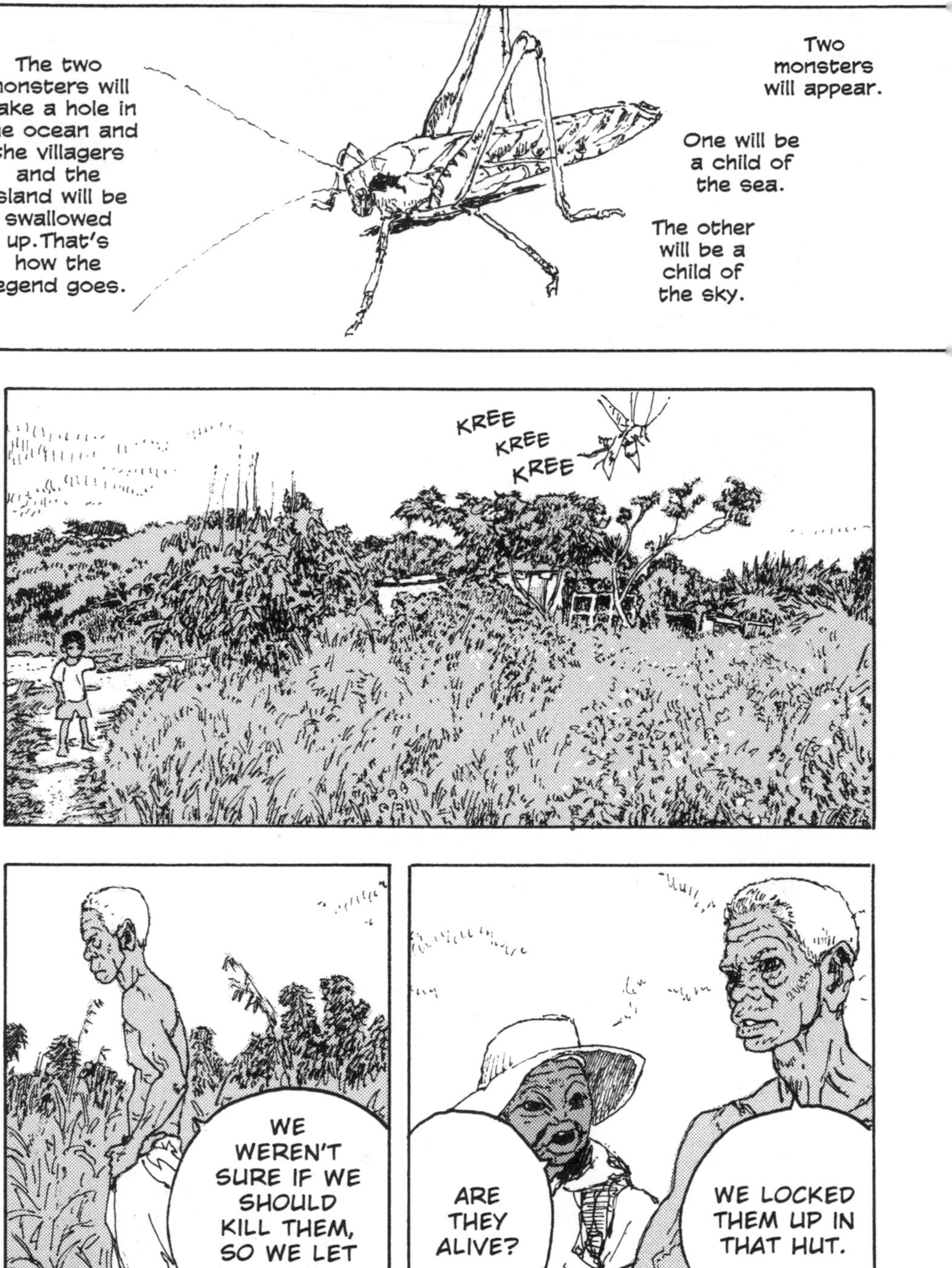
Two monsters will appear.
One will be a child of the sea.
The other will be a child of the sky.
The two monsters will make a hole in the ocean and the villagers and the island will be swallowed up. That's how the legend goes.
KREE KREE KREE
WE LOCKED THEM UP IN THAT HUT.
ARE THEY ALIVE?
WE WEREN'T SURE IF WE SHOULD KILL THEM, SO WE LET THEM LIVE.

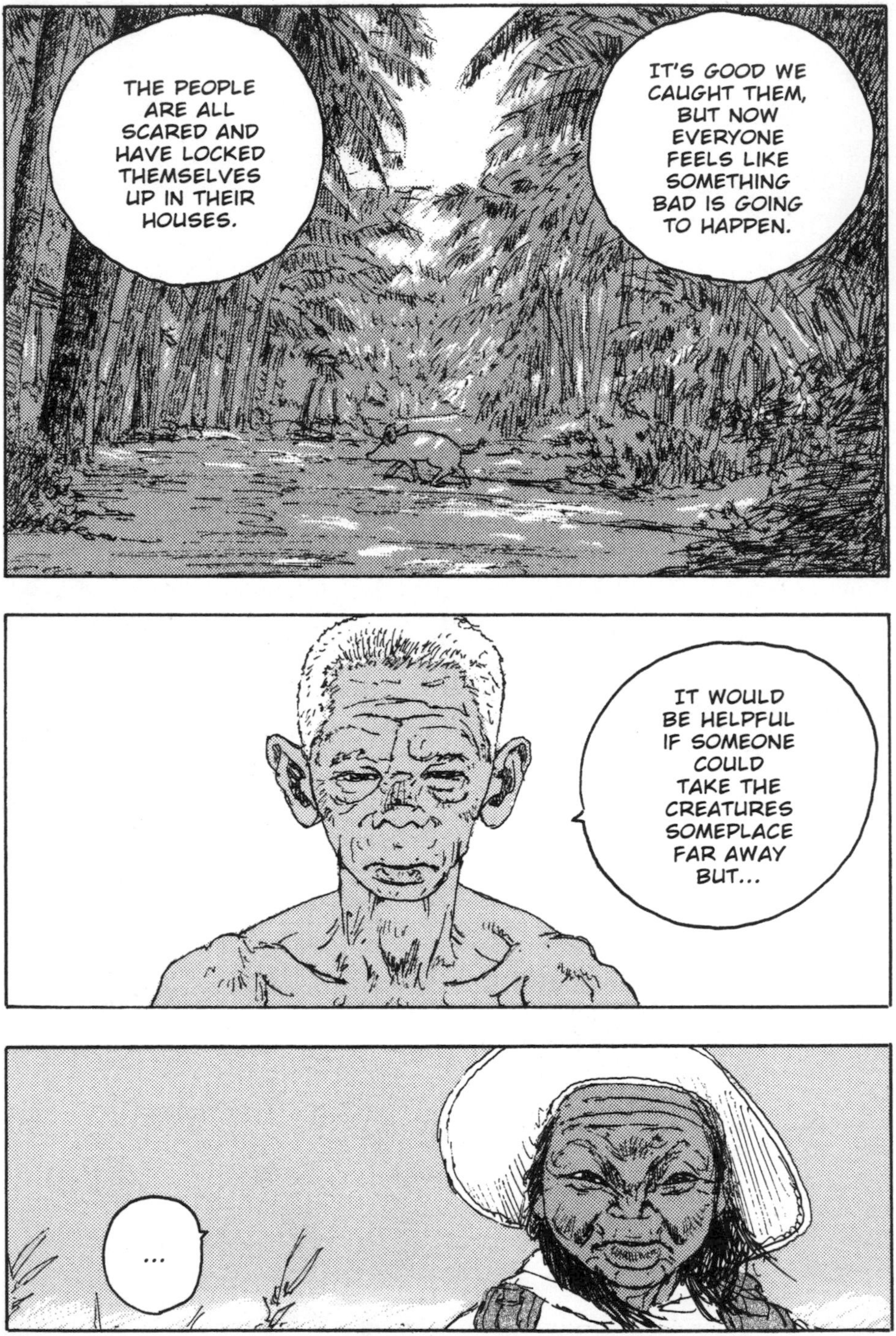
IT'S GOOD WE CAUGHT THEM, BUT NOW EVERYONE FEELS LIKE SOMETHING BAD IS GOING TO HAPPEN.
THE PEOPLE ARE ALL SCARED AND HAVE LOCKED THEMSELVES UP IN THEIR HOUSES.
IT WOULD BE HELPFUL IF SOMEONE COULD TAKE THE CREATURES SOMEPLACE FAR AWAY BUT...
...

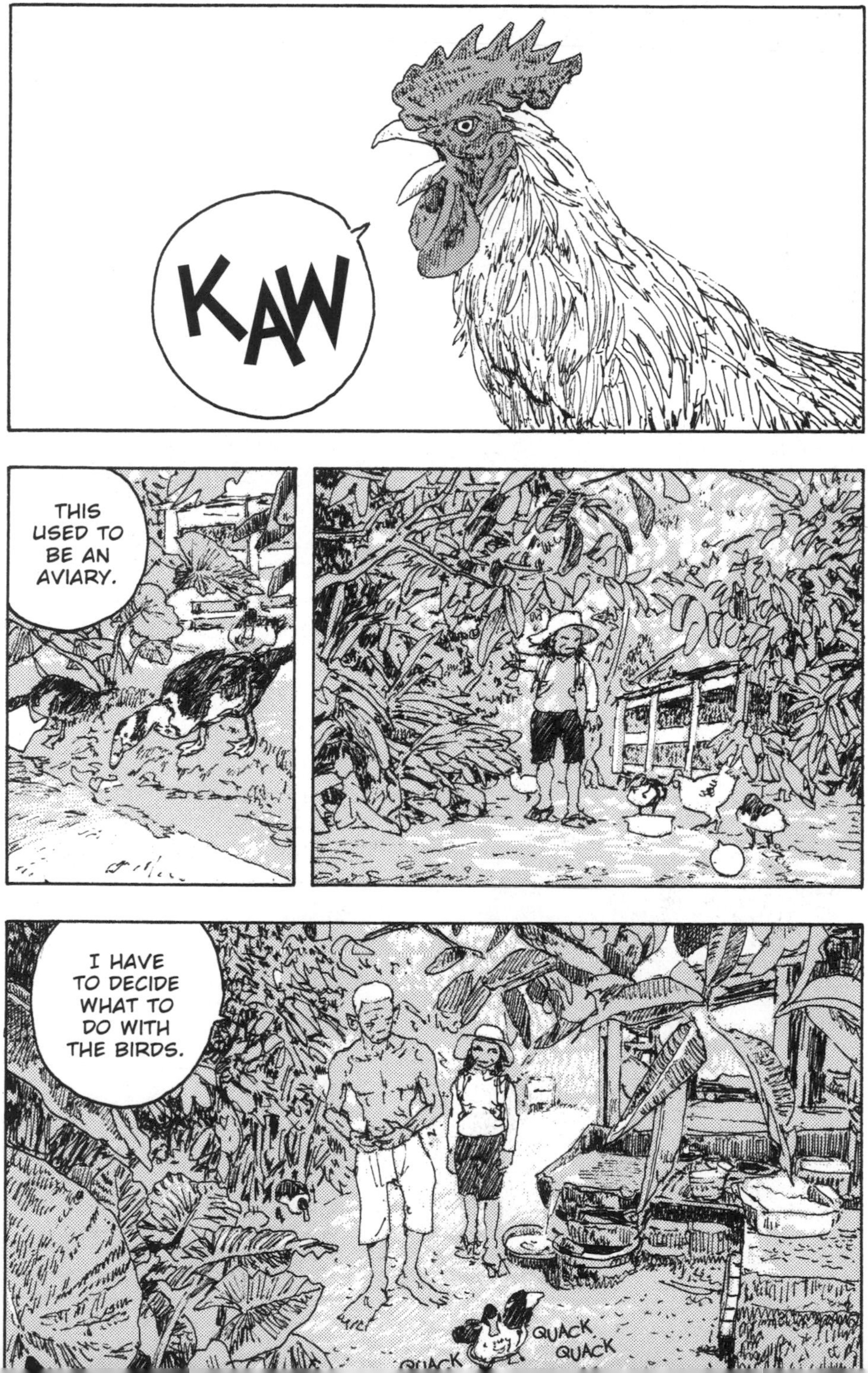
KAW
THIS USED TO BE AN AVIARY.
I HAVE TO DECIDE WHAT TO DO WITH THE BIRDS.
QUACK QUACK
QUACK

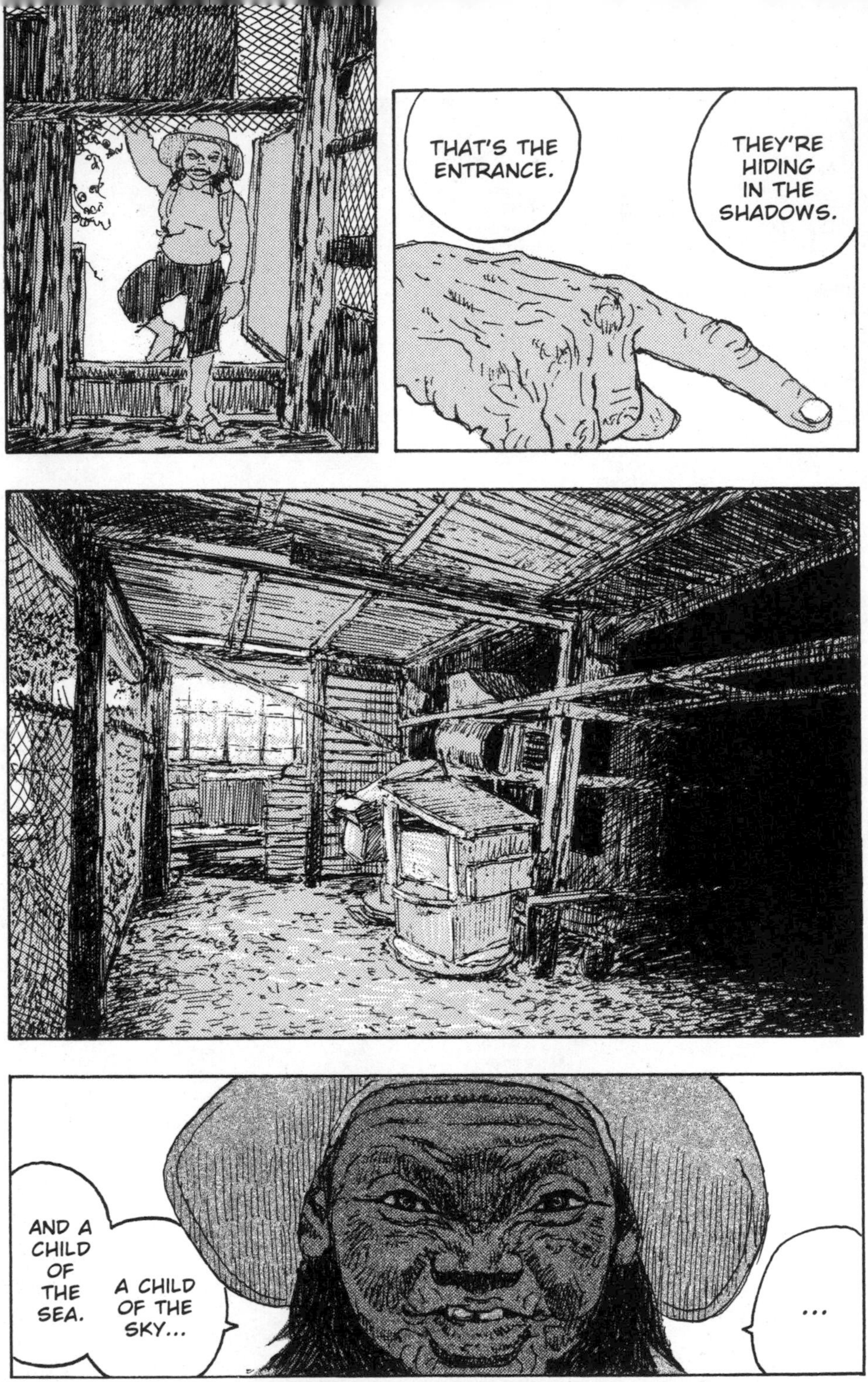
THEY'RE HIDING IN THE SHADOWS.
THAT'S THE ENTRANCE.
...
A CHILD OF THE SKY...
AND A CHILD OF THE SEA.

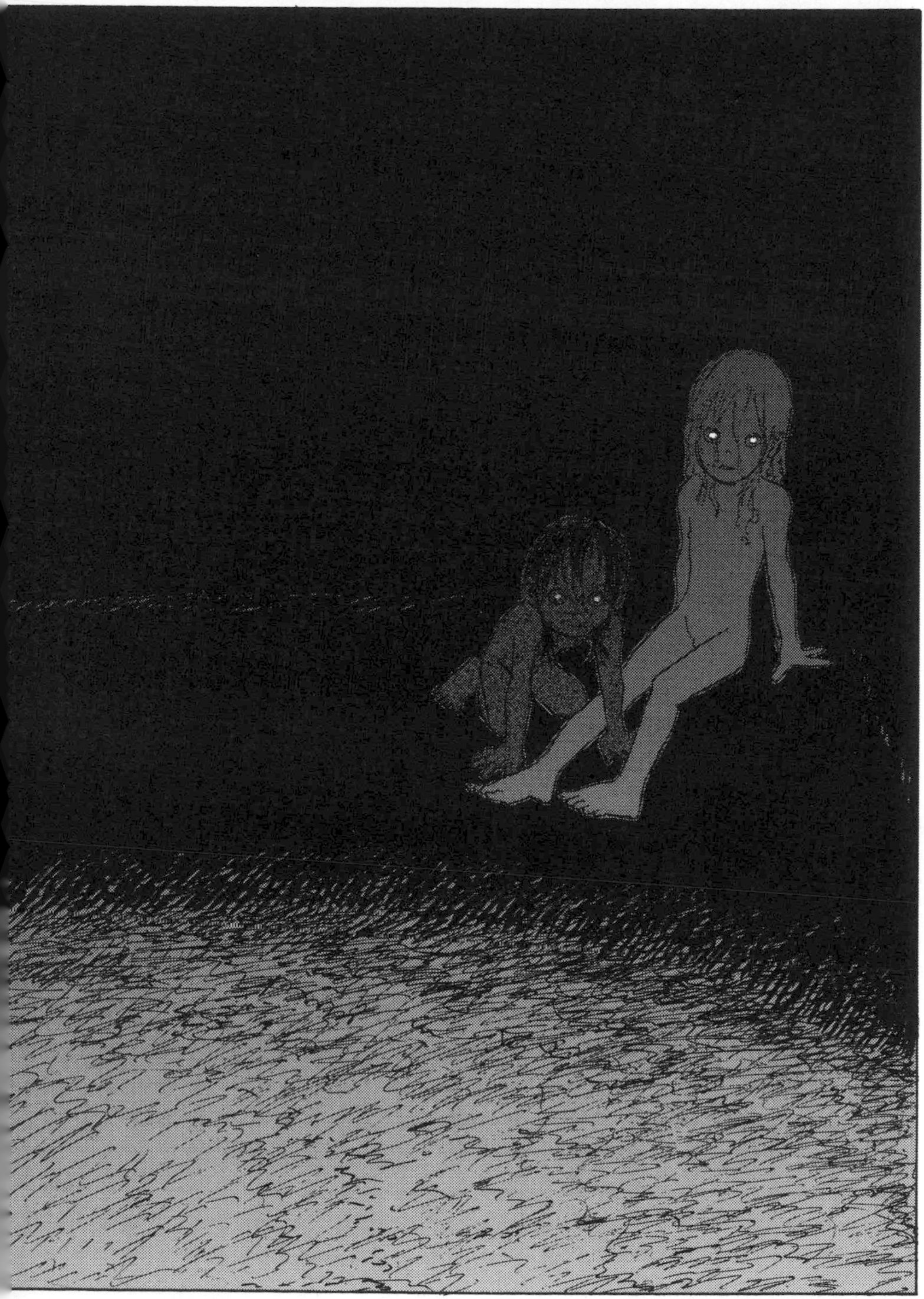

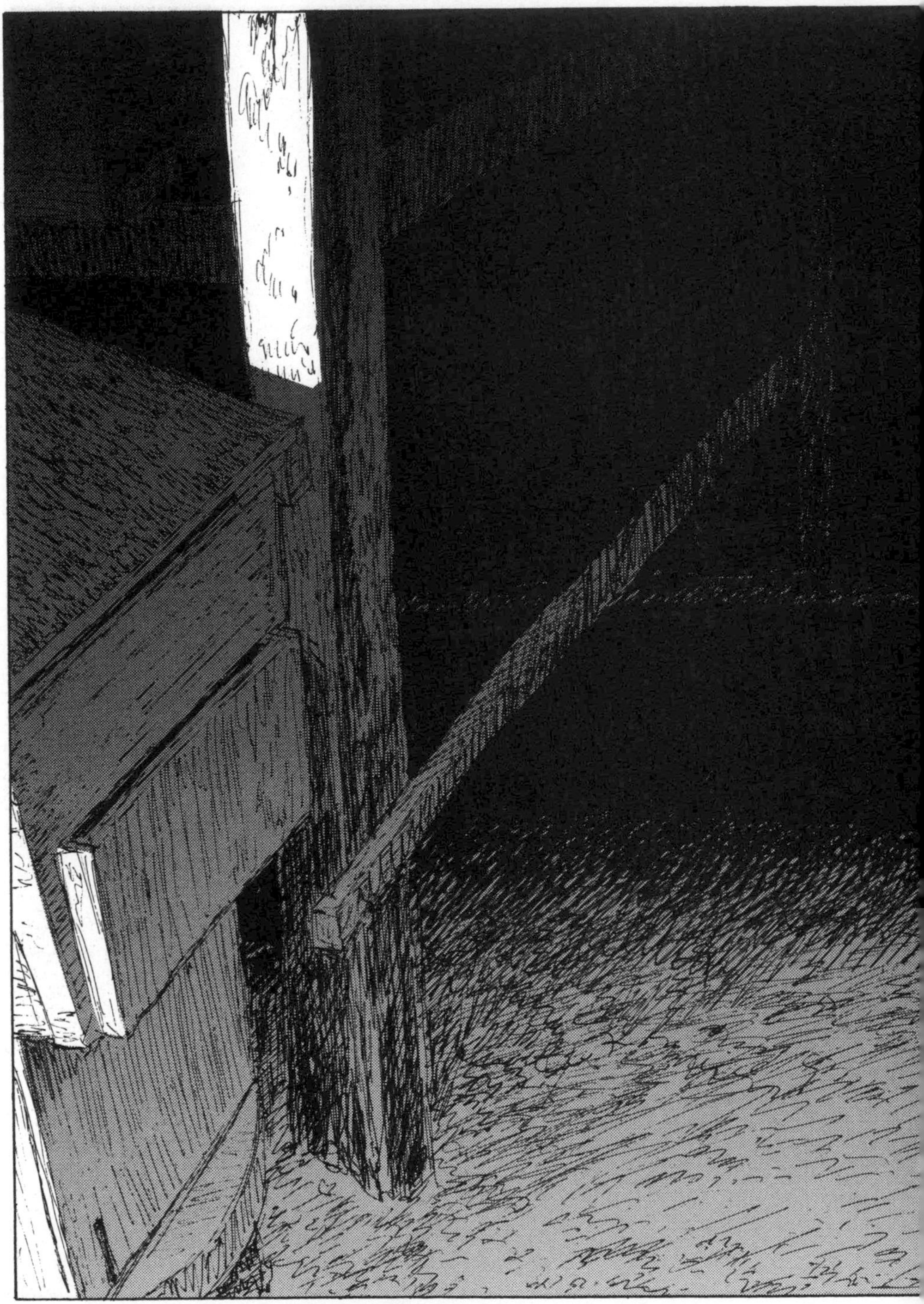

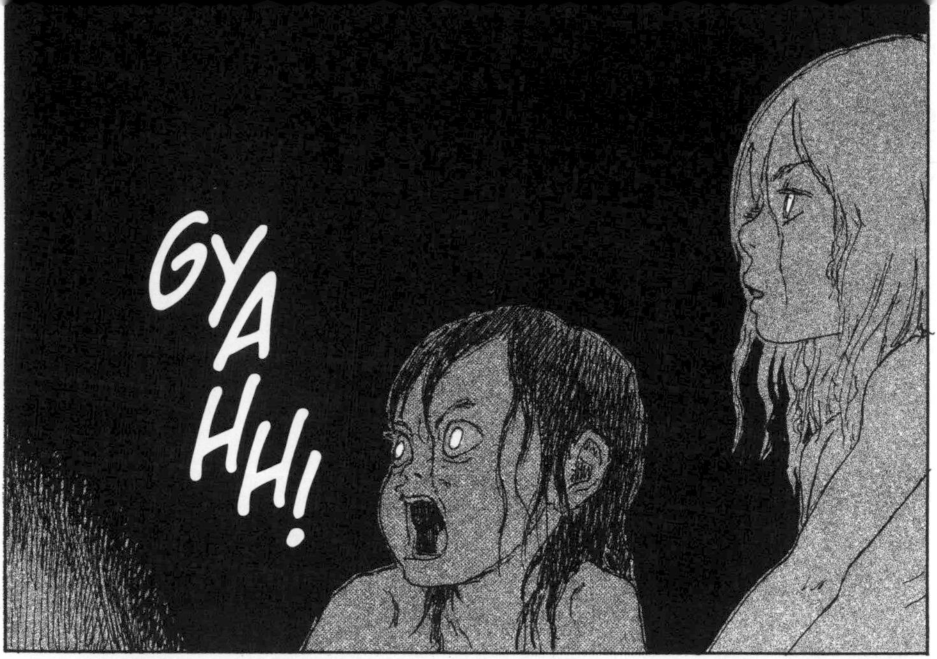
GYAHH!
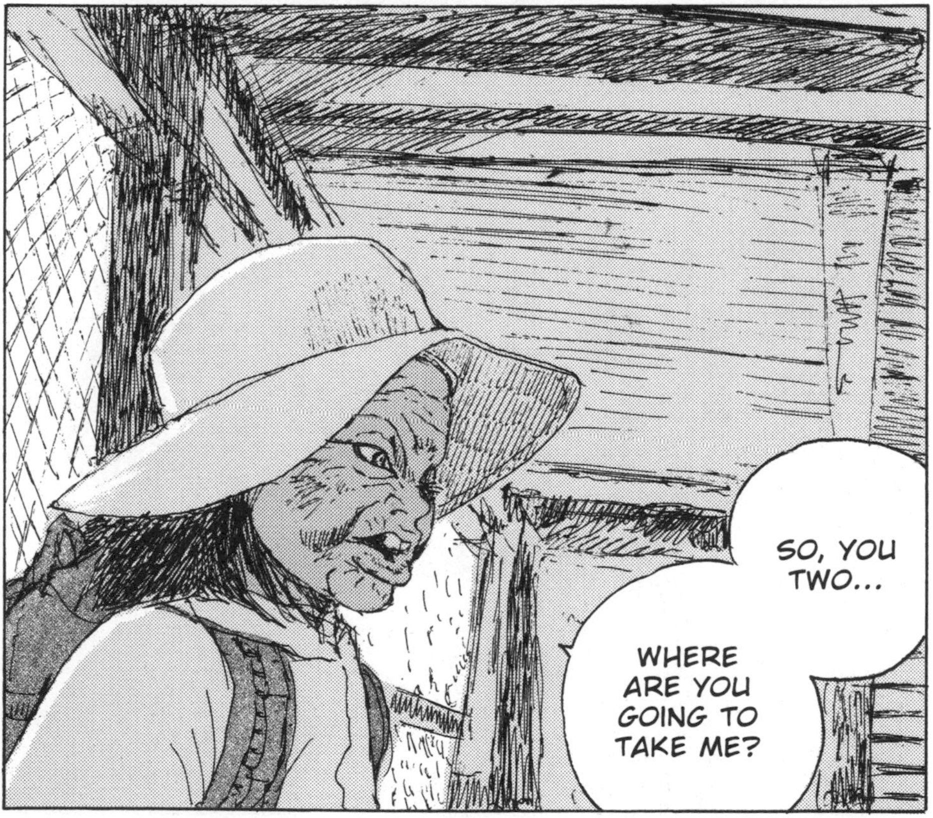
SO, YOU TWO...
WHERE ARE YOU GOING TO TAKE ME?

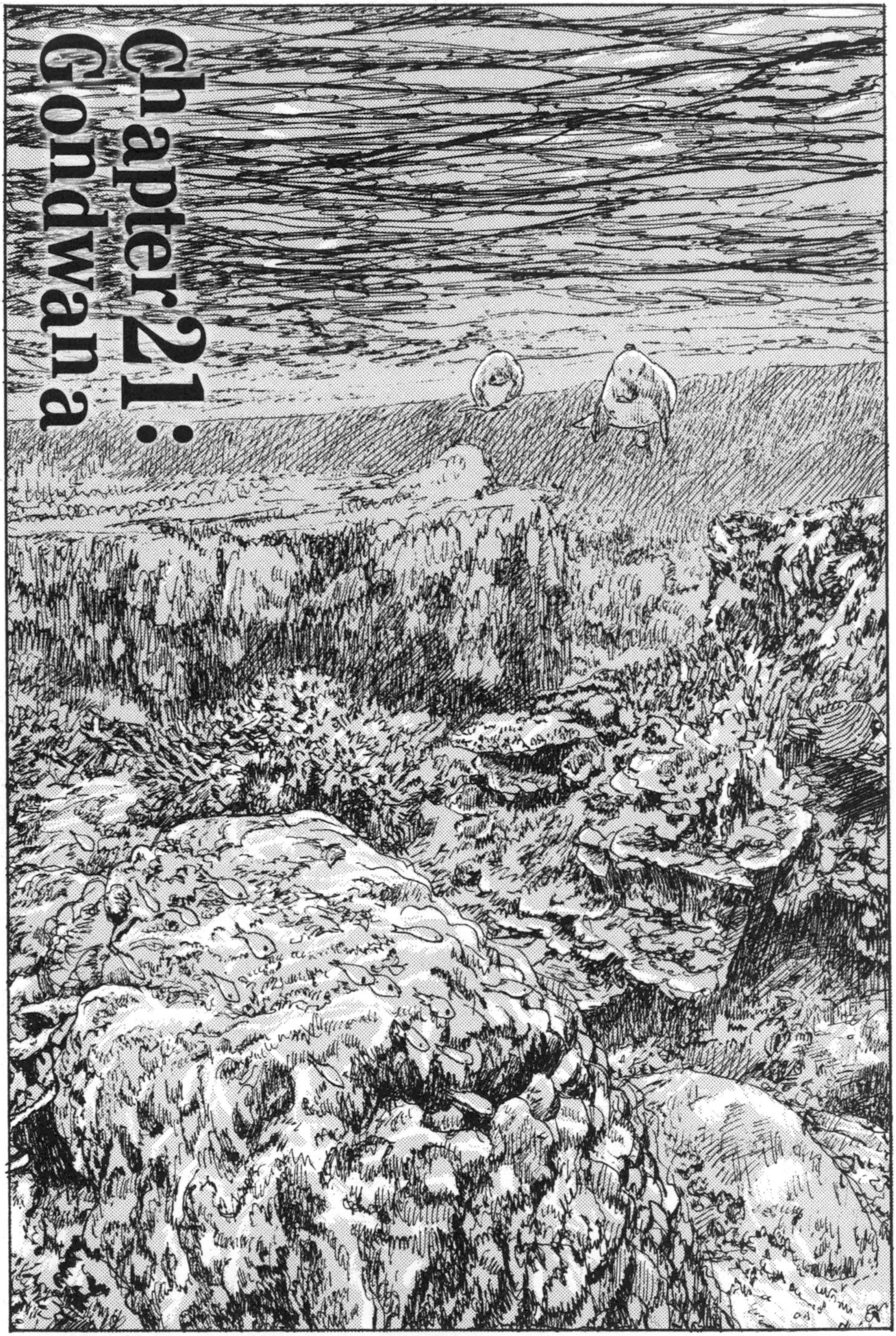
Chapter 21:
Gondwana

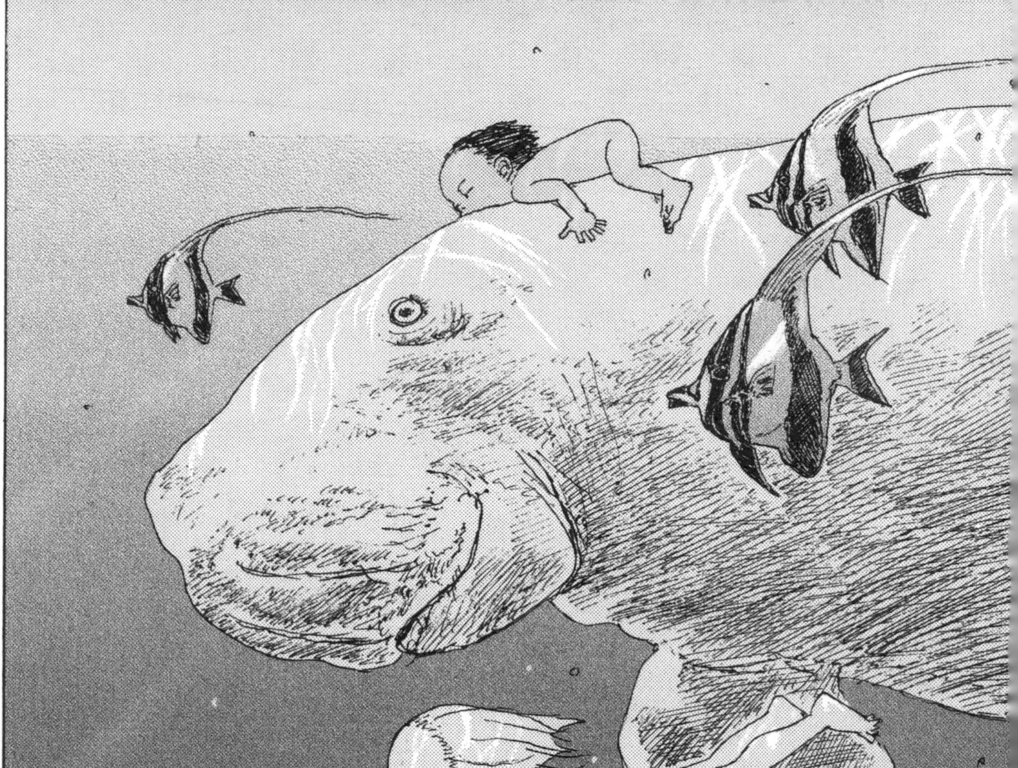
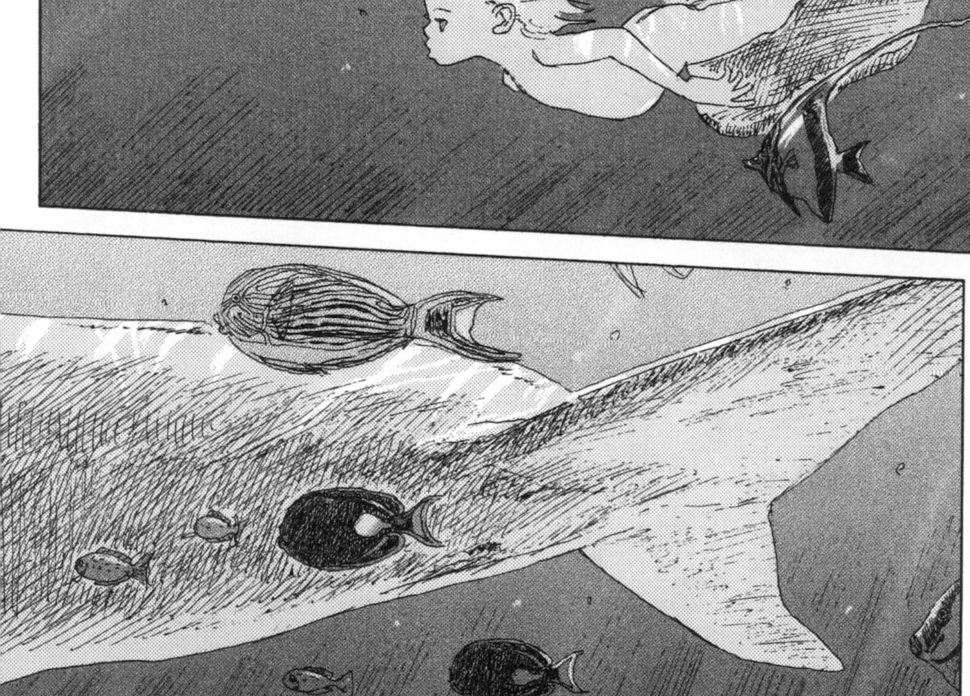

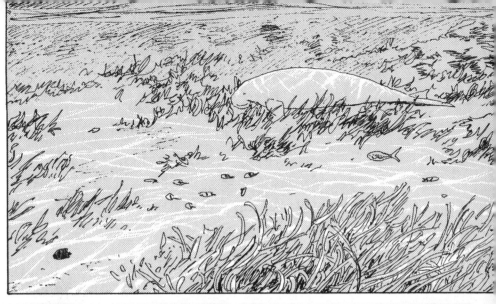

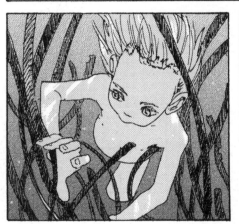

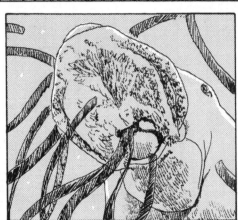

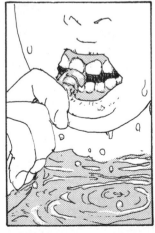

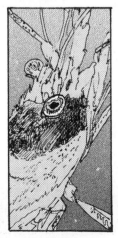

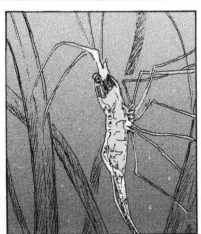

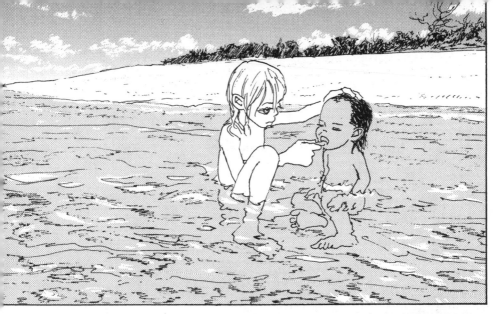

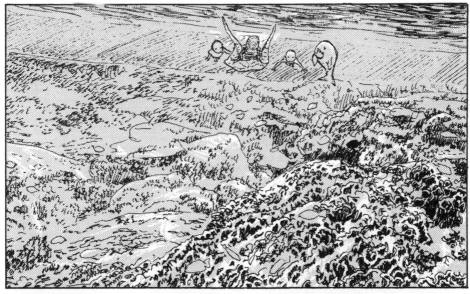

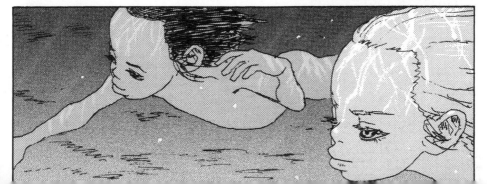

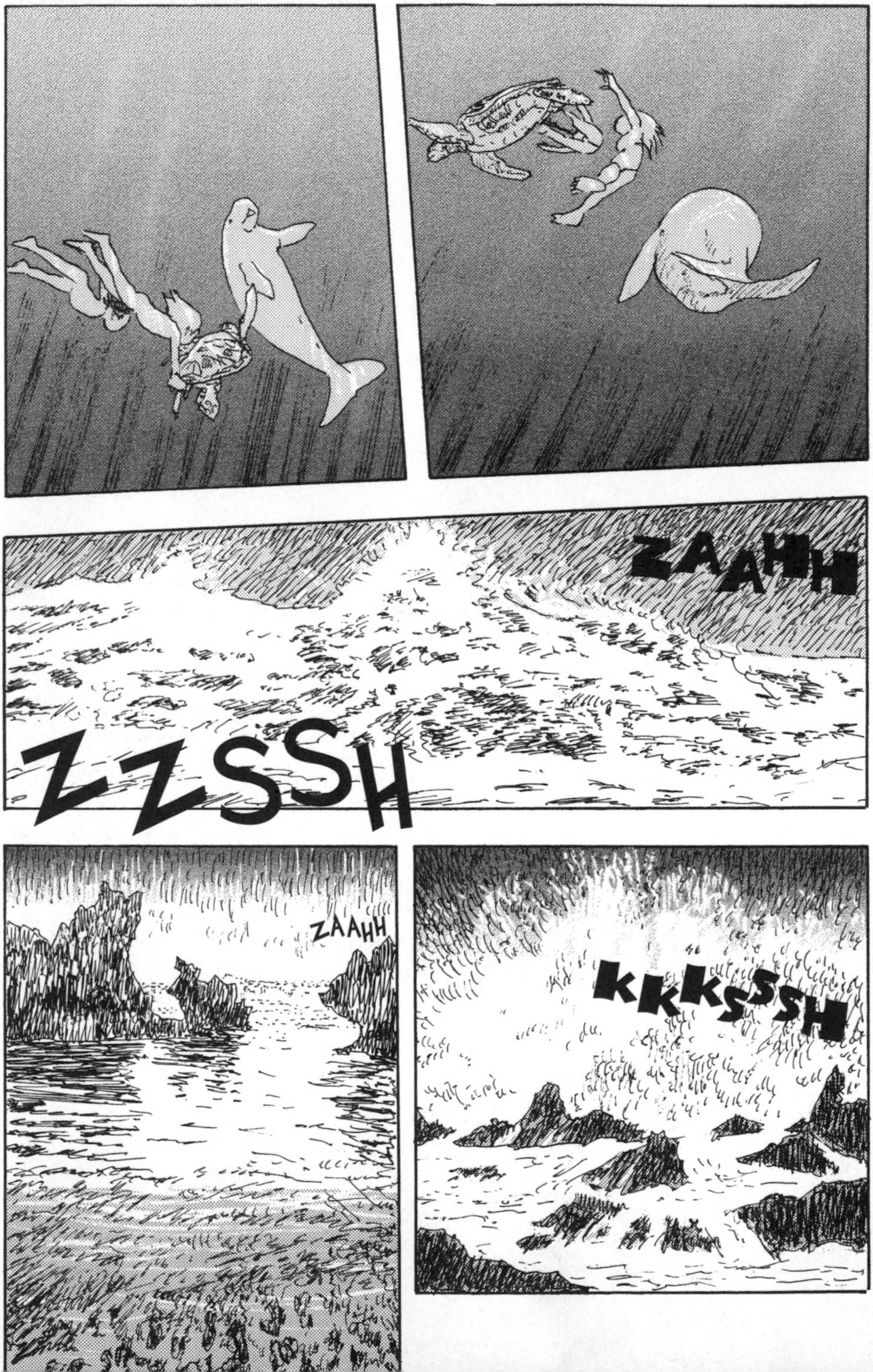
ZAAHH
ZZSSH
KKKSSSH
ZAAHH

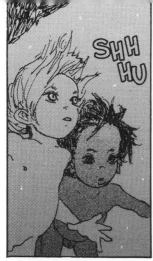

SHH HU

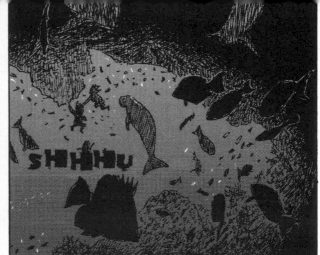

SHHHU

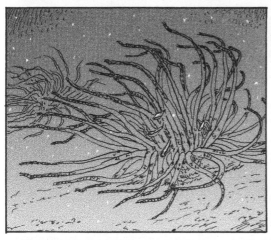

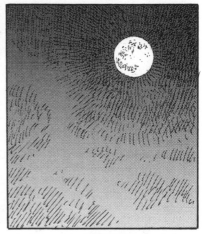

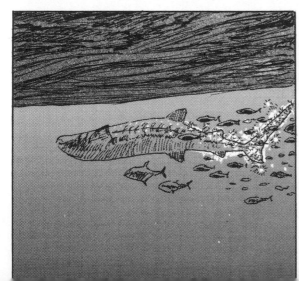

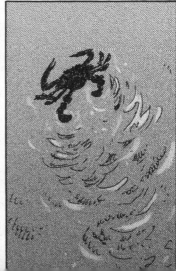

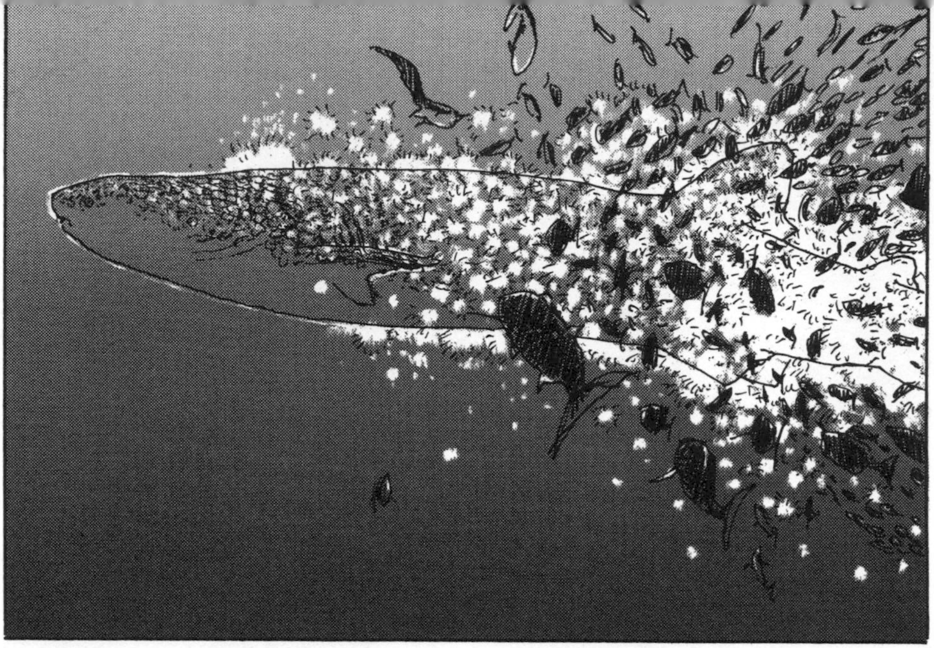
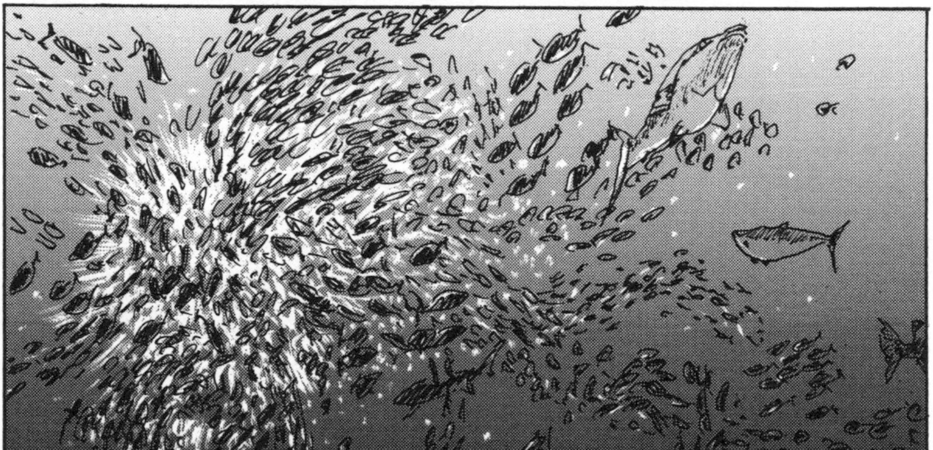
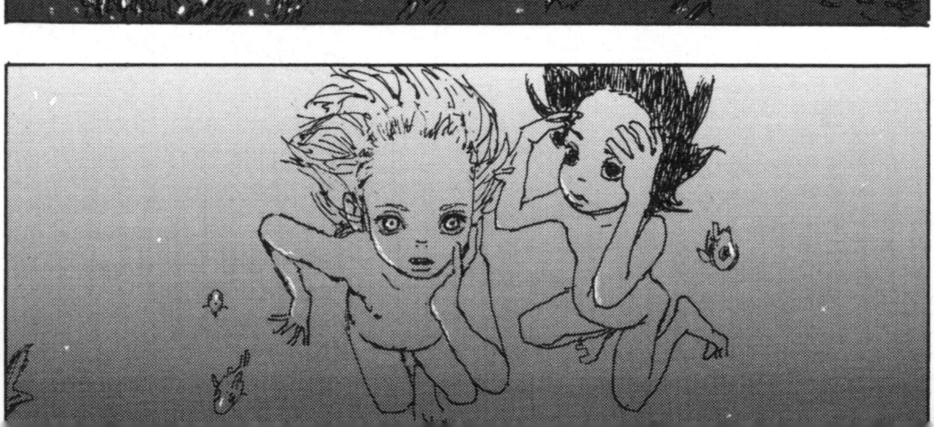

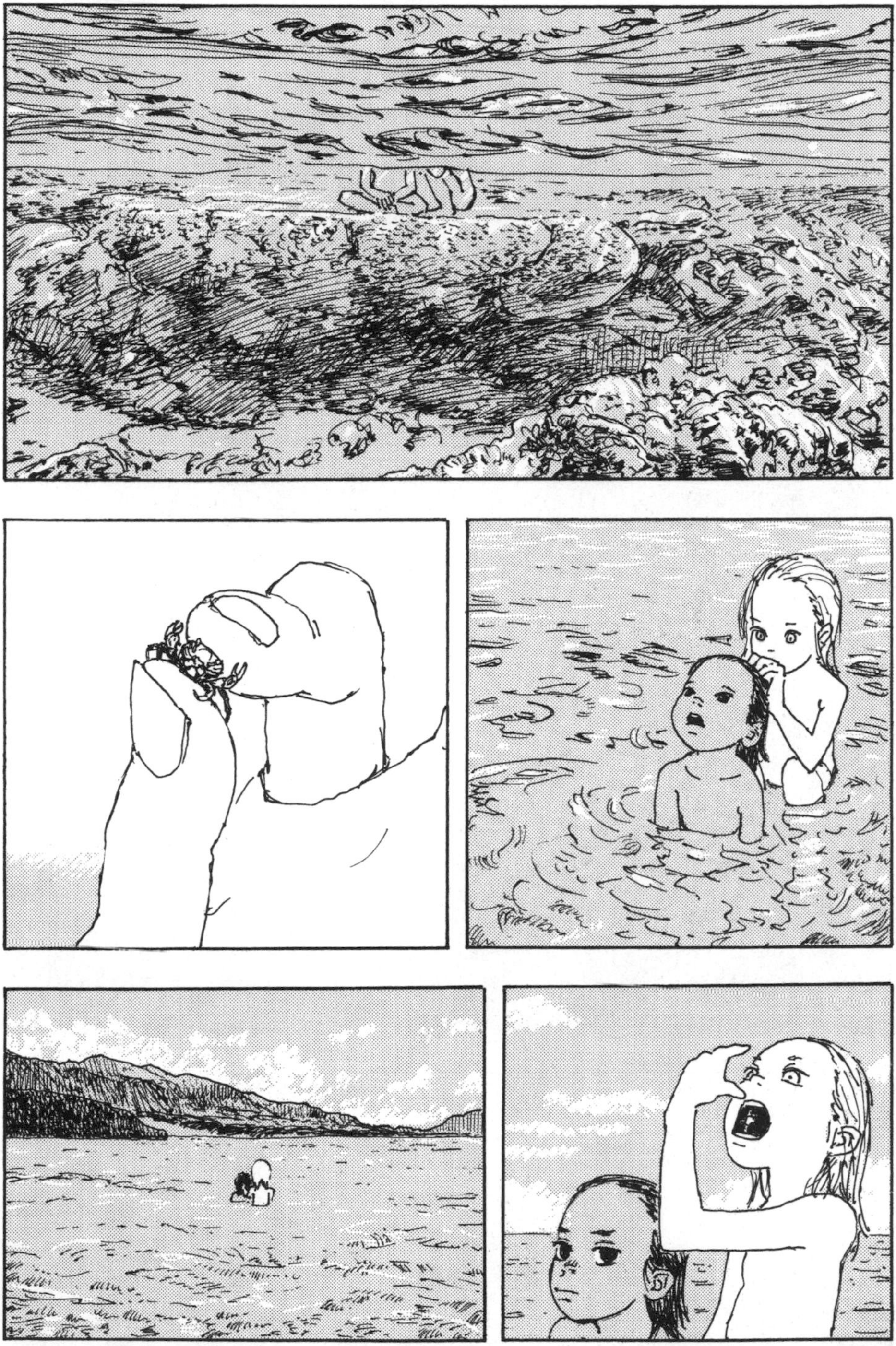

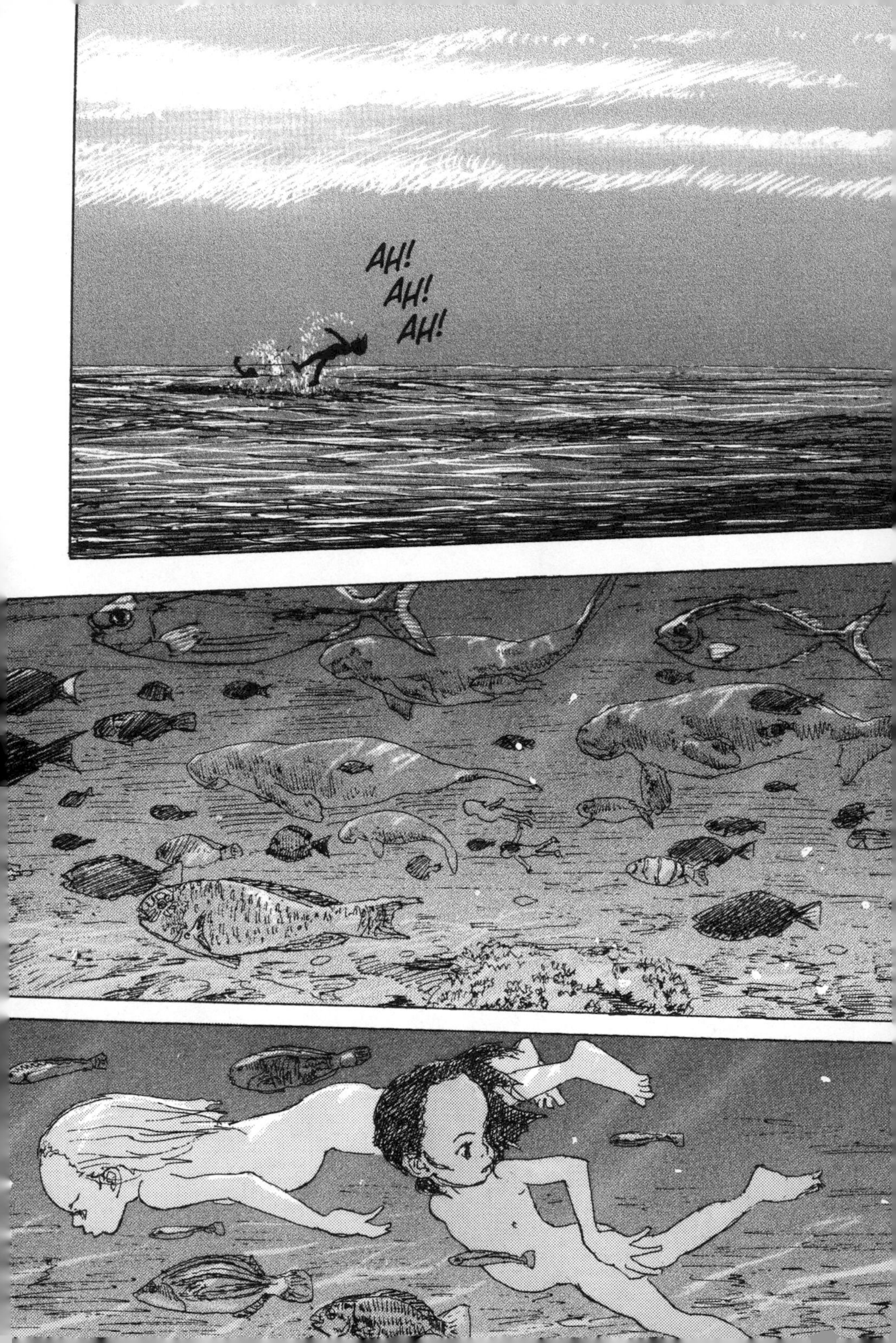
AH!
AH!
AH!

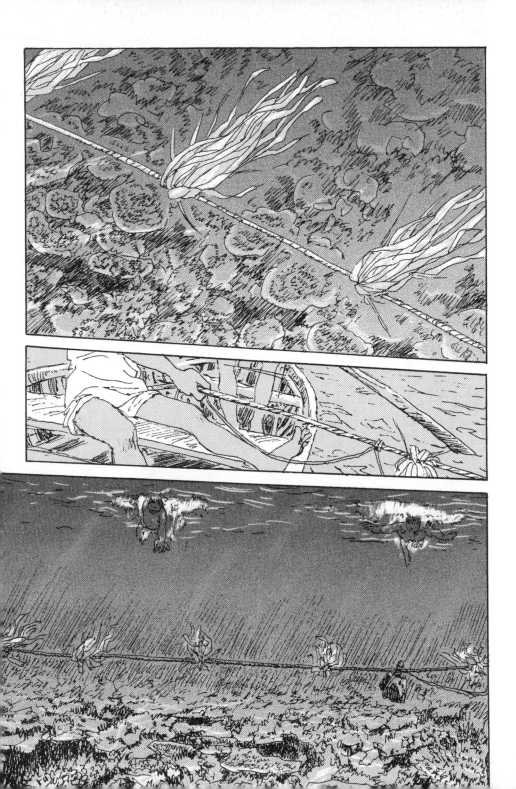

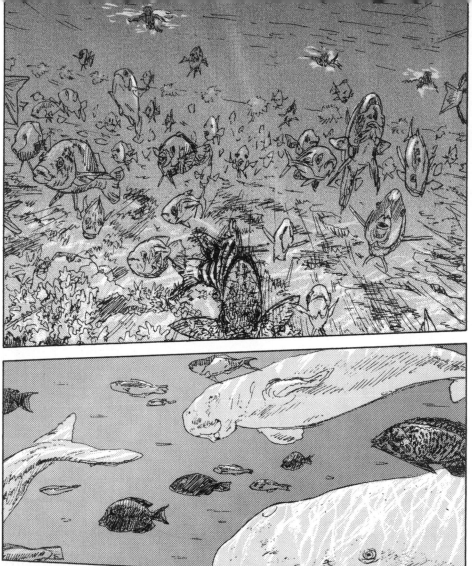

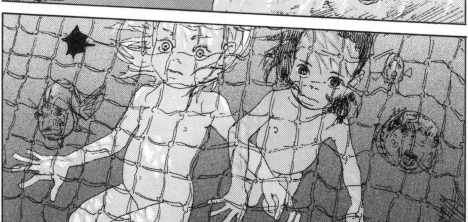

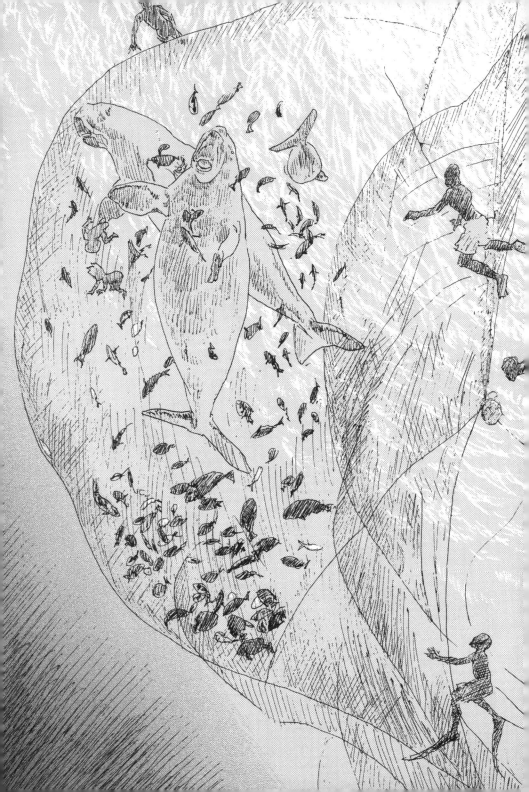

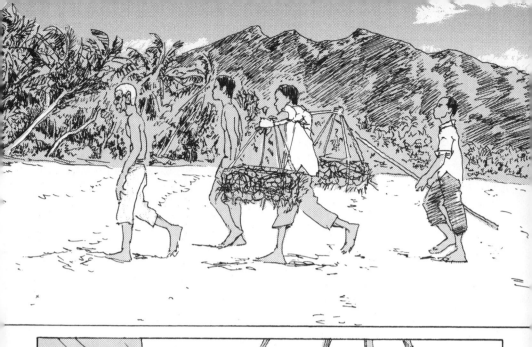

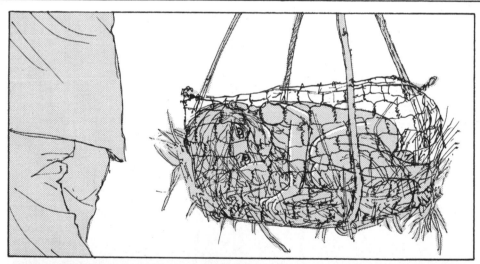

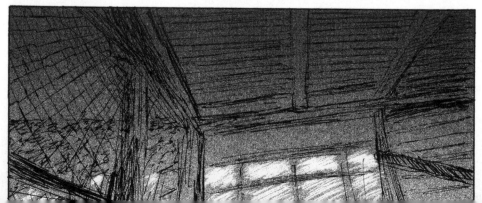

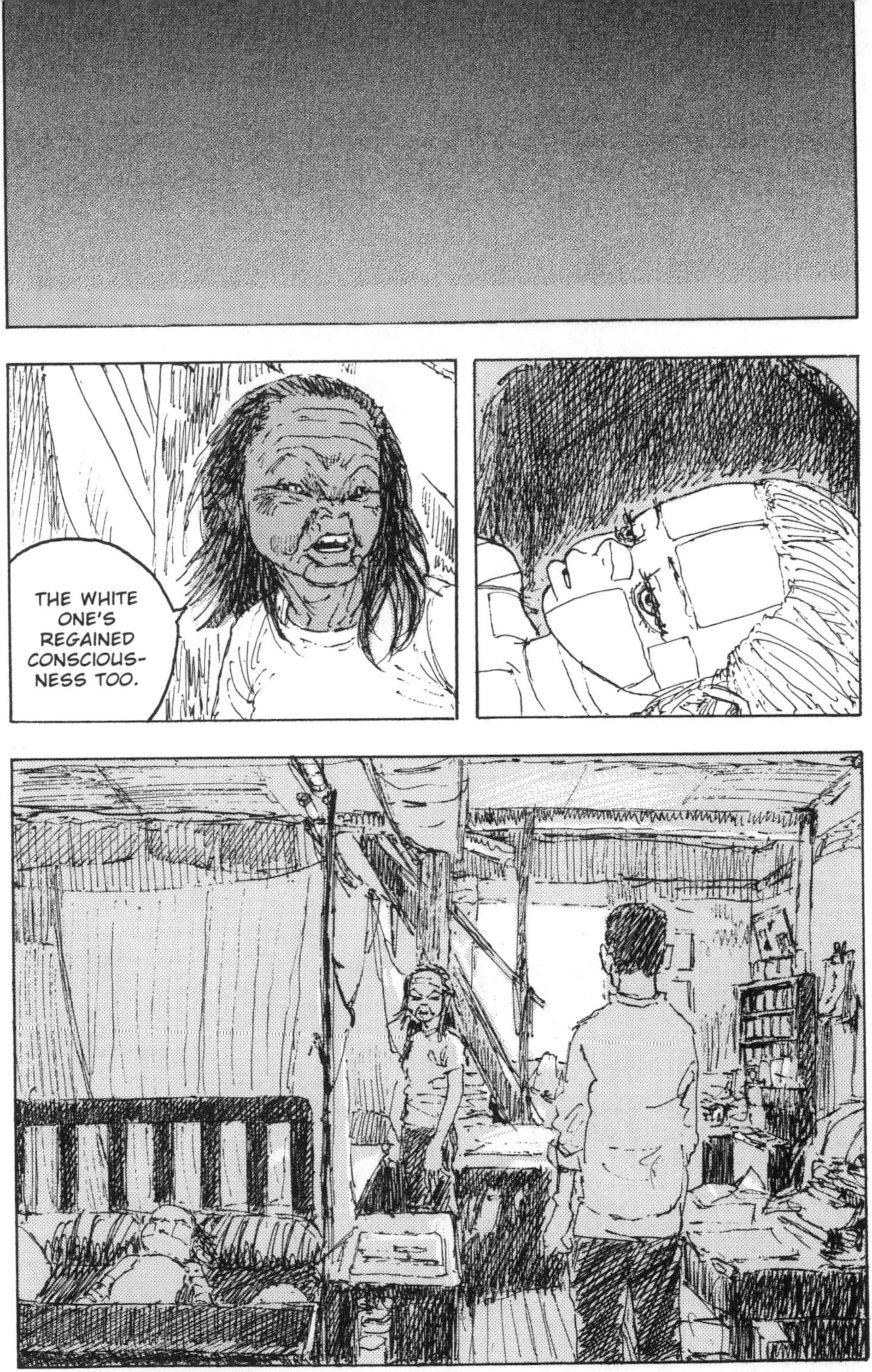
THE WHITE ONE'S REGAINED CONSCIOUSNESS TOO.

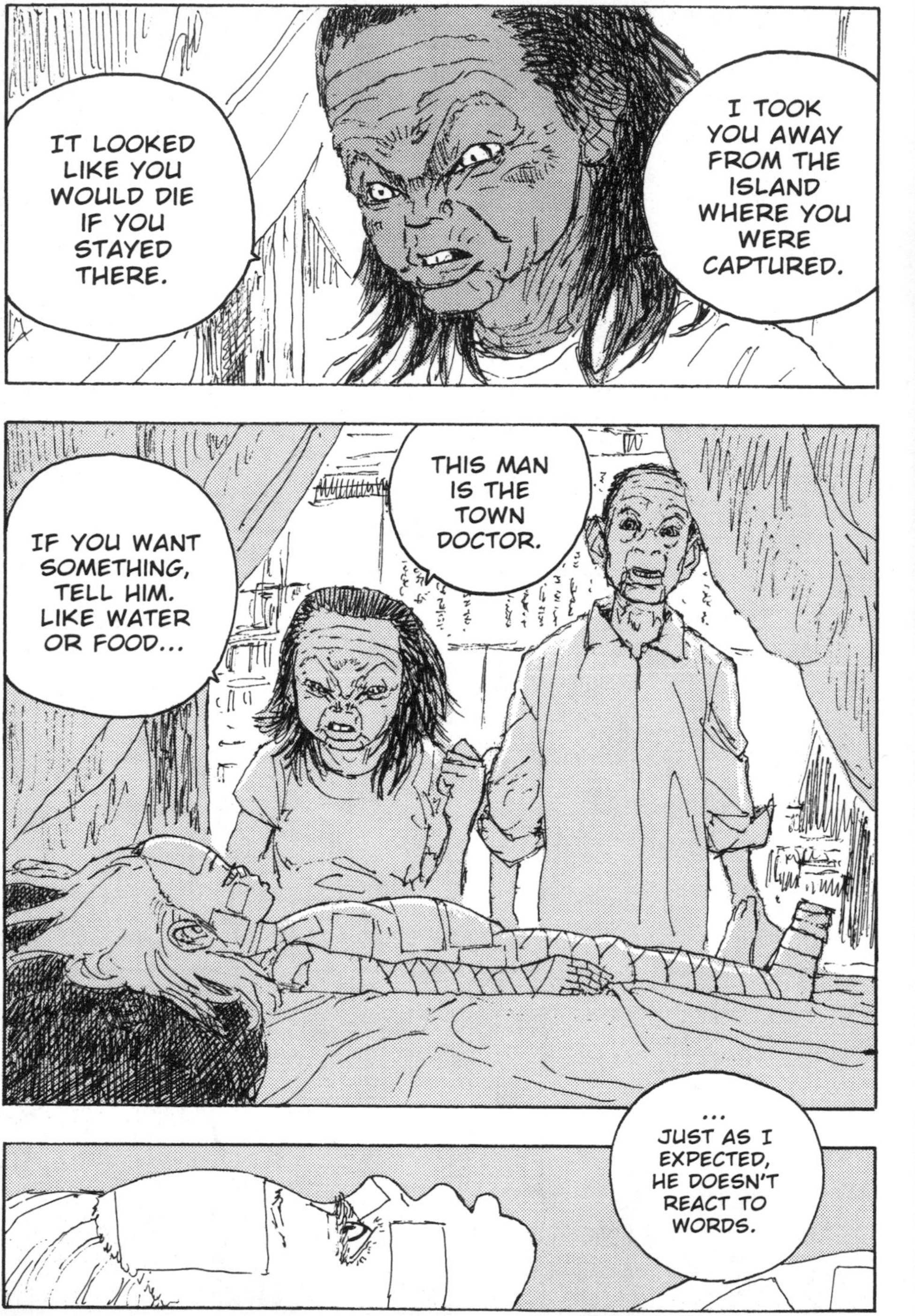
I TOOK YOU AWAY FROM THE ISLAND WHERE YOU WERE CAPTURED.
IT LOOKED LIKE YOU WOULD DIE IF YOU STAYED THERE.
THIS MAN IS THE TOWN DOCTOR.
IF YOU WANT SOMETHING, TELL HIM. LIKE WATER OR FOOD...
... JUST AS I EXPECTED, HE DOESN'T REACT TO WORDS.

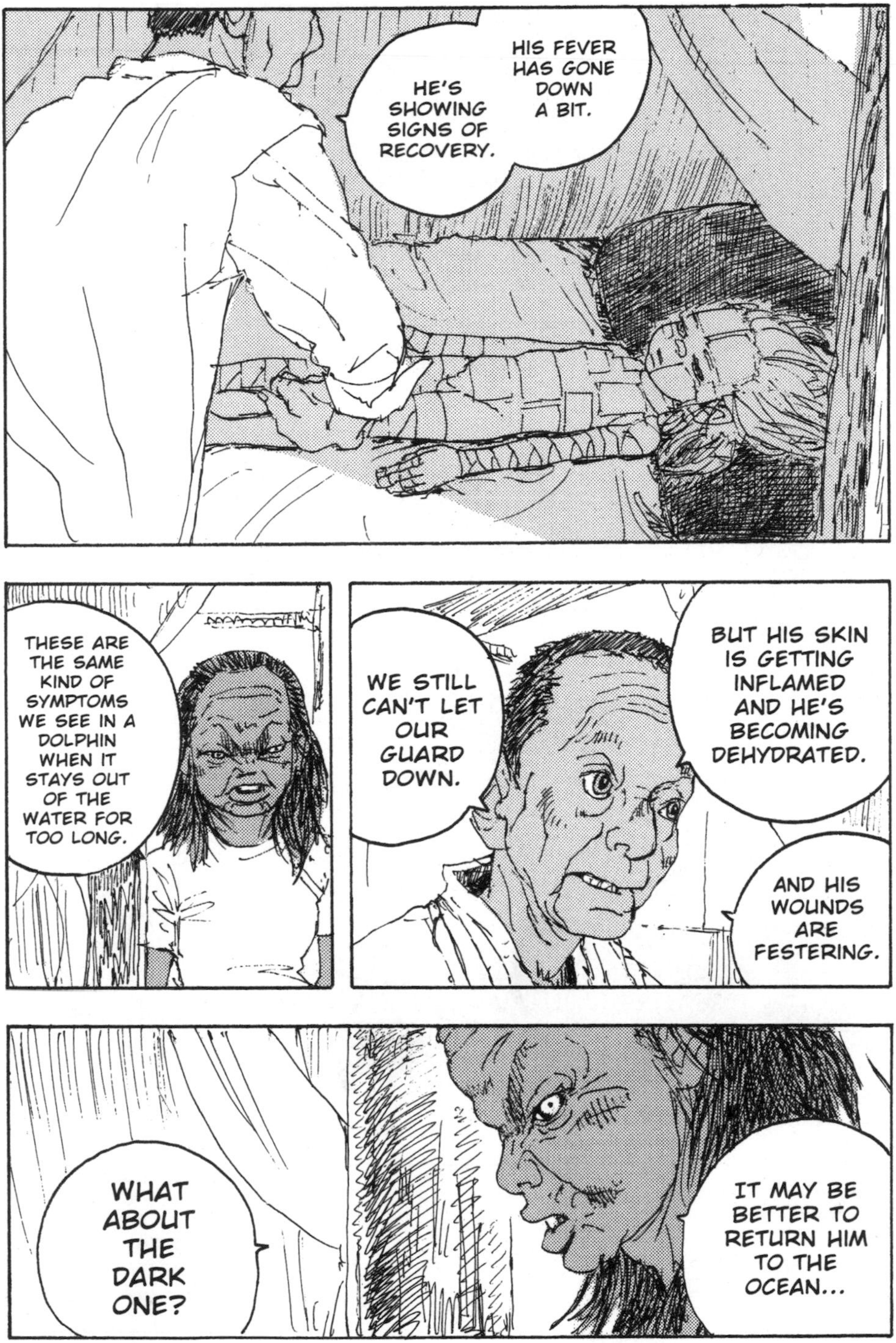
HIS FEVER HAS GONE DOWN A BIT.
HE'S SHOWING SIGNS OF RECOVERY.
BUT HIS SKIN IS GETTING INFLAMED AND HE'S BECOMING DEHYDRATED.
AND HIS WOUNDS ARE FESTERING.
WE STILL CAN'T LET OUR GUARD DOWN.
THESE ARE THE SAME KIND OF SYMPTOMS WE SEE IN A DOLPHIN WHEN IT STAYS OUT OF THE WATER FOR TOO LONG.
IT MAY BE BETTER TO RETURN HIM TO THE OCEAN...
WHAT ABOUT THE DARK ONE?

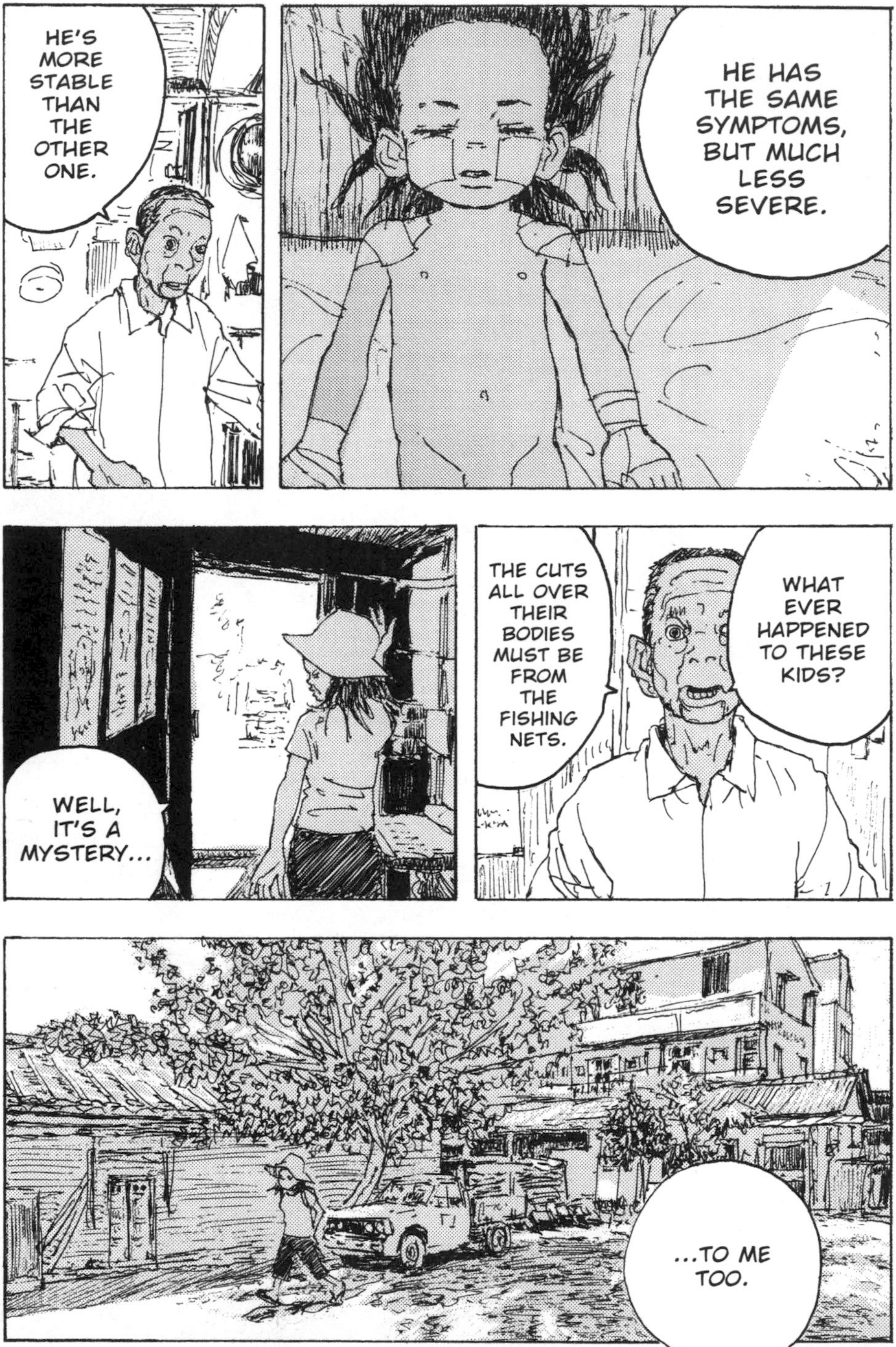
HE HAS THE SAME SYMPTOMS, BUT MUCH LESS SEVERE.
HE'S MORE STABLE THAN THE OTHER ONE.
WHAT EVER HAPPENED TO THESE KIDS?
THE CUTS ALL OVER THEIR BODIES MUST BE FROM THE FISHING NETS.
WELL, IT'S A MYSTERY...
...TO ME TOO.

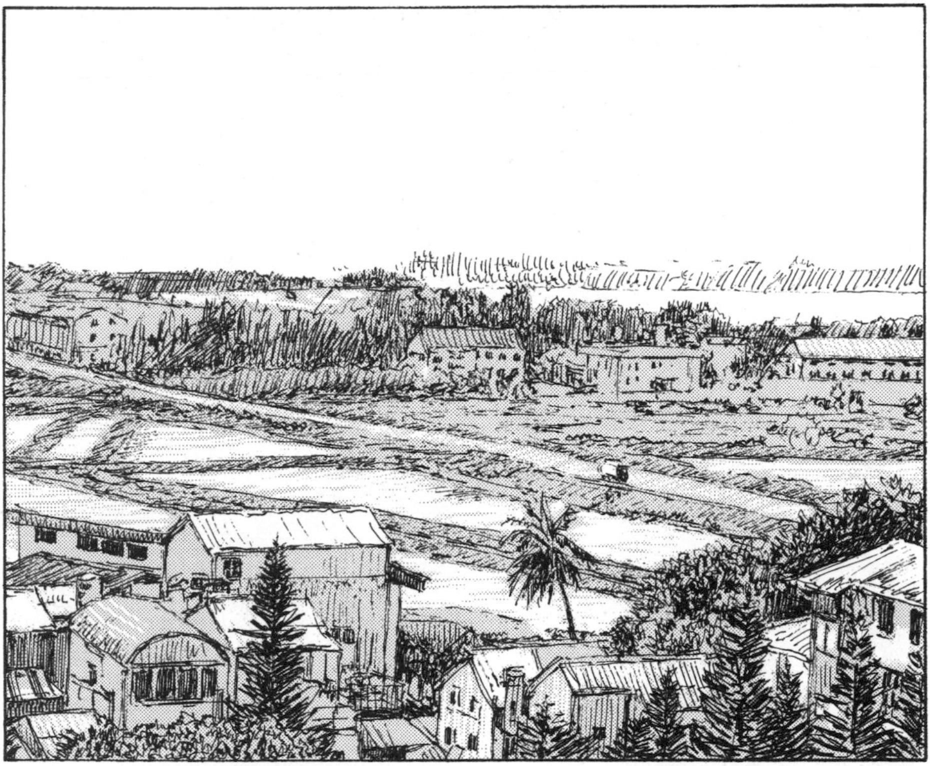

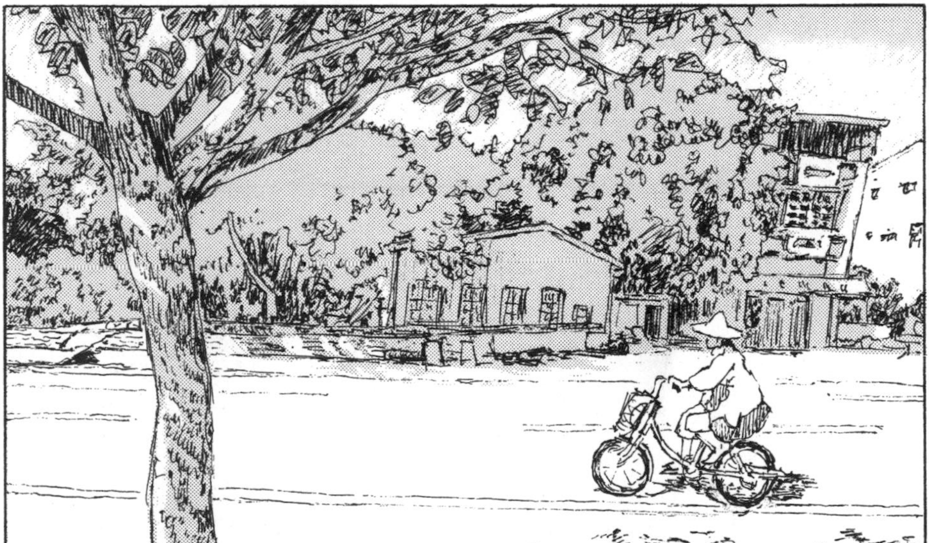

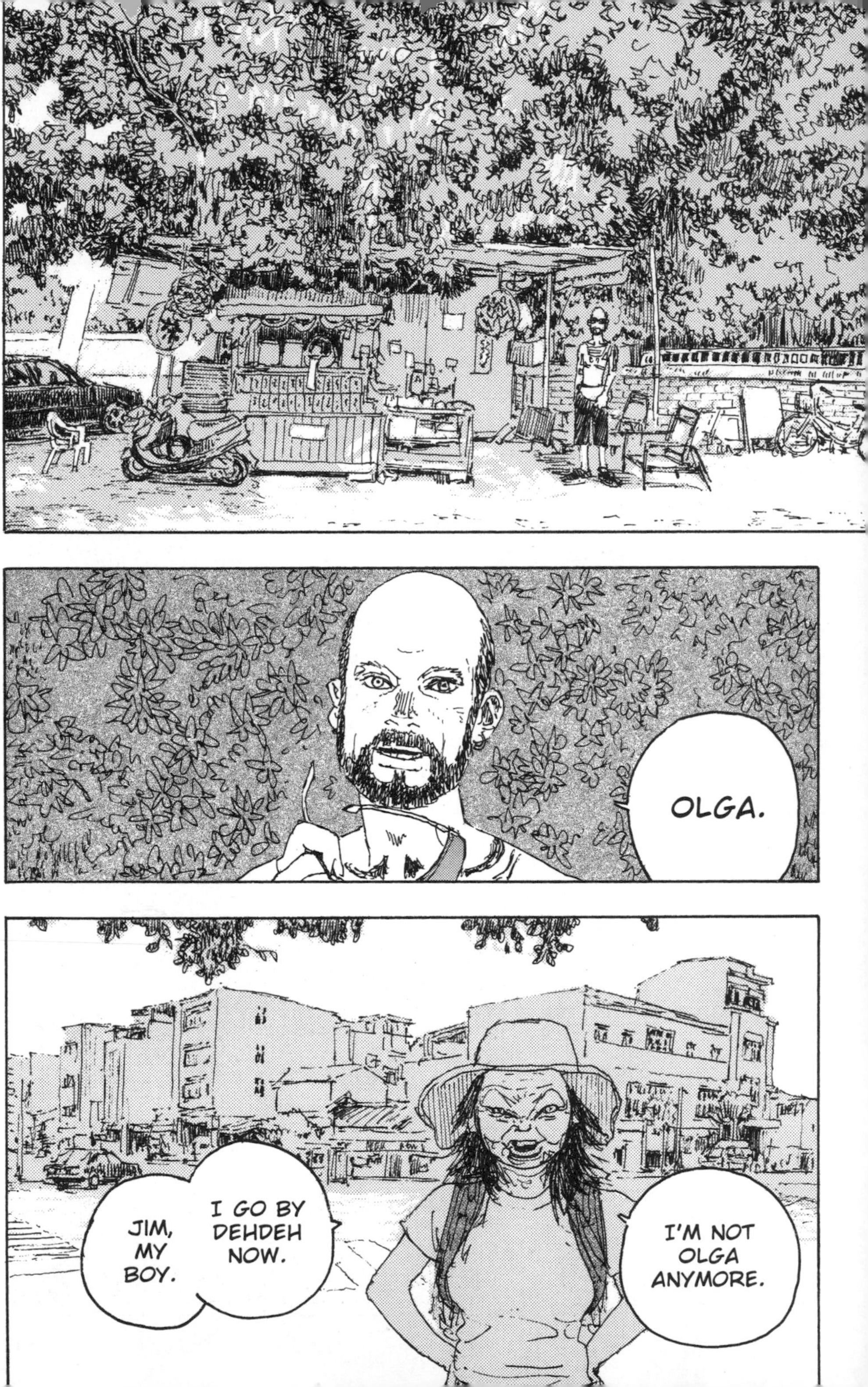
OLGA.
I'M NOT OLGA ANYMORE.
I GO BY DEHDEH NOW.
JIM, MY BOY.

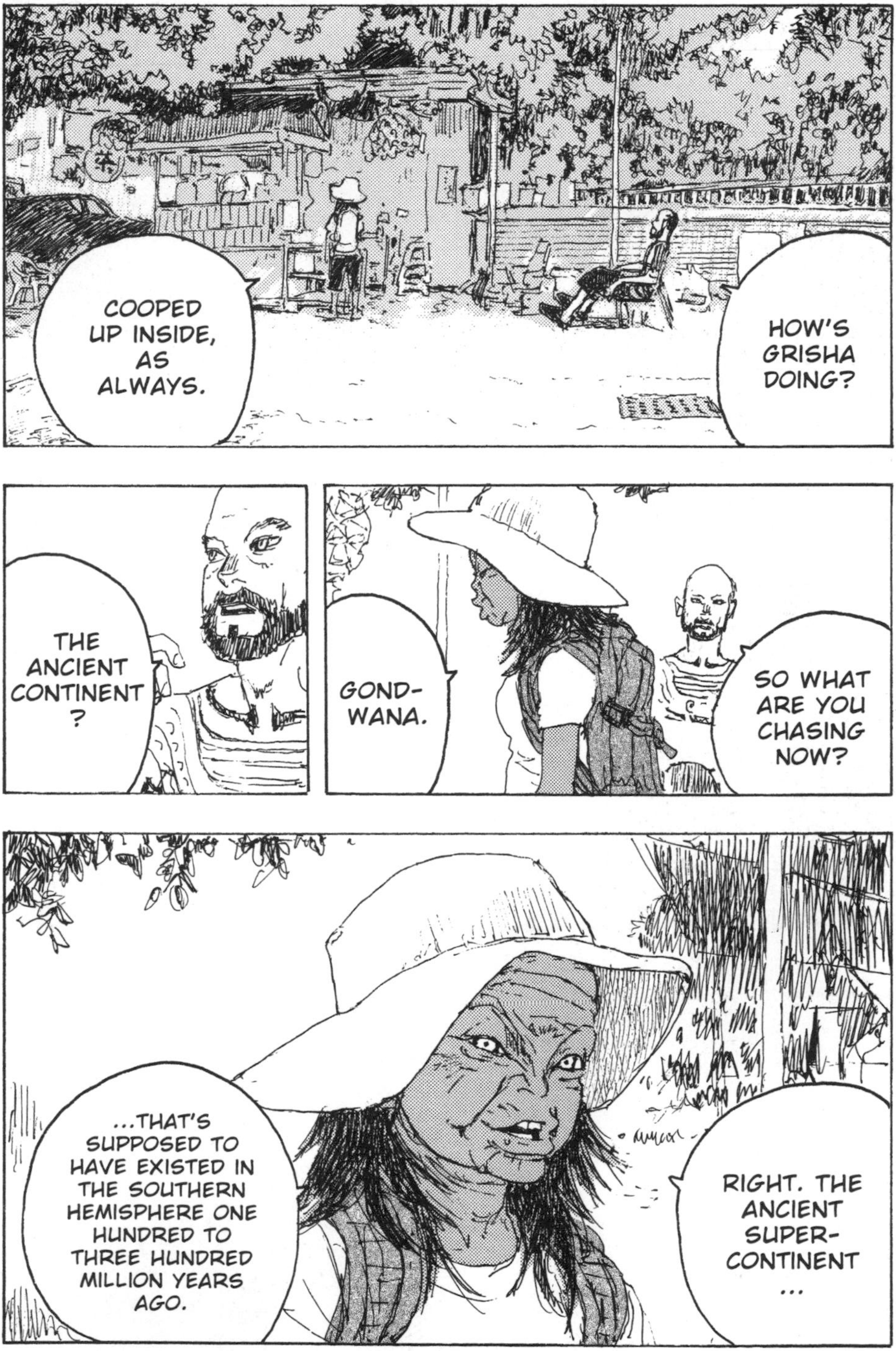

HOW'S GRISHA DOING?
COOPED UP INSIDE, AS ALWAYS.
SO WHAT ARE YOU CHASING NOW?
GOND-WANA.
THE ANCIENT CONTINENT ?
RIGHT. THE ANCIENT SUPER-CONTINENT ...
...THAT'S SUPPOSED TO HAVE EXISTED IN THE SOUTHERN HEMISPHERE ONE HUNDRED TO THREE HUNDRED MILLION YEARS AGO.

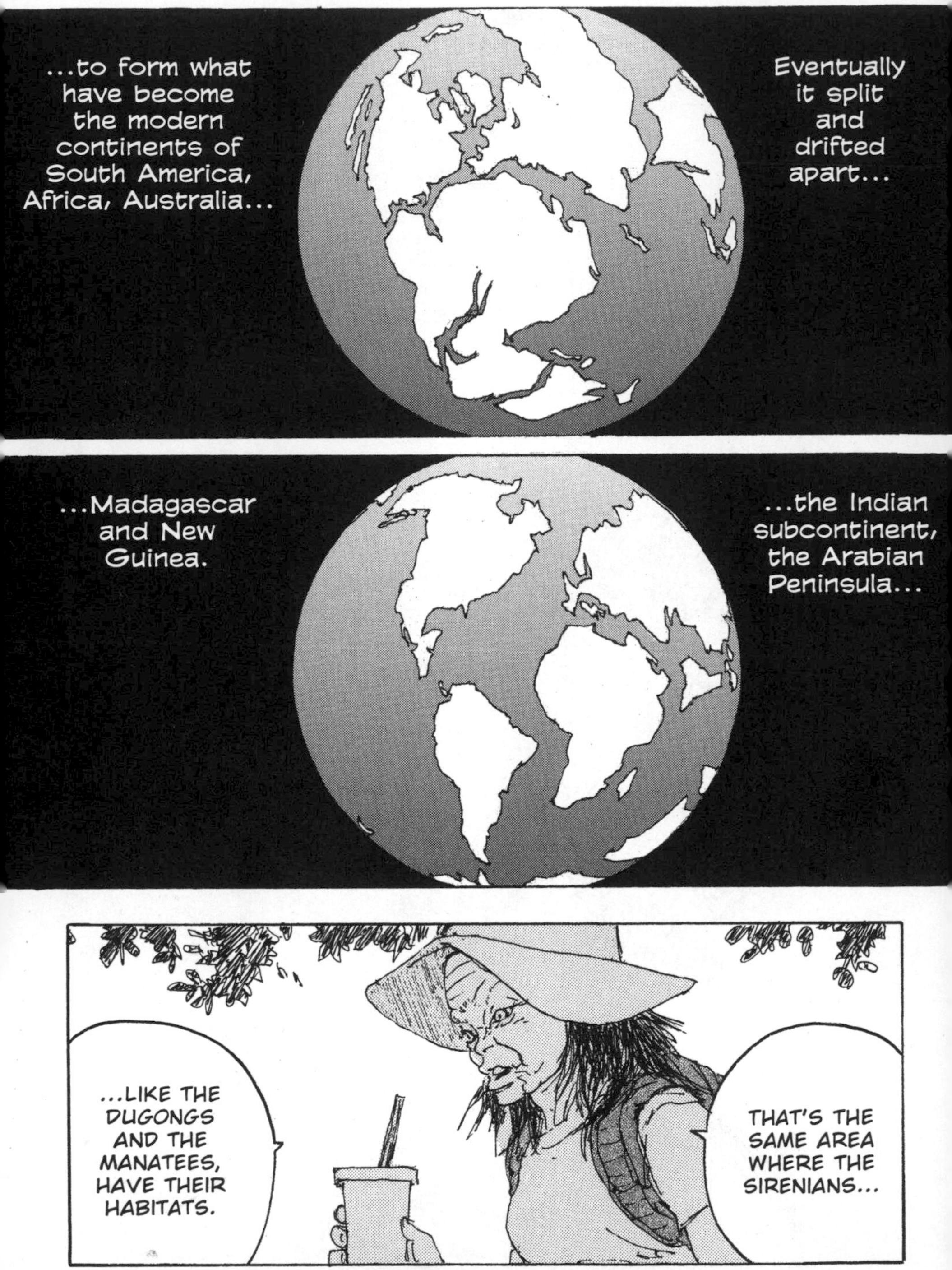
Eventually it split and drifted apart...
...to form what have become the modern continents of South America, Africa, Australia...
...the Indian subcontinent, the Arabian Peninsula...
...Madagascar and New Guinea.
THAT'S THE SAME AREA WHERE THE SIRENIANS...
...LIKE THE DUGONGS AND THE MANATEES, HAVE THEIR HABITATS.

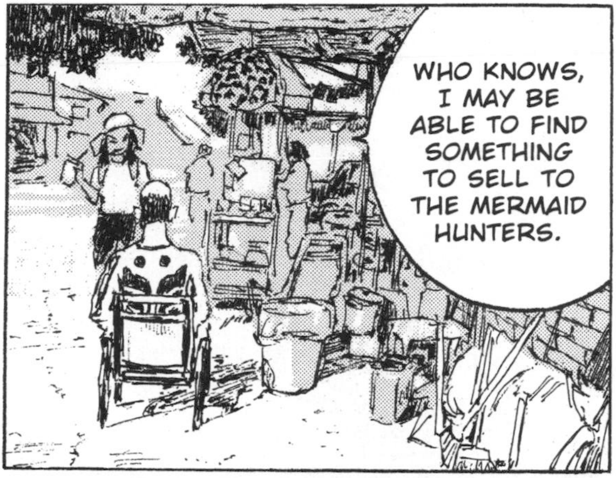
WHO KNOWS, I MAY BE ABLE TO FIND SOMETHING TO SELL TO THE MERMAID HUNTERS.
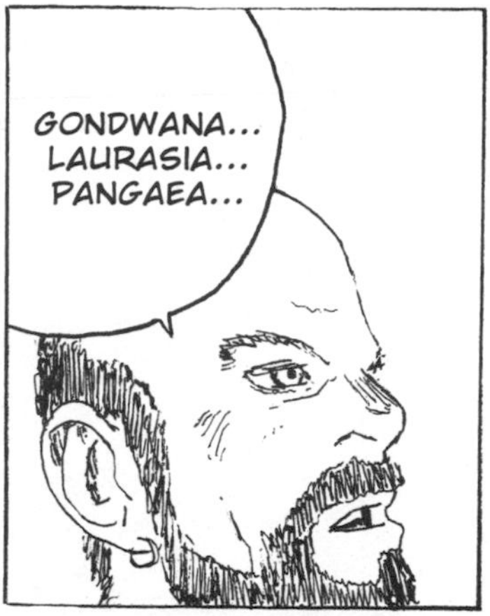
GONDWANA... LAURASIA... PANGAEA...
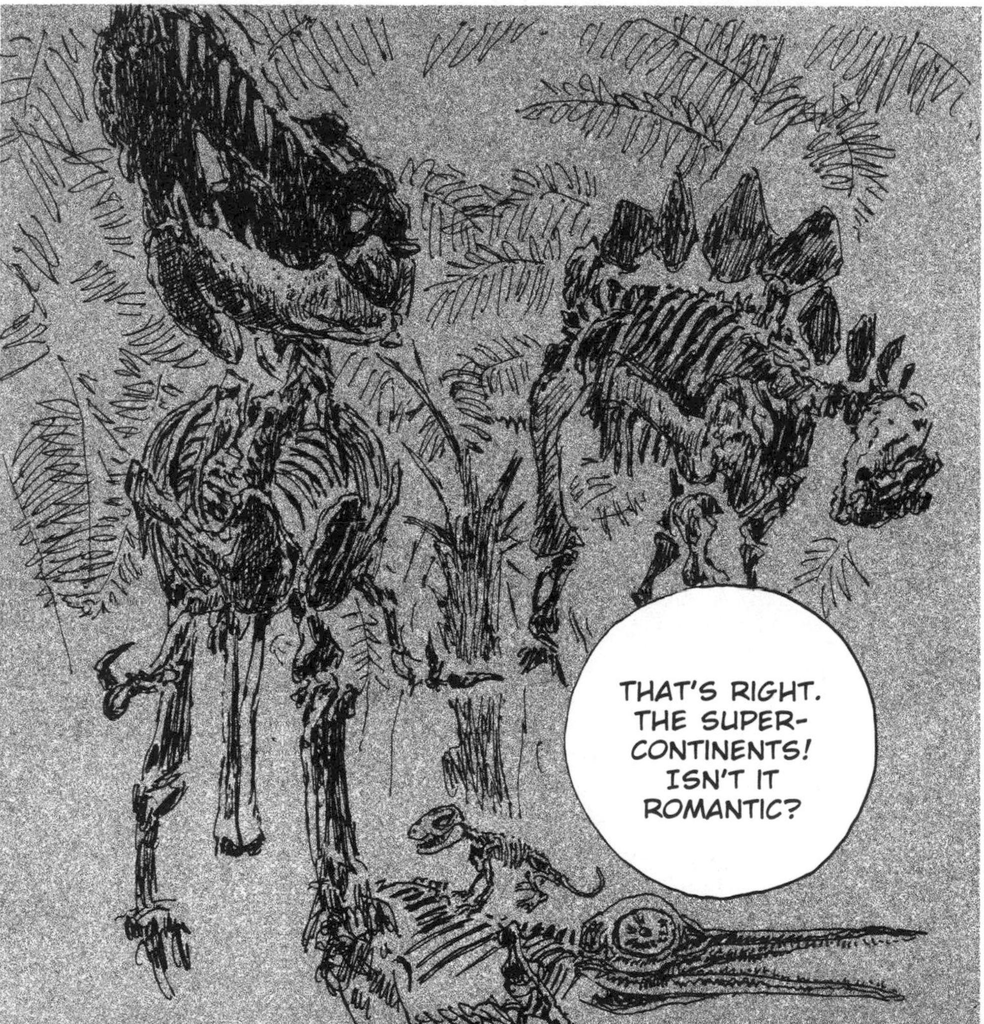
THAT'S RIGHT. THE SUPER-CONTINENTS! ISN'T IT ROMANTIC?

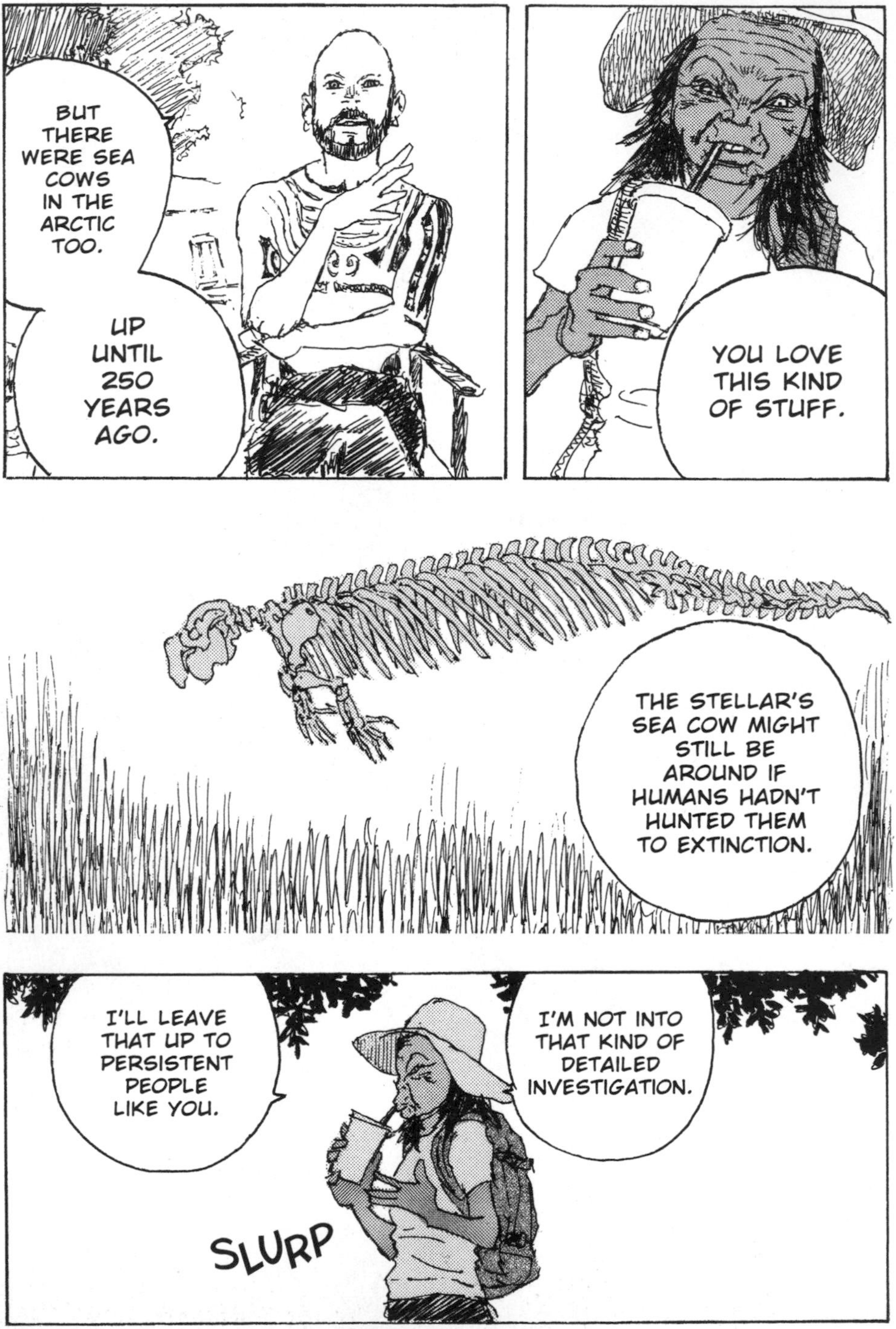
YOU LOVE THIS KIND OF STUFF.
BUT THERE WERE SEA COWS IN THE ARCTIC TOO.
UP UNTIL 250 YEARS AGO.
THE STELLAR'S SEA COW MIGHT STILL BE AROUND IF HUMANS HADN'T HUNTED THEM TO EXTINCTION.
I'M NOT INTO THAT KIND OF DETAILED INVESTIGATION.
I'LL LEAVE THAT UP TO PERSISTENT PEOPLE LIKE YOU.
SLURP

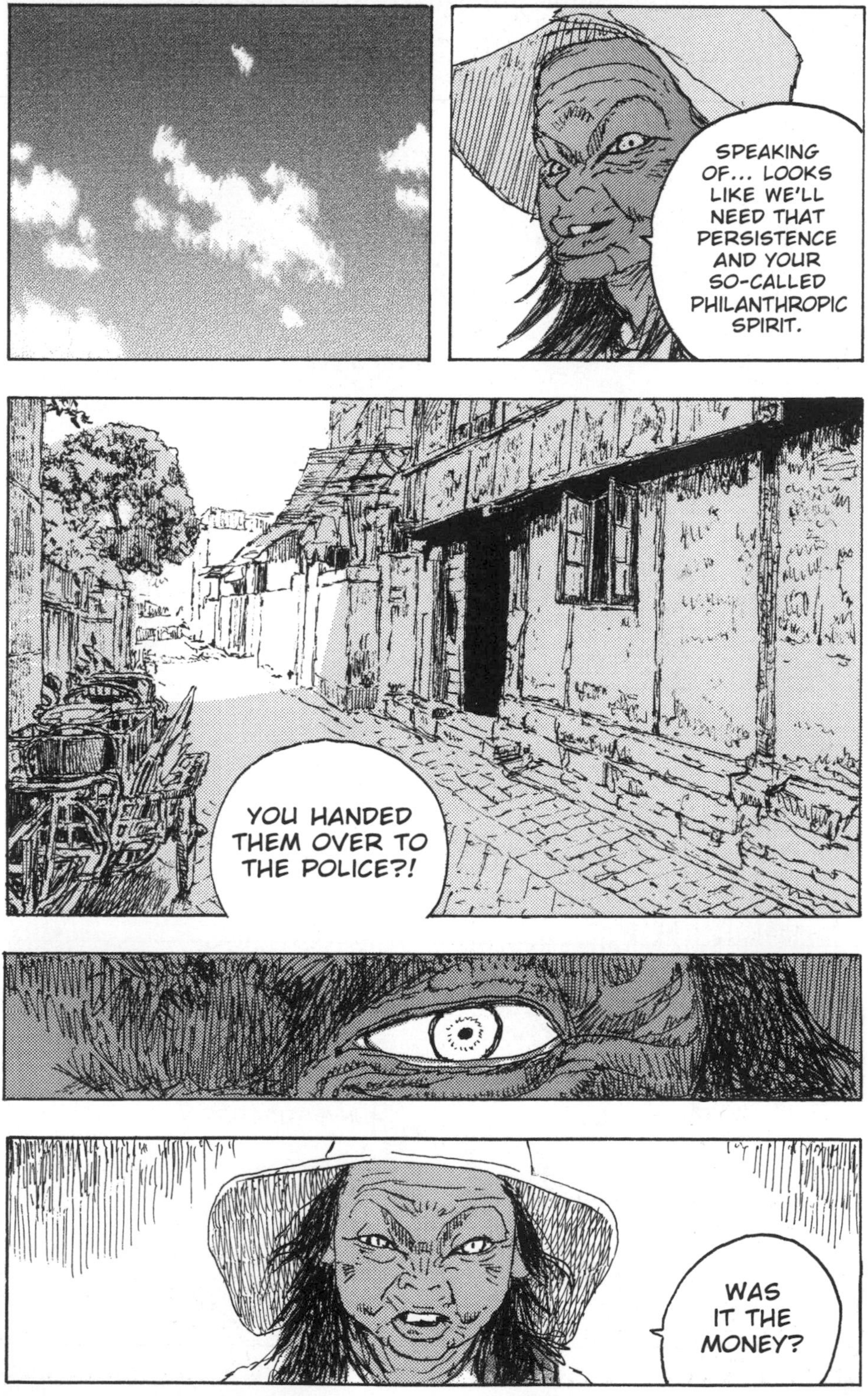
SPEAKING OF... LOOKS LIKE WE'LL NEED THAT PERSISTENCE AND YOUR SO-CALLED PHILANTHROPIC SPIRIT.
YOU HANDED THEM OVER TO THE POLICE?!
WAS IT THE MONEY?

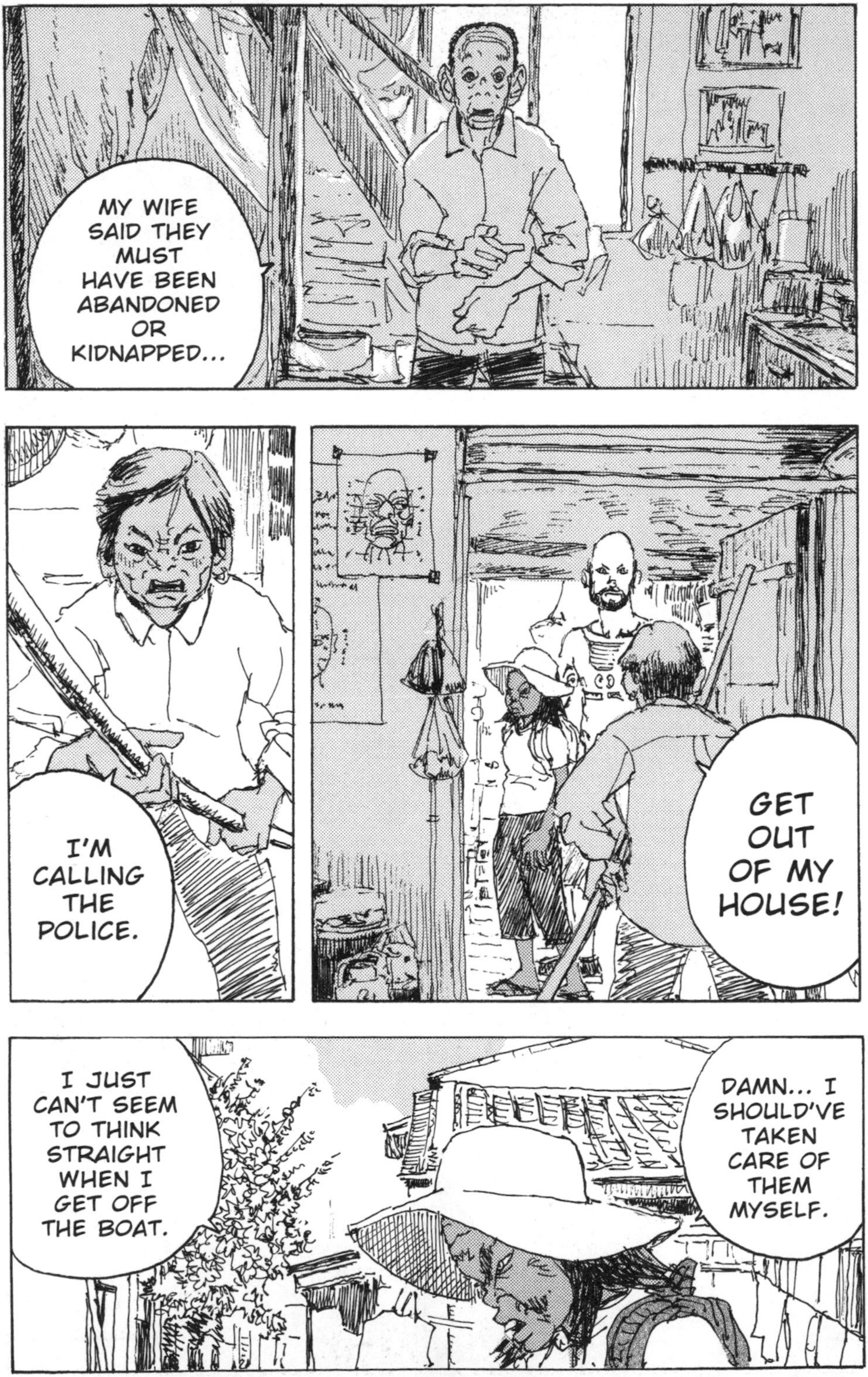
MY WIFE SAID THEY MUST HAVE BEEN ABANDONED OR KIDNAPPED...
GET OUT OF MY HOUSE!
I'M CALLING THE POLICE.
DAMN... I SHOULD'VE TAKEN CARE OF THEM MYSELF.
I JUST CAN'T SEEM TO THINK STRAIGHT WHEN I GET OFF THE BOAT.

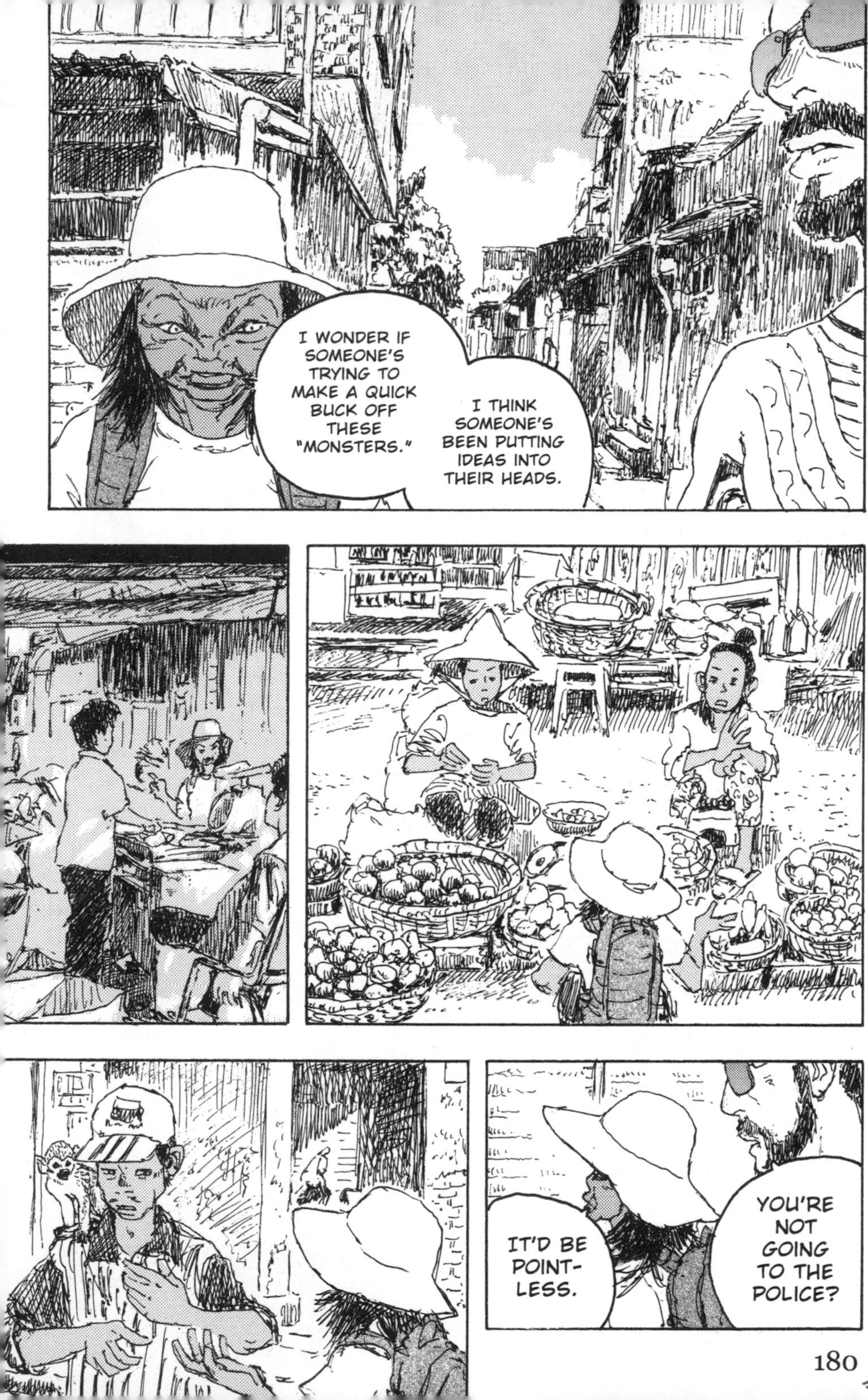
I THINK SOMEONE'S BEEN PUTTING IDEAS INTO THEIR HEADS.
I WONDER IF SOMEONE'S TRYING TO MAKE A QUICK BUCK OFF THESE "MONSTERS."
YOU'RE NOT GOING TO THE POLICE?
IT'D BE POINT-LESS.

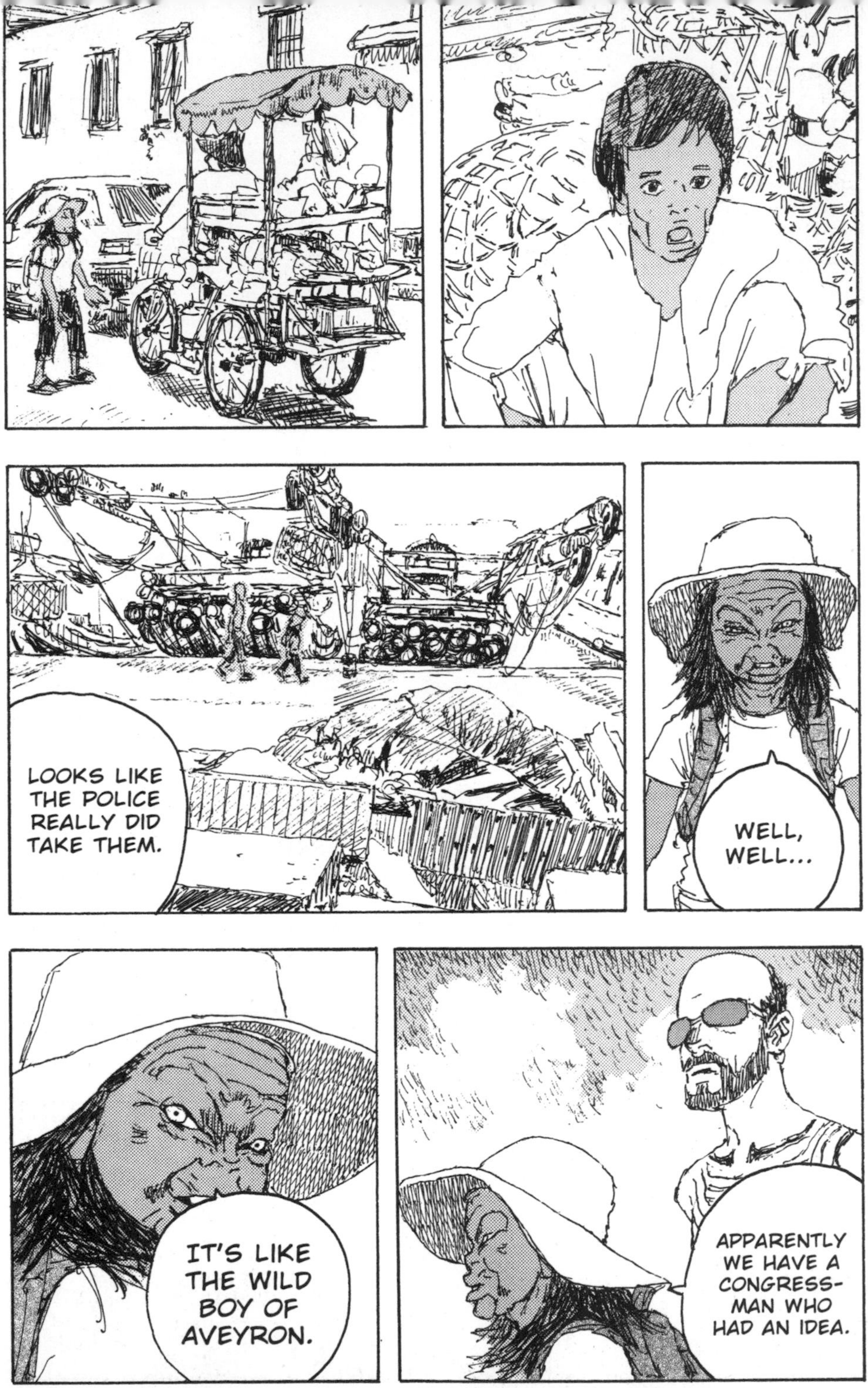
WELL, WELL...
LOOKS LIKE THE POLICE REALLY DID TAKE THEM.
APPARENTLY WE HAVE A CONGRESS-MAN WHO HAD AN IDEA.
IT'S LIKE THE WILD BOY OF AVEYRON.

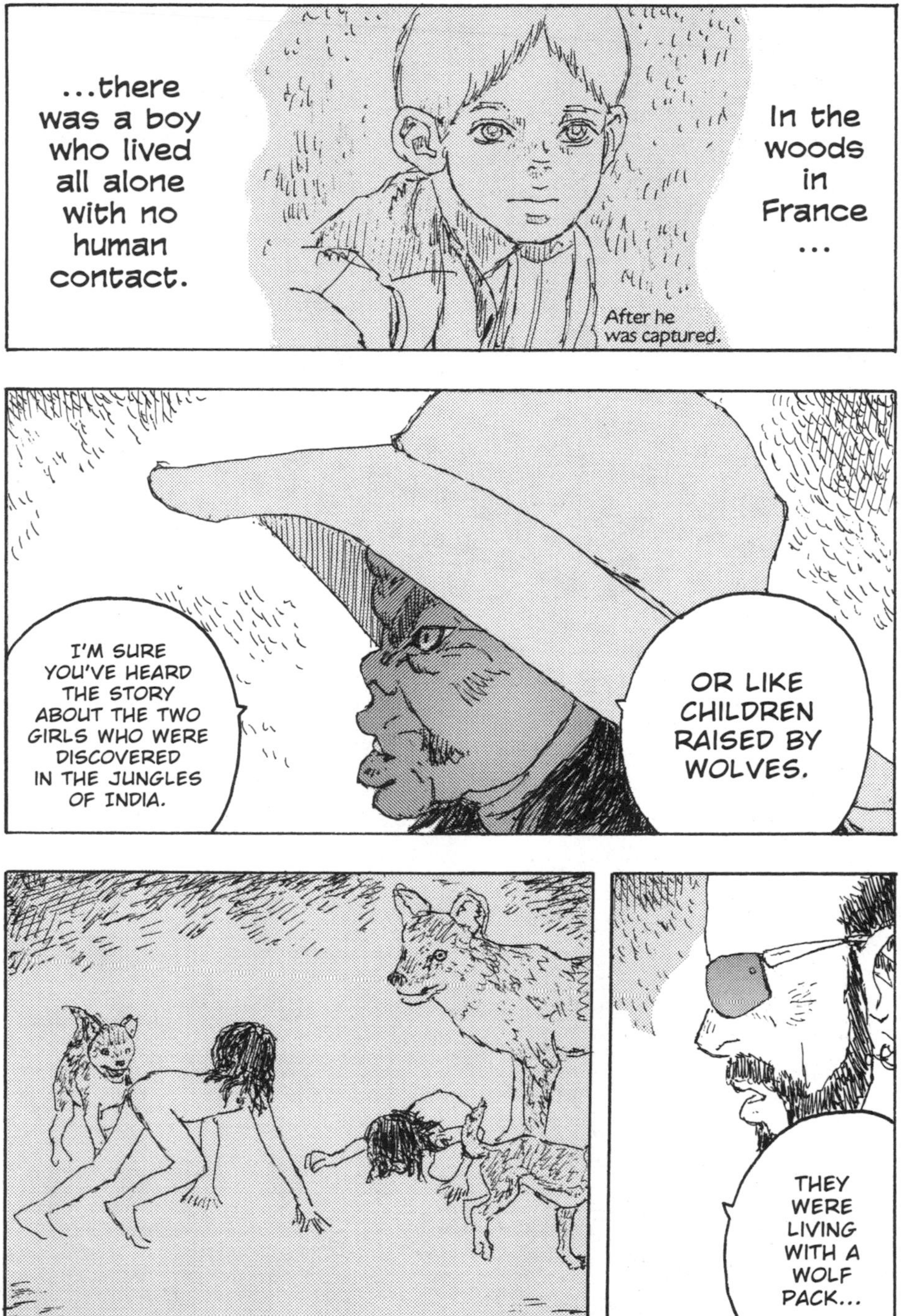
In the woods in France ...
...there was a boy who lived all alone with no human contact.
After he was captured.
OR LIKE CHILDREN RAISED BY WOLVES.
I'M SURE YOU'VE HEARD THE STORY ABOUT THE TWO GIRLS WHO WERE DISCOVERED IN THE JUNGLES OF INDIA.
THEY WERE LIVING WITH A WOLF PACK...

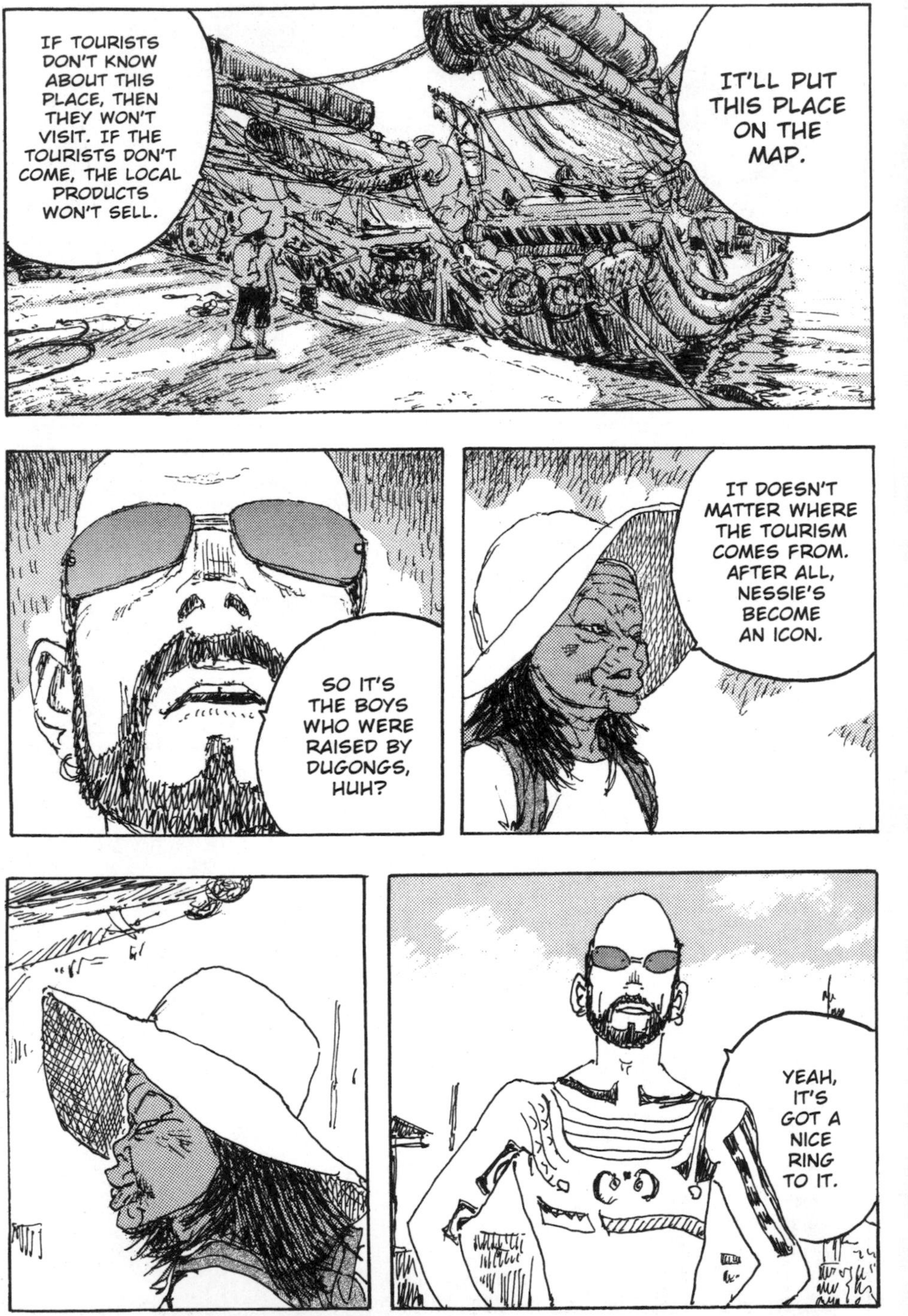
IT'LL PUT THIS PLACE ON THE MAP.
IF TOURISTS DON'T KNOW ABOUT THIS PLACE, THEN THEY WON'T VISIT. IF THE TOURISTS DON'T COME, THE LOCAL PRODUCTS WON'T SELL.
IT DOESN'T MATTER WHERE THE TOURISM COMES FROM. AFTER ALL, NESSIE'S BECOME AN ICON.
SO IT'S THE BOYS WHO WERE RAISED BY DUGONGS, HUH?
YEAH, IT'S GOT A NICE RING TO IT.

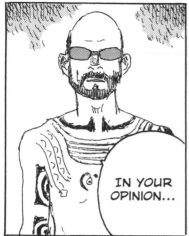

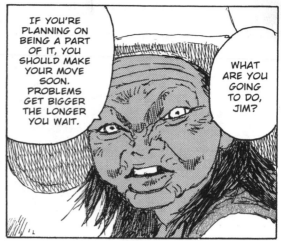

IF YOU'RE PLANNING ON BEING A PART OF IT, YOU SHOULD MAKE YOUR MOVE SOON. PROBLEMS GET BIGGER THE LONGER YOU WAIT.

WHAT ARE YOU GOING TO DO, JIM?

IN YOUR OPINION...

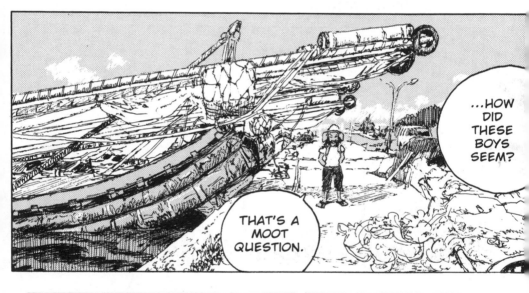

...HOW DID THESE BOYS SEEM?

THAT'S A MOOT QUESTION.

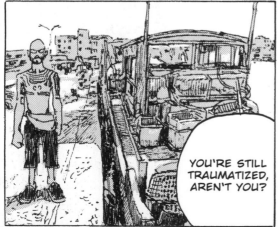

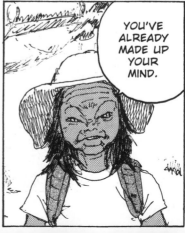

YOU'VE ALREADY MADE UP YOUR MIND.

YOU'RE STILL TRAUMATIZED, AREN'T YOU?

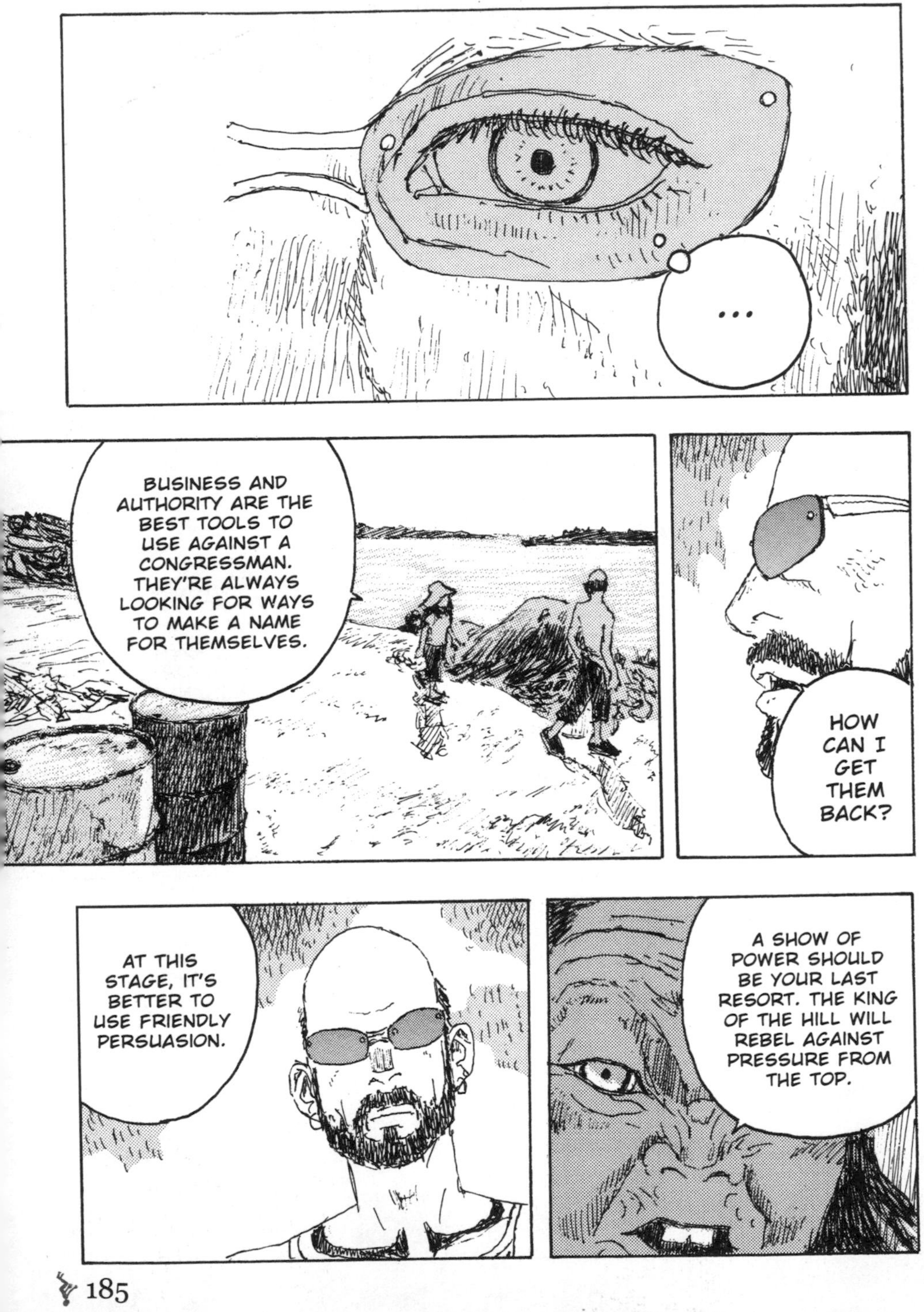
...
HOW CAN I GET THEM BACK?
BUSINESS AND AUTHORITY ARE THE BEST TOOLS TO USE AGAINST A CONGRESSMAN. THEY'RE ALWAYS LOOKING FOR WAYS TO MAKE A NAME FOR THEMSELVES.
A SHOW OF POWER SHOULD BE YOUR LAST RESORT. THE KING OF THE HILL WILL REBEL AGAINST PRESSURE FROM THE TOP.
AT THIS STAGE, IT'S BETTER TO USE FRIENDLY PERSUASION.

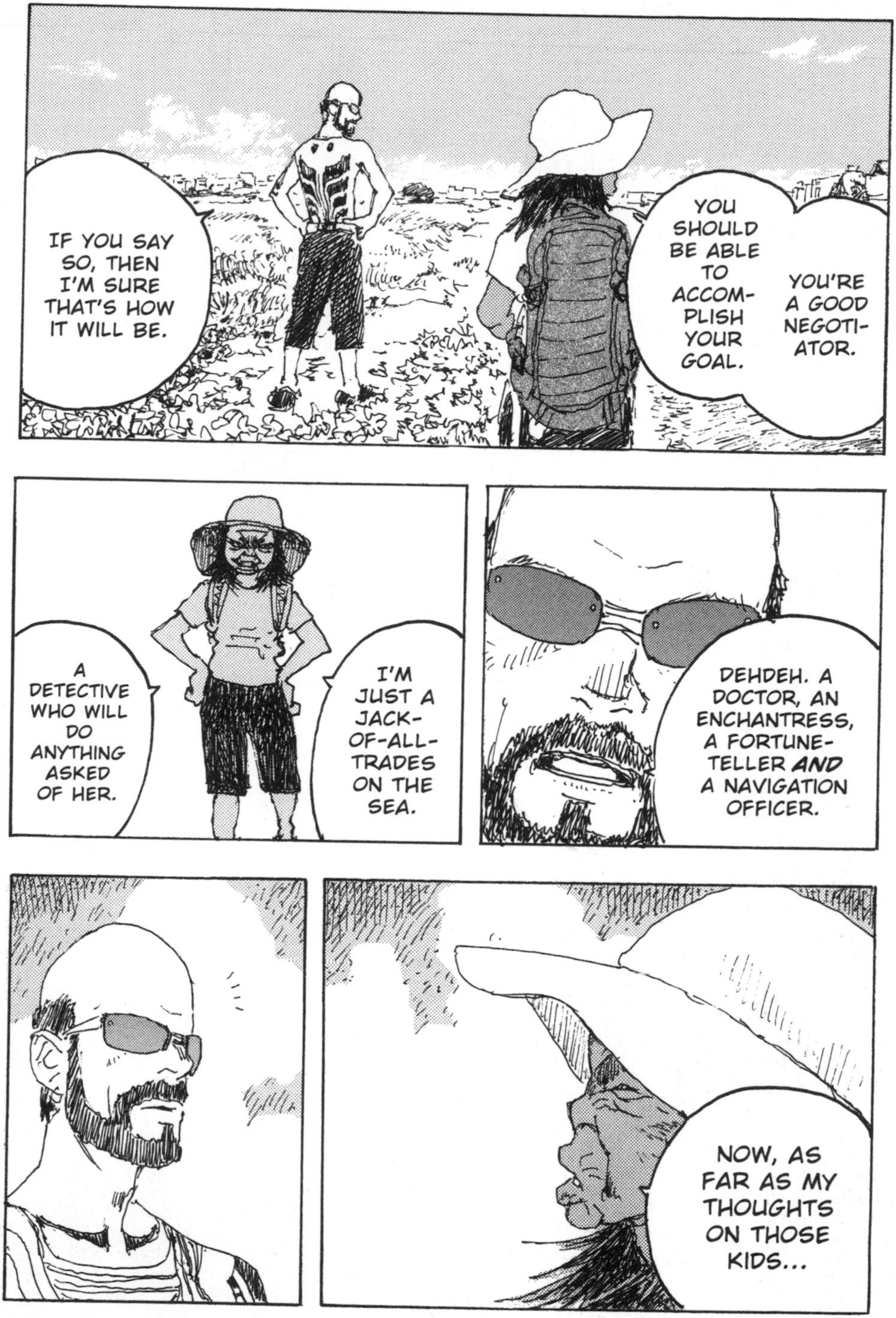
YOU'RE A GOOD NEGOTIATOR.
YOU SHOULD BE ABLE TO ACCOMPLISH YOUR GOAL.
IF YOU SAY SO, THEN I'M SURE THAT'S HOW IT WILL BE.
DEHDEH. A DOCTOR, AN ENCHANTRESS, A FORTUNE-TELLER *AND* A NAVIGATION OFFICER.
I'M JUST A JACK-OF-ALL-TRADES ON THE SEA.
A DETECTIVE WHO WILL DO ANYTHING ASKED OF HER.
NOW, AS FAR AS MY THOUGHTS ON THOSE KIDS...

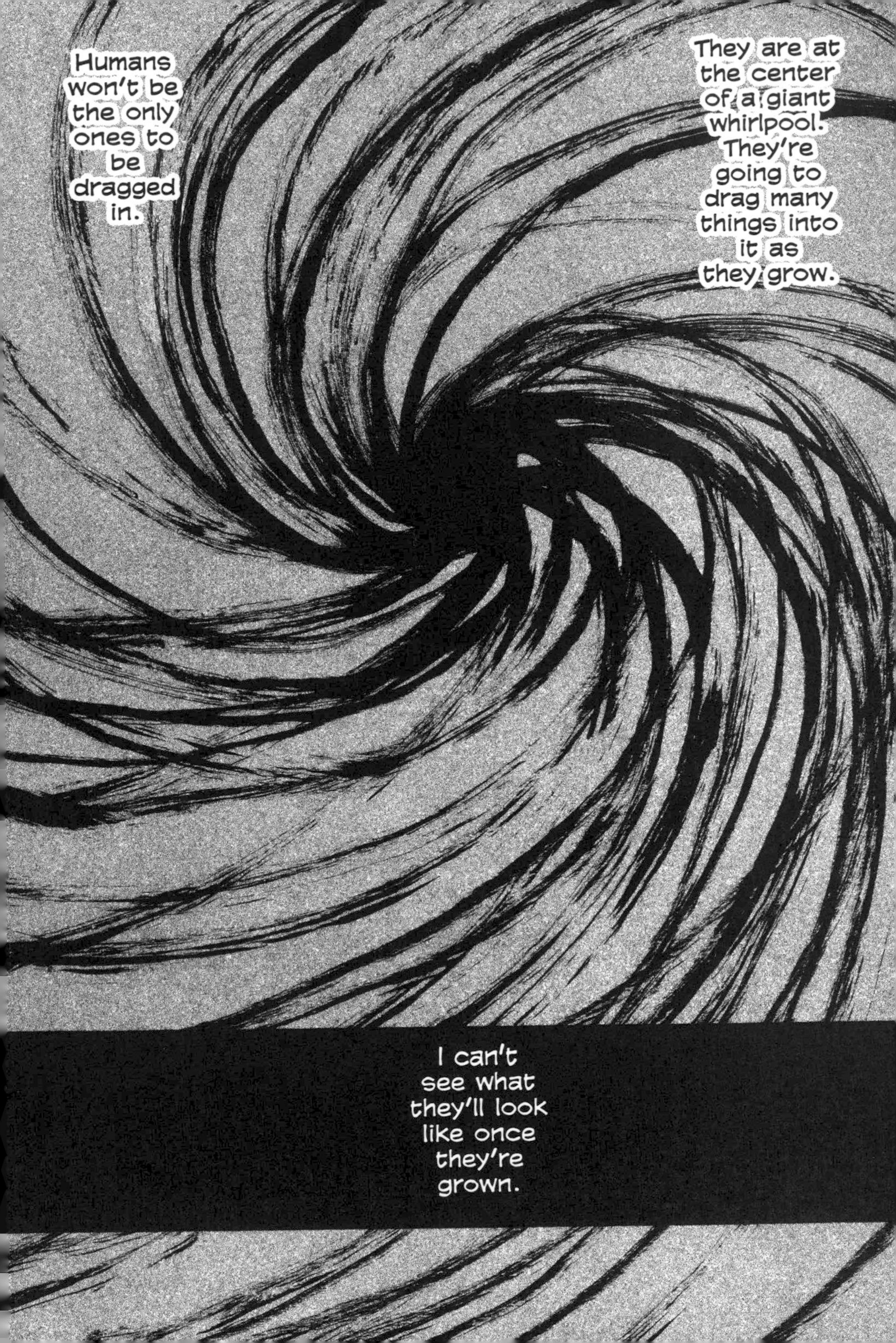
They are at the center of a giant whirlpool. They're going to drag many things into it as they grow.
Humans won't be the only ones to be dragged in.
I can't see what they'll look like once they're grown.

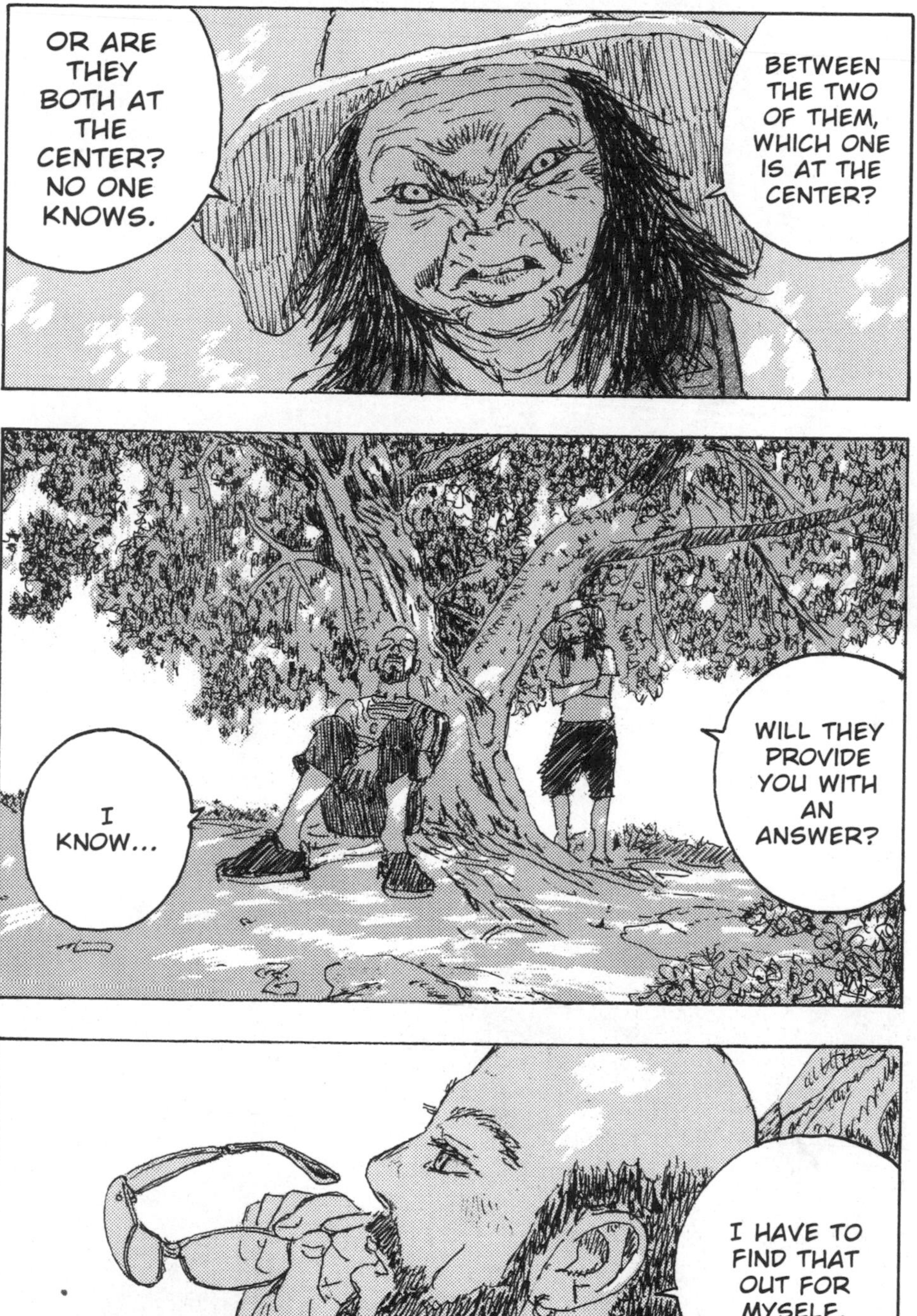
BETWEEN THE TWO OF THEM, WHICH ONE IS AT THE CENTER?
OR ARE THEY BOTH AT THE CENTER? NO ONE KNOWS.
WILL THEY PROVIDE YOU WITH AN ANSWER?
I KNOW...
I HAVE TO FIND THAT OUT FOR MYSELF.

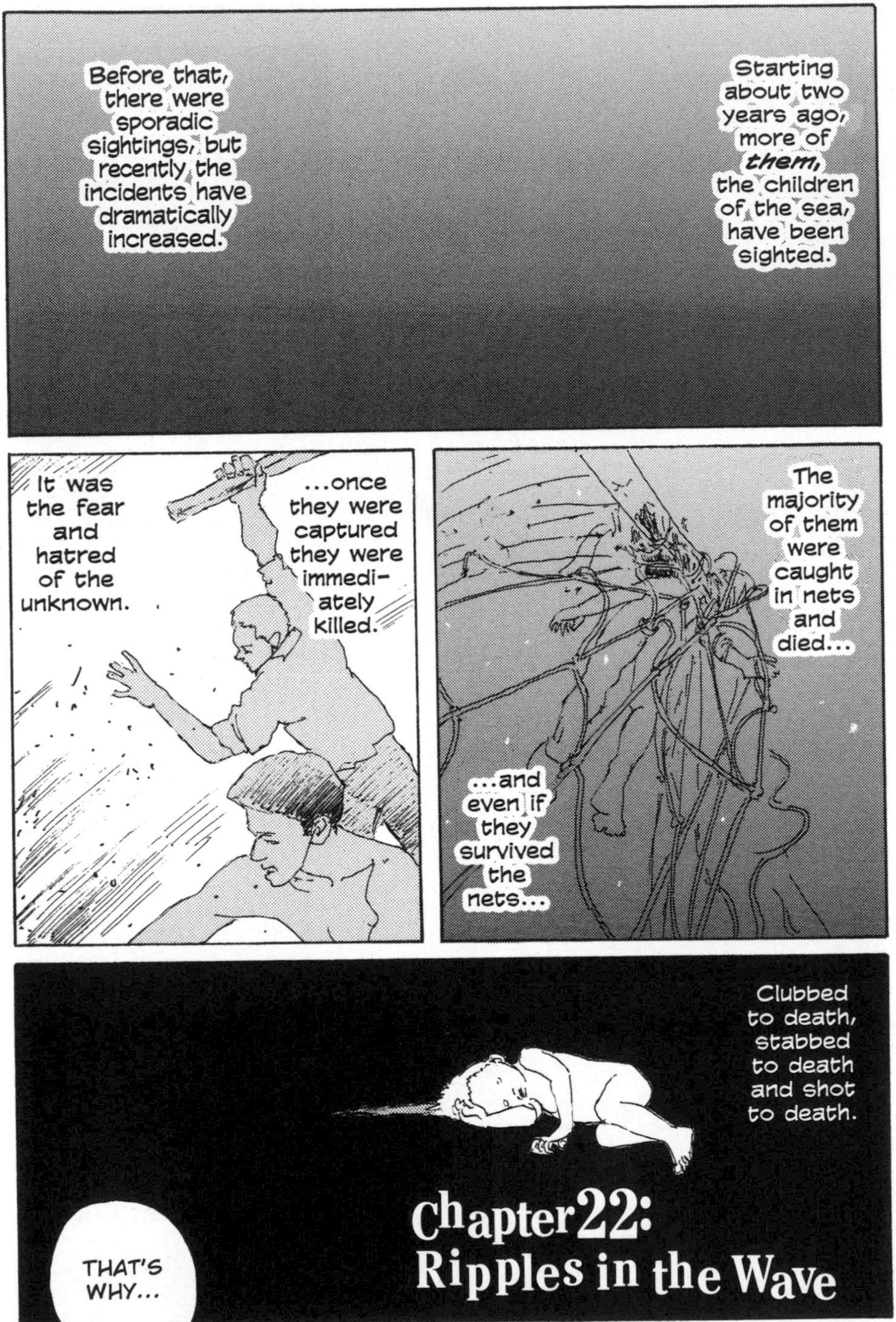
Starting about two years ago, more of ***them,*** the children of the sea, have been sighted.
Before that, there were sporadic sightings, but recently the incidents have dramatically increased.
The majority of them were caught in nets and died...
...and even if they survived the nets...
...once they were captured they were immediately killed.
It was the fear and hatred of the unknown.
Clubbed to death, stabbed to death and shot to death.
Chapter 22: Ripples in the Wave
THAT'S WHY...

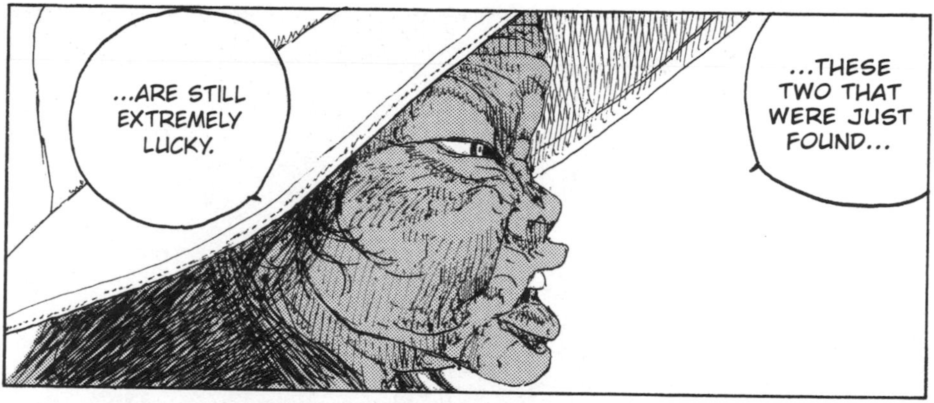
...THESE TWO THAT WERE JUST FOUND...
...ARE STILL EXTREMELY LUCKY.

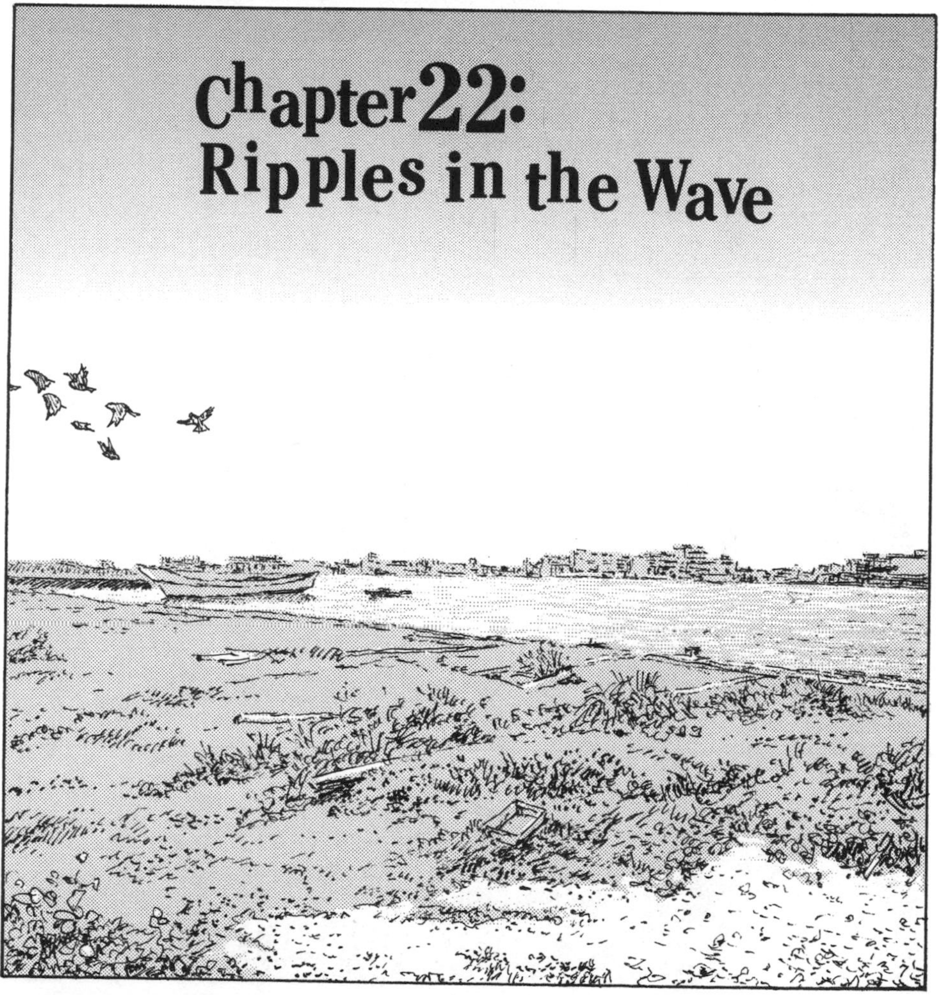
Chapter 22: Ripples in the Wave

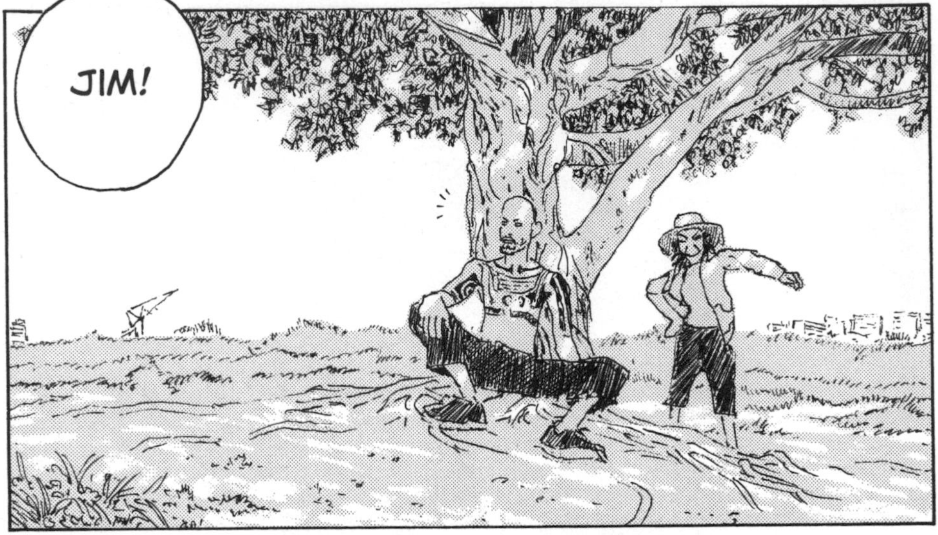
JIM!

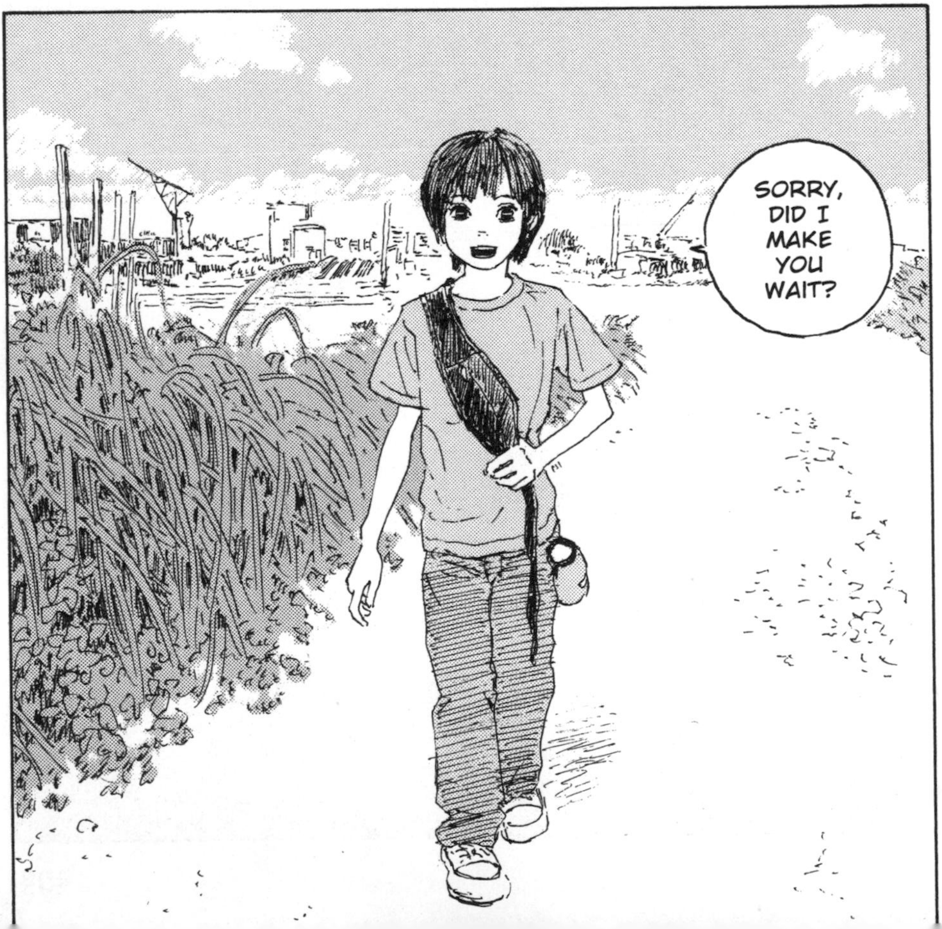
SORRY, DID I MAKE YOU WAIT?

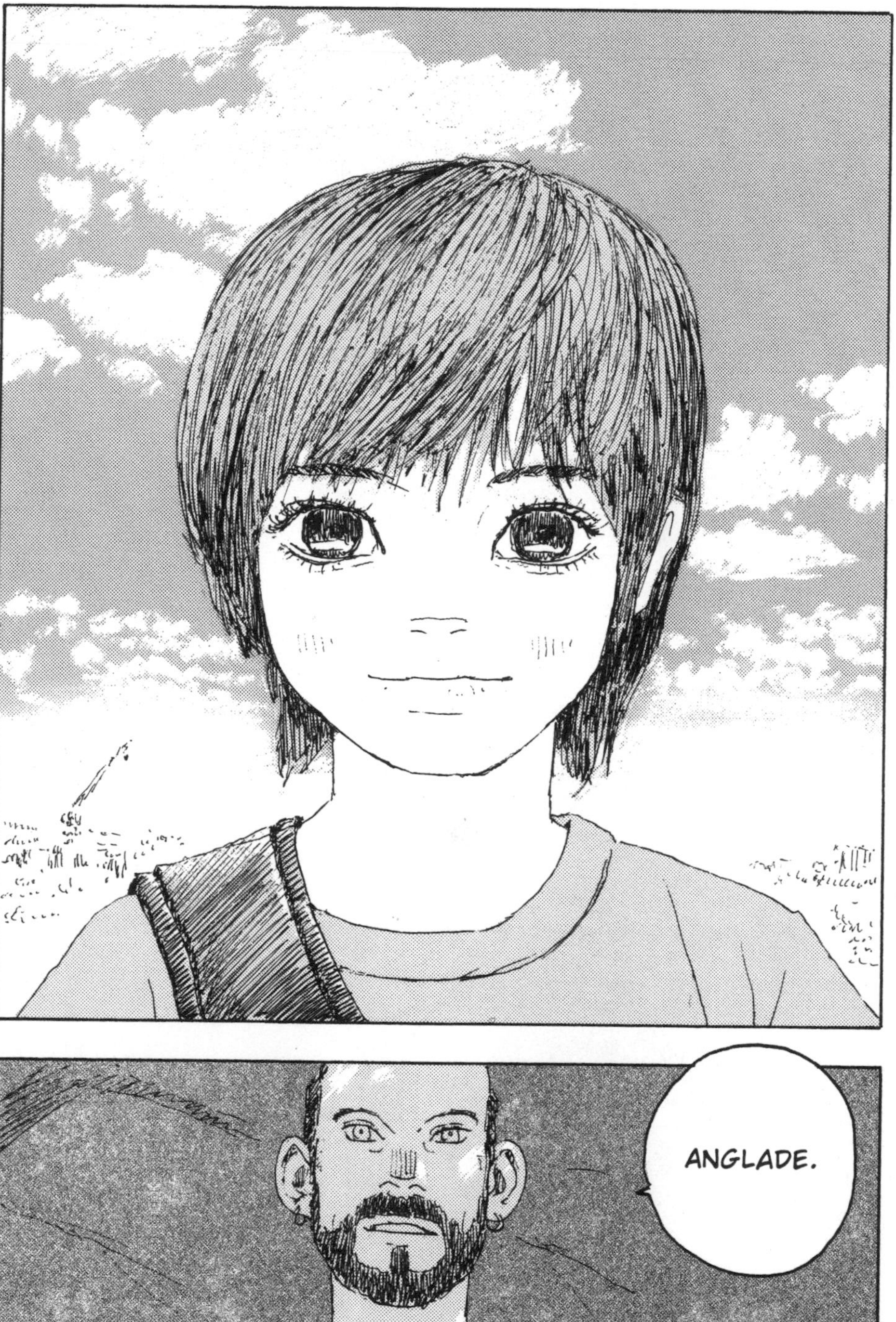
ANGLADE.

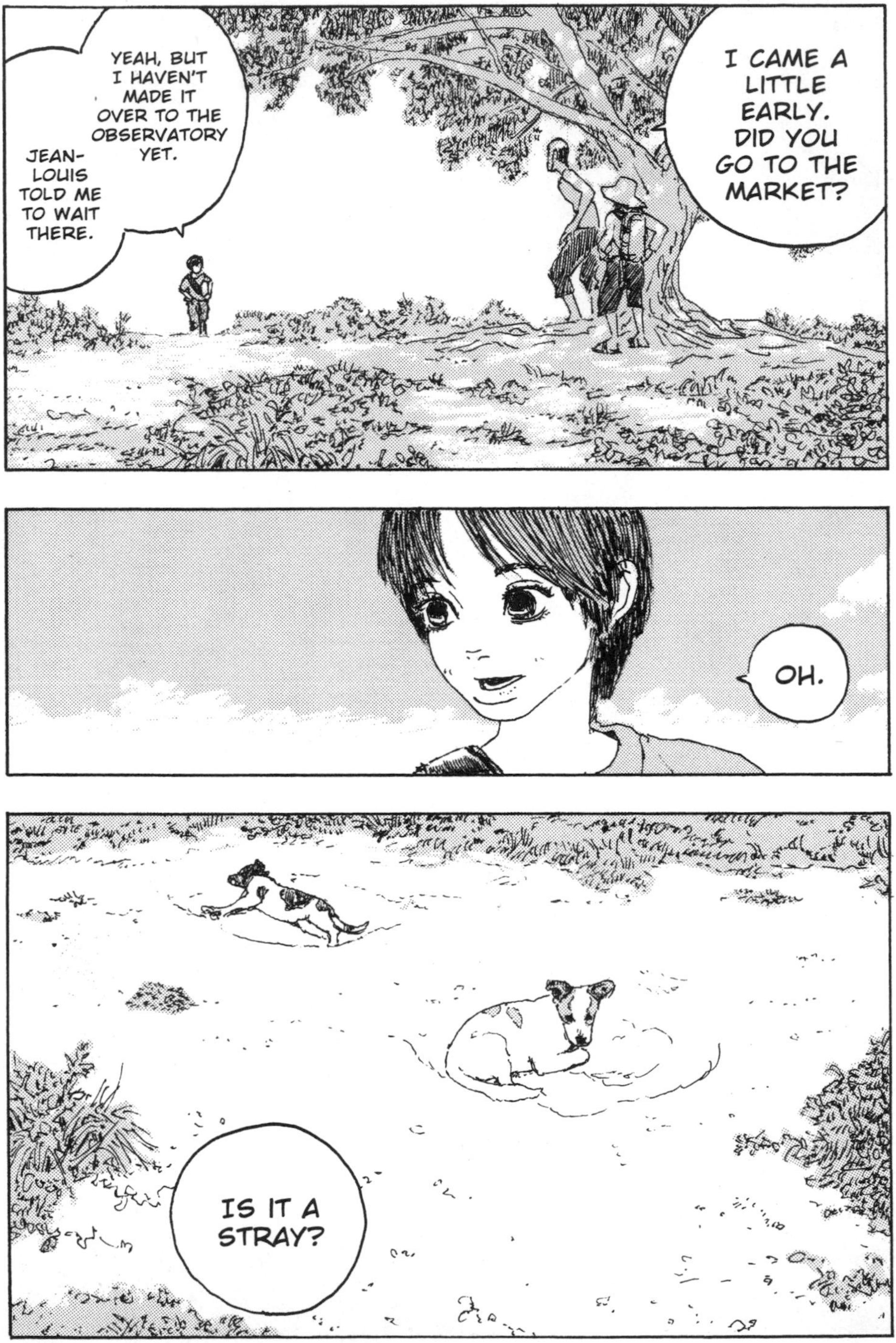
I CAME A LITTLE EARLY. DID YOU GO TO THE MARKET?
YEAH, BUT I HAVEN'T MADE IT OVER TO THE OBSERVATORY YET.
JEAN-LOUIS TOLD ME TO WAIT THERE.
OH.
IS IT A STRAY?

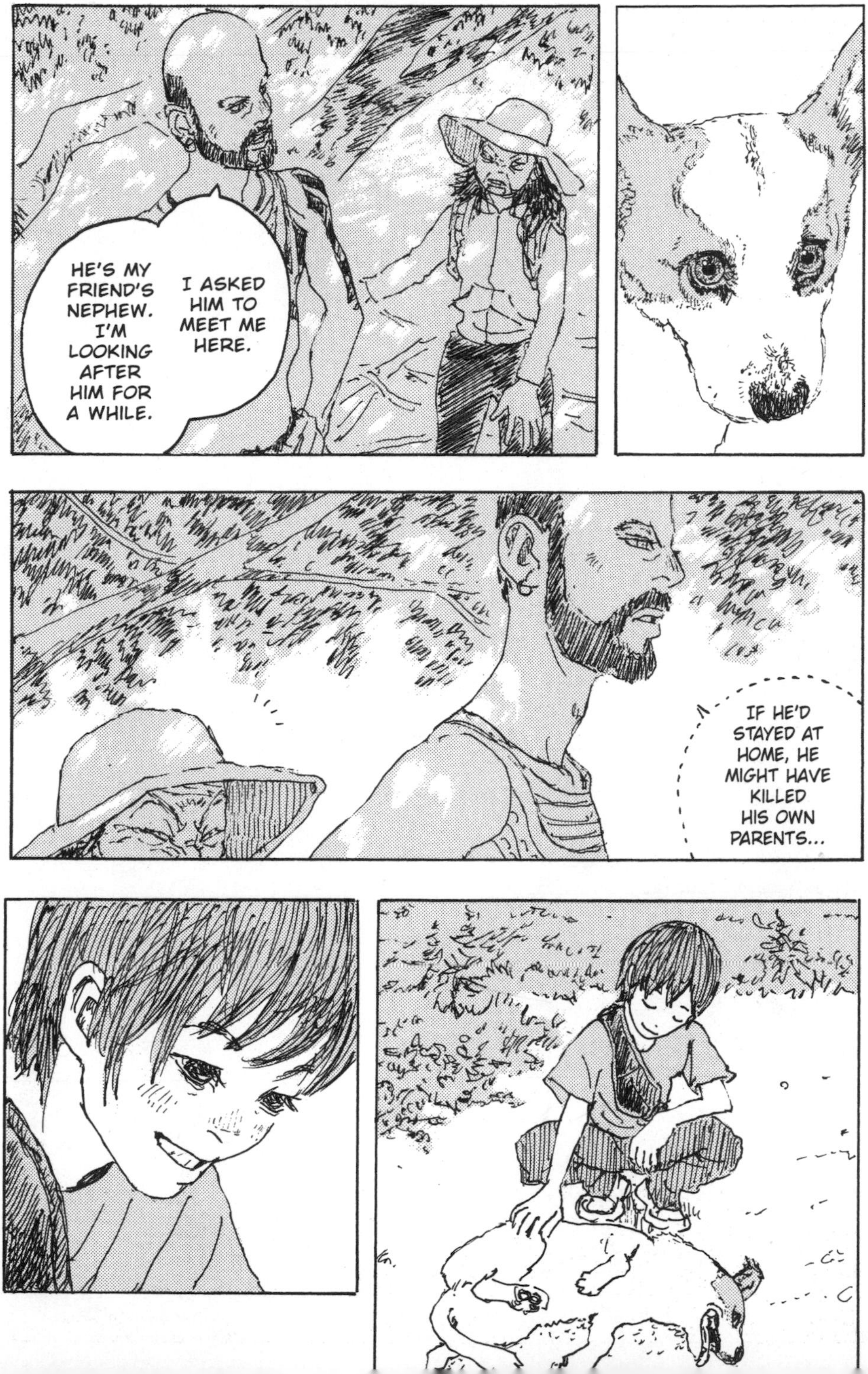
HE'S MY FRIEND'S NEPHEW. I'M LOOKING AFTER HIM FOR A WHILE.
I ASKED HIM TO MEET ME HERE.
IF HE'D STAYED AT HOME, HE MIGHT HAVE KILLED HIS OWN PARENTS...

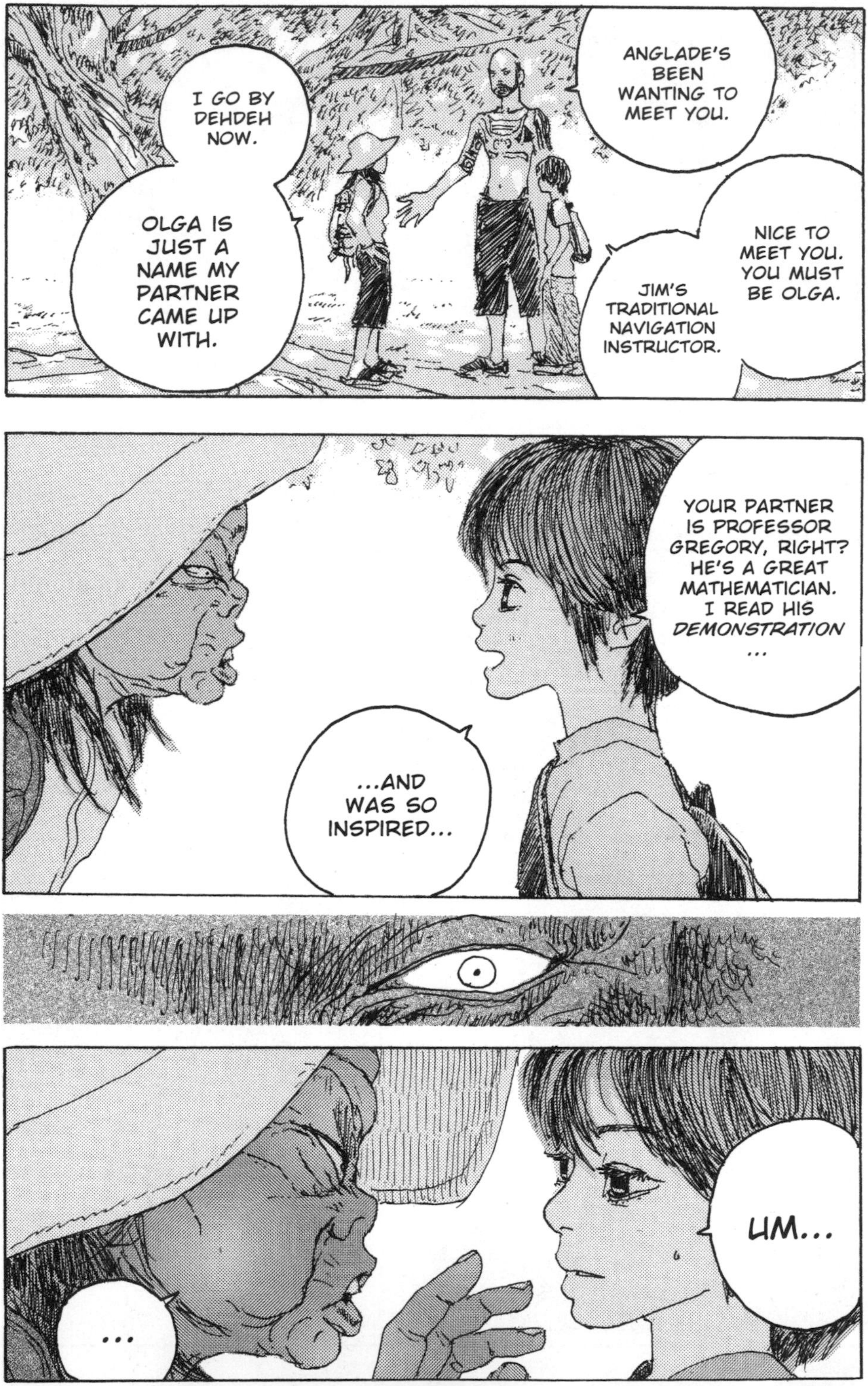
ANGLADE'S BEEN WANTING TO MEET YOU.
NICE TO MEET YOU. YOU MUST BE OLGA.
JIM'S TRADITIONAL NAVIGATION INSTRUCTOR.
I GO BY DEHDEH NOW.
OLGA IS JUST A NAME MY PARTNER CAME UP WITH.
YOUR PARTNER IS PROFESSOR GREGORY, RIGHT? HE'S A GREAT MATHEMATICIAN. I READ HIS *DEMONSTRATION* ...
...AND WAS SO INSPIRED...
UM...
...

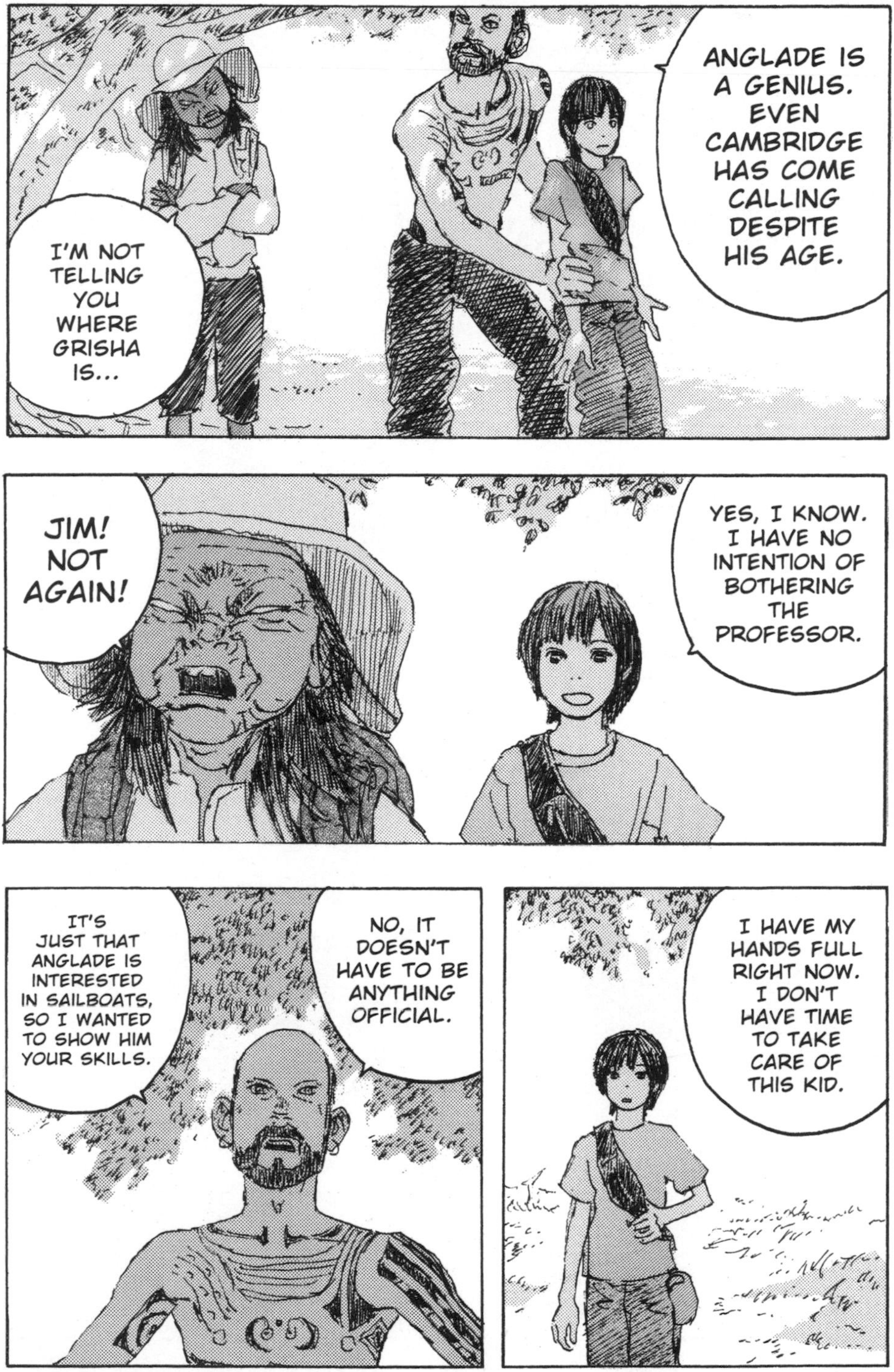
ANGLADE IS A GENIUS. EVEN CAMBRIDGE HAS COME CALLING DESPITE HIS AGE.
I'M NOT TELLING YOU WHERE GRISHA IS...
YES, I KNOW. I HAVE NO INTENTION OF BOTHERING THE PROFESSOR.
JIM! NOT AGAIN!
I HAVE MY HANDS FULL RIGHT NOW. I DON'T HAVE TIME TO TAKE CARE OF THIS KID.
NO, IT DOESN'T HAVE TO BE ANYTHING OFFICIAL.
IT'S JUST THAT ANGLADE IS INTERESTED IN SAILBOATS, SO I WANTED TO SHOW HIM YOUR SKILLS.

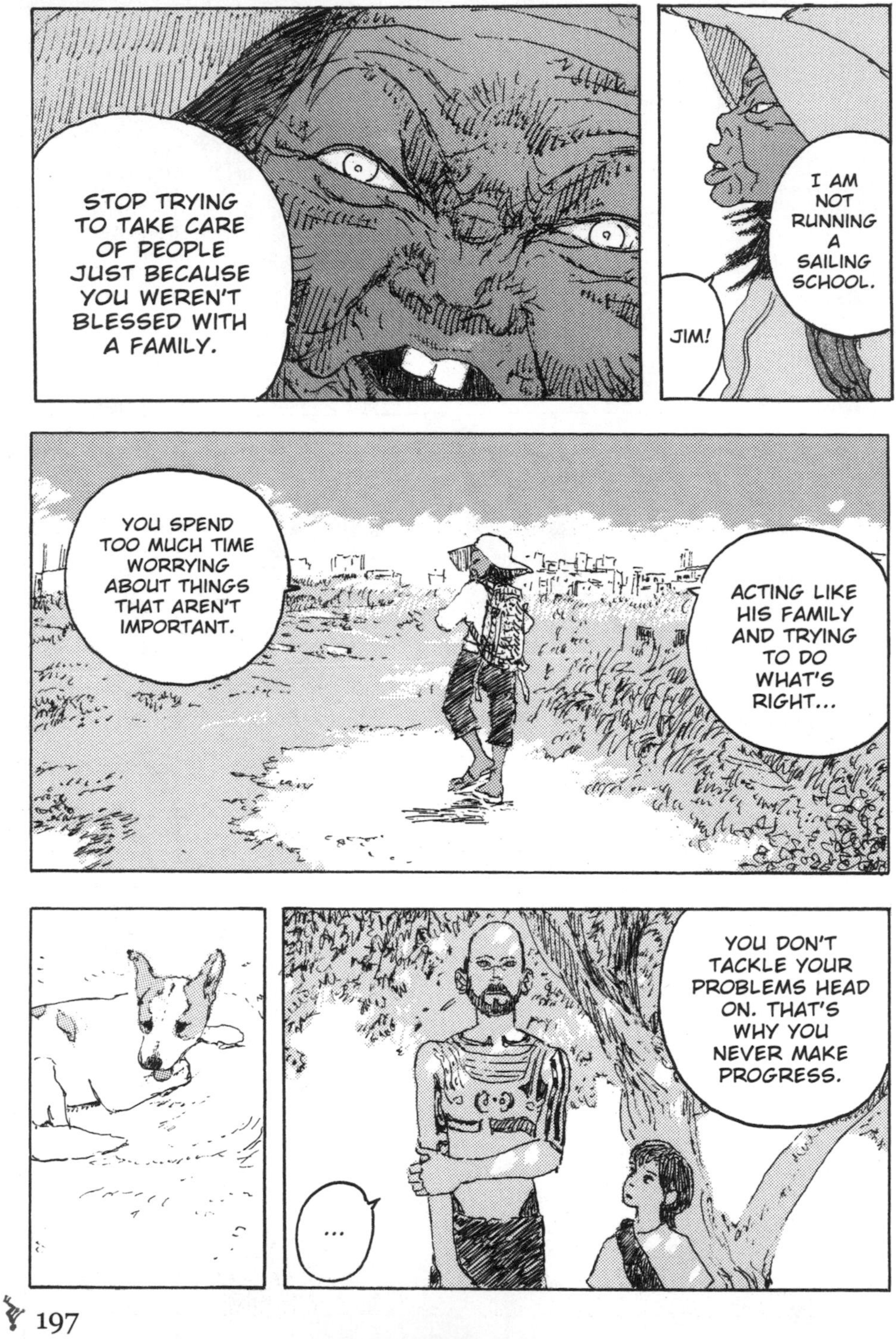
I AM NOT RUNNING A SAILING SCHOOL.
JIM!
STOP TRYING TO TAKE CARE OF PEOPLE JUST BECAUSE YOU WEREN'T BLESSED WITH A FAMILY.
ACTING LIKE HIS FAMILY AND TRYING TO DO WHAT'S RIGHT...
YOU SPEND TOO MUCH TIME WORRYING ABOUT THINGS THAT AREN'T IMPORTANT.
YOU DON'T TACKLE YOUR PROBLEMS HEAD ON. THAT'S WHY YOU NEVER MAKE PROGRESS.
...

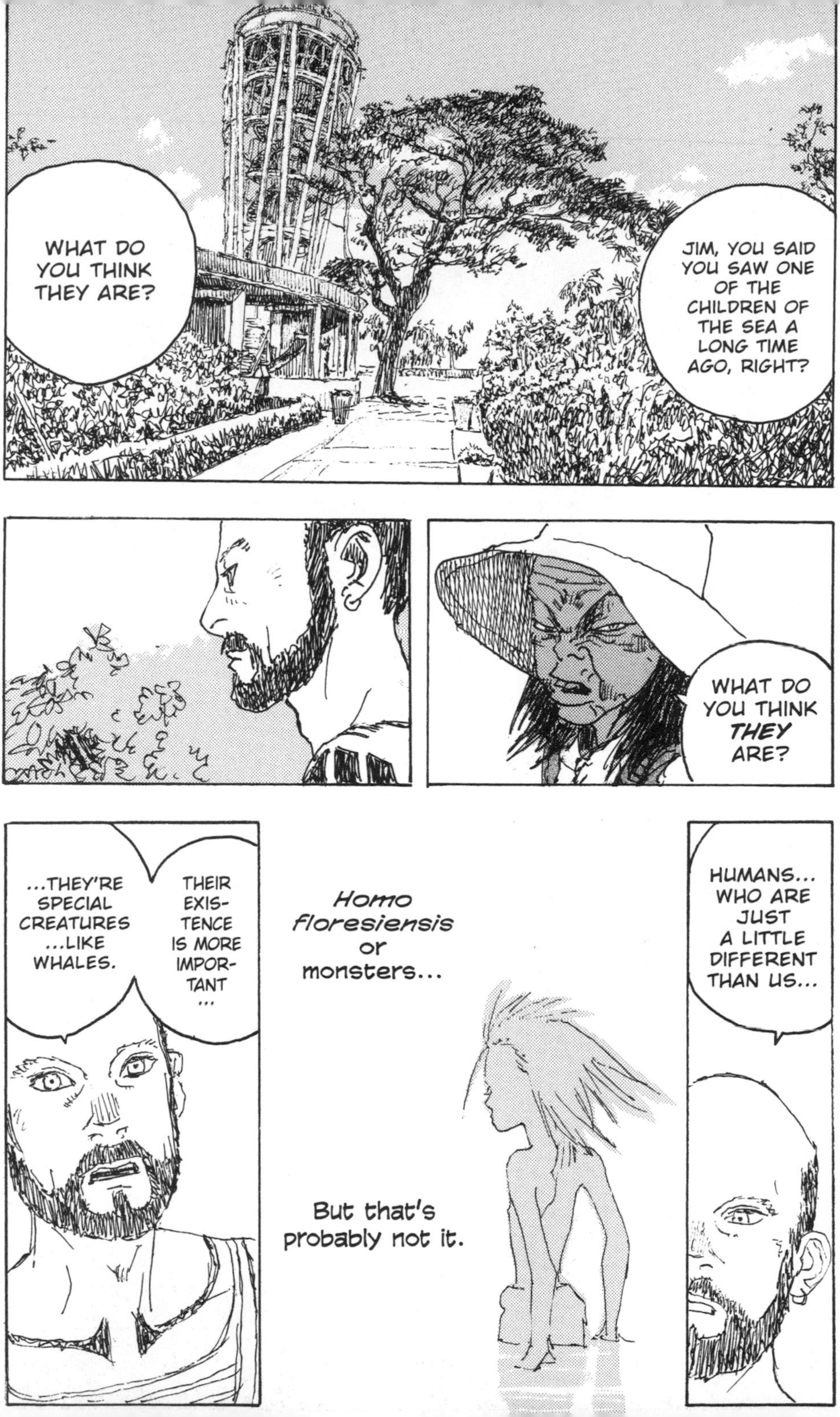
JIM, YOU SAID YOU SAW ONE OF THE CHILDREN OF THE SEA A LONG TIME AGO, RIGHT?
WHAT DO YOU THINK THEY ARE?
WHAT DO YOU THINK *THEY* ARE?
HUMANS... WHO ARE JUST A LITTLE DIFFERENT THAN US...
Homo floresiensis or monsters...
But that's probably not it.
THEIR EXIS-TENCE IS MORE IMPOR-TANT...
...THEY'RE SPECIAL CREATURES ...LIKE WHALES.

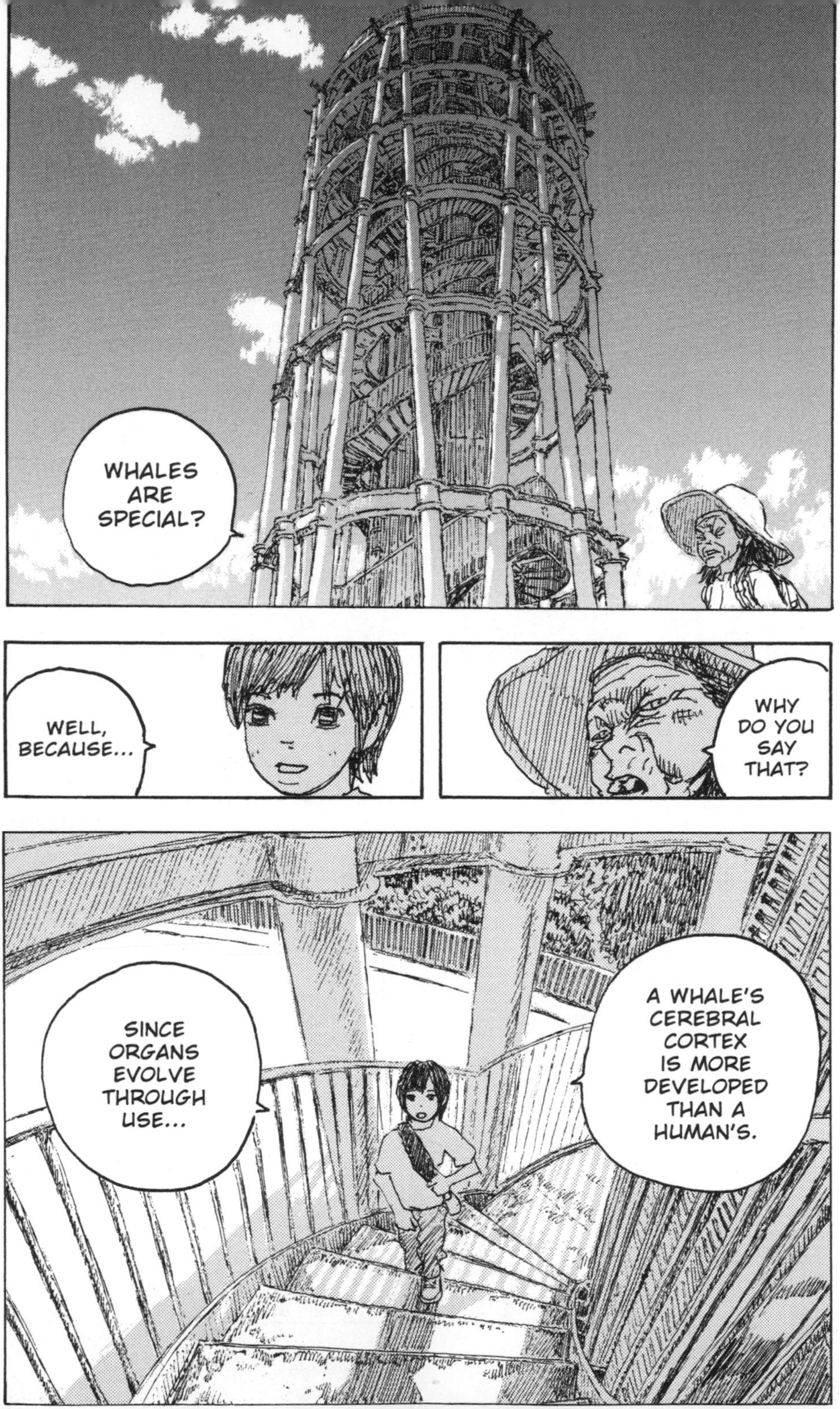
WHALES ARE SPECIAL?
WHY DO YOU SAY THAT?
WELL, BECAUSE...
A WHALE'S CEREBRAL CORTEX IS MORE DEVELOPED THAN A HUMAN'S.
SINCE ORGANS EVOLVE THROUGH USE...

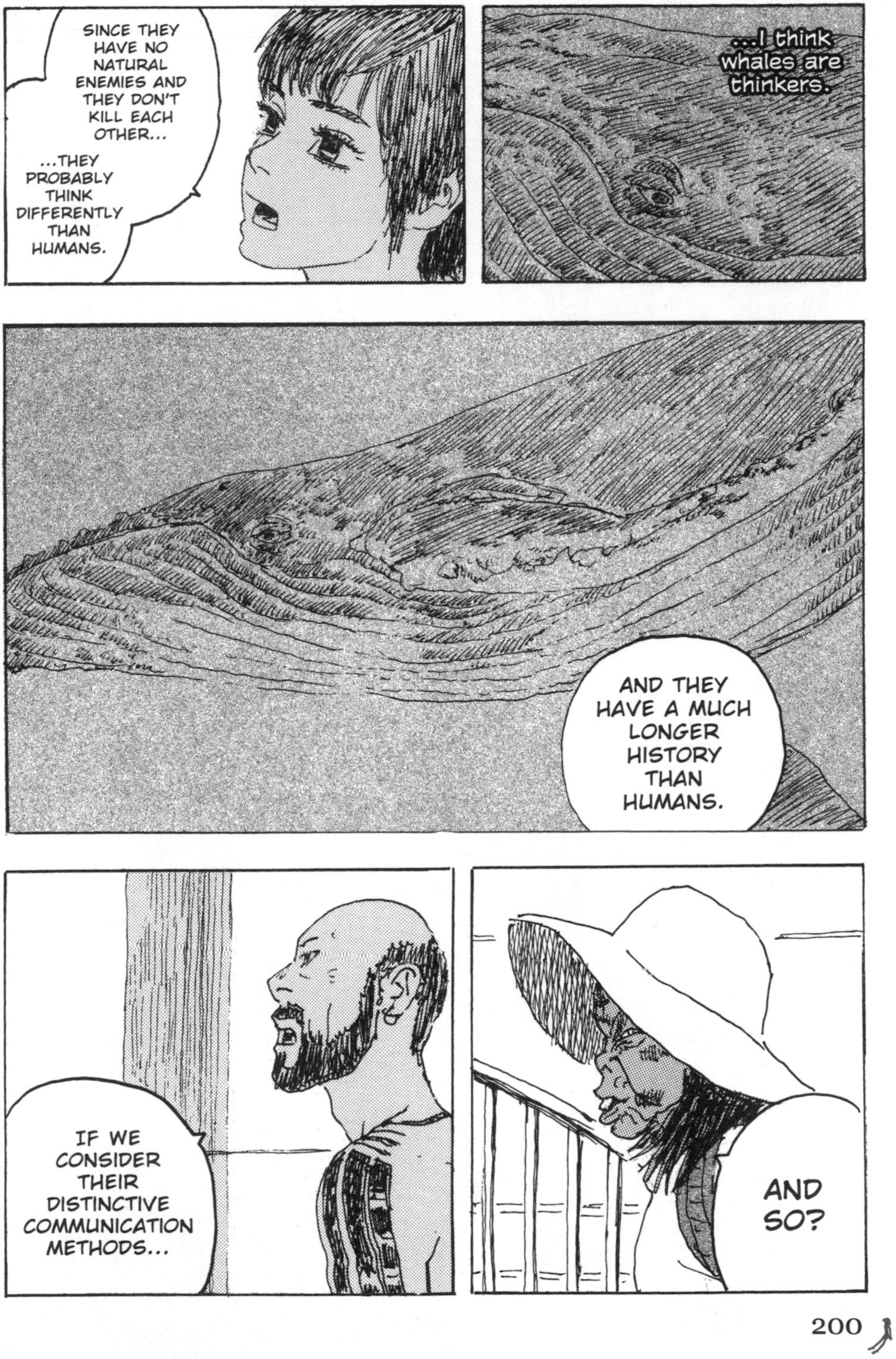
...I think whales are thinkers.
SINCE THEY HAVE NO NATURAL ENEMIES AND THEY DON'T KILL EACH OTHER...
...THEY PROBABLY THINK DIFFERENTLY THAN HUMANS.
AND THEY HAVE A MUCH LONGER HISTORY THAN HUMANS.
AND SO?
IF WE CONSIDER THEIR DISTINCTIVE COMMUNICATION METHODS...

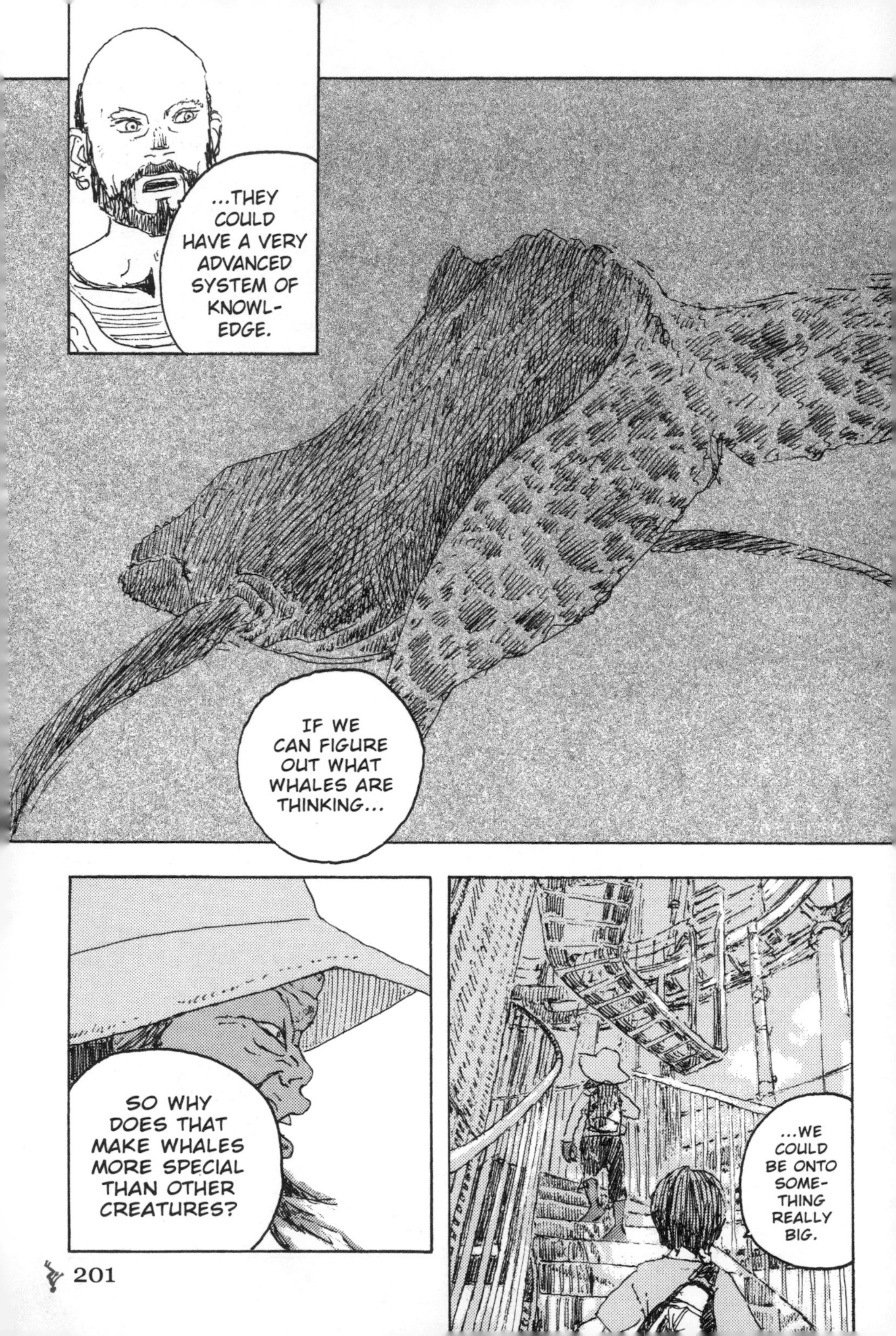
...THEY COULD HAVE A VERY ADVANCED SYSTEM OF KNOWL-EDGE.
IF WE CAN FIGURE OUT WHAT WHALES ARE THINKING...
...WE COULD BE ONTO SOME-THING REALLY BIG.
SO WHY DOES THAT MAKE WHALES MORE SPECIAL THAN OTHER CREATURES?

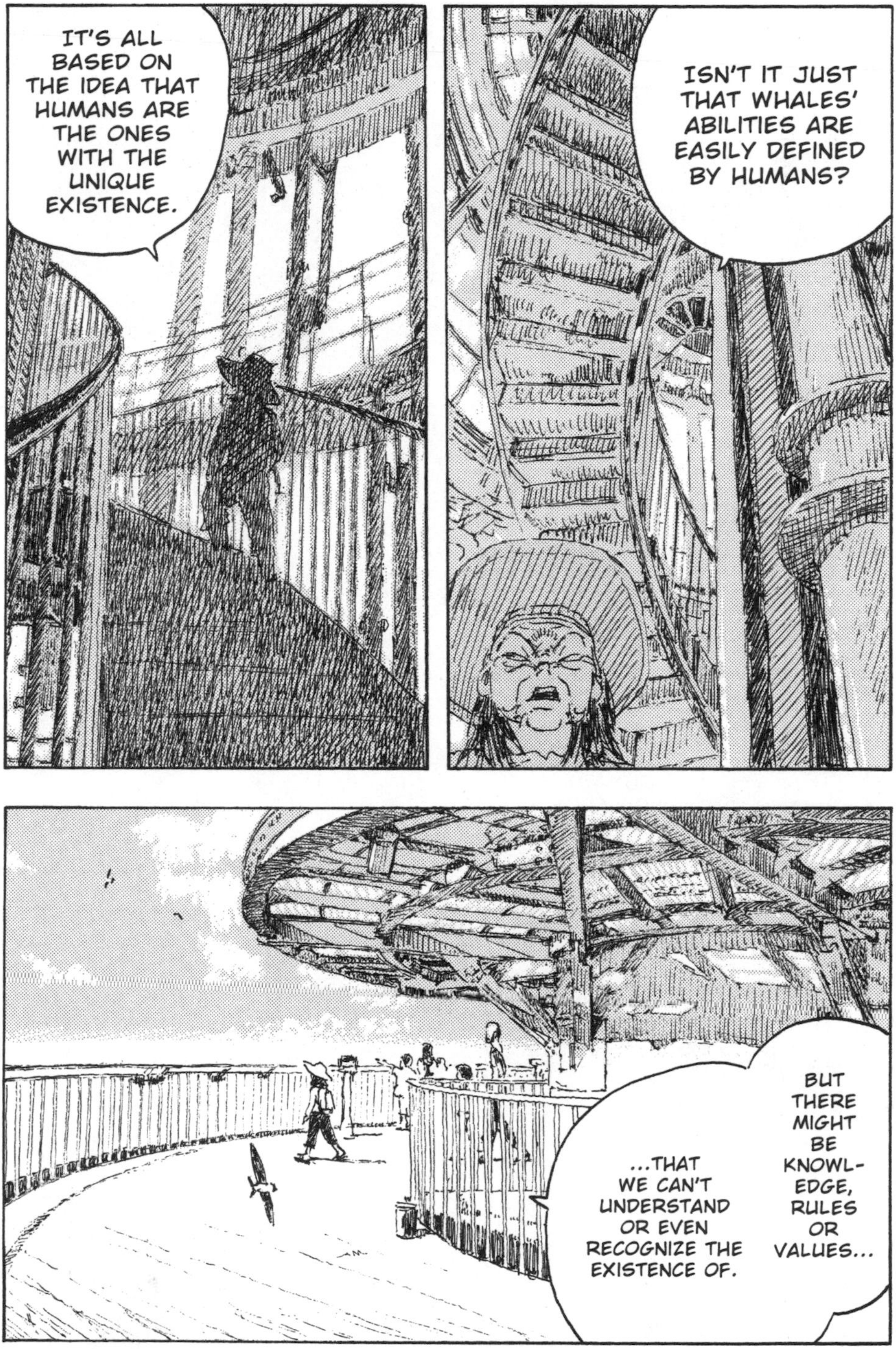
ISN'T IT JUST THAT WHALES' ABILITIES ARE EASILY DEFINED BY HUMANS?
IT'S ALL BASED ON THE IDEA THAT HUMANS ARE THE ONES WITH THE UNIQUE EXISTENCE.
BUT THERE MIGHT BE KNOWL-EDGE, RULES OR VALUES...
...THAT WE CAN'T UNDERSTAND OR EVEN RECOGNIZE THE EXISTENCE OF.

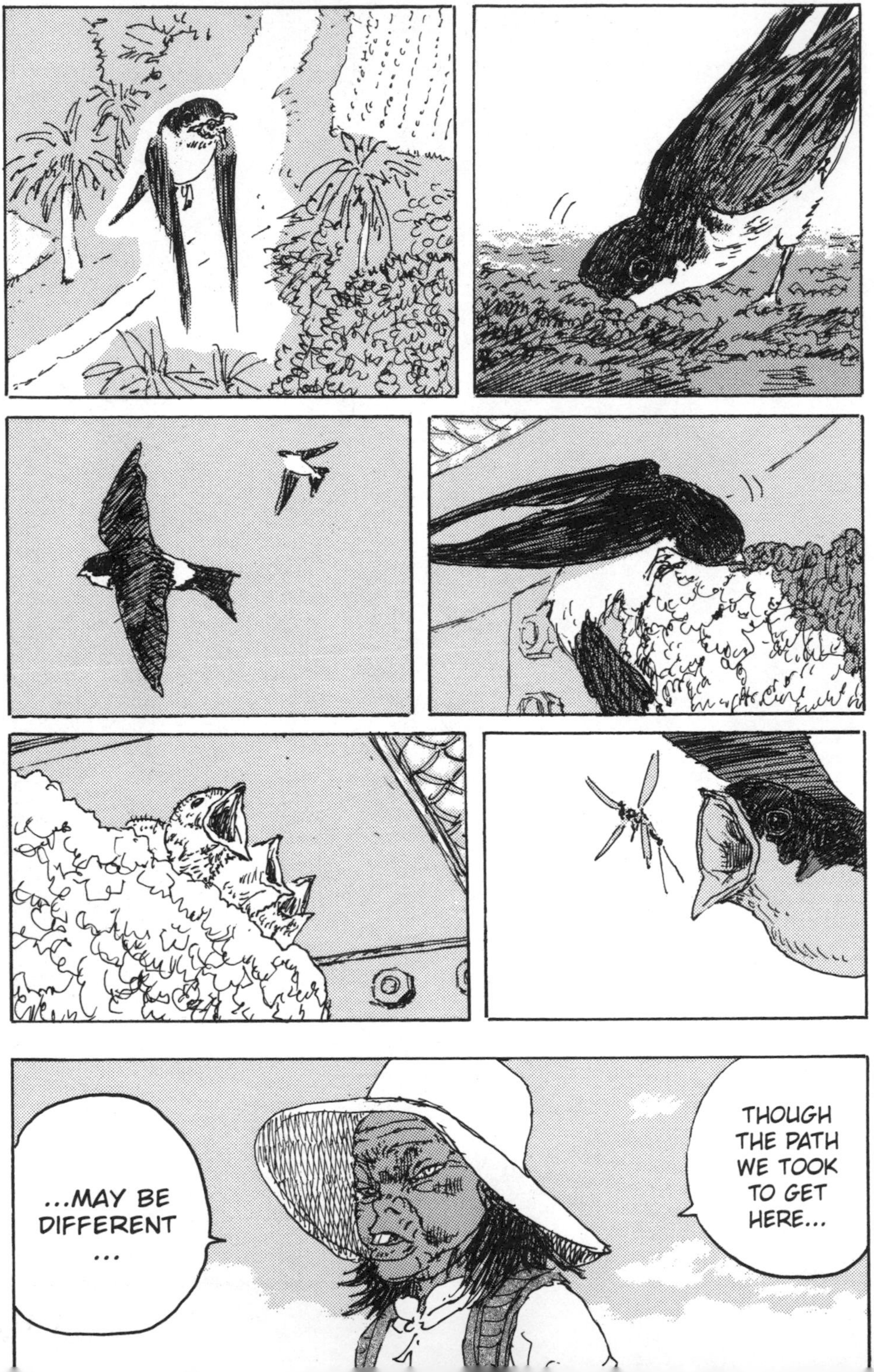
THOUGH THE PATH WE TOOK TO GET HERE...
...MAY BE DIFFERENT ...

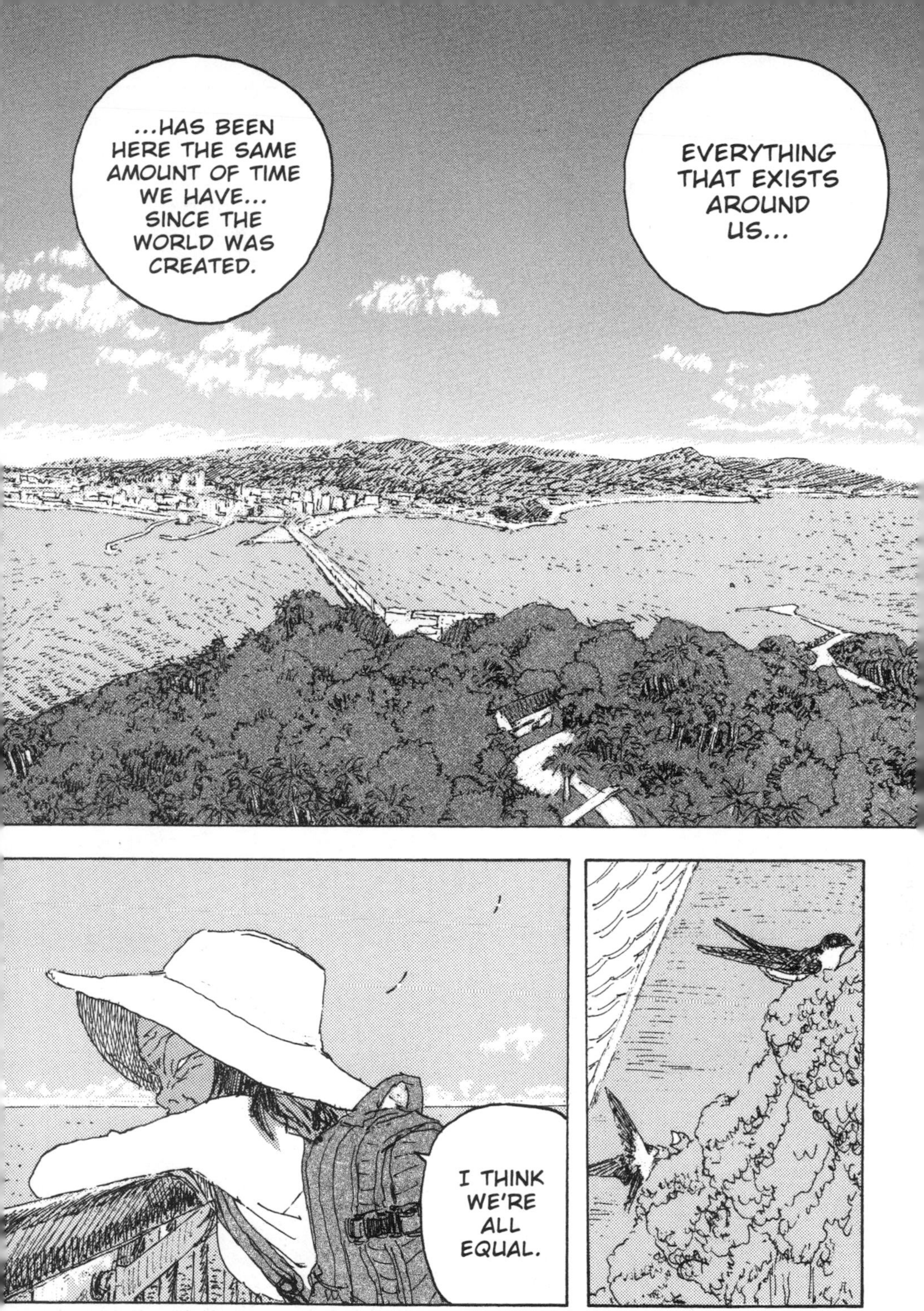
EVERYTHING THAT EXISTS AROUND US...
...HAS BEEN HERE THE SAME AMOUNT OF TIME WE HAVE... SINCE THE WORLD WAS CREATED.
I THINK WE'RE ALL EQUAL.

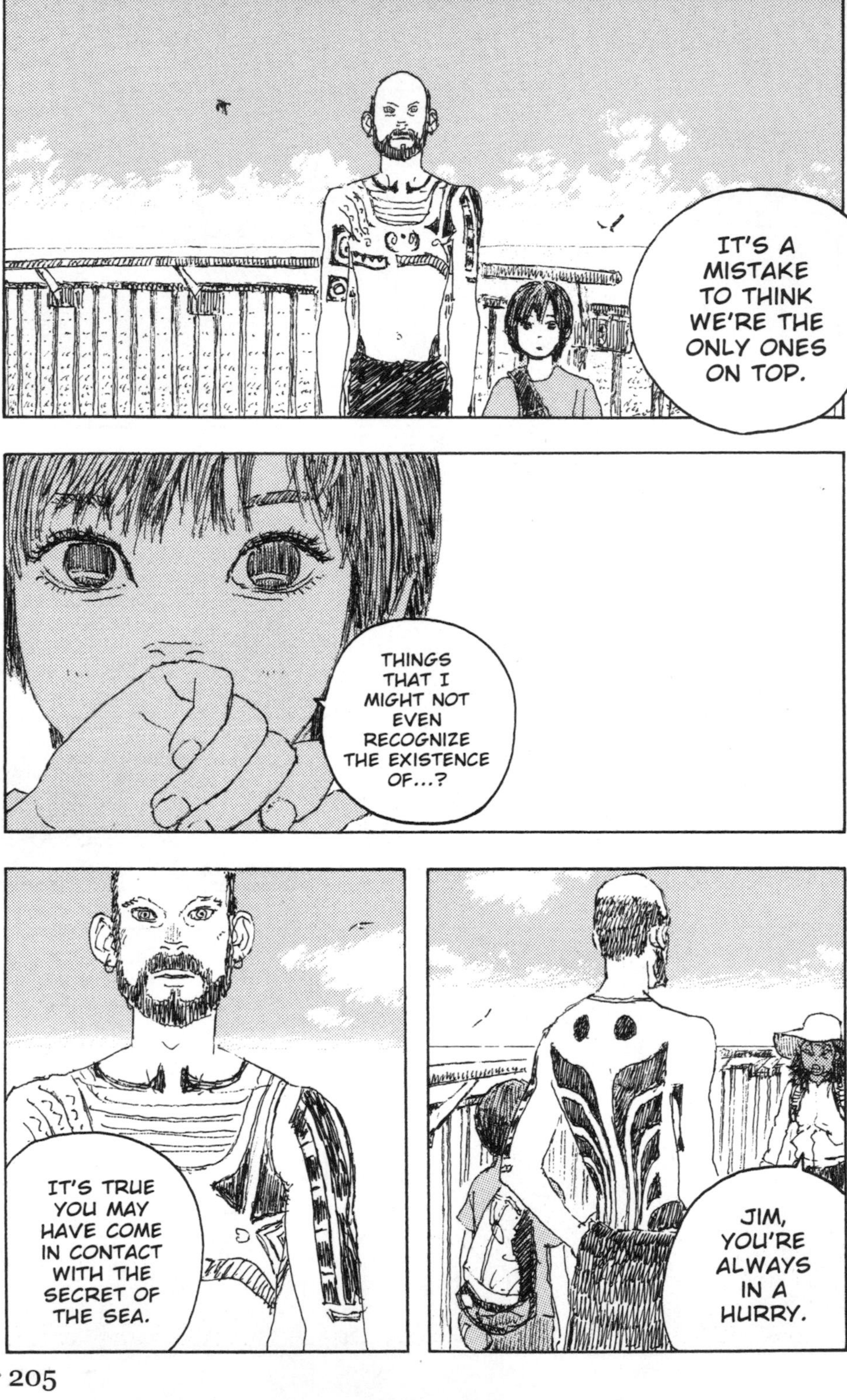
IT'S A MISTAKE TO THINK WE'RE THE ONLY ONES ON TOP.
THINGS THAT I MIGHT NOT EVEN RECOGNIZE THE EXISTENCE OF...?
JIM, YOU'RE ALWAYS IN A HURRY.
IT'S TRUE YOU MAY HAVE COME IN CONTACT WITH THE SECRET OF THE SEA.

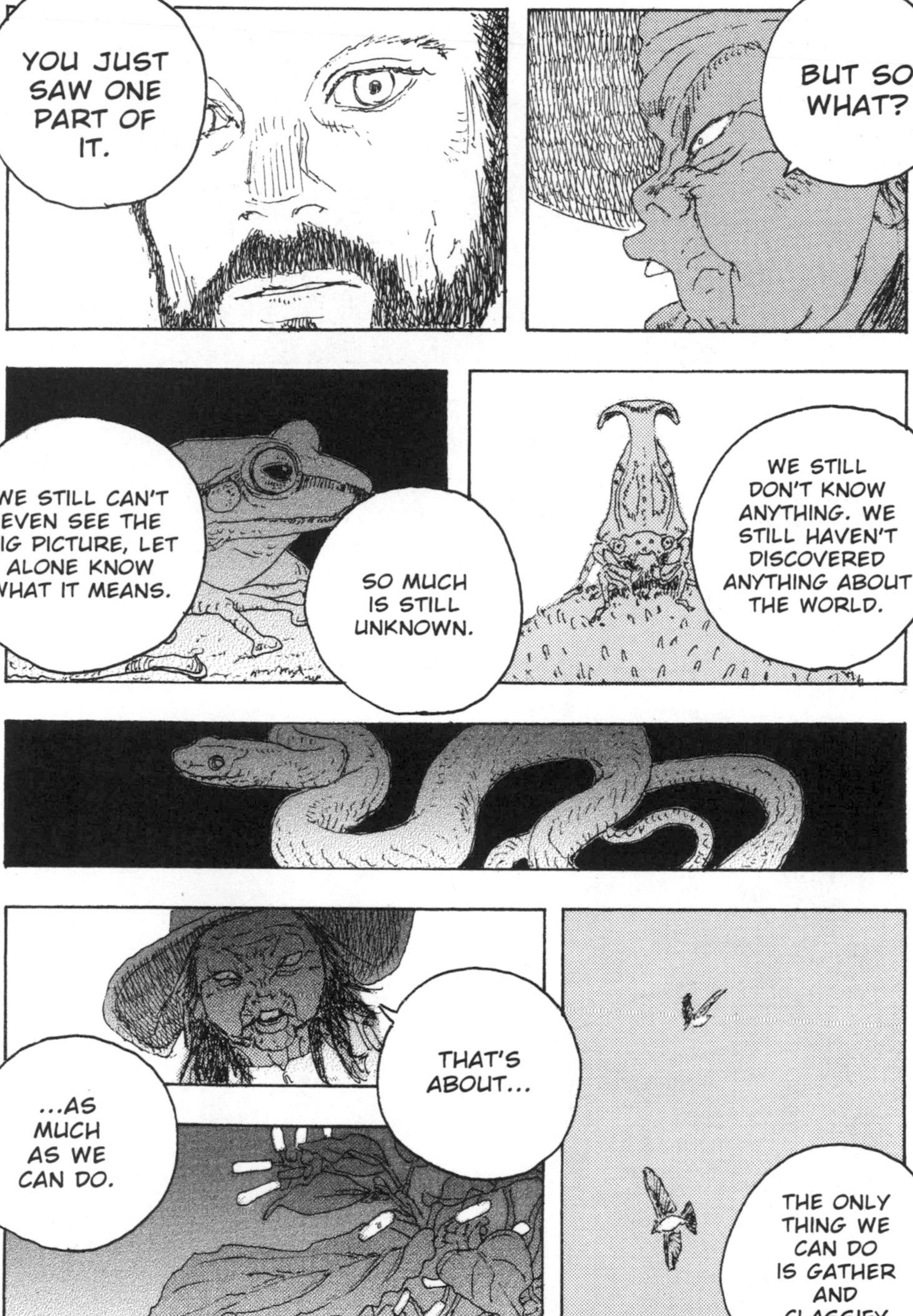
BUT SO WHAT?
YOU JUST SAW ONE PART OF IT.
WE STILL DON'T KNOW ANYTHING. WE STILL HAVEN'T DISCOVERED ANYTHING ABOUT THE WORLD.
SO MUCH IS STILL UNKNOWN.
WE STILL CAN'T EVEN SEE THE BIG PICTURE, LET ALONE KNOW WHAT IT MEANS.
THE ONLY THING WE CAN DO IS GATHER AND CLASSIFY THINGS.
THAT'S ABOUT...
...AS MUCH AS WE CAN DO.

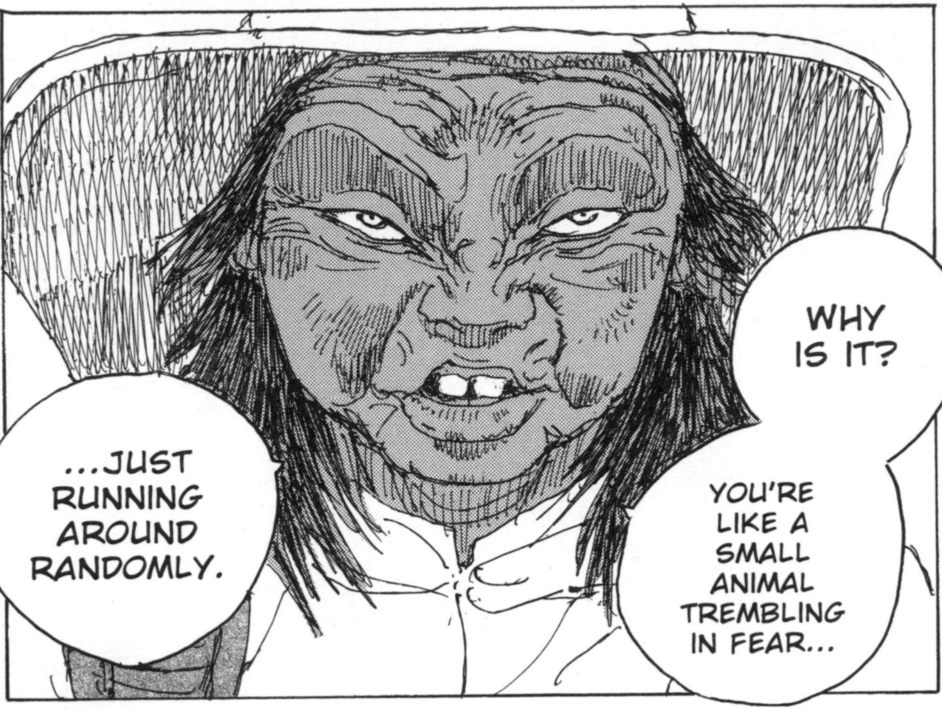
WHY IS IT?
YOU'RE LIKE A SMALL ANIMAL TREMBLING IN FEAR...
...JUST RUNNING AROUND RANDOMLY.

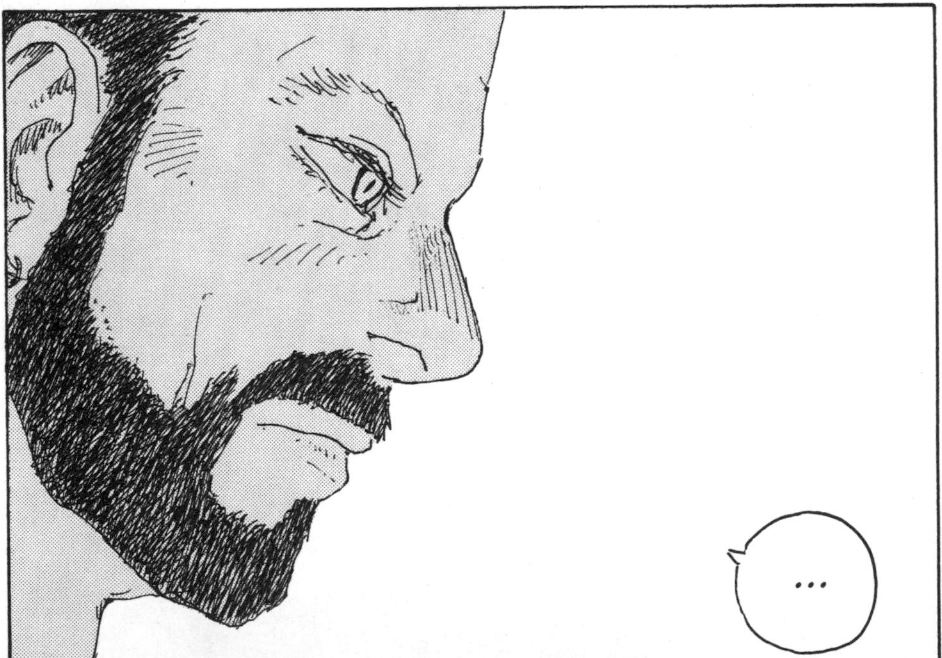
...

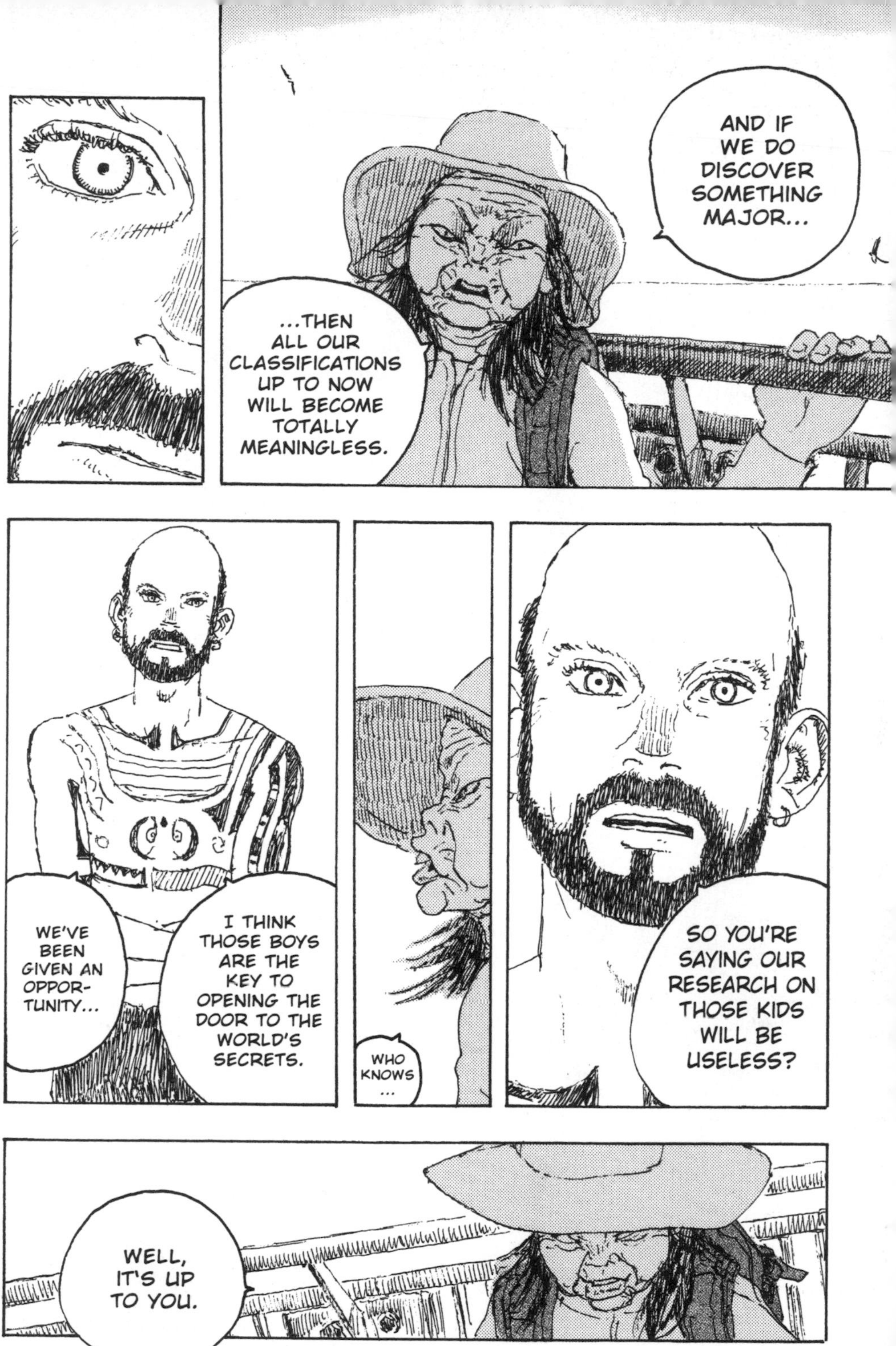
AND IF WE DO DISCOVER SOMETHING MAJOR...
...THEN ALL OUR CLASSIFICATIONS UP TO NOW WILL BECOME TOTALLY MEANINGLESS.
SO YOU'RE SAYING OUR RESEARCH ON THOSE KIDS WILL BE USELESS?
WHO KNOWS...
I THINK THOSE BOYS ARE THE KEY TO OPENING THE DOOR TO THE WORLD'S SECRETS.
WE'VE BEEN GIVEN AN OPPOR-TUNITY...
WELL, IT'S UP TO YOU.

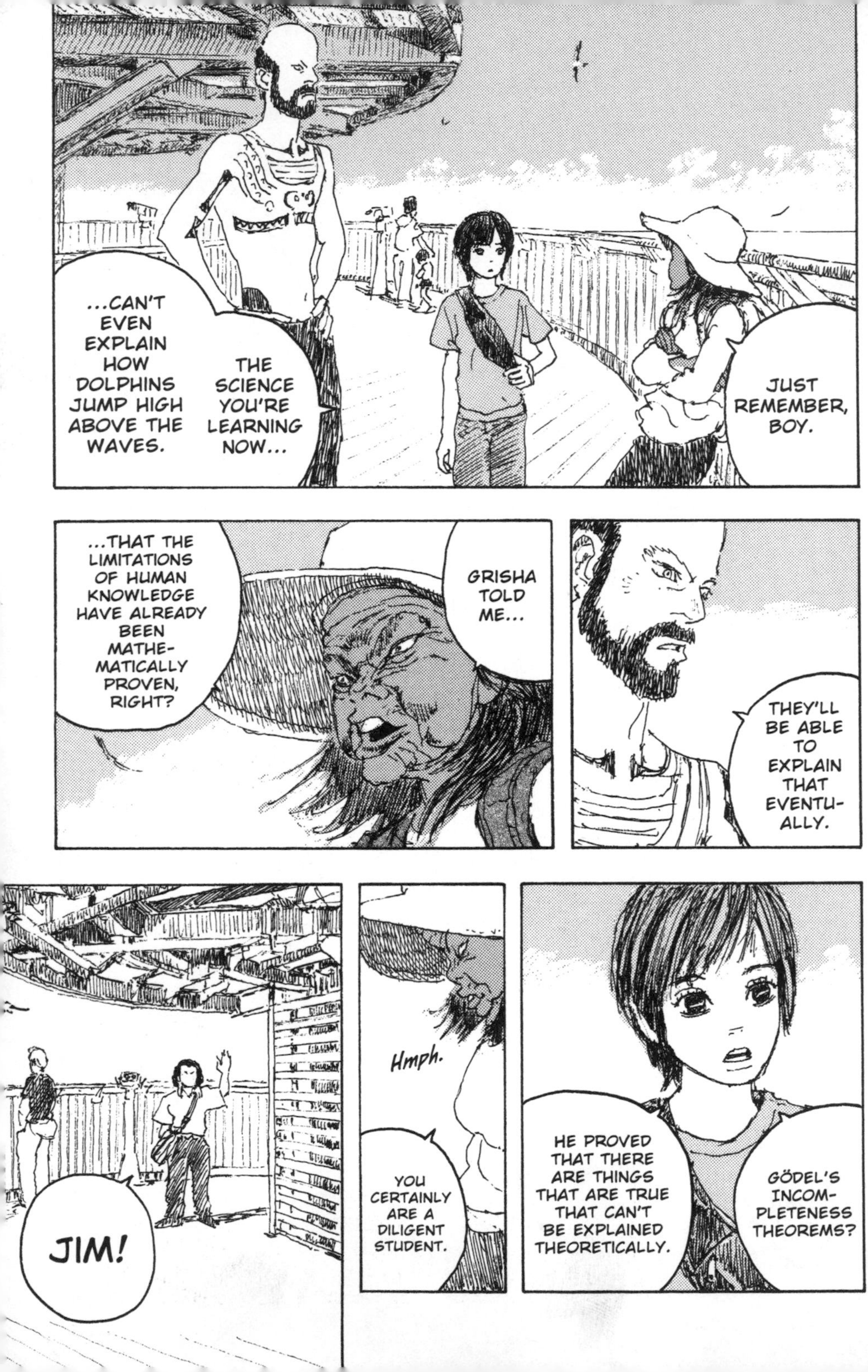
JUST REMEMBER, BOY.
THE SCIENCE YOU'RE LEARNING NOW...
...CAN'T EVEN EXPLAIN HOW DOLPHINS JUMP HIGH ABOVE THE WAVES.
THEY'LL BE ABLE TO EXPLAIN THAT EVENTUALLY.
GRISHA TOLD ME...
...THAT THE LIMITATIONS OF HUMAN KNOWLEDGE HAVE ALREADY BEEN MATHEMATICALLY PROVEN, RIGHT?
GÖDEL'S INCOMPLETENESS THEOREMS?
HE PROVED THAT THERE ARE THINGS THAT ARE TRUE THAT CAN'T BE EXPLAINED THEORETICALLY.
Hmph.
YOU CERTAINLY ARE A DILIGENT STUDENT.
JIM!

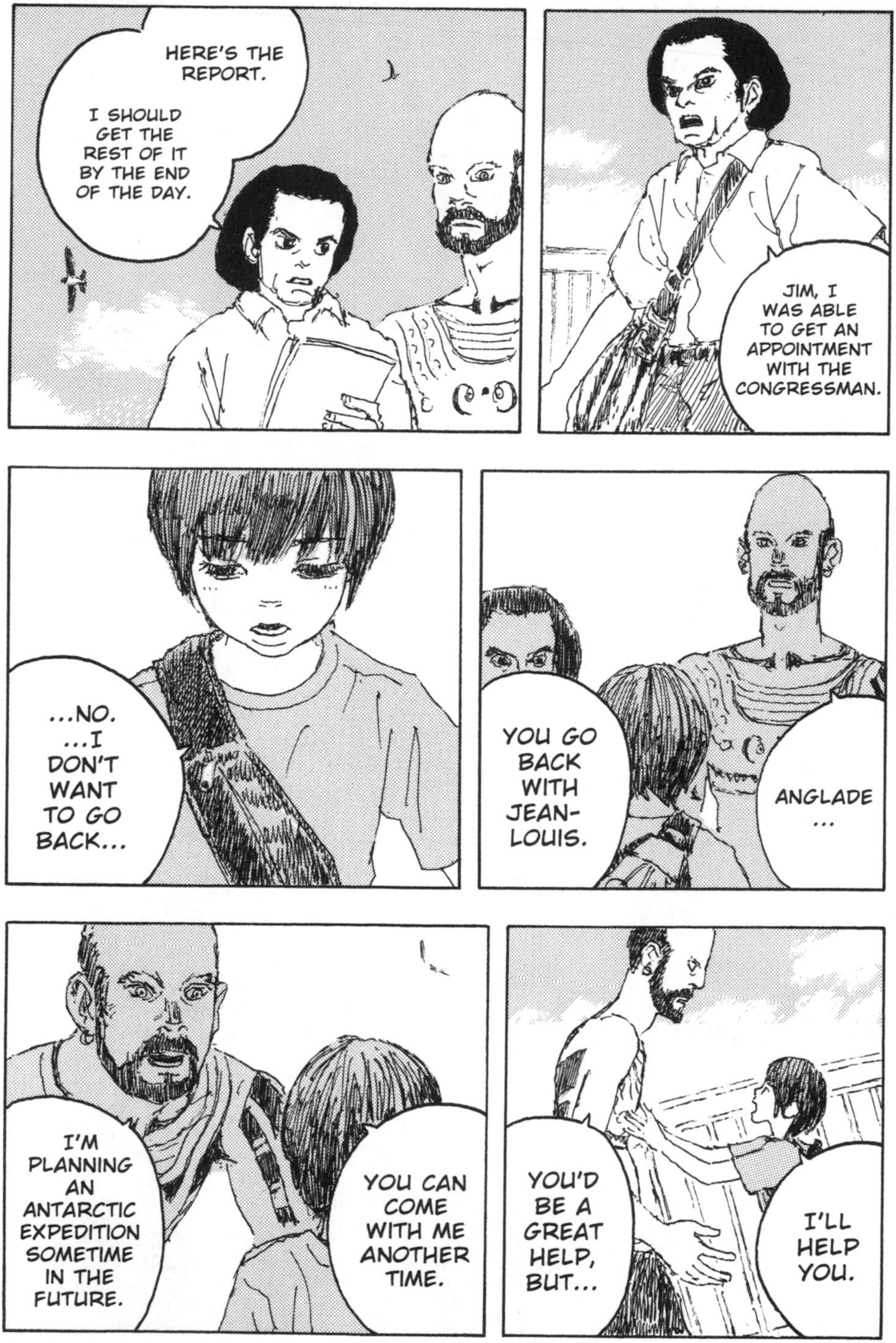
JIM, I WAS ABLE TO GET AN APPOINTMENT WITH THE CONGRESSMAN.
HERE'S THE REPORT.
I SHOULD GET THE REST OF IT BY THE END OF THE DAY.
ANGLADE ...
YOU GO BACK WITH JEAN-LOUIS.
...NO. ...I DON'T WANT TO GO BACK...
I'LL HELP YOU.
YOU'D BE A GREAT HELP, BUT...
YOU CAN COME WITH ME ANOTHER TIME.
I'M PLANNING AN ANTARCTIC EXPEDITION SOMETIME IN THE FUTURE.

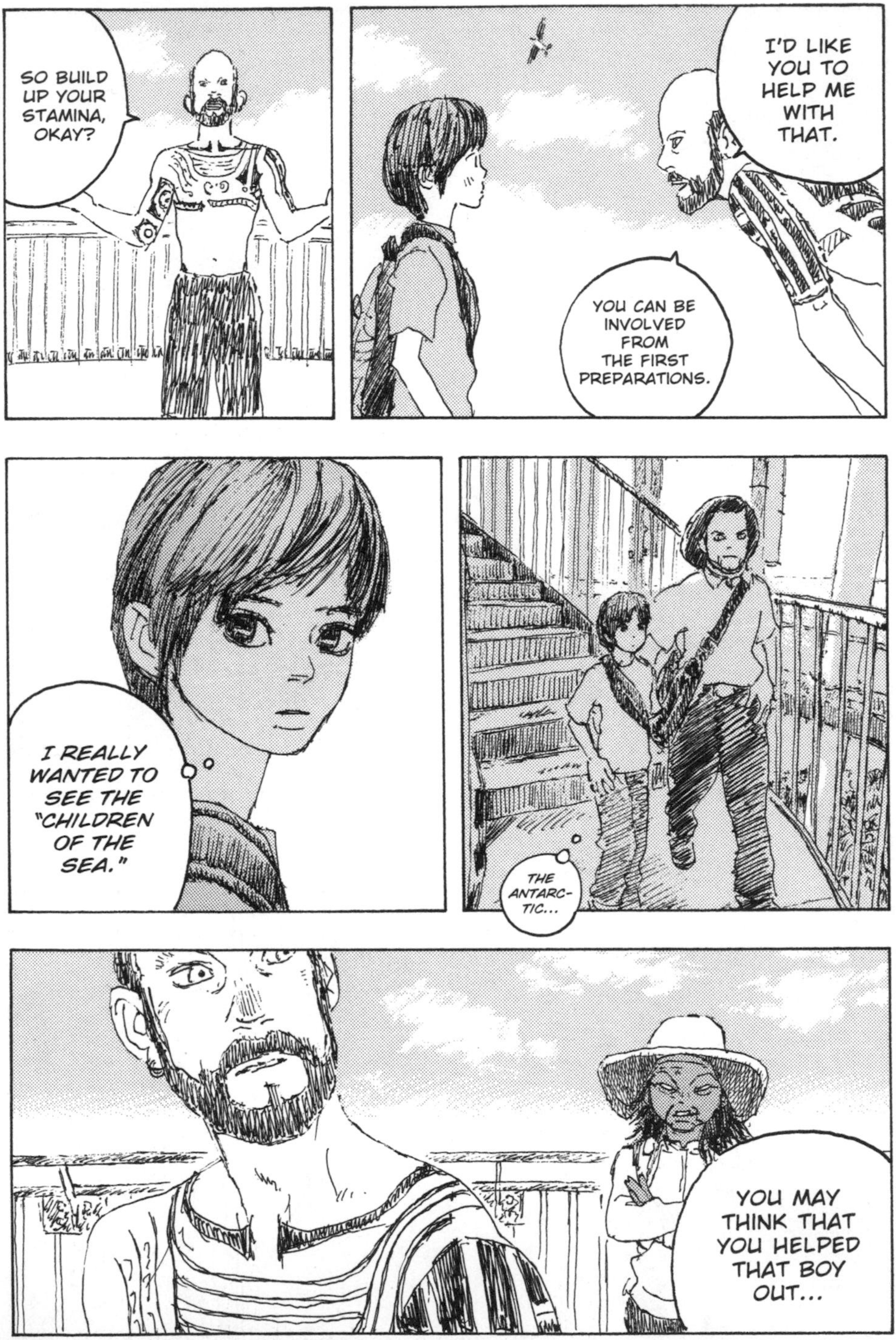
I'D LIKE YOU TO HELP ME WITH THAT.
YOU CAN BE INVOLVED FROM THE FIRST PREPARATIONS.
SO BUILD UP YOUR STAMINA, OKAY?
THE ANTARCTIC...
I REALLY WANTED TO SEE THE "CHILDREN OF THE SEA."
YOU MAY THINK THAT YOU HELPED THAT BOY OUT...

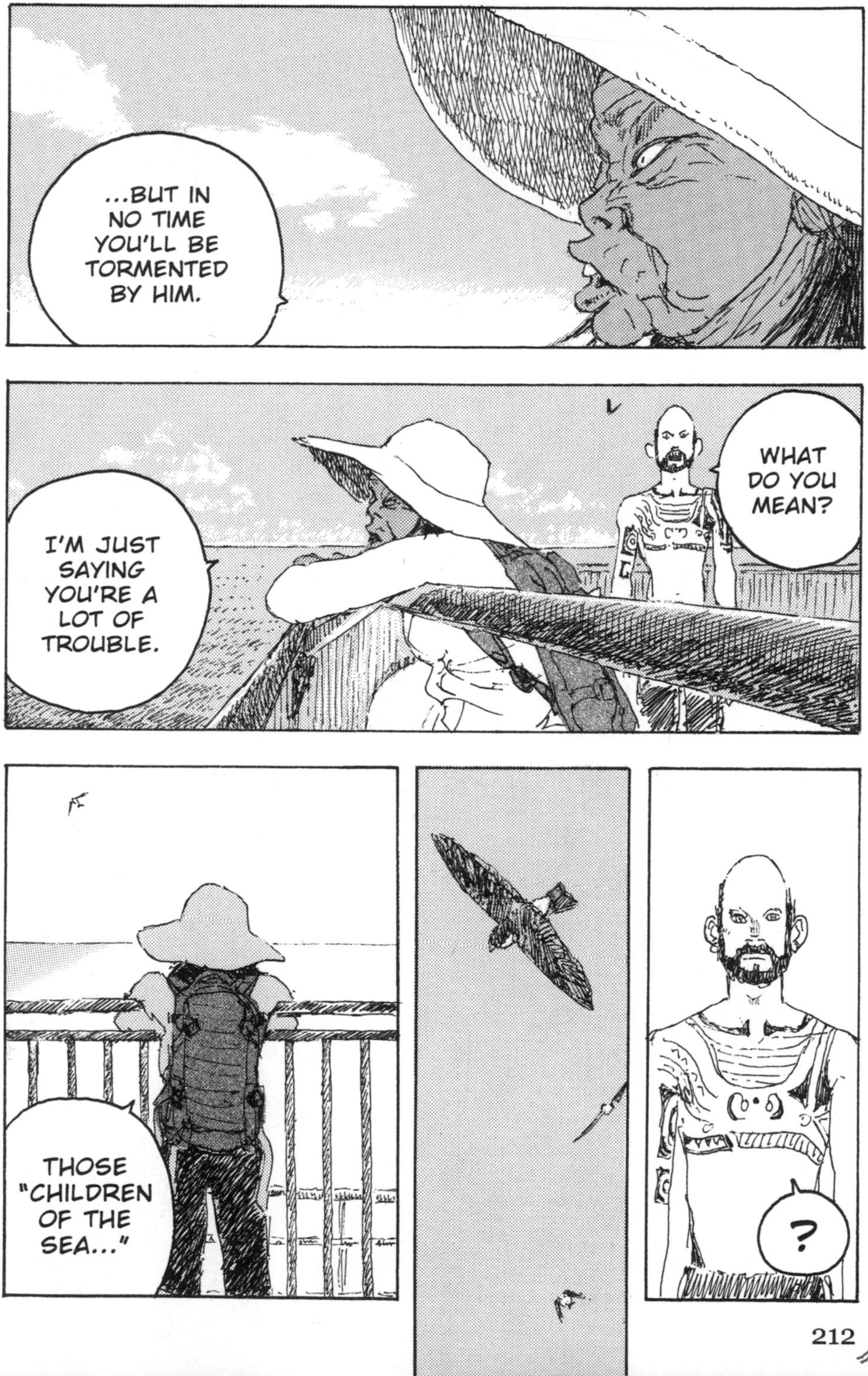
...BUT IN NO TIME YOU'LL BE TORMENTED BY HIM.
WHAT DO YOU MEAN?
I'M JUST SAYING YOU'RE A LOT OF TROUBLE.
?
THOSE "CHILDREN OF THE SEA..."

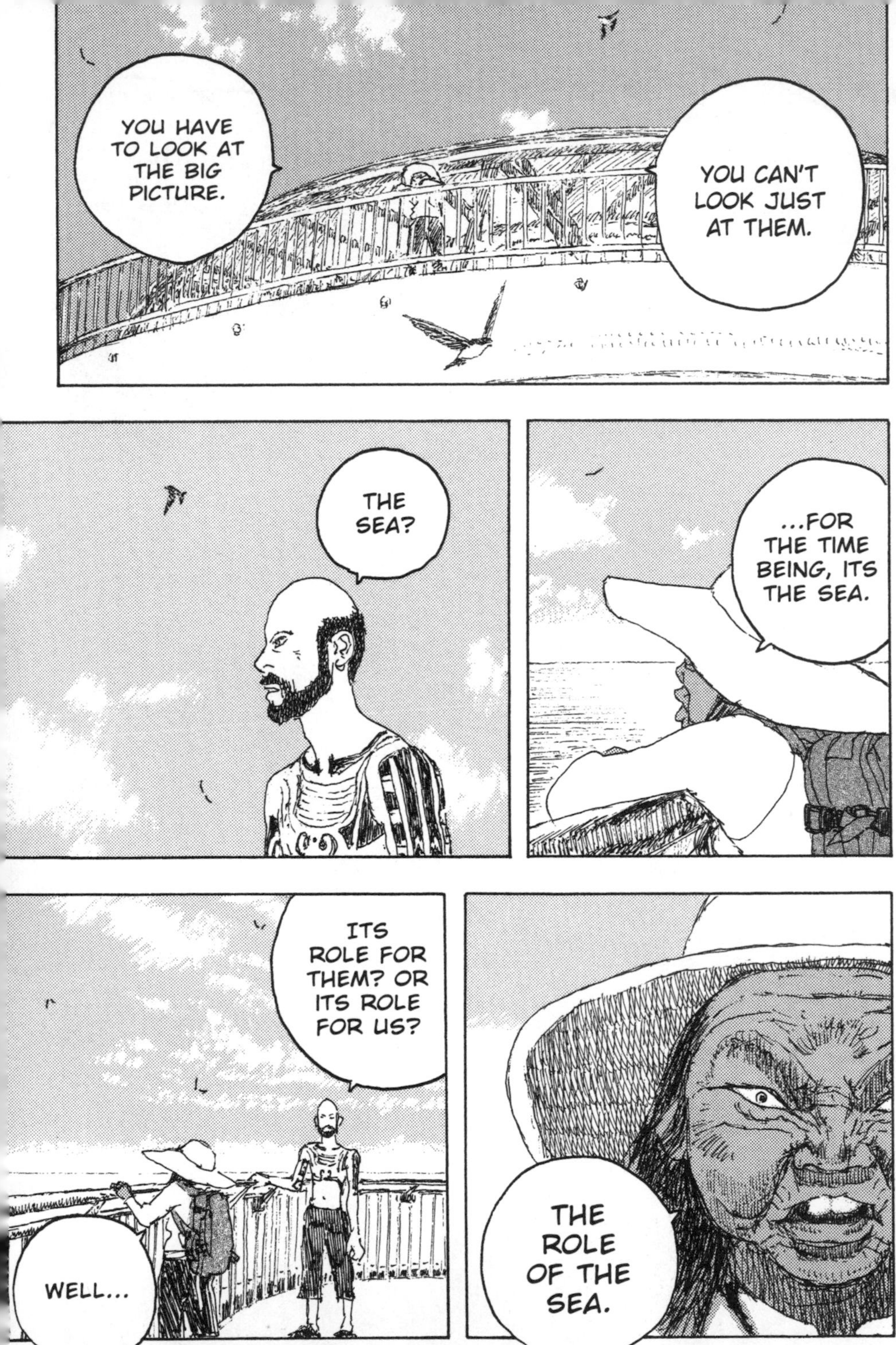
YOU CAN'T LOOK JUST AT THEM.
YOU HAVE TO LOOK AT THE BIG PICTURE.
...FOR THE TIME BEING, ITS THE SEA.
THE SEA?
THE ROLE OF THE SEA.
ITS ROLE FOR THEM? OR ITS ROLE FOR US?
WELL...

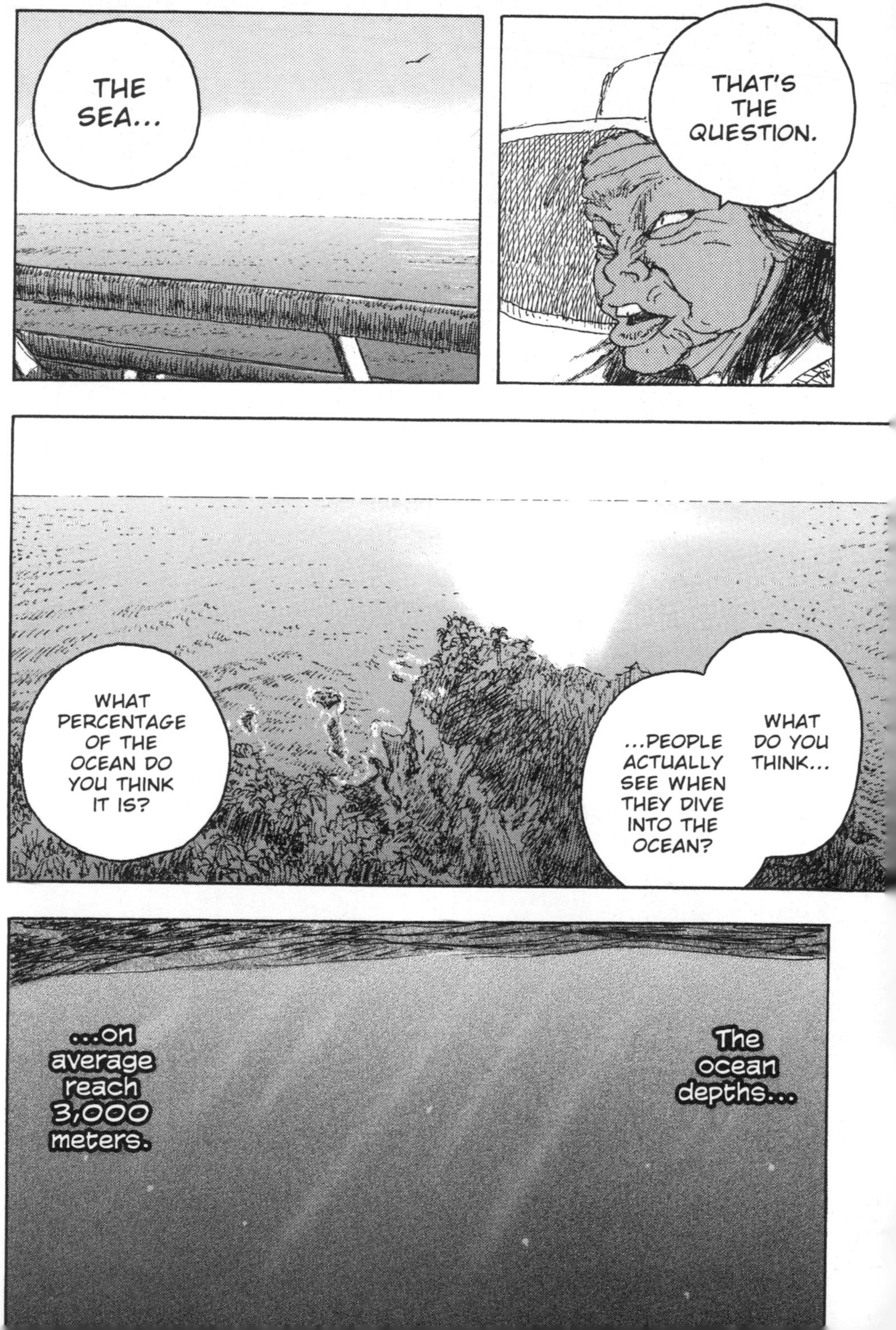
THAT'S THE QUESTION.
THE SEA...
WHAT DO YOU THINK...
...PEOPLE ACTUALLY SEE WHEN THEY DIVE INTO THE OCEAN?
WHAT PERCENTAGE OF THE OCEAN DO YOU THINK IT IS?
The ocean depths...
...on average reach 3,000 meters.

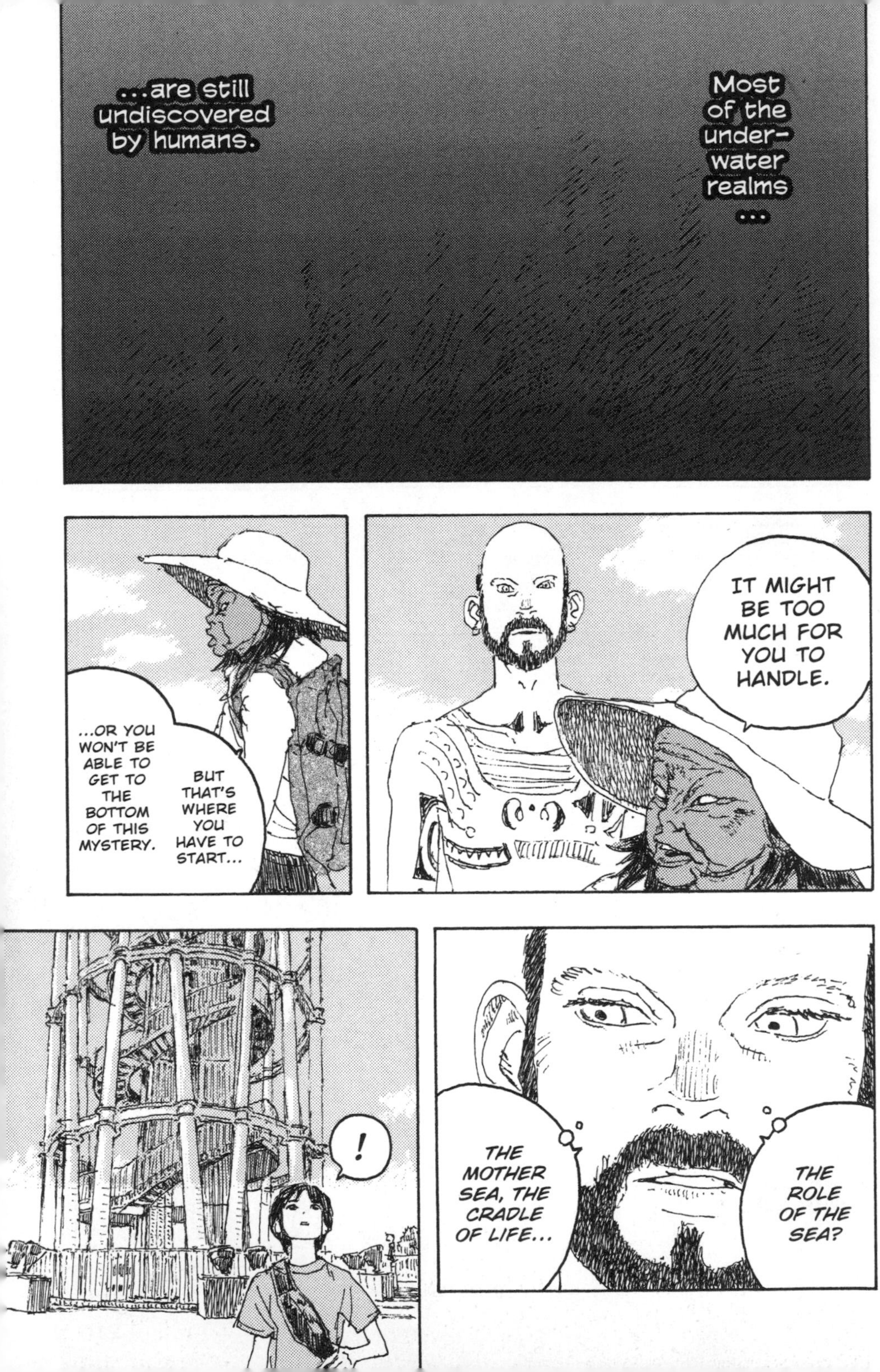
Most of the under-water realms...
...are still undiscovered by humans.
IT MIGHT BE TOO MUCH FOR YOU TO HANDLE.
BUT THAT'S WHERE YOU HAVE TO START...
...OR YOU WON'T BE ABLE TO GET TO THE BOTTOM OF THIS MYSTERY.
THE ROLE OF THE SEA?
THE MOTHER SEA, THE CRADLE OF LIFE...
!

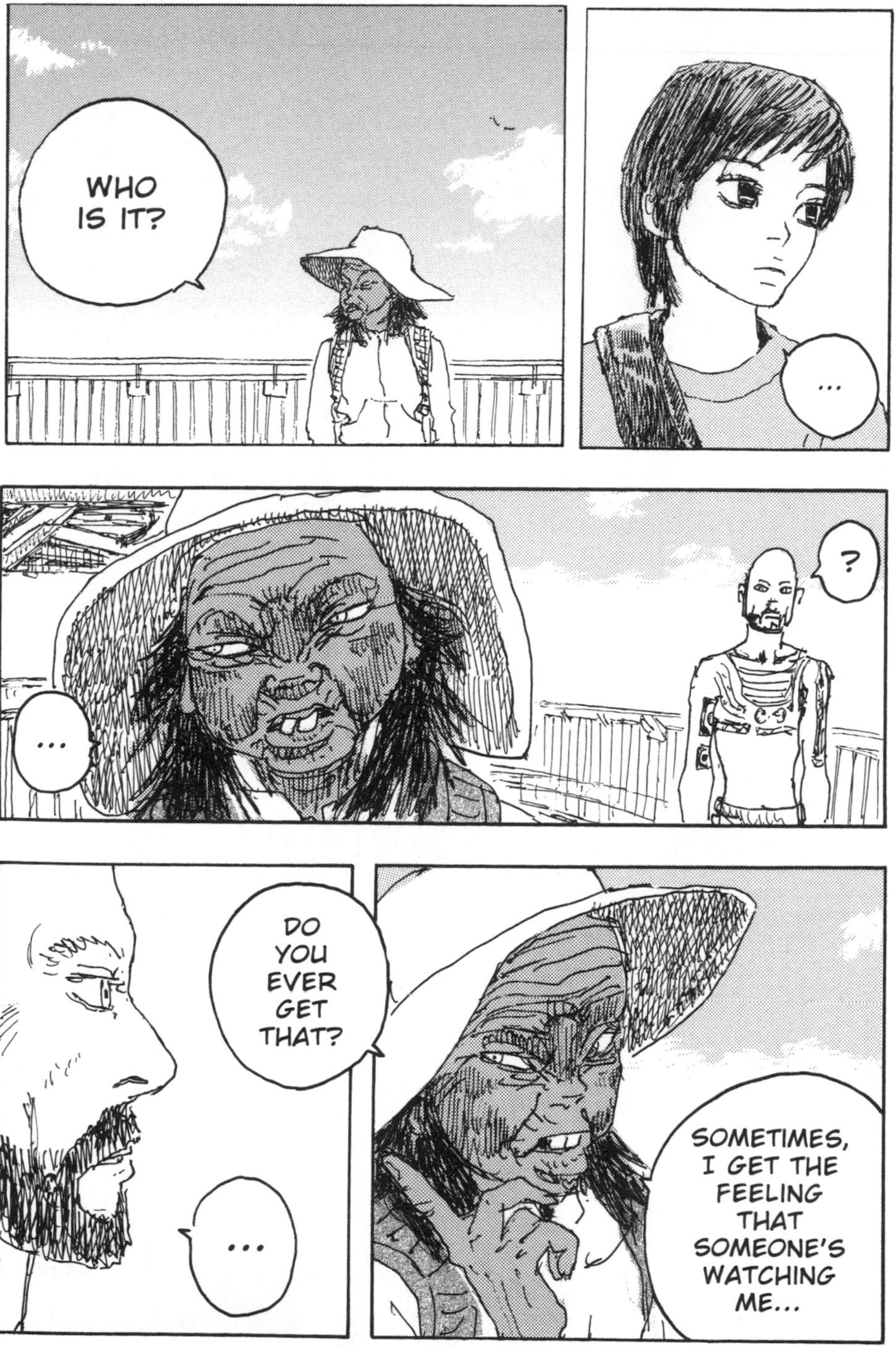
...
WHO IS IT?
?
...
SOMETIMES, I GET THE FEELING THAT SOMEONE'S WATCHING ME...
DO YOU EVER GET THAT?
...

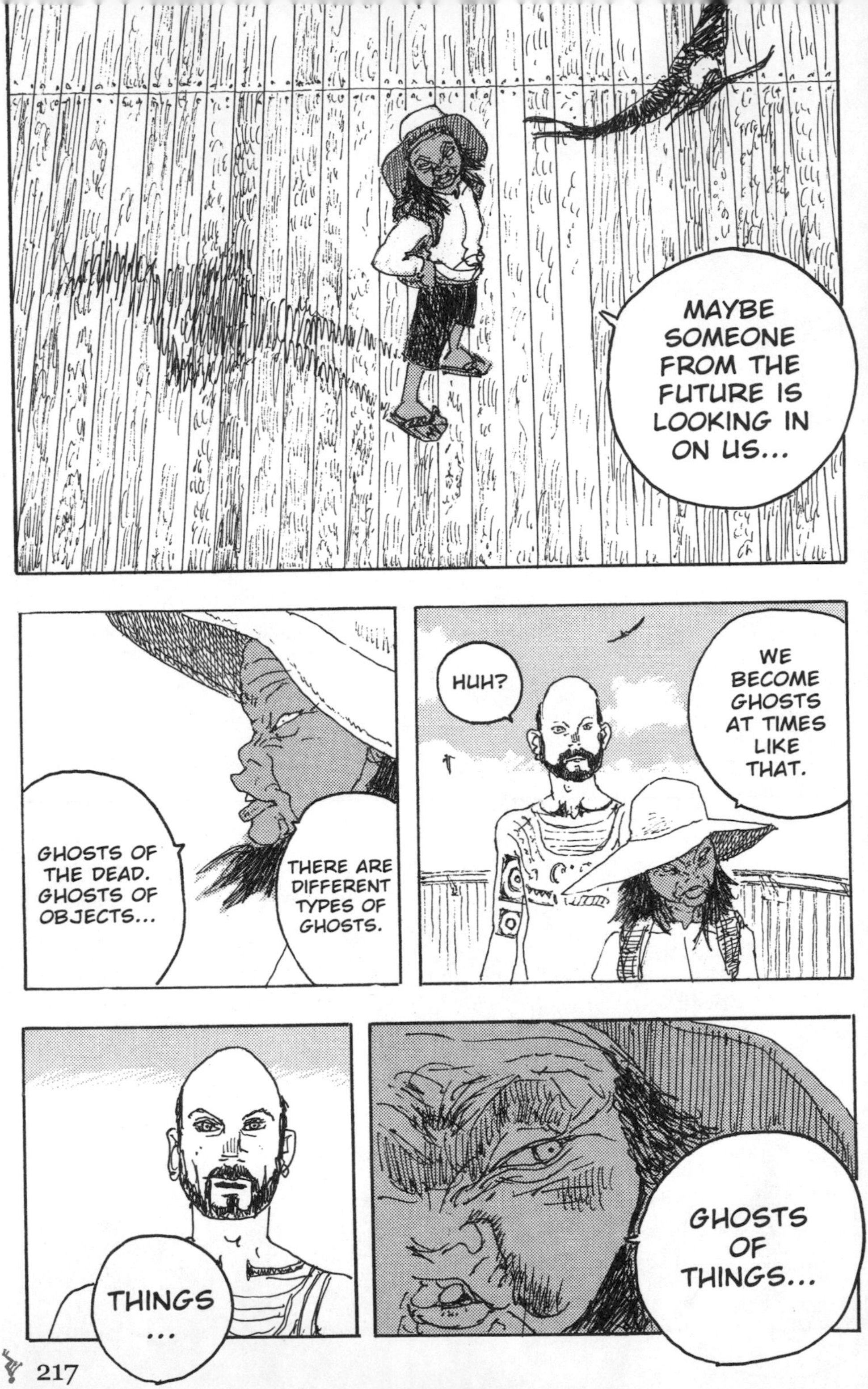
MAYBE SOMEONE FROM THE FUTURE IS LOOKING IN ON US...
WE BECOME GHOSTS AT TIMES LIKE THAT.
HUH?
THERE ARE DIFFERENT TYPES OF GHOSTS.
GHOSTS OF THE DEAD. GHOSTS OF OBJECTS...
GHOSTS OF THINGS...
THINGS ...

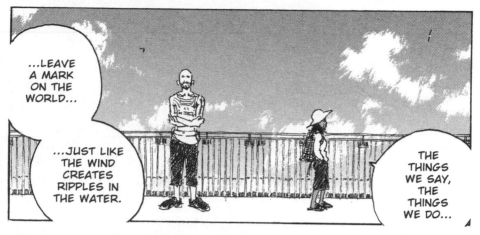

THE THINGS WE SAY, THE THINGS WE DO...
...LEAVE A MARK ON THE WORLD...
...JUST LIKE THE WIND CREATES RIPPLES IN THE WATER.
IT CHANGES SHAPE AS IT SPREADS OUT.
IT CHANGES INTO A SEGMENT OF WHALE SONG...
...AS IT'S PASSED ON THROUGH THE VIBRATIONS OF ELEMENTARY PARTICLES.

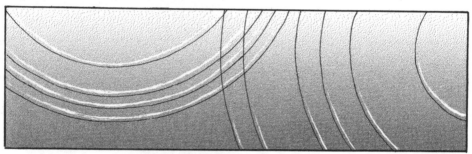

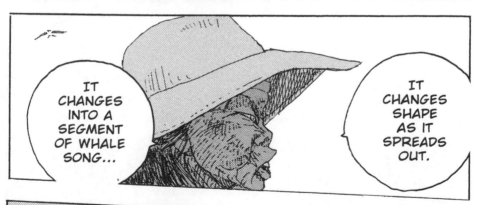

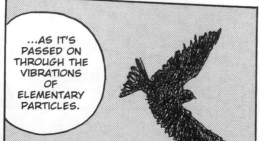

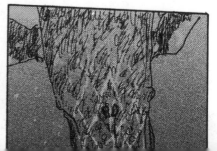

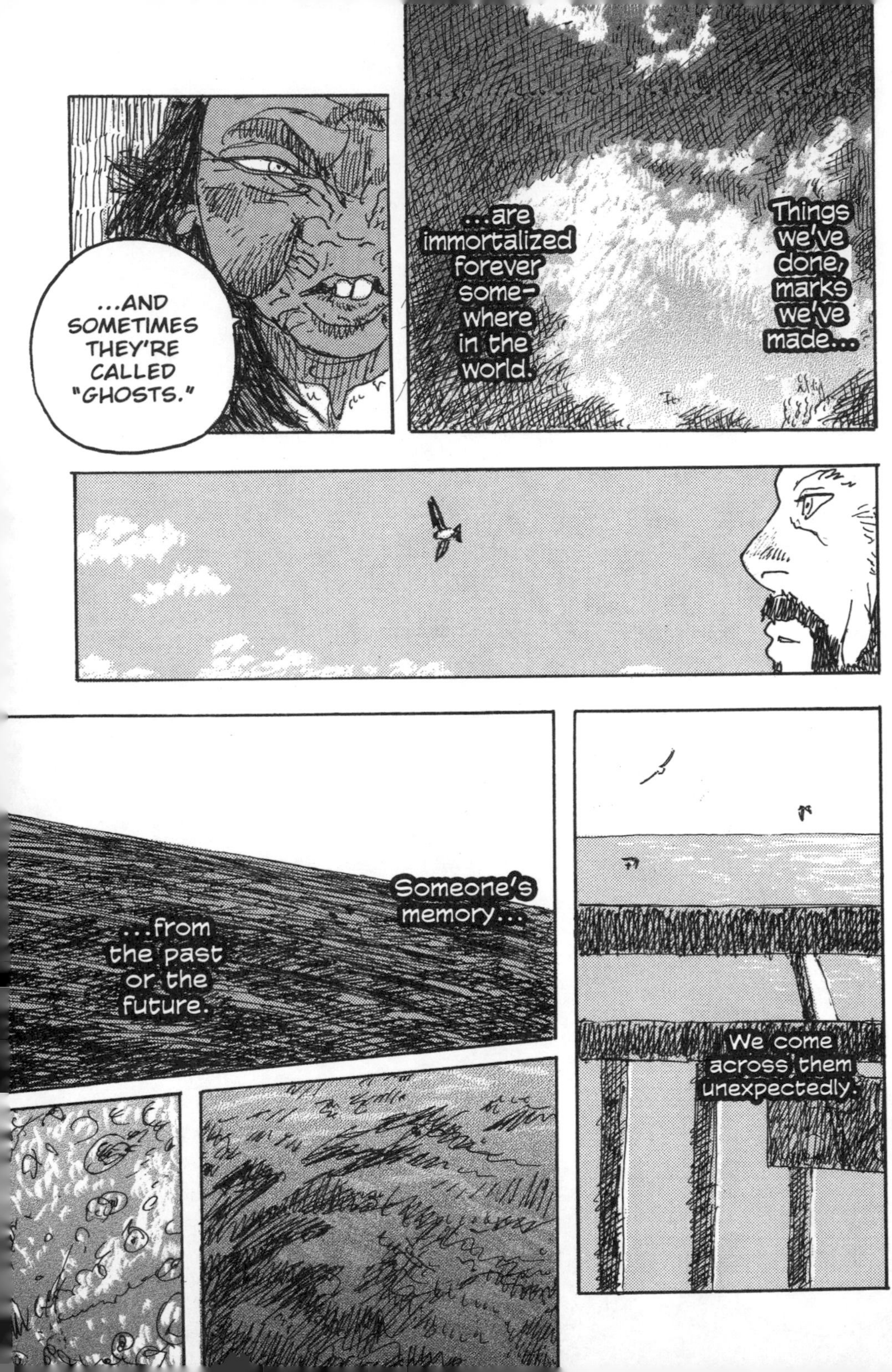
Things we've done, marks we've made...
...are immortalized forever some-where in the world.
...AND SOMETIMES THEY'RE CALLED "GHOSTS."
We come across them unexpectedly.
Someone's memory...
...from the past or the future.

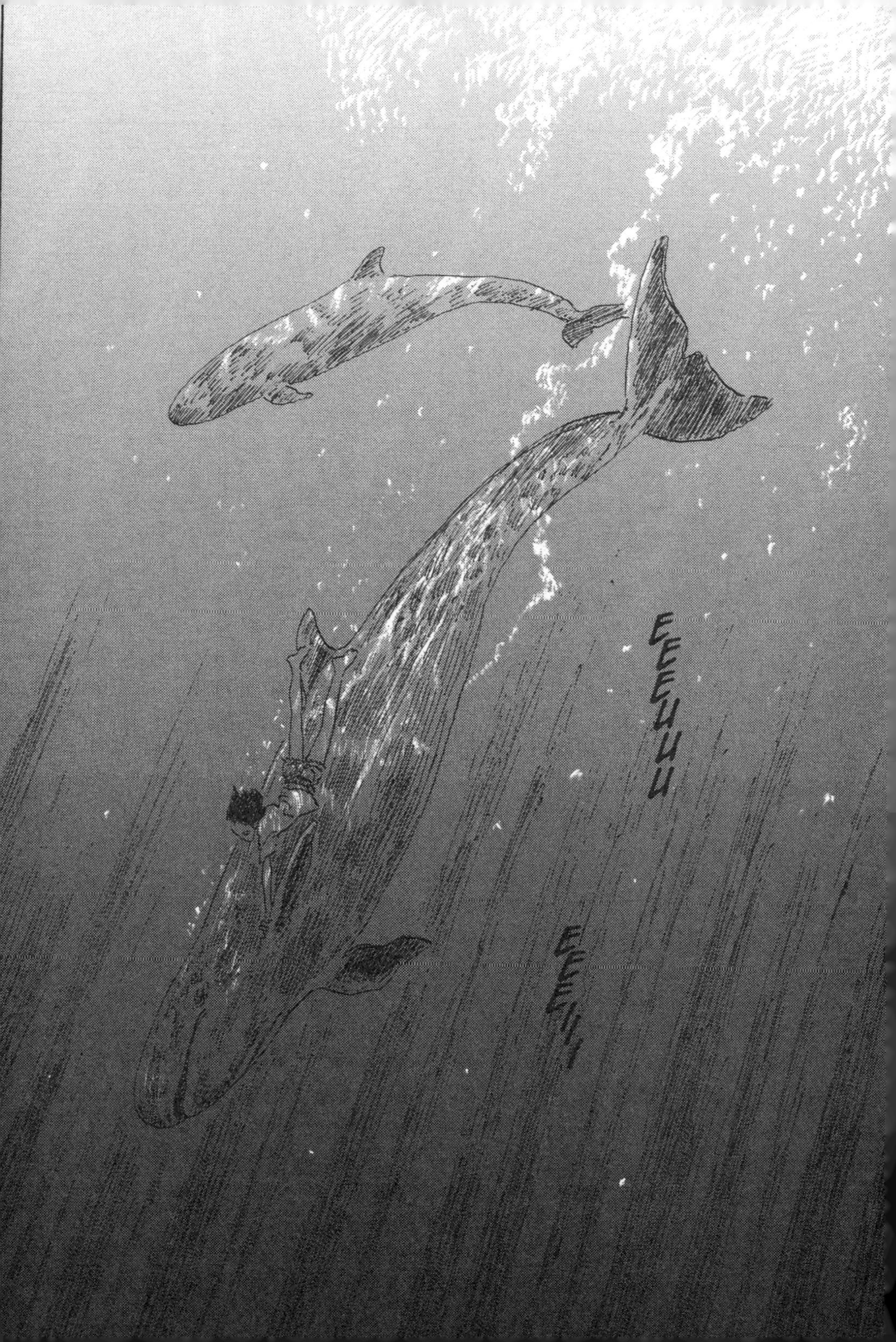
EEEUUU
EEEU

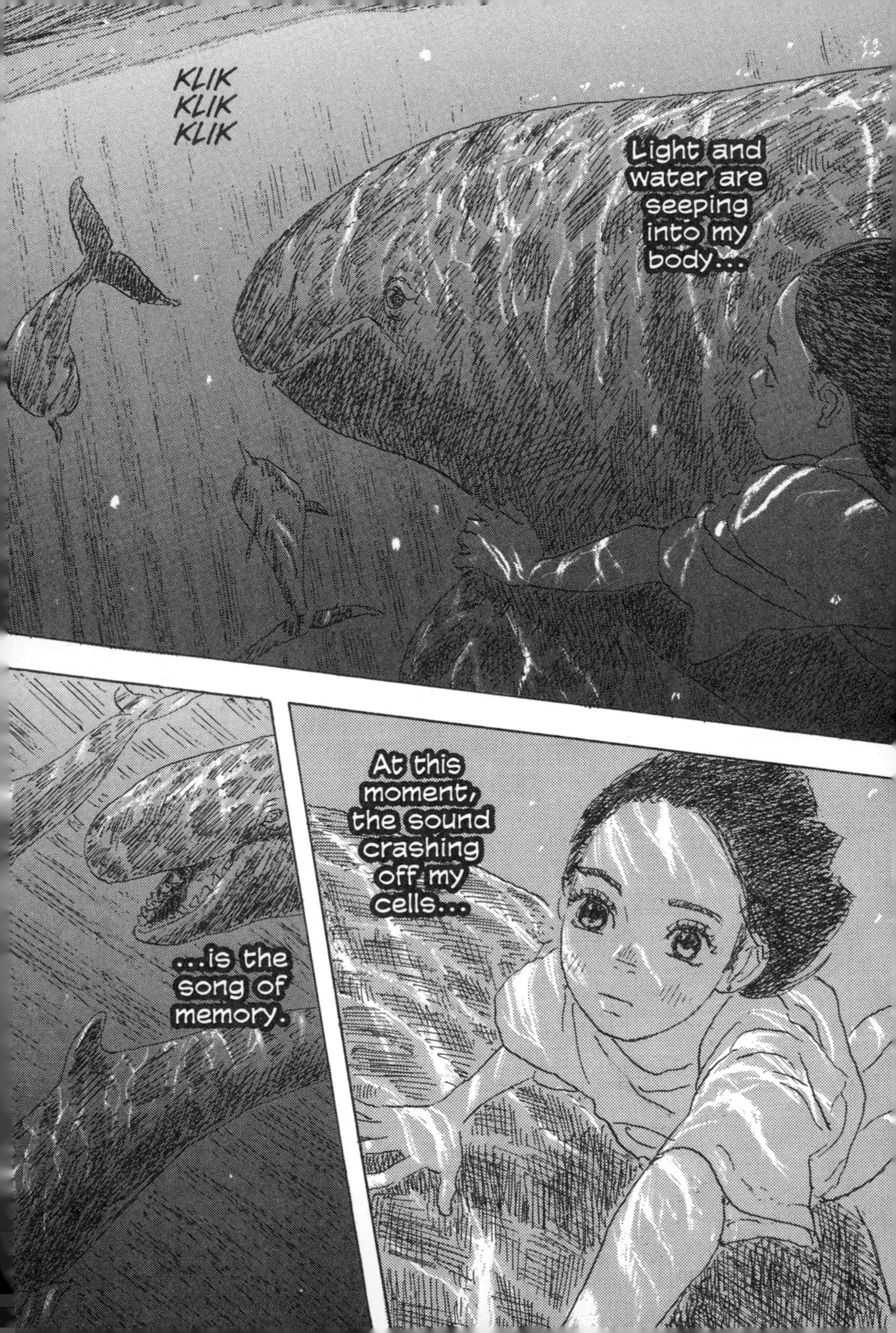
Light and water are seeping into my body...
KLIK KLIK KLIK
At this moment, the sound crashing off my cells...
...is the song of memory.

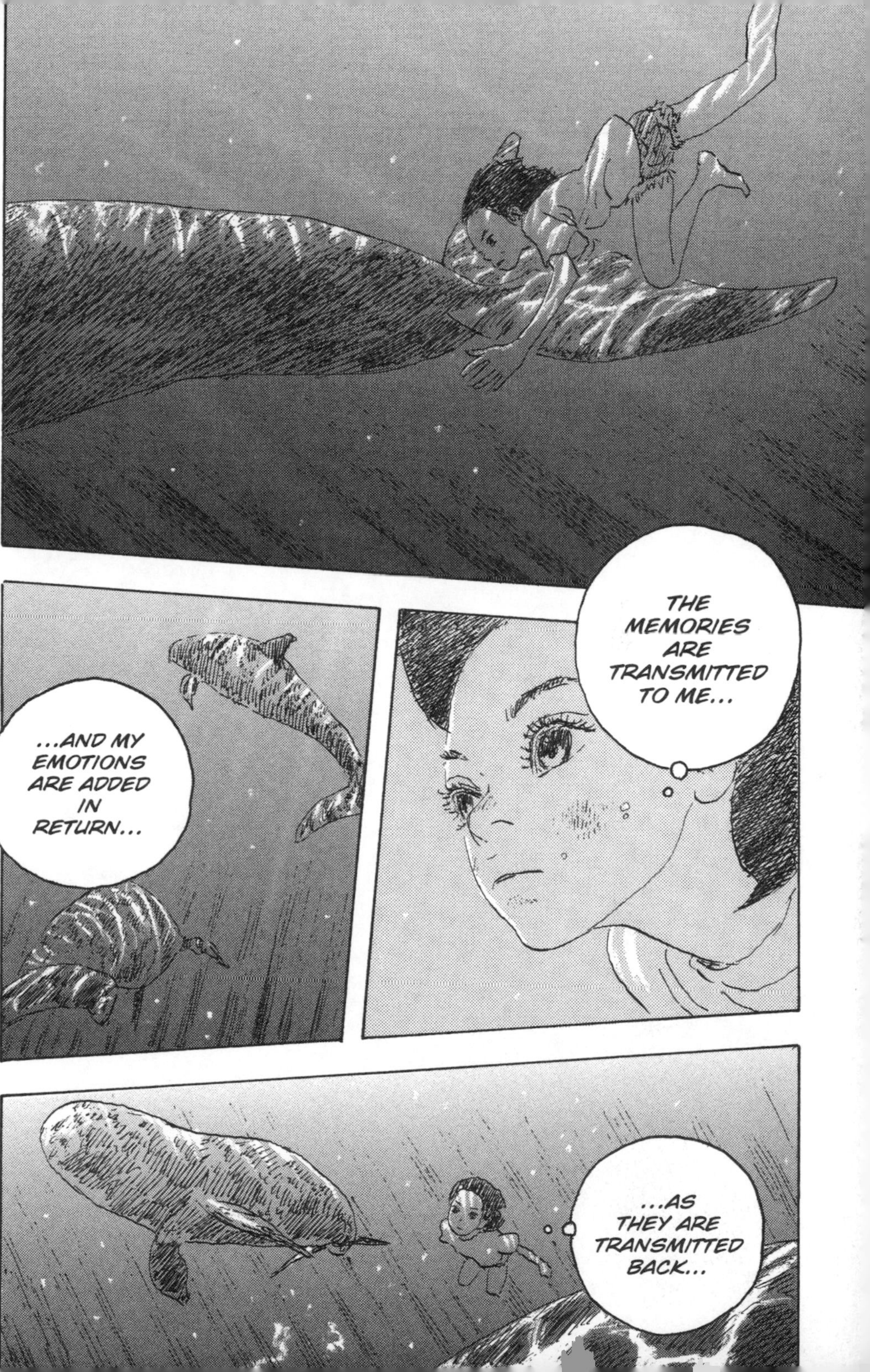
THE MEMORIES ARE TRANSMITTED TO ME...
...AND MY EMOTIONS ARE ADDED IN RETURN...
...AS THEY ARE TRANSMITTED BACK...

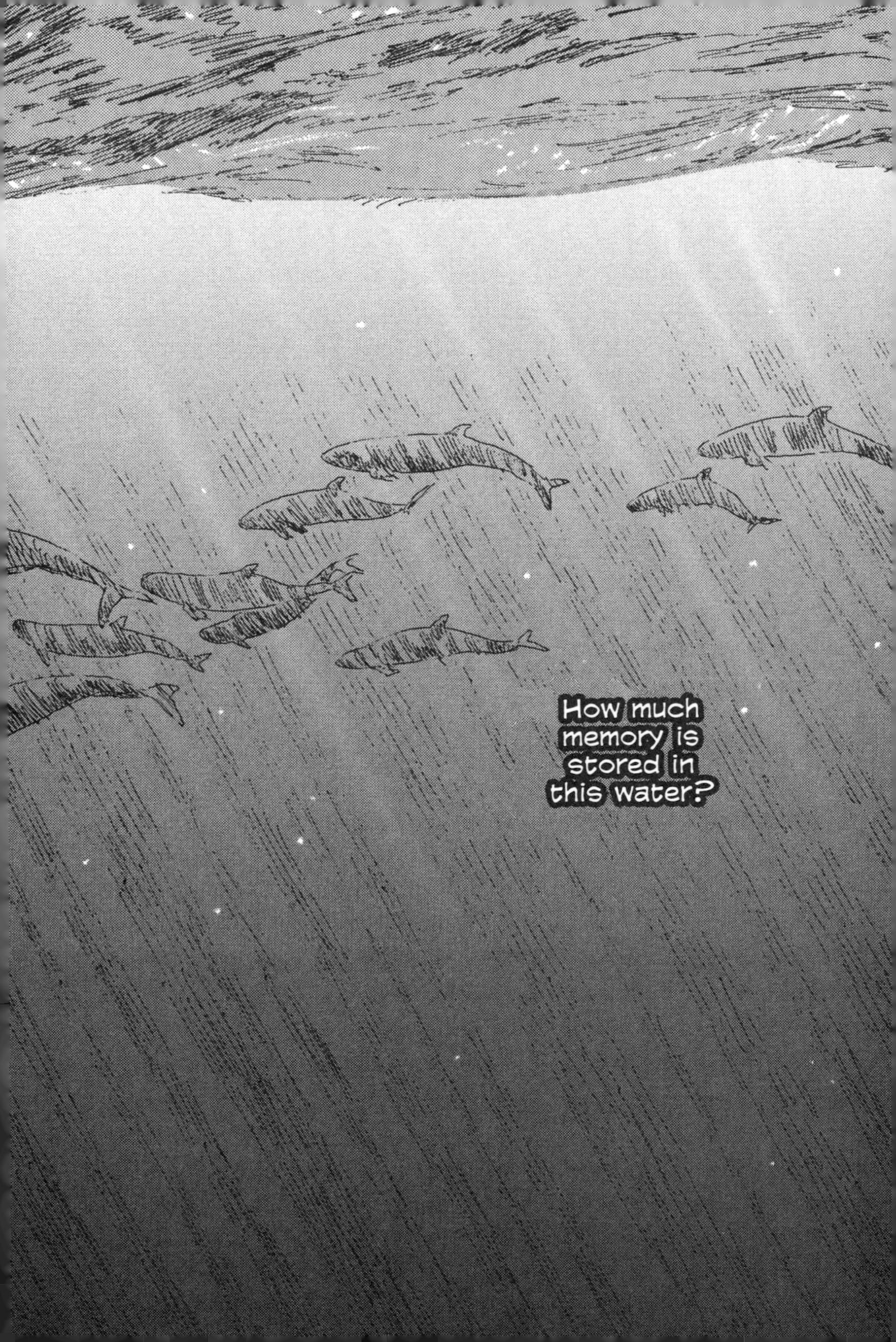
How much memory is stored in this water?

I JUST HAVE TO FOLLOW THIS MEMORY. RIGHT, SORA?
YES.
...
I FOUND YOU.
UMI...

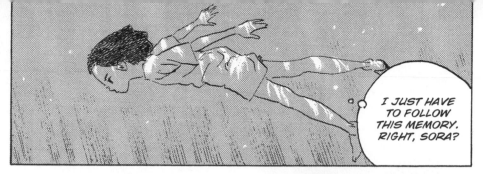

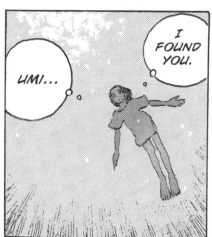

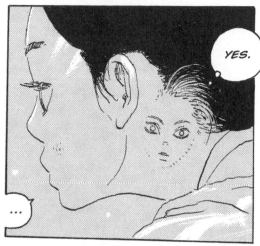

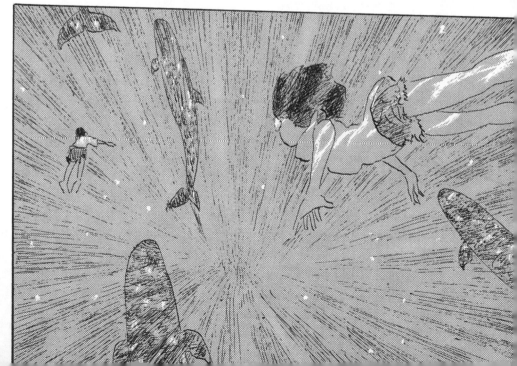

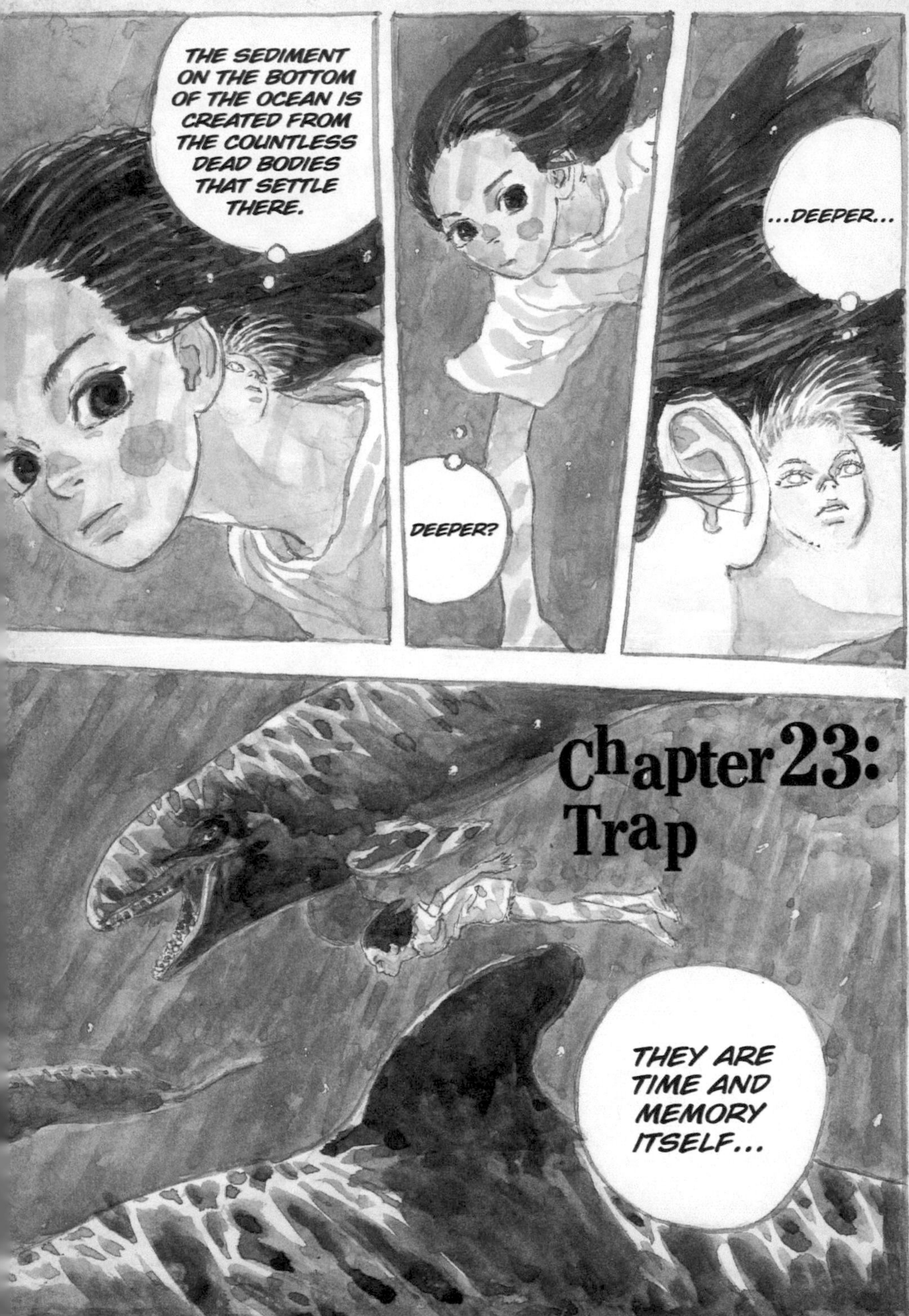
...DEEPER...
DEEPER?
THE SEDIMENT ON THE BOTTOM OF THE OCEAN IS CREATED FROM THE COUNTLESS DEAD BODIES THAT SETTLE THERE.
Chapter 23: Trap
THEY ARE TIME AND MEMORY ITSELF...

Chapter 23: Trap

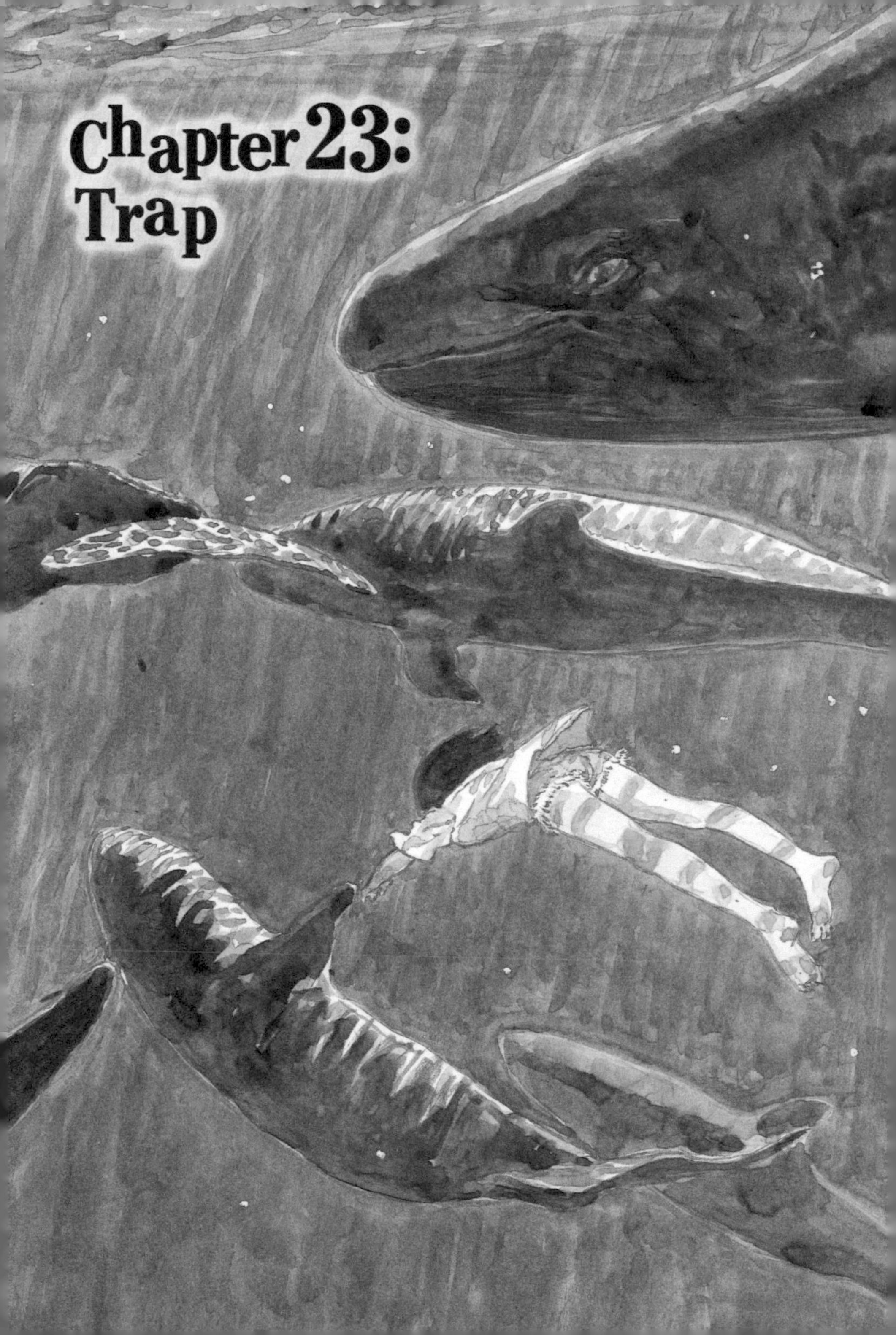

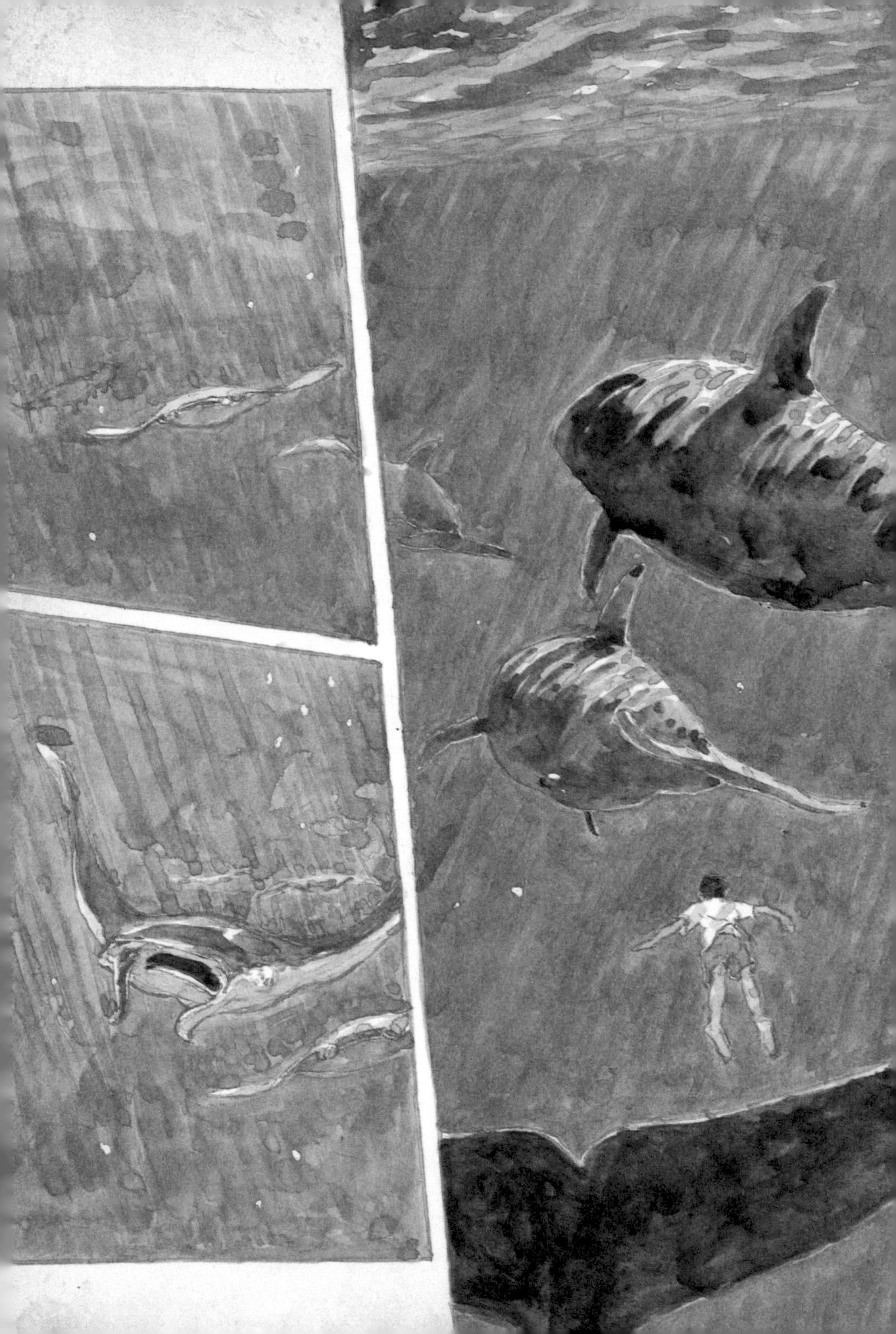

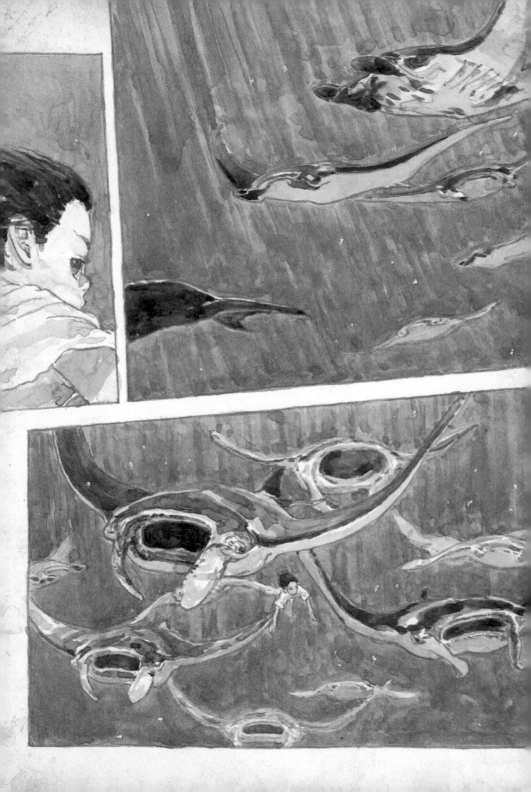

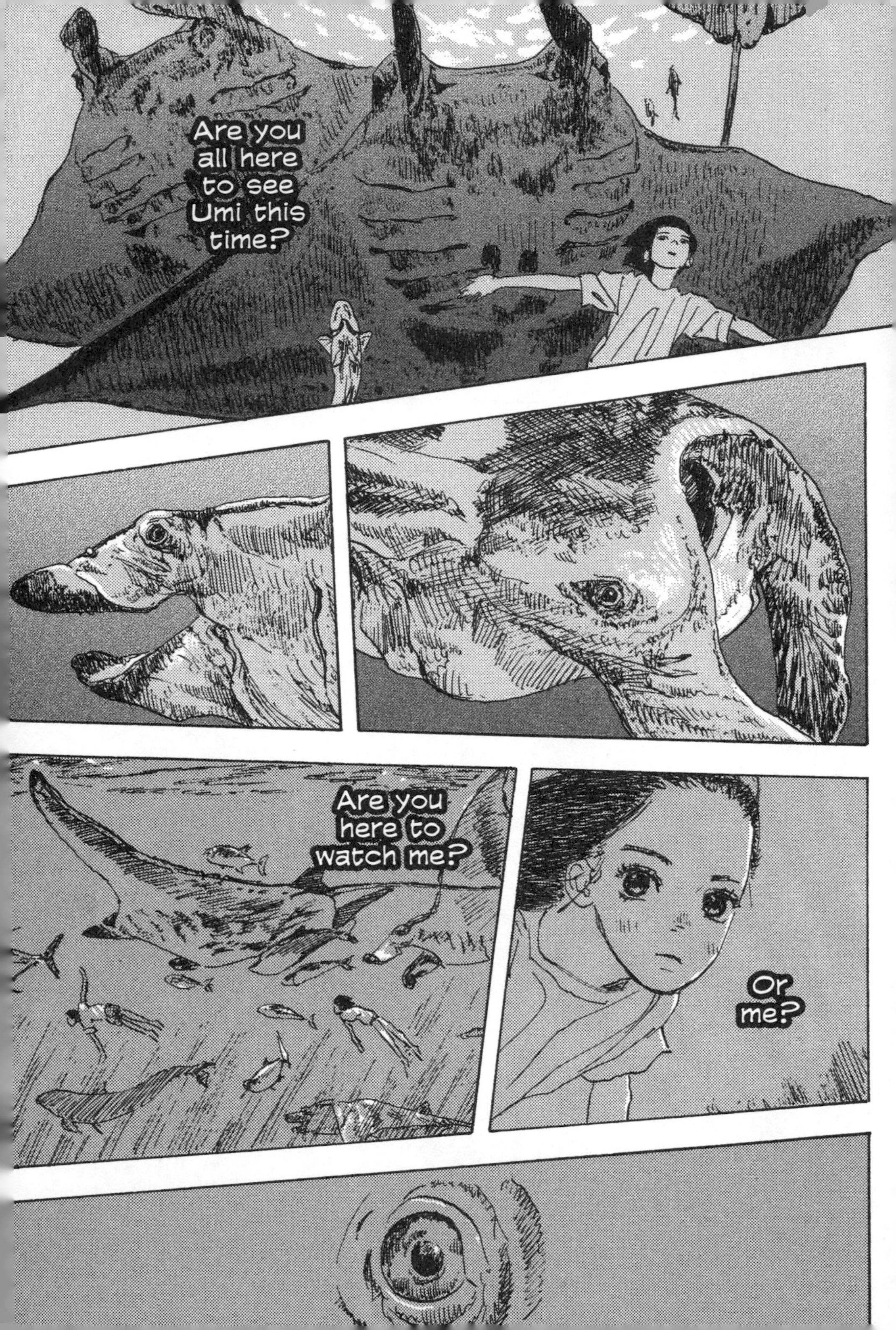
Are you all here to see Umi this time?
Or me?
Are you here to watch me?

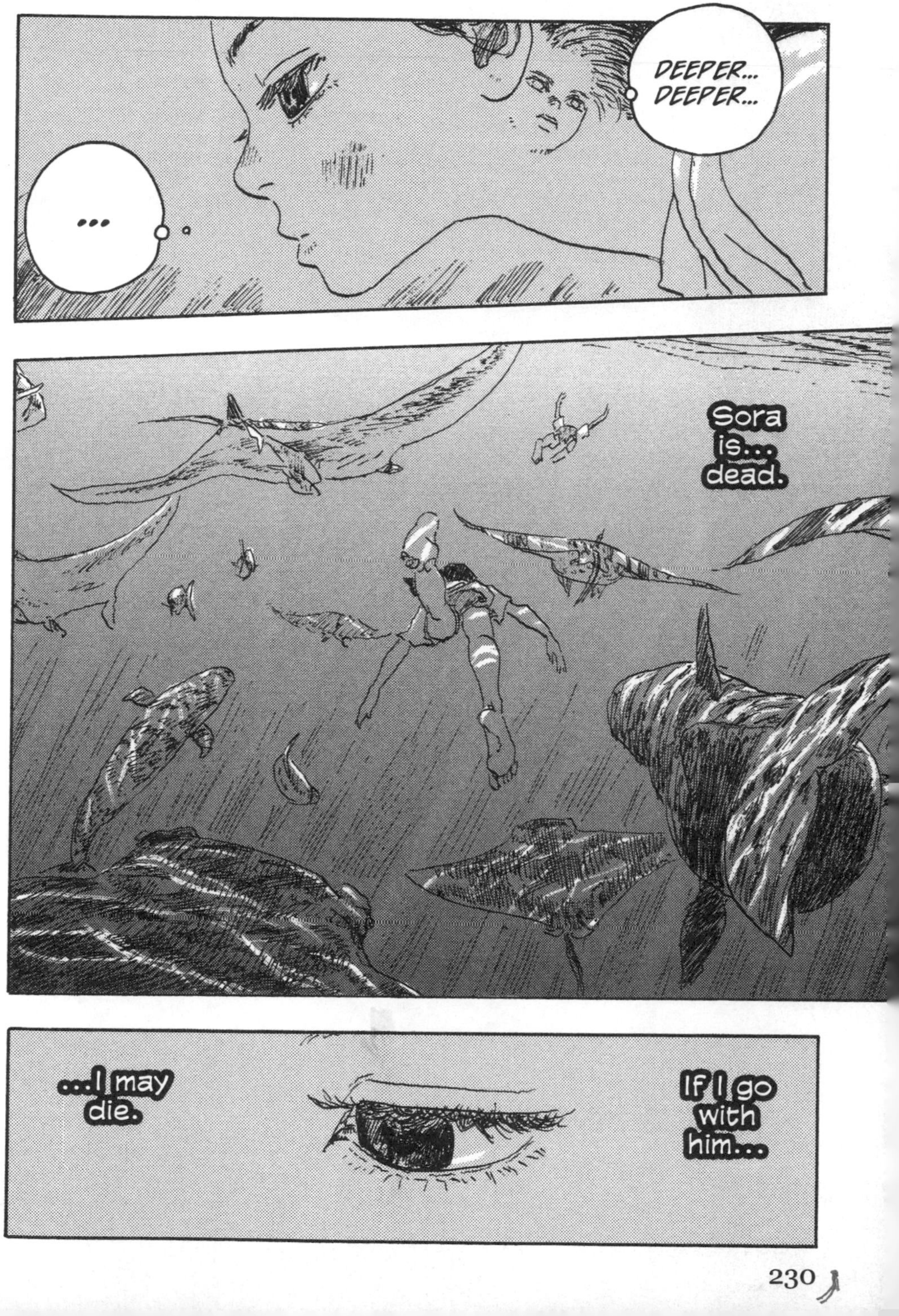
DEEPER... DEEPER...
...
Sora is... dead.
If I go with him...
...I may die.

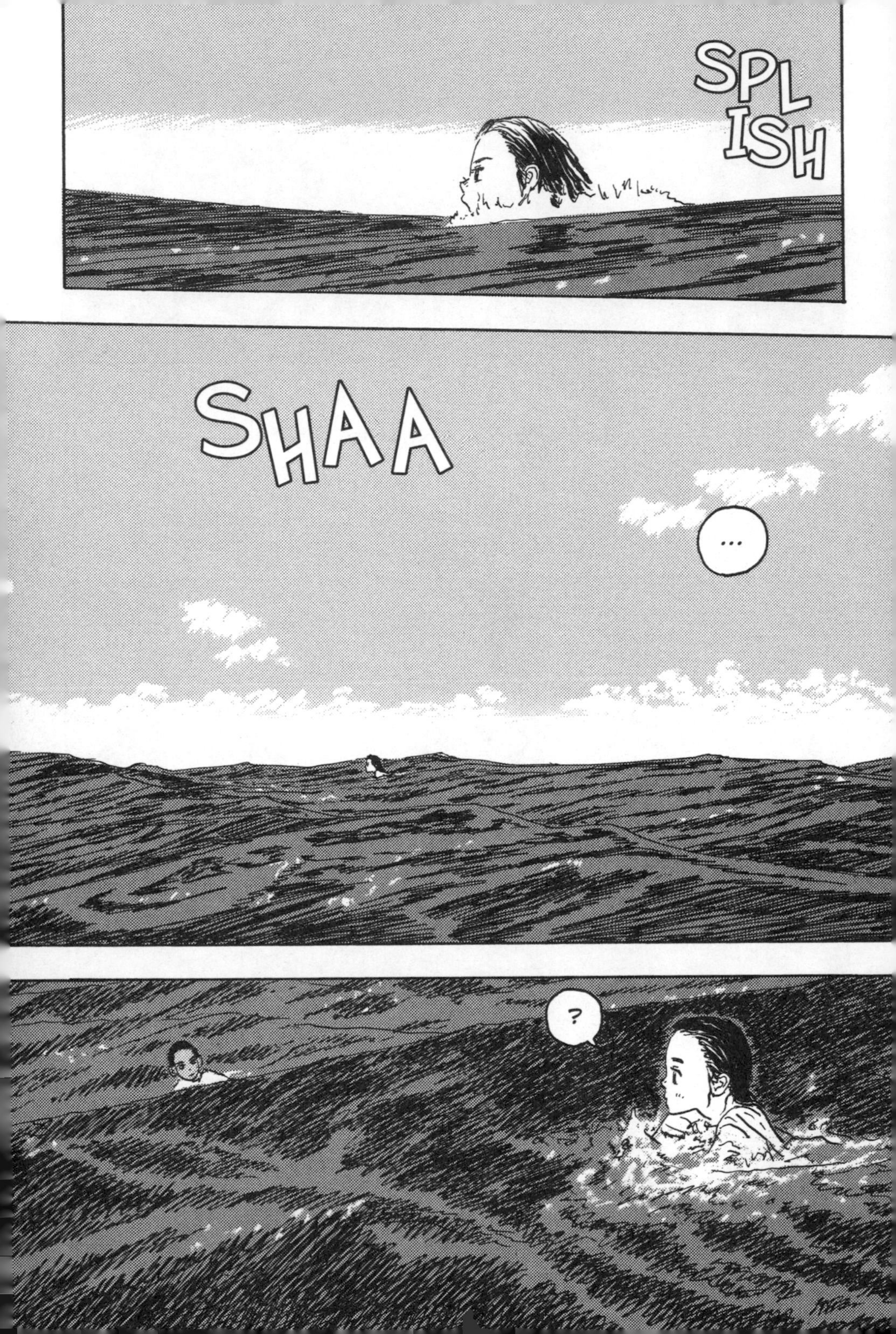
SPLISH
SHAA
...
?

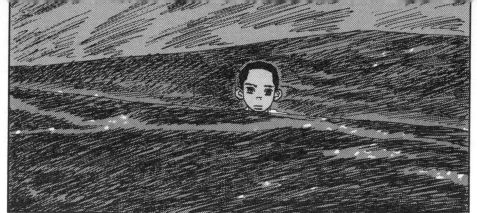

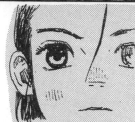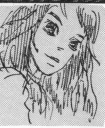

You should be careful about Umi...

...

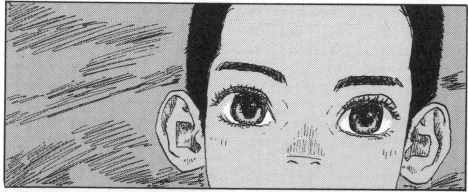

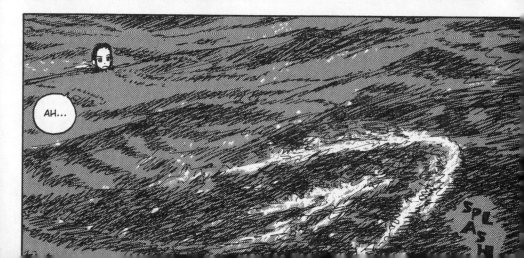

AH...

SPLASH

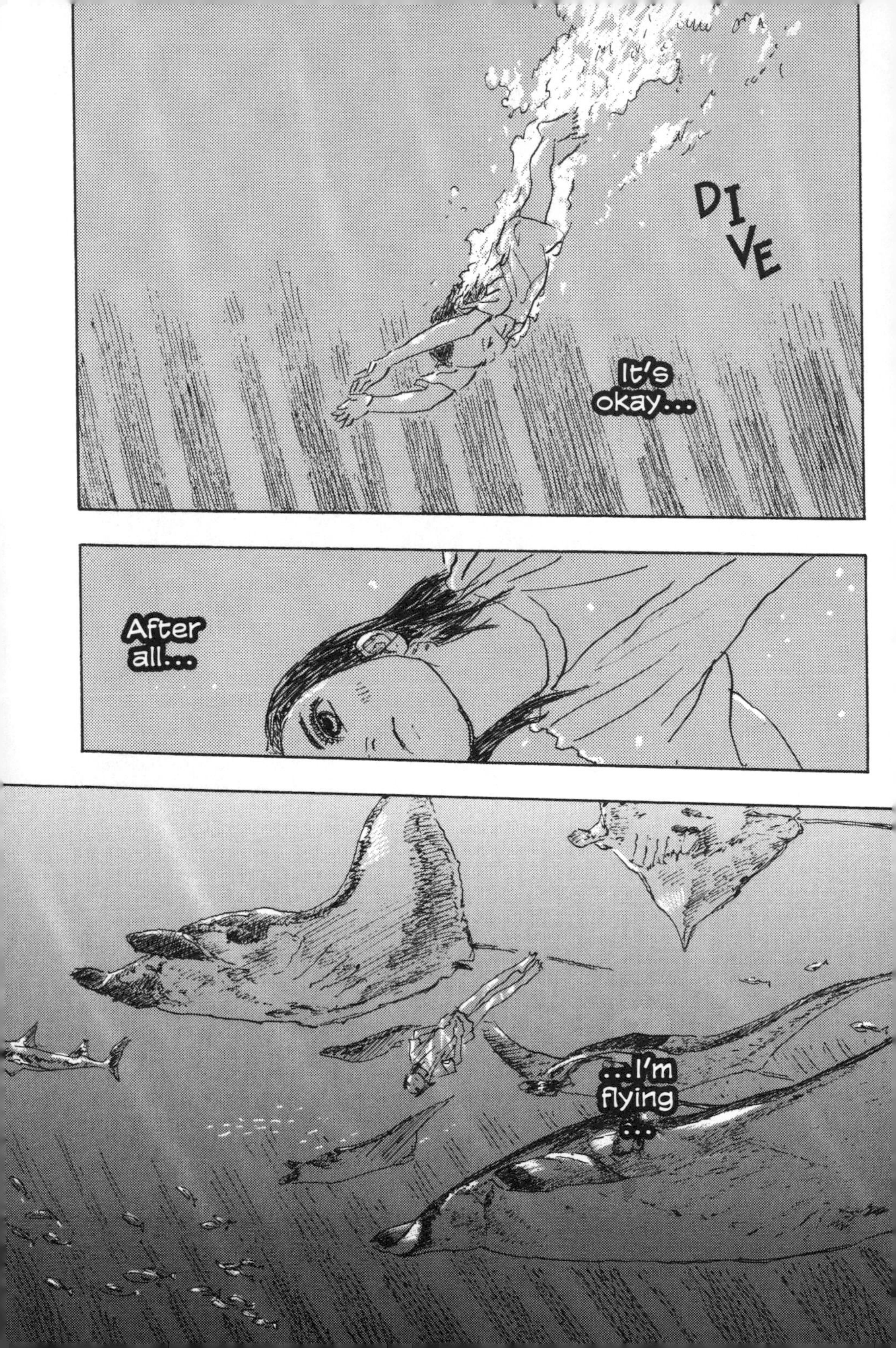
DIVE
It's okay...
After all...
...I'm flying...

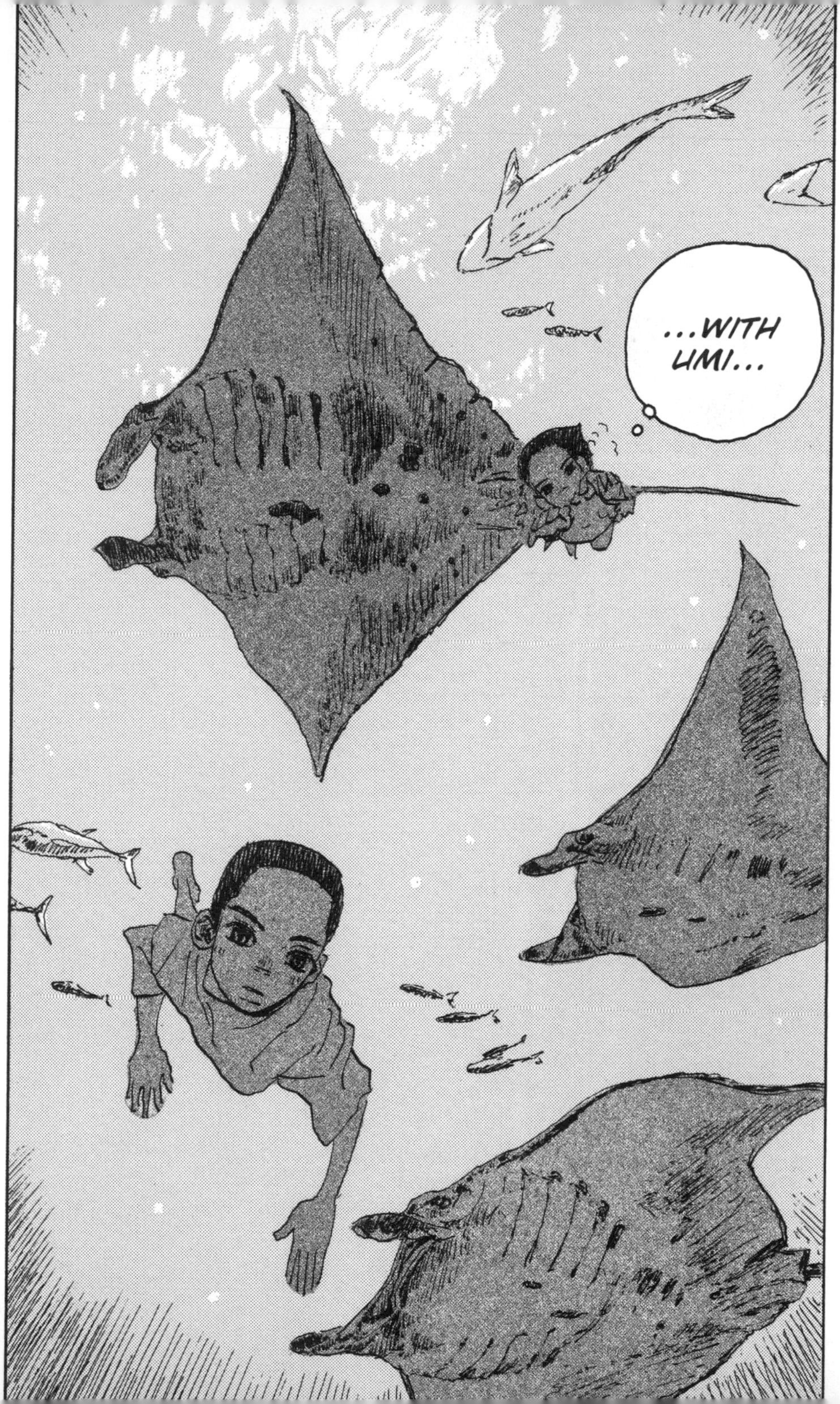
...WITH UMI...

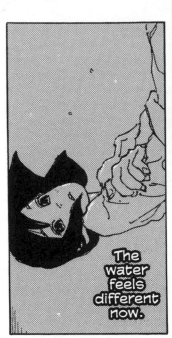

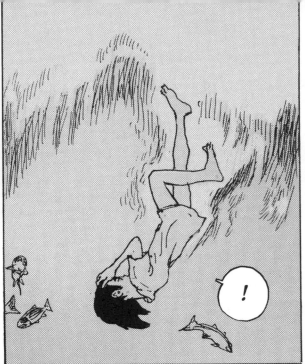

The water feels different now.

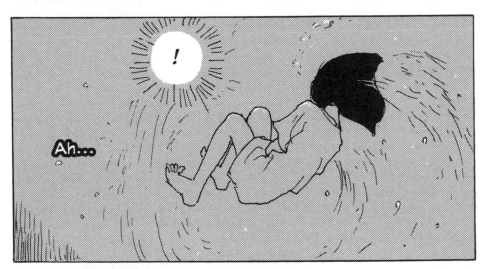

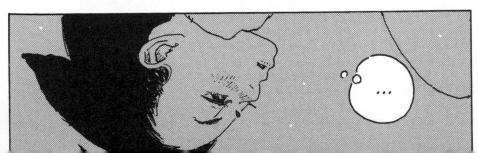

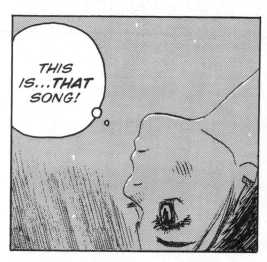

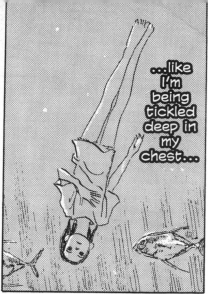

...like I'm being tickled deep in my chest...
THIS IS...THAT SONG!
The humpback whales' song...
From far away...
I'm in the layer of water where the whale songs are transmitted.
THE SONG THAT TIME...
THE SONG I HEARD THE FIRST TIME I MET SORA.

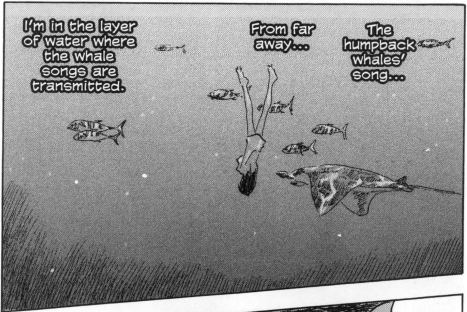

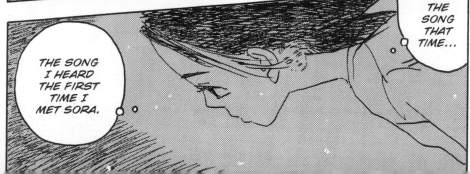

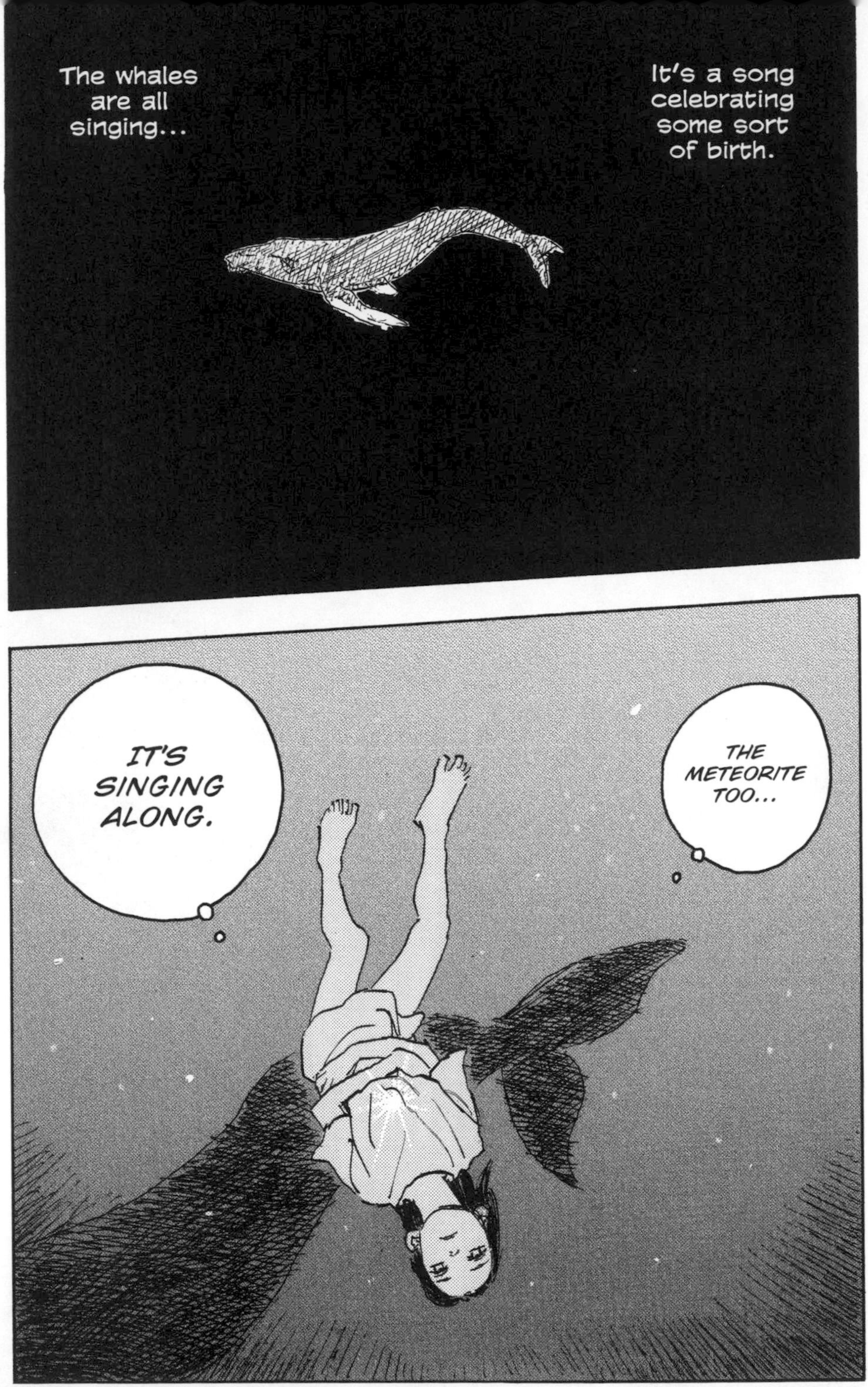
It's a song celebrating some sort of birth.
The whales are all singing...
THE METEORITE TOO...
IT'S SINGING ALONG.

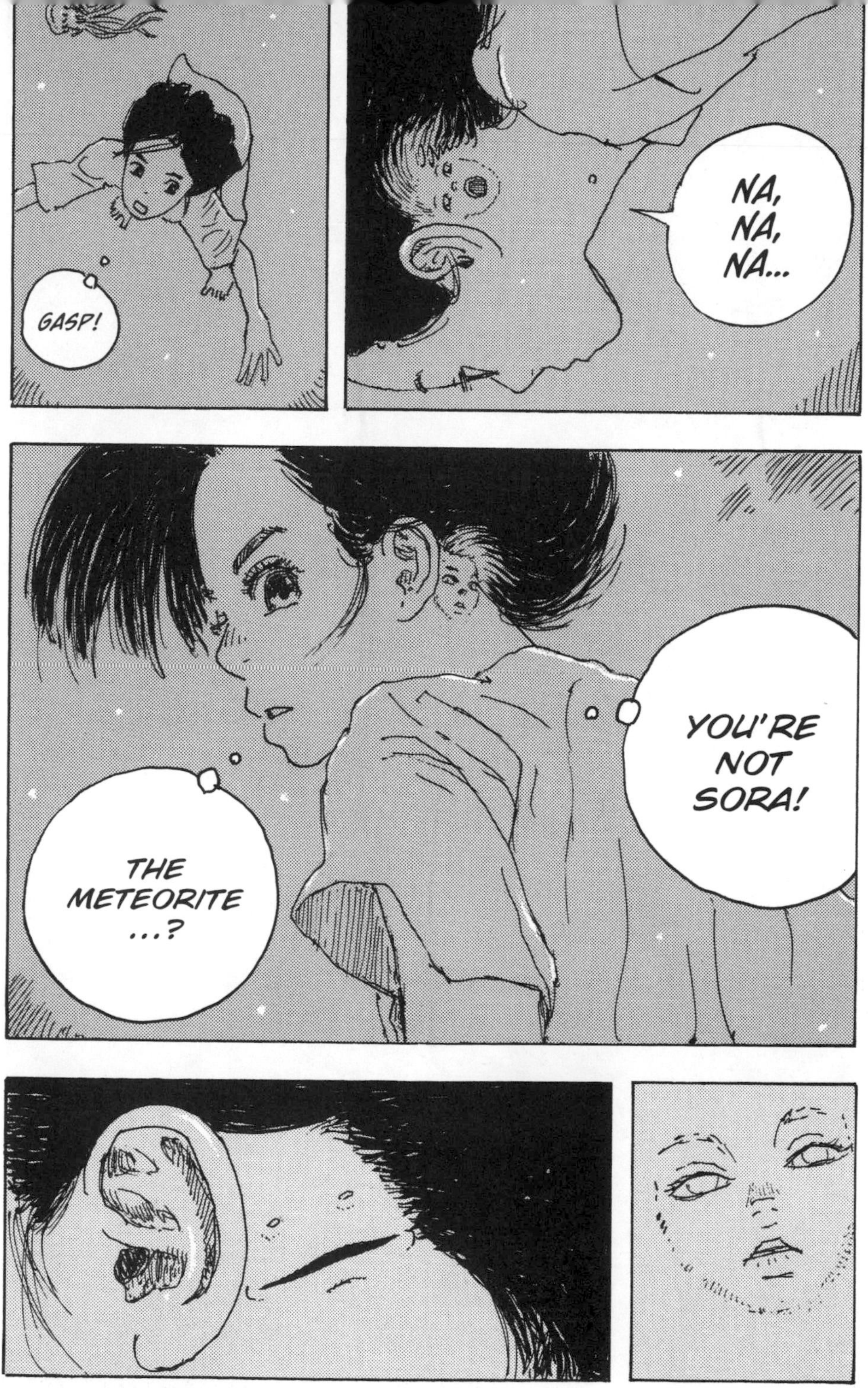
NA, NA, NA...
GASP!
YOU'RE NOT SORA!
THE METEORITE ...?

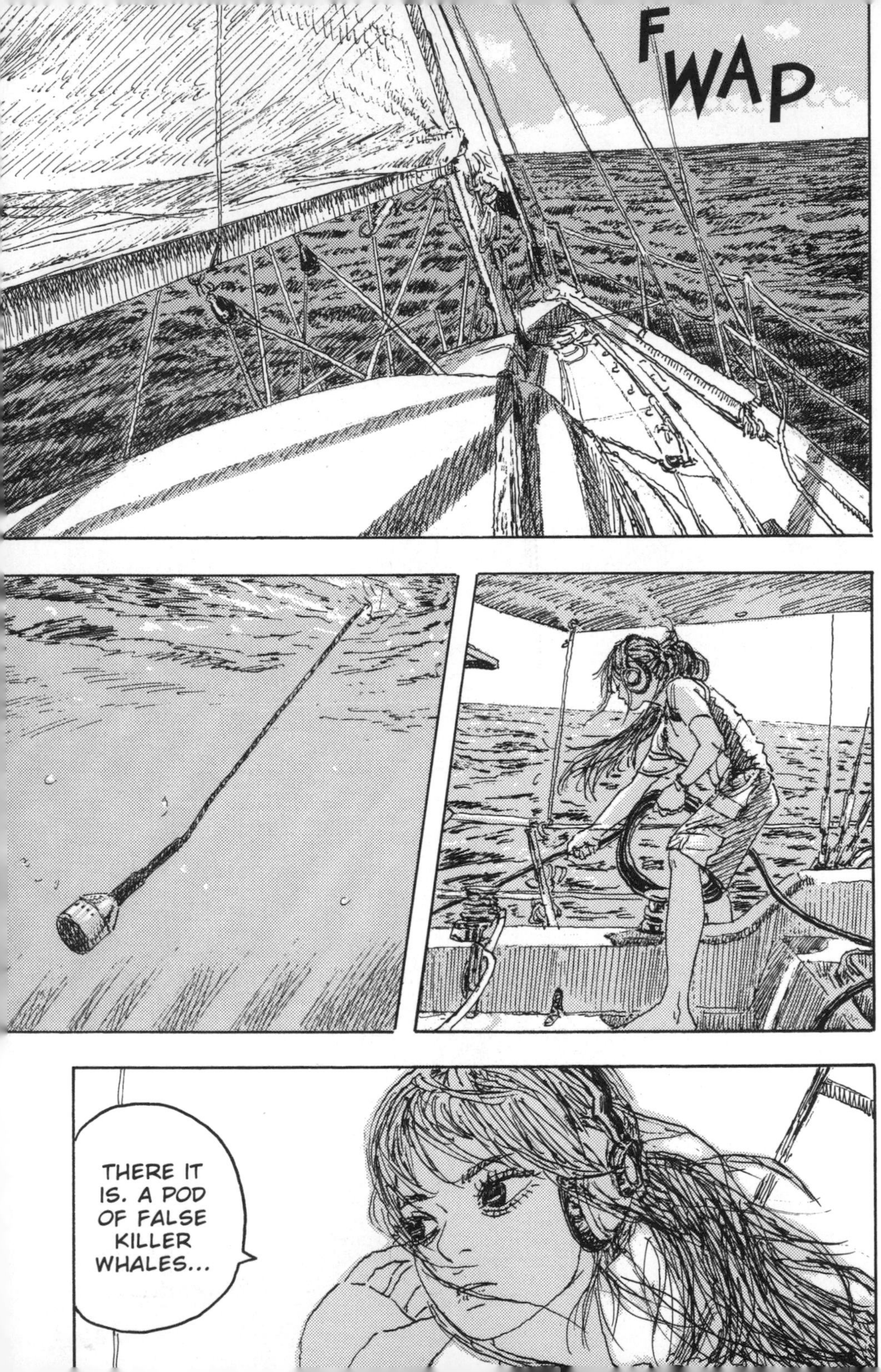
FWAP
THERE IT IS. A POD OF FALSE KILLER WHALES...

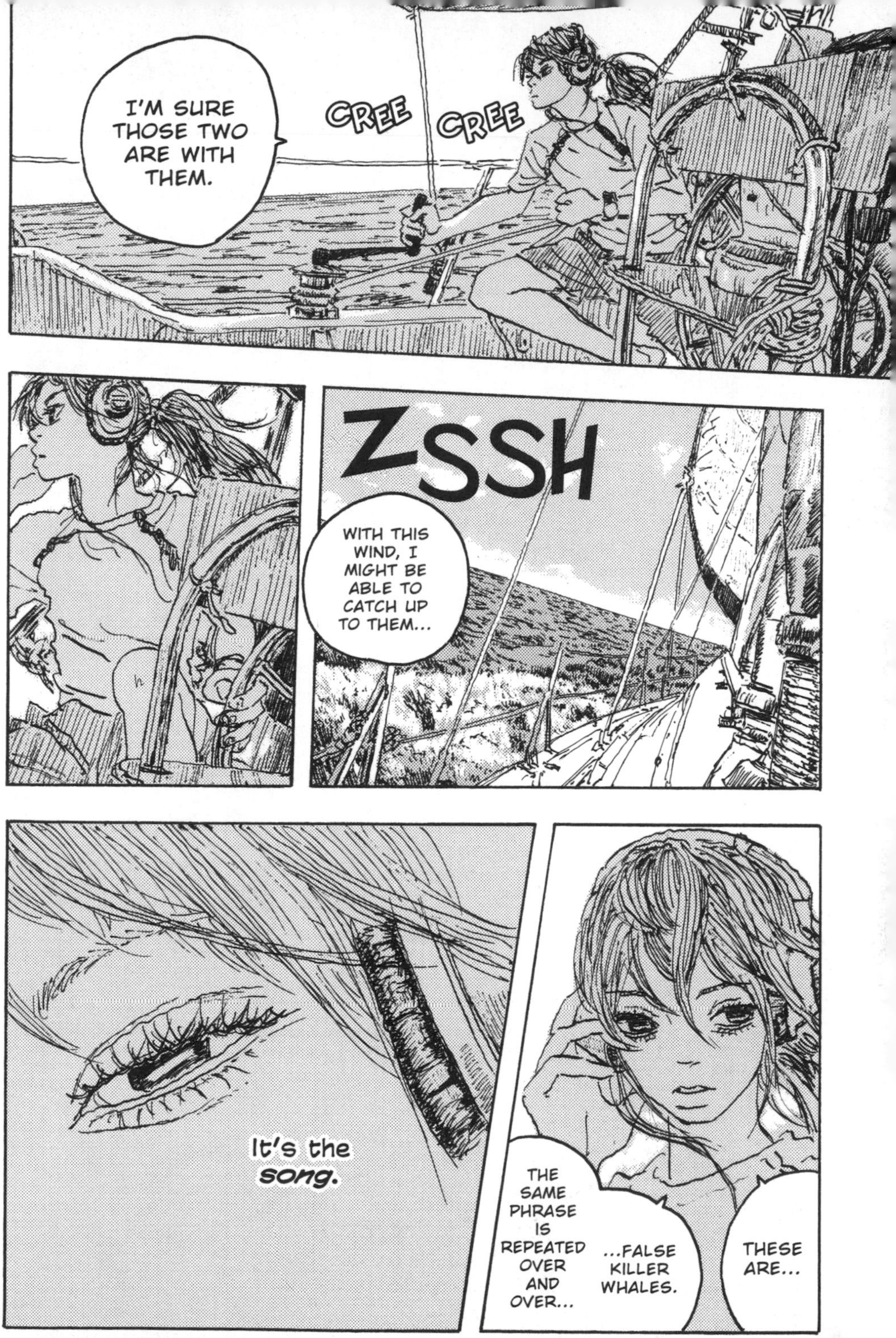

CREE
CREE
I'M SURE THOSE TWO ARE WITH THEM.
ZSSH
WITH THIS WIND, I MIGHT BE ABLE TO CATCH UP TO THEM...
THESE ARE...
...FALSE KILLER WHALES.
THE SAME PHRASE IS REPEATED OVER AND OVER...
It's the *song*.

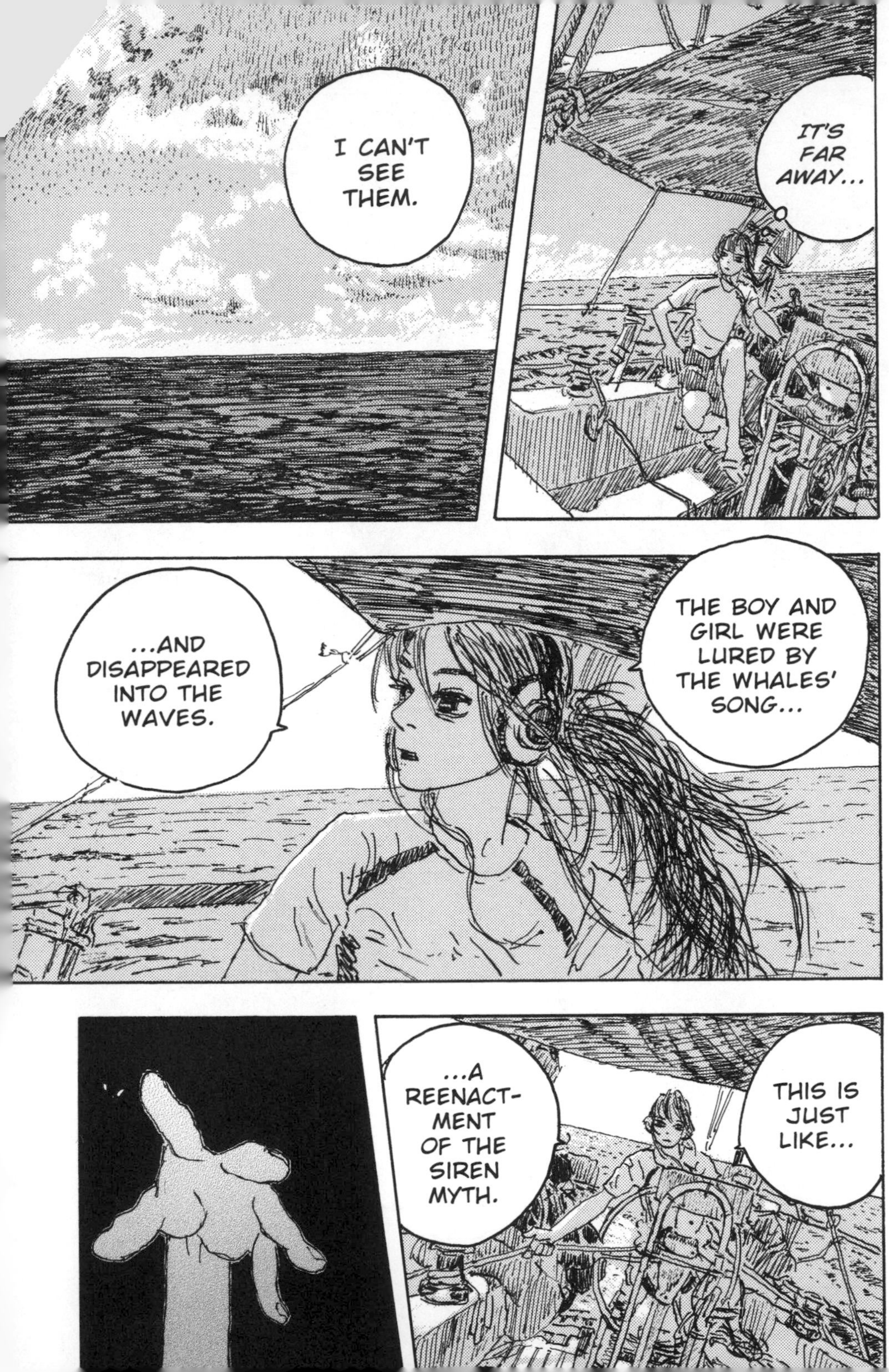
IT'S FAR AWAY...
I CAN'T SEE THEM.
THE BOY AND GIRL WERE LURED BY THE WHALES' SONG...
...AND DISAPPEARED INTO THE WAVES.
THIS IS JUST LIKE...
...A REENACTMENT OF THE SIREN MYTH.

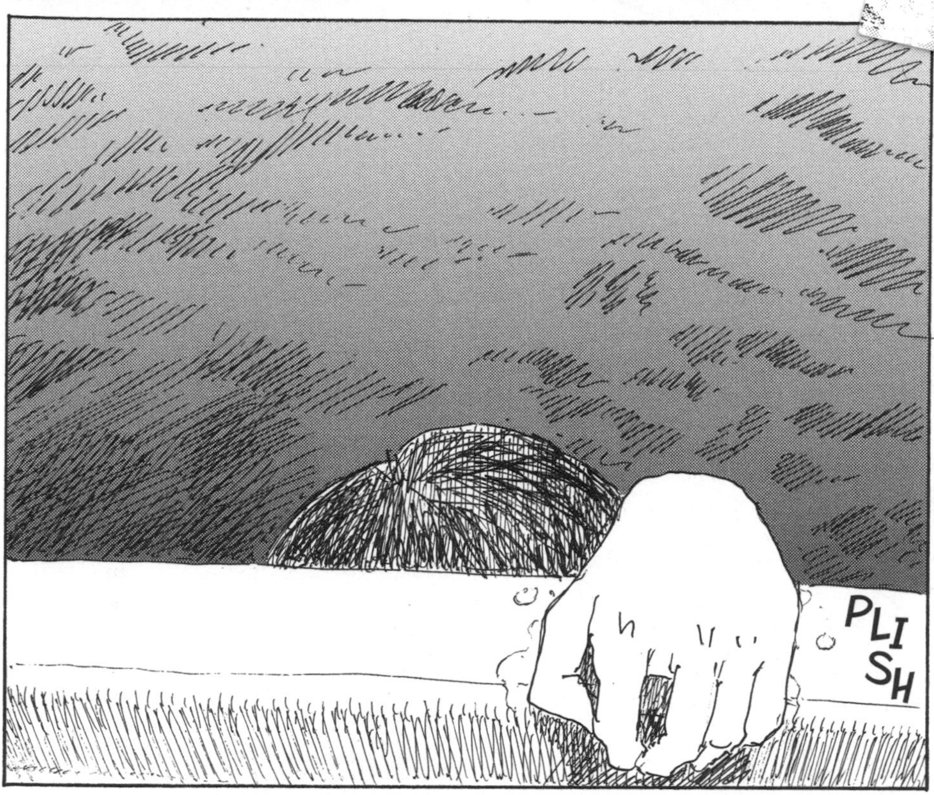
PLISH
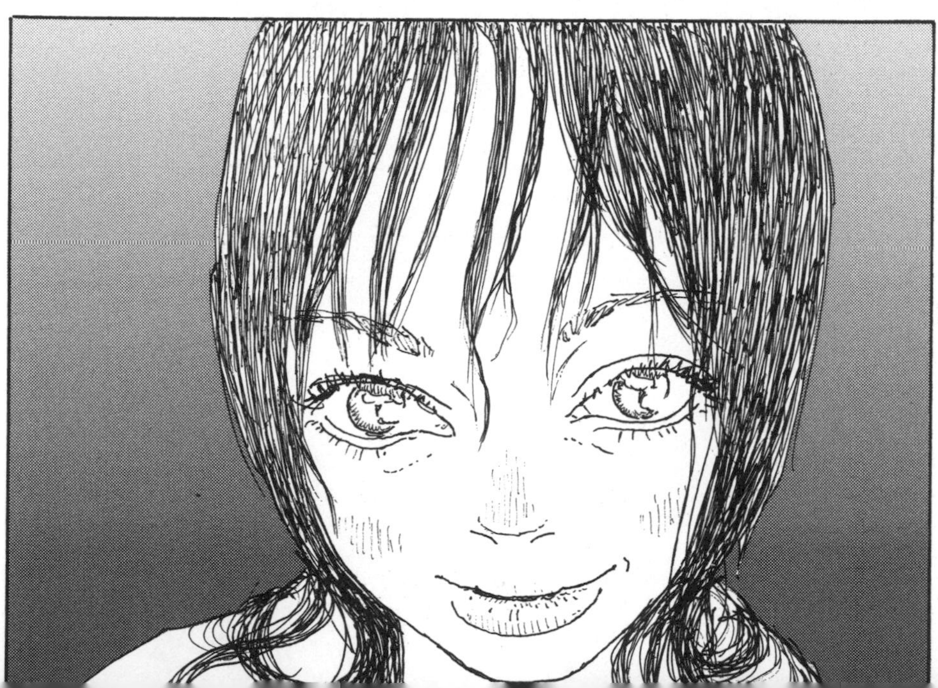

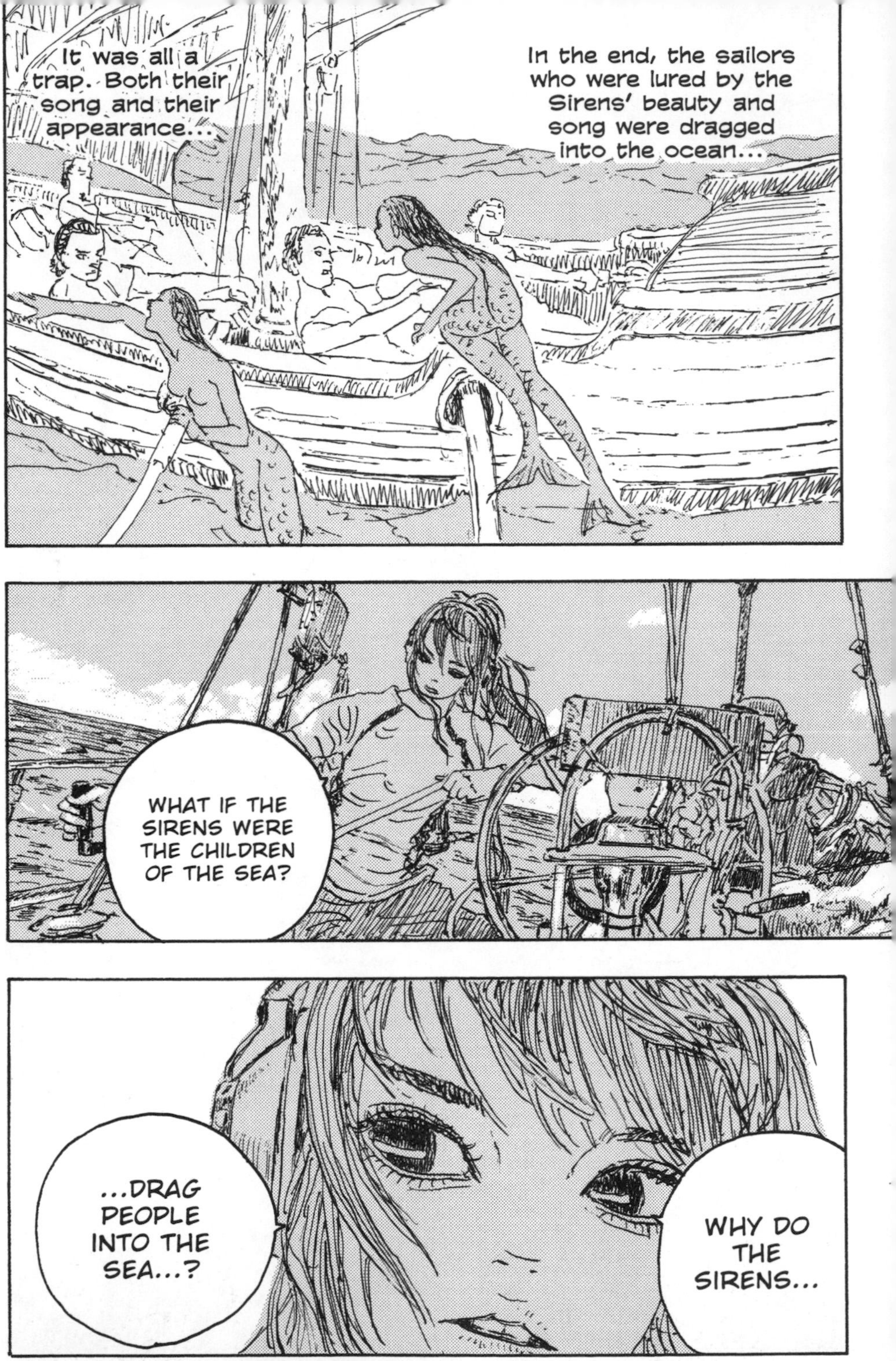
In the end, the sailors who were lured by the Sirens' beauty and song were dragged into the ocean...
It was all a trap. Both their song and their appearance...
WHAT IF THE SIRENS WERE THE CHILDREN OF THE SEA?
WHY DO THE SIRENS...
...DRAG PEOPLE INTO THE SEA...?

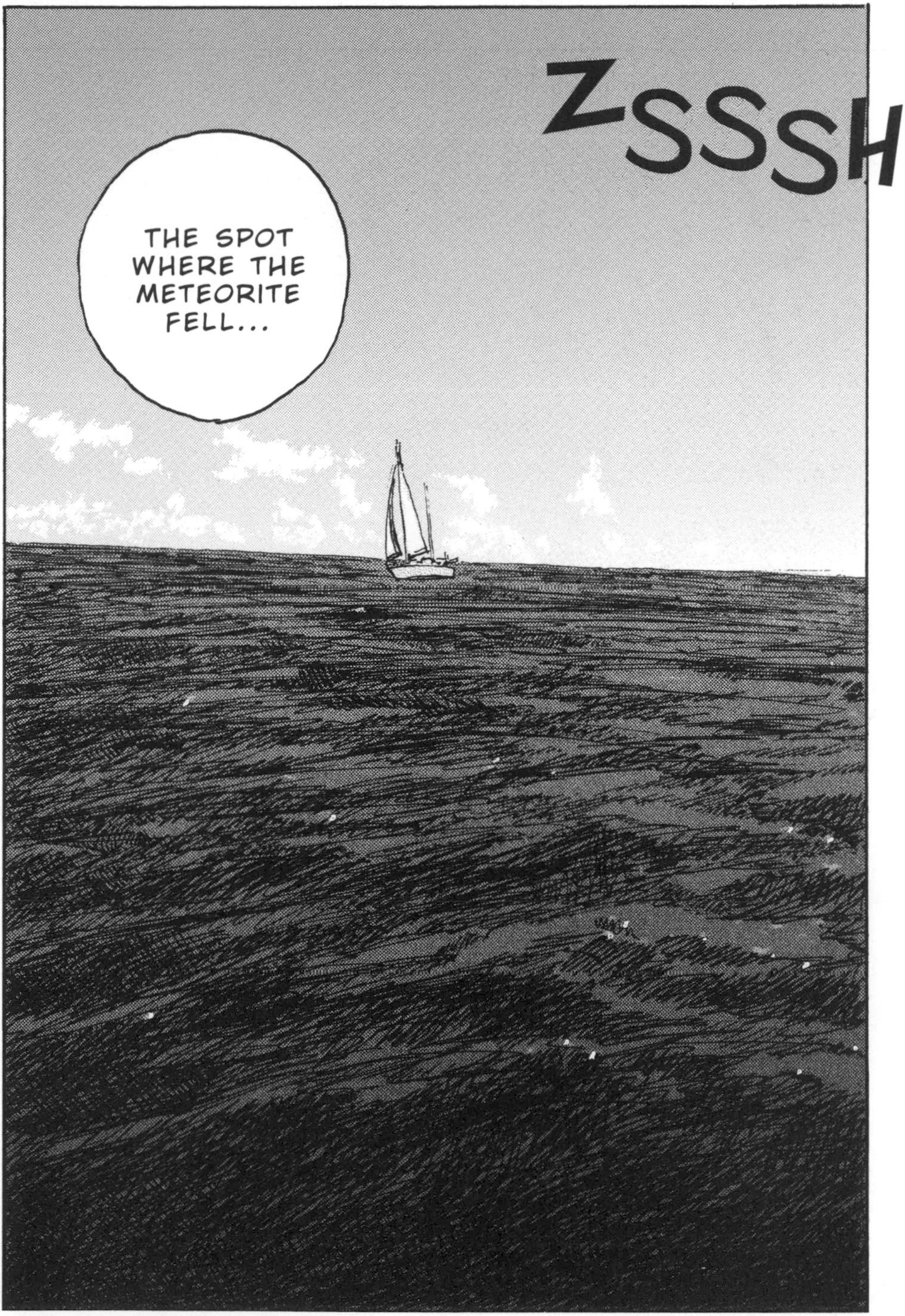
ZSSSH
THE SPOT WHERE THE METEORITE FELL...

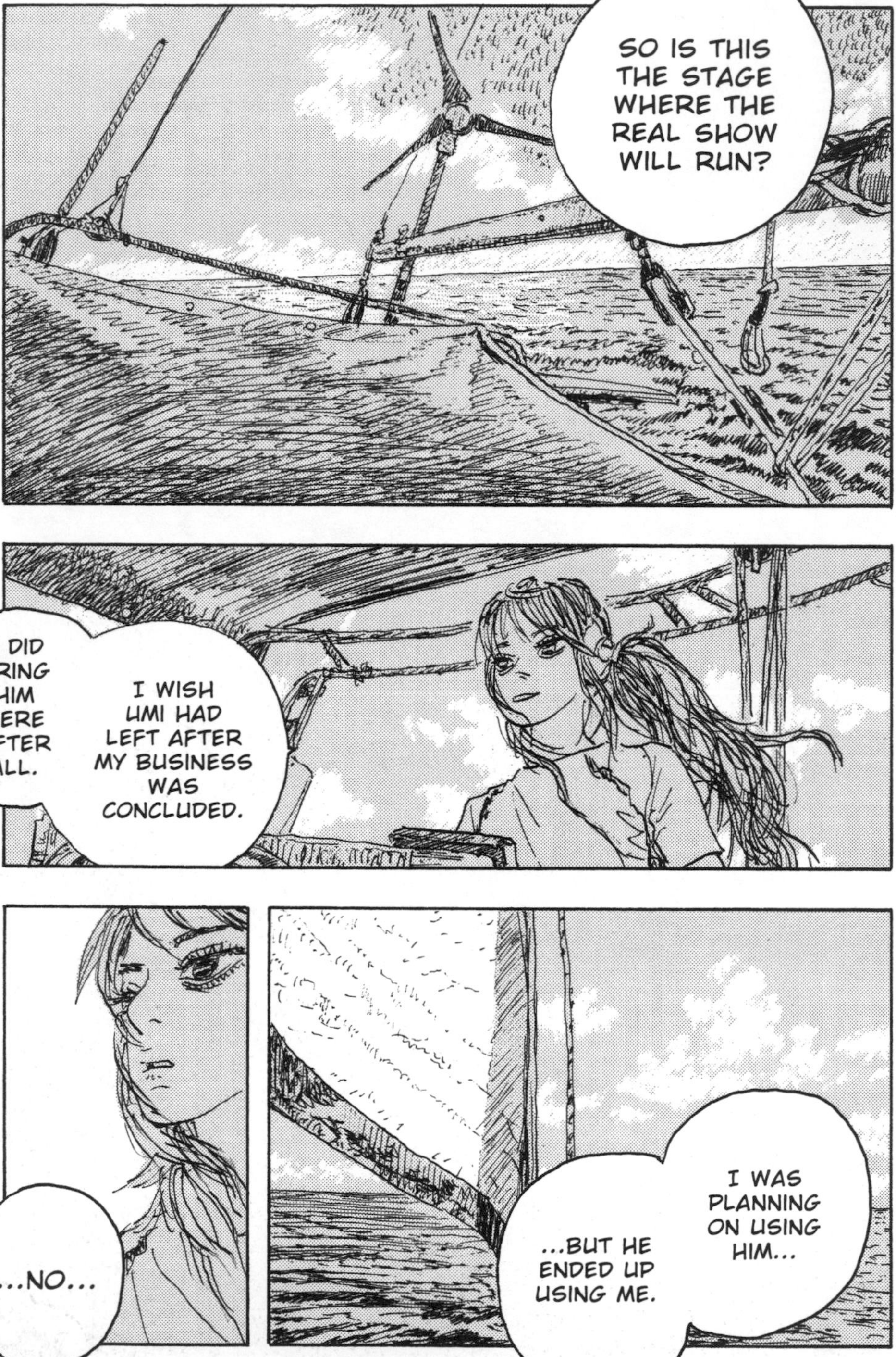
SO IS THIS THE STAGE WHERE THE REAL SHOW WILL RUN?
I WISH UMI HAD LEFT AFTER MY BUSINESS WAS CONCLUDED.
I DID BRING HIM HERE AFTER ALL.
I WAS PLANNING ON USING HIM...
...BUT HE ENDED UP USING ME.
...NO...

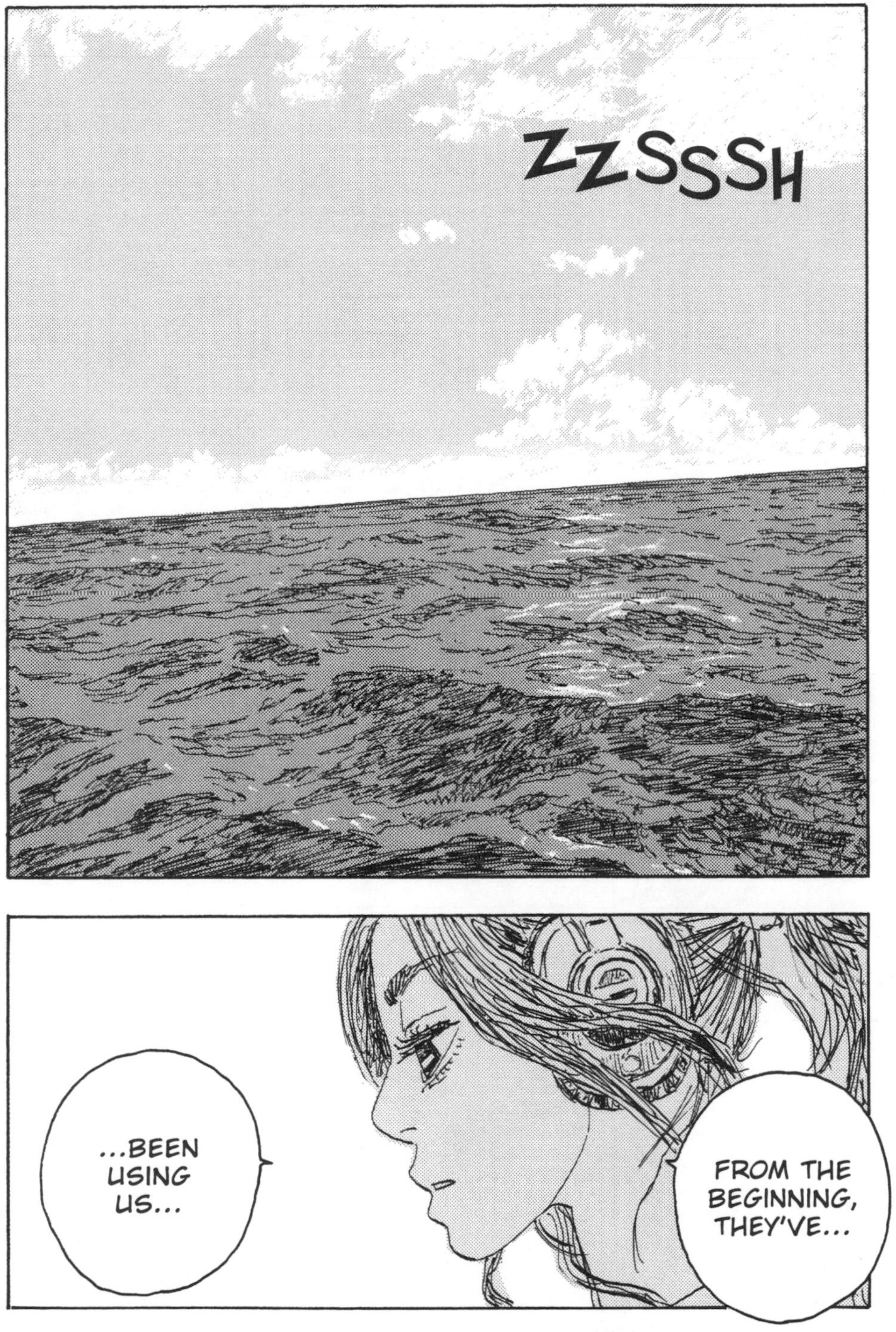
ZZSSSSH
FROM THE BEGINNING, THEY'VE...
...BEEN USING US...

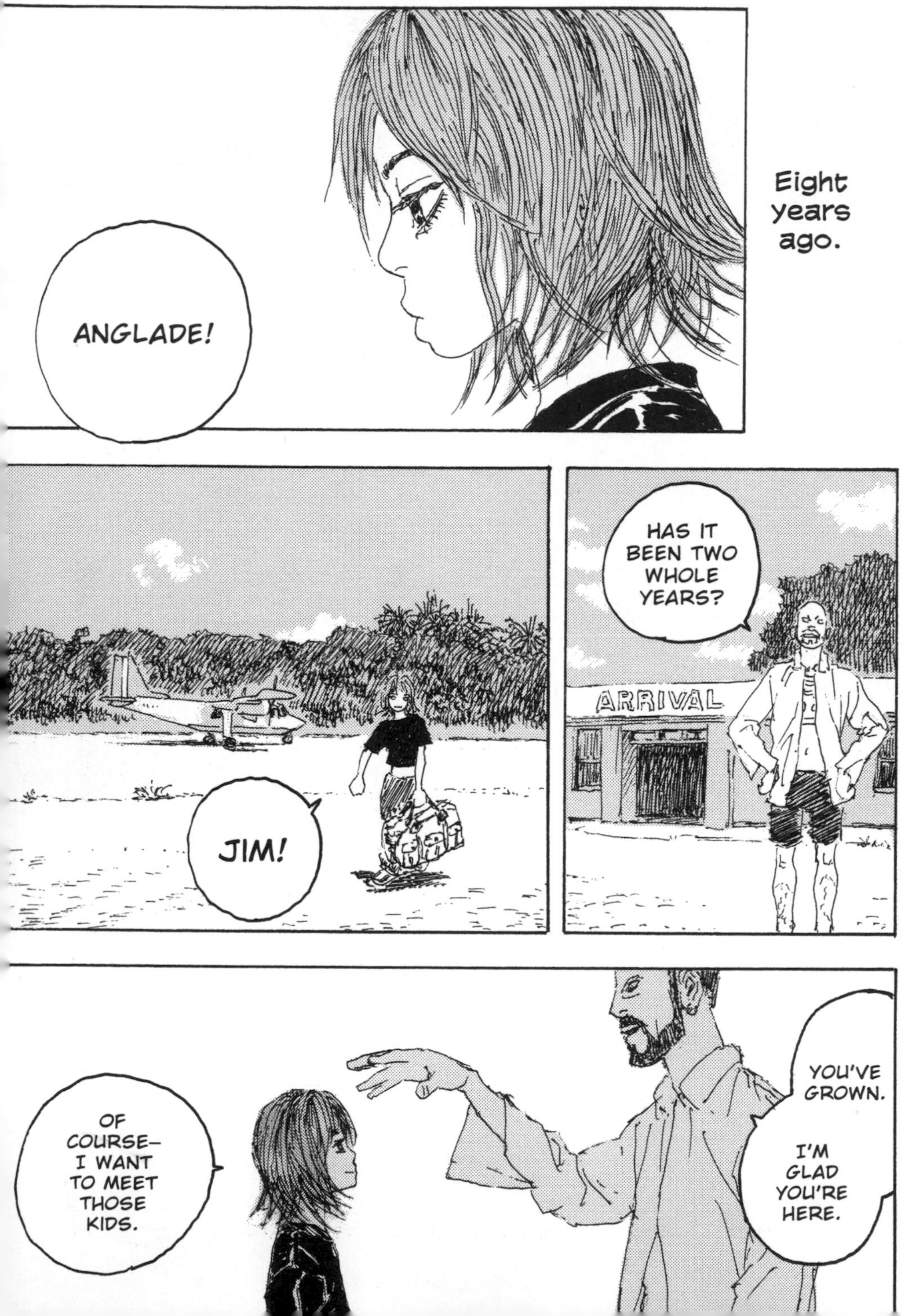
Eight years ago.
ANGLADE!
HAS IT BEEN TWO WHOLE YEARS?
ARRIVAL
JIM!
YOU'VE GROWN.
I'M GLAD YOU'RE HERE.
OF COURSE— I WANT TO MEET THOSE KIDS.

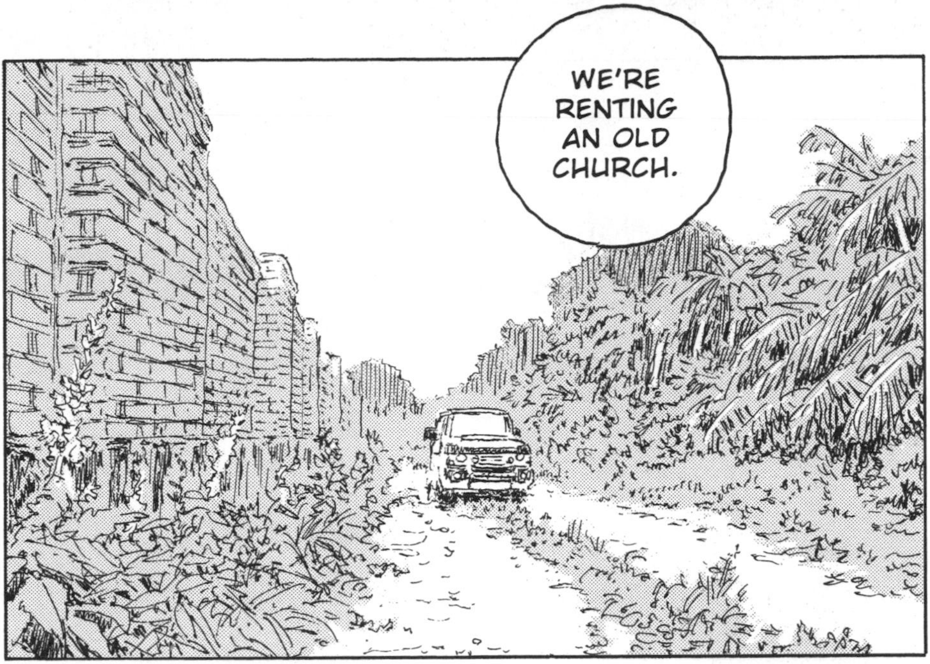
WE'RE RENTING AN OLD CHURCH.

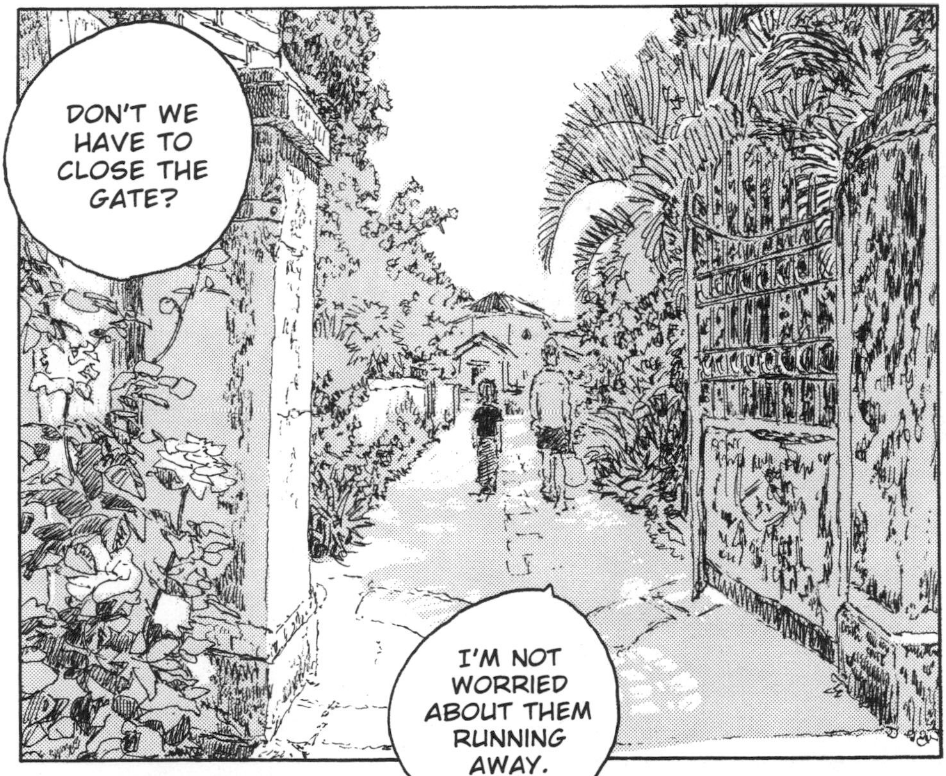
DON'T WE HAVE TO CLOSE THE GATE?
I'M NOT WORRIED ABOUT THEM RUNNING AWAY.

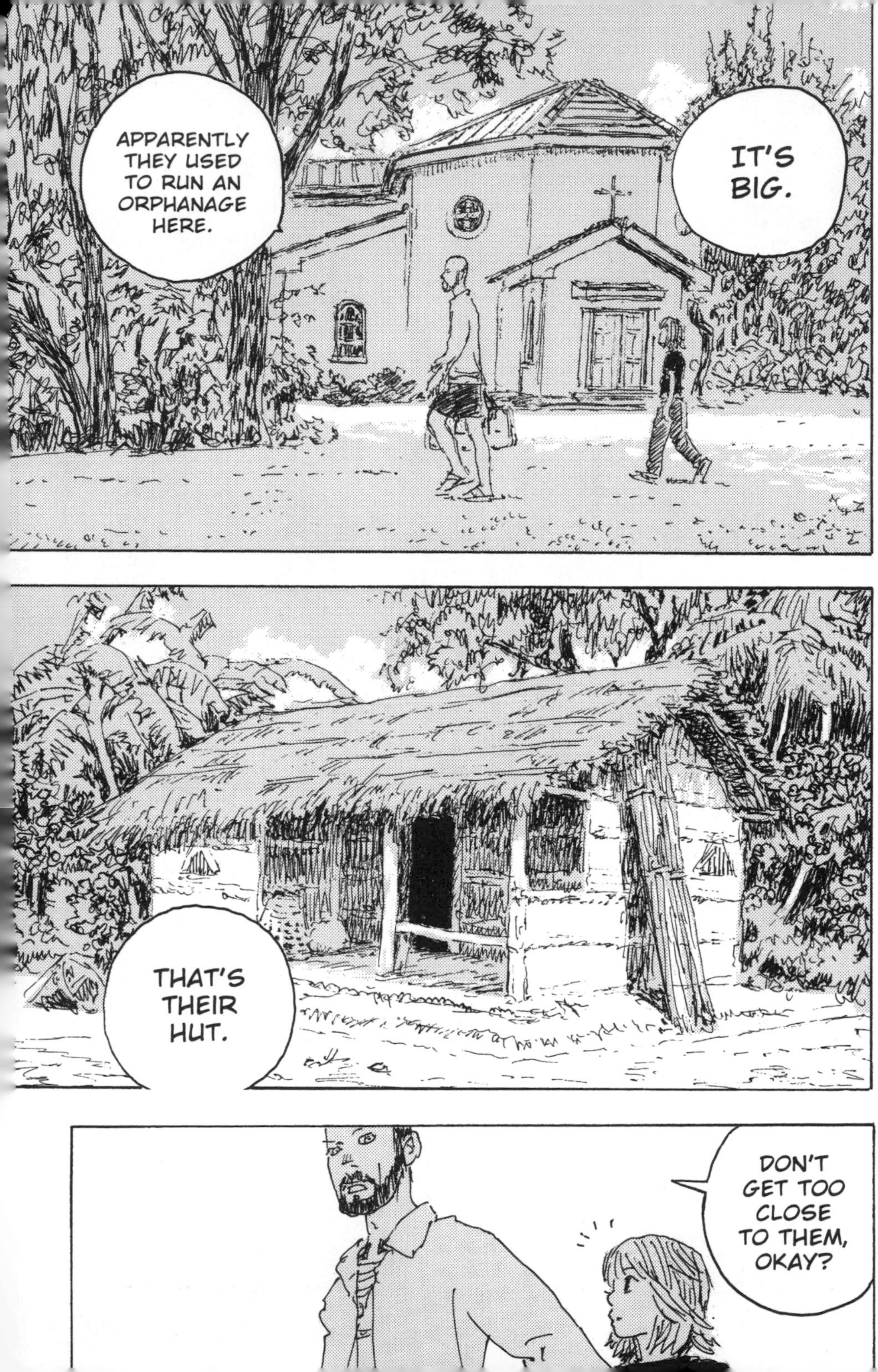
IT'S BIG.
APPARENTLY THEY USED TO RUN AN ORPHANAGE HERE.
THAT'S THEIR HUT.
DON'T GET TOO CLOSE TO THEM, OKAY?

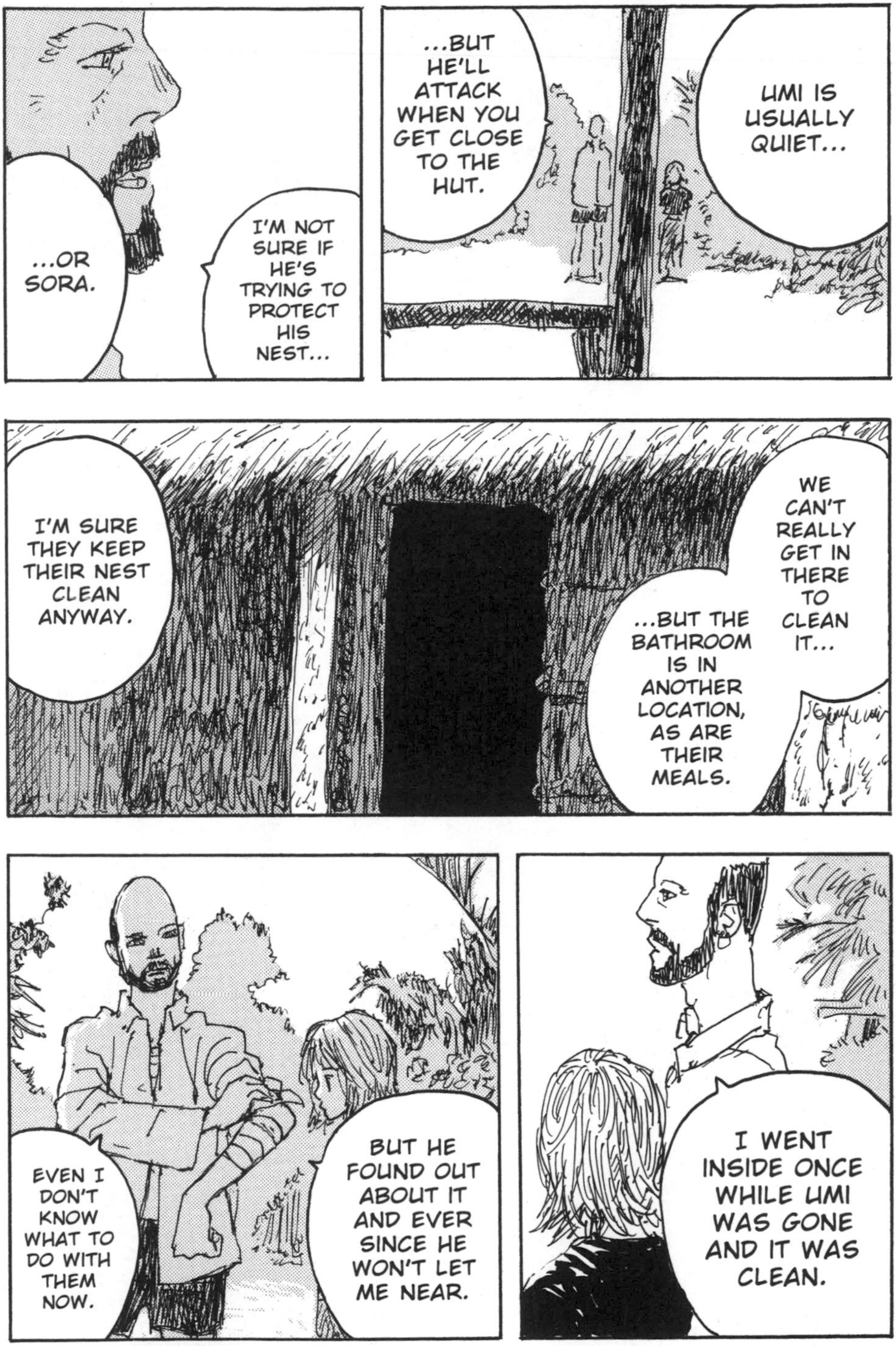
UMI IS USUALLY QUIET...
...BUT HE'LL ATTACK WHEN YOU GET CLOSE TO THE HUT.
I'M NOT SURE IF HE'S TRYING TO PROTECT HIS NEST...
...OR SORA.
WE CAN'T REALLY GET IN THERE TO CLEAN IT...
...BUT THE BATHROOM IS IN ANOTHER LOCATION, AS ARE THEIR MEALS.
I'M SURE THEY KEEP THEIR NEST CLEAN ANYWAY.
I WENT INSIDE ONCE WHILE UMI WAS GONE AND IT WAS CLEAN.
BUT HE FOUND OUT ABOUT IT AND EVER SINCE HE WON'T LET ME NEAR.
EVEN I DON'T KNOW WHAT TO DO WITH THEM NOW.

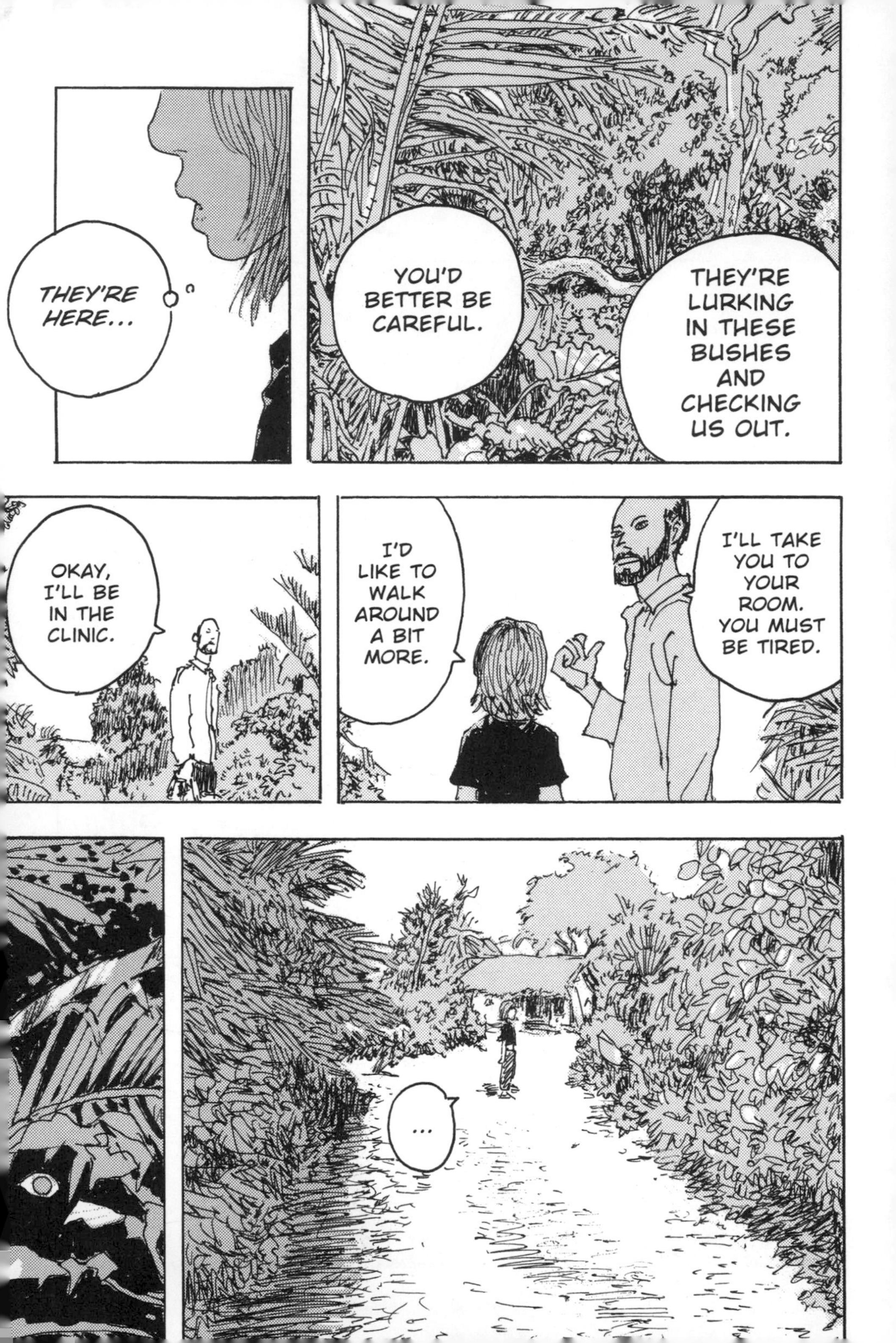
THEY'RE LURKING IN THESE BUSHES AND CHECKING US OUT.
YOU'D BETTER BE CAREFUL.
THEY'RE HERE...
I'LL TAKE YOU TO YOUR ROOM. YOU MUST BE TIRED.
I'D LIKE TO WALK AROUND A BIT MORE.
OKAY, I'LL BE IN THE CLINIC.
...

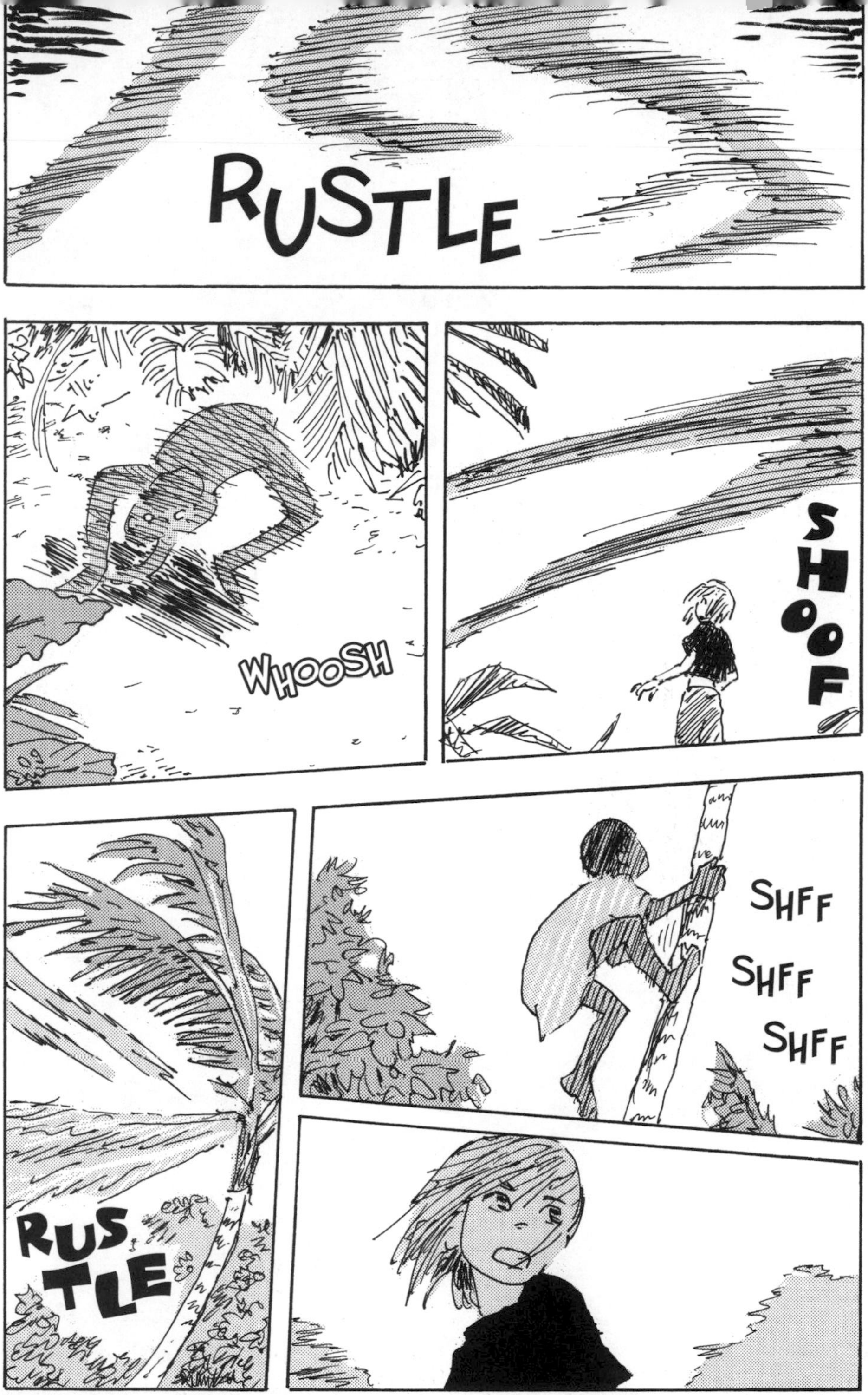
RUSTLE
SHOOF
WHOOSH
SHFF
SHFF
SHFF
RUSTLE

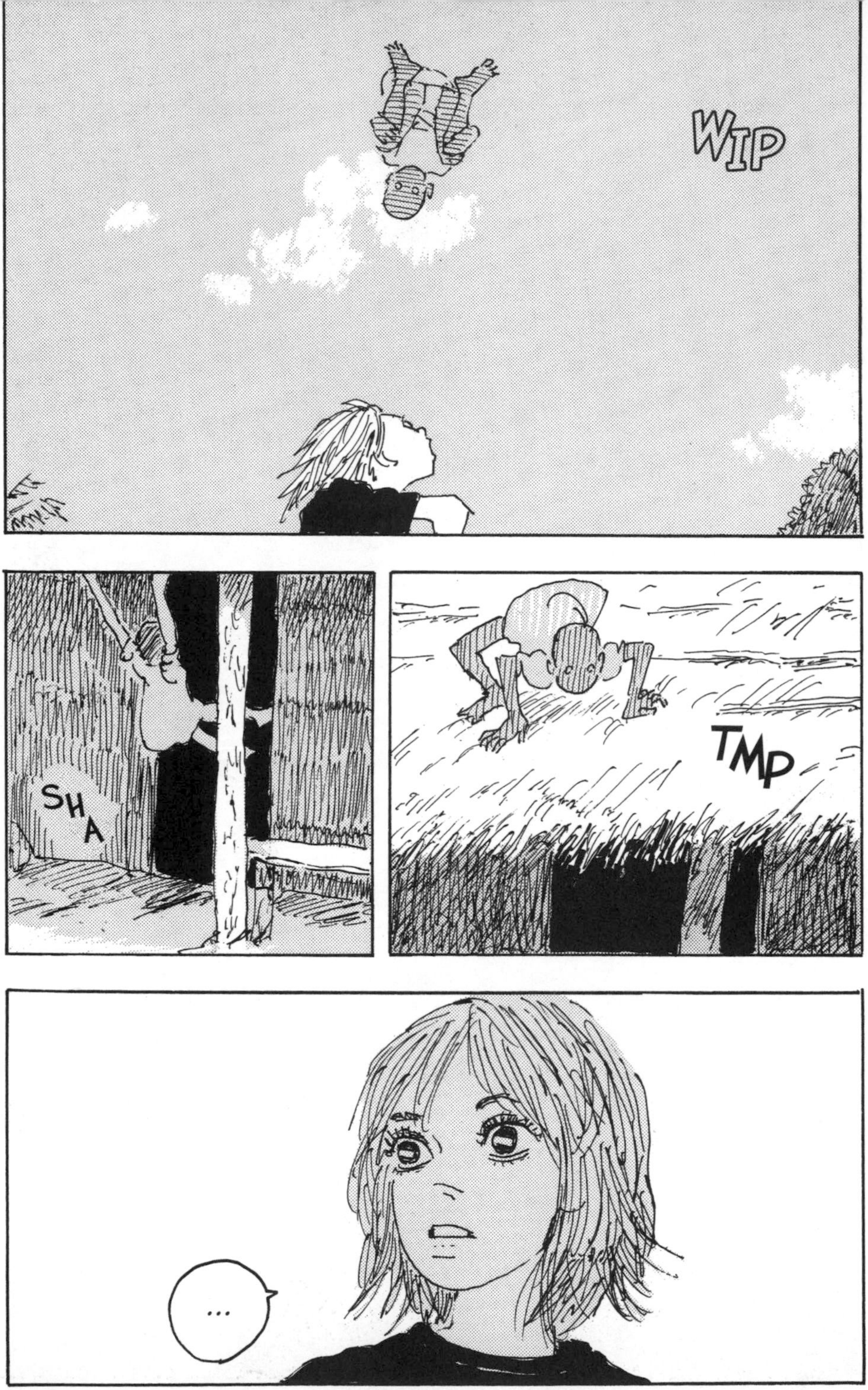
WIP
TMP
SHA
...

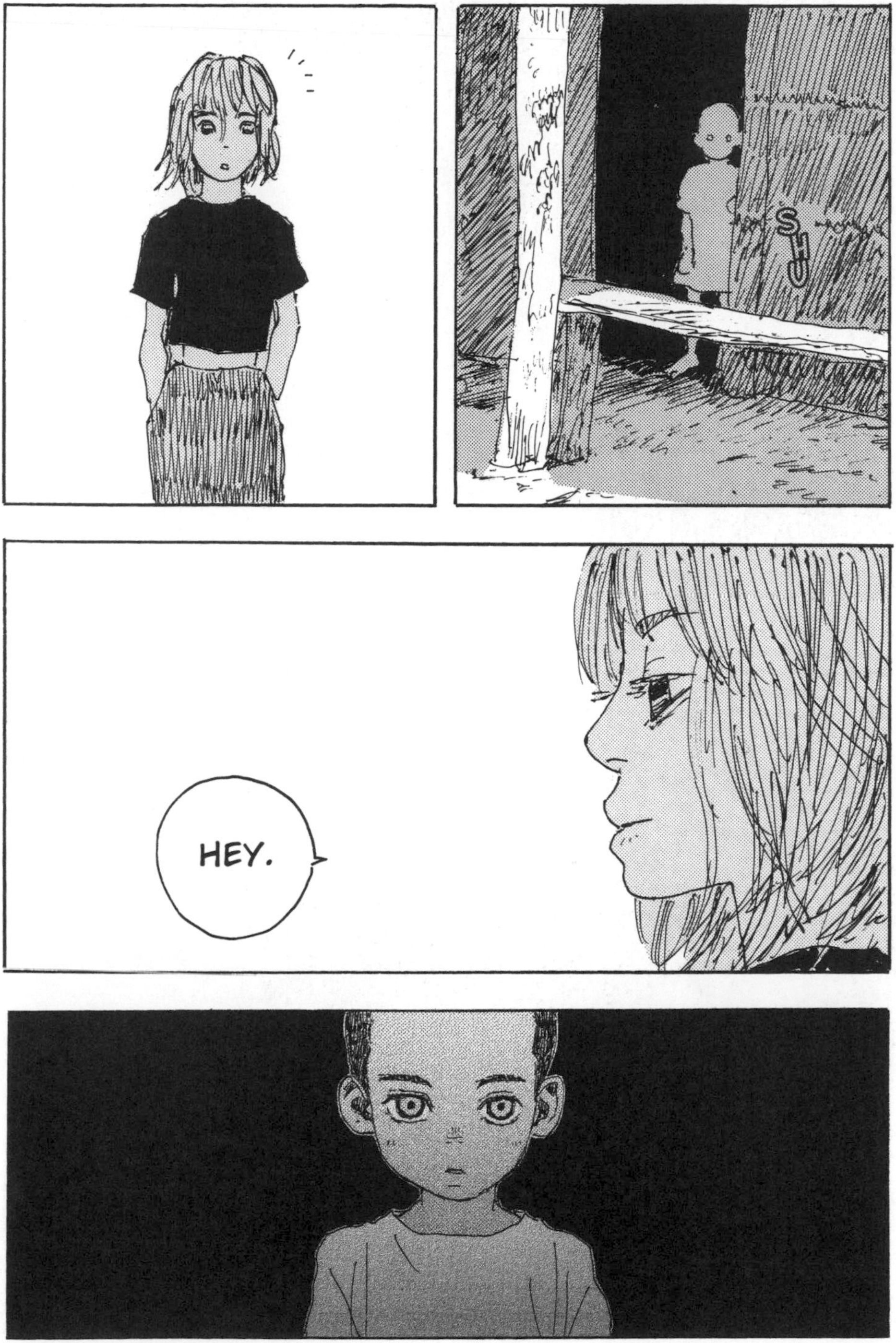
SHU
HEY.

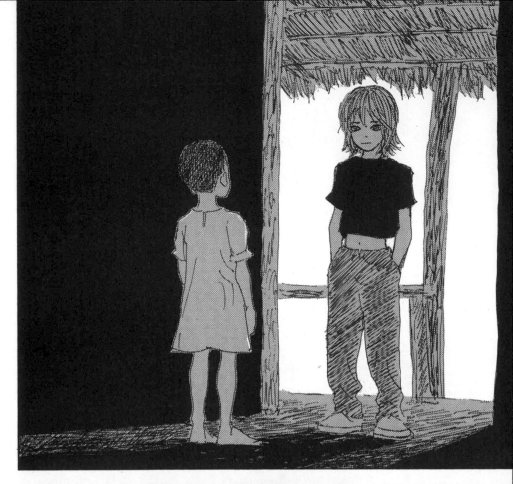

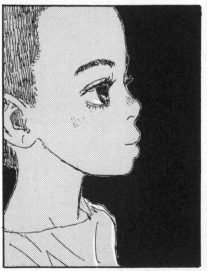

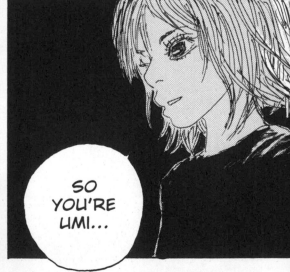

SO
YOU'RE
UMI...

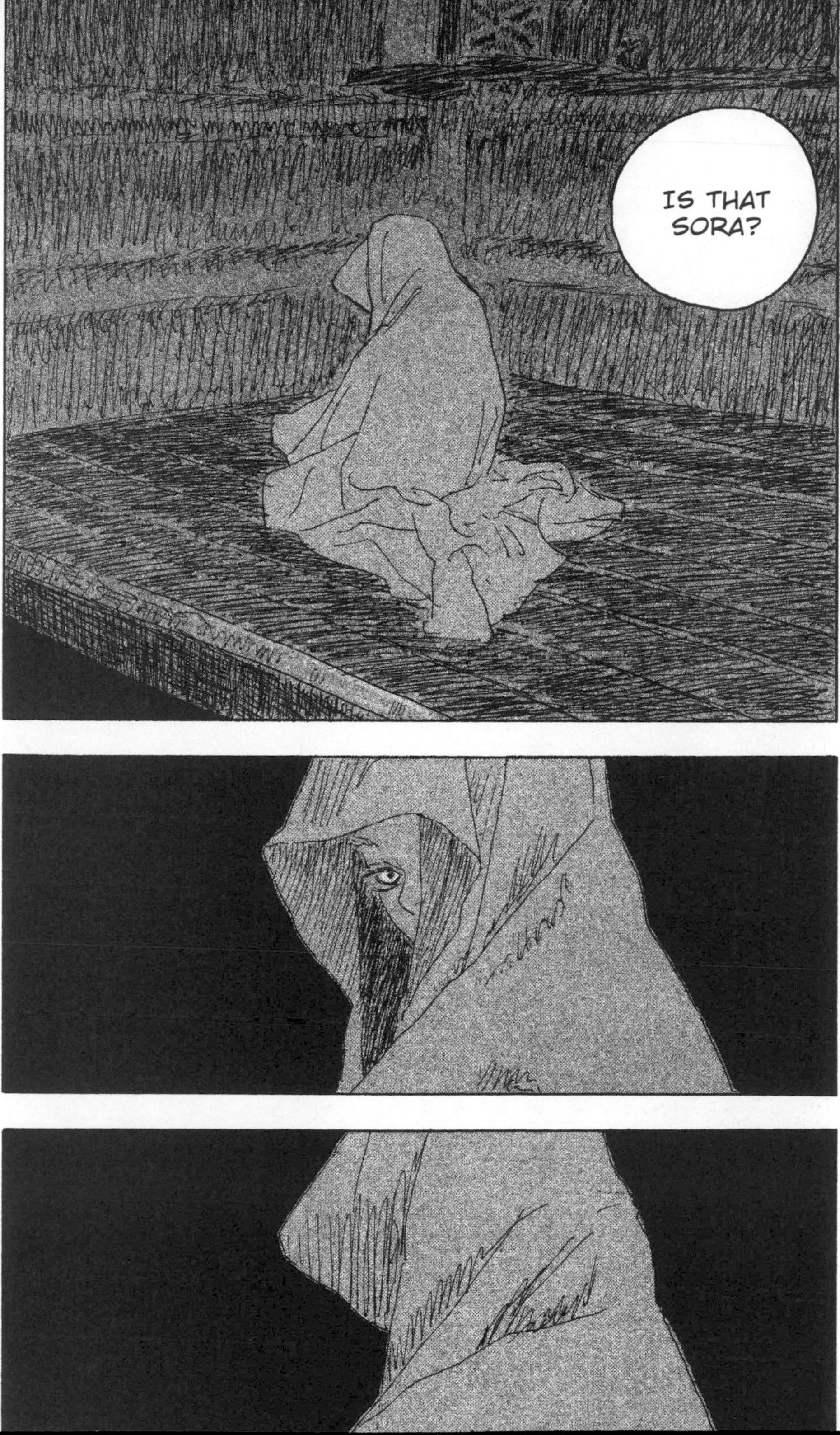
IS THAT SORA?

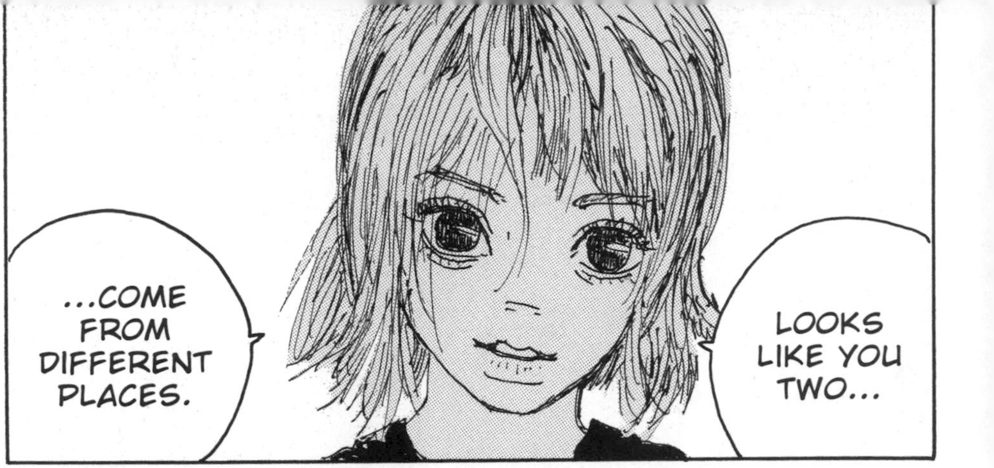
LOOKS LIKE YOU TWO...
...COME FROM DIFFERENT PLACES.
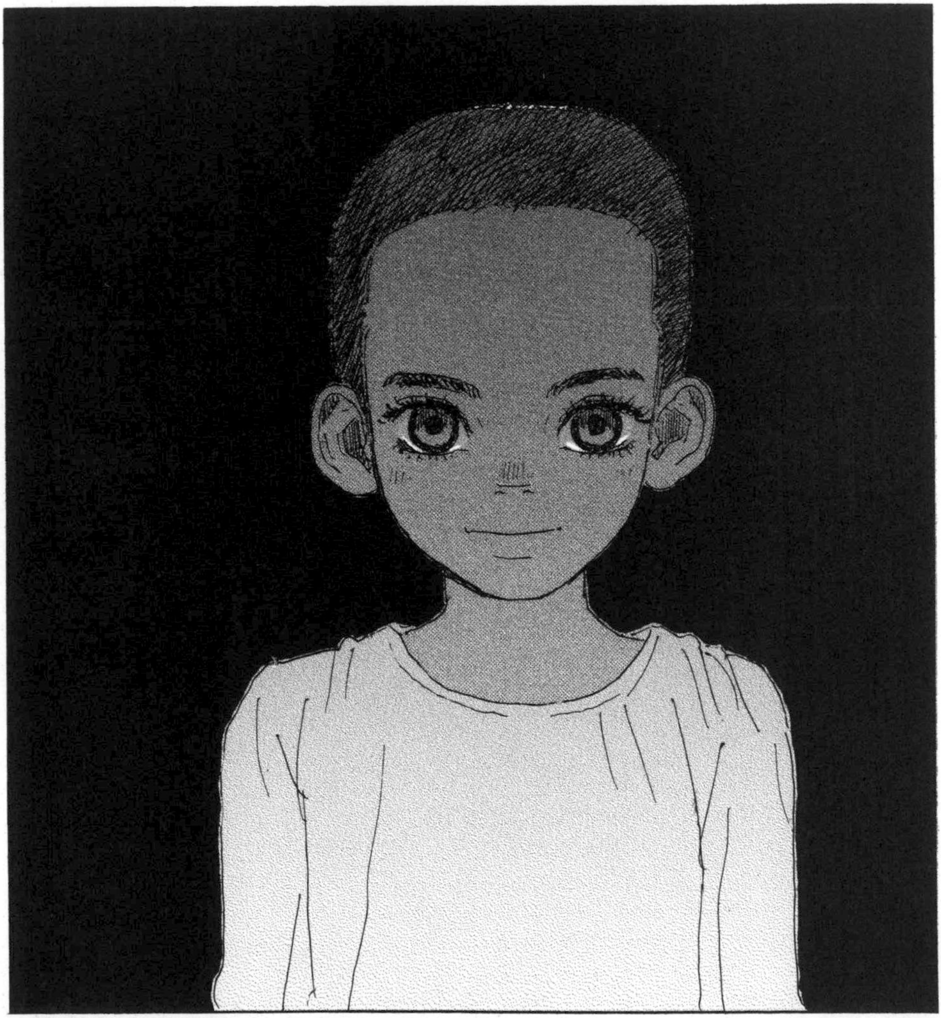

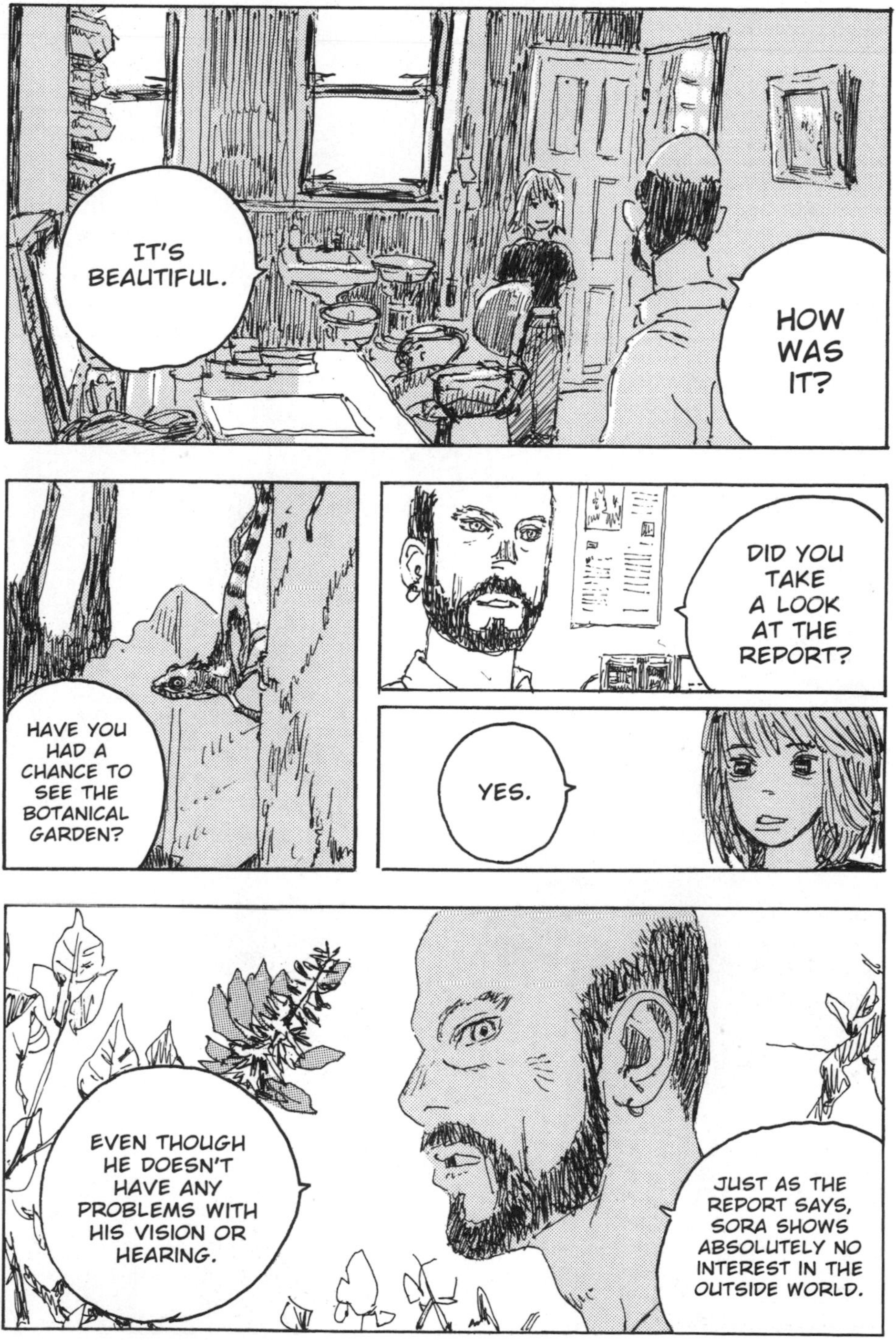
HOW WAS IT?
IT'S BEAUTIFUL.
DID YOU TAKE A LOOK AT THE REPORT?
YES.
HAVE YOU HAD A CHANCE TO SEE THE BOTANICAL GARDEN?
JUST AS THE REPORT SAYS, SORA SHOWS ABSOLUTELY NO INTEREST IN THE OUTSIDE WORLD.
EVEN THOUGH HE DOESN'T HAVE ANY PROBLEMS WITH HIS VISION OR HEARING.

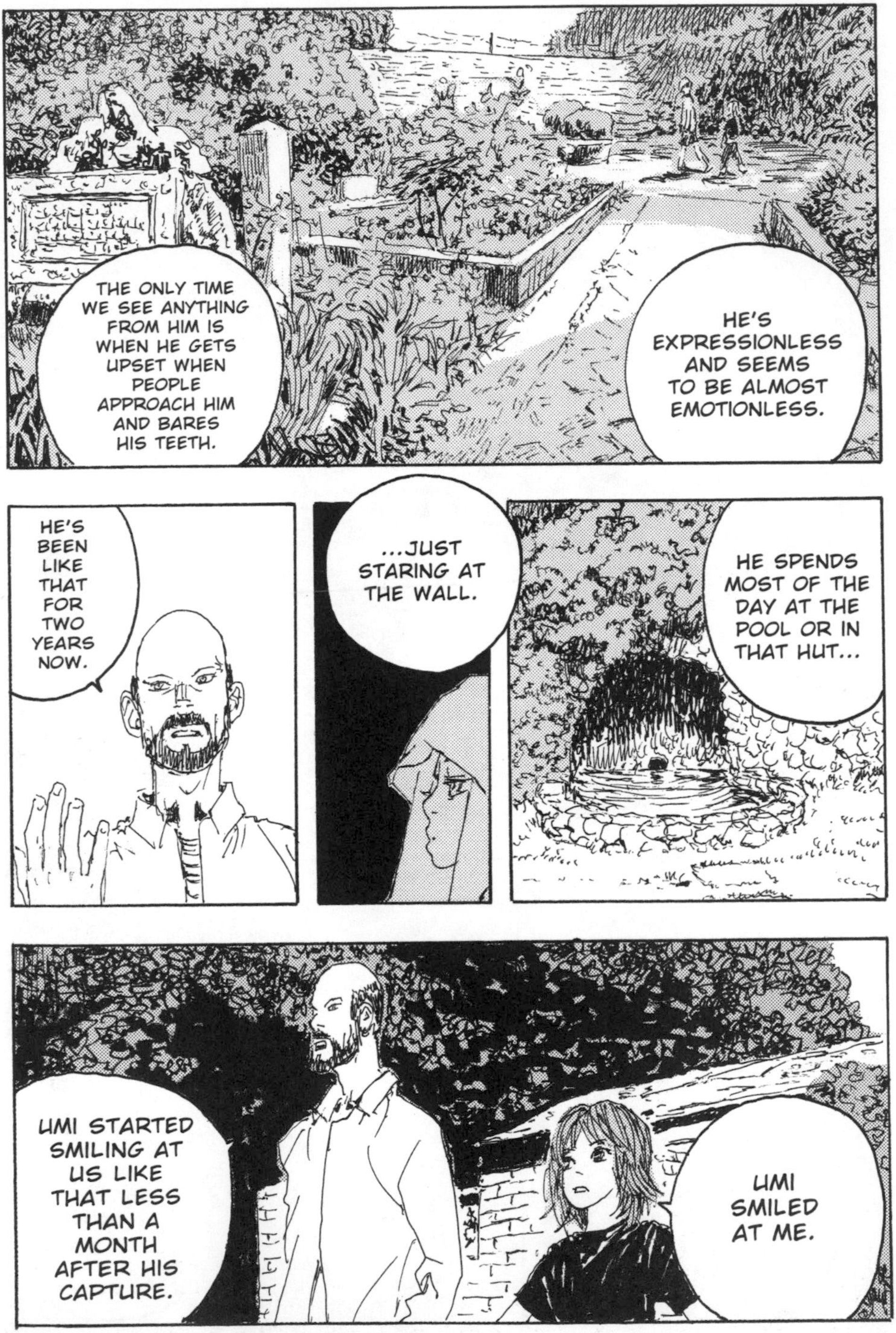
HE'S EXPRESSIONLESS AND SEEMS TO BE ALMOST EMOTIONLESS.
THE ONLY TIME WE SEE ANYTHING FROM HIM IS WHEN HE GETS UPSET WHEN PEOPLE APPROACH HIM AND BARES HIS TEETH.
HE SPENDS MOST OF THE DAY AT THE POOL OR IN THAT HUT...
...JUST STARING AT THE WALL.
HE'S BEEN LIKE THAT FOR TWO YEARS NOW.
UMI SMILED AT ME.
UMI STARTED SMILING AT US LIKE THAT LESS THAN A MONTH AFTER HIS CAPTURE.

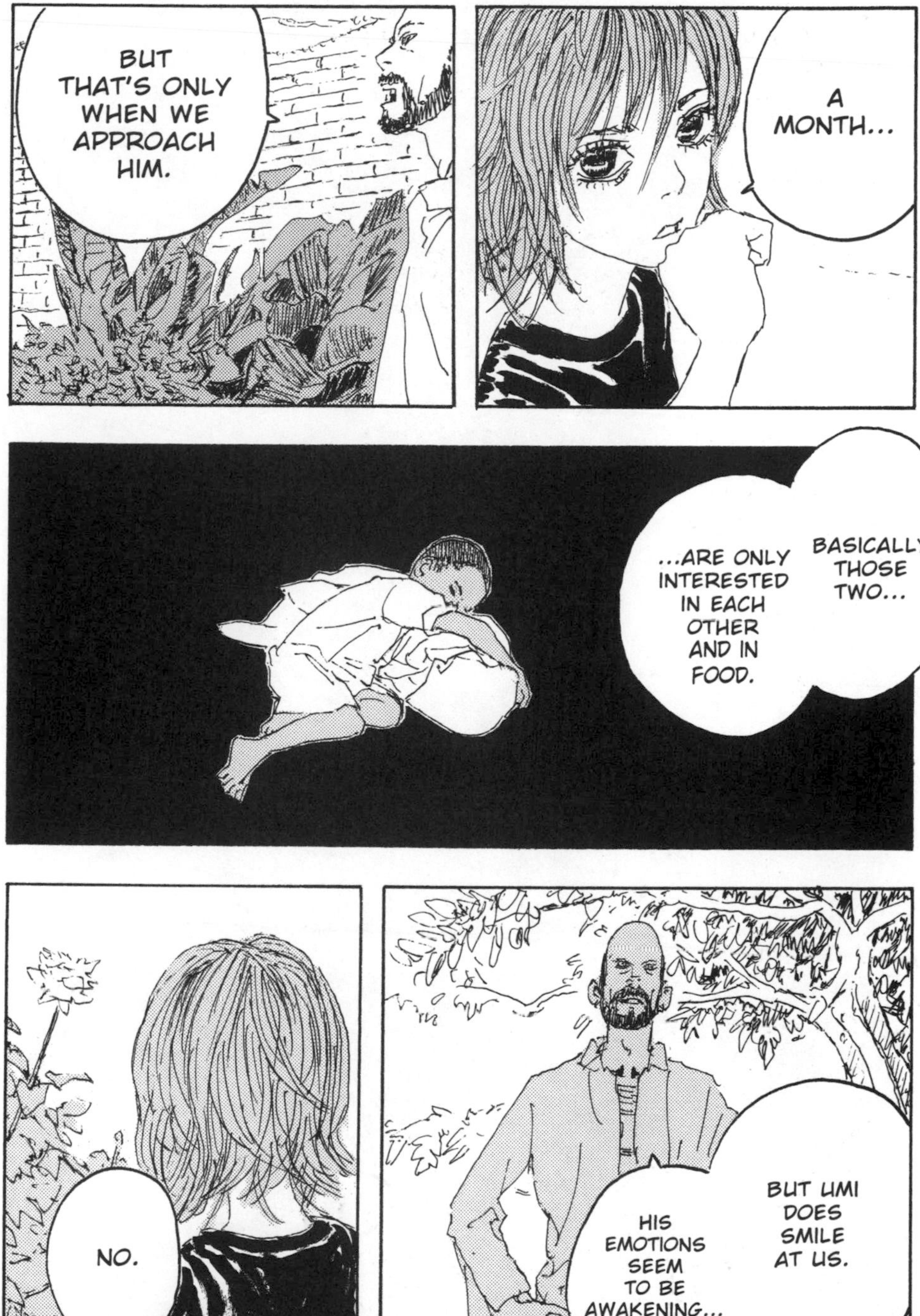
A MONTH...
BUT THAT'S ONLY WHEN WE APPROACH HIM.
BASICALLY THOSE TWO...
...ARE ONLY INTERESTED IN EACH OTHER AND IN FOOD.
BUT UMI DOES SMILE AT US.
HIS EMOTIONS SEEM TO BE AWAKENING...
NO.

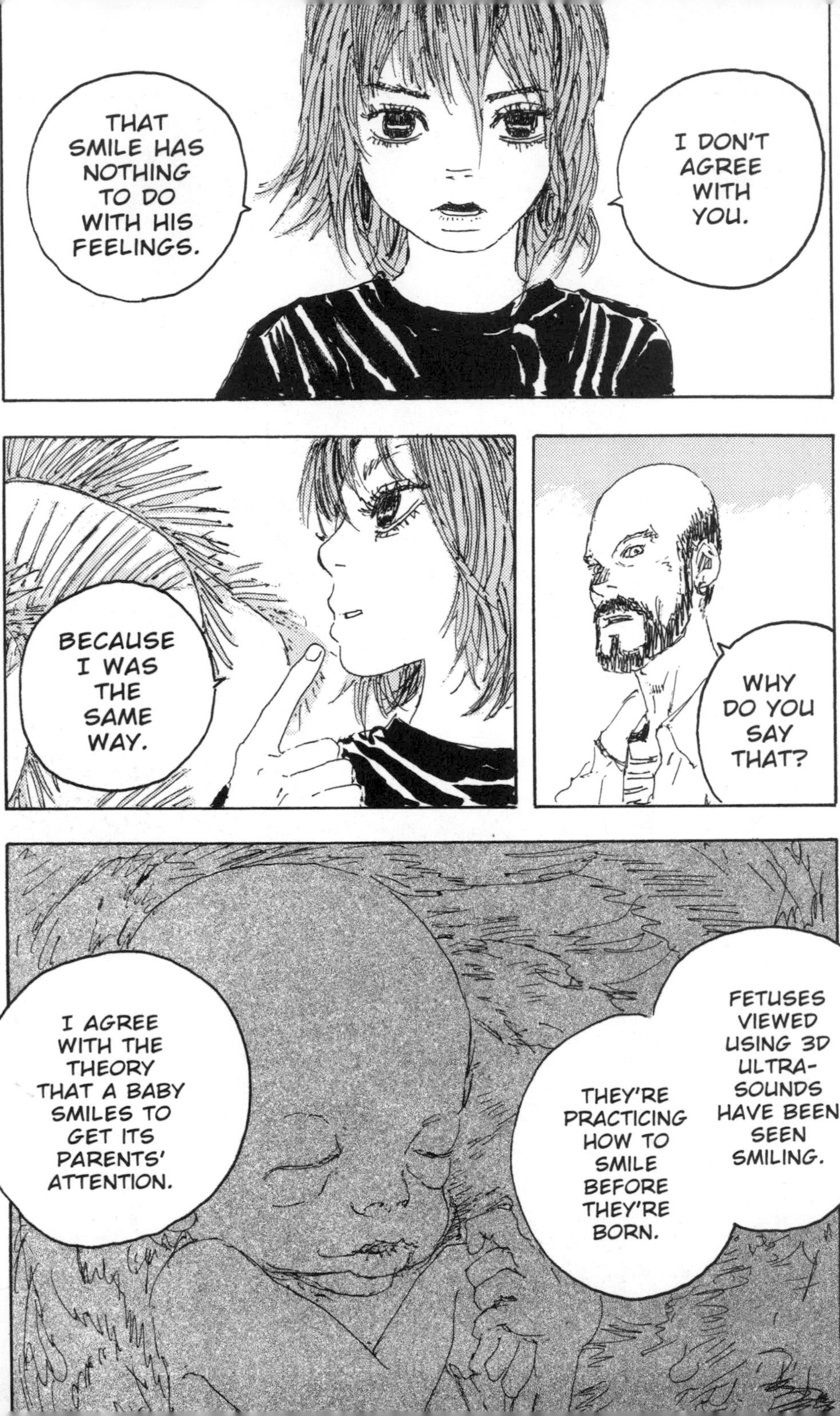
I DON'T AGREE WITH YOU.
THAT SMILE HAS NOTHING TO DO WITH HIS FEELINGS.
WHY DO YOU SAY THAT?
BECAUSE I WAS THE SAME WAY.
FETUSES VIEWED USING 3D ULTRA-SOUNDS HAVE BEEN SEEN SMILING.
THEY'RE PRACTICING HOW TO SMILE BEFORE THEY'RE BORN.
I AGREE WITH THE THEORY THAT A BABY SMILES TO GET ITS PARENTS' ATTENTION.

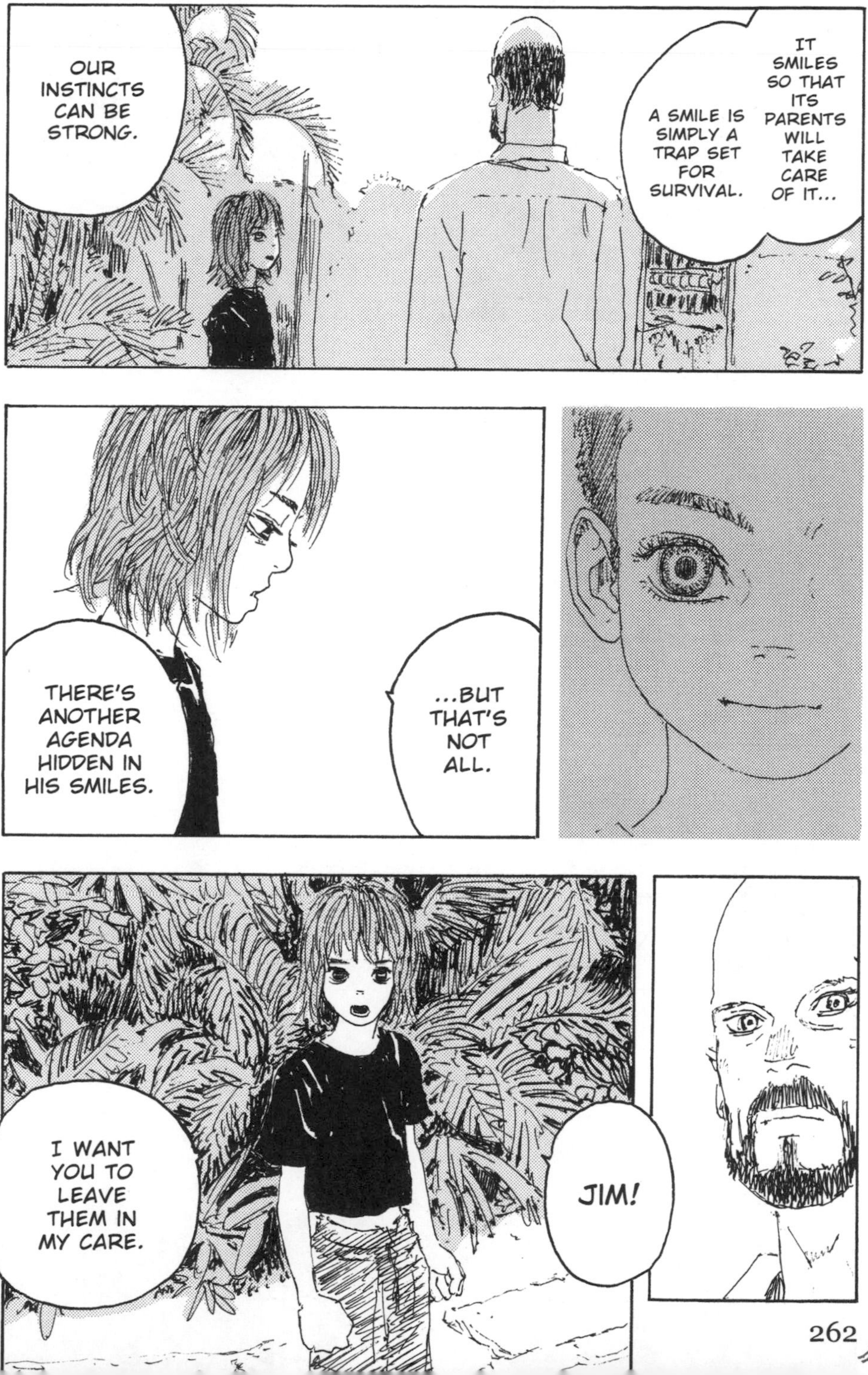
IT SMILES SO THAT ITS PARENTS WILL TAKE CARE OF IT...
A SMILE IS SIMPLY A TRAP SET FOR SURVIVAL.
OUR INSTINCTS CAN BE STRONG.
...BUT THAT'S NOT ALL.
THERE'S ANOTHER AGENDA HIDDEN IN HIS SMILES.
JIM!
I WANT YOU TO LEAVE THEM IN MY CARE.

Chapter 24: Internal Organs

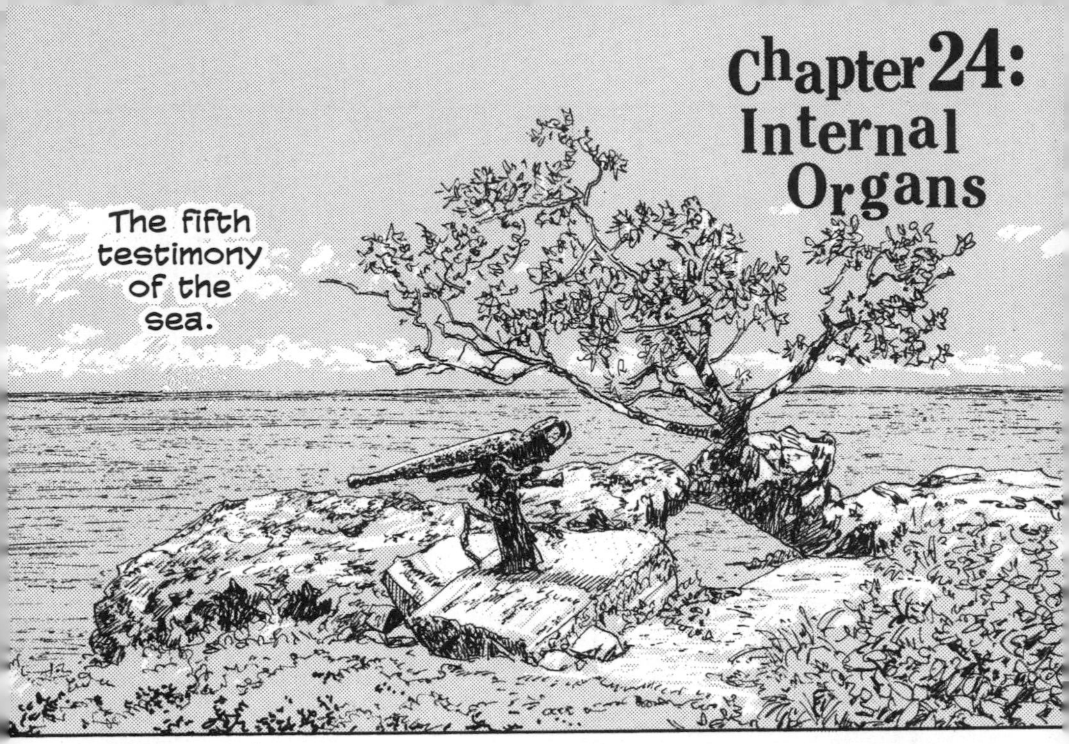
The fifth testimony of the sea.

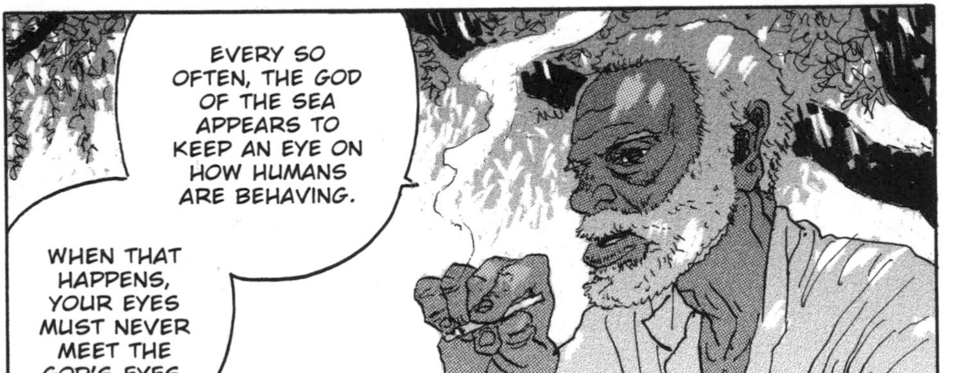
EVERY SO OFTEN, THE GOD OF THE SEA APPEARS TO KEEP AN EYE ON HOW HUMANS ARE BEHAVING.
WHEN THAT HAPPENS, YOUR EYES MUST NEVER MEET THE GOD'S EYES.

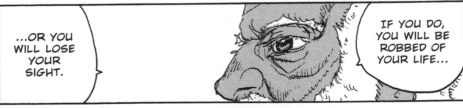

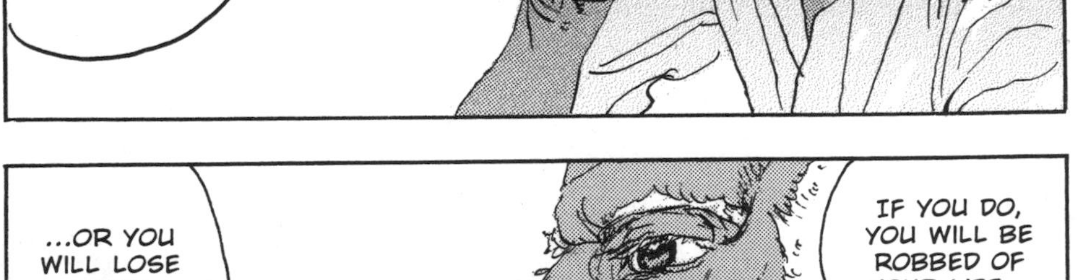
IF YOU DO, YOU WILL BE ROBBED OF YOUR LIFE...
...OR YOU WILL LOSE YOUR SIGHT.

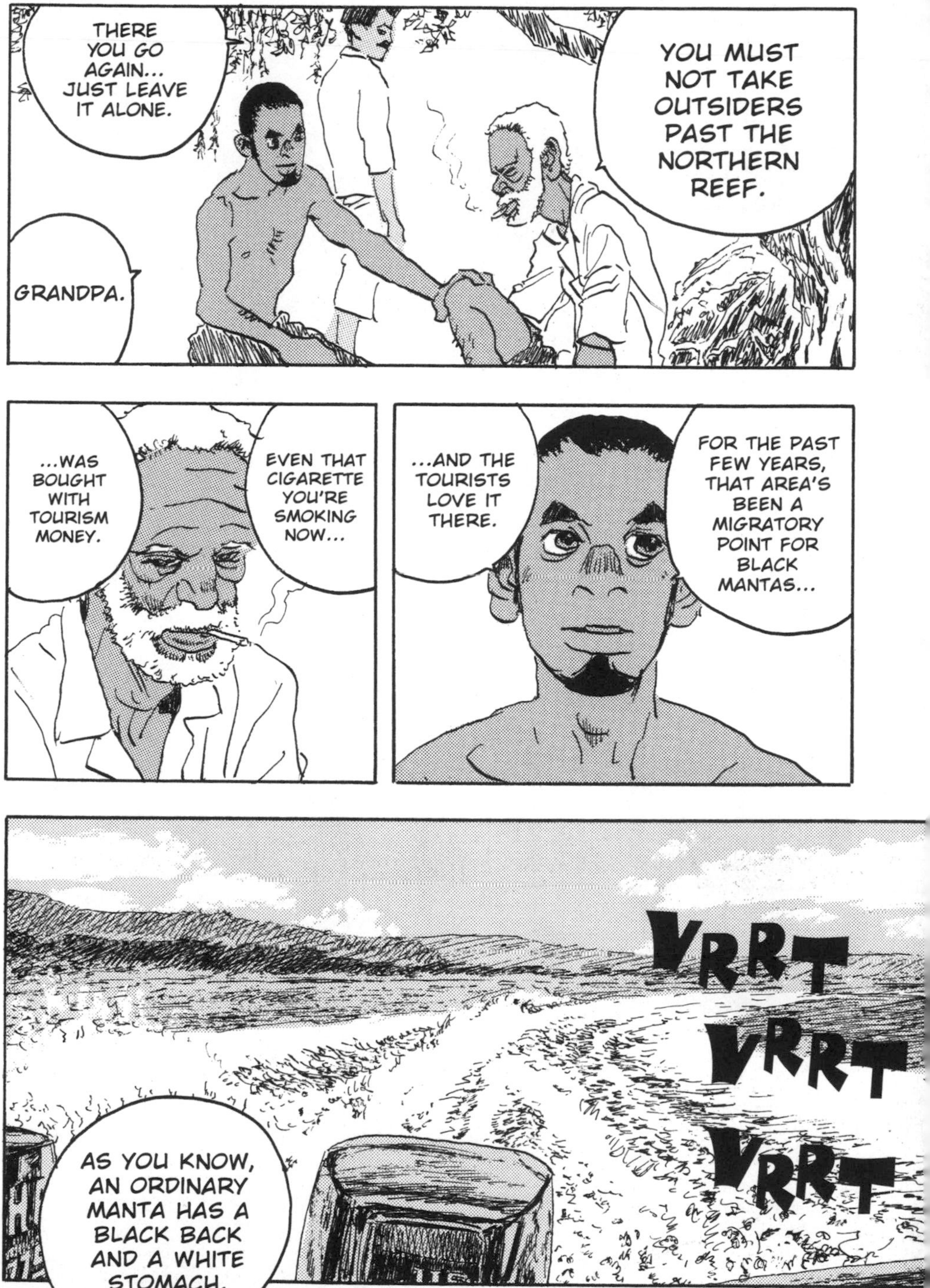
YOU MUST NOT TAKE OUTSIDERS PAST THE NORTHERN REEF.
THERE YOU GO AGAIN... JUST LEAVE IT ALONE.
GRANDPA.
FOR THE PAST FEW YEARS, THAT AREA'S BEEN A MIGRATORY POINT FOR BLACK MANTAS...
...AND THE TOURISTS LOVE IT THERE.
EVEN THAT CIGARETTE YOU'RE SMOKING NOW...
...WAS BOUGHT WITH TOURISM MONEY.
VRRT
VRRT
VRRT
AS YOU KNOW, AN ORDINARY MANTA HAS A BLACK BACK AND A WHITE STOMACH.

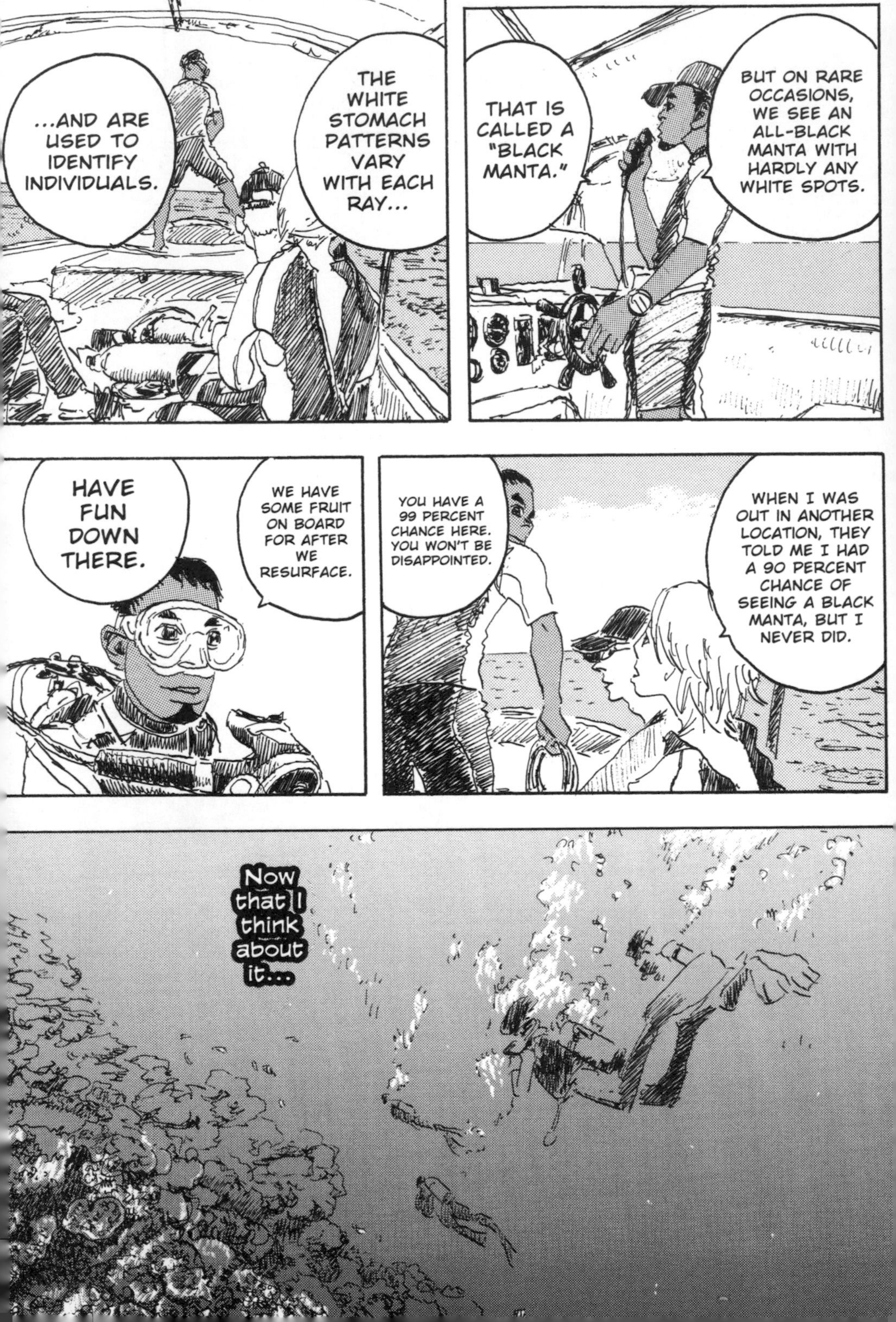
BUT ON RARE OCCASIONS, WE SEE AN ALL-BLACK MANTA WITH HARDLY ANY WHITE SPOTS.
THAT IS CALLED A "BLACK MANTA."
THE WHITE STOMACH PATTERNS VARY WITH EACH RAY...
...AND ARE USED TO IDENTIFY INDIVIDUALS.
WHEN I WAS OUT IN ANOTHER LOCATION, THEY TOLD ME I HAD A 90 PERCENT CHANCE OF SEEING A BLACK MANTA, BUT I NEVER DID.
YOU HAVE A 99 PERCENT CHANCE HERE. YOU WON'T BE DISAPPOINTED.
WE HAVE SOME FRUIT ON BOARD FOR AFTER WE RESURFACE.
HAVE FUN DOWN THERE.
Now that I think about it...

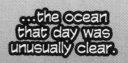
...the ocean that day was unusually clear.

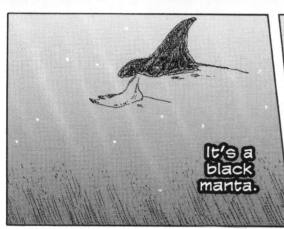
It's a black manta.

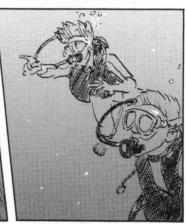

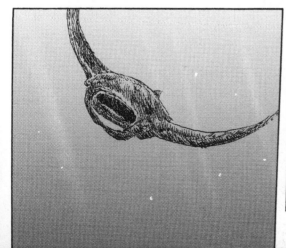

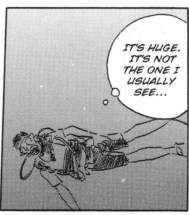
IT'S HUGE. IT'S NOT THE ONE I USUALLY SEE...

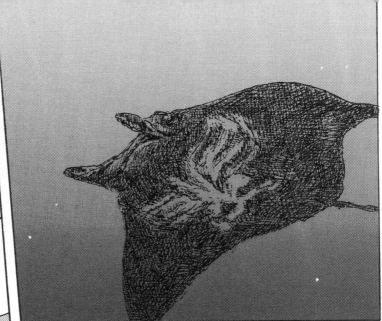

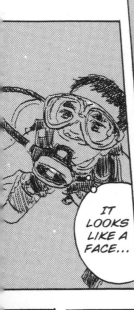

IT LOOKS LIKE A FACE...

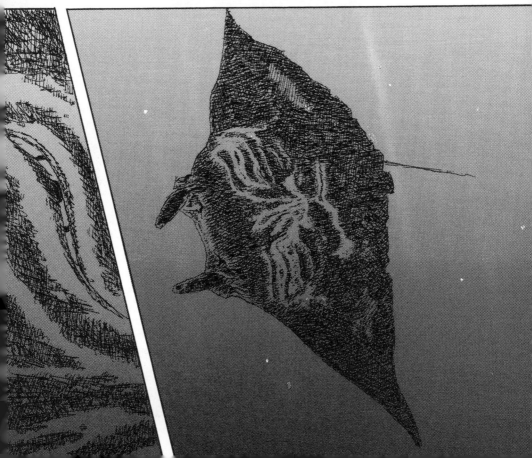

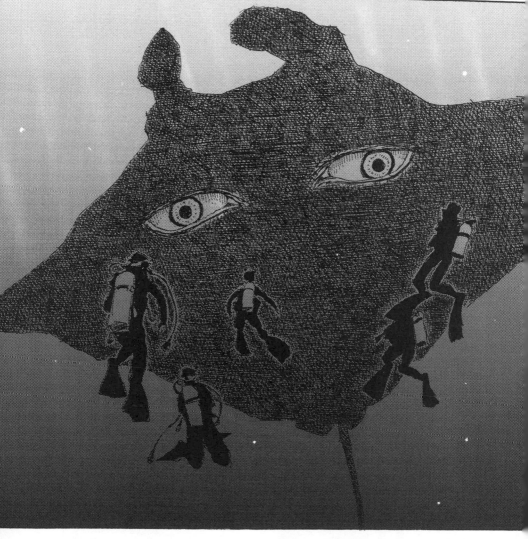

Ah...

Of the five people diving that day,
one went missing, two drowned and
the other two lost their eyesight.

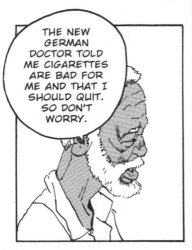

SORRY, GRAMPS.
I CAN'T BUY YOU CIGARETTES ANYMORE.
THE NEW GERMAN DOCTOR TOLD ME CIGARETTES ARE BAD FOR ME AND THAT I SHOULD QUIT. SO DON'T WORRY.
But ever since then...
...my brain felt like it was going to explode...
...if I didn't keep spitting out the things that came gushing into my head.
AND THAT'S WHY I STARTED TO MAKE THESE THINGS.
AND FOR WHATEVER REASON, MANY PEOPLE WANT TO BUY THEM...

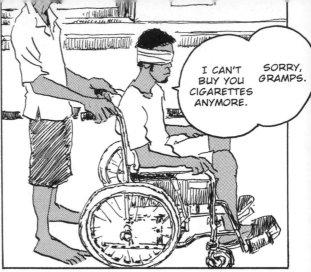

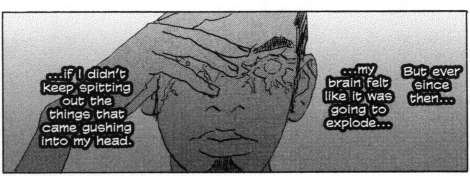

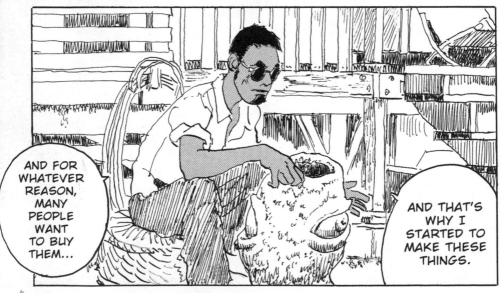

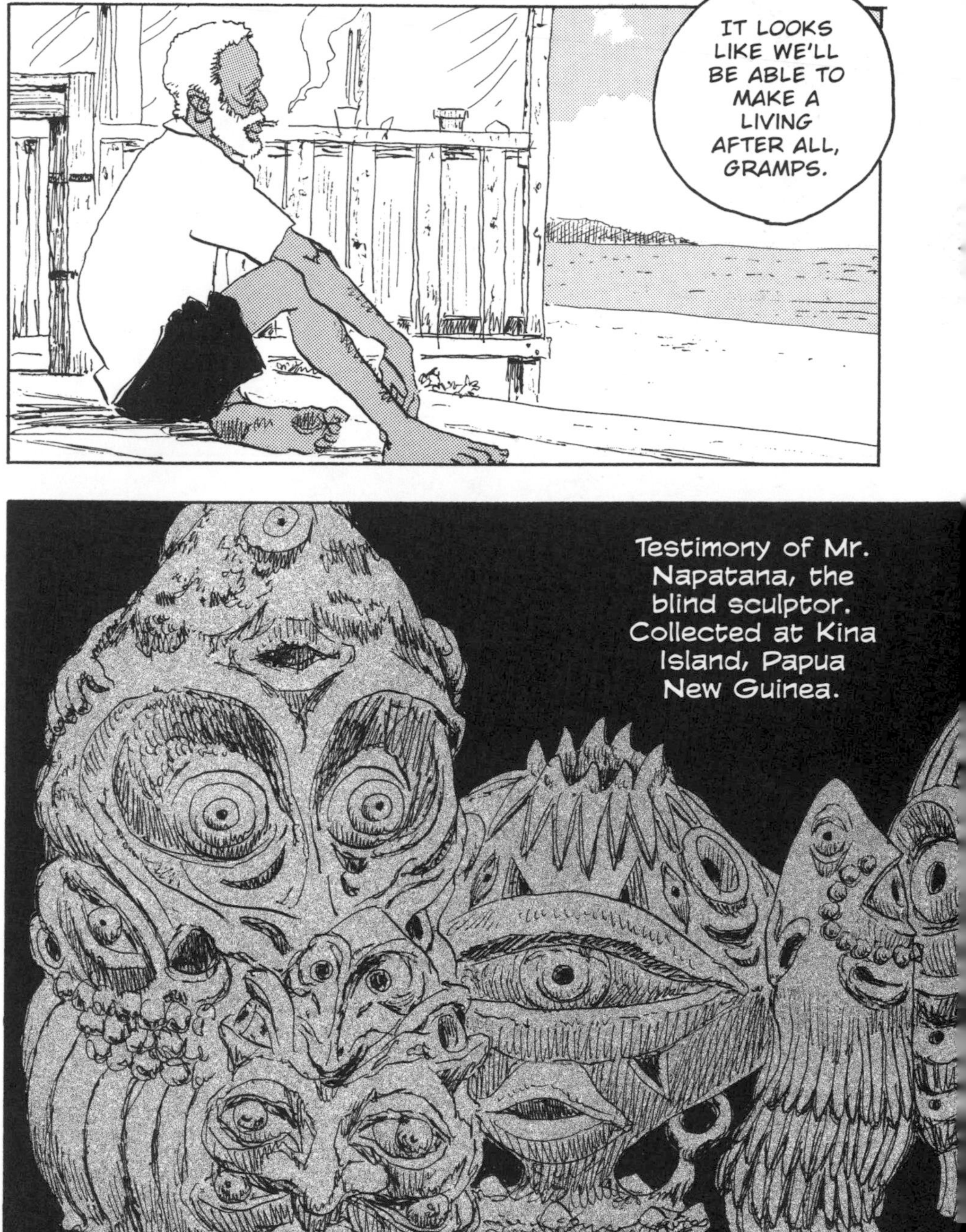

IT LOOKS LIKE WE'LL BE ABLE TO MAKE A LIVING AFTER ALL, GRAMPS.
Testimony of Mr. Napatana, the blind sculptor. Collected at Kina Island, Papua New Guinea.

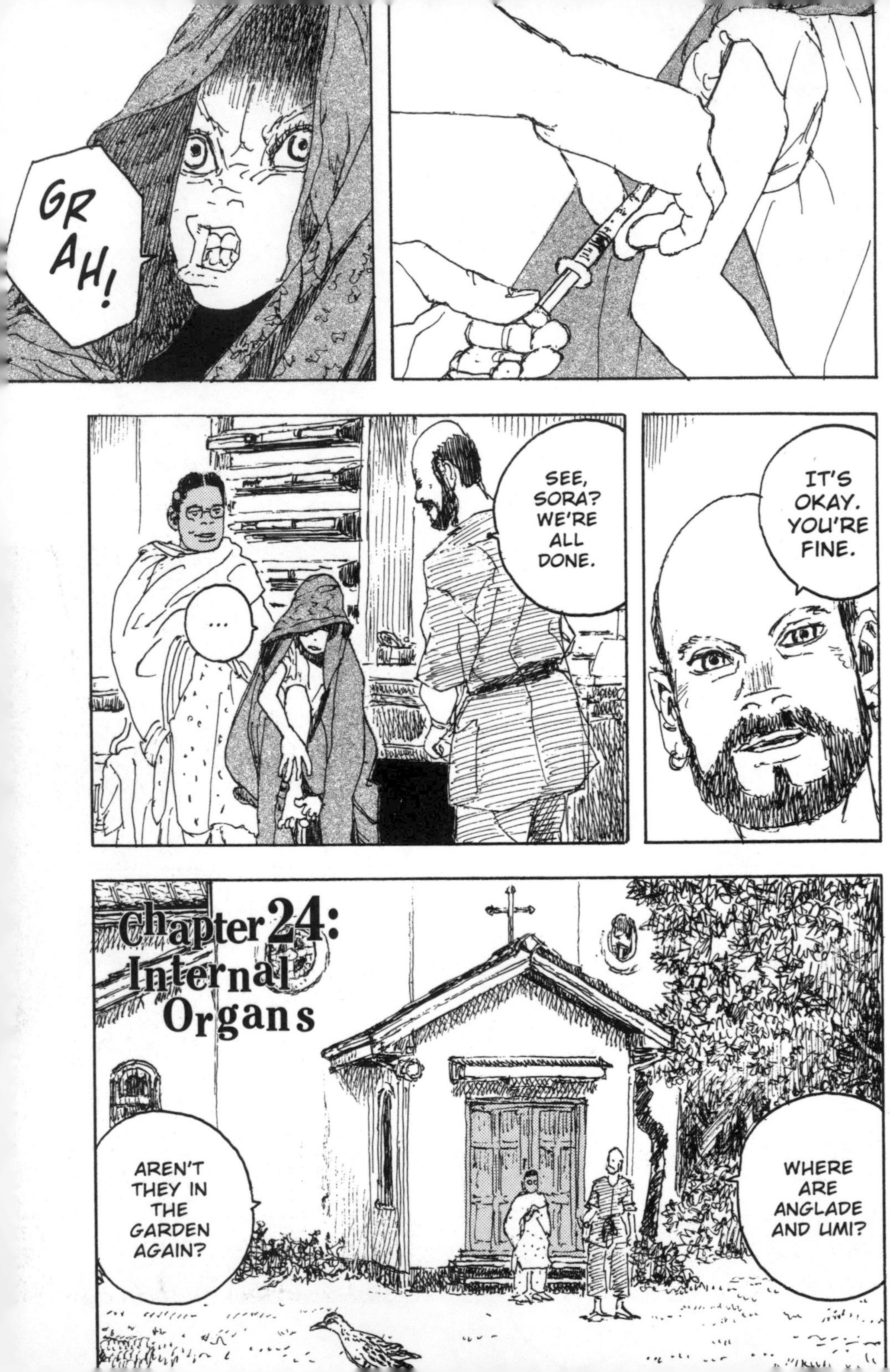
GRAH!
IT'S OKAY. YOU'RE FINE.
SEE, SORA? WE'RE ALL DONE.
...
Chapter 24: Internal Organs
WHERE ARE ANGLADE AND UMI?
AREN'T THEY IN THE GARDEN AGAIN?

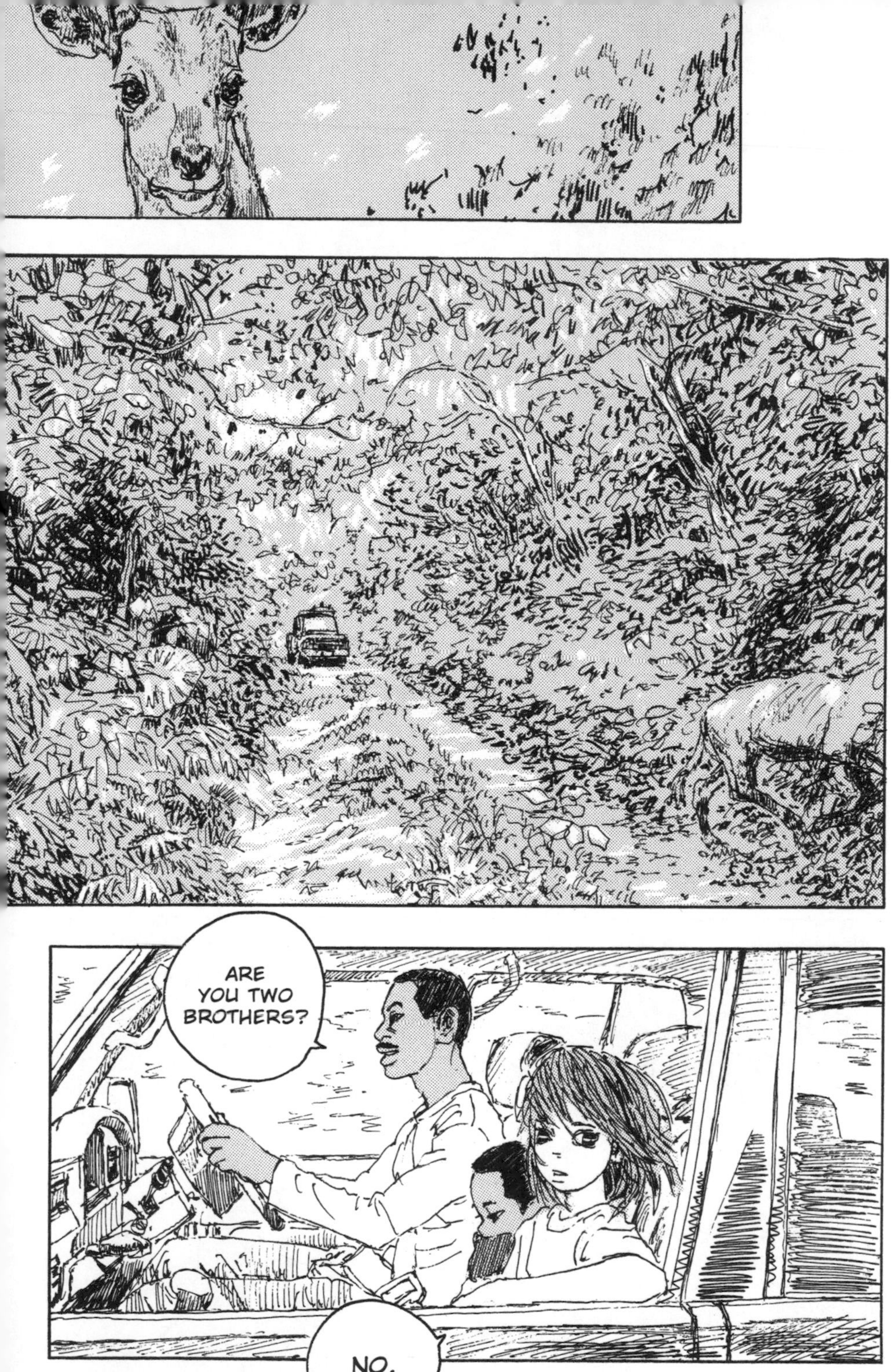
ARE YOU TWO BROTHERS?
NO.

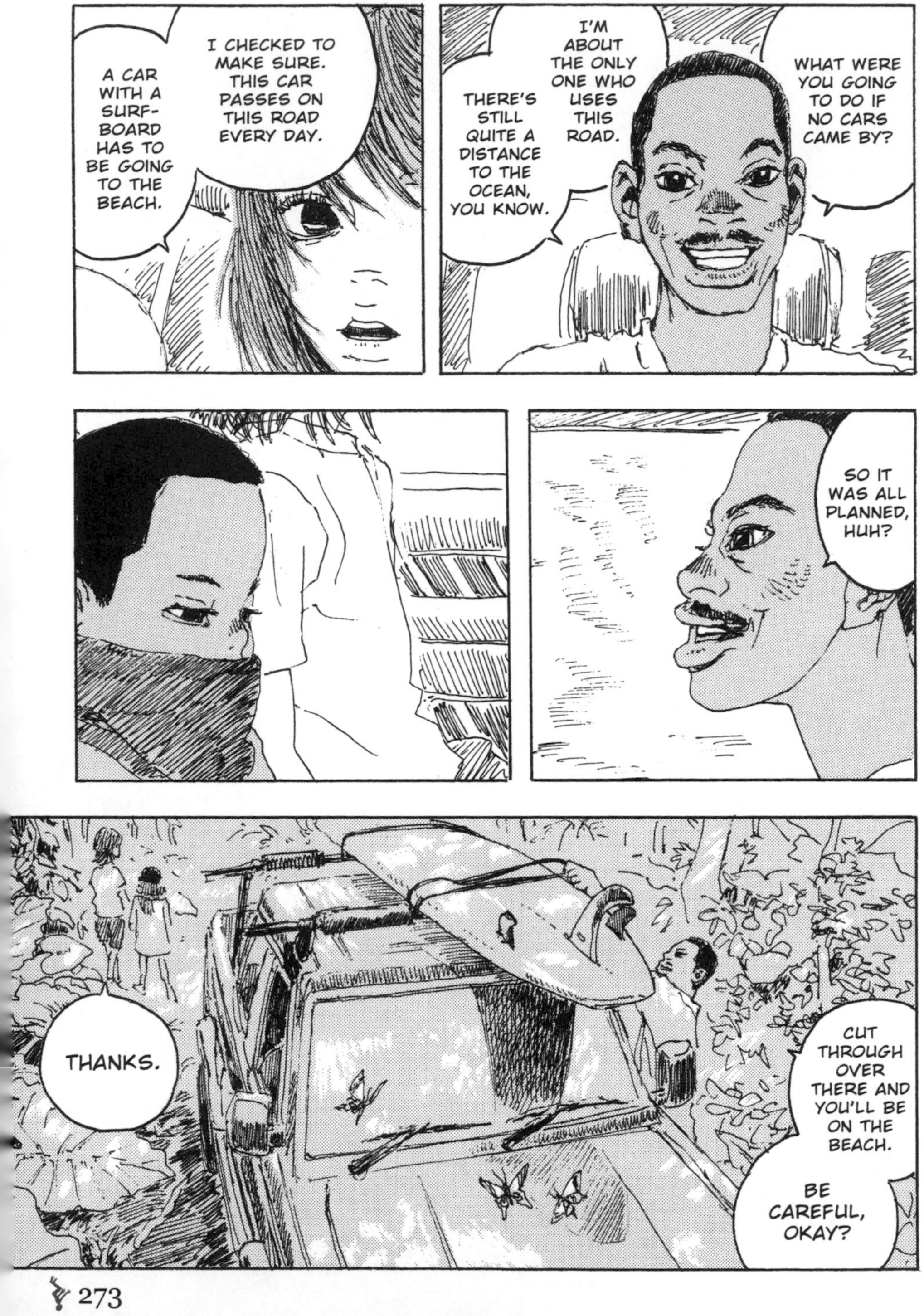
WHAT WERE YOU GOING TO DO IF NO CARS CAME BY?
I'M ABOUT THE ONLY ONE WHO USES THIS ROAD.
THERE'S STILL QUITE A DISTANCE TO THE OCEAN, YOU KNOW.
I CHECKED TO MAKE SURE. THIS CAR PASSES ON THIS ROAD EVERY DAY.
A CAR WITH A SURF-BOARD HAS TO BE GOING TO THE BEACH.
SO IT WAS ALL PLANNED, HUH?
CUT THROUGH OVER THERE AND YOU'LL BE ON THE BEACH.
BE CAREFUL, OKAY?
THANKS.

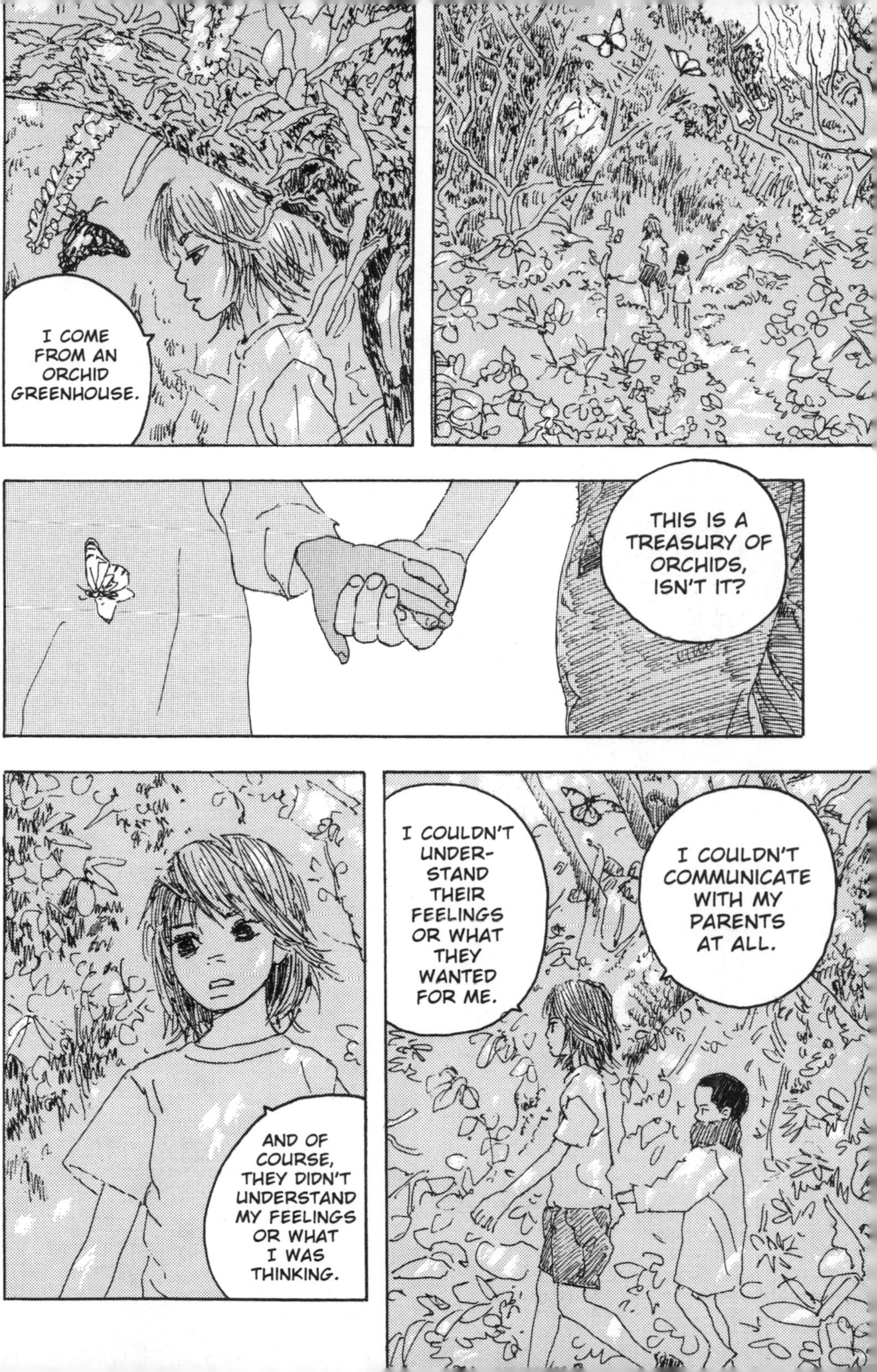
I COME FROM AN ORCHID GREENHOUSE.
THIS IS A TREASURY OF ORCHIDS, ISN'T IT?
I COULDN'T COMMUNICATE WITH MY PARENTS AT ALL.
I COULDN'T UNDER-STAND THEIR FEELINGS OR WHAT THEY WANTED FOR ME.
AND OF COURSE, THEY DIDN'T UNDERSTAND MY FEELINGS OR WHAT I WAS THINKING.

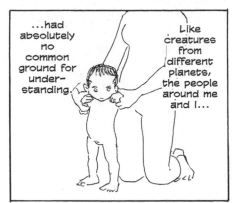

Now that I think about it, I used something other than words to think.
I expressed my emotions differently then too.
Like creatures from different planets, the people around me and I...
...had absolutely no common ground for under-standing.
I lived all by myself in a separate world.
Until I turned six years old.
That day, I snuck out of the room I was locked in and wandered into a neighboring greenhouse.
KLINK
KLINK
PLINK PLINK
TINK TINK

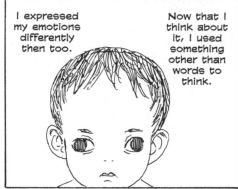

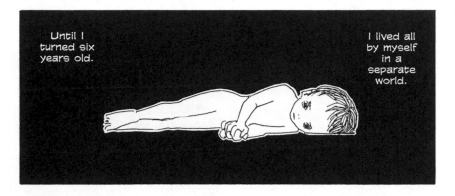

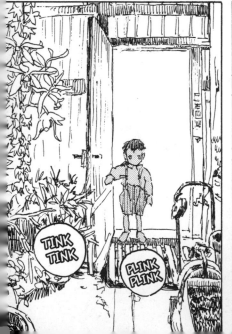

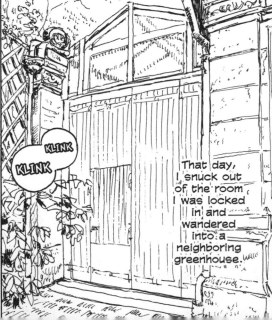

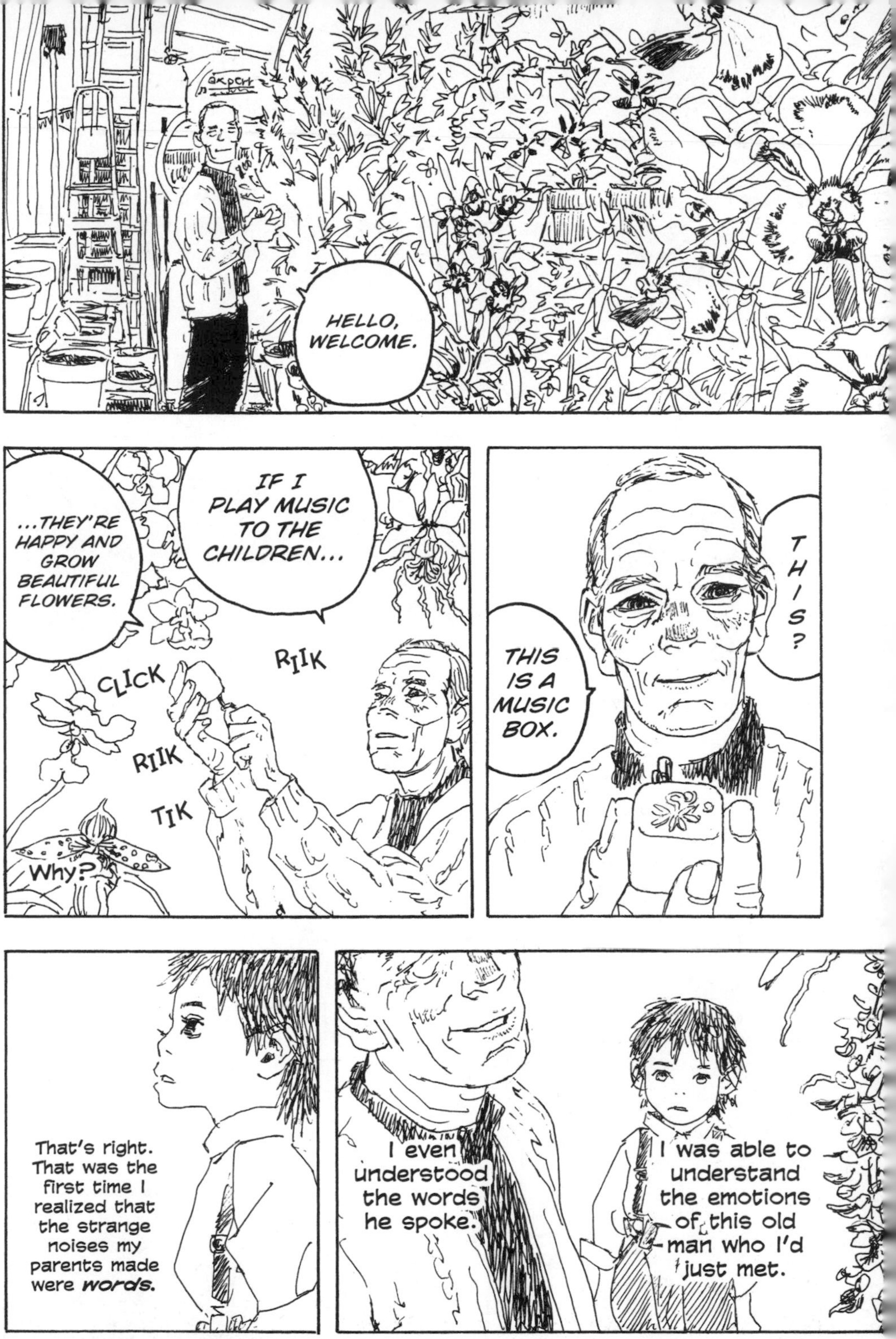
HELLO, WELCOME.
THIS?
THIS IS A MUSIC BOX.
IF I PLAY MUSIC TO THE CHILDREN...
...THEY'RE HAPPY AND GROW BEAUTIFUL FLOWERS.
RIIK
CLICK
RIIK
TIK
Why?
I was able to understand the emotions of this old man who I'd just met.
I even understood the words he spoke.
That's right. That was the first time I realized that the strange noises my parents made were *words*.

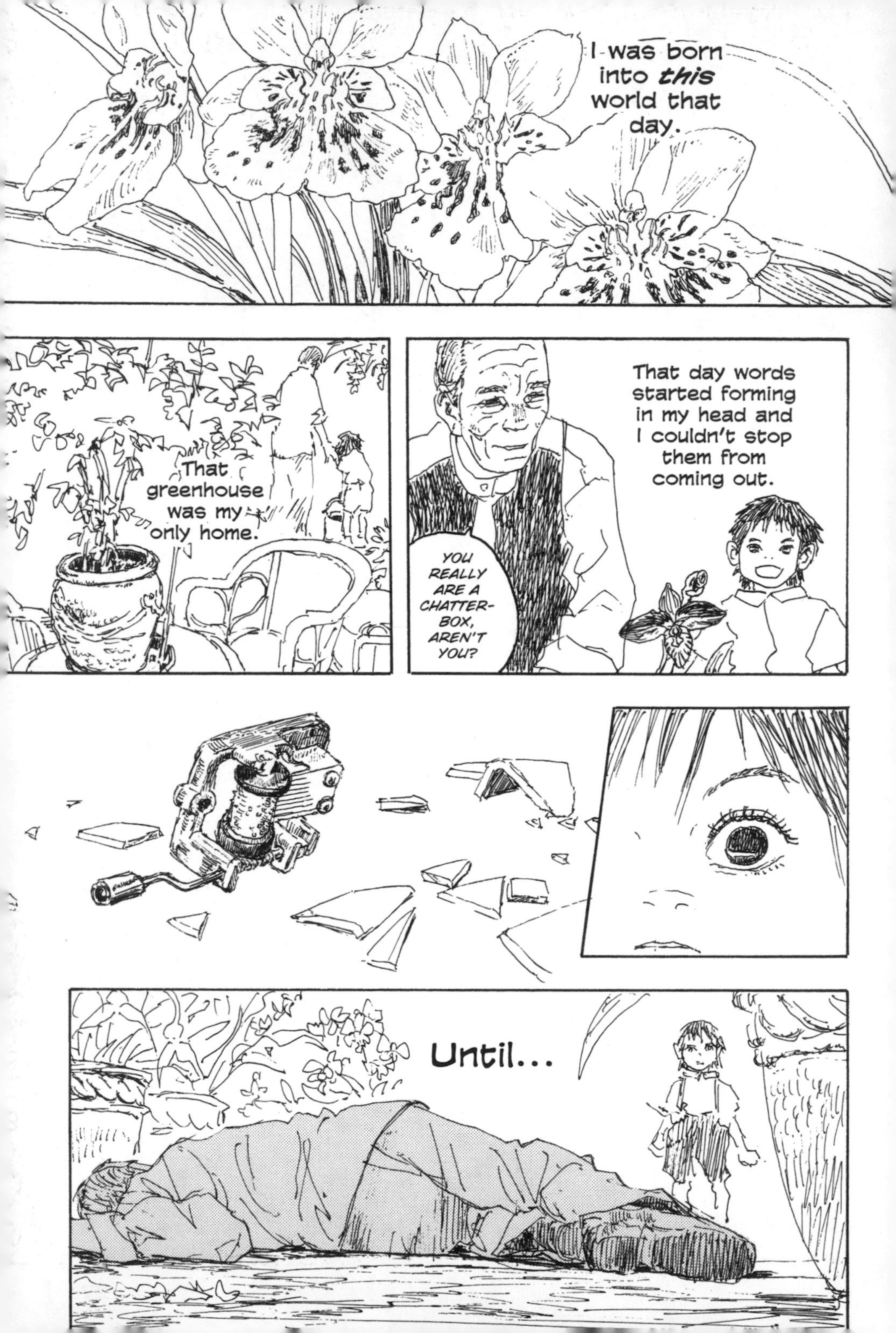
I was born into *this* world that day.
That day words started forming in my head and I couldn't stop them from coming out.
YOU REALLY ARE A CHATTER-BOX, AREN'T YOU?
That greenhouse was my only home.
Until...

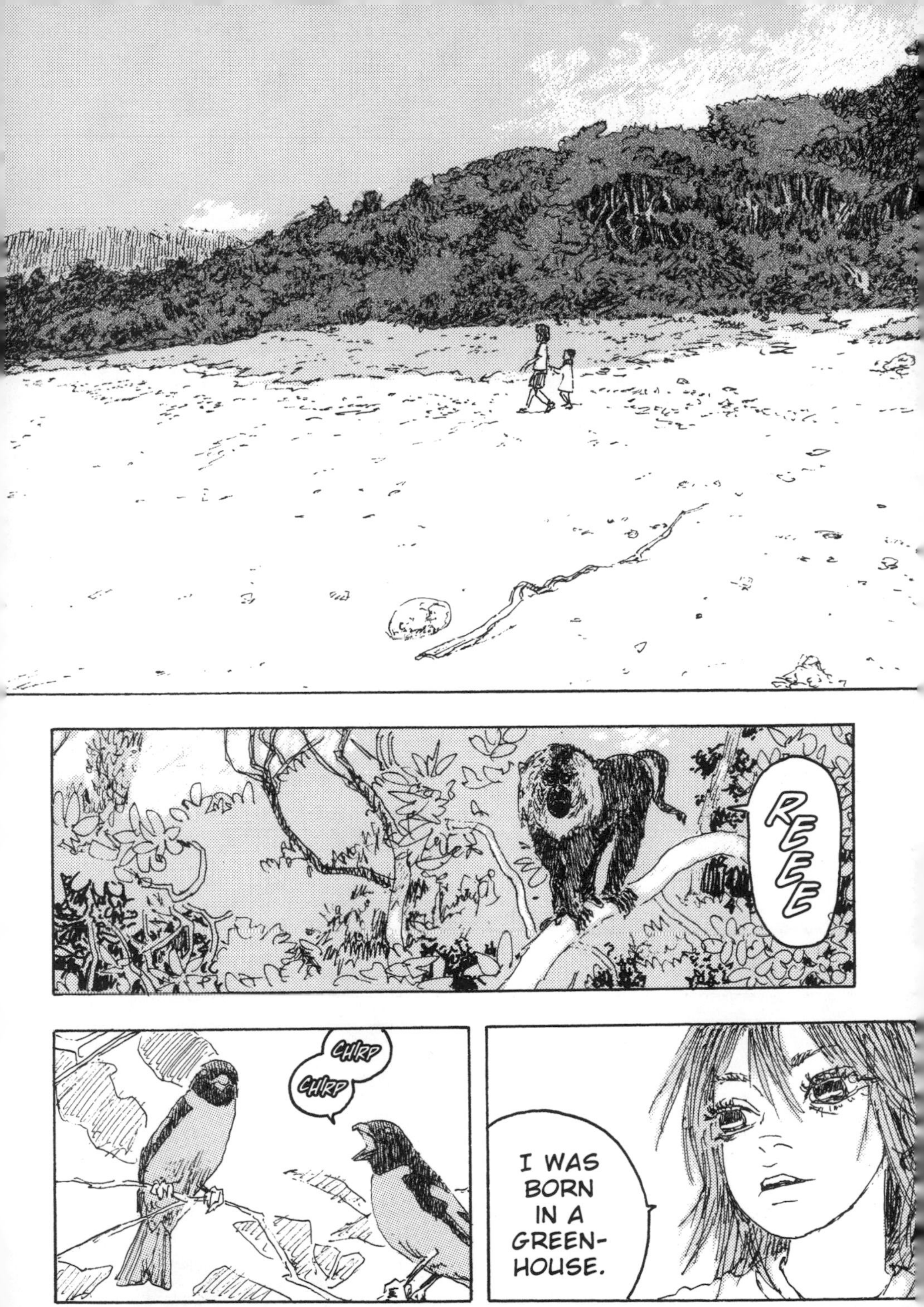
REEE
I WAS BORN IN A GREENHOUSE.
CHIRP
CHIRP

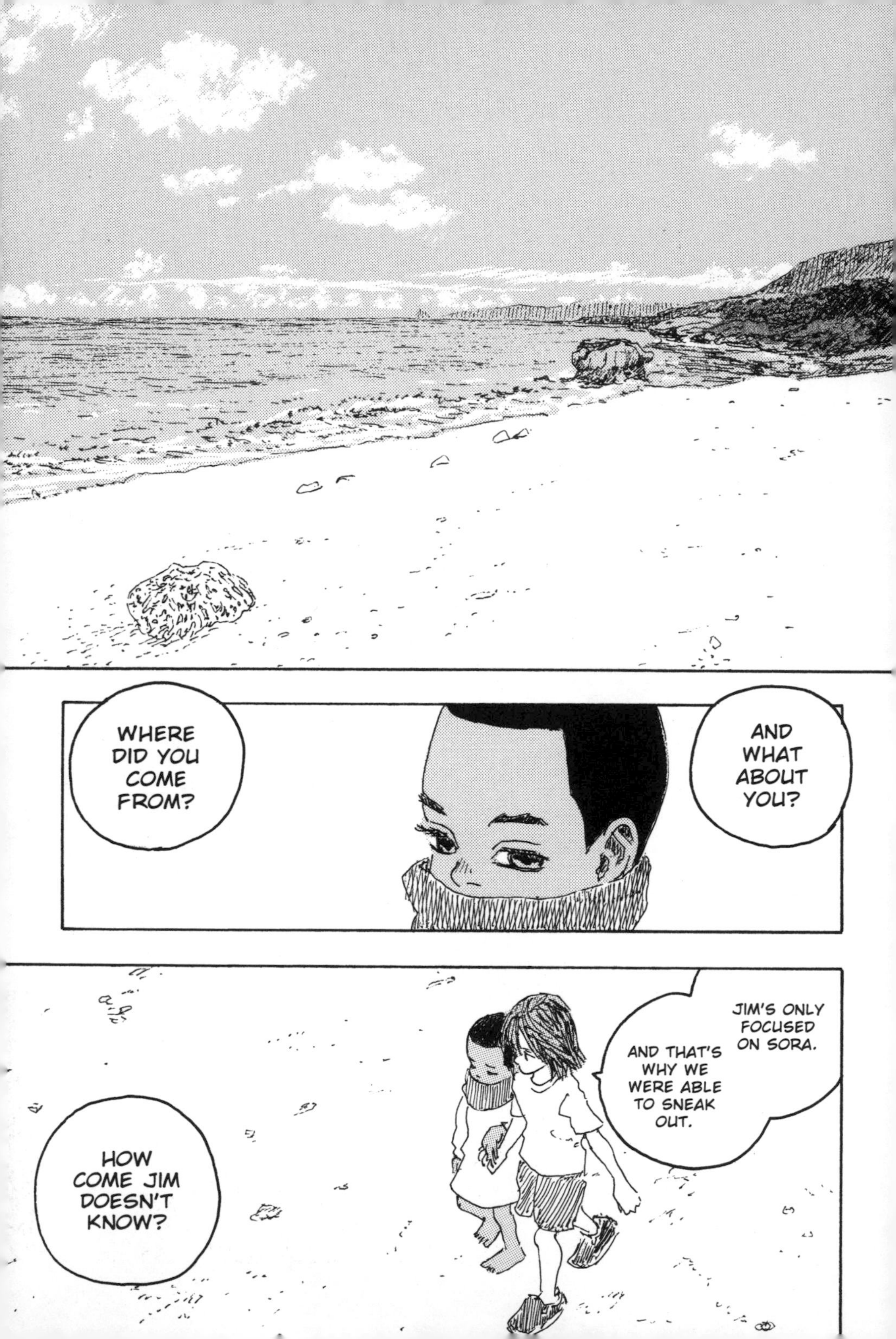
WHERE DID YOU COME FROM?
AND WHAT ABOUT YOU?
HOW COME JIM DOESN'T KNOW?
JIM'S ONLY FOCUSED ON SORA.
AND THAT'S WHY WE WERE ABLE TO SNEAK OUT.

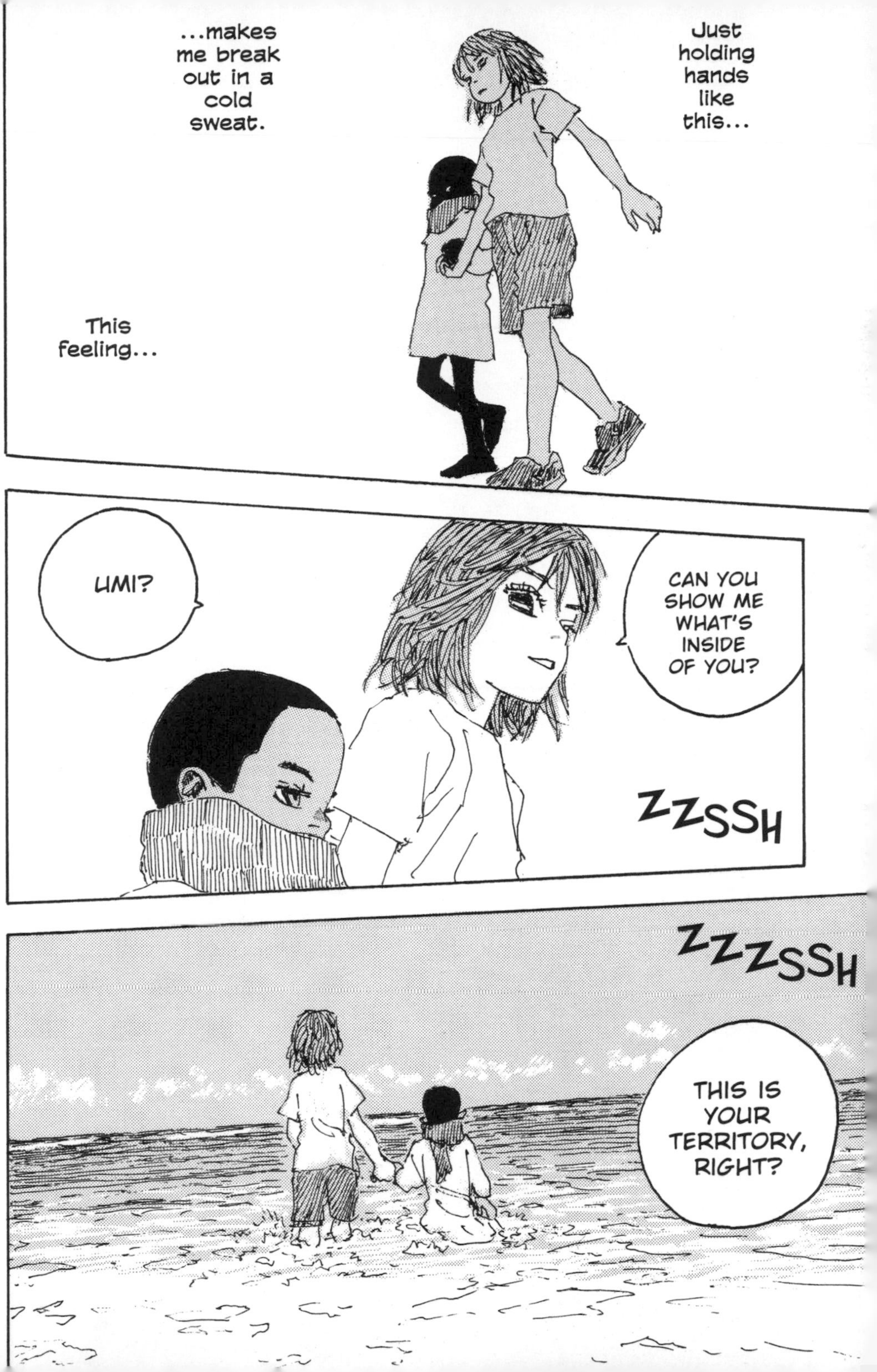
Just holding hands like this...
...makes me break out in a cold sweat.
This feeling...
CAN YOU SHOW ME WHAT'S INSIDE OF YOU?
UMI?
ZZSSH
ZZZSSH
THIS IS YOUR TERRITORY, RIGHT?

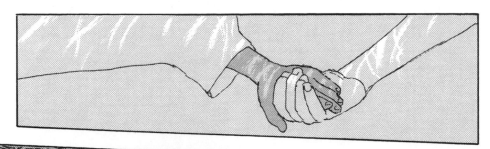

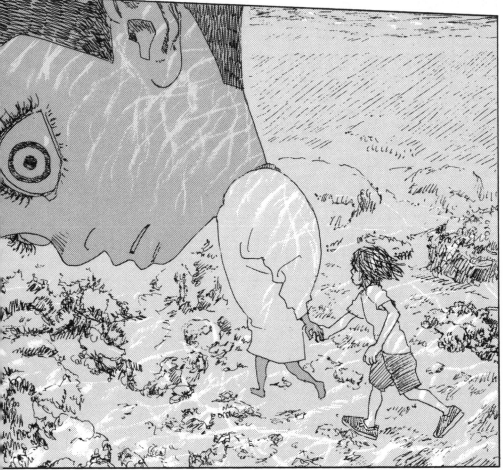

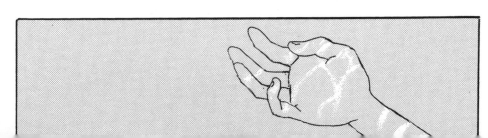

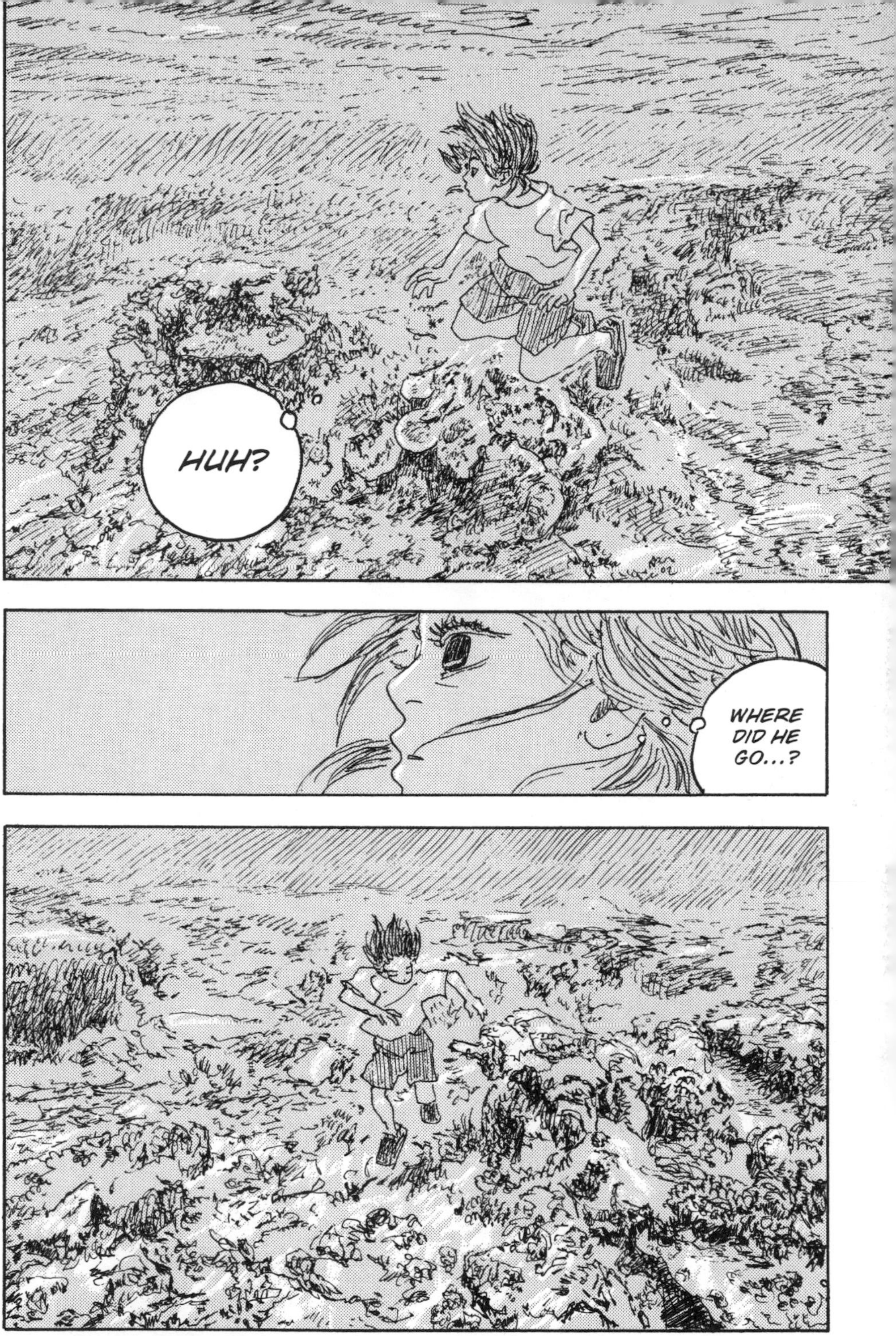
HUH?
WHERE DID HE GO...?

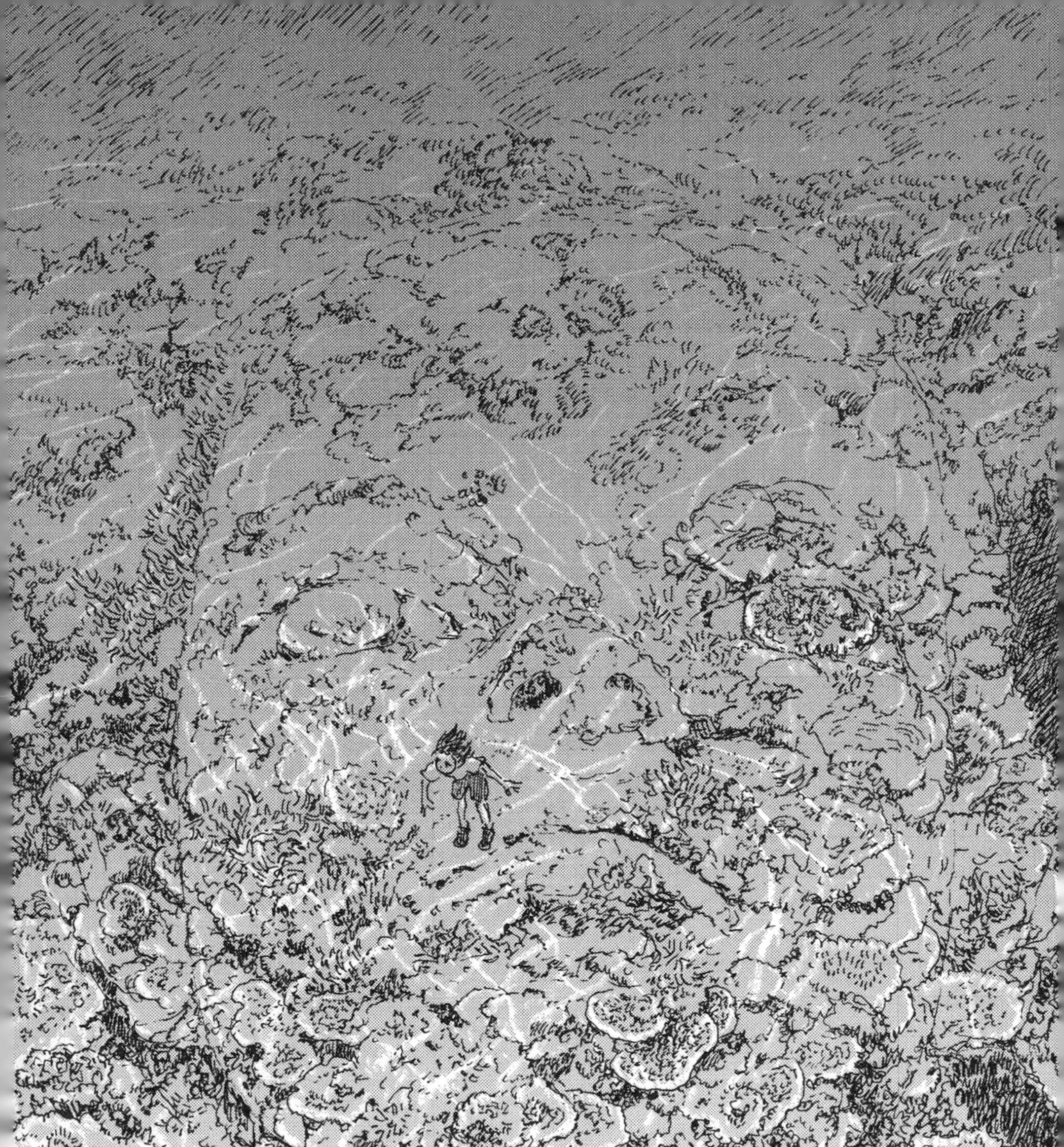
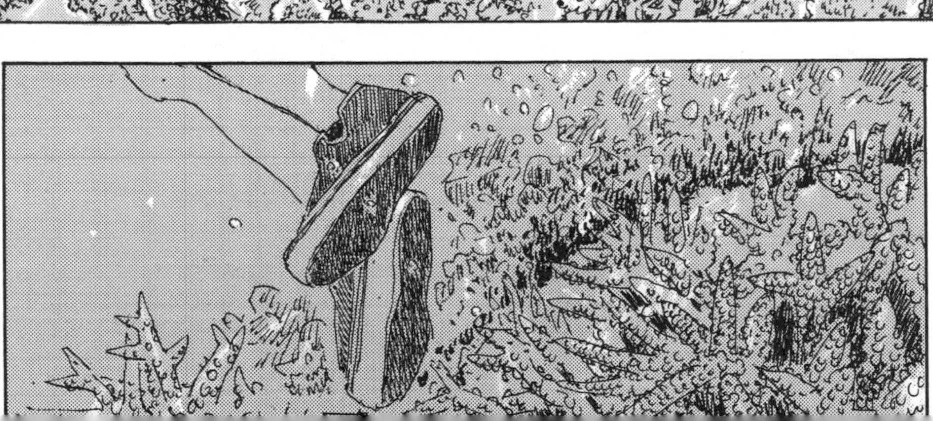

AH HH
AH...

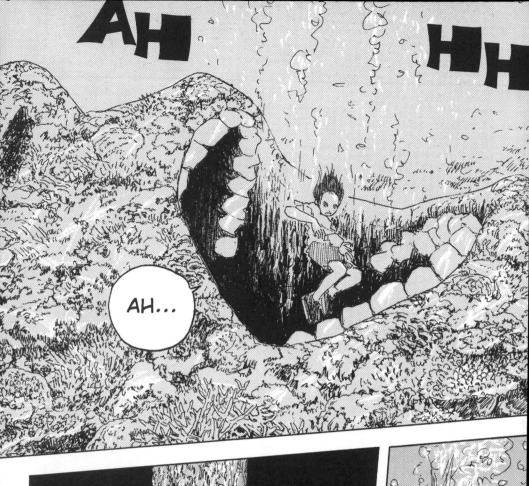

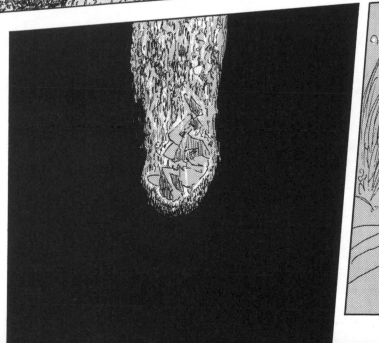

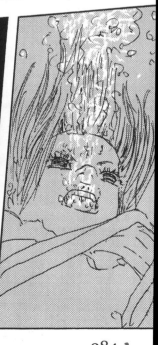

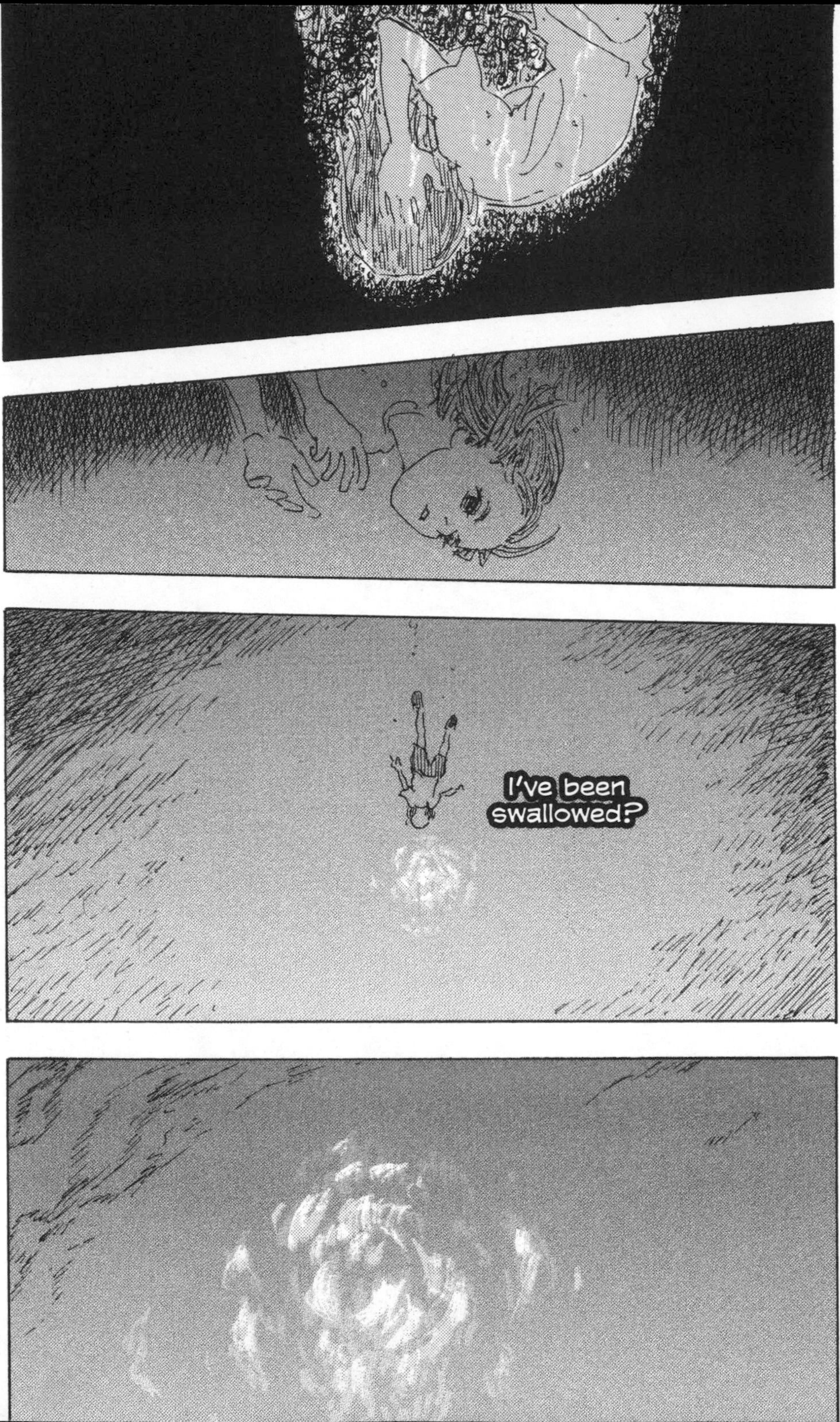
I've been swallowed?

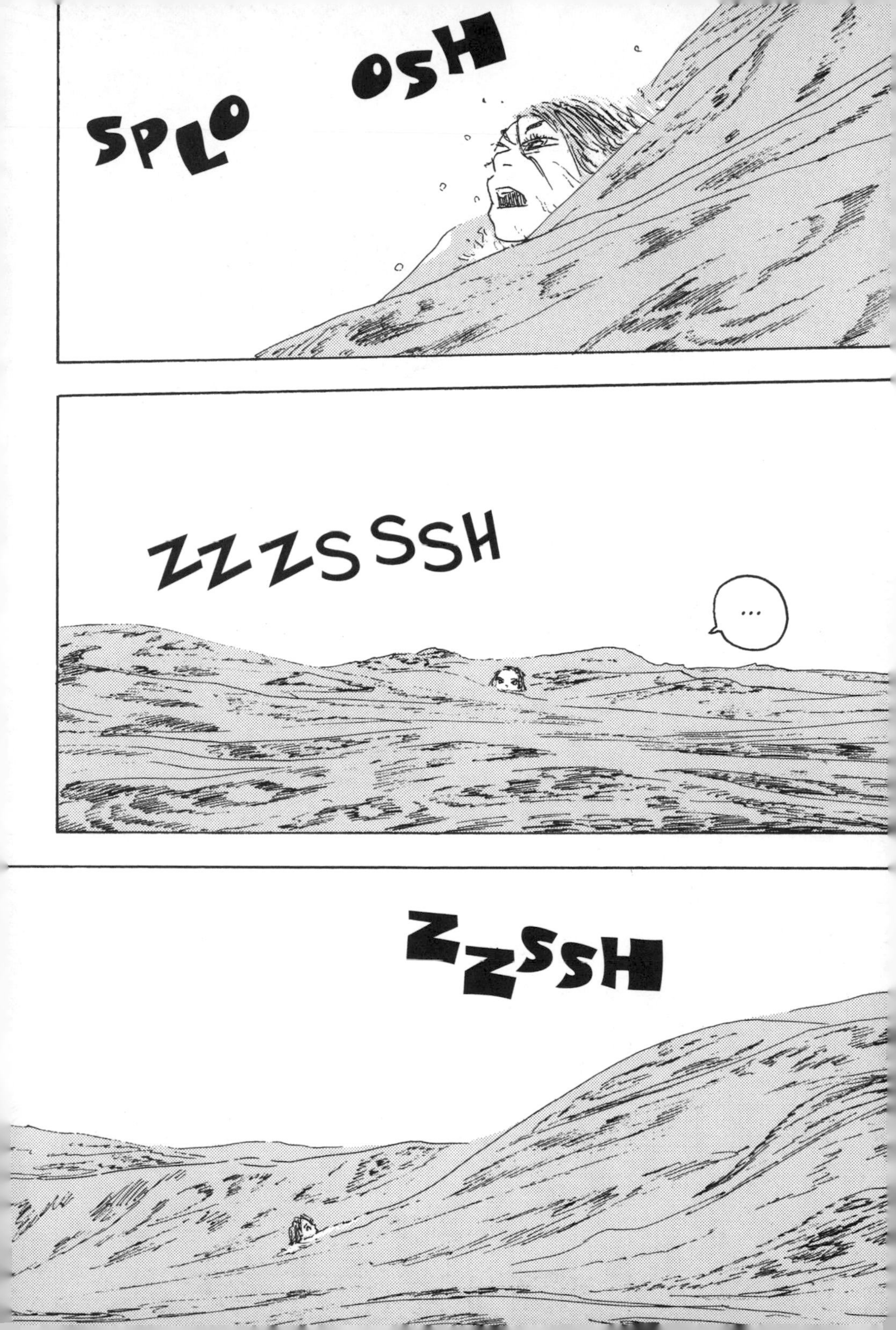
SPLOOSH
ZZZSSSH
...
ZZSSH

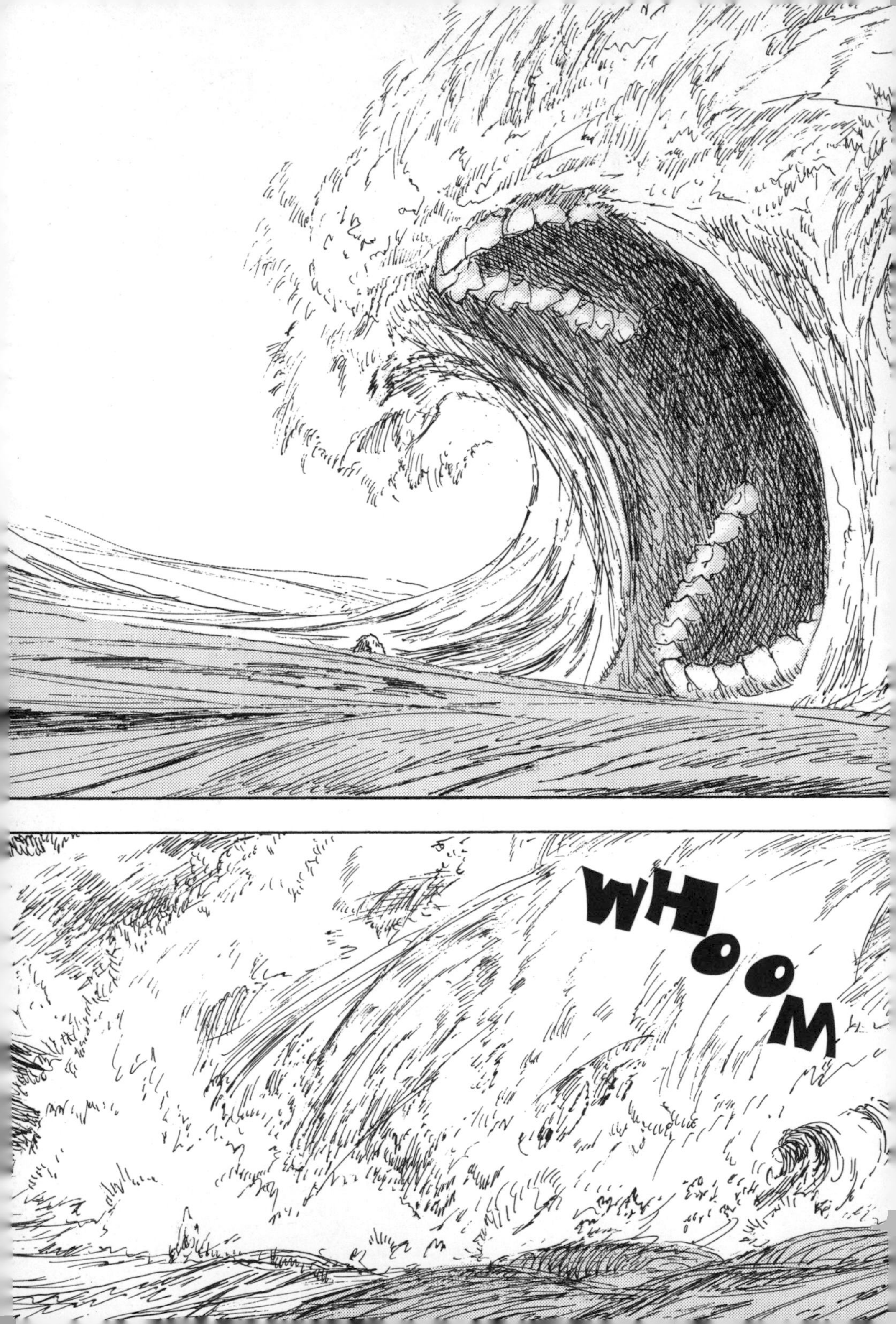
WHOOM

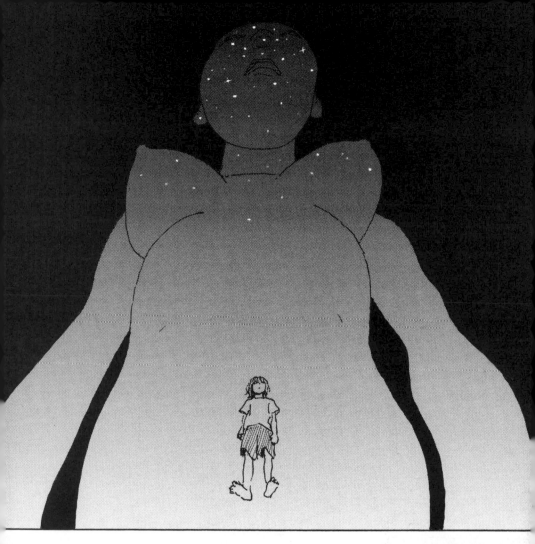

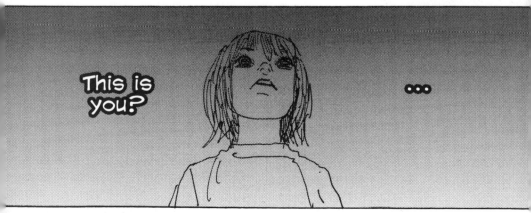

This is you?

...

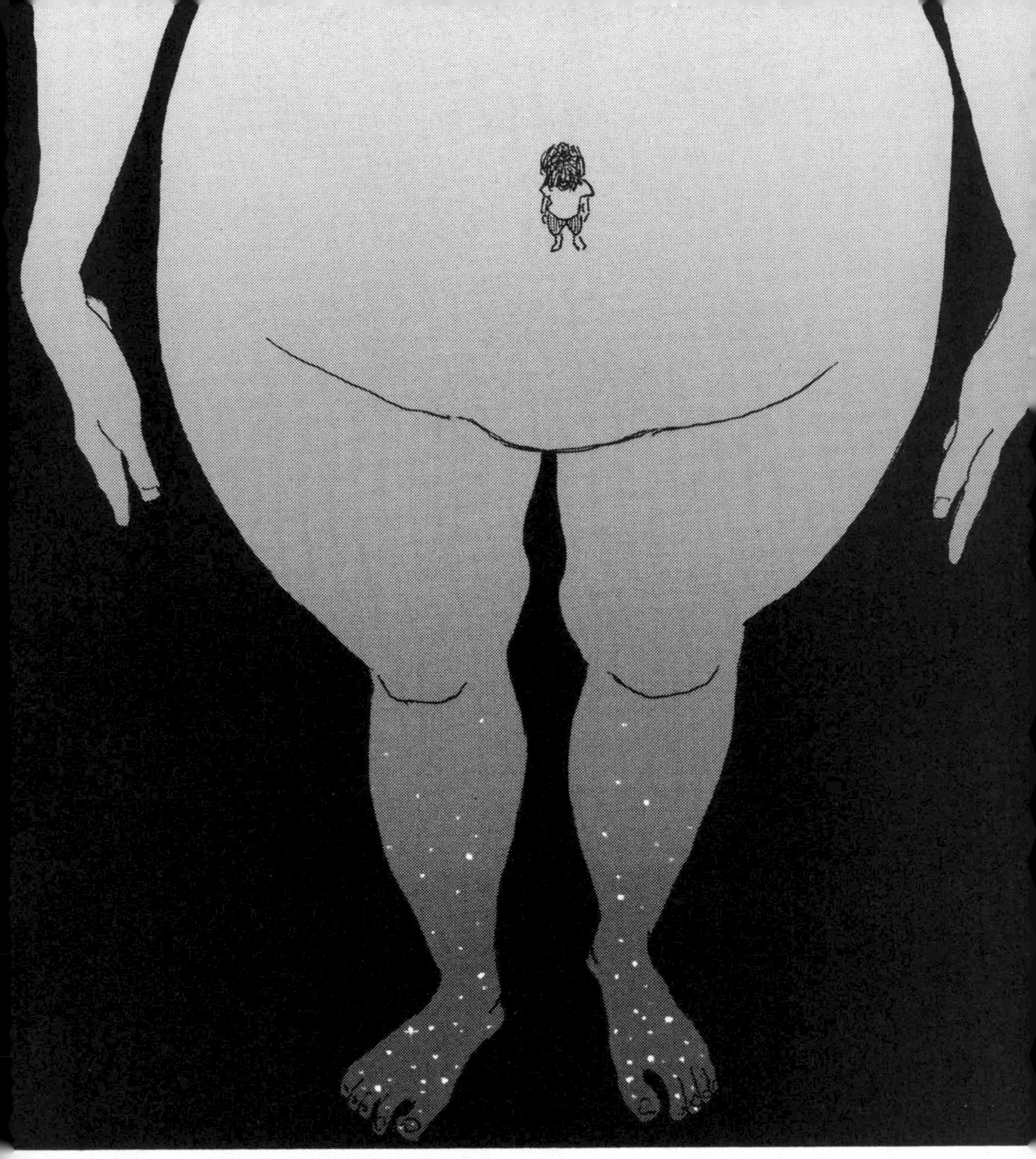

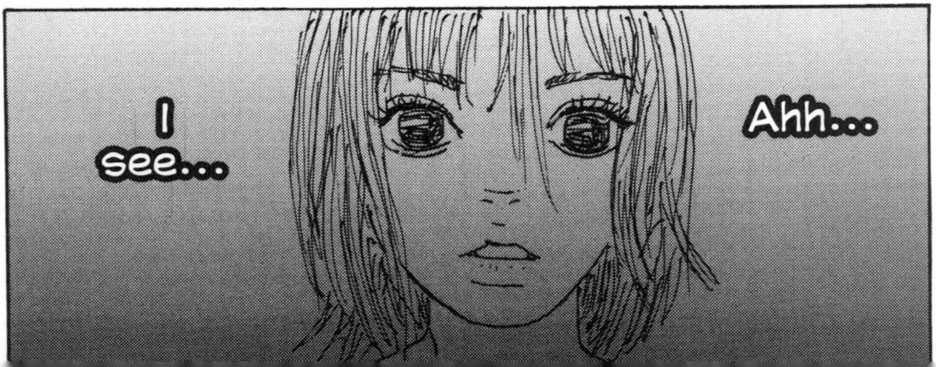
Ahh...
I see...

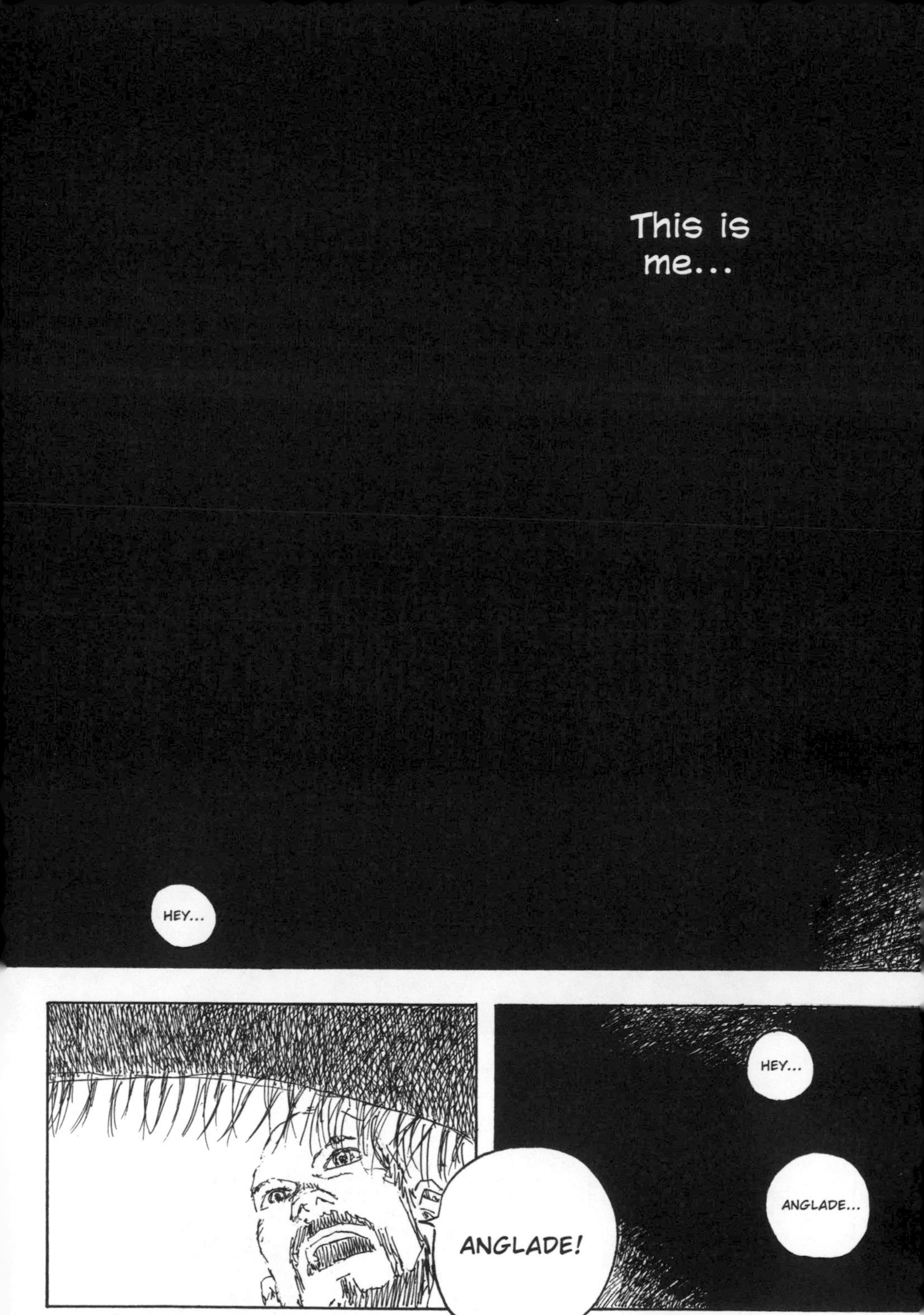
This is me...
HEY...
HEY...
ANGLADE...
ANGLADE!

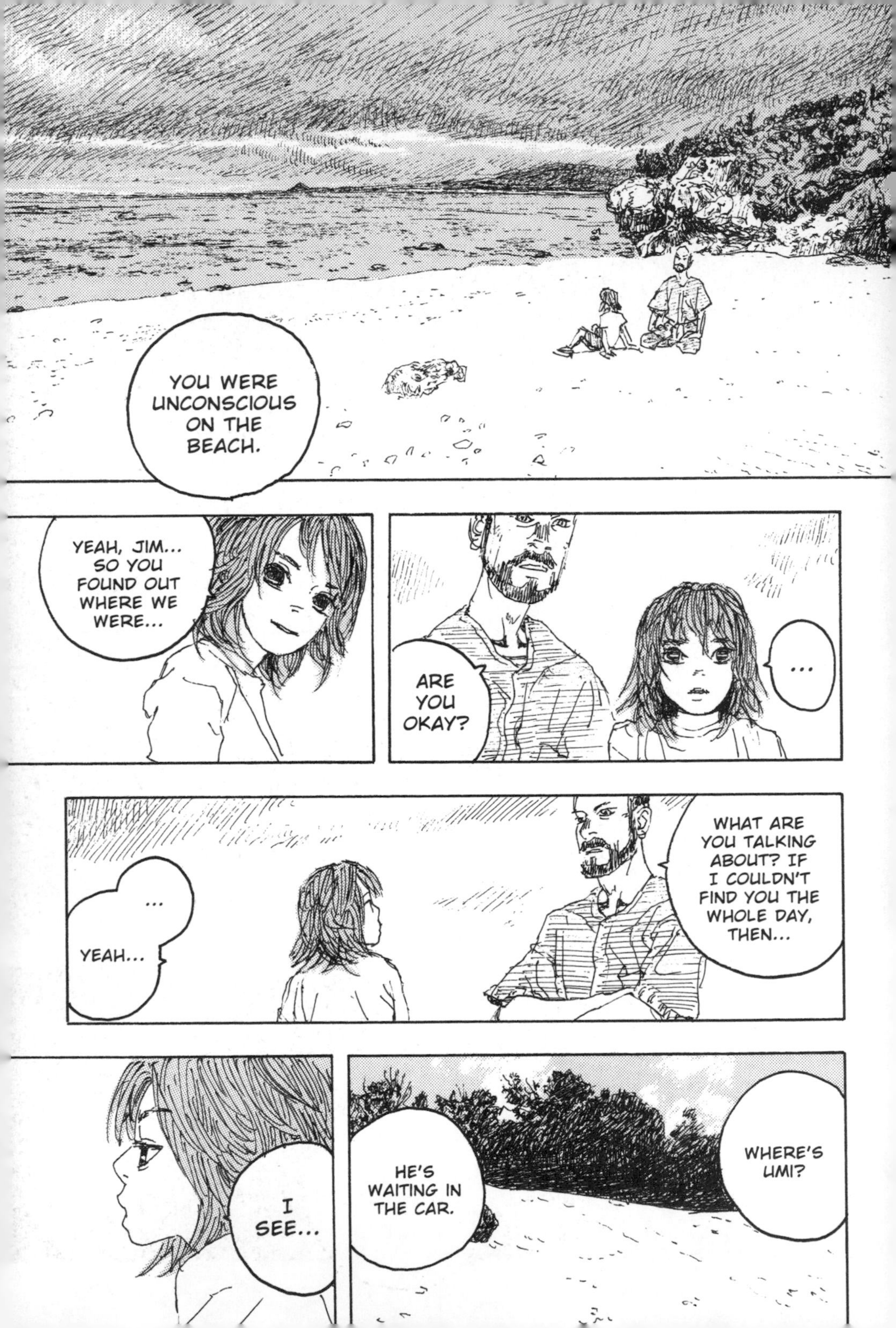
YOU WERE UNCONSCIOUS ON THE BEACH.
...
ARE YOU OKAY?
YEAH, JIM... SO YOU FOUND OUT WHERE WE WERE...
WHAT ARE YOU TALKING ABOUT? IF I COULDN'T FIND YOU THE WHOLE DAY, THEN...
... YEAH...
WHERE'S UMI?
HE'S WAITING IN THE CAR.
I SEE...

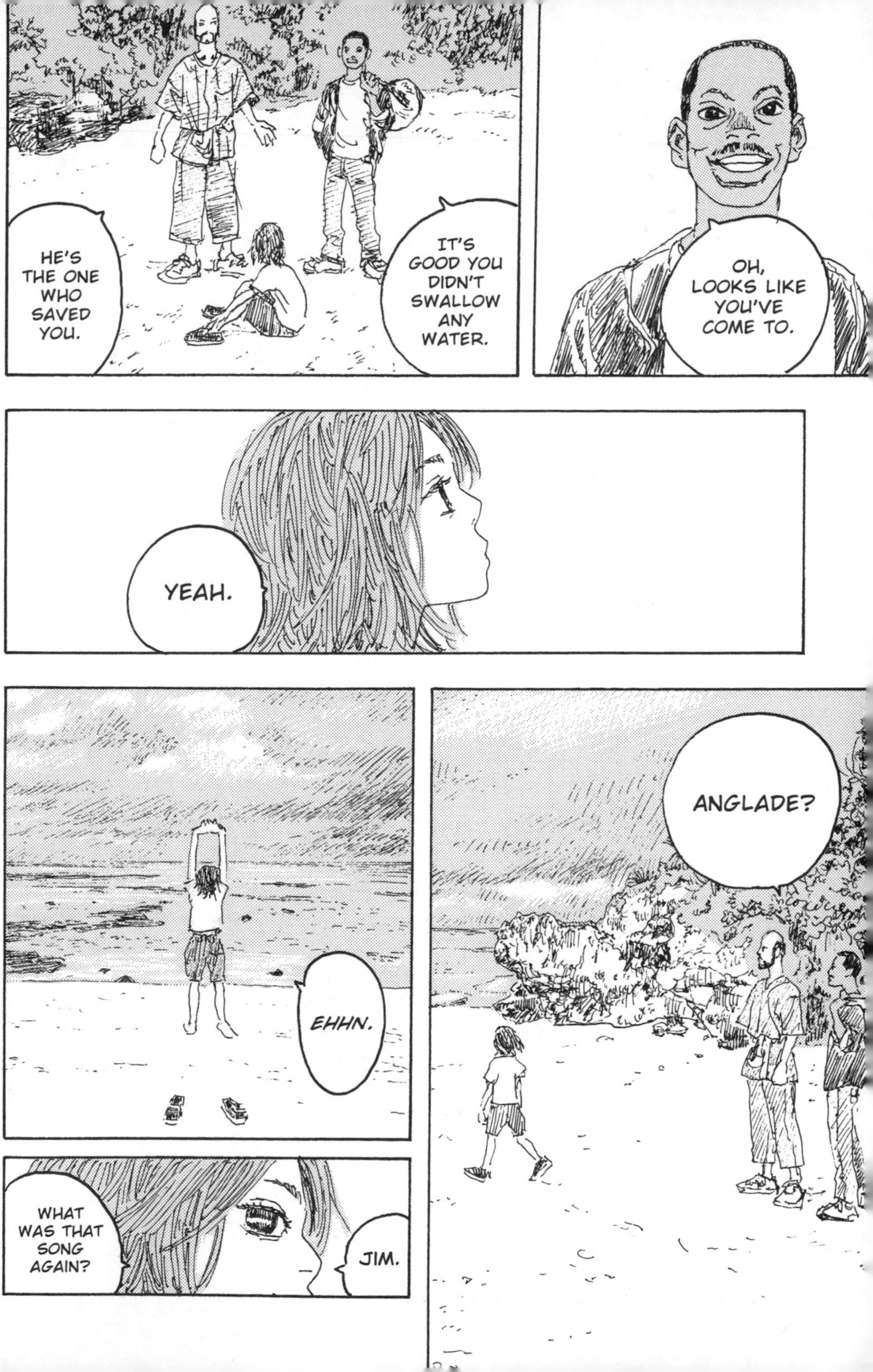
OH, LOOKS LIKE YOU'VE COME TO.
IT'S GOOD YOU DIDN'T SWALLOW ANY WATER.
HE'S THE ONE WHO SAVED YOU.
YEAH.
ANGLADE?
EHHN.
JIM.
WHAT WAS THAT SONG AGAIN?

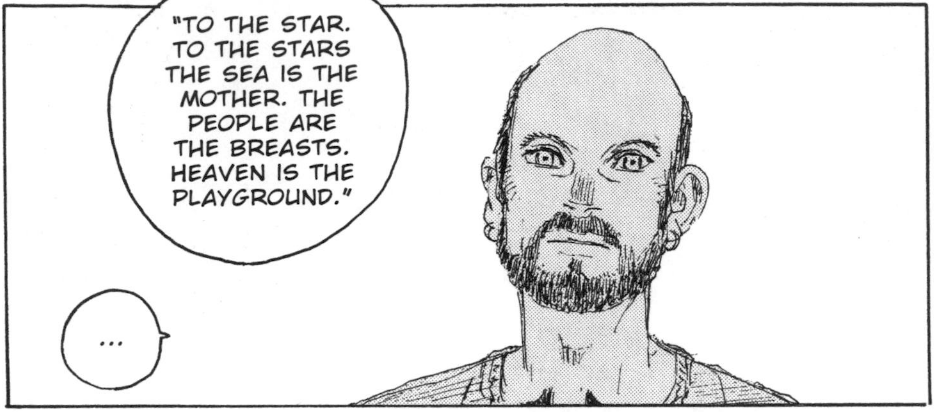
"TO THE STAR. TO THE STARS THE SEA IS THE MOTHER. THE PEOPLE ARE THE BREASTS. HEAVEN IS THE PLAYGROUND."
...

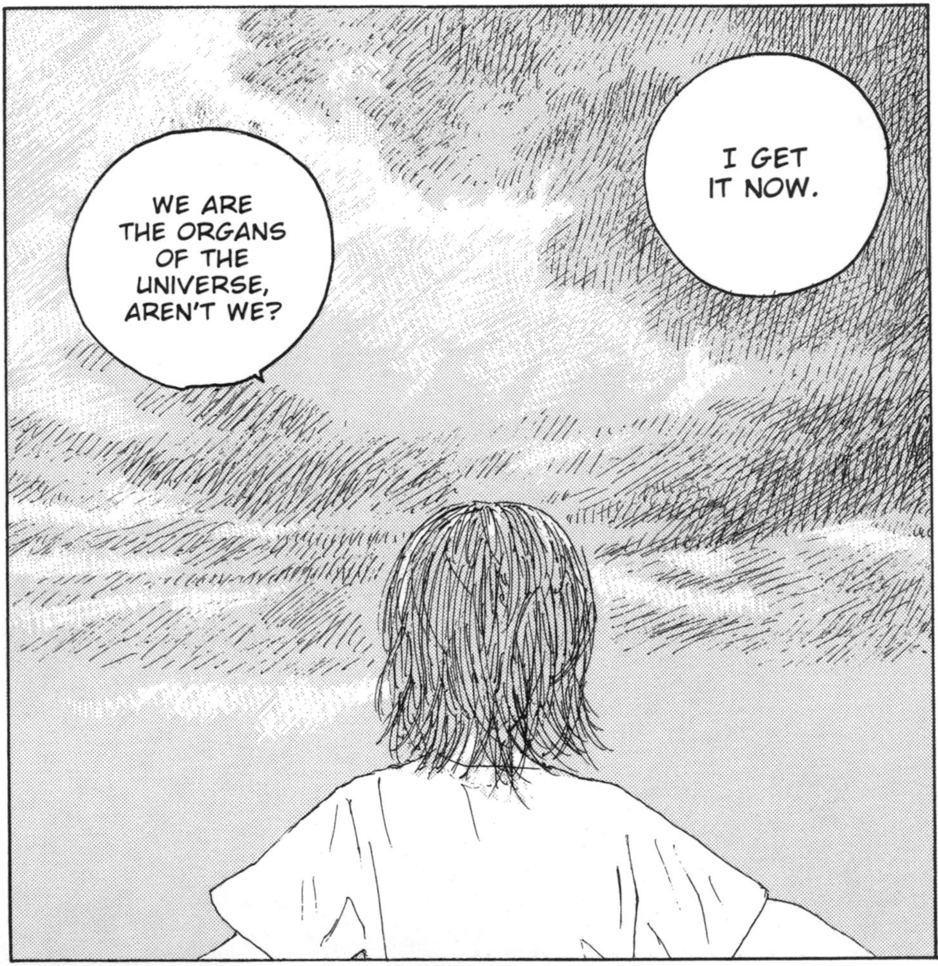
I GET IT NOW.
WE ARE THE ORGANS OF THE UNIVERSE, AREN'T WE?

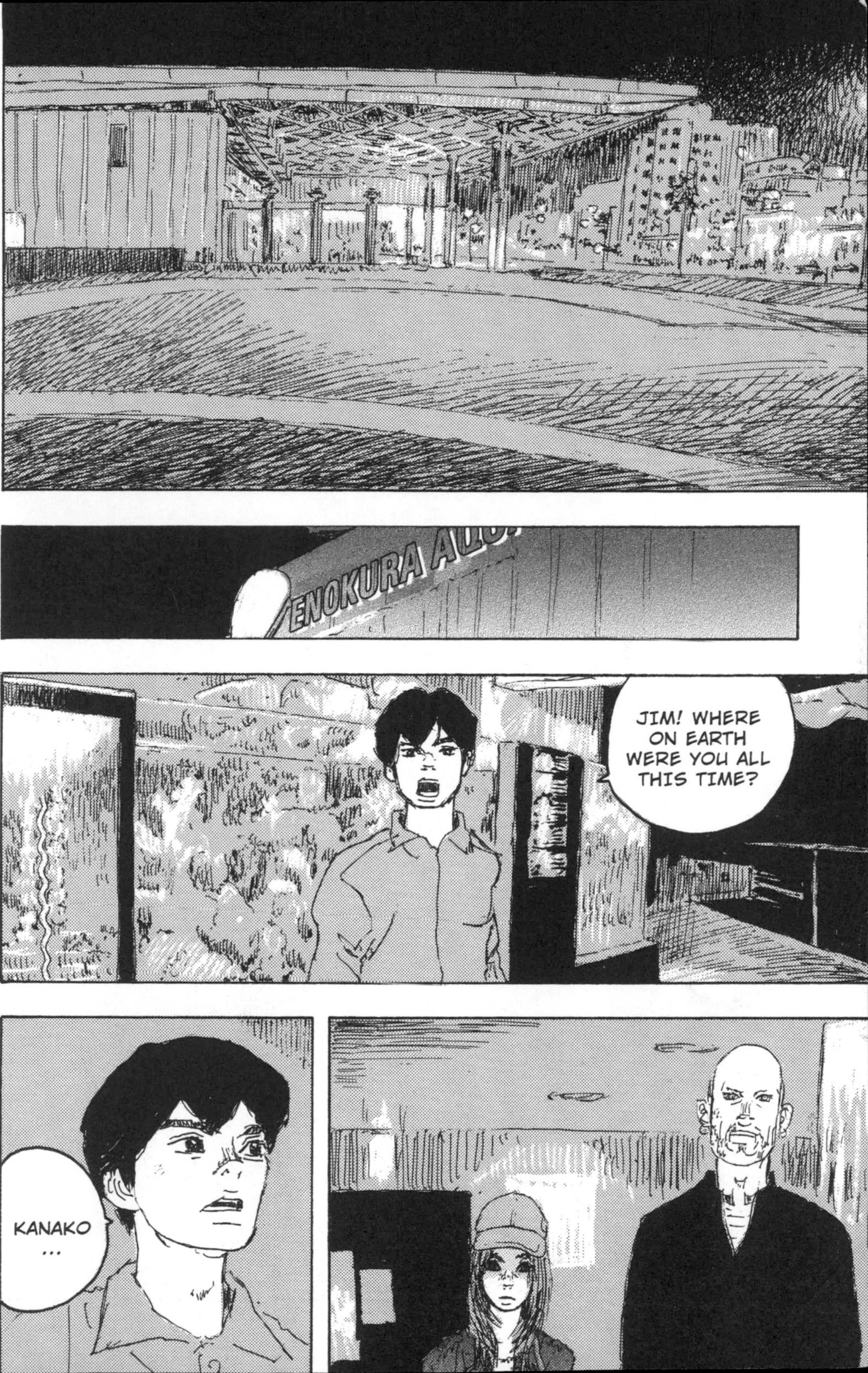
ENOKURA
JIM! WHERE ON EARTH WERE YOU ALL THIS TIME?
KANAKO ...

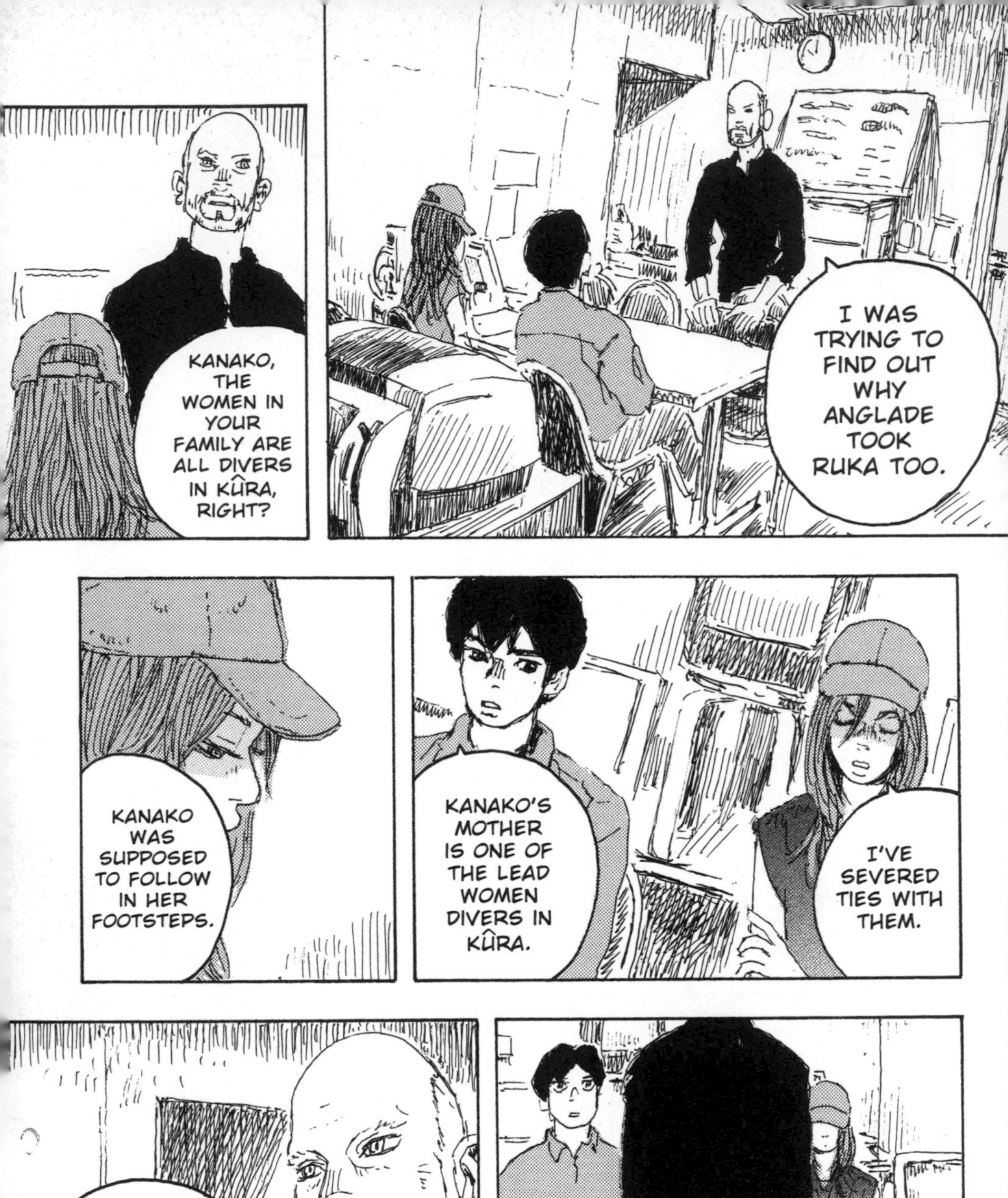
I WAS TRYING TO FIND OUT WHY ANGLADE TOOK RUKA TOO.
KANAKO, THE WOMEN IN YOUR FAMILY ARE ALL DIVERS IN KÛRA, RIGHT?
KANAKO'S MOTHER IS ONE OF THE LEAD WOMEN DIVERS IN KÛRA.
I'VE SEVERED TIES WITH THEM.
KANAKO WAS SUPPOSED TO FOLLOW IN HER FOOTSTEPS.
WAS SHE A DIVER SINCE CHILDHOOD?
YES, SHE WAS.
IN THAT CASE, I'M SURE RUKA INHERITED THAT TALENT.

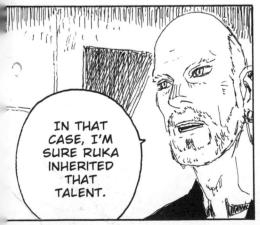

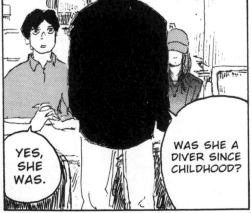

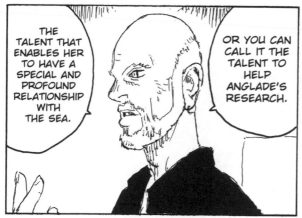

DIVING TALENT?
OR YOU CAN CALL IT THE TALENT TO HELP ANGLADE'S RESEARCH.
THE TALENT THAT ENABLES HER TO HAVE A SPECIAL AND PROFOUND RELATIONSHIP WITH THE SEA.
YOU MUST KNOW WHAT I'M TALKING ABOUT.
...
ANGLADE IS PART OF A GROUP INTERESTED IN THE OCEAN.
I'M CONNECTED TO ANOTHER GROUP WITH DIFFERENT PHILOSOPHIES.
RIGHT NOW, EACH GROUP ...
...IS TRYING TO FIND A HYPOTHETICAL PERSON WHO'S BEEN INVOLVED IN THE UNUSUAL CHANGES WE'VE SEEN IN THE OCEAN THE LAST FEW YEARS.

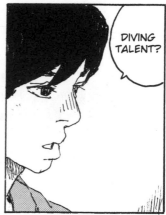

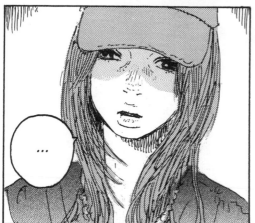

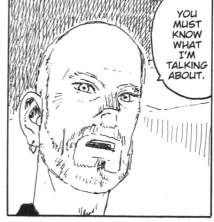

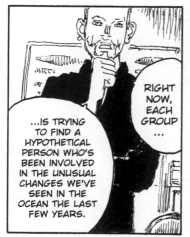

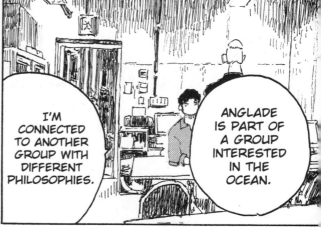

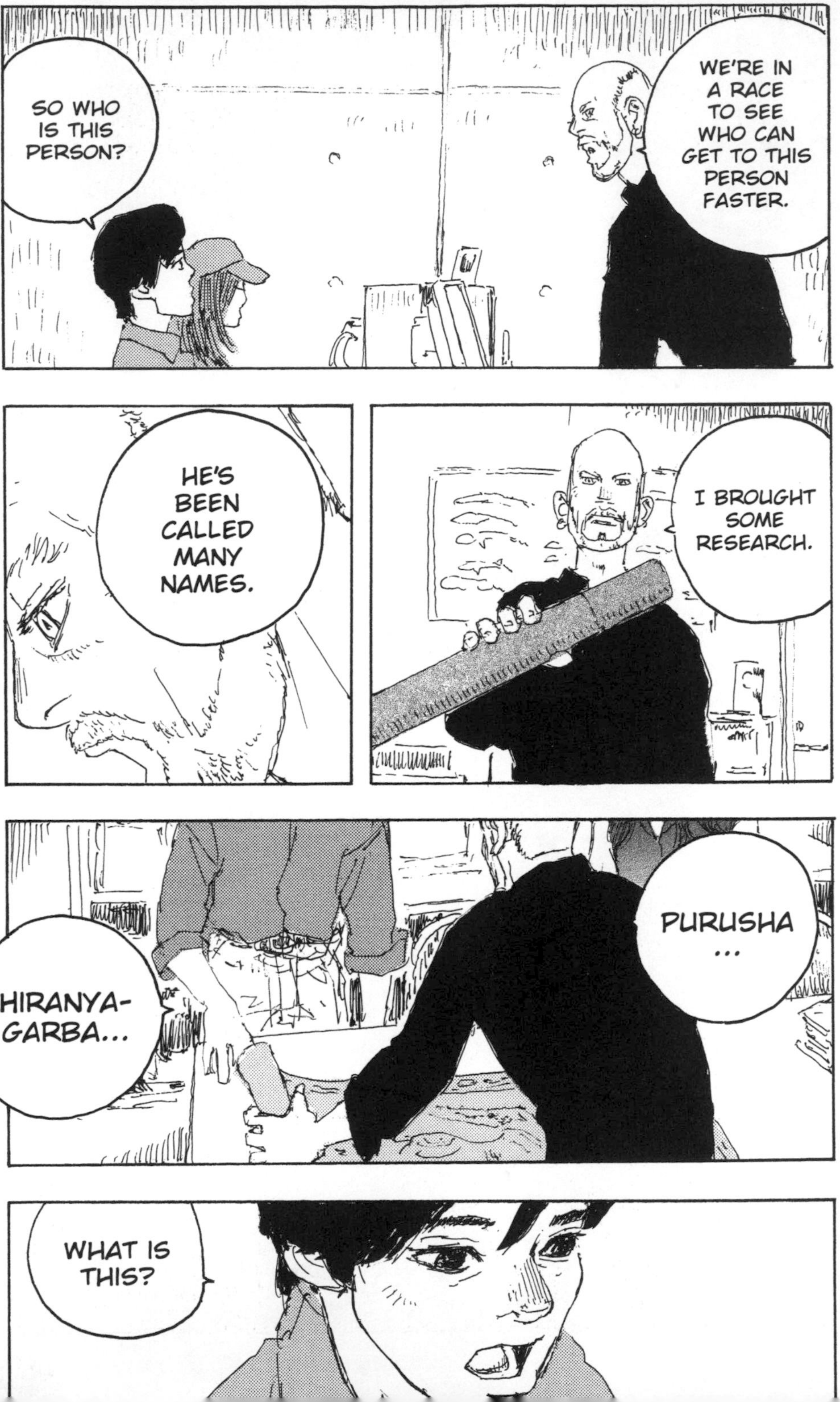
WE'RE IN A RACE TO SEE WHO CAN GET TO THIS PERSON FASTER.
SO WHO IS THIS PERSON?
I BROUGHT SOME RESEARCH.
HE'S BEEN CALLED MANY NAMES.
PURUSHA...
HIRANYA-GARBA...
WHAT IS THIS?

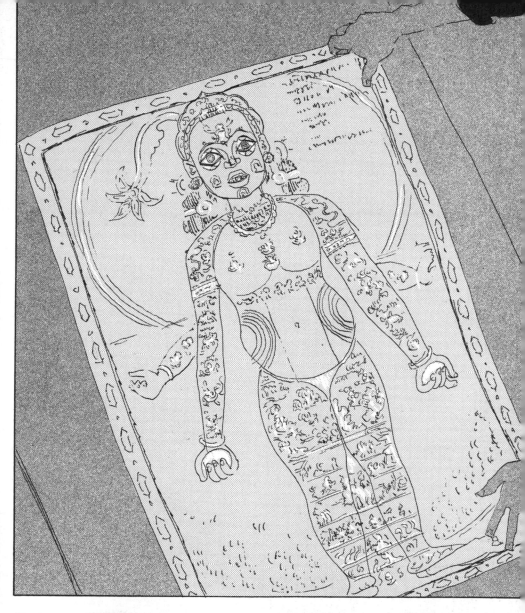

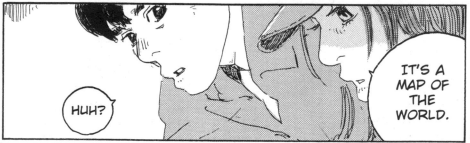

HUH?

IT'S A MAP OF THE WORLD.

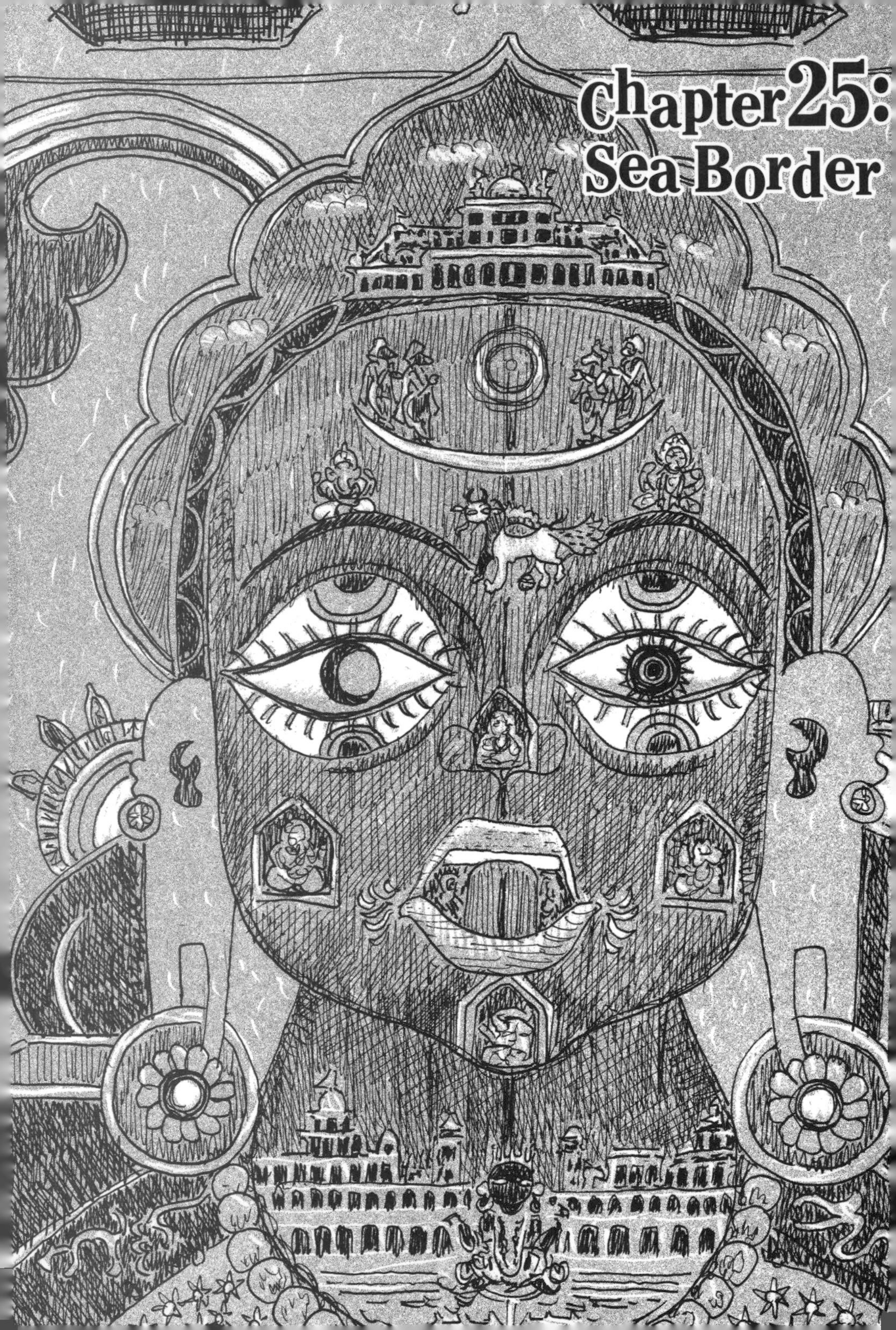
Chapter 25:
Sea Border

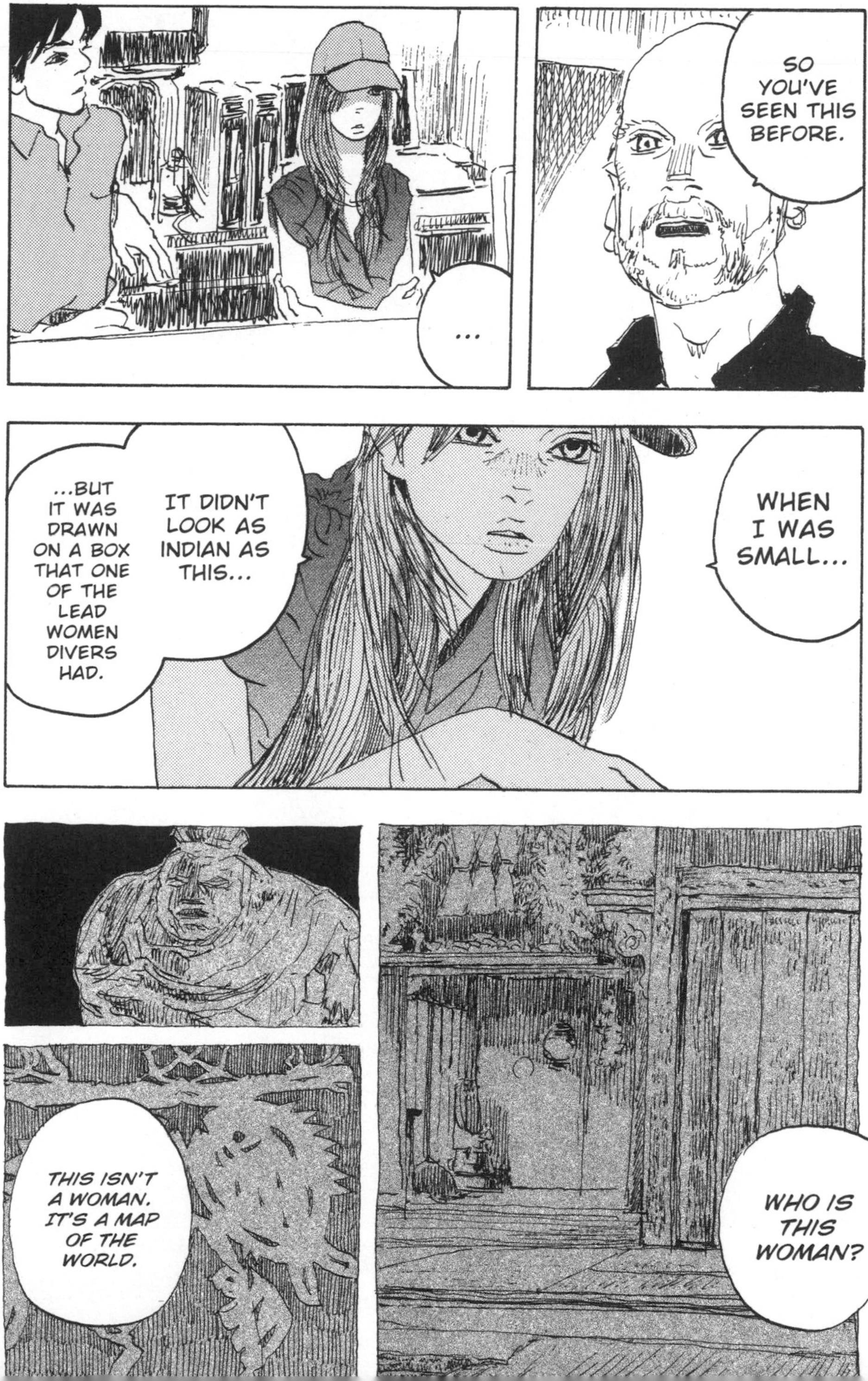
SO YOU'VE SEEN THIS BEFORE.
...
WHEN I WAS SMALL...
IT DIDN'T LOOK AS INDIAN AS THIS...
...BUT IT WAS DRAWN ON A BOX THAT ONE OF THE LEAD WOMEN DIVERS HAD.
WHO IS THIS WOMAN?
THIS ISN'T A WOMAN. IT'S A MAP OF THE WORLD.

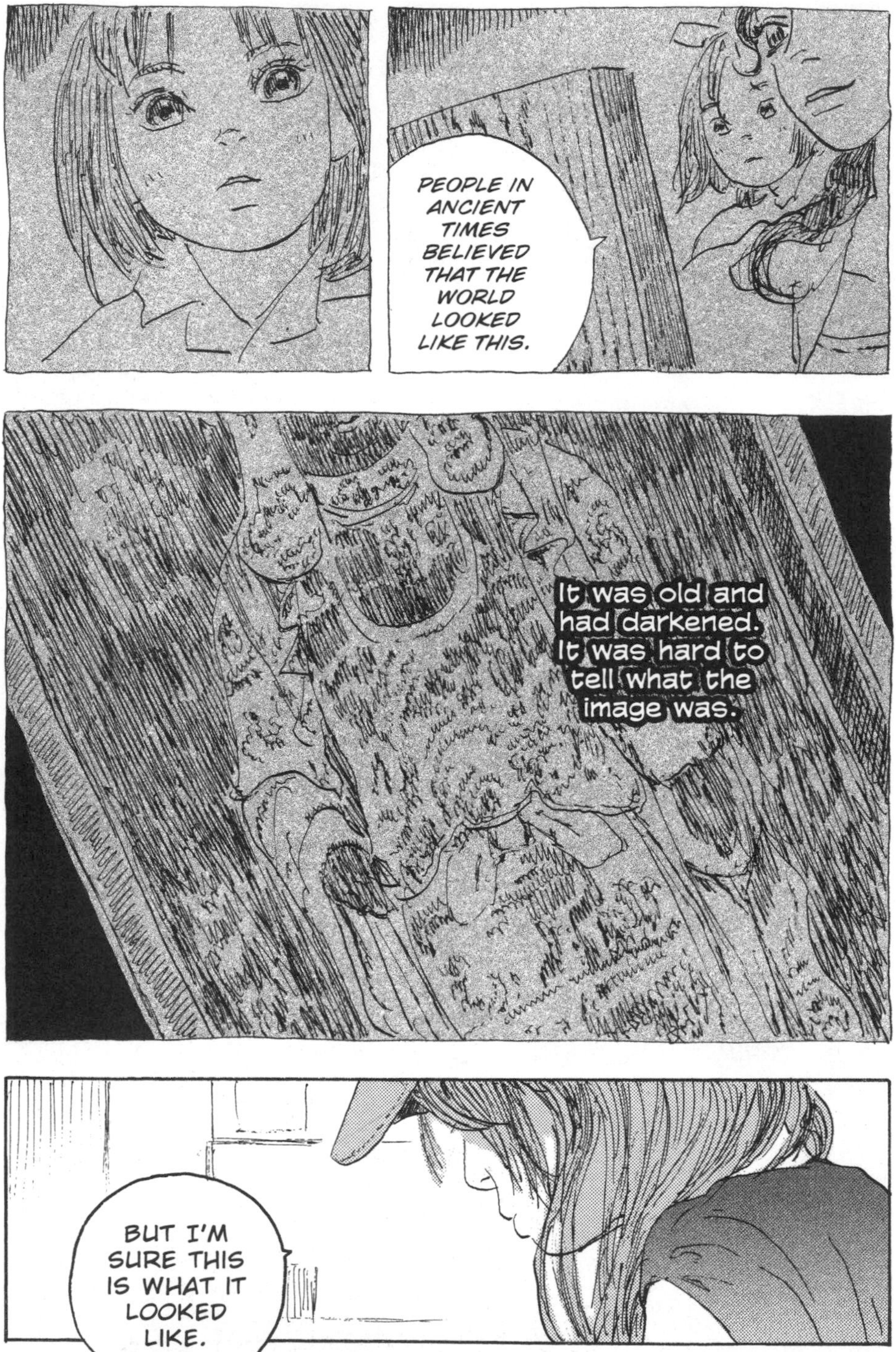
PEOPLE IN ANCIENT TIMES BELIEVED THAT THE WORLD LOOKED LIKE THIS.
It was old and had darkened. It was hard to tell what the image was.
BUT I'M SURE THIS IS WHAT IT LOOKED LIKE.

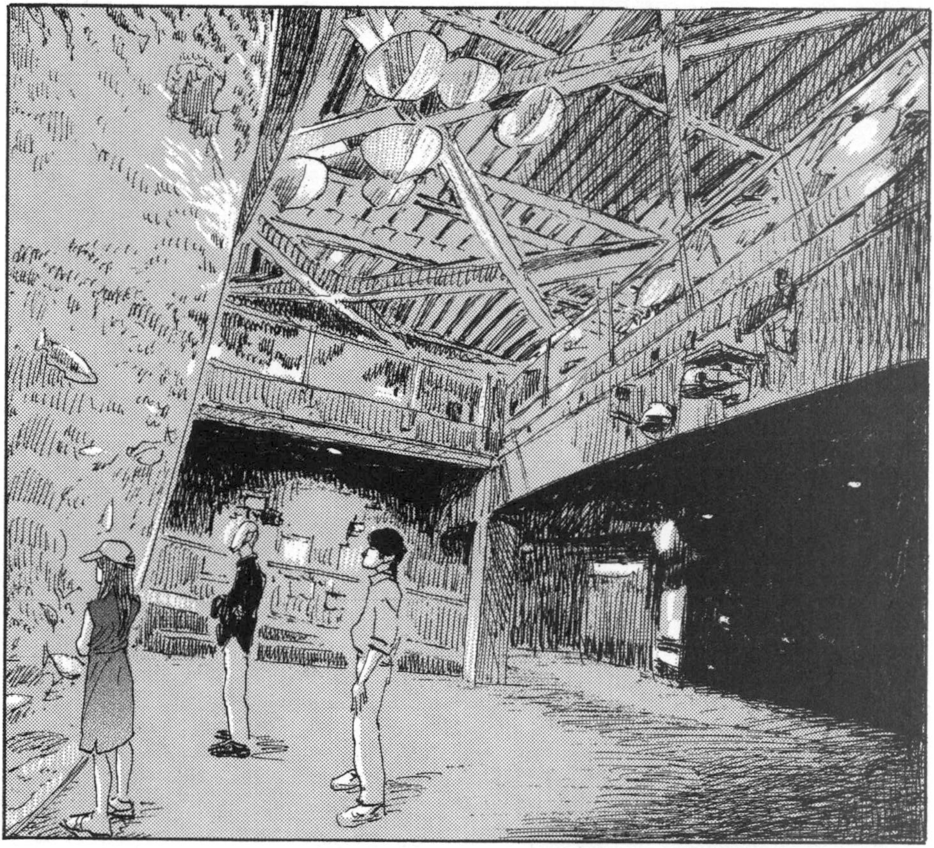

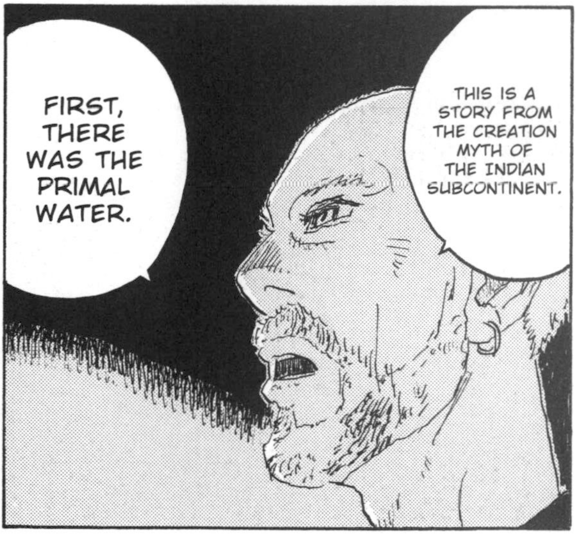
THIS IS A STORY FROM THE CREATION MYTH OF THE INDIAN SUBCONTINENT.
FIRST, THERE WAS THE PRIMAL WATER.

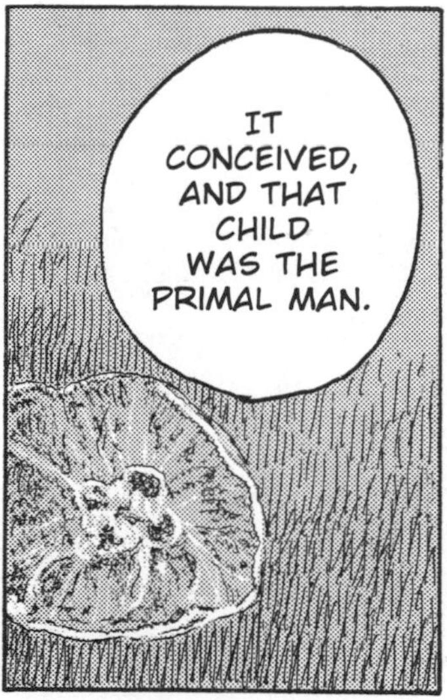
IT CONCEIVED, AND THAT CHILD WAS THE PRIMAL MAN.

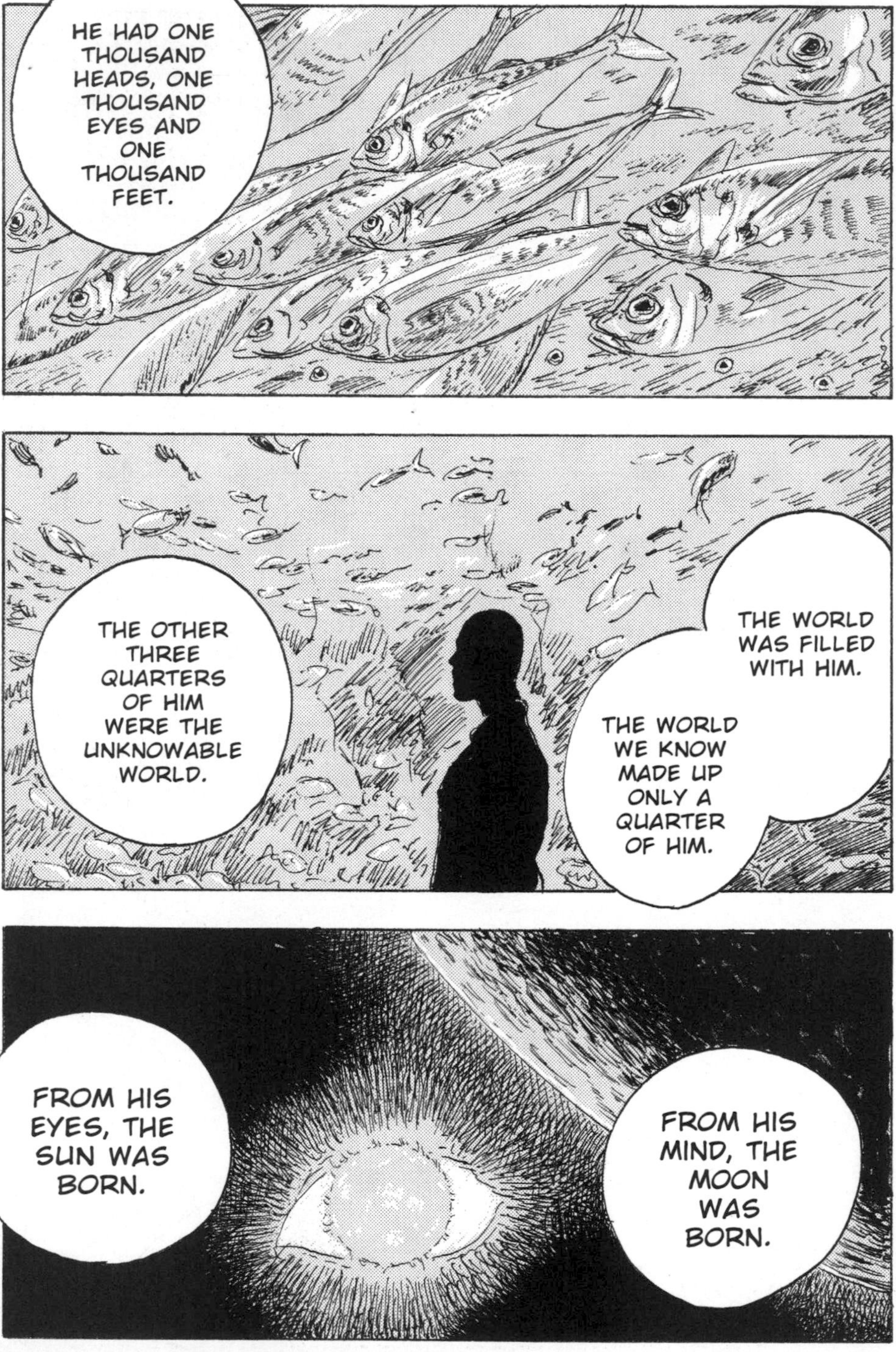
HE HAD ONE THOUSAND HEADS, ONE THOUSAND EYES AND ONE THOUSAND FEET.
THE WORLD WAS FILLED WITH HIM.
THE WORLD WE KNOW MADE UP ONLY A QUARTER OF HIM.
THE OTHER THREE QUARTERS OF HIM WERE THE UNKNOWABLE WORLD.
FROM HIS MIND, THE MOON WAS BORN.
FROM HIS EYES, THE SUN WAS BORN.

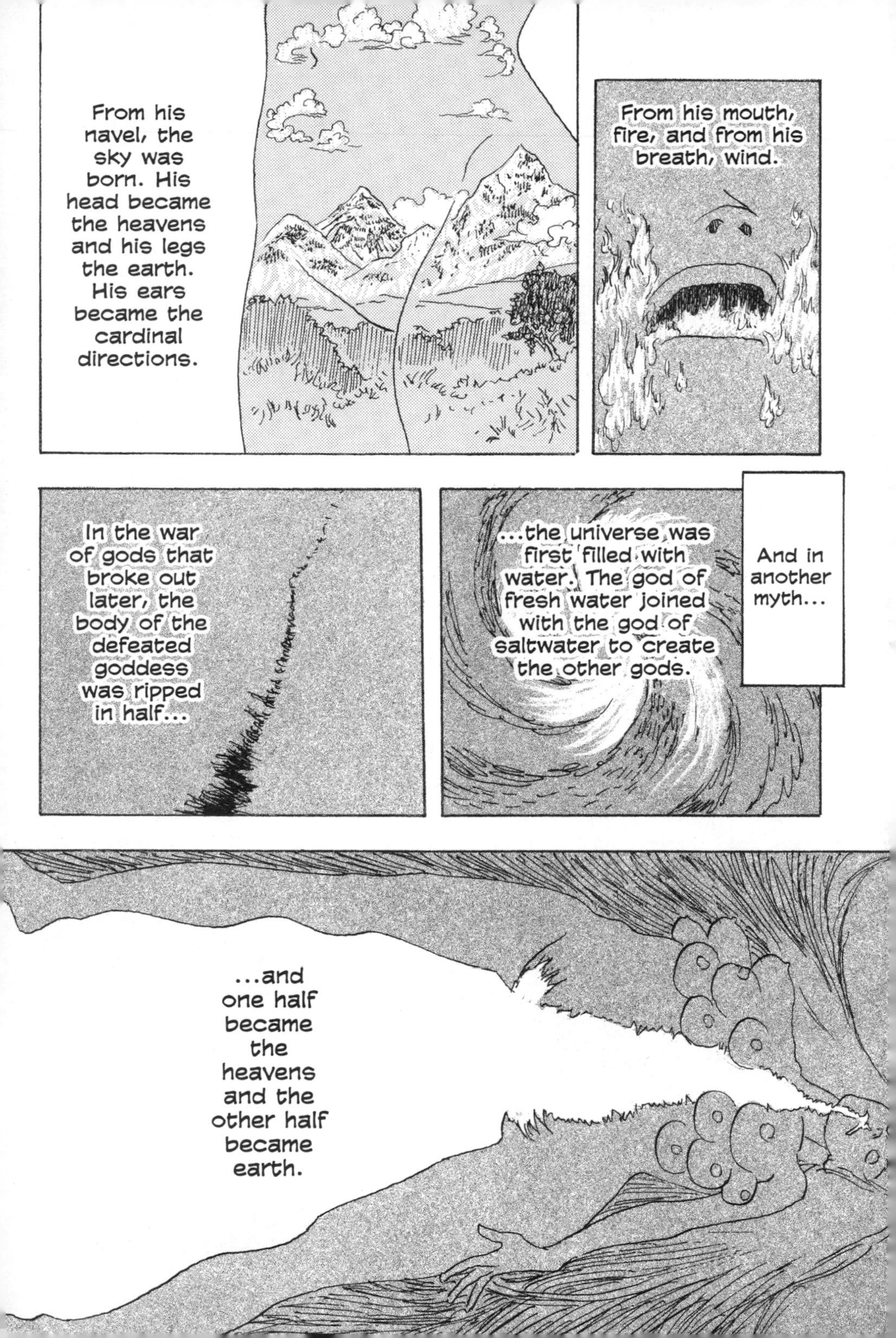
From his mouth, fire, and from his breath, wind.
From his navel, the sky was born. His head became the heavens and his legs the earth. His ears became the cardinal directions.
And in another myth...
...the universe was first filled with water. The god of fresh water joined with the god of saltwater to create the other gods.
In the war of gods that broke out later, the body of the defeated goddess was ripped in half...
...and one half became the heavens and the other half became earth.

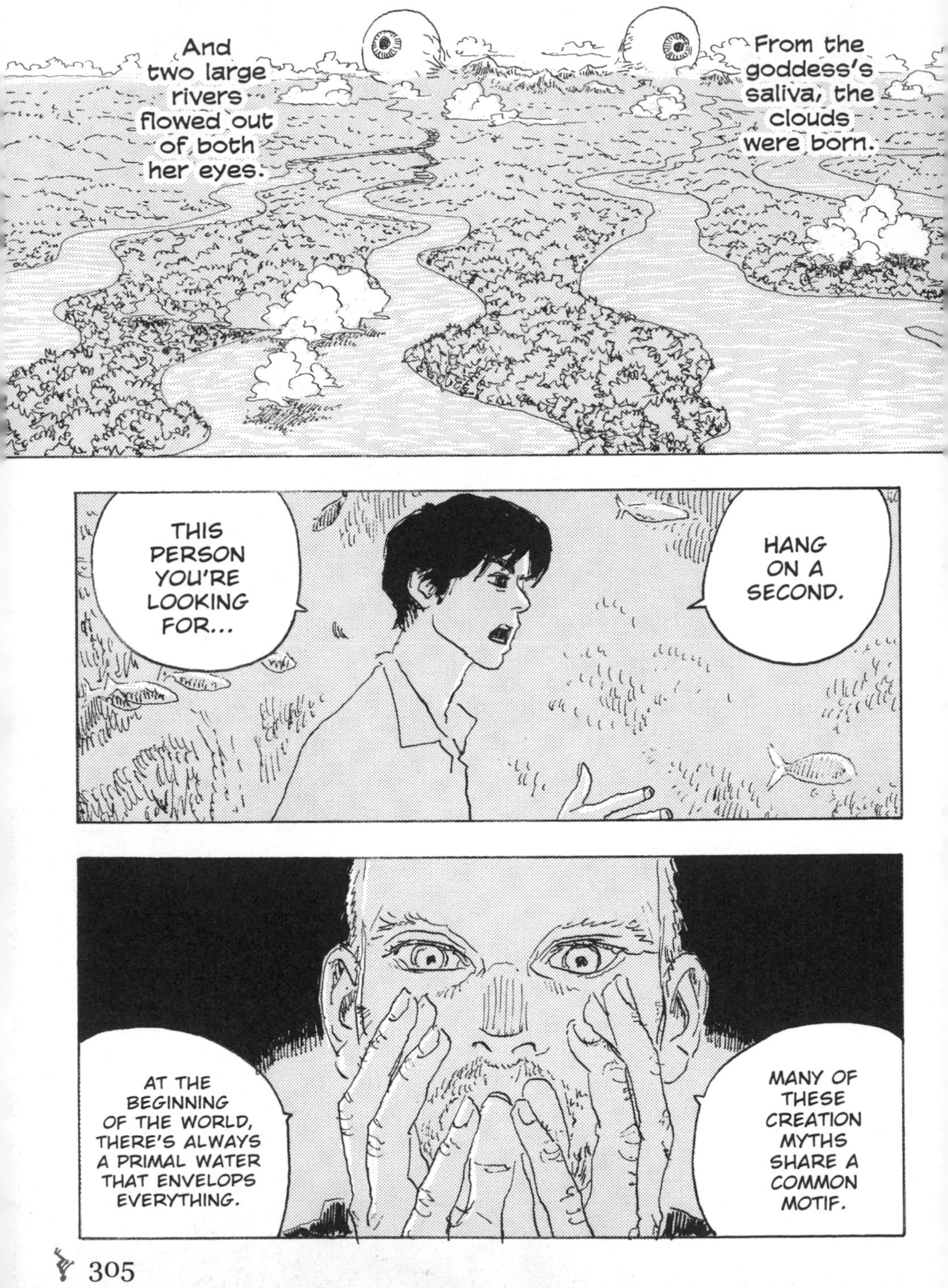
From the goddess's saliva, the clouds were born.
And two large rivers flowed out of both her eyes.
HANG ON A SECOND.
THIS PERSON YOU'RE LOOKING FOR...
MANY OF THESE CREATION MYTHS SHARE A COMMON MOTIF.
AT THE BEGINNING OF THE WORLD, THERE'S ALWAYS A PRIMAL WATER THAT ENVELOPS EVERYTHING.

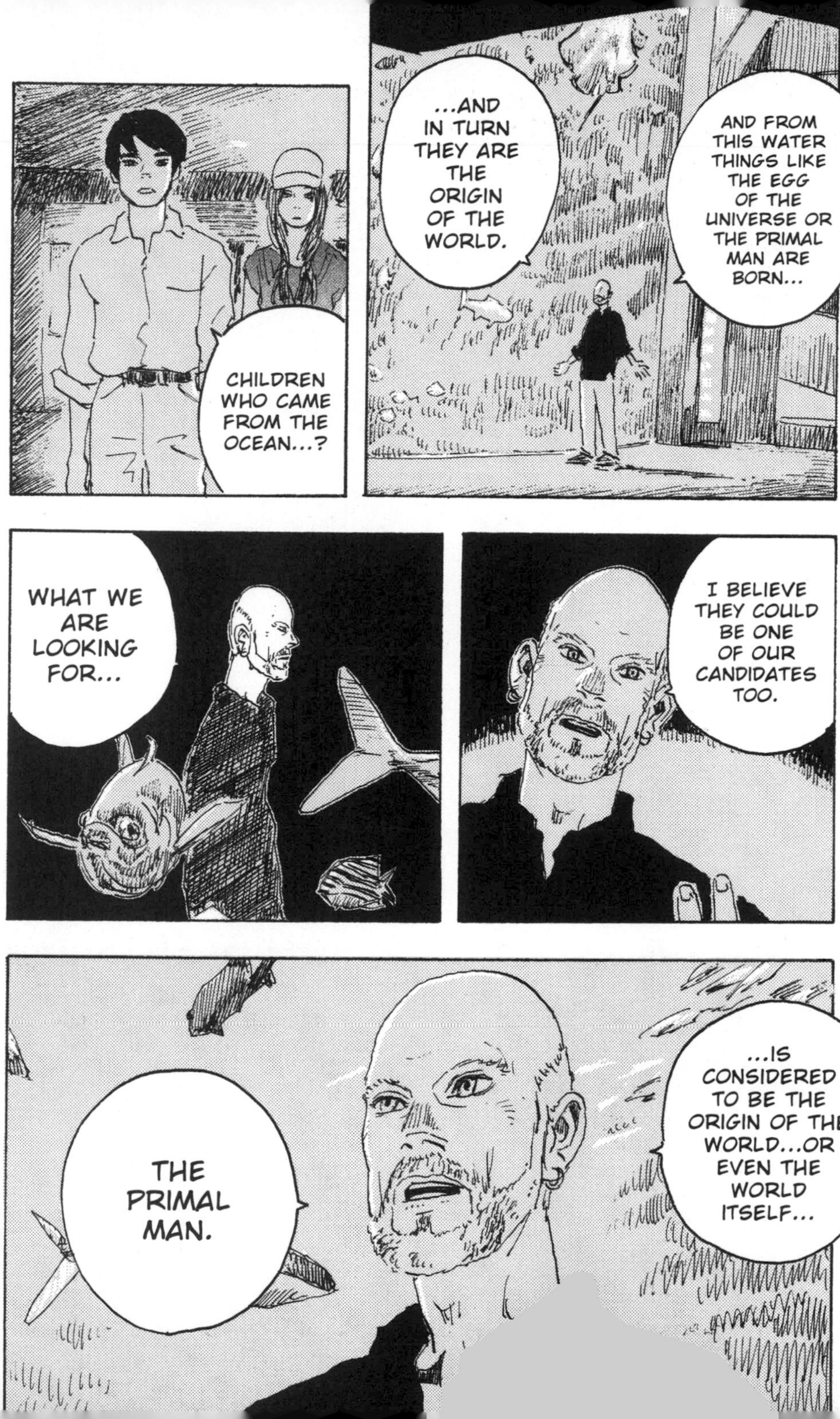
AND FROM THIS WATER THINGS LIKE THE EGG OF THE UNIVERSE OR THE PRIMAL MAN ARE BORN...
...AND IN TURN THEY ARE THE ORIGIN OF THE WORLD.
CHILDREN WHO CAME FROM THE OCEAN...?
I BELIEVE THEY COULD BE ONE OF OUR CANDIDATES TOO.
WHAT WE ARE LOOKING FOR...
...IS CONSIDERED TO BE THE ORIGIN OF THE WORLD...OR EVEN THE WORLD ITSELF...
THE PRIMAL MAN.

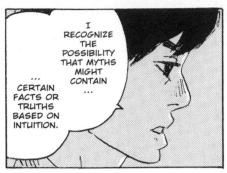

...
I RECOGNIZE THE POSSIBILITY THAT MYTHS MIGHT CONTAIN ...
... CERTAIN FACTS OR TRUTHS BASED ON INTUITION.
AS HUMAN BEINGS, COMPARING THE MYSTERY OF THE WORLD...
...AND LIFE TO THE MYSTERY OF THE HUMAN BODY IS NATURAL...
BUT THAT'S A DIFFERENT STORY FROM WHETHER OR NOT THE PRIMAL MAN EXISTED.
OF COURSE, WE THOUGHT SO TOO.
EVEN NOW, WE DON'T THINK THAT MYTHS ARE BASED ON FACTS.
BUT...
WE SAW IT...
In...

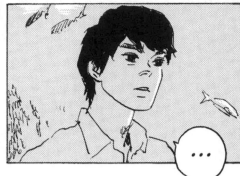

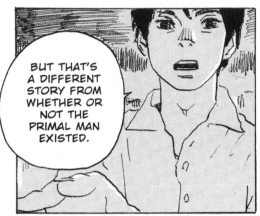

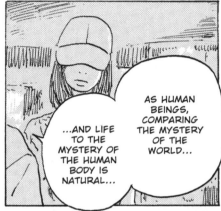

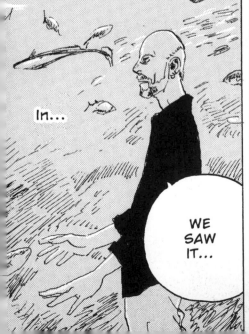

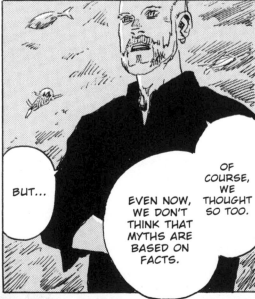

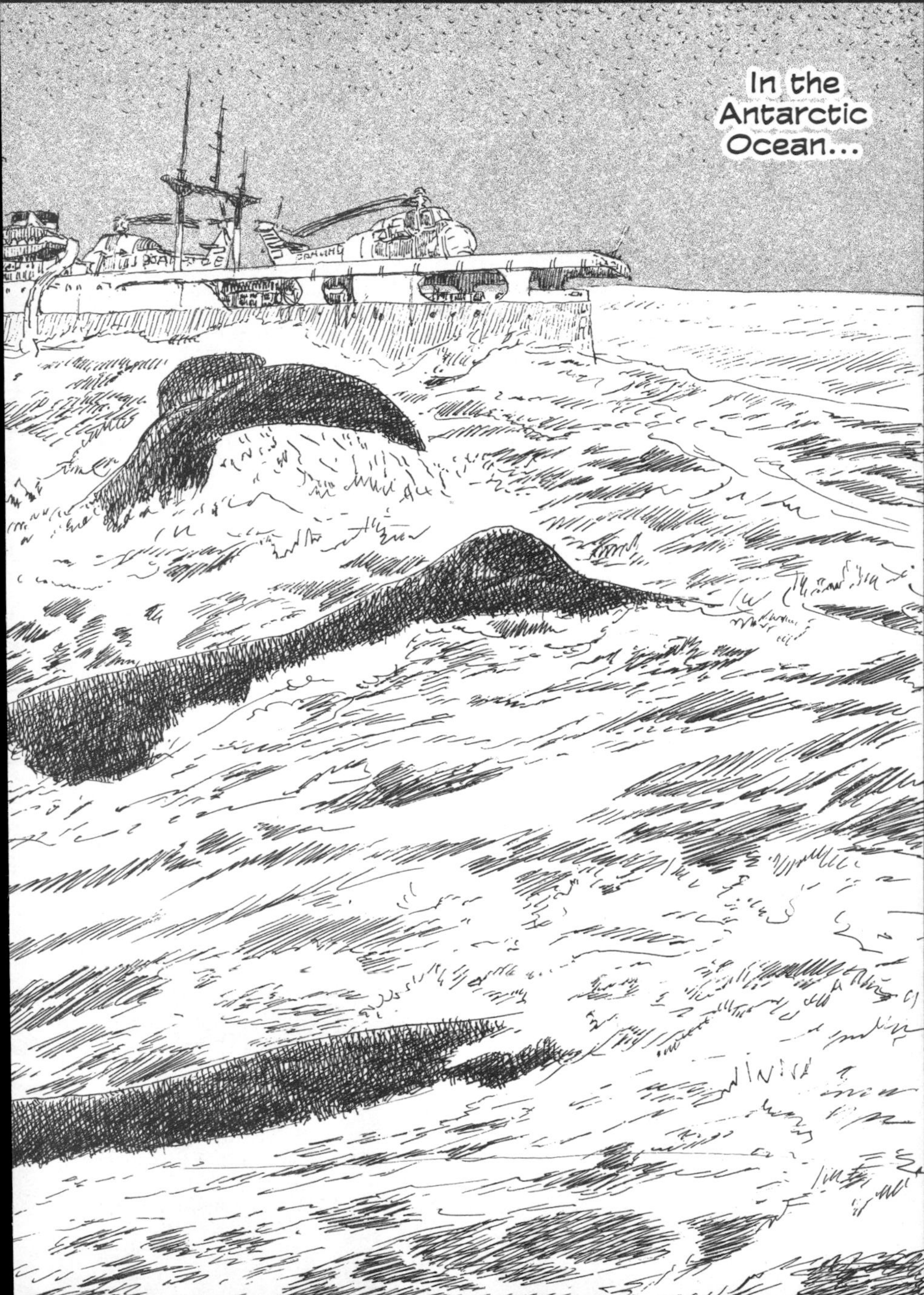
In the Antarctic Ocean...

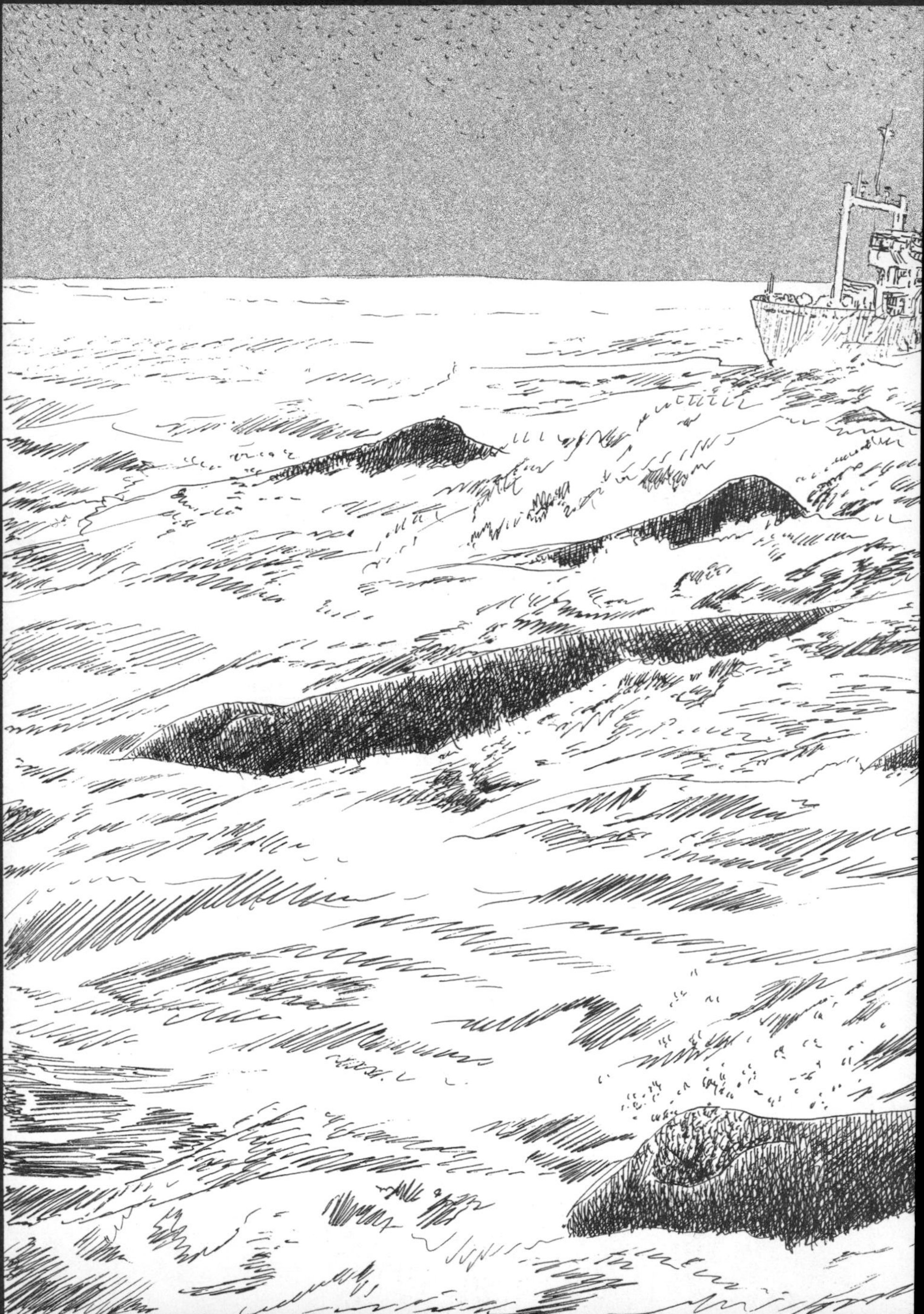

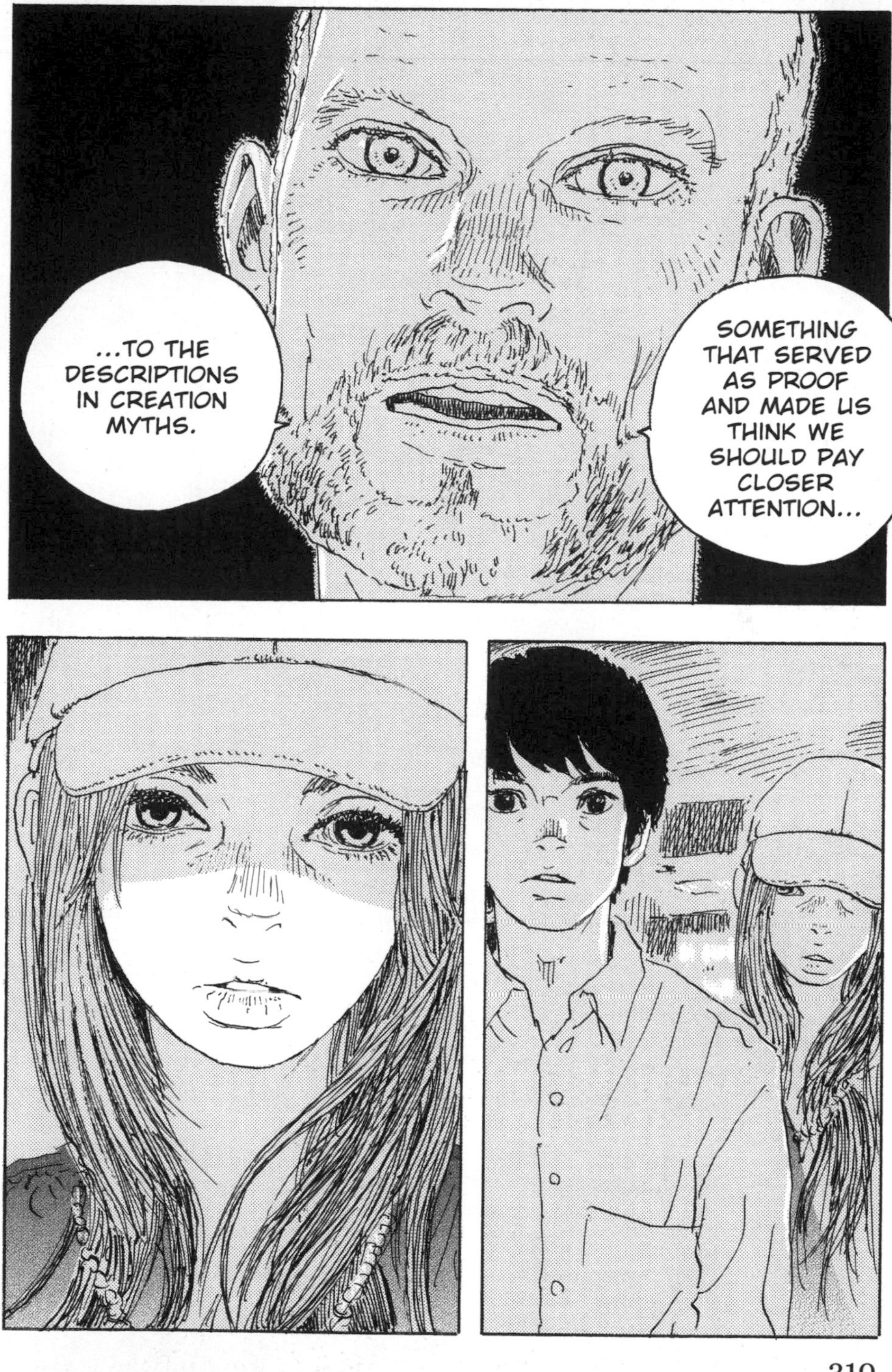
SOMETHING THAT SERVED AS PROOF AND MADE US THINK WE SHOULD PAY CLOSER ATTENTION...
...TO THE DESCRIPTIONS IN CREATION MYTHS.

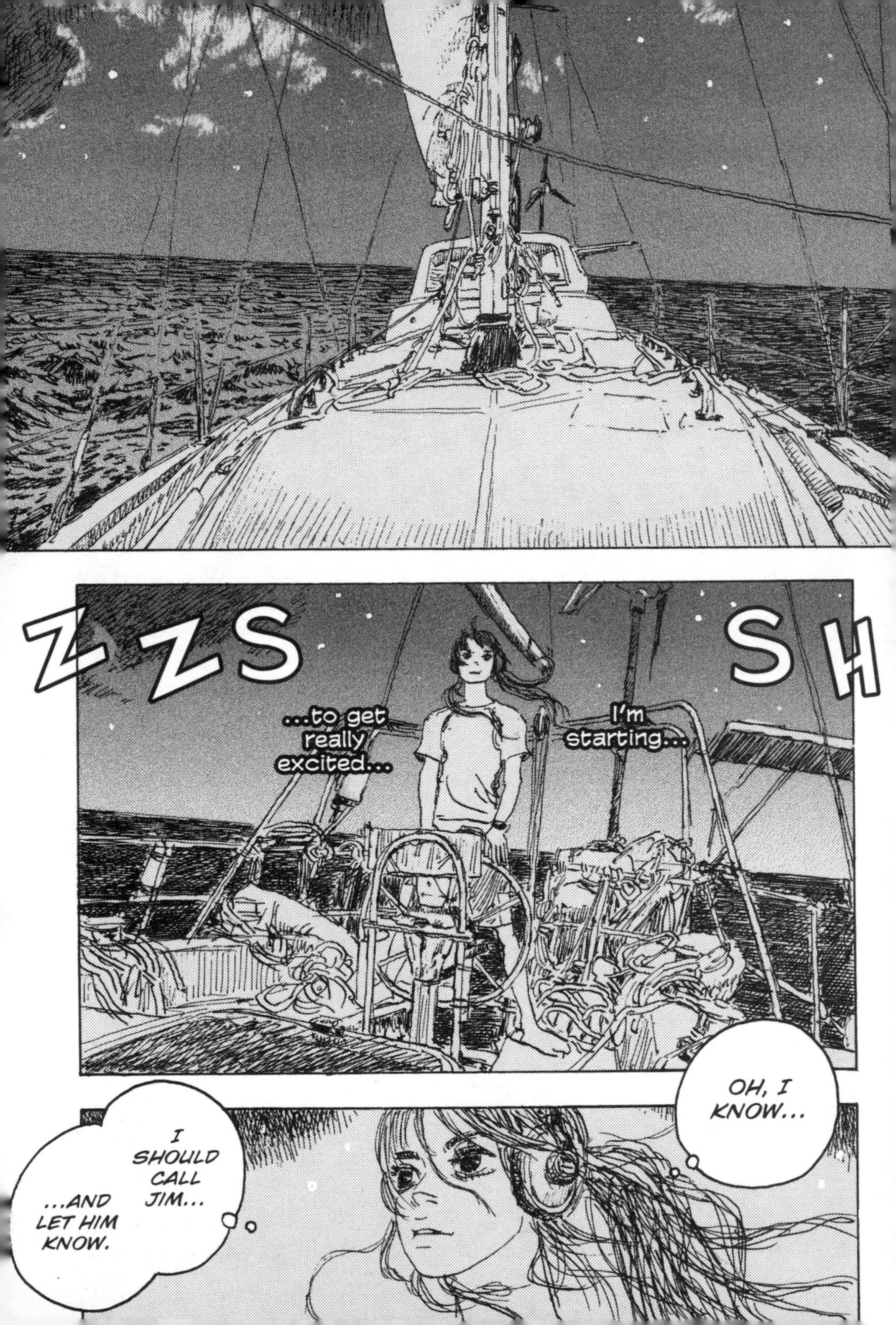
ZZS SH
I'm starting...
...to get really excited...
OH, I KNOW...
I SHOULD CALL JIM...
...AND LET HIM KNOW.

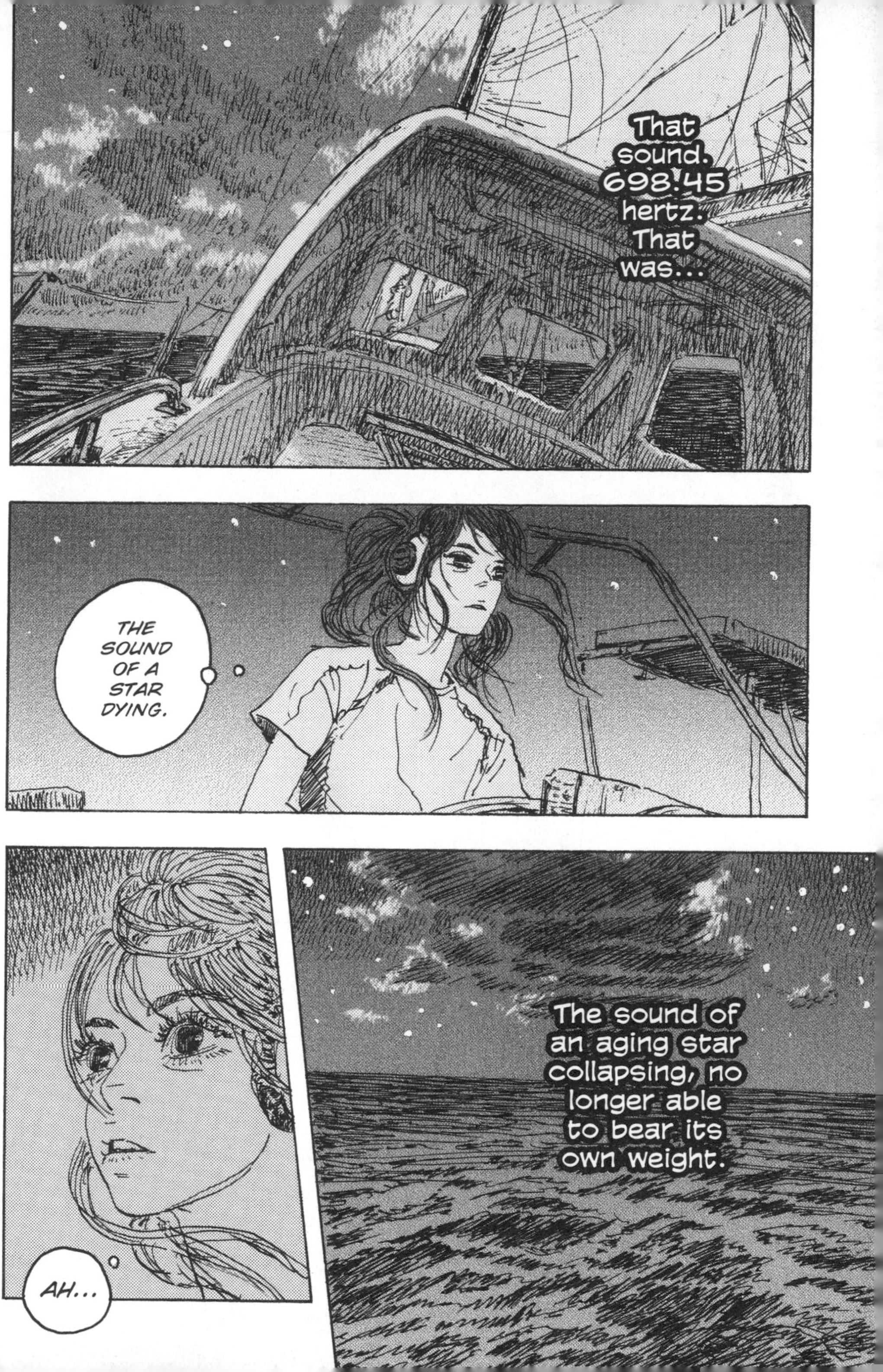
That sound. 698.45 hertz. That was...
THE SOUND OF A STAR DYING.
The sound of an aging star collapsing, no longer able to bear its own weight.
AH...

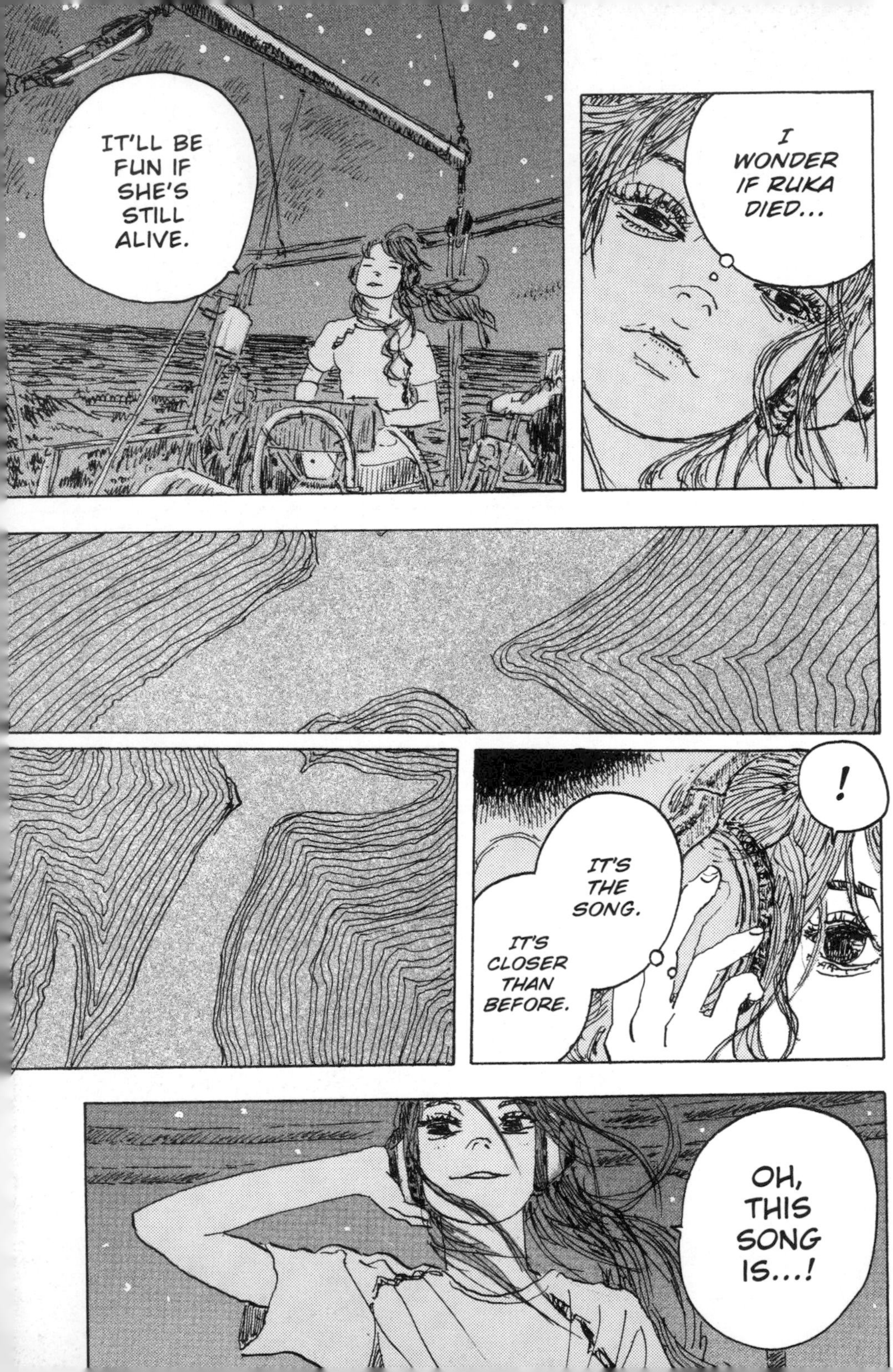
I WONDER IF RUKA DIED...
IT'LL BE FUN IF SHE'S STILL ALIVE.
!
IT'S THE SONG.
IT'S CLOSER THAN BEFORE.
OH, THIS SONG IS...!

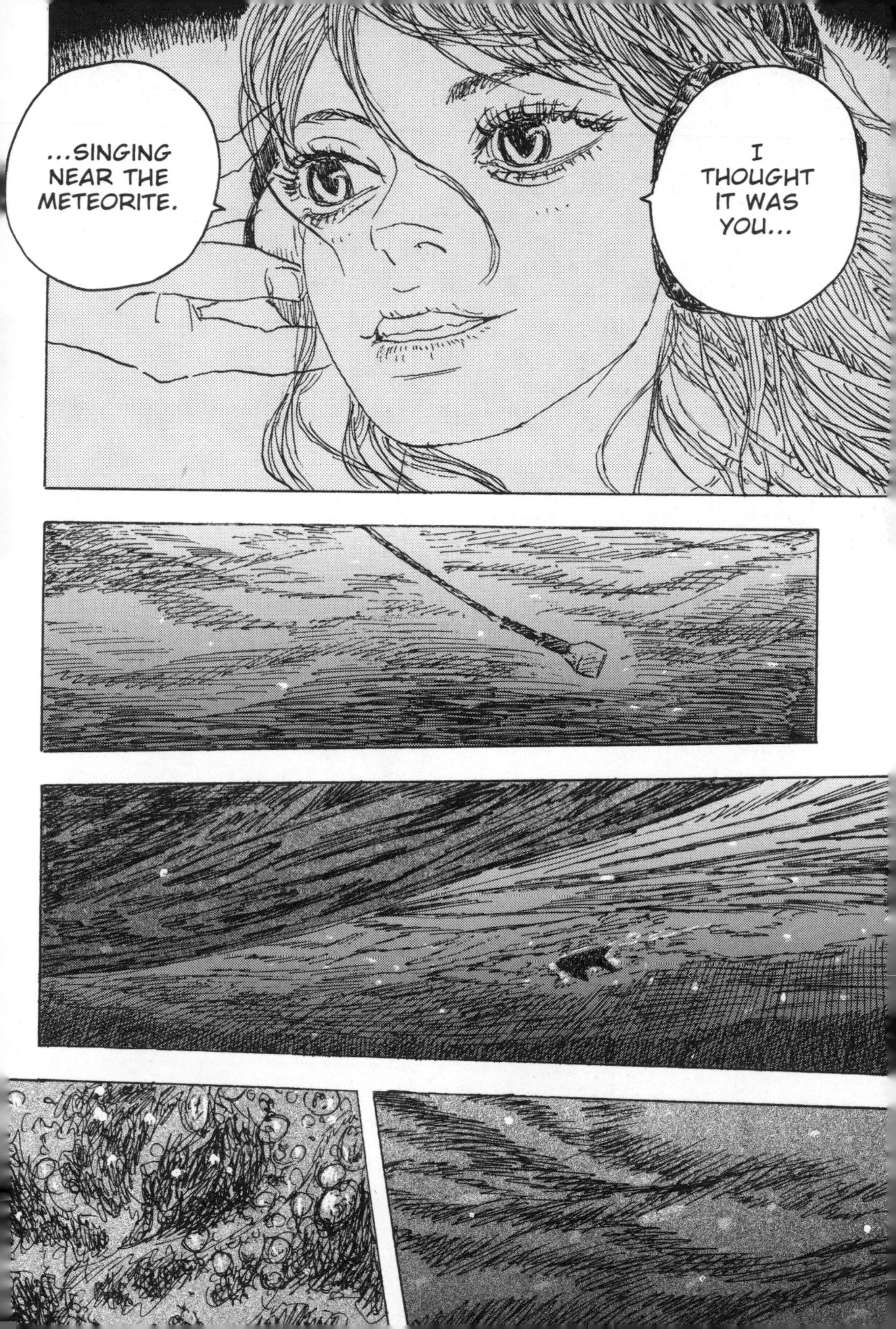
I THOUGHT IT WAS YOU...
...SINGING NEAR THE METEORITE.

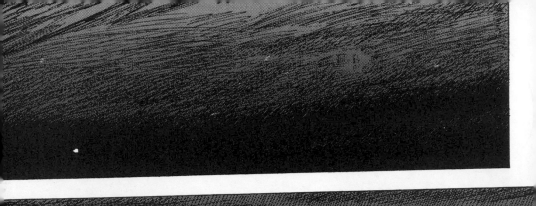

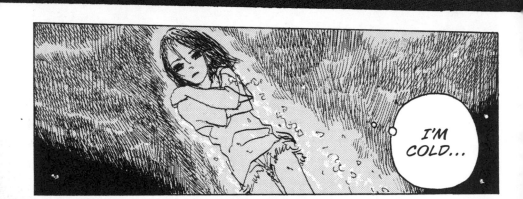

I'M
COLD...

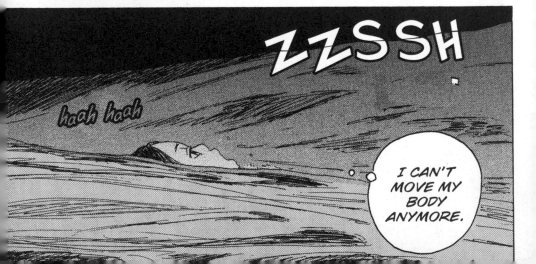

ZZSSH

haah haah

I CAN'T
MOVE MY
BODY
ANYMORE.

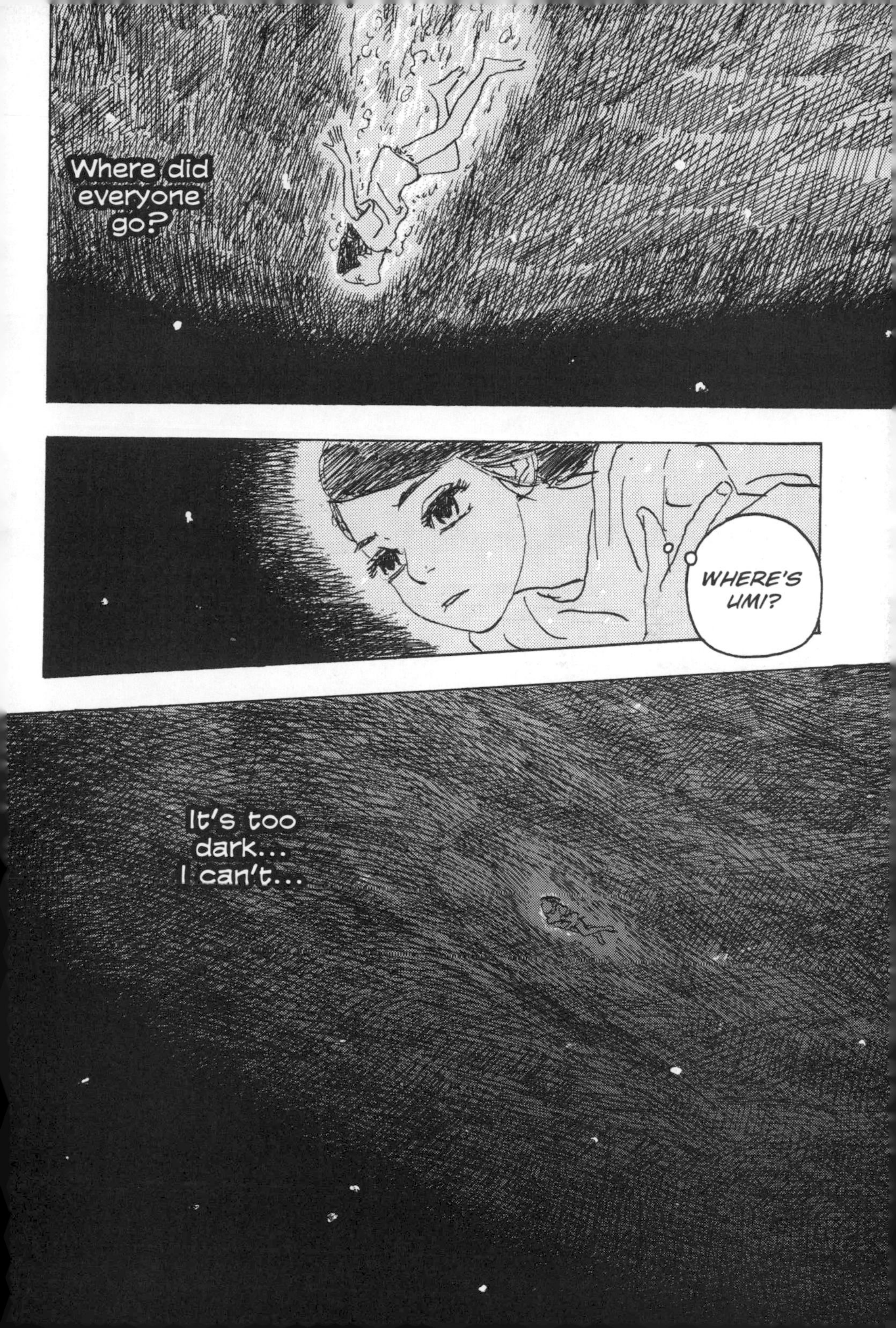
Where did everyone go?
WHERE'S UMI?
It's too dark... I can't...

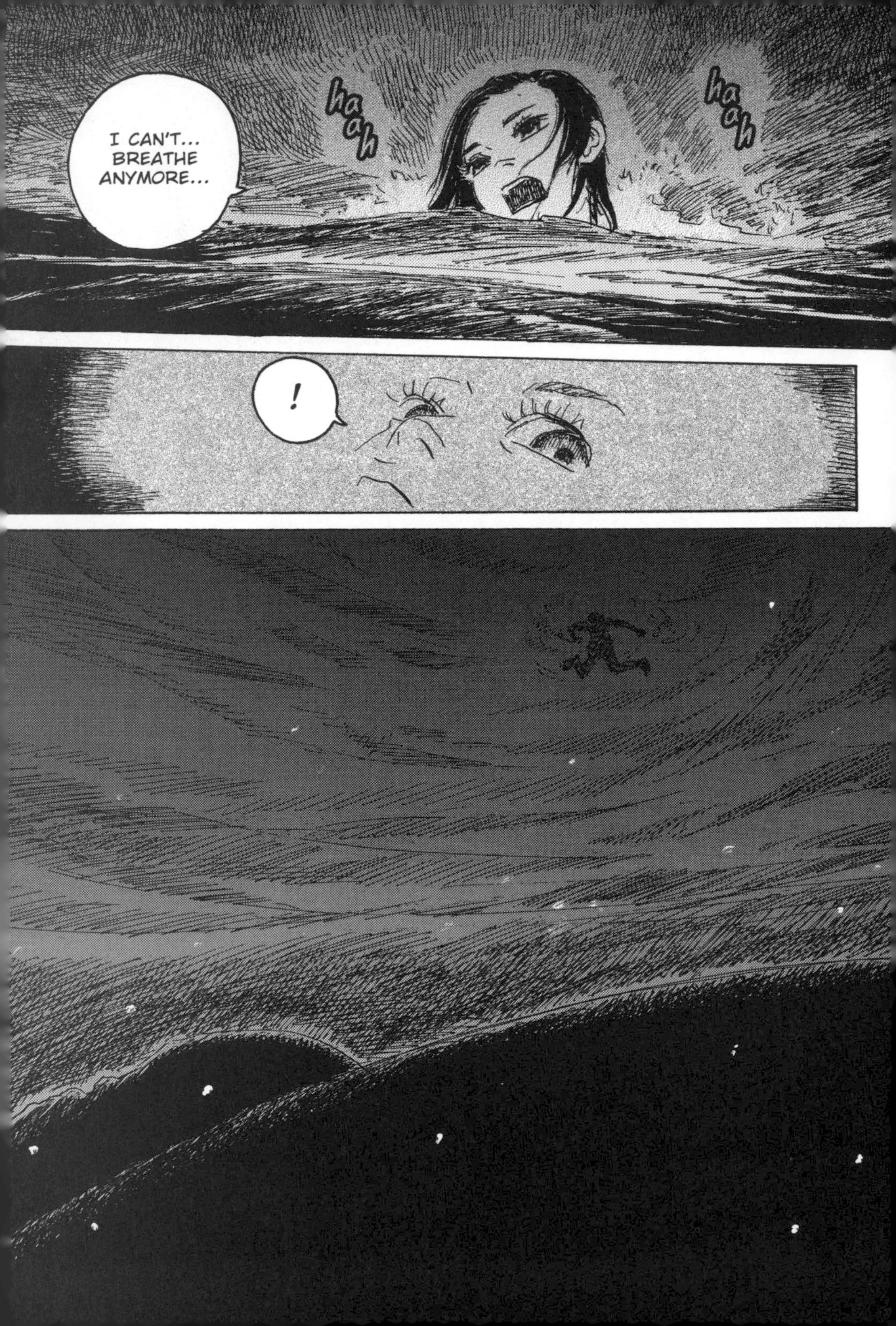
haah
haah
I CAN'T... BREATHE ANYMORE...
!

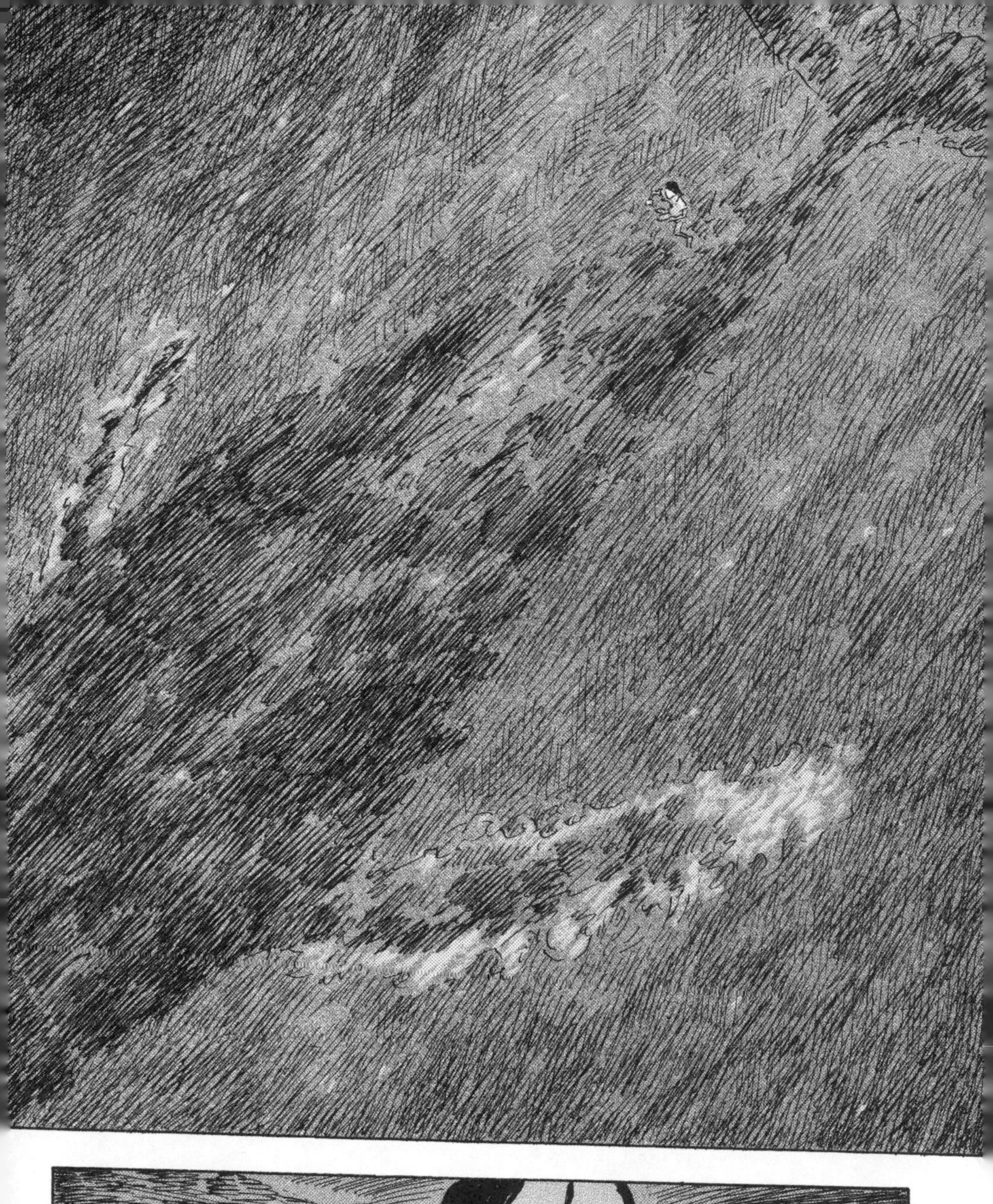

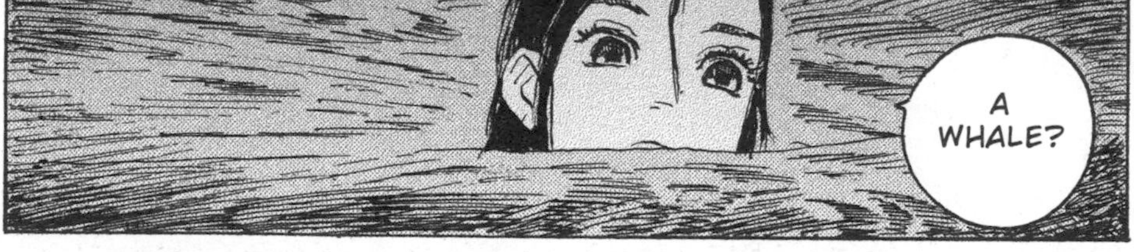
A WHALE?

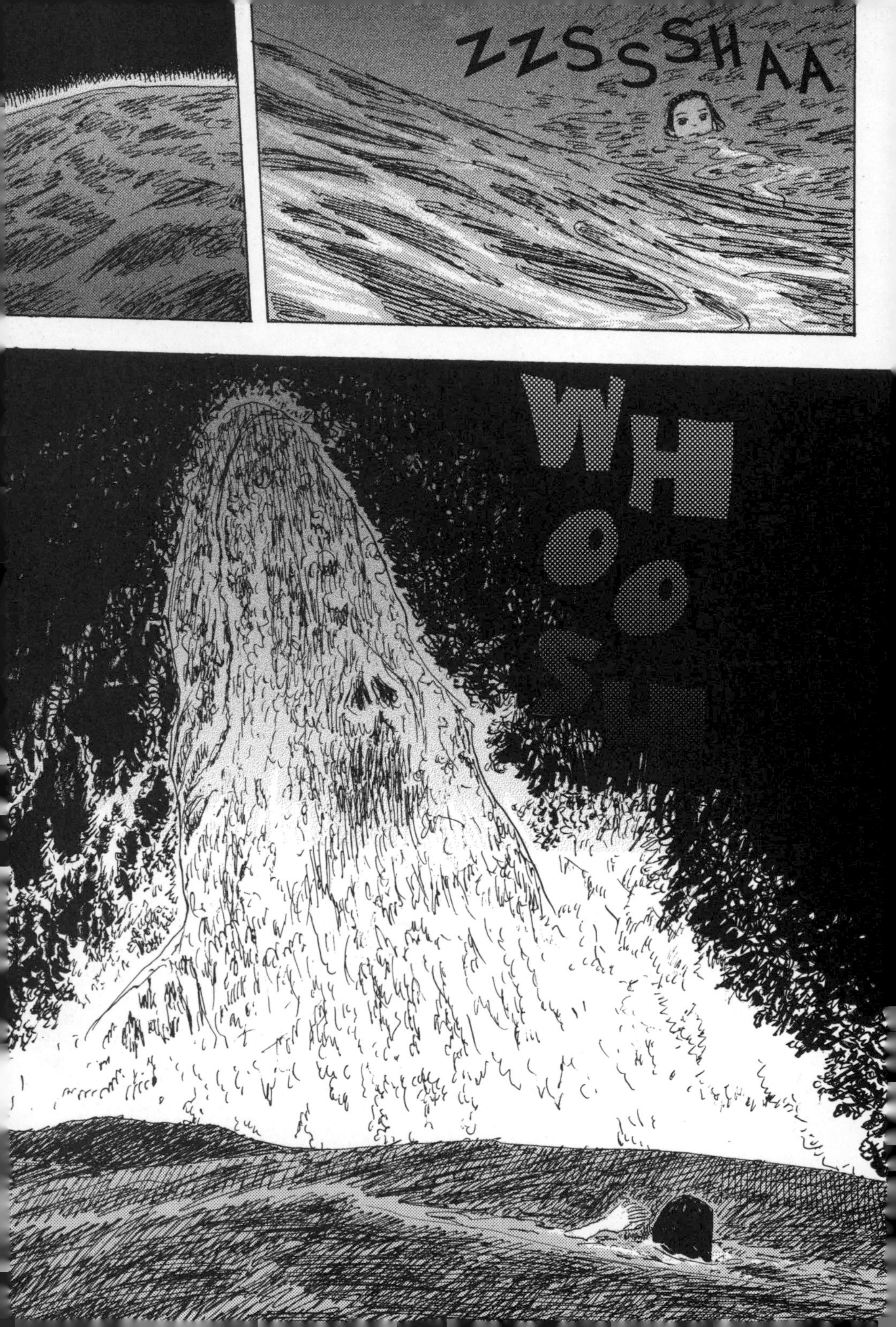
ZZSSSHAA
WHOOSH

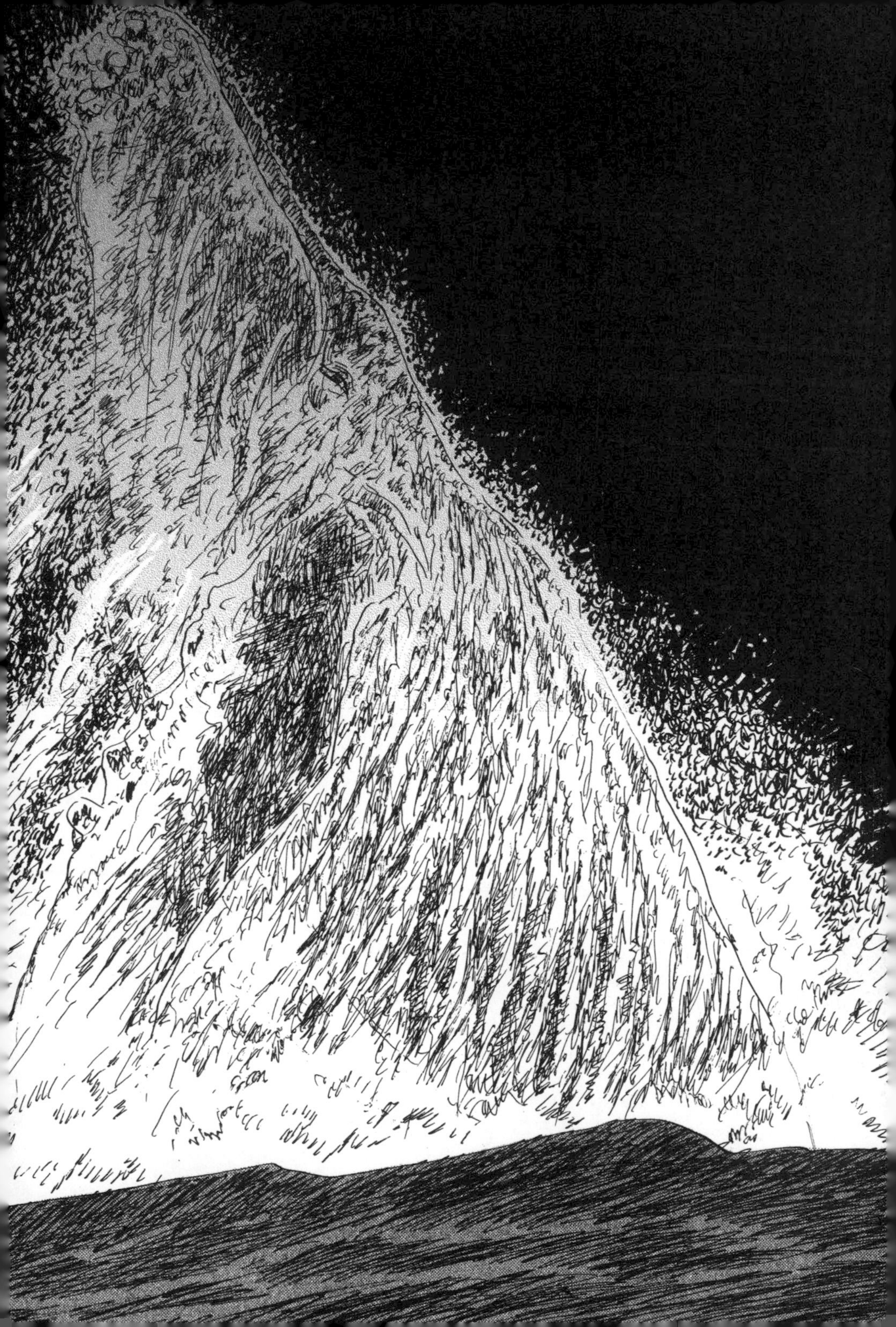

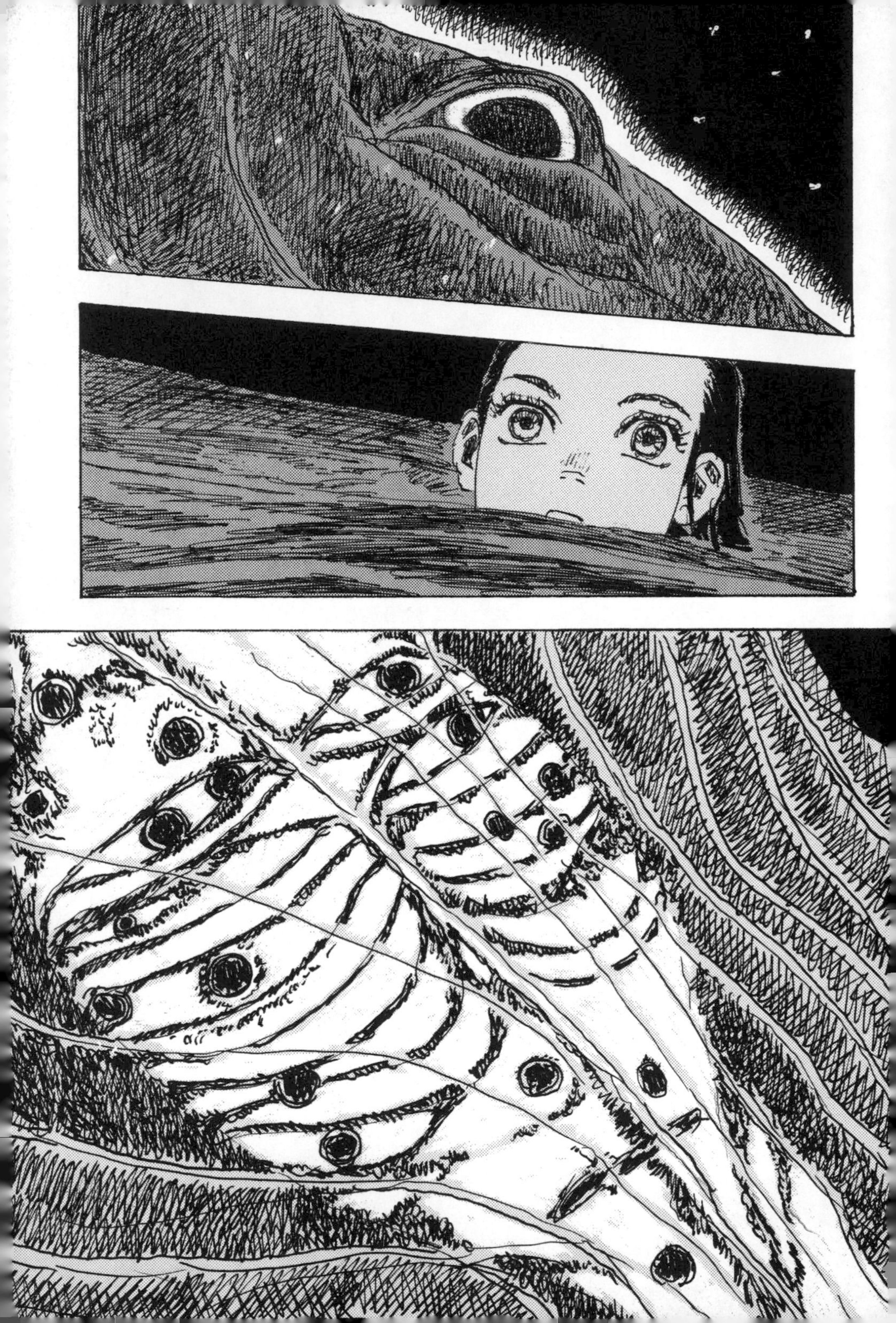

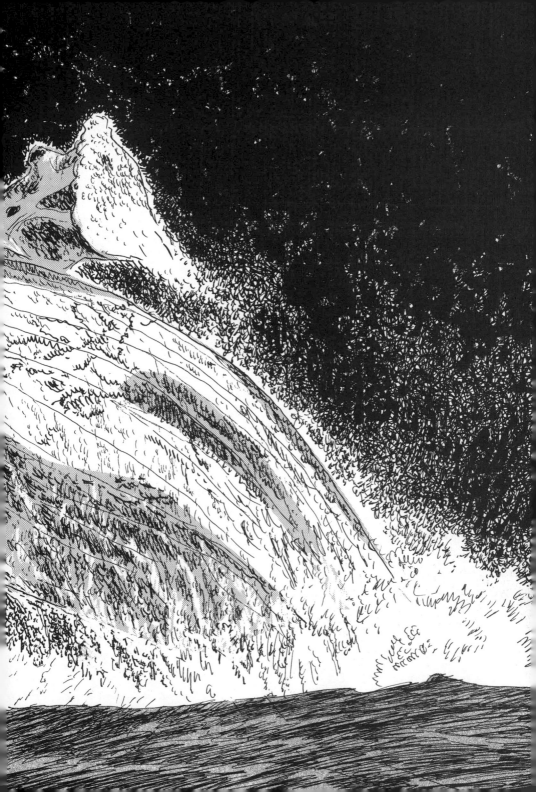

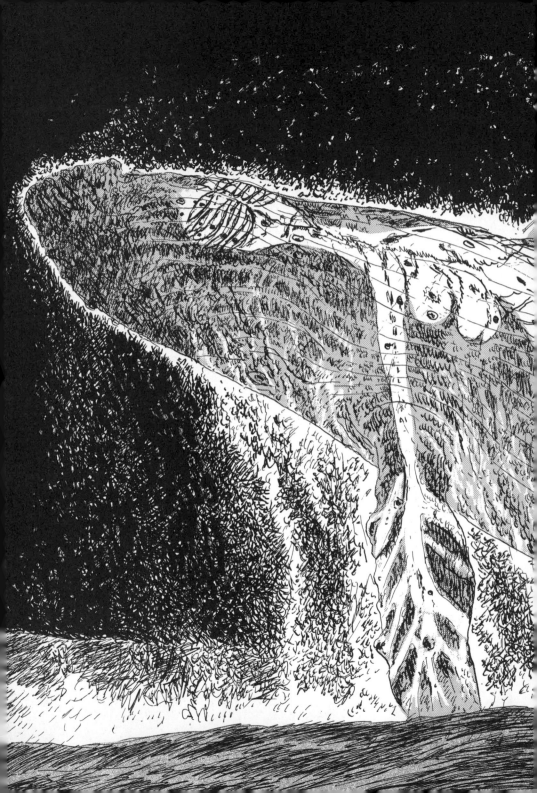

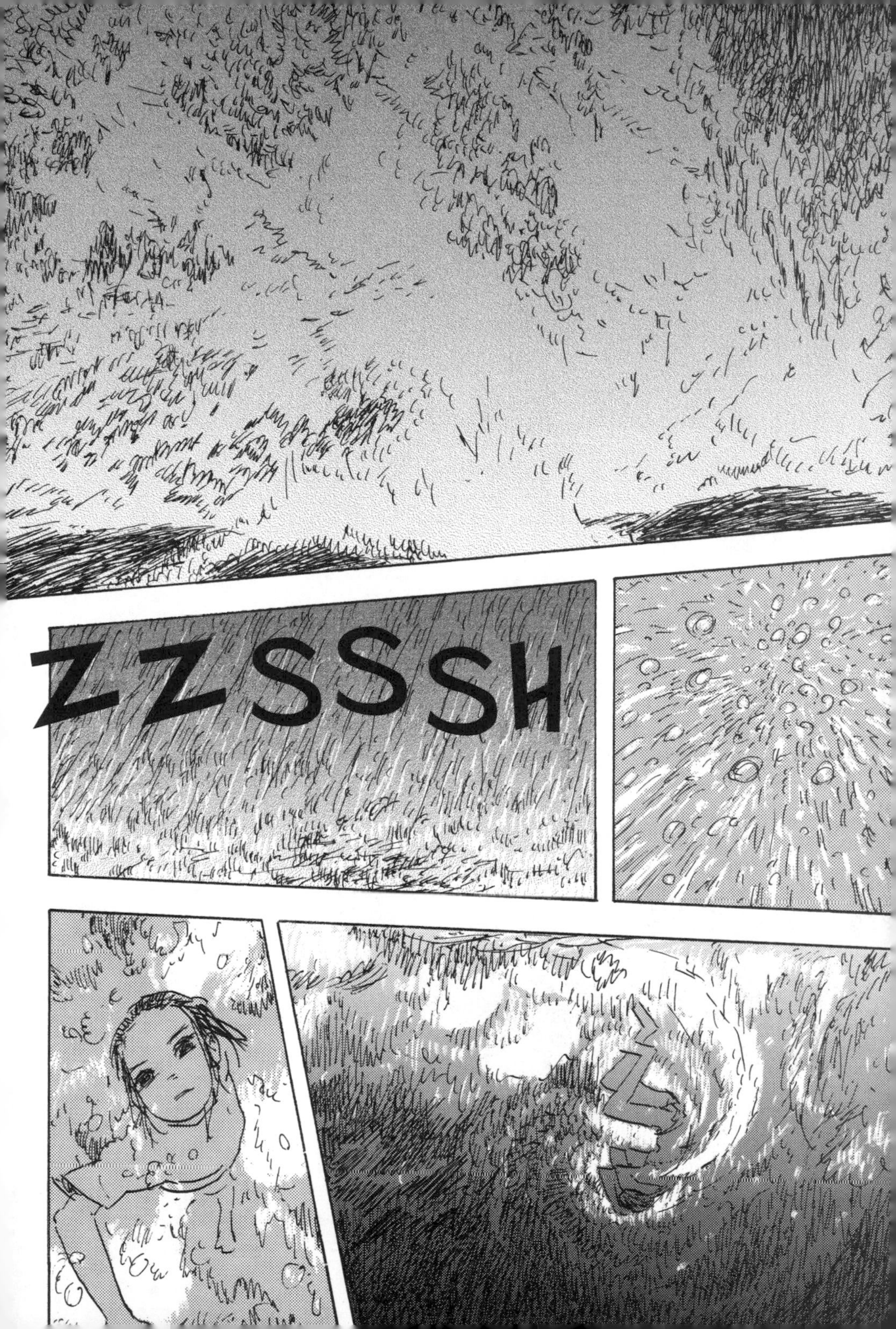
ZZSSSH

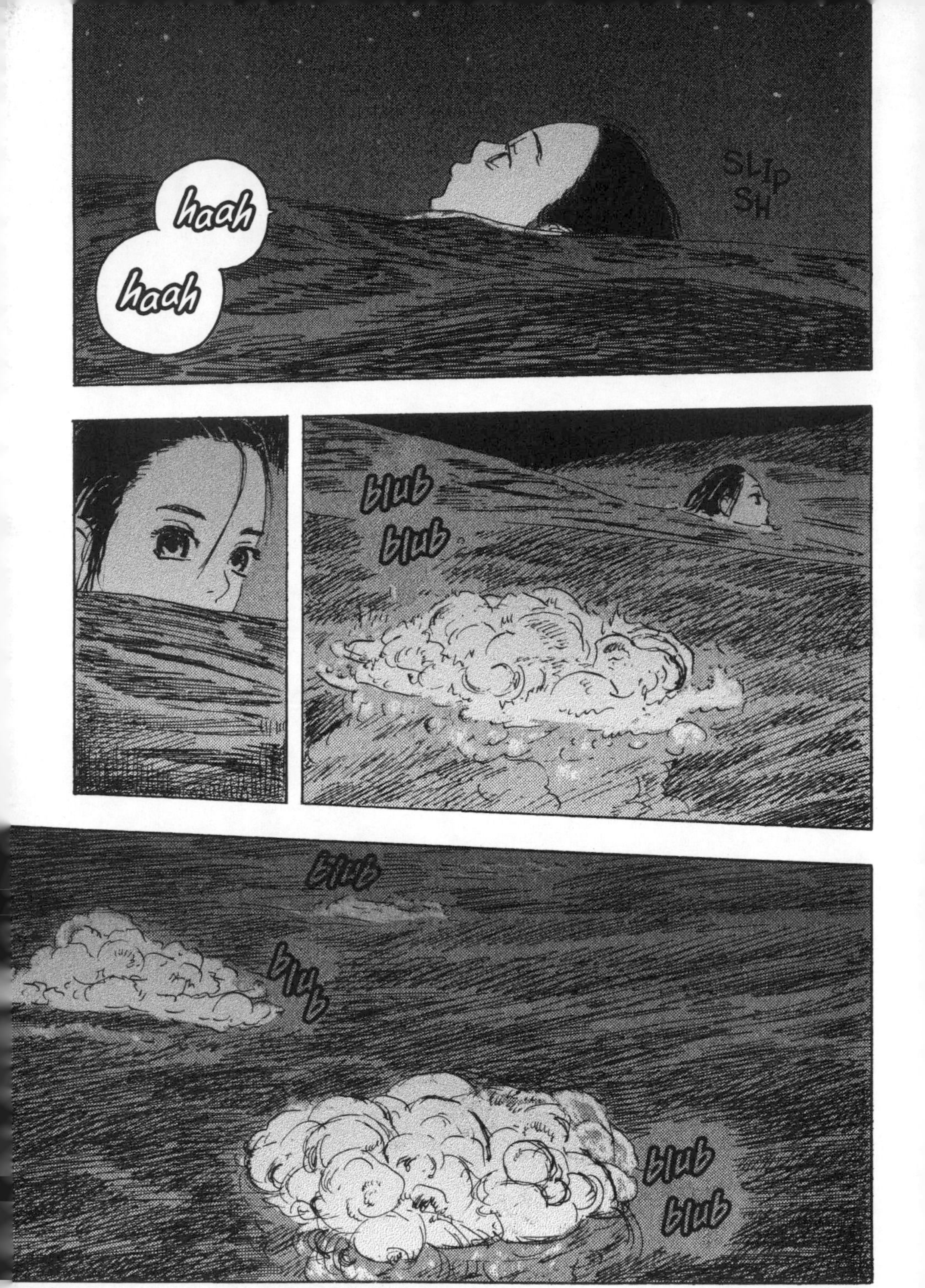
SLIP SH
haah
haah
blub
blub
blub
blub
blub
blub

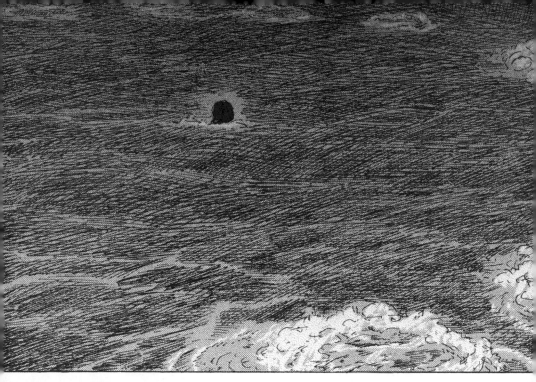

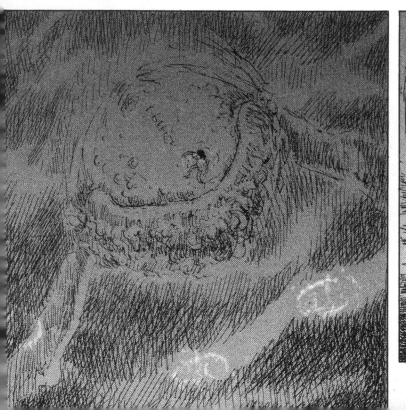

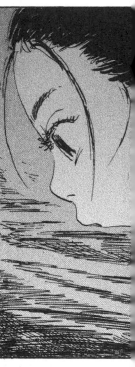

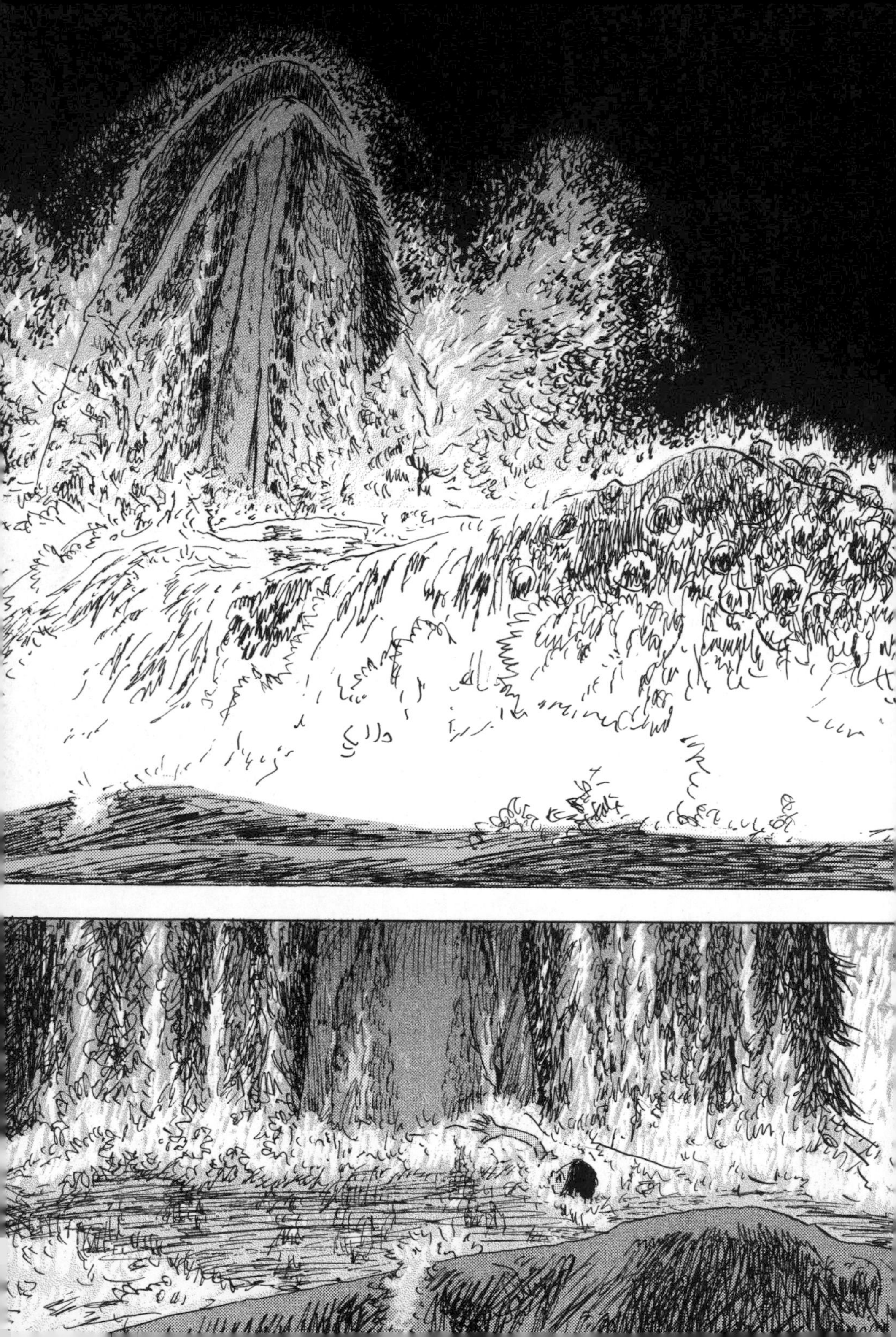

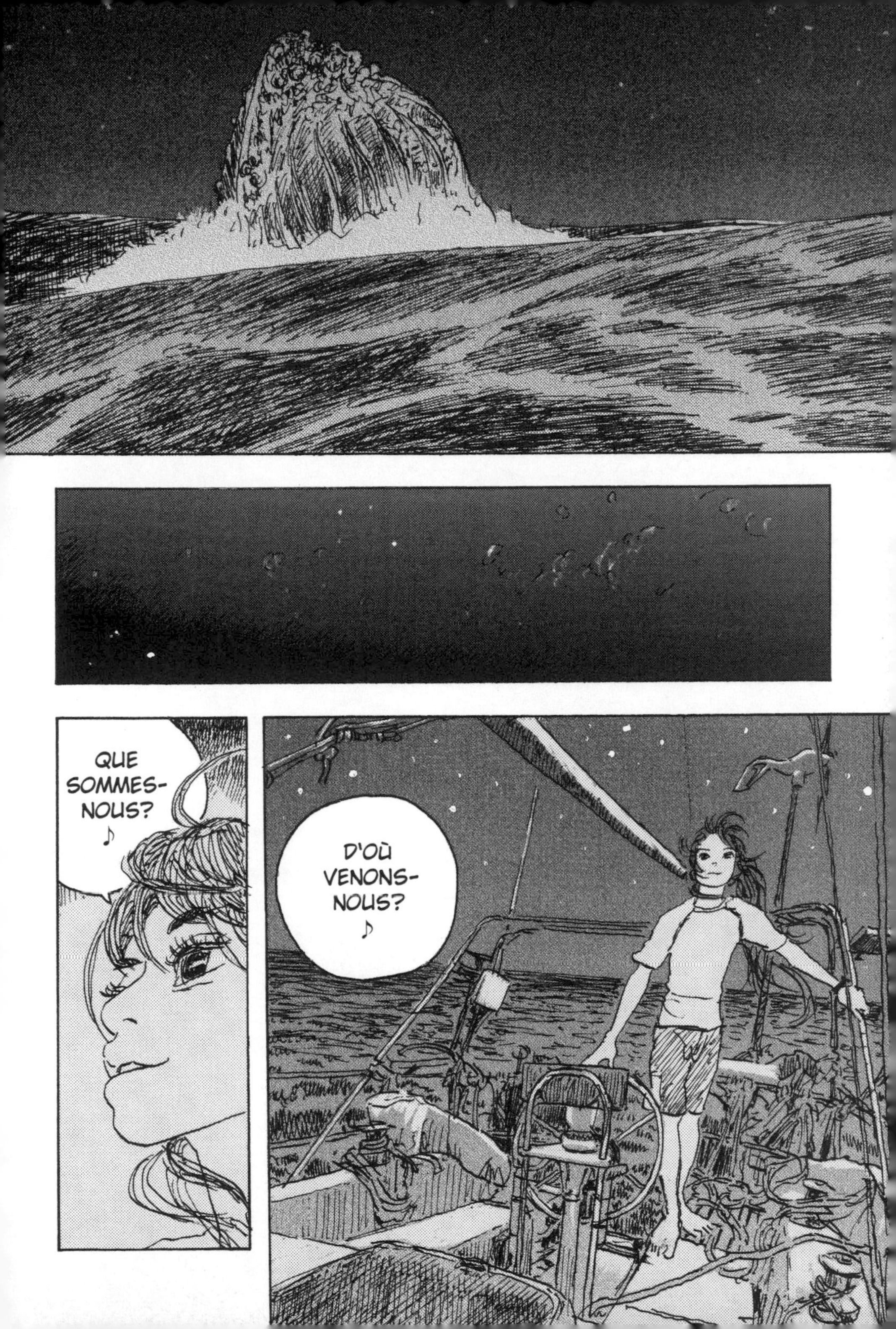
D'OÙ VENONS-NOUS? ♪
QUE SOMMES-NOUS? ♪

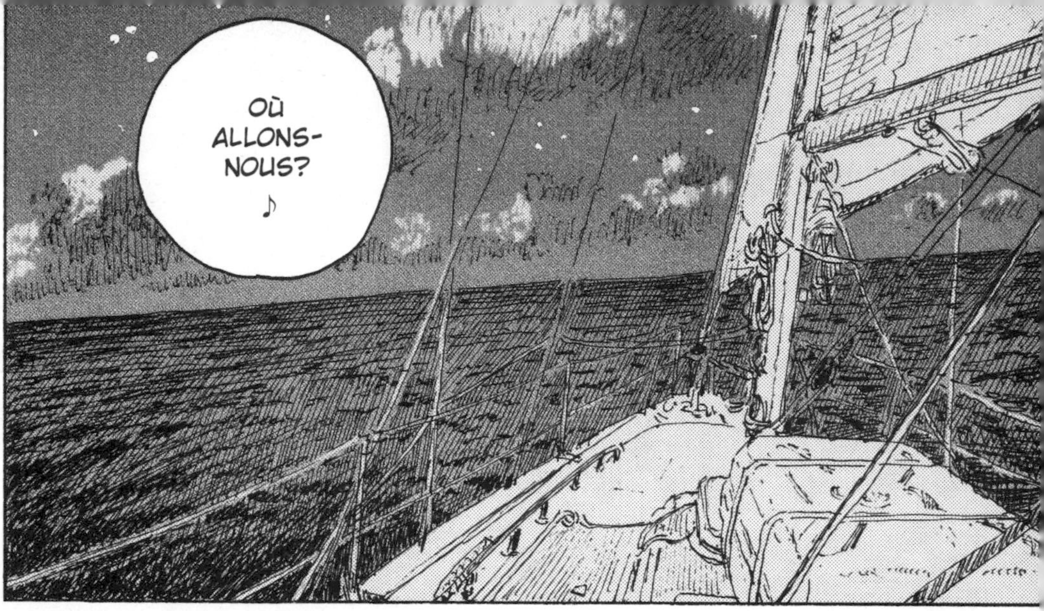
OÙ ALLONS-NOUS? ♪

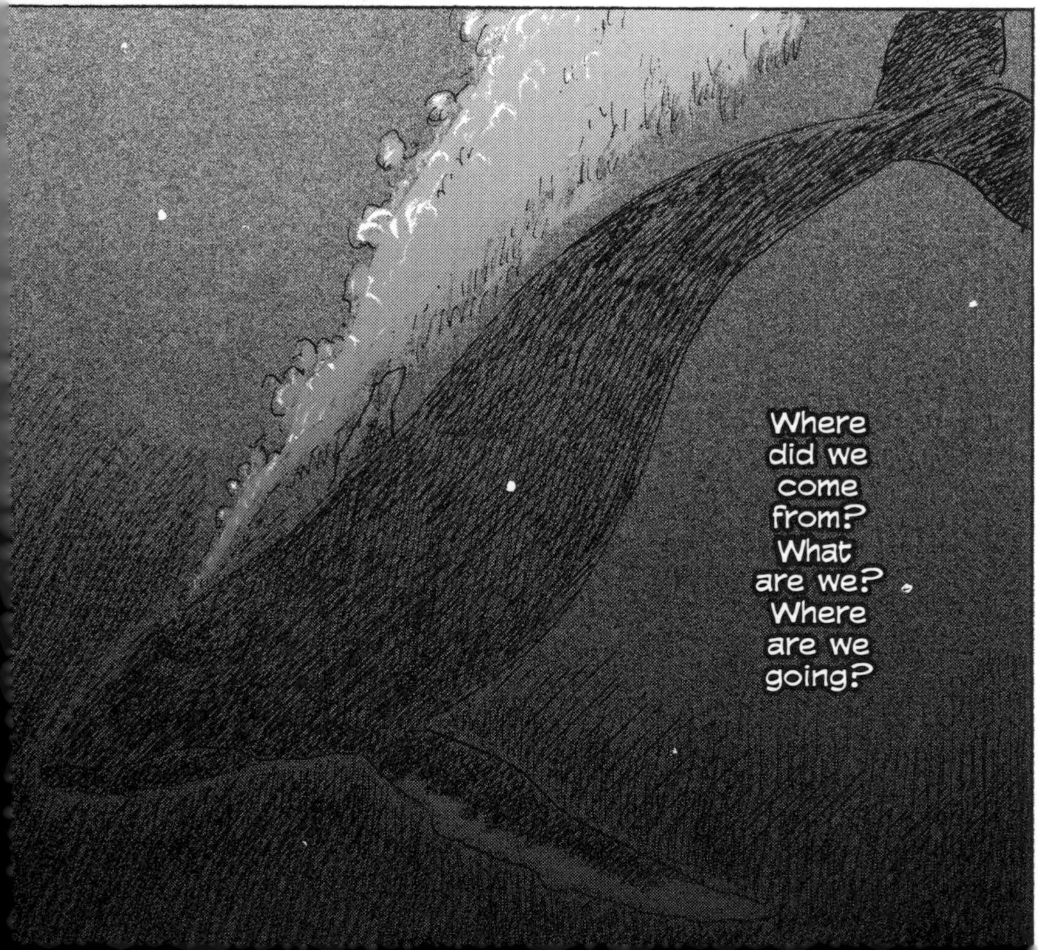
Where did we come from? What are we? Where are we going?

MMM...
Ruka...
CREE
Ruka, the *song* is coming...

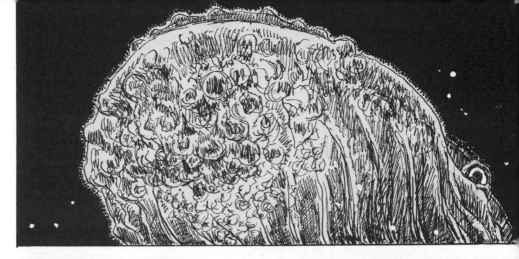

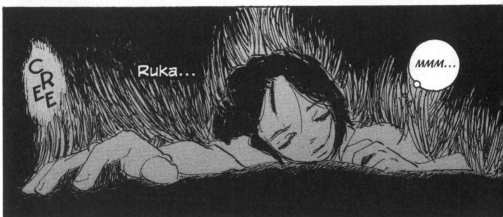

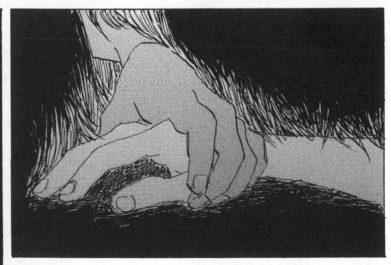

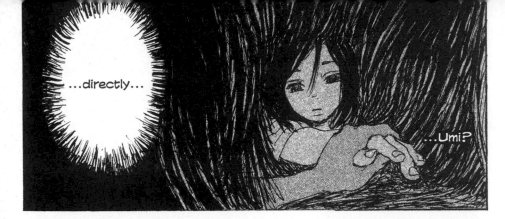

...directly...

...Umi?

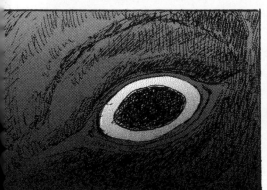

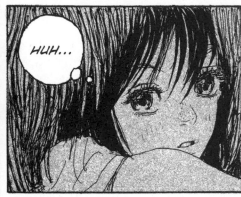

HUH...

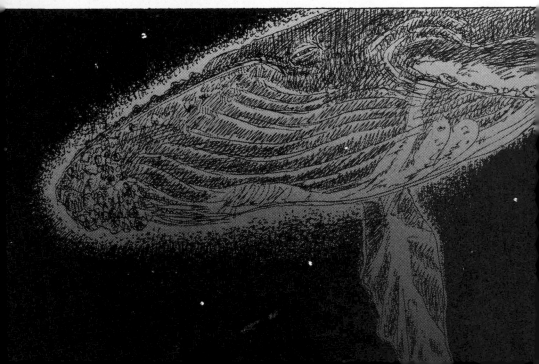

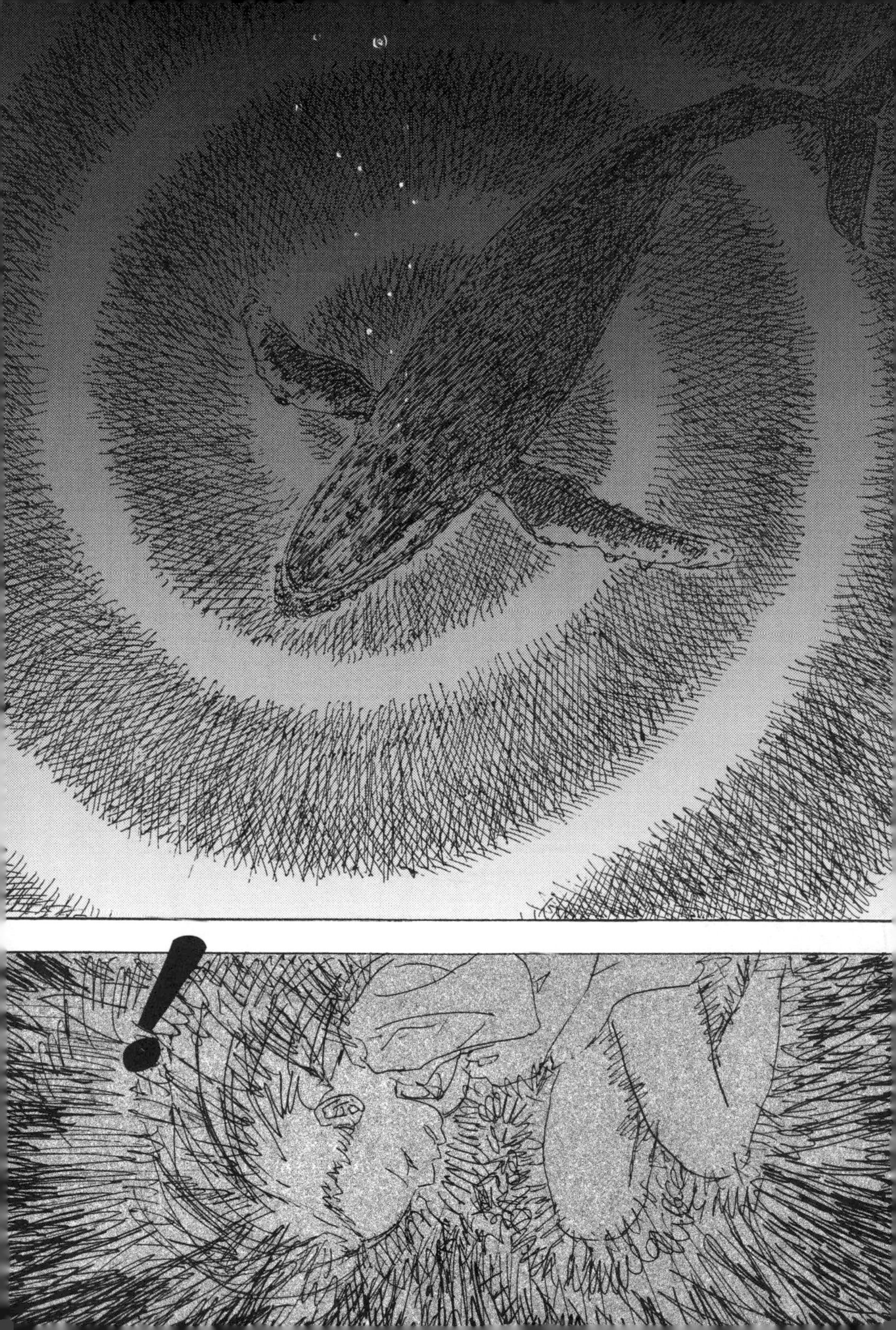
!

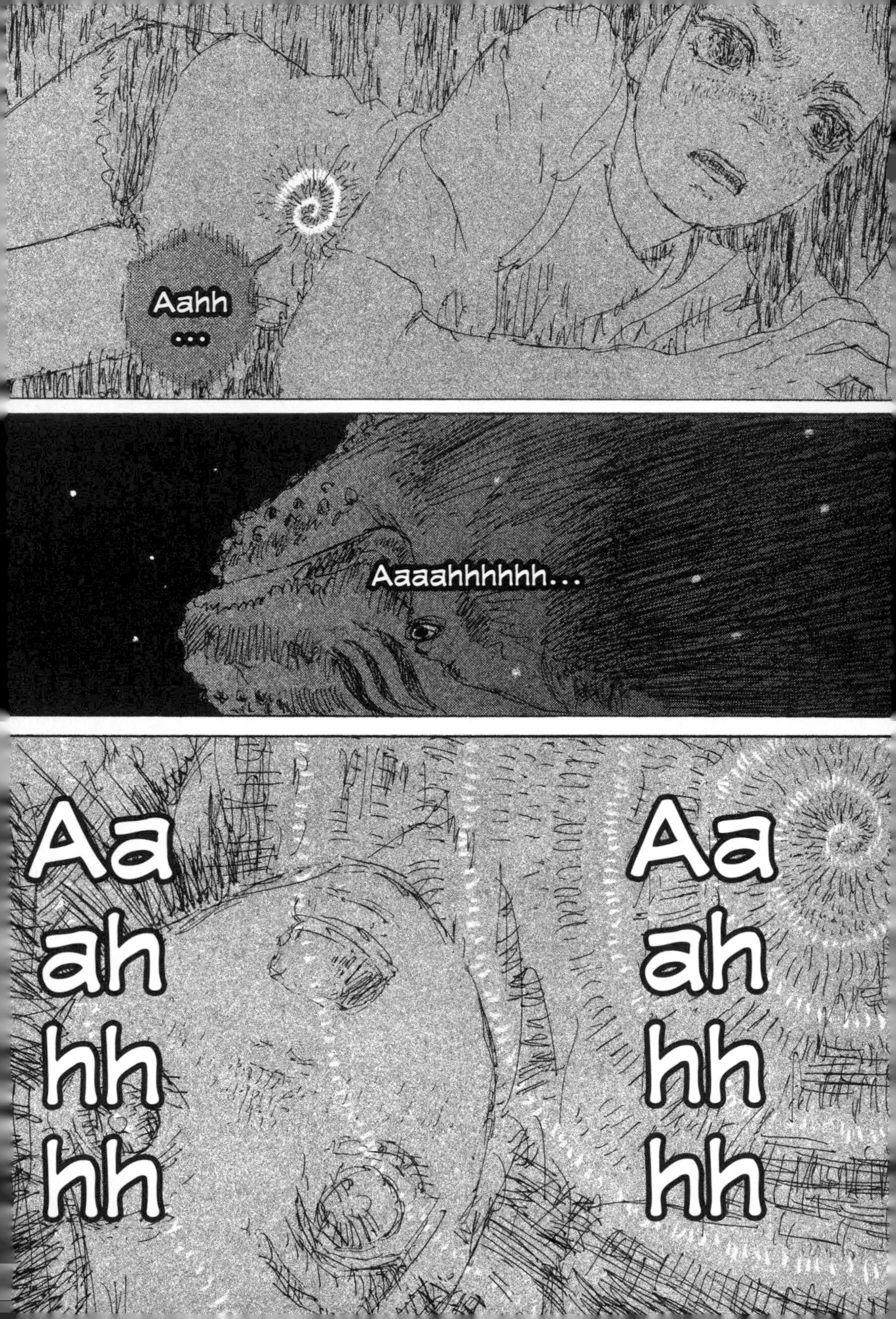
Aahh...
Aaaahhhhh...
Aaahhhhh
Aaahhhhh

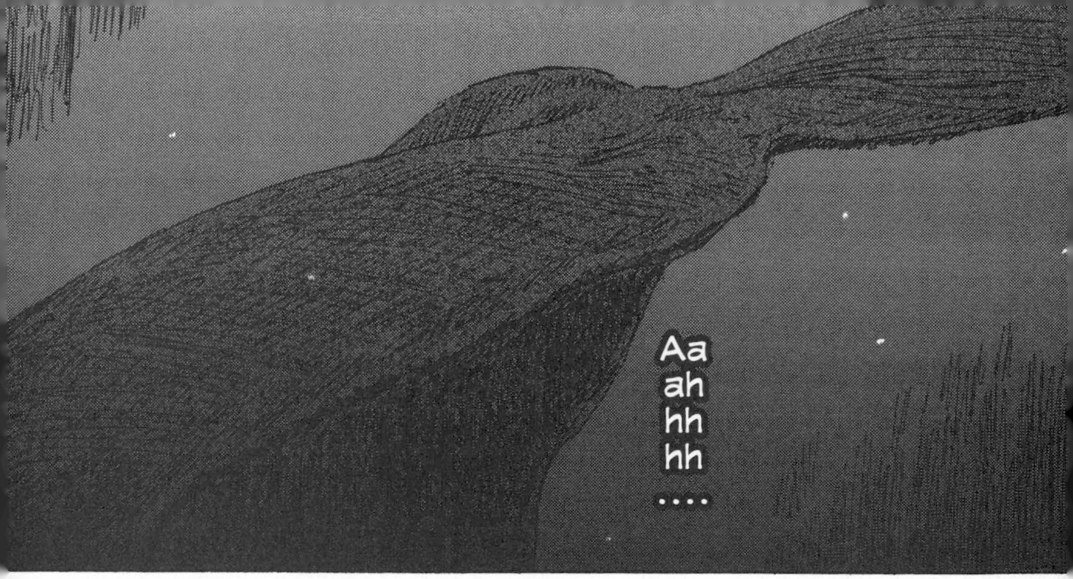
Aaahhhh....
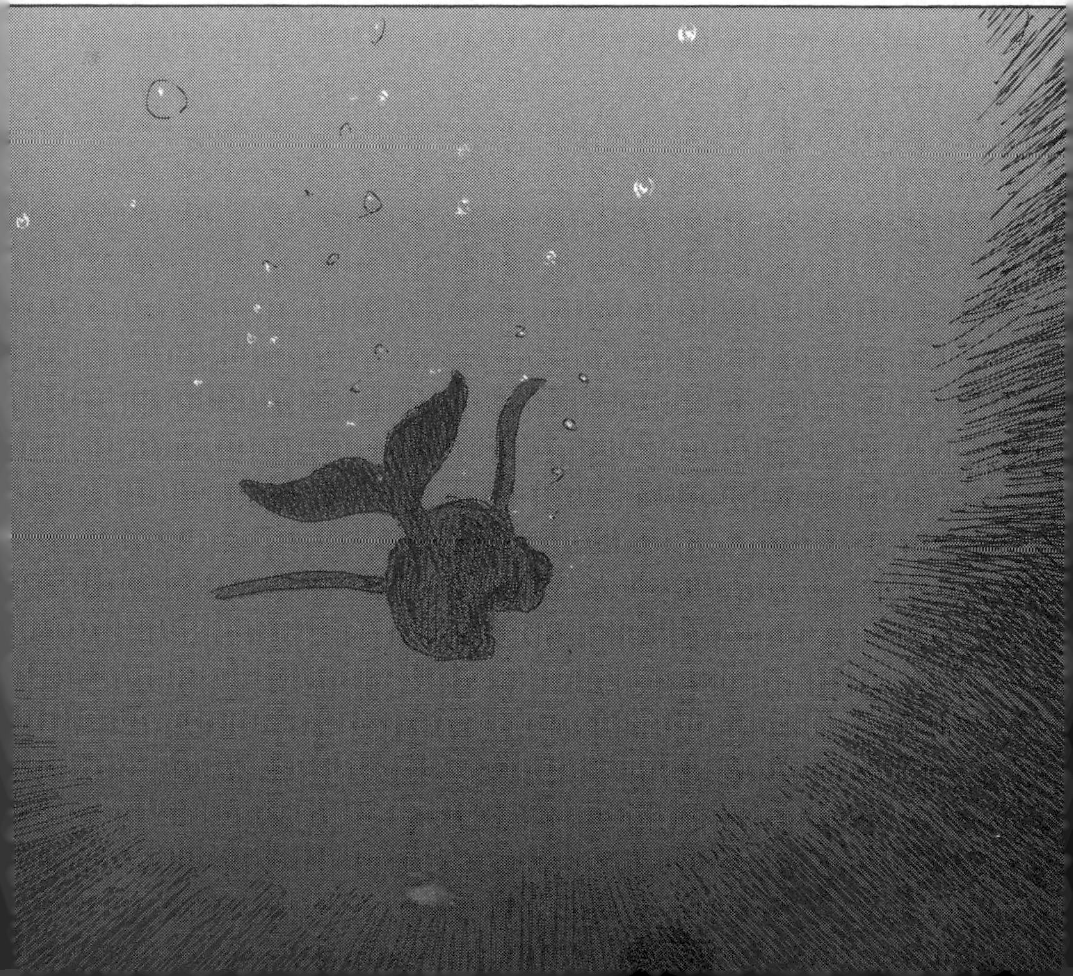

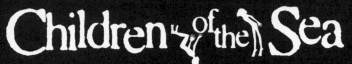

Children of the Sea

VOLUME 3
END NOTES

Page 148, panel 1: Child of the sea, child of the sky

Umi's name means "sea"; Sora's name means "sky."

Page 295, panel 2: Women divers

Ama (海女) means "women of the sea," although with different kanji it can also mean "men of the sea" or "people of the sea." Ama still dive for shellfish and seaweed without oxygen tanks, although they have added wet suits in recent years.

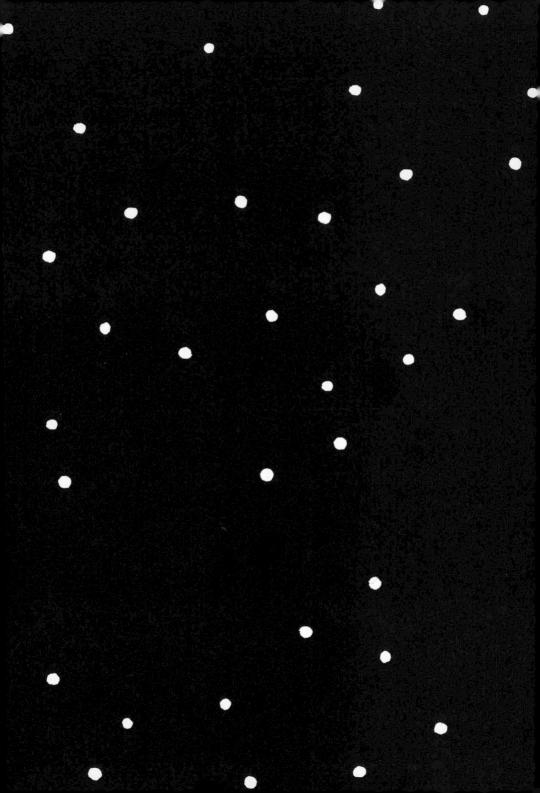

CHILDREN OF THE SEA

Volume 3
VIZ Signature Edition

STORY AND ART BY DAISUKE IGARASHI

© 2007 Daisuke IGARASHI/Shogakukan
All rights reserved.
Original Japanese edition "KAIJU NO KODOMO" published by SHOGAKUKAN Inc.

Original Japanese cover design by chutte

Cooperation and assistance from Enoshima Aquarium

TRANSLATION = JN Productions
TOUCH-UP ART & LETTERING = Jose Macasocol
DESIGN = Fawn Lau
EDITOR = Pancha Diaz

VP, PRODUCTION = Alvin Lu
VP, SALES & PRODUCT MARKETING = Gonzalo Ferreyra
VP, CREATIVE = Linda Espinosa
PUBLISHER = Hyoe Narita

Printed in the U.S.A.

Published by VIZ Media, LLC
P.O. Box 77010
San Francisco, CA 94107

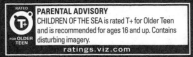

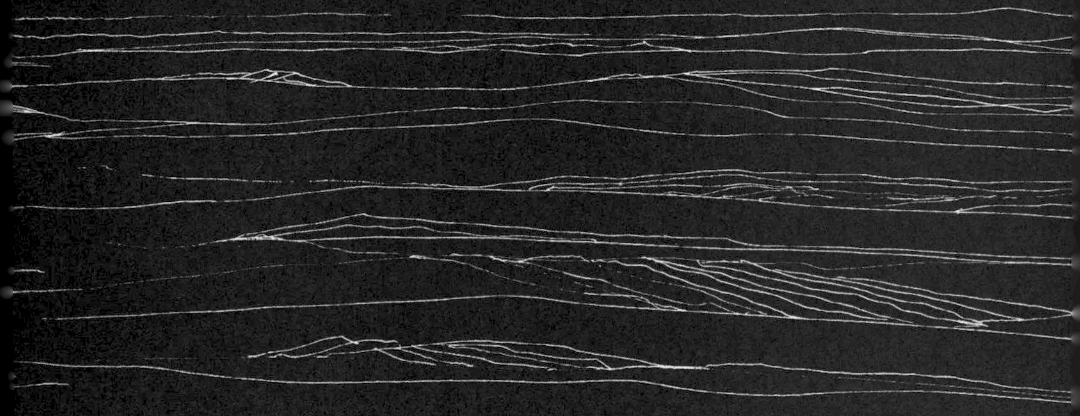

PARENTAL ADVISORY
CHILDREN OF THE SEA is rated T+ for Older Teen
and is recommended for ages 16 and up. Contains
disturbing imagery.
ratings.viz.com

www.viz.com

www.sigikki.com

10 9 8 7 6 5 4 3 2 1
First printing, June 2010

This is the **LAST PAGE** of this book.

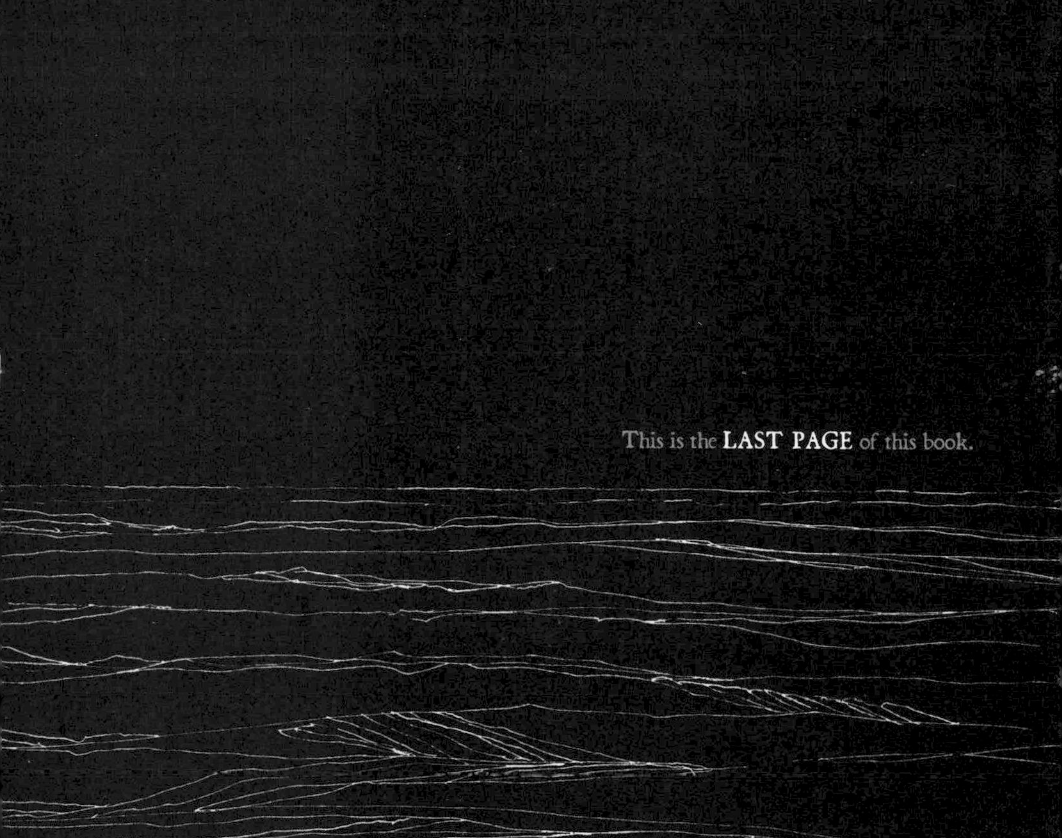

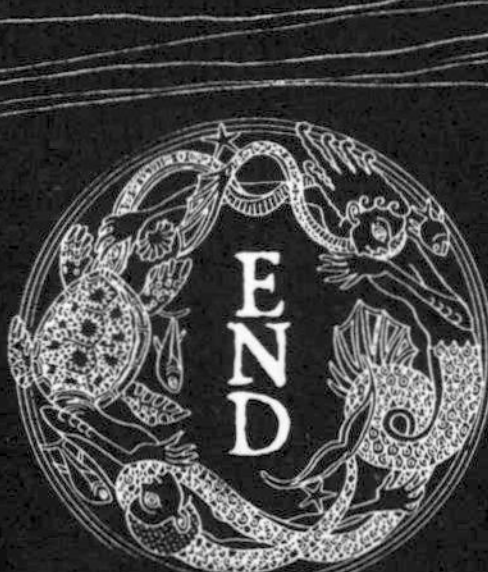
END

CHILDREN OF THE SEA
is printed from RIGHT TO LEFT in the original Japanese format in order to present **DAISUKE IGARASHI'S** stunning artwork the way it was meant to be seen.